THE
COMPLETE
SOUTHERN
COOKBOOK

More than 800 of the Most Delicious,
Down-home Recipes

By TAMMY ALGOOD

RUNNING PRESS
PHILADELPHIA · LONDON

9 8 7 6 5 4 3 2 1
Digit on the right indicates the number of this printing

Library of Congress Control Number: 2010928983
ISBN: 978-0-7624-3864-8
Cover and interior design by Amanda Richmnd
Typography: Archer and Verlag

Running Press Book Publishers
2300 Chestnut Street
Philadelphia, PA 19103-4371

Visit us on the web!
www.runningpresscooks.com

To Mama and Mother,
who showed me how to be a Southern lady

and to George,
the love of my life!

TABLE OF CONTENTS

ACKNOWLEDGMENTS

Quite literally dozens of people made this book possible and to them I'm overflowing with gratitude. First, my deepest thanks to my friend Bryan Curtis who has very patiently guided me through this entire process. He has remarkably kept me focused on our vision and on track at every turn. I consider him a wise brother, and I cherish his sense of humor and enthusiasm. I have learned so much from him and appreciate his hard work and time. Without him, this book would still be in my head.

To Geoff Stone at Running Press, who has been a longtime friend, I give special thanks. His incredible attention to detail and knowledge of the industry is inspiring. He has been trustworthy, dedicated, and loyal to me and this book from the beginning. I have nothing but the deepest respect for him and his staff.

With those two thanks in mind, I have to express my sincere appreciation to my dear friend Laura Leach, whose husband, Dave, introduced me to both Bryan and Geoff. God certainly used our connection to take me to this point. Don't think for a moment that I didn't notice! Cheers to you, my friend!

Thank you to quite literally the dozens of my "guinea pig" friends who tasted again and again recipe after recipe, helping me fine-tune each one without ever complaining! They are culinary heroes to me and you know who you are!

I stand in awe of my wonderful parents, who instilled in me the values of home, love, dedication, loyalty, and a work ethic. I love you with my whole heart.

Lastly, I have to raise a glass to my wonderful husband, George, who has been the calm in the middle of the book storm. Without his unfailing support, this book would never have been written. He is the finest man I know, and I love him.

INTRODUCTION

Lots of images float through my mind when the word "Southern" is mentioned. I think of magnolia trees, Spanish moss, rocking chairs, and endless sunshine. I see visions of ballgames, church services, and tire swings. But, it would be difficult for me to talk very long about the Southern way of life without taking a trip through the kitchen. That is where everything we love most in our homes is centered.

The kitchen is where we begin the day with a hearty breakfast, where we bring lovingly harvested foods to prepare, and where we rifle through the details of our day. It's where as kids we had snacks after school and where we would sit and do homework. Although we had a nice dining room, we ate the majority of our meals at the kitchen table. The Southern kitchen is a place of memories unlike any other room in the house. More than likely, the back door opens into the kitchen, just begging folks to "come on in!"

I have always considered it a privilege to have been born and raised in the South. That starting place was Starkville, Mississippi, a sleepy Southern town that has only recently grown to any significant size. My daddy was a well-respected dairy specialist at Mississippi State University, and my beautiful mother stayed home to raise four children and run our busy household.

We were a typical middle class Southern family. My brother, Steve, was the oldest and my sister Rita, the youngest. My identical twin sister, Tina, and I took the middle spots. Life was filled with school, chores, friends, 4-H activities, and church.

My grandparents moved down the street from us when I was nine years old. It was the most wonderful thing I could ever imagine and weekends were spent doing all kinds of things with my grandmother (Mama). I loved being at Mama's house, learning how to sew, cook, do needlework, and garden. There was no school in the world better than standing beside her apron strings.

As I grew older, I never lost that love of home and naturally wanted to major in home economics in college. My love of home and cooking and gardening evolved into my job as a food marketing specialist with the University of Tennessee Extension, where I help farmers sell what they grow. Seeing their love of the land and dependence on Mother Nature for a living deepens my appreciation for the dedication and hard work that goes into getting our precious food to the market. For decades, I have been trumpeting the message of buying local at farmers' markets and more recently through community supported agriculture (CSA's), where wholesome, natural food is delivered fresh from the farm. Shopping locally not only provides you with better, healthier food but it also supports a community. And a strong community is ingrained in the Southern culture where hospitality reigns.

If there is one thing Southerners know well, it's the whole concept of hospitality. Somewhere deep in our souls we know that we may not have the largest fanciest house, but we can feed you. When I got married, my husband, George, and I decided to entertain at our house on a regular basis, and it has grown to be something we both enjoy. I adore the entire process of selecting the menu, ironing the linens, setting the table, lighting the candles, selecting the wine, and opening the door to family and friends. It is Southern life at its finest and what led me down the path to this book. Southern living is so much more than the area of the country where we live. It is a lifestyle that cherishes home and community and is a way of thinking that celebrates one's heritage. Southerners have always demonstrated love and caring through the food placed on our tables, and we probably always will.

Life in the South is simple and uncomplicated, and so is our food. It is frequently pulled from the garden and eaten raw with the occasional steaming, boiling, or roasting. We didn't grow up using exotic ingredients, but built our food traditions around the items growing in our own backyards, or those of our neighbors. Old family recipes are incredibly basic while a taste of new Southern cooking dresses it up a bit. Both old and new Southern recipe traditions are included in this book, and my hope is that you will learn how to enjoy a taste of true Southern culture through our cuisine.

At the very beginning of this book idea, I thought about how cooking follows seasons. We all tend to load up on certain foods that are on the market in abundance at particular times of the year. You know, those times when fresh sweet corn, peaches, zucchini, or tomatoes arrive on local farm markets or when gardens are begging to be harvested. At that moment, you don't want to have to spend valuable time flipping through appetizer, soup, salad, dessert, and side dish sections of a cookbook. You have excess food to prepare or perhaps a craving for something in particular. Therefore the book is arranged alphabetically by the main ingredient for convenience. Time is on your side with this book because you have everything at your fingertips in one chapter. It is useable and arranged to give you everything you need, including storage and preservation information in one place. It is a Southern friend to you no matter where your kitchen is located. These recipes are for those who still appreciate the art form of enhancing the lives of those you love the Southern way ... one meal at a time. So welcome to the South. I think you'll enjoy the trip!

KITCHEN NOTES

My goal is for you to find culinary success with every recipe included in this book. In order for that to happen, there are a few ingredient listings that need to be explained.

Butter: Unsalted butter is my preference simply based on taste. It contains absolutely no salt, which is used as a preservative. Since it doesn't have the shelf life of salted butter, store extra supplies in the freezer. When cutting butter into flour to make a dough, it is best to use chilled butter rather than soft butter.

Eggs: In any recipe calling for eggs, I base it on carton sizes labeled "large." That's the only size I generally purchase and find it is typically the most economical.

Herbs: I grow my own herbs and find it to be one of the finest and most constant gardening rewards. For that reason, I utilize fresh herbs quite frequently because it's what I have right outside my kitchen. That doesn't mean dried herbs cannot be used if you don't have the luxury of a garden. See the herb chapter for substitutions.

Lemon or Lime Juice: Southerners are practical, if nothing else, and I am no exception. I realize that not everyone keeps fresh lemons and limes on hand all the time. So fresh lemon or lime juice is only specifically called for in recipes where you'll be zesting the citrus and I know it will be available. If you purchase reconstituted juice instead, that's fine to use, but again, fresh is best.

Milk: I grew up with a "Dairy Specialist Daddy," so whole milk is what I have consumed and used my entire life. That's also what I prefer for cooking purposes and what I used in testing all the recipes. If you buy reduced-fat milk, by all means use it.

Salt: There are times I call for "kosher salt" and other times I simply list "salt" as an ingredient. There's a very good reason for the difference. Kosher salt dissolves quicker than regular iodized salt, and I can't help but like that. I use it when I want the salt to disperse quickly, as with hash browns or on French fries, so I taste salt but don't have a mouthful of it with the first bite. Regular iodized salt is what I generally use for baking.

Wine: I did not grow up seeing wine used in cooking. It is something I've grown to appreciate as I've been cooking on my own. Price on some level reflects quality, but that shouldn't be your only basis for selecting a wine. That's the beauty of shopping at a local winery . . . you get to taste the product before you buy, so you'll know if you like it instantly. Taste should always be your guide. If you really like a $7 bottle of Chardonnay, great! Use what you like.

Don't use any wine in cooking that you wouldn't like to drink because what you are adding is that particular flavor. If it's been open and in your refrigerator, taste it. If you like the way it tastes, use it for cooking. If you don't like the flavor, discard it.

With that in mind, never substitute anything labeled "cooking wine" that is sold in the supermarket (located by vinegars) for wine listed as an ingredient. Cooking wine is loaded with salt to make it "undrinkable" and as a result, it is not acceptable for use, in my opinion. Regular wine that you like to drink is best.

If for some reason you can't find a particular ingredient listed in this book, consult the many sources of food ingredients that are located online. This book is designed to be user friendly. So for instance, if you have questions about the okra called for in a shrimp recipe, flip over to the okra chapter for more information. Lastly, to have success with any recipe, read it through completely before starting.

CANNING INSTRUCTIONS

Many are intimidated by the process of home canning, but it's just like following a recipe. There are two methods that are considered safe: boiling water bath canning and pressure canning. Each is used for specific foods and the two methods are not interchangeable.

Boiling Water Bath

BOILING WATER BATHS ARE SIMPLY LARGE covered containers of boiling water that covers the submerged jars by at least one inch. You will need a boiling water bath canner, new flat canning lids, clean canning jars, rust-free screw bands, canning funnel, ladle, timer, long-handled wooden spoons, tongs for handling hot lids or a magnetic lid lifter, jar lifter, saucepans, bubble wand or rubber spatula, and hot pads or oven mitts.

The jars are placed on a rack that allows the boiling water to circulate beneath the jars. This method is used for canning foods where the boiling point of water (212°F at sea level) is sufficient for destroying any potentially harmful bacteria. It is used for high acid foods such as fruits (including tomatoes), pickles, relishes, jams, jellies, preserves, and marmalades. Processing times will vary according to the size of the jar and the kind of food in the jar. Always follow the processing times listed in the recipe.

Here are the general steps for the boiling water bath. Always read the instructions for your equipment as steps may vary.

STEP 1 Fill your canner halfway with water for pint jars and slightly more than halfway for larger jars. Place the canner over high heat to preheat.

STEP 2 Wash and rinse your canning jars with boiling water for 10 minutes to sterilize them.

STEP 3 Keep the jars hot until ready to fill. This is best done by submerging the empty jars in a large stockpot of simmering water.

STEP 4 Prepare your recipe. Fill the jars with a canning funnel leaving the recommended headspace. Remove any air bubbles by gently inserting a bubble wand or a small rubber spatula along the side of the canning jar between the food and the jar. Do not mix the filled jars. Slowly turn the jar and move the spatula or bubble wand up and down to allow bubbles to escape. This step is not necessary when canning liquids such as juice.

STEP 5 Clean the rim of the jars with a damp paper towel.

STEP 6 Place the flat seals on the jar and screw on the ring bands until just tight.

STEP 7 Place the jars on the rack and gently lower the rack into the boiling water. (The water should cover the jars by at least two inches and there should be room for the water to flow around each jar.) If you are not using a rack made especially for canning, lower the jars into the water with a jar lifter. Keep the jars upright at all times.

STEP 8 Cover the pot and add more boiling water if needed to sufficiently cover. When the water returns to a vigorous boil, start the timer and process for the recommended time, adjusting for altitude. (Add 2 minutes of boiling time per every 1,000 feet above sea level.)

STEP 9 When finished processing, turn off the heat and remove the jars with a jar lifter, being careful not to tilt the jars. Allow them to cool on a wire rack in a draft free location. Don't crowd the jars as air needs to circulate to help them cool. Leave them undisturbed at room temperature for 12 to 24 hours. You will likely hear popping sounds at the jars cool and seal.

STEP 10 Make sure the flat lids are all concave. If any lid is not concave, that jar will need to be reprocessed until a proper seal is achieved or stored in the refrigerator and used immediately.

STEP 11 If desired, remove the screw bands before storing. (It's not necessary but sometimes they get rusty if you leave them on.) Do not retighten the screw bands after processing. Label the jars before storing in a dark cool place.

Pressure Canning

PRESSURE CANNERS ARE NECESSARY FOR canning foods that are low in acid because they need to be canned at temperatures higher than the boiling point of water. That includes vegetables, meats, poultry, and seafood that need temperatures of 240°F in order to destroy potentially harmful micro-organisms. Again, the exact processing times will vary, so follow the processing time listed in the recipe. Pressure canners are made of heavy metal and have locking lids that prevent steam from escaping until you open the vent. You will have either a dial or a weighted pressure gauge on the lid to let you know the amount of pressure inside the canner.

Here are some general steps for pressure canning, but because each model is different, follow the manufacturer's instructions for use.

STEP 1 Place at least 2 to 3 inches of hot water in the pressure canner. (Some canners require more water, so follow your manufacturer's directions.)

STEP 2 Wash and rinse your canning jars with boiling water for 10 minutes to sterilize them.

STEP 3 Keep the jars hot until ready to fill. This is best done by submerging the empty jars in a large stockpot of simmering water.

STEP 4 Prepare your recipe. Fill the jars with a canning funnel, leaving the recommended headspace. Remove any air bubbles by gently inserting a bubble wand or a small rubber spatula along the side of the canning jar between the food and the jar. Do not mix the filled jars. Slowly turn the jar and move the spatula or bubble wand up and down to allow bubbles to escape.

STEP 5 Clean the rim of the jars with a damp paper towel.

STEP 6 Place the flat lids on the jar and screw on the ring bands until just tight.

STEP 7 Place the filled jars on the rack using a jar lifter. Keep the jars upright at all times. Fasten the canner lid securely.

STEP 8 Leave weight off the vent port or open the petcock. Place over high heat and heat until steam flows freely from the vent port or open petcock. Let the steam flow continuously for 10 minutes.

STEP 9 Place the weight on the vent port or close the petcock. The canner will pressurize during the next 3 to 5 minutes. Start timing when the pressure reading on the dial gauge indicates that the recommended pressure has been reached or when the weighted gauge begins to jiggle as the manufacturer describes.

STEP 10 Regulate the heat under the canner to maintain a steady pressure. Avoid sudden changes in pressure. When the time required for processing is complete, turn off the heat and remove the canner from the heat source. Let the canner depressurize and do not remove the lid.

STEP 11 After the canner has depressurized, remove the weight from the vent port or open the petcock. Wait 10 minutes, unfasten the lid, and remove it carefully. (Note: When removing the lid, always lift it away from your face.)

STEP 12 Remove the jars with a jar lifter, being careful not to tilt the jars. Allow them to cool on a wire rack in a draft free location. Don't crowd the jars as air needs to circulate to help them cool. Leave them undisturbed at room temperature for 12 to 24 hours. You will likely hear popping sounds at the jars cool and seal.

STEP 13 Make sure the flat lids are all concave. If any lid is not concave, that jar will need to be reprocessed until a proper seal is achieved or stored in the refrigerator and used immediately.

STEP 14 Remove the screw bands before storing. (It's not necessary but sometimes they get rusty if you leave them on.) Do not retighten the screw bands after processing. Label the jars before storing in a cool, dark place.

Terms and Equipment

Canning Jars: Use only canning jars that are made for home canning. These have been tempered for multiple uses. Do not use commercial jars, such as mayonnaise or jelly jars because these are designed for one time use only. Also, don't use antique canning jars for home canning. Proper canning jars come in a variety of sizes and have two-piece lids (flat tops and screw or ring bands). Jars and lids should be sterilized in hot water before used in canning. Keep them hot until ready to use.

Headspace: The area of unfilled space between the top of the food and the bottom of the jar lid is the headspace. This is critical for proper canning and sealing of the jars. The headspace allows room for the food to expand as it is heated. Generally, the higher the temperature, the greater the food will expand, so there is typically more headspace in pressure canned foods than those canned in a water bath.

Canning Funnel: I will not can without my handy canning funnel. It is specifically designed to fit the rim of canning jars and is wide at the top. It keeps the mess at bay when ladling hot food into the jars.

Bubble Wand: A bubble wand is a flat long stick that is used for removing bubbles from the jars before they are sealed. It is just the right size for running down the inside of the jar and gets the job done in a snap. You can also use a rubber spatula, but just make sure it is plastic, not metal. You may have to adjust the headspace after removing trapped air bubbles.

Jar Lifter: A jar lifter looks like really strange tongs. It is extremely helpful in lowering the filled jars into your canner and also for removing them after processing. Make sure the rounded end is securely positioned below the screw band. Also, be careful not to tilt the jars when placing in the canner and when removing them.

Timer: Don't depend on your memory when timing the canning process. Invest in a good kitchen timer. Timing begins with a pressure canner when the correct amount of pressure is reached. Timing begins with a boiling water bath as soon as the water returns to a boil. Keep a lid on the container when using the boiling water bath method.

Cooling Rack: Filled jars can be quite heavy, so make sure you have a heavy-duty wire rack for cooling the jars. Leave at least one inch of space between the jars when placing on the rack and make sure they are away from any drafty areas. Allow the jars to sit undisturbed for 12 to 24 hours to cool completely. Most will make a popping sound as they cool. Never cover the jars while they are cooling.

Sealing: The jar is properly sealed if the lid is concave and will not push down or pop back up when pressed in the center with your finger. Only perform this test after the jars have cooled completely.

Storage: After the jars have cooled, label the lids with the contents and canning date. Home canned foods that are properly sealed can be stored at room temperature and they prefer cool, dark, dry places. Keep them away from storage places near stoves or ovens. For best quality, use within one year.

ALMONDS

I **REMEMBER THE FIRST TIME I SAW JORDAN ALMONDS. IT WAS AT A HUGE SOUTHERN WEDDING** reception and I was completely entranced. I thought they looked like tiny Easter eggs encased in pastel candy coatings. They were served in sparkling crystal dishes with small sterling silver spoons and were delicious.

For those of us with a sweet tooth, almonds are the nuts that make candy special. Take for instance, the two most popular candy bars in our household: Hershey's with Almonds and Almond Joy.

I grew up loving both of these thanks to the nutty crunch of almonds. Santa always knew to leave those bars in our Christmas stockings. We could sing the popular jingle, and for the record, we always felt like a nut! Tina and I would eat all around the whole almond on top of an Almond Joy, saving the almond bite for last.

Obviously, we were not the only ones to fall in love with sweet almonds. They became popular in the South thanks to their incredible keeping quality. These treats were common holiday gifts that were roasted, toasted, blanched, ground, sliced, chopped, smoked, and candied.

And even though we love to coat catfish with almonds, roll cheese balls in it, and throw the slivers on salads and rice, it's the confectionary use that shines best on the Southern dinner table.

Nutrition: Almonds are an excellent source of protein and are rich in phosphorus, calcium, magnesium, potassium, folic acid, riboflavin, vitamin E, and dietary fiber. A one-ounce serving, which is around twenty-two whole almonds, contains 180 calories.

Paste: Almond paste is a combination of blanched ground almonds, sugar, glycerin, and occasionally almond extract. It is used in cake and cookie recipes. Marzipan is a mixture of almond paste, sugar, egg whites, and usually food colorings. It is frequently shaped into a variety of forms and used as a garnish.

Yields: One pound of almonds yields three cups whole, three-and-one-half cups chopped or slivered, four cups ground, or five cups sliced.

Storage: Store almonds in the refrigerator or any cool place where the temperature is below 35°F. They freeze well if placed in an airtight container. Use frozen almonds within one year for best quality. There is no need to thaw before using.

Origin: China is the original home of almonds, which were carried in the saddlebags of caravans down the ancient Silk Road.

ALMOND BRITTLE

The old saying about necessity being the mother of invention is proven with this recipe. I was in the mood to make candy one Saturday and had been craving peanut brittle. I didn't want to have to run to the grocery store for the peanuts, so I substituted slivered almonds. You'll love the subtle flavor difference.

YIELD: 4 CUPS

1 pound blanched, slivered almonds
2 cups sugar
$\frac{1}{2}$ cup water
2 tablespoons light corn syrup
1 pound (4 sticks) unsalted butter

Preheat the oven to 350°F. Spread the almonds in a single layer in a jelly-roll pan and toast for 10 minutes. Transfer to a large saucepan. Lightly grease the jelly-roll pan and set aside.

Add the sugar, water, corn syrup, and butter and place over medium-high heat, stirring often. Bring to a boil, reduce the heat to medium, and stir gently until the mixture reaches exactly 290°F on a candy thermometer. Pour the candy onto the prepared jelly-roll pan and cool completely on a wire rack.

When cool, crack into pieces of candy. Store in an airtight container lined with wax paper between the layers.

Celebration
February 16 is National Almond Day.

CHOCOLATE ALMOND BALLS

Homemade candy will tempt every sweet friend you know. The flavor of this candy will improve after twenty-four hours, so make it ahead of time.

YIELD: 5 $\frac{1}{2}$ DOZEN CANDIES

3 (6-ounce) packages semisweet chocolate chips
1 (14-ounce) can sweetened condensed milk
3 tablespoons amaretto
$\frac{1}{2}$ teaspoon pure almond extract
1 cup chopped almonds

In a heavy saucepan over low heat, combine the chocolate and the milk. Stir until the chips are completely melted. Add the amaretto and the extract. Cool to room temperature and then cover and refrigerate 2 hours.

Shape the dough into $\frac{3}{4}$-inch balls and roll in the chopped almonds. Place on a baking sheet lined with wax paper. Refrigerate until firm, and then store in a tightly covered container.

EARLY USE: Ancient Romans used ground almonds instead of flour or starch to thicken soups, stews, and gravies. Jordan almonds were "invented" by the Fabian family in ancient Rome around 177 BC. It became a common practice to give sugar-coated almonds to guests at weddings because almonds were believed to bring good fortune and good luck to all concerned.

CINNAMON-SWIRLED ALMOND POUND CAKE

If you've never used almond paste, you'll get hooked on it with this recipe. Look for it in the baking aisle of the supermarket. Refrigerate or freeze the unused portion of the tube.

YIELD: 12 SERVINGS

1 cup sliced almonds

1 tablespoon ground cinnamon

3 tablespoons almond paste

1 (18.25-ounce) package white cake mix

1 (3.4-ounce) package vanilla instant pudding mix

1 (8-ounce) container sour cream

4 eggs, lightly beaten

$\frac{1}{2}$ cup vegetable oil

$\frac{1}{2}$ cup amaretto

$\frac{1}{2}$ cup water

Preheat the oven to 350°F. Grease and flour a 10-inch tube pan and set aside.

Place the almonds and cinnamon in the bowl of a food processor. Process until finely chopped.

Place one-third of the almond mixture in the bottom of the prepared pan. Add the almond paste to the remaining almond mixture and stir until well combined.

In the bowl of an electric mixer, combine the cake mix, pudding mix, sour cream, eggs, oil, amaretto, and water. Beat on low speed to combine and then increase to medium speed and beat 2 minutes.

Spoon one-third of the batter into the prepared pan. Evenly sprinkle half the almond paste mixture over the batter. Repeat and end with the last of the batter on top.

Bake 55 minutes, or until a tester inserted in the center comes out clean. Cool in the pan 10 minutes and then cool completely on a wire rack before serving.

HEIRLOOM ALMOND CRUST

This recipe could be considered a family heirloom. I found it in a recipe notebook my mother gave me years ago. It was clipped from the newspaper and the tape holding it in the book had yellowed and dried. The star beside it made me want to give it a try. It's fabulous! Use it for any cheesecake or tart.

YIELD: 1 CRUST

3 cups ground almonds

$\frac{1}{4}$ cup sugar

$\frac{1}{2}$ teaspoon pure almond extract

6 tablespoons unsalted butter, melted

In a mixing bowl, combine the almonds and sugar. Make a well in the center and add the extract and butter. Mix well. Press into the bottom and up the sides of a greased springform, tart, or pie pan. Refrigerate until ready to use.

TREES: Almond trees produce flowers before they produce leaves and require bees for pollination. They are strikingly similar to peach and nectarine trees. Almonds grow in clusters and are covered by a gray-green, velvety but tough hull. At maturity, the hull will split open along one side to reveal the almond in its shell. At this point, the almonds start to dry naturally on the tree. That makes them a dehydrated food that contains only 5 percent water at harvest. The shells are not wasted. They are used to make lots of products, including charcoal briquettes.

JAZZED ALMOND PUFFS

These pastries are very delicate and a great brunch or party appetizer addition.

YIELD: 12 SERVINGS

2 cups all-purpose flour, divided

$\frac{1}{2}$ pound (2 sticks) plus 4 tablespoons unsalted butter, divided

1 cup plus 2 tablespoons water, divided

2 teaspoons pure almond extract, divided

3 eggs

$\frac{1}{2}$ cup slivered almonds

2 cups confectioners' sugar

3 tablespoons milk

Preheat the oven to 350°F.

Place 1 cup of the flour in a medium bowl. With a pastry blender, cut in 1 stick of the butter until the mixture resembles coarse meal. Drizzle with 2 tablespoons of the water and mix well with a fork. Divide the dough in half and pat each half into a 13 x 10-inch rectangle on an ungreased baking sheet. Set aside.

In a medium saucepan over medium-high heat, combine 1 stick of the butter with the remaining 1 cup of the water. Bring to a boil and remove from the heat. Add 1 teaspoon of the extract and the remaining 1 cup of the flour.

Stir vigorously for 1 minute. Beat in the eggs until the mixture is smooth. Spread half of the mixture over each rectangle, covering completely. Sprinkle each with $\frac{1}{4}$ cup of the almonds. Bake 1 hour, or until the top is crisp and lightly browned. Cool on a wire rack at least 30 minutes.

Meanwhile, soften the remaining 4 tablespoons of the butter. In a medium bowl, combine the confectioners' sugar, the softened butter, the remaining 1 teaspoon of the extract, and the milk. Mix well and spread over cooled pastry. Cut into squares or fingers and serve at room temperature.

LOW-COUNTRY ALMOND SHORTBREAD

George and I stopped at a tiny bakery while on vacation in the Low Country, and I have attempted to re-create the experience here. It was raining like the dickens outside, but we didn't care because this buttery shortbread tasted like heaven.

YIELD: 8 SERVINGS

$\frac{1}{2}$ pound (2 sticks) unsalted butter, softened

$\frac{1}{2}$ cup confectioners' sugar

1 teaspoon pure vanilla extract

1 teaspoon pure almond extract

Pinch of salt

2 cups cake flour

$\frac{1}{2}$ cup finely ground almonds

$\frac{1}{4}$ cup slivered almonds

Line a baking sheet with parchment paper and set aside.

In the bowl of an electric mixer, cream the butter and confectioners' sugar on medium speed until light and fluffy. Add the vanilla extract, almond extract, and salt, blending well.

Reduce mixer speed to low and add the flour and ground almonds. Mix well. Spread the dough on the prepared pan and sprinkle the top with the slivered almonds, pressing gently into the dough. Refrigerate at least 20 minutes.

Preheat the oven to 350°F. Place the pan upside down on a solid surface to remove the dough. Remove the parchment and place back on the baking sheet.

Cut the dough with a 2-inch cutter and place on the baking sheet. Bake 13 to 15 minutes, or just until the edges start to brown. Cool in the pan on a wire rack. Store leftovers in an airtight container.

SLOW-BAKED ALMOND PUDDING

I love making this dessert for dinner parties because it demands to be made ahead of time. The first time you make it will not be your last. It is beautiful.

YIELD: 8 TO 10 SERVINGS

$^1/_4$ cup packed light brown sugar
$^3/_4$ cup toasted slivered almonds
1 (14-ounce) can sweetened condensed milk
$^1/_2$ cup cream
5 eggs
$^1/_2$ teaspoon pure almond extract
Toasted almonds for garnish

Preheat the oven to 325°F. Sprinkle the sugar in the bottom of an ungreased 8-inch round cake pan and set aside.

In a blender, grind the almonds. Add the milk, cream, eggs, and extract, blending well. Pour into the prepared pan and place in a larger pan. Pour hot water to a depth of 1 inch in the larger pan.

Bake 45 to 50 minutes, or until a knife inserted in the center comes out clean. Refrigerate 3 hours and invert on a serving plate. Slice and serve with a garnish of toasted almonds.

EXTRACT: Almond extract is produced by combining almond oil with ethyl alcohol. It has a very intense flavor. Store it in a cool, dark place.

OIL: When almonds are pressed, the result is a mild oil that can range from very inexpensive to pricey. It has a delicate flavor and aroma that is divine when used as a salad dressing or tossed in wild rice.

WHITE CHOCOLATE ALMOND SQUARES

This dessert is so lovely. I love the simplicity of it and the total focus on almonds.

YIELD: 16 SQUARES

12 ounces white chocolate, broken into pieces
$^1/_2$ pound (2 sticks) unsalted butter
3 eggs
$^3/_4$ cup all-purpose flour
1 teaspoon pure almond extract
$^1/_2$ cup slivered almonds

Preheat the oven to 325°F. Lightly grease an 8-inch square baking pan and set aside.

Melt the chocolate and butter in a large saucepan over low heat, stirring constantly. Remove from the heat just when the chocolate melts.

With an electric mixer, beat in the eggs until the mixture is smooth. Add the flour and extract. Spread the batter evenly in the prepared pan. Top with the almond slivers. Bake 30 to 35 minutes, or just until the center is set. Cool completely in the pan on a wire rack before cutting into squares.

TREES: Almond trees produce flowers before they produce leaves and require bees for pollination. They are strikingly similar to peach and nectarine trees. Almonds grow in clusters and are covered by a gray-green, velvety but tough hull. At maturity, the hull will split open along one side to reveal the almond in its shell. At this point, the almonds start to dry naturally on the tree. That makes them a dehydrated food that contains only 5 percent water at harvest.

APPLES

(AND APPLESAUCE AND APPLE CIDER)

DESPITE VARIOUS EXOTIC FRUIT FADS, SOUTHERNERS HAVE NEVER LOST THEIR APPETITE for apples. Oh sure, there was a brief fling with mangoes and some ardent glances at kiwifruit, but we've continually returned to this lunchbox favorite time and time again.

Apples carry us through many seasons, but particularly shine in the fall. Southerners bob for them at Halloween parties, pass them under our chins at county fair competitions, and give them to strict teachers in order to score a little extra credit.

We squeeze them into cider, cook them down into sauce, strain them into jelly, fold them in quick bread, and bake them in tarts. If that isn't enough, we'll wrap them in caramel, dip them in candy, and fry them in pies.

All this good fruit cheer is right around nearly everyone's corner. If you're thinking "ho-hum" right now, you've probably been lulled into that thought by a mealy, ubiquitous "shipped in from some other place" supermarket apple.

Believe me, there are full-of-flavor, juicy, homegrown fruits to be found at the local orchard in your community. Their crisp, refreshing texture matches fall weather, and the fresh season is wonderfully long. Apples are so autumn.

I would be hard pressed to pick a favorite variety. The type I purchase depends on how I will use the fruit. I prefer Arkansas Blacks for eating raw. Braeburn and Golden Delicious can't be beat when fried. Gala, Mutsu, and Granny Smith apples are perfect in pies. Jonagolds and Pink Ladys roast beautifully. McIntosh and Winesaps make great applesauce.

Yes, you could say that apples are quite the charmers around the South, and I have the recipes to prove it!

Equivalents: One pound equals four cups of chopped or diced fruit. That pound will consist of three medium-size apples. At least a couple of pounds will be needed to fill a nine-inch pie. Want more? One peck equals ten and a half pounds and one bushel equals forty-two pounds.

Nutrition: A medium apple contains about eighty calories and is more than eighty percent water. It is loaded with pectin and provides as much dietary fiber as a bowl of bran cereal.

Selection: Apples should always feel firm and not appear wrinkled or shriveled. Avoid any that have obvious bruises, soft spots, or cracks in the outer skin.

APPLAUSE APPLESAUCE

The key to good applesauce is using a mixture of apples. If you don't have access to the particular types listed, just make sure you have a combination of sweet and tart.

YIELD: 4 SERVINGS

2 Winesap apples, cored, peeled, and cut into wedges

2 Jonathan apples, cored, peeled, and cut into wedges

2 Lodi apples, cored, peeled, and cut into wedges

2 McIntosh apples, cored, peeled, and cut into wedges

$\frac{1}{2}$ cup water

$\frac{1}{4}$ cup sugar (or more to taste)

$\frac{1}{2}$ teaspoon ground cinnamon

Combine the apples and water in a Dutch oven over medium heat. Cover and cook about 20 minutes, stirring occasionally, or until the apples are very soft.

Pass through a food mill into a serving bowl. Stir in the sugar and cinnamon. Add more sugar if necessary. Serve warm, at room temperature, or cold.

Storage: Apples can be stored at room temperature, but the shelf life lengthens considerably when kept in the refrigerator. Place them in a plastic bag with several holes punched in it for air circulation. Add a tablespoon of water and place in the crisper drawer. If you've got too many to fit in the drawer, place them in the bottom of the refrigerator.

APPLE CIDER CREAM CHEESE FROSTING

While this frosting is made for Apple Cider Cupcakes, don't stop there. Spread it on gingerbread or carrot cake for something unusual.

YIELD: ABOUT 2 CUPS

2 cups apple cider

1 (8-ounce) package cream cheese, softened

$\frac{2}{3}$ cup confectioners' sugar

In a small saucepan, bring the cider to a gentle boil and reduce to $\frac{1}{4}$ cup, around 15 minutes. Cool completely. Mix with the cream cheese and sugar until the desired spreading consistency is obtained. Spread on cooled pastries.

TIP: Sprinkle apples with any type of citrus juice to slow down browning (a natural oxidation process) when they are cut. If you don't want to flavor the apples, you can soak the cut portions in a bowl of water with a couple of tablespoons of citrus juice or two crushed vitamin C tablets added to the water.

Celebrations

October is National Apple Month.
The 2nd week of August is National Apple Week.
June 17 is National Apple Streusel Day.
September 17 is National Apple Dumpling Day.
September 30 is National Hot Mulled Cider Day.
October 21 is National Caramel Apple Day.
October 31 is National Candy Apple Day.
December 3 is National Apple Pie Day.

APPLE CIDER CUPCAKES

A school lunch box could quite possibly never be the same after one of these fall treats gets packed inside. Or, take them to tailgate parties and serve with warm cider.

YIELD: 18 CUPCAKES

3 cups apple cider
$^3/_4$ cup vegetable shortening
$1^3/_4$ cups sugar
2 eggs
2 cups all-purpose flour
1 teaspoon baking soda
1 teaspoon ground cinnamon
Pinch of salt
Apple Cider Cream Cheese Frosting (page 22)

In a large saucepan, bring the cider to a gentle boil and cook around 15 minutes to reduce by half. Set aside to cool.

Preheat the oven to 375°F. Grease and flour a muffin pan or fill with paper liners.

In the bowl of an electric mixer, combine the shortening and sugar until light and fluffy, about 2 minutes. Add the eggs, one at a time, beating well after each addition.

In a separate bowl, combine the flour, baking soda, cinnamon, and salt. Add to the shortening mixture alternately with the reduced cider, beginning and ending with the dry ingredients.

Divide the batter evenly among the muffin cups and bake 25 minutes, or until a tester inserted in the center comes out clean. Transfer to a wire rack to cool completely, and then frost with Apple Cider Cream Cheese Frosting.

APPLE DAPPLE CAKE

Warm brown sugar syrup is poured over this cake before serving, making it simply luscious!

YIELD: 12 SERVINGS

3 eggs
$1^1/_4$ cups vegetable oil
3 teaspoons pure vanilla extract, divided
2 cups granulated sugar
3 cups all-purpose flour, divided
1 teaspoon baking soda
1 teaspoon salt
1 teaspoon ground cinnamon
$^1/_4$ teaspoon ground nutmeg
3 cups chopped Golden Delicious apples
1 cup chopped pecans
1 cup shredded coconut
6 tablespoons unsalted butter, melted
1 cup packed brown sugar
$^1/_4$ cup milk

Preheat the oven to 350°F. Grease and flour a Bundt pan and set aside.

In the bowl of an electric mixer, beat together the eggs, oil, 2 teaspoons of the extract, and the granulated sugar. Mix well.

In a separate bowl, stir together $2^3/_4$ cups of the flour, the baking soda, salt, cinnamon, and nutmeg. Add to the egg mixture, beating well.

Combine the remaining flour with the apples, pecans, and coconut. Fold into the batter and pour into the prepared pan. Bake 1 hour and 10 minutes. Let cool in the pan 5 minutes, and then cool completely on a wire rack.

Meanwhile, in a small saucepan over medium heat, combine the butter, brown sugar, milk, and the remaining extract. Boil 3 minutes and set aside to cool 10 minutes. Place the cake on a serving platter. Slowly pour the warm syrup over the cake.

BROWN SUGAR
AND APPLE DUMPLINGS

Everyone will think you spent lots of time in the kitchen on these, but refrigerated biscuit dough makes it easy!

YIELD: 5 SERVINGS

$\frac{1}{2}$ cup packed brown sugar

1 teaspoon ground cinnamon

$\frac{1}{3}$ cup golden raisins

1 cup heavy whipping cream, divided

4 large Golden Delicious apples, cored, peeled, and coarsely chopped

1 (12-ounce) can refrigerated large flaky biscuits, at room temperature

1 egg, lightly beaten

Preheat the oven to 375°F. Lightly grease a baking sheet and set aside.

In a small bowl, combine the brown sugar and cinnamon, mixing well. Remove 3 tablespoons of the sugar mixture and transfer the remainder to a large saucepan. Place over low heat and add the raisins and 3 tablespoons of the cream. Stir until the sugar completely dissolves, about 3 minutes. Stir in the apples and set aside to cool.

In a medium bowl combine half of the reserved sugar mixture with the remaining cream. Beat until soft peaks form. Cover and refrigerate.

On a lightly floured surface, roll out each biscuit to a 7-inch round. Brush lightly with the egg. Fill each center evenly with the apple mixture. Pull up four sides of the dough to cover the filling and twist, making an apple shape. Press any seams to seal.

Transfer to the prepared baking sheet and brush the tops with the remaining egg. Sprinkle the tops with the remaining cinnamon sugar. Bake until golden brown, 15 to 17 minutes. Serve warm with the whipped cream.

DRIED AND FRIED
APPLE PIES

Fried pies are semicircles of pastry filled with fruit and, as the name suggests, fried. In the South, they are a regular snack. Dried fruit is typically used as the filling because they evolved from using preserved fruit after fresh was no longer available.

YIELD: 11 PIES

$\frac{1}{2}$ pound dried apples

3 cups water

1 teaspoon ground cinnamon

1 to $1\frac{1}{2}$ cups plus $1\frac{1}{2}$ teaspoons sugar, divided

$2\frac{1}{2}$ cups all-purpose flour

$1\frac{1}{2}$ teaspoons salt

$\frac{1}{2}$ cup vegetable shortening

$\frac{3}{4}$ cup evaporated milk

Vegetable oil

In a large saucepan over low heat, combine the apples and the water. Bring to a simmer, cover, and cook 30 to 45 minutes, or until the apples have the consistency of preserves. Check after 30 minutes because the cooking time will vary depending on the dryness of the apples.

Remove from heat and stir in the cinnamon. Stir in 1 cup of the sugar. Taste and add up to $\frac{1}{2}$ cup more sugar if necessary. Cool completely.

Meanwhile, in a mixing bowl, stir together the flour, the salt, and the remaining $1\frac{1}{2}$ teaspoons of sugar. Cut in the shortening with a pastry blender or 2 forks until the mixture resembles coarse meal. Add the milk and stir just until moistened. Gather the dough into a ball and flatten into a thick disk. Refrigerate 30 minutes.

Divide the dough in half. On a lightly floured surface, roll half of the dough to $\frac{1}{8}$-inch thickness and cut into 6-inch rounds. Place 2 tablespoons of the apples in the center of each round. Dampen the edges, fold over, and seal the edges with the tines of a fork. Repeat with the remaining pastry.

Pour the oil to the depth of $\frac{1}{2}$ inch in a large skillet. Place over medium-high heat and bring to 350°F. Fry 3 to 4 minutes on each side, or until golden brown. Fry no more than two pies at once. Drain on paper towels and serve warm or at room temperature.

DRIED APPLE STACK CAKE

I like to make this cake the day before it will be served. That gives time for the juices from the apples to soak into the cake layers.

YIELD: 10 SERVINGS

$\frac{1}{2}$ cup vegetable shortening

2 cups sugar, divided

$\frac{1}{2}$ cup sorghum syrup

$\frac{1}{2}$ cup buttermilk

1 egg, beaten

1 teaspoon pure vanilla extract

$3\frac{1}{4}$ cups all-purpose flour

$\frac{1}{2}$ teaspoon baking soda

$\frac{1}{2}$ teaspoon salt

$\frac{1}{2}$ teaspoon ground ginger

4 cups dried apples

$3\frac{1}{2}$ cups water

$\frac{1}{2}$ teaspoon ground cinnamon

$\frac{1}{2}$ teaspoon ground nutmeg

Preheat the oven to 350°F. Lightly grease a 9-inch cast-iron or ovenproof skillet and set aside.

In the bowl of an electric mixer, cream the shortening 2 minutes. Gradually add $\frac{1}{2}$ cup of the sugar and the sorghum, beating until smooth. Add the buttermilk, egg, and extract, mixing well.

In a separate bowl, combine the flour, baking soda, salt, and ginger. Gradually add to the buttermilk mixture, beating just until moistened.

Place $\frac{1}{2}$ cup of the batter in the prepared skillet. Bake 8 to 9 minutes, or until golden brown. Transfer immediately to a wire rack and repeat with the remaining batter.

Meanwhile, place the dried apples and water in a large saucepan over medium-high heat. Bring to a boil, cover, and reduce the heat to low. Simmer 30 minutes, or until the apples are tender. Stir in the remaining sugar, the cinnamon, and nutmeg, stirring until well blended.

Stack a layer of the cake on a serving plate. Spread the apple filling over the top. Repeat with the remaining layers and the remaining filling. Cover and refrigerate overnight before serving.

FLAVOR SAVER FRIED APPLES

There are several apple varieties that can be used in this recipe. Just be sure to use a mixture!

YIELD: 4 TO 6 SERVINGS

3 tablespoons unsalted butter

2 Golden Delicious, Jonagold, or Jonathan apples, cored and cut into $\frac{1}{2}$-inch slices

2 Braeburn, Pink Lady, or Winesap apples, cored and cut into $\frac{1}{2}$-inch slices

$\frac{1}{4}$ cup sugar

In a large skillet over medium-high heat, melt the butter. Add the apples and fry 4 minutes, stirring occasionally. Add the sugar and continue cooking 18 to 20 minutes, stirring frequently. Serve warm.

OLD-TIME APPLE PIE

My daddy always likes this pie served with a slice of Cheddar cheese on top.

YIELD: 8 SERVINGS

2 pounds Granny Smith apples, peeled, cored and cut into $\frac{1}{2}$-inch slices

2 pounds Molly's Delicious or Braeburn apples, peeled, cored, and cut into $\frac{1}{2}$-inch slices

$\frac{1}{4}$ cup all-purpose flour

$\frac{1}{2}$ cup sugar, divided

2 tablespoons apple jelly

1 tablespoon lemon juice

$\frac{1}{2}$ teaspoon ground cinnamon

$\frac{1}{4}$ teaspoon ground nutmeg

$\frac{1}{4}$ teaspoon salt

Crust for a Double Pie Pastry (page 400)

1 tablespoon unsalted butter, cut into small pieces

1 egg, lightly beaten

Place the apples in a large mixing bowl and set aside.

In a separate bowl, stir together the flour, $\frac{1}{3}$ cup of the sugar, the jelly, juice, cinnamon, nutmeg, and salt. Sprinkle over the apples, tossing gently to coat. Let stand 30 minutes, gently tossing every 10 minutes.

Meanwhile, preheat the oven to 425°F. Place one pie pastry in the bottom of a 9-inch pie plate. Gently press the dough into place.

Spoon the apples into the pastry, pressing tightly and mounding in the center. Pour any juices over the apples and sprinkle with the remaining sugar. Dot the top with the butter.

Place the remaining pie pastry over the top of the apples. Fold the edges under, sealing to the bottom crust and crimp as desired. Brush the top of the pie and edges with the beaten egg. Cut 5 slits in the top for steam to escape.

Place the pie on a jelly-roll pan and bake 15 minutes. Lower the oven temperature to 350°F and bake 35 minutes. Cover loosely with aluminum foil to prevent excessive browning. Bake 30 minutes longer. Cool on a wire rack 2 hours before serving.

JEZEBEL SAUCE

You will find all kinds of reasons to serve this sauce. Use it with chicken fingers, grilled fish, roasted pork, mozzarella sticks, fried shrimp, fried pickle chips, brie, or poured over a block of cream cheese (the old favorite).

YIELD: 1$\frac{1}{2}$ CUPS

1 (5-ounce) jar apple jelly

1 (5-ounce) jar pineapple preserves

$\frac{1}{3}$ cup prepared horseradish

$\frac{1}{2}$ tablespoon dry mustard

$\frac{1}{4}$ teaspoon black pepper

$\frac{1}{4}$ teaspoon crushed red pepper

In a medium bowl, whisk together the jelly, preserves, horseradish, mustard, black pepper, and red pepper. Whisk until smooth. Cover and refrigerate until ready to use.

Note: This recipe can easily be doubled.

PAIRING: Good partners with apples on a cheese tray include sharp Cheddar, Asiago, Gruyére, Stilton, and Gouda.

SOUTHERN APPLE FRITTERS

This recipe is perfect for a brunch crowd because it makes a bunch!

YIELD: 3 DOZEN

Vegetable oil
3 cups all-purpose flour
$\frac{1}{2}$ cup granulated sugar
2 teaspoons baking powder
$\frac{1}{2}$ teaspoon salt
1 cup milk
1 egg
4 tablespoons unsalted butter, melted
2 cups finely chopped Golden Delicious apples
$\frac{1}{4}$ cup orange juice
2 teaspoons grated orange zest
1 teaspoon pure vanilla extract
Confectioners' sugar

Pour the oil to a depth of 2 inches in a Dutch oven. Place over medium-high heat and bring the temperature to 350°F.

Meanwhile, in a mixing bowl, combine the flour, sugar, baking powder, and salt. Make a well in the center.

In a separate bowl, whisk together the milk, egg, and butter. Stir in the apples, juice, zest, and extract. Add to the flour mixture, stirring just until moistened.

Drop by rounded tablespoons in the hot oil. Fry $1\frac{1}{2}$ minutes on each side or until golden brown. Drain on paper towels and cool slightly. Sprinkle with confectioners' sugar and serve warm.

BOTANY: Apples are members of the rose family and grow on the world's oldest cultivated fruit tree. There are over seven thousand varieties in the world today and around twenty-five hundred grown in the U.S.

TEMPERATURES: Apples need cool nights and sunny days to ripen at their best.

HARVESTING: Apples need only a half twist back and forth to loosen the stem gently without causing any damage to the tree. If you pick apples from a local orchard, harvest only in the areas designated by the grower.

FREEZING: Apple cider freezes extremely well. Pour it into ice cube trays and freeze until solid. Then transfer to a freezer container. Use within nine months for best quality.

PEEL: To peel or not to peel? The answer to that question demands another question. What are you going to do with the apples? The skins are generally left on in fruit salads, but I don't want them left on in every recipe. That means it's up to you and a matter of personal preference. If you have a lot of apples to peel, hand-cranked peelers that attach to countertops are great. There are electric versions that are more expensive.

GADGETS: If you just want to core the fruit, an apple corer is an inexpensive necessity. It has a handle on one end and a cutting ring on the other end. It's fast and efficient.
If you want to wedge and core the fruit, an apple wedger performs both in a cinch. It looks like a wheel with spokes and with one push, you've accomplished both tasks.

APRICOTS

SOUTHERNERS LOVE TO SIT AROUND AND SING, PICK BANJOS AND GUITARS, PLUCK FIDDLES, and play harmonicas. It is a fun pastime and everyone is welcome to participate. If you don't have as much talent in those areas as others, you play "second fiddle" and let the others take center stage.

Have you noticed there always seems to be certain fruits that are permanently stuck in the job of second fiddle? It's not that there's anything wrong with them, but others demand the spotlight and won't let it go.

I think that's the way most people see apricots. You probably buy them dried, canned, or in the form of a jam or preserve, but when was the last time you purchased them fresh? Part of the problem is that apricots hit the market around the same time as fresh Southern peaches and nectarines. Try as they may, apricots just can't compete with those fruit divas . . . or can they?

I have made it a point over the past several years to reacquaint myself with this unique fruit when it hits the market in the summer. It has surprised me with a flavor that is very different from its cousin, the peach.

Apricots are smaller than peaches but are similar in that they have a pit. Unlike cling and semi-cling peaches, the pits of apricots are always easy to remove. In fact, I've found that the pit practically falls out of the fruit when you cut it in half.

When the season ends, I have no problem purchasing frozen or canned apricots, but my favorite form other than fresh is dried. With the moisture removed, they taste like candy and have a color similar to Southern sunsets.

Some have described apricots as a plum beneath a nectarine's coat, but I think they stand well on their own. Make your own pledge to seek them out this coming year when the fresh season begins and you'll see what I mean.

Nutrition: Apricots are a good source of vitamin C and potassium. One fresh raw apricot contains only thirty-six calories.

Selection: Apricots should have a uniform color throughout and be plump and relatively firm. They are very delicate fruits and must be handled carefully. The skin color can range from pale yellow to deep orange depending on the variety.

Storage: Keep fresh apricots in the refrigerator crisper drawer in a plastic bag with a few holes punched in it for air circulation. They are highly perishable and should be used within five days of purchase.

Yields: One pound of fresh apricots will yield about three cups of sliced fruit. Depending on the size and variety, you'll need from eight to twelve apricots to equal one pound. It takes six pounds of fresh apricots to have one pound of dried fruit.

APRICOT AND GOAT CHEESE BITES

This is one uniquely delicious appetizer thanks to the sweet apricots and tangy goat cheese. It always gets rave reviews.

YIELD: 18 APPETIZER SERVINGS

2 (15.25-ounce) cans apricot halves, drained and chopped

2 tablespoons pear or white balsamic vinegar

2 tablespoons minced onion

$1/4$ teaspoon sea salt

1 teaspoon chopped fresh thyme

32 baguette slices, cut on the diagonal

3 tablespoons walnut oil

1 cup soft goat cheese

In a medium saucepan over medium heat, combine the apricots, vinegar, onions, and salt. Cook 15 to 20 minutes, or until the mixture is thick. Stir in the thyme and set aside to cool.

Meanwhile, preheat the broiler. Brush the baguette slices with the oil. Broil 2 minutes, or until lightly browned.

To serve, spread each baguette slice with $1/2$ tablespoon of the goat cheese and $1/2$ tablespoon of the apricot mixture.

Note: The apricot mixture can be made the day ahead and refrigerated. Bring to room temperature thirty minutes before using.

APRICOT SAGE BUTTER

Excellent on pork at dinner or a toasted bagel at breakfast!

YIELD: $1/3$ CUP

4 tablespoons unsalted butter, softened

2 tablespoons apricot preserves

1 teaspoon minced fresh sage

$1/2$ teaspoon kosher salt

Combine the butter, preserves, sage, and salt. Cover and refrigerate at least 1 hour before using. Keeps up to 1 week in the refrigerator.

SWEET APRICOT NECTAR COOKIES

If you've never used apricot nectar before, you'll love how it adds extra flavor to these cookies. Look for it in the juice aisle of the supermarket. It is usually sold in cans.

YIELD: 3 DOZEN COOKIES

$2^3/4$ cups all-purpose flour

1 teaspoon baking soda

$3/4$ cup granulated sugar

$1/4$ cup packed brown sugar

$1/2$ pound (2 sticks) unsalted butter, softened

1 egg

$1/4$ cup apricot nectar

$1/2$ cup apricot preserves

$3/4$ cup dried apricots, chopped

Preheat the oven to 300°F. In a medium bowl, combine the flour and baking soda. In the bowl of an electric mixer, beat the granulated and brown sugars with the butter until fluffy.

Add the egg, nectar, and preserves, beating until smooth. Add the flour mixture and apricots, blending on low speed just until combined.

Drop by rounded tablespoons onto ungreased cookie sheets about 2 inches apart. Bake 22 to 24 minutes, or until lightly browned around the edges. Let cool on the baking sheets 5 minutes, and then transfer to wire racks to cool completely.

FRIED APRICOT FRITTERS

These fritters are beyond good. They can be served at breakfast, brunch, or dessert.

YIELD: 6 SERVINGS

2 cups all-purpose flour

Pinch of salt

2 eggs, beaten

1 cup light beer, at room temperature

2 tablespoons unsalted butter, melted

1 tablespoon plus $\frac{1}{3}$ cup Kirsch, divided

12 apricot halves, canned or fresh

Vegetable oil

2 cups crushed butter cookies or crumbled macaroons

Confectioners' sugar

In a large mixing bowl, whisk together the flour, salt, eggs, beer, butter, and 1 tablespoon of the Kirsch. Set aside for 3 hours.

One hour before preparing, drain the apricots if using canned and peel the apricots if using fresh. Place in a large zip-top plastic bag and add the remaining Kirsch. Set aside for 1 hour.

Pour the oil to a depth of 1 inch in a deep, heavy skillet. Place over medium-high heat and bring to 350°F.

Remove the fruit from the Kirsch and roll in the crumbs. Dip in the batter and carefully lower into the hot oil with tongs. Fry until golden brown on all sides, about 4 minutes. Drain on paper towels. Dust with confectioners' sugar and serve warm.

GOSPEL SINGING APRICOT BREAD

This moist, slightly sweet bread will make you give lots of thanks for the apricot harvest.

YIELD: 1 LOAF

$1\frac{1}{2}$ cups thinly sliced dried apricots

$1\frac{1}{2}$ cups water

$2\frac{1}{2}$ cups all-purpose flour

2 teaspoons baking powder

1 teaspoon baking soda

1 teaspoon salt

$\frac{1}{2}$ cup honey

2 tablespoons unsalted butter, softened

1 egg, beaten

1 teaspoon pure almond extract

$\frac{1}{2}$ teaspoon orange zest

1 cup chopped almonds

In a medium saucepan, combine the apricots and water. Place over medium-high heat and bring to a boil. Reduce the heat to low and simmer 10 minutes. Cool 15 minutes.

Meanwhile, preheat the oven to 350°F. Grease a loaf pan and set aside.

In the bowl of an electric mixer, combine the flour, baking powder, baking soda, and salt, blending well. Make a well in the center and set aside.

In a separate bowl, stir together the honey and butter. Add the egg, almond extract, and apricot mixture and then stir into the dry mixture with mixer on medium-low speed. Add the zest and almonds, mixing well.

Transfer to the prepared pan and bake $1\frac{1}{2}$ hours, or until a tester inserted in the center comes out clean. Cool 10 minutes in the pan, and then cool completely on a wire rack.

BREAD-AND-BUTTER CUSTARD

This is one of the first recipes I made on television when I moved to Nashville. It's foolproof, which is why I serve it regularly.

YIELD: 6 TO 8 SERVINGS

8 slices (½-inch thick) French bread
½ cup apricot preserves
3 tablespoons unsalted butter, softened
3 cups milk
1 cup cream
2 teaspoons orange zest
½ cup sugar
3 eggs
4 egg yolks
Confectioners' sugar

Preheat the oven to 325°F. Lightly grease a shallow 2-quart baking dish that will fit into a baking pan about 3 inches deep. Set the baking pans aside.

Arrange half of the bread slices in the prepared baking dish. Trim the slices if necessary to prevent overlapping, but it's not necessary to fill the space completely. Spread the preserves over the bread.

Arrange the remaining bread slices on top of the preserves. Spread with the butter and place the baking dish in the baking pan. Set aside.

In a heavy saucepan over medium heat, combine the milk, cream, and orange zest. Heat until bubbles form along the edge of pan, but do not allow the mixture to boil. Set aside. Bring a teakettle full of water to a boil.

In a large bowl, combine the sugar, eggs and yolks. Whisk until well blended. Gradually add the hot milk, stirring continuously until blended. Carefully pour half of the hot custard mixture around, but not over, the bread slices. Let absorb 2 minutes.

Pour the rest of the custard around the bread.

using a large spatula, press the slices down even with the top of custard and hold for a few seconds to help the bread absorb more custard.

Pour the boiling water into baking pan to reach two-thirds up the sides of the baking dish. Bake about 45 minutes, or until just set. Test by inserting a knife into the center of the custard. It should come out clean. Do not overbake.

Remove the baking dish from the water bath and cool slightly on a wire rack. Serve warm with a dusting of confectioners' sugar over the top.

"HIT THE SAUCE" APRICOT JAM

You will find oh so many uses for this jam. I dry apricots in my dehydrator and keep a jar of this in my refrigerator all summer long.

YIELD: 1½ CUPS

1 cup firmly packed chopped dried apricots
1½ cups boiling water
¼ cup dry white wine
¼ cup apricot or peach brandy
1 cup sugar
1 cinnamon stick

Place the apricots in a mixing bowl and add the boiling water. Stir in the wine and brandy, mixing well. Cover and refrigerate at least 1 hour or up to 8 hours.

Transfer the apricot mixture to a heavy saucepan and add the sugar and cinnamon. Place over high heat and bring to a boil. Reduce the heat to low and simmer, stirring occasionally, until thick, around 45 minutes. Cool, discard the cinnamon stick, and refrigerate.

ASPARAGUS

NOTHING TASTES MORE LIKE SPRING IN THE SOUTH THAN FRESH ASPARAGUS. IT HAS HAD A following throughout history like few other vegetables. Poets have sung praises to it, artists have painted it, and healers have prescribed it. I am inspired by it.

I had never seen asparagus growing until I moved to Tennessee and actually saw it first in the late summer. I was amazed that it was really asparagus because it appeared to be a cloud-like fern. When I returned to the same farm later in the fall, it had turned a beautiful golden color. I just kept saying, "This is asparagus?"

Oh what a difference a few months will make, because by March, it was a gourmet feast. I helped the grower harvest it with a sharp knife and I couldn't believe I was in the same place. It began my love affair with this perennial vegetable.

If fresh asparagus seems costly even when it is in season, remember that the grower must wait at least three years before asparagus beds are ready to yield. The taste is worth the price as far as I am concerned, since canned and frozen asparagus just can't compare.

While it takes a while to establish an asparagus bed, it doesn't waste time in the spring as it begins to nose its way out of the ground. I honestly believe you could watch it grow. With the right weather, it can grow as much as six inches in one day, causing growers to harvest spears daily during the short, but sweet season.

The tougher ends need a longer cooking time than the tender tips, especially if you purchase thick stalks. I do not own an asparagus steamer simply because I don't like one-use pots. However, if you have room in your kitchen for one, they are great for cooking asparagus. They are tall and skinny and look like holders for those really long pencils you used to win at the fair.

I accomplish the same thing by using a thick rubber band to hold the spears together and stand them in a tall pot containing a cup of boiling water.

Nutrition: Asparagus contains significant amounts of vitamins C, A, and B6 as well as thiamine and potassium. In addition, it has more folic acid per serving than any other vegetable. While high in fiber, it is low in calories, weighing in at only four calories per spear.

Selection: When buying asparagus, you will first have to decide between thick and thin because you want the spears to cook evenly. Either one is fine and a matter of personal preference rather than an indicator of quality. Select those that are nearly completely green all the way down the stalk. As the asparagus ages, you will see the whiteness at the end begin to extend further up the stalk. Then look at the tips, which should be compact. Avoid those with tips that have begun to unfurl or look like grass gone to seed.

Yields: One pound of trimmed asparagus is equivalent to two cups cut, which serves four side dishes.

COUNTRY HAM AND ASPARAGUS MINI-MUFFINS

This recipe uses just the extremely tender asparagus tips. Matching it with hearty country ham is a great combination for brunch.

YIELD: 18 MINI-MUFFINS

1 (3-ounce) package cream cheese, softened

4 tablespoons unsalted butter, softened

$^3/_4$ cup plus 1 tablespoon all-purpose flour, divided

$^1/_4$ cup plain cornmeal

$^3/_4$ cup shredded Swiss cheese

1 egg

$^1/_3$ cup cream

$^1/_2$ cup finely chopped country ham

18 (1-inch-long) fresh asparagus tips

In the bowl of an electric mixer, combine the cream cheese and butter until well blended. Stir in $^3/_4$ cup of the flour and the cornmeal. Cover and refrigerate 1 hour.

Lightly grease 18 miniature muffin cups and then preheat the oven to 425°F.

Shape the dough into 18 balls. Press evenly into the bottom and up the sides of each muffin cup. Set aside.

In a small bowl, stir together the Swiss cheese and the remaining 1 tablespoon of flour. In a separate bowl, whisk together the egg and cream. Stir in the Swiss cheese mixture and ham. Spoon evenly into the muffin cups.

Bake 7 minutes. Top each muffin with an asparagus tip. Reduce the oven temperature to 300°F. Cover with aluminum foil. Bake 17 minutes, or until set. Serve warm.

"CREAM OF THE CROP" ASPARAGUS SOUP

As many a farmer will tell you, spring comes to most parts of the South in "fits and starts." That means that while the days may warm up nicely, the evenings can stay brisk, at best. That's why I love this soup. It's warm for those remaining chilly nights, but tastes like spring!

YIELD: 6 SERVINGS

2 pounds fresh asparagus, trimmed

3 tablespoons unsalted butter

2 cups chopped onion

$1^1/_2$ teaspoons salt

3 tablespoons all-purpose flour, divided

2 cups vegetable or chicken stock

2 cups warm milk

2 teaspoons minced fresh dill

$^1/_2$ teaspoon chopped fresh tarragon

$^1/_2$ teaspoon white pepper

Remove the tips from the asparagus and set aside. Cut the spears in 1-inch pieces and set aside. Melt the butter in a large skillet over medium heat. Add the onions, asparagus spears, and salt. Sauté 9 minutes.

Reduce the heat to low and sprinkle with 2 tablespoons of the flour. Cook 2 minutes, stirring constantly. Cook another 4 minutes, stirring frequently.

Add the stock and increase the heat to medium high. Stir constantly until the mixture comes to a boil. Reduce the heat to low and simmer 5 minutes. Sprinkle with the remaining 1 tablespoon of flour and cook another 8 minutes, stirring frequently.

Add the milk and use an immersion blender to purée the soup (or cool and purée in a regular blender). Add the dill, tarragon, and pepper. Stir in the reserved asparagus tips and heat another 2 minutes. Serve immediately in warm soup bowls.

FRIED "SPEAR-IT" STICKS

Asparagus is not immune from getting battered and fried. These spears are unforgettable!

YIELD: 6 SERVINGS

1 egg, lightly beaten
1 tablespoon cold water
$\frac{1}{2}$ cup dry seasoned breadcrumbs
$\frac{1}{4}$ cup shredded Parmesan cheese
1 teaspoon paprika
1 pound cooked fresh asparagus
Vegetable oil for frying

In a shallow bowl, whisk together the egg and water. In a separate shallow dish, combine the breadcrumbs, cheese, and paprika. Dip the asparagus in the egg mixture and then dredge in the crumbs. Place on a wax paper-lined baking sheet and refrigerate 1 hour.

Pour the oil in a large skillet to a depth of $\frac{1}{2}$ inch. Place over medium-high heat and fry the spears until golden brown, turning as necessary, about 3 minutes. Drain on paper towels and serve warm.

GRILLED ASPARAGUS

Spring has arrived and it's time to dust off the grill. The theme is green for your dinner side dish and your decoration backdrop of spring trees, emerging herbs, and lush lawn grass.

YIELD: 4 SERVINGS

1 pound fresh asparagus, trimmed
3 tablespoons olive oil
$\frac{1}{4}$ cup lemon juice
$\frac{1}{2}$ teaspoon seasoned salt
$\frac{1}{4}$ teaspoon black pepper

Preheat the grill to medium-high heat (375°F). Drizzle the asparagus with the oil. Grill, covered, for 2 minutes on each side, or until crisp-tender.

While the asparagus is grilling, combine the juice, salt, and pepper in a small bowl. When the asparagus is done, drizzle with the juice mixture. Serve immediately or cover and refrigerate at least 2 hours before serving.

"HUG YOUR SOUL" ASPARAGUS CASSEROLE

Fresh asparagus is served warm, tender, and wrapped in a creamy Parmesan sauce in this casserole. What a tasty way to add vegetables to your dinner menu!

YIELD: 10 SERVINGS

3 pounds fresh asparagus, trimmed
4 tablespoons unsalted butter, divided
2 tablespoons all-purpose flour
$1\frac{1}{2}$ cups milk
$\frac{3}{4}$ cup shredded Parmesan cheese, divided
$\frac{1}{4}$ teaspoon seasoned salt
$\frac{2}{3}$ cup soft breadcrumbs
$\frac{1}{4}$ teaspoon paprika

Place a large saucepan of water over medium-high heat and bring to a boil. Add the asparagus and cook 3 minutes.

Meanwhile, preheat the oven to 350°F and lightly grease a 13 x 9-inch baking dish. Drain the asparagus and arrange evenly in the prepared dish. Set aside.

Melt 3 tablespoons of the butter in the same saucepan over medium heat. Whisk in the flour until smooth. Cook 1 minute, whisking constantly.

Gradually add the milk. Whisk constantly until

thick and bubbly, about 4 minutes. Stir in $\frac{1}{2}$ cup of the cheese and the salt. Blend well. Pour over the asparagus and set aside.

Melt the remaining tablespoon of butter and combine with the remaining $\frac{1}{4}$ cup of cheese, the breadcrumbs, and paprika. Sprinkle evenly over the casserole. Bake 25 to 30 minutes, or until bubbly. Serve warm.

LEMON BUTTER ASPARAGUS

This recipe is incredibly simple and the best!

YIELD: 2 SERVINGS

$\frac{1}{2}$ pound fresh asparagus, trimmed

2 tablespoons unsalted butter, cubed

1 tablespoon dry white wine

1 tablespoon fresh lemon juice

1 teaspoon grated lemon zest

$\frac{1}{4}$ teaspoon kosher salt

Place the asparagus in a microwave-safe dish. Dot with the butter and drizzle with the wine and lemon juice. Sprinkle evenly with the zest and salt.

Cover loosely and microwave on high 3 minutes, or until the asparagus turns bright green. Let stand 5 minutes before serving.

> "I stick to asparagus which still seems to inspire gentle thought."
>
> —CHARLES LAMB

MARINATED FRESH ASPARAGUS

This recipe is a revelation. The meatiness of this vegetable is accented by the tangy marinade that somehow manages to be strong and subtle at the same time.

YIELD: 6 SERVINGS

$1\frac{1}{2}$ pounds fresh asparagus, trimmed

1 yellow or orange bell pepper, seeded and chopped

1 bunch green onions, chopped

1 celery stalk, finely chopped

$\frac{3}{4}$ cup canola oil

$\frac{1}{2}$ cup red wine vinegar

$\frac{1}{2}$ cup sugar

1 garlic clove, minced

$\frac{1}{4}$ teaspoon paprika

Bring a large pot of water to a boil over high heat. Add the asparagus, cover, and cook 6 minutes, or until crisp-tender. Drain well. Place in a single layer in a 13 x 9-inch baking dish.

In a large jar with a tight-fitting lid, combine the peppers, onions, celery, oil, vinegar, sugar, garlic, and paprika. Shake well to emulsify. Pour over the asparagus, cover and refrigerate at least 4 hours. Drain and serve at room temperature.

Celebration
May is National Asparagus Month.

STEAMED ASPARAGUS WITH PEPPER-WALNUT SAUCE

Purists will love the way asparagus is served here. The sauce gives its simple flavor a layer of complexity and a little extra finesse.

YIELD: 4 SERVINGS

$\frac{1}{4}$ teaspoon salt

$\frac{1}{2}$ pound fresh asparagus, trimmed

2 tablespoons walnut oil

$\frac{1}{2}$ cup chopped roasted red bell peppers

$\frac{1}{4}$ cup chopped walnuts

1 garlic clove, minced

$\frac{1}{4}$ teaspoon black pepper

In a large skillet over medium-high heat, bring $\frac{1}{2}$ inch of water to a boil. Add the salt and lay the asparagus in the water. Cook 2 to 3 minutes, or until the asparagus is bright green. Drain promptly and place in a single layer in a serving dish.

Add the oil to a dry skillet over medium heat. When hot, add the peppers, walnuts, and garlic. Cook 2 minutes, or until thoroughly heated. Sprinkle with the black pepper. Spoon over the asparagus and serve immediately.

BOTANY: Asparagus is a member of the lily family and a distant relative to onions, leeks, garlic, tulips, and gladioli. It first earned fame as a medicine believed to have the power to cure toothaches, heart trouble, and dropsy. It was a regular treatment to take the pain out of bee stings. Then someone discovered it was good to eat (probably someone using it to cure a toothache!) and the rest is history.

ORIGIN: The exact origin of asparagus is unknown because it grows wild in so many places. However, many food historians believe it is a native of the eastern area around the Mediterranean Sea.

VARIETIES: There are more than one hundred fifty varieties of asparagus growing throughout the world. The most common color is green, followed by purple, and lastly white. White asparagus is simply asparagus that has not been allowed to have sunlight. Once a bed is established, it can remain productive for more than thirty years.

NAME: Ancient Greeks are responsible for the name "aspharagos," which means "sprout" or "shoot."

PRESERVING: Asparagus lends itself to many popular preservation methods. It can be frozen, dried, pickled, and canned. Before freezing, it must be water blanched. Small, thin spears need to only be blanched two minutes. Thicker, large stalks require four minutes. Add a minute to each amount of time if you are steam blanching.

BACON

ALL I HAVE TO DO TO GET MY HUSBAND INTO THE KITCHEN IN A HURRY IS FRY BACON. THE heady aroma of it sizzling away in the skillet is better than any dinner bell ever made. It works every time no matter what time of day. I can hardly get it to the table without him grabbing a slice. Bacon is a man magnet.

Maybe you save this salty goodie as a breakfast regular on the weekends. Perhaps you enjoy it occasionally on a burger, between layers of melted cheese in a sandwich, or sprinkled on a salad. No matter how you use it, you might notice that bacon is in the midst of a revival thanks to its enormous versatility and unmatched flavor.

Southerners have been craving these crispy strips for decades because it simply tastes good. It began to be popular here much the same way as country ham. Years ago, cured and smoked bacon was one of the few meats available after "hog killing time" occurred and fresh meats were no longer available.

It remains popular because bacon enhances everything it touches, making it more than a guilty pleasure. It makes us salivate and feel hungry for it even if we are full. Add to it the wonderful drippings that are leftover in the pan and you've got the basis for any recipe popular south of the Mason-Dixon line.

My mother used to save the rendered fat or bacon drippings in a stainless steel can labeled "drippings." My grandmother saved them in an old coffee can. Because we used the drippings in practically everything we made, they never lasted long. Today, I keep drippings in my refrigerator because I don't use them quite as frequently. Both the bacon and drippings are absolutely essential to true Southern cooking and should be more than a breakfast stand-by.

Frying: To pan fry bacon correctly, you must not overcrowd the pan. Bacon that overlaps will not cook evenly. Once the strips are in the skillet, place it over medium heat. If you are using cast iron, there is no need to move the bacon to different places around the pan as it cooks because cast iron doesn't have hot spots. Turn the bacon regularly and use a splatter guard to keep the mess at bay.

Selection: When shopping for bacon, flip the package over and look at the product through the package window opening. For the best flavor, the bacon should have an equal distribution of fat to lean. If the lean portions are distributed throughout the slices, it will tend to be crispy when cooked. If it is concentrated in fewer, but larger sections, it will tend to be chewy when cooked. Select according to your taste.

Storage: Bacon needs to remain refrigerated and used within eight days of opening. It freezes beautifully if you end up with more bacon than you can use within that time frame. Use frozen bacon within a month for best quality.

BACON CHEESE DIP

The combination of cheese, pepper jelly, and salty bacon is a winner!

YIELD: 8 SERVINGS

1 (8-ounce) package cream cheese, softened

1 cup grated raclette or sharp Cheddar cheese

$\frac{1}{2}$ cup mayonnaise

2 green onions, chopped

$\frac{1}{2}$ cup pepper jelly, melted

7 buttery crackers, crushed

8 bacon slices, cooked and crumbled

Preheat the oven to 350°F. Lightly grease an 8-inch square baking dish and set aside.

In the bowl of an electric mixer, combine the cream cheese, raclette, mayonnaise, onions, and jelly. Transfer to the prepared baking dish.

Top with the crushed crackers and crumbled bacon. Bake 15 minutes. Serve warm with crackers. **Note:** This recipe can easily be doubled.

BACON-WRAPPED BRUSSELS SPROUTS

If you think you don't like Brussels sprouts, this recipe will change your mind. Use the same recipe for wrapping chicken livers, fresh pineapple, water chestnuts, scallops, fresh figs, or shrimp.

YIELD: 8 APPETIZER SERVINGS

10 peppered bacon slices

2 tablespoons soy sauce

10 Brussels sprouts, cut in half lengthwise

Preheat the oven to 400°F. Lightly grease a wire rack and place over a baking sheet. Set aside.

Place 5 bacon slices between paper towels. Microwave on high power 1$\frac{1}{2}$ minutes. Repeat with the remaining bacon. Cut the slices in half crosswise.

Sprinkle the cut sides of the Brussels sprouts evenly with the soy sauce. Wrap a bacon slice around each sprout half, securing with a wooden pick. Place on the wire rack with the cut side up. Bake 20 to 25 minutes, or until the sprouts are tender. Serve warm.

"BRING HOME THE BACON" TOMATOES

One bite and these appetizers will fly off your party tray. It's a version of the famous BLT sandwich that is stuffed in a tomato shell.

YIELD: 6 TO 8 SERVINGS

15 large cherry tomatoes (not grape tomatoes)

$\frac{1}{4}$ teaspoon garlic salt

8 bacon slices

2 tablespoons thinly sliced green onions, white parts only

2 tablespoons dry plain breadcrumbs

$\frac{1}{4}$ cup finely chopped iceberg lettuce

3 tablespoons mayonnaise

$\frac{1}{8}$ teaspoon black pepper

Cut a thin slice off the bottom of each tomato so it will sit level. Cut a $\frac{1}{4}$-inch slice from the stem end of each tomato. With a melon baller or a small spoon, scoop out the seeds and pulp and discard.

Sprinkle the inside of each tomato lightly with the salt. Invert on layers of paper towels to drain. Let drain 15 minutes.

Meanwhile, in a large skillet over medium heat, fry the bacon until crisp, around 8 minutes. Drain on paper towels and crumble when cool enough to handle.

In a medium bowl, combine the onions, bread-crumbs, lettuce, mayonnaise, and pepper. Stir in the bacon crumbles. Spoon the mixture into the tomatoes. Refrigerate until ready to serve.

....

BROWN SUGAR–PEPPERED BACON

Brunch is smiling over this recipe. So is your revamped BLT because this is so totally irresistible that you will use it everywhere.

YIELD: 12 SERVINGS

1 pound thick sliced peppered bacon
1 tablespoon black pepper
1½ cups packed brown sugar

Preheat the oven to 425°F. Line a broiler pan with foil and arrange the bacon in a single layer in the pan.

Sprinkle the bacon slices evenly with the pepper. Evenly cover with the sugar. Bake 25 minutes, or until the bacon has reached your desired degree of doneness. Let stand 3 minutes on a wire rack to set the sugar before serving or using.

....

HALF-TIME BACON PINWHEELS

Don't pop these in the oven until the second quarter of the televised game is half over or you'll have kitchen chaos on your hands. These really score!

YIELD: 3 DOZEN PINWHEELS

8 bacon slices, cooked and crumbled

1 (4-ounce) can mushroom stems and pieces, drained and chopped
¼ cup mayonnaise
¼ teaspoon garlic powder
¼ teaspoon onion powder
¼ teaspoon white pepper
1 (8-ounce) can refrigerated crescent rolls
1 (8-ounce) package cream cheese, softened

Preheat the oven to 375°F. Lightly grease a baking sheet and set aside.

In a medium bowl, combine the bacon, mushrooms, mayonnaise, garlic powder, onion powder, and pepper. Blend well and set aside.

Separate the crescent dough into 4 rectangles on a hard surface. Press the perforations to seal. Spread one-fourth of the cream cheese over each rectangle, leaving a ¼-inch margin on one of the long sides.

Spread one-fourth of the bacon mixture over the cream cheese. Tightly roll jelly-roll style beginning at the long side without the margin. Pinch the edges to seal. Repeat with the remaining dough.

Cut the rolls into ½-inch slices and place the cut side down on the prepared pan. Bake 9 minutes, or until lightly browned. Serve warm or at room temperature.

....

KENTUCKY BABY HOT BROWNS

Hot browns are steeped in Kentucky Derby tradition. This is an appetizer version of the famous dish and perfect after sipping mint juleps.

YIELD: 24 APPETIZERS

24 party bread slices (pumpernickel or rye)
3 tablespoons unsalted butter

3 tablespoons all-purpose flour

1/2 cup shredded sharp Cheddar cheese

1 cup milk

1 1/2 cups diced cooked turkey

1/4 teaspoon seasoned salt

1/4 teaspoon red pepper

1/2 cup shredded Parmesan cheese

8 bacon slices, cooked and crumbled

Preheat the oven to 500°F. Arrange the bread on a lightly greased baking sheet. Bake 3 minutes.

Melt the butter in a large saucepan over medium heat. Whisk in the flour and cook, stirring constantly, about 1 minute, or until smooth.

Stir in the Cheddar and whisk until melted. Gradually whisk in the milk and increase the heat to medium. Whisk constantly for 3 minutes. Stir in the turkey, salt, and pepper and spoon evenly over the bread slices. Sprinkle the tops evenly with the Parmesan and crumbled bacon. Bake 2 minutes, or until golden brown. Serve warm.

PARMESAN BACON STICKS

These yummy sticks take a while to slowly bake in the oven, but the time is worth it.

YIELD: 15 APPETIZER SERVINGS

1 pound bacon, cut in half lengthwise

1 (4-ounce) package hard bread sticks, about 30

1/2 cup shredded Parmesan cheese

Preheat the oven to 250°F. Wrap the bacon strips around the bread sticks. Place on an ungreased jelly-roll pan so that none of the sticks are touching. Sprinkle evenly with the cheese. Bake 90 minutes. Drain on paper towels. Serve immediately or at room temperature.

"RISE AND DINE" BACON MONKEY BREAD

This pull-apart bread is very popular in the South for celebratory brunches, weekend breakfasts, and Christmas morning. This one is easy to prepare thanks to refrigerated biscuit dough.

YIELD: 12 TO 15 SERVINGS

1 pound bacon, cooked and crumbled

1/2 cup shredded Parmesan cheese

1 white onion, peeled and chopped

2 tablespoons chopped fresh parsley

3 (10-ounce) cans refrigerated buttermilk biscuit dough

1/4 pound (1 stick) unsalted butter, melted

Preheat the oven to 350°F. Lightly grease a 10-inch tube or Bundt pan and set aside.

In a small bowl, combine the bacon, cheese, onions, and parsley. Set aside.

Cut the biscuits in 4 wedges and dip each piece in the butter. Layer one-third in the prepared pan. Sprinkle with half of the bacon mixture. Repeat the process, ending with the biscuits.

Bake 40 minutes, or until golden brown. Cool in the pan on a wire rack 10 minutes. Invert onto a serving platter and serve immediately.

"SERVE IT ON THE SIDE" BACON CUPS

Every now and then, you crave something different for brunch or breakfast and nothing is better than bacon and cheese.

YIELD: 12 CUPS

3 tablespoons unsalted butter

3 tablespoons all-purpose flour

¾ cup milk

¾ cup shredded sharp Cheddar cheese

1 tablespoon Dijon mustard

6 bacon slices, cooked and crumbled

4 eggs, separated

Preheat the oven to 350°F. Lightly grease a 12-cup muffin pan and set aside.

In a medium saucepan over medium heat, melt the butter. Stir in the flour and cook 1 minute. Gradually add the milk, stirring until well blended. Cook and stir constantly until the mixture comes to a boil. Immediately remove from the heat and add the cheese, mustard, and bacon. Stir until the cheese completely melts. Set aside to cool 5 minutes.

Meanwhile, beat the egg whites at high speed of an electric mixer until stiff, about 5 minutes.

Add the egg yolks, one at a time, to the bacon mixture. Gently fold in the egg whites.

Spoon evenly into the prepared muffin cups. Bake 25 minutes, or until puffed and set. Serve warm.

SIZZLING BACON TWISTS

Serve these twisted strips as an accompaniment with green salads or soup. They can be made ahead of time if you can keep everyone out of the batch!

YIELD: 8 TO 10 SERVINGS

1 pound bacon

¼ cup ground pecans

Preheat the oven to 375°F and place the rack in the upper third of the oven.

Meanwhile, cover one side of each bacon slice with the ground pecans. Twist each slice into a tight spiral. Arrange the twists on the rack of a broiler pan and press the ends onto the pan. Make sure the twists do not touch. Some will unravel a bit as they cook. Sprinkle any remaining pecans over the top.

Bake 30 minutes or until the bacon is done. Drain on paper towels and serve warm or at room temperature.

TAILGATE BACON DIP

Southerners are great at tailgating. We don't just tailgate at football games, but during baseball season as well. That means we are always looking for good food that packs and travels well but is delicious enough so no leftovers have to be packed and carried back home. This dip fills the bill nicely.

YIELD: 1 ½ CUPS

8 bacon slices

1 (8-ounce) container sour cream

1 green onion, sliced

1 tablespoon minced fresh parsley

2 teaspoons prepared horseradish

1 teaspoon Worcestershire sauce

¼ teaspoon black pepper

In a large skillet over medium heat, fry the bacon until crisp, around 8 minutes. Drain on paper towels and crumble when cool enough to handle.

Meanwhile, stir together the sour cream, onions, parsley, horseradish, Worcestershire, and pepper until well blended. Add the bacon, cover, and refrigerate at least 2 hours before serving. Serve with pretzel chips or crackers.

BANANAS

GROWING UP, WE REGULARLY FEASTED ON A LUNCH OF SLICED BANANAS ON WHITE BREAD slathered with mayonnaise. Ok, perhaps it doesn't sound nearly as good as it tastes, but don't knock it until you've tried it!

It was a special occasion indeed when a banana pudding was served and we gobbled it up like there was no tomorrow. A banana split was quite literally something beyond our wildest childhood dreams. Banana slices were put on our breakfast corn flakes and every now and then we ate them whole and frozen when it was blistering hot outside.

The same story of banana feasting could be said for nearly every Southern household, but it was Elvis who brought it to center stage with his love of peanut butter and banana sandwiches. This wasn't just peanut butter with sliced bananas on it. In true Southern style it had the outside slices smeared in butter and then grilled. You just have to try it!

Bananas remain one of the South's most popular fruits, looking like rays of sunshine and packaged in a great disposable container. Typically, I use more bananas in the winter months. They seem more obvious when there are fewer seasonal fresh fruits available, but you'll rarely find supplies dwindle on the market.

Ask a couple of people when bananas are ready to eat and you'll probably get a couple of different answers. Some like them with just a hint of green, while others want them to be only mellow and yellow.

I tend to lean to the dark side, preferring those that are beautifully mottled and speckled with brown sugar spots. And just when bananas appear as if they have just about had it, I start tying apron strings, greasing pans, and dusting flour. That's when most of the starch reserves have converted to sugar, the consistency is creamy and soft, and they are perfect for use in loads of desserts and breads.

Nutrition: Potassium is the main nutritional punch you receive from bananas because our bodies store only a small reserve. An average banana contains around ninety-five calories and is a good source of dietary fiber, vitamin C, and iron.

Selection: Look for plump, firm bananas that are free of obvious bruises. Bananas are harvested while still immature and "green" so they can withstand shipping.

Storage: Room temperature storage is what bananas like best. If you purchase them in plastic produce bags, remove them from the bag, which inhibits breathing. Normally, the outer skin will turn from yellowish green to a full yellow color to yellow with brown dots. You can store overripe ones in the refrigerator until you are ready to use them, if necessary. The outer peel will darken, but who eats the peel? The flesh will be fine.

ALL-SEASON BANANA BREAD

Who doesn't enjoy a moist quick bread that can be in the oven baking in a snap? Toasted and buttered slices for breakfast will begin any day perfectly.

YIELD: 1 LOAF

1½ cups all-purpose flour

1 cup plus 2 tablespoons granulated sugar, divided

2 teaspoons ground cinnamon, divided

1 teaspoon baking soda

½ teaspoon salt

1 cup mashed ripe bananas (3 medium)

2 eggs

½ cup vegetable oil

¼ cup honey

¼ cup water

2½ tablespoons packed brown sugar

Preheat the oven to 350°F. Lightly grease and flour a loaf pan and set aside.

In a medium bowl, combine the flour, 1 cup of the granulated sugar, 1 teaspoon of the cinnamon, the baking soda, and salt. Set aside.

In the bowl of an electric mixer, combine the bananas, eggs, oil, honey, and water until smooth. Add the flour mixture and stir to blend. Transfer to the prepared pan.

In a small bowl, combine the remaining 2 tablespoons sugar, the remaining 1 teaspoon cinnamon, and the brown sugar. Sprinkle evenly over the batter.

Bake 55 to 60 minutes, or until a tester inserted in the center comes out clean. Cool in the pan 30 minutes. Turn the pan on its side and slide out the bread, being careful not to dislodge the topping. Turn the bread right side up to cool completely on a wire rack before slicing and serving.

BANANA PUDDIN' PIE

When Southerners find something they like, as in Banana Pudding, they find creative ways to serve it in different forms.

YIELD: 8 TO 10 SERVINGS

½ cup sugar

2 tablespoons all-purpose flour

2 teaspoons cornstarch

¼ teaspoon salt

3 cups milk

4 egg yolks

8 tablespoons unsalted butter, divided

1 tablespoon dark rum

7 whole graham crackers, finely crushed

18 vanilla wafer cookies

6 bananas, peeled and cut into ¼-inch slices, divided

Whipped cream

In a heavy saucepan, whisk together the sugar, flour, cornstarch, and salt. Over medium-high heat, gradually whisk in the milk and yolks. Continue stirring 7 minutes. Bring to a boil for 1 minute, stirring constantly.

Remove from heat and stir in 4 tablespoons of the butter and the rum. Stir until the butter has completely melted. Transfer to a bowl and press plastic wrap on the surface to prevent a skin from forming. Refrigerate at least 4 hours.

Melt the remaining 4 tablespoons of butter. Combine the crushed graham crackers and melted butter until moist crumbs form. Press into the bottom of a 9-inch pie pan. Arrange the cookies with the rounded side out around the sides of the dish to form the outer crust. Set aside.

Spread 1 cup of the pudding mixture over the bottom of the crust. Place half of the banana slices over the pudding in overlapping circles. Cover the bananas with the remaining pudding mixture. Cover and refrigerate.

When ready to serve, place the remaining banana slices on top of the pie and cover with whipped cream. Serve cold.

Note: This pie can be made the day ahead. Simply top with the last bananas and spread on the whipped cream at the last minute.

BANANAS FOSTER TART— SANS FLAME!

This dessert doesn't require lighting the liquor like regular Bananas Foster, but tastes just as marvelous. So if the lighting gives you a nervous stomach, this is your alternative!

YIELD: 10 SERVINGS

2 bananas, cut into $^1/_4$-inch slices

$4^1/_2$ teaspoons light rum

1 teaspoon grated orange zest

1 recipe Single Pie Pastry (page 402), baked and cooled

$^2/_3$ cup chopped pecans

$^2/_3$ cup packed brown sugar

$^1/_4$ cup cream

4 tablespoons unsalted butter

$^1/_2$ teaspoon banana extract

In a small bowl, combine the bananas and rum, tossing to coat. Sprinkle the zest on the bottom of the baked crust. Arrange the bananas in a single layer over the zest. Sprinkle with the pecans and set aside.

In a medium saucepan over medium-high heat, combine the brown sugar, cream, and butter. Cook 3 minutes, or until the mixture comes to a boil. Cook 4 minutes, stirring constantly, or until the

mixture has thickened and turned golden brown.

Remove from the heat and stir in the extract. Spoon the mixture over the bananas. Cool 30 minutes before serving. Serve warm or at room temperature. Store leftovers in the refrigerator.

BROWN SUGAR BANANA SCONES

What could be better on a cold winter morning than these warm scones and butter? Brown sugar and pecans are pressed into the dough just before baking, giving these delicious scones a crunchy topping.

YIELD: 12 SERVINGS

3 cups all-purpose flour

$^1/_2$ cup plus 1 tablespoon packed brown sugar, divided

2 teaspoons baking powder

$^1/_2$ teaspoon salt

$^1/_4$ teaspoon baking soda

3 tablespoons unsalted butter

$^1/_4$ cup buttermilk

1 teaspoon rum or banana extract

2 egg whites

2 bananas, mashed

$^1/_3$ cup chopped pecans

Preheat the oven to 400°F. Lightly grease a baking sheet with cooking spray and set aside.

In a medium bowl, combine the flour, $^1/_2$ cup of the brown sugar, the baking powder, salt, and baking soda. With a pastry blender or 2 forks, cut in the butter until the mixture resembles coarse meal.

In a separate bowl, combine the buttermilk, extract, and egg whites. Whisk together well. Add to the flour mixture along with mashed bananas. Stir well.

The dough will be wet and sticky, but turn onto a well-floured surface and knead lightly 5 times. Pat into a 9-inch circle on the prepared baking sheet. Sprinkle with the pecans and the remaining tablespoon of brown sugar, pressing gently into the dough.

With a sharp knife, cut the dough into 12 wedges. Cut into, but not all the way through, the dough. Bake 20 minutes, or until golden brown. Completely cut into wedges and serve warm.

CARAMEL-BANANA BREAD PUDDING

Don't have time to make a caramel sauce? No problem! Store-bought sauce makes this pudding come together in a snap.

YIELD: 8 SERVINGS

$1\frac{1}{2}$ cups caramel sauce or syrup

$\frac{1}{4}$ teaspoon sea salt

8 slices white, buttermilk, or potato sandwich bread

3 bananas, peeled and thinly sliced on the diagonal

4 eggs

$1\frac{1}{2}$ cups half-and-half

$\frac{1}{3}$ cup milk

$2\frac{1}{2}$ tablespoons sugar, divided

1 teaspoon banana or rum extract

2 tablespoons unsalted butter, melted

Preheat the broiler. Lightly grease 8 ($\frac{3}{4}$-cup) ramekins.

In a small bowl, combine the caramel sauce and sea salt. Spoon 1 generous tablespoon into each ramekin and set aside.

Place the bread on a lightly greased jelly-roll pan. Spread 1 generous tablespoon of the sauce over each bread slice. Broil 1 to 2 minutes or until the caramel is bubbly. Watch carefully to avoid burning. Cool on a wire rack.

When cool, cut each bread slice into 6 squares. Set 1 banana slice on each bread square. Arrange on the edges, side by side into prepared ramekins so it fits snugly.

In a medium bowl, whisk together the eggs, half-and-half, milk, $1\frac{1}{2}$ tablespoons of the sugar, and extract. Pour enough custard into each ramekin to reach the top. Let stand about 30 minutes, or until the bread absorbs the custard.

Meanwhile, position the rack in bottom third of the oven and preheat to 400°F. Pour the remaining custard into the ramekins. Brush the exposed bread pieces with the melted butter. Sprinkle the tops with the remaining tablespoon of sugar.

Set the ramekins in a large roasting pan. Pour enough hot water into the pan so that it comes halfway up the sides of the ramekins. Bake 45 minutes, or until a tester inserted in the center comes out clean. Remove the ramekins from the pan and cool on a wire rack. Serve warm.

Note: This can be made up to 8 hours in advance. Cover and refrigerate until ready to use. Bring to room temperature before serving.

Celebrations

February 23 is National Banana Bread Day.
March 2 is National Banana Crème Pie Day.
August 10 is National Banana Split Day.
August 27 is Banana Lover's Day.

HUMMINGBIRD CAKE

This cake showcases everything good about Southern desserts. It is rich, decadent, and as sweet as the flower nectar that attracts hummingbirds.

YIELD: 12 SERVINGS

3 cups all-purpose flour

2 cups sugar

1 teaspoon ground cinnamon

1 teaspoon baking soda

$^{1}/_{2}$ teaspoon salt

$^{3}/_{4}$ cup vegetable oil

1 (8-ounce) can crushed pineapple, undrained

1 teaspoon pure vanilla extract

$^{1}/_{2}$ teaspoon banana extract

2 cups mashed bananas

1 cup chopped pecans

Pecan Cream Cheese Frosting (page 341)

Preheat the oven to 350°F. Flour and grease 2 (9-inch) round cake pans and set aside.

Meanwhile, in a large bowl, combine the flour, sugar, cinnamon, baking soda, and salt. Blend well and set aside.

In a separate bowl, combine the oil, pineapple, vanilla extract, banana extract, bananas, and pecans. Add to the dry ingredients, mixing until well combined.

Divide the batter evenly between the prepared pans. Bake 25 to 30 minutes, or until a tester inserted in the center comes out clean.

Cool in the pan on wire racks 10 minutes. Carefully remove from the pans and cool completely. Spread the Pecan Cream Cheese Frosting in between the layers, on the sides, and top.

MORNING STAR BANANA FLAPJACKS

The term "flapjacks" goes all the way back to the 1600s with roots in South Africa. Start your day with a reminder of the Deep South with this pairing of bananas, pecans, and Buttered Rum Praline Syrup (page 339). Sprinkle extra toasted pecans over the top, if desired, before serving.

YIELD: 4 TO 6 SERVINGS

2 cups biscuit mix

1 cup buttermilk

1 cup mashed bananas

2 eggs

$^{1}/_{4}$ cup chopped pecans

Lightly grease a griddle or skillet and place over medium-high heat.

Meanwhile, in a large bowl, combine the biscuit mix, buttermilk, bananas, eggs, and pecans. Stir just until moistened.

Using a $^{1}/_{4}$ cup measure, pour the batter on the griddle. Cook until the tops are covered with bubbles and the edges look dry, about 2 minutes. Flip and cook until golden brown, about 1 minute longer. Repeat with the remaining batter. Serve warm with Buttered Rum Praline Syrup.

SPEEDING UP RIPENING: If you simply can't wait for the bananas to ripen on their own, you can speed up the process. Place the bananas in a brown paper bag along with either a tomato or an apple. Loosely close the bag and let stand at room temperature overnight. Rather than pulling a banana from the bunch, it's best to cut it off with a sharp knife. Even the slightest squeeze can cause a nasty bruise.

NEW ORLEANS BANANAS FOSTER

Thank Brennan's Restaurant for this dessert luxury named for Richard Foster, a faithful patron. I was very nervous the first time I made this thanks to the flambéing, but it's not as hard as it may seem. Just make sure you tilt the pan away from you and constantly swirl it for the best results.

YIELD: 4 SERVINGS

3 tablespoons unsalted butter

¾ cup packed brown sugar

3 tablespoons banana liqueur

¼ teaspoon ground cinnamon

4 bananas, peeled, cut in half lengthwise and cut in half crosswise

3 tablespoons dark rum

Vanilla ice cream

Place a large heavy skillet over medium heat and add the butter. Stir in the brown sugar, liqueur, and cinnamon. Stir constantly until the sugar dissolves, about 3 minutes.

Place the bananas in the sugar mixture cut side down. Cook until soft and slightly brown, about 4 minutes. Add the rum, but do not stir. Heat 2 minutes.

Carefully, light the sauce while tilting the pan. Swirl the pan until the flames die out, about 2 minutes.

Place a scoop of ice cream in 4 serving bowls. Place 2 banana slices on each scoop. Evenly distribute the warm sauce over the bananas. Serve immediately.

SOUTHERN CHARM BANANA PUDDING

You'll see many shortcut versions of this cool Southern dessert, but the extra time spent on this one will be noticed, tasted, and appreciated immediately.

YIELD: 8 SERVINGS

3½ tablespoons all-purpose flour

1¾ cups sugar, divided

Dash of salt

3 eggs, separated

3 cups milk

2 teaspoons pure vanilla extract, divided

1 (12-ounce) package vanilla wafers

6 bananas

In a heavy saucepan over medium heat, combine the flour, 1⅓ cups of the sugar, salt, egg yolks, and milk. Cook around 10 minutes, stirring constantly until smooth and thick. Stir in 1 teaspoon of the extract and set aside.

Preheat the oven to 325°F.

Layer one-third of the wafers in a 3-quart baking dish. Slice 2 bananas and layer over the wafers. Pour one-third of the custard over the bananas. Repeat twice.

Beat the egg whites at high speed of an electric mixer until foamy. Gradually add the remaining sugar a tablespoon at a time. Beat until stiff peaks form. Blend in the remaining extract. Spread over the custard, sealing to the edge. Bake 25 to 30 minutes, or until golden brown.

Note: This recipe can be made without the meringue if you want. You can also make just the pudding portion, if desired.

BETTER BANANA CREAM PIE

Meringue is such a wonderful thing. It can't be piled on enough for me. There are times when I double the meringue ingredients just to make it sky high. This creamy, rich pie is a great way to end any meal.

YIELD: 8 SERVINGS

2 cups milk

1 cup sugar, divided

Dash of salt

$\frac{1}{4}$ cup cornstarch

3 eggs, separated

1 cup half-and-half

2 tablespoons unsalted butter

1 teaspoon pure vanilla extract

$\frac{1}{2}$ teaspoon banana extract, divided

1 recipe Single Pie Pastry (page 402), baked and cooled

2 bananas, peeled and thinly sliced

$\frac{1}{4}$ teaspoon cream of tartar

Place the milk in a small saucepan over medium-high heat.

In a separate saucepan, combine $\frac{2}{3}$ cup of the sugar, the salt, cornstarch, egg yolks, and half-and-half. Place over medium heat.

When the milk begins to form bubbles around the edges, around 5 minutes, pour into the sugar mixture, whisking until smooth. Continue to whisk constantly another 5 to 7 minutes, or until the mixture is thick.

Remove from the heat and add the butter, vanilla extract, and $\frac{1}{4}$ teaspoon of the banana extract. Stir well to blend. Pour one-third into the pastry shell. Layer half of the banana slices on top. Repeat and pour the remaining custard on top. Set aside.

Preheat the oven to 350°F.

Beat the egg whites and cream of tartar on high speed of an electric mixer until foamy. Gradually add the remaining sugar, 1 tablespoon at a time. Fold in the remaining banana extract. Spread over the top of the pie, sealing to the edge.

Bake 12 to 15 minutes, or until golden brown. Cool completely on a wire rack before serving.

BOTANY: Bananas do not grow on trees, as commonly believed, but rather on rapidly sprouting fibrous plants that are actually giant perennial herbs of the lily family. Banana plants love weather that is hot and humid. They will take at least a couple of years to produce the first crop. Flowers of the banana plant are purple and beautifully exotic. The so-called "trunk" of the banana plant is not made of wood but is a soft stalk composed of leaves growing very closely together and one inside another. As a result, the stalks can be quite weak, due to being around 85 percent water. The plants reach heights of up to thirty feet, making it the tallest plant on earth that doesn't have a tough, woody stem.

ORIGIN: Bananas are believed to have originated in the Malaysian jungles of Southeast Asia. Their history can be traced all the way back to Alexander the Great's conquest of India, where he first discovered the fruit in 327 BC.

FRUIT: Banana plants produce one bunch of bananas about every fifteen months. Each bunch is composed of close to a dozen "hands," with each having around eighteen "fingers" or what we know as the actual banana. On the tree, bananas appear to be growing upside down from how we would normally expect them to grow.

BARBECUE

BARBECUE HAS A FOOD CULTURE AND FOLLOWING ALL ITS OWN. THERE ARE AFICIONADOS who will only use certain meat cuts, dry rubs, and sauces. It generally takes them all day or longer to get the job done and they take their barbecuing very seriously. The necessary tongs, brushes, thermometers, and equipment are close to a bevy of smokers, grills, and cookers. It requires patience, careful attention, and a watchful and educated eye, nose, and touch for the proper doneness of the food. When it's done, the meal is a feast.

There are others who will throw practically anything on the grill and cover it with whatever store-bought sauce is in the refrigerator. Their concoctions can be done in the time it would take a reasonable person to drink a couple of beers. They generally have one rule: Grill it, don't kill it! Oh, when it's done, the meal is a feast.

Then you get into barbecue sauce and the extremes are just as pronounced. There are competitions galore throughout the South to showcase who is best. The debate is just as vigorous as you see with rival football teams, if not more so. Go east to the Carolinas and you have vinegar-based sauces. Head west to Texas and the sauces are tomato based. Travel to the Mississippi River and you've got a blend of the two.

These sauces are even served differently. Carolina sauce is usually called a finishing sauce for pork, and is used after the meat is completely cooked. Texans like their beef and use barbecue sauce for basting during the cooking process. Those of us in the middle call barbecue sauce a "mopping" sauce thanks to the mop-like instrument used to put it on the meat. It all can become rather confusing.

Who has makes it best? The one you like. George can equally waiver between the barbecue types and sauces. Me? I just want the Southern sun to beam down benevolent rays, the table to be set really cute, and the sides ready to serve while I sit and enjoy the scent of it all. These recipes are a mix of quick and not so quick, as well as Carolina, Texas, and Tennessee styles. Roll up your sleeves, break out the paper napkins, and dig in!

Dry Rubs: Dry rubs are considered by many to be the most important part of the whole barbecue process. These spice mixtures are rubbed on the meat before cooking and give it a punch of taste. It's your first opportunity to add flavor to the meat you are going to cook. Don't use a lot of seasoning combinations with really strong flavors or the meat will taste overspiced. You can easily double or even triple dry rub recipes. I keep mine in a small canning jar so I'll have it ready to use at any moment.

Sauce: Many backyard barbecue enthusiasts consider the sauce the crucial element of success. It is the final and all-important sensory embellishment that will have guests licking greedily from their fingers. Typically, sauces are either tomato or vinegar based. They can be thin or thick, with the thicker ones often used as a dipping sauce. Thinner ones are great for marinating the meat or for basting while it cooks. The sauce should complement the meat, not overwhelm it.

ANOINTED BARBECUED BRISKET

Begin early in the morning. By dinnertime, you'll be a hero.

YIELD: 6 TO 8 SERVINGS

1 (6-pound) beef brisket roast, trimmed
1 tablespoon vegetable oil

Dry Rub:
$1/4$ cup paprika
2 tablespoons cayenne
2 tablespoons black pepper
2 tablespoons dried or granulated garlic

Prepare the grill on one side of a smoker and set a water pan on the other side. When the grill is hot, add pieces of hickory wood that have been soaked at least an hour in water. Bring the heat to 225°F.

Bring the roast to room temperature. Rub evenly with the oil and set aside. In a small bowl, mix the dry rub by combining the paprika, cayenne, pepper, and garlic. Rub all over the roast.

Set the roast over the water pan for indirect heat, cover, and maintain the temperature. Smoke 10 to 12 hours, or until the desired degree of doneness, checking after 8 hours. Remove from the grill and let stand 10 minutes, covered. Slice thinly against the grain and serve with Carolina Finishing Sauce (page 51).

Note: Leftovers make great sandwiches the following day.

CAROLINA BABY BACK RIBS

This is the Rolls Royce of ribs. Use your own barbecue sauce or baste with Texas Thunder Barbecue Sauce (page 53).

YIELD: 6 SERVINGS

2 sides baby back ribs

Dry Rub:
$1/4$ cup chili powder
1 tablespoon black pepper
1 tablespoon brown sugar
2 teaspoons garlic powder
1 teaspoon crushed red pepper
1 teaspoon dried thyme
1 recipe Texas Thunder Barbecue Sauce (page 53)

Place the ribs with the underside up in a large baking pan. Loosen the membrane along the end of the ribs. Grasp the membrane with a paper towel and pull the membrane off the ribs. Set aside.

In a small bowl, mix the dry rub by combining the chili powder, black pepper, brown sugar, garlic powder, red pepper, and thyme. Rub over both sides of the ribs, using all of the dry rub. Cover and refrigerate 8 hours or overnight.

Preheat the grill to medium (325°F). Place the ribs on the oiled rack with the meaty side up in the center of the grill. Cover and grill 75 minutes, or until the meat begins to shrink from the ends of the bones. Turn occasionally and baste with Texas Thunder Barbecue Sauce every 15 minutes, stopping 15 minutes before the ribs are done. Cool 5 minutes before cutting. Serve with additional sauce, if desired.

CAROLINA FINISHING SAUCE

This sauce is so named because it is used after the meat has been roasted, smoked, or grilled. It doesn't compete with the meat, but enhances the flavor beautifully.

YIELD: 1½ CUPS

½ pound (2 sticks) unsalted butter
Juice of 1 lemon
1½ tablespoons Worcestershire sauce
1 tablespoon honey
1½ teaspoons salt
1 teaspoon black pepper
½ cup cider vinegar

In a medium saucepan over medium-high heat, melt the butter. Add the lemon juice, Worcestershire, honey, salt, and pepper. Stir until the honey melts and the mixture is smooth. Remove from the heat and stir in the vinegar. Set aside to cool completely before using. Refrigerate any leftovers.

WEATHER: Estimating the exact cooking time is sometimes difficult. The times given are to be used as a guide. The rate at which meat will cook varies greatly due to the outside elements, such as if it's raining, cold, windy, humid, or hot. Low temperatures mean long cooking times, and these elements can certainly change during the process. The cooking time also depends on the diligence of the cook and the type of grill you are using. A good instant-read meat thermometer is your best friend in determining whether the meat is done and ready to enjoy.

LAWN CHAIR BARBECUED CHICKEN

Pull up a lawn chair and relax. This chicken cooks in just enough time for you to enjoy the evening weather before dinner.

YIELD: 4 TO 6 SERVINGS

1 (3-pound) whole chicken, split
½ teaspoon kosher salt
½ teaspoon black pepper
½ cup Texas Thunder Barbecue Sauce
   (page 53)
⅓ cup orange marmalade
1 teaspoon Worcestershire sauce
1 teaspoon prepared horseradish

Prepare the hot grill. Meanwhile, bring the chicken to room temperature. Sprinkle it all over with the salt and pepper.

In a small bowl, combine the barbecue sauce, marmalade, Worcestershire, and horseradish. Set aside.

Grill the chicken over the hot grill for about 10 minutes to sear and mark the outside. Baste after 5 minutes with the sauce. Move the chicken to the indirect heat side of the grill. Maintain a medium-hot temperature and cover.

Continue basting every 10 minutes until the chicken is done, around 40 to 50 minutes. The internal temperature should be 180°F. Let chicken rest 10 minutes before cutting into pieces. Serve warm.

Celebrations
May is National Barbecue Month.
July 4 is National Barbecued Spareribs Day

OVEN-ROASTED BARBECUED SPARERIBS

Spareribs are long, narrow cuts taken from the breastbone of the hog. Ask your butcher to remove the fatty brisket end. Oven roasting tenderizes these ribs beautifully. This is the way to enjoy barbecue when the weather outside is nasty.

YIELD: 6 SERVINGS

1 (4-pound) slab spareribs

1 (12-ounce) can full-flavored beer

1/4 cup soy sauce

2 tablespoons brown sugar

2 tablespoons lemon juice

2 tablespoons chili sauce

2 tablespoons ketchup

1/2 teaspoon onion or garlic salt

1/2 teaspoon black pepper

1 recipe Texas Thunder Barbecue Sauce (page 53)

Place the ribs in a shallow dish. In a mixing bowl, combine the beer, soy sauce, brown sugar, lemon juice, chili sauce, ketchup, onion salt, and pepper. Blend well and pour over the ribs. Cover and refrigerate 8 hours or overnight.

Place the oven rack in the middle and bottom of the oven. Preheat the oven to 350°F. Line a jelly-roll pan with aluminum foil. Lightly grease a wire rack and place in the jelly-roll pan.

Remove the ribs from the marinade and place meaty side up on the prepared rack. Place in the center of the oven. Add 1 to 2 cups of water to the marinade dish and put on the bottom rack of the oven.

Roast 90 minutes or until the meat begins to shrink from the bone. Do not turn the ribs over. Baste with Texas Thunder Barbecue Sauce or your favorite barbecue sauce every 20 minutes. Let stand 5 minutes before slicing and serving.

TENNESSEE'S BEST BUTT

We love smoking Boston pork butts. They make the best pulled pork sandwiches. The cider and brandy basting mixture is heavenly. Cross the state line and serve it with Carolina Finishing Sauce (page 51)

YIELD: 8 SERVINGS

5 tablespoons brown sugar

1/4 cup minced onion

3 garlic cloves, minced

2 tablespoons paprika

2 tablespoons lemon pepper

1 tablespoon chili powder

1 tablespoon summer savory

2 teaspoons seasoned salt

1/4 teaspoon crushed red pepper

1/8 teaspoon ground cloves

1/8 teaspoon ground nutmeg

1 (6-pound) pork butt, trimmed

1 Golden Delicious or Granny Smith apple, cored and cut in half

3 cups apple cider

1/2 cup apple brandy

In a medium bowl, mix together the brown sugar, onion, garlic, paprika, lemon pepper, chili powder, savory, salt, red pepper, cloves, and nutmeg. Blend well and rub all over the pork. Cover and refrigerate 8 hours or overnight.

Prepare the smoker. Place the pork on a smoker rack over the filled water pan. Place the apple halves in the water pan. Cover and smoke 6 to 8 hours, turning every hour. After 2 hours, begin basting every hour with the mixture of cider and brandy. When done, the meat should register 160°F in the center. Let the meat stand, covered, at least 20 minutes before trimming away the bone and excess fat. Coarsely chop and serve.

TEXAS THUNDER BARBECUE SAUCE

There are quite literally hundreds of barbecue sauce recipes floating around, but this one is the recipe we use constantly.

YIELD: 3 CUPS

2 tablespoons unsalted butter

1 white or yellow onion, peeled and sliced

4 garlic cloves, minced

2 cups ketchup

1 cup packed brown sugar

$^3/_4$ cup cider vinegar

$^1/_2$ cup soy sauce

2 tablespoons Worcestershire sauce

2 teaspoons canola oil

1 teaspoon crushed red pepper

1 teaspoon dry mustard

$^1/_2$ teaspoon liquid smoke

Place the butter in a large skillet over medium heat. Add the onions. Cook 6 minutes, or until golden brown, stirring frequently. Transfer to a large saucepan and place over medium heat. Stir in the garlic, ketchup, brown sugar, vinegar, soy sauce, Worcestershire, oil, red pepper, dry mustard, and liquid smoke. Bring to a simmer and reduce the heat to low. Cover and simmer 30 minutes. Pour through a mesh strainer and discard the solids. Refrigerate the sauce until ready to use.
Note: Always store in the refrigerator and use within two weeks for best quality.

BURNT ENDS: The charred burnt ends of barbecue used to be plunged into the bean pot, but now the trend is to mix it in with the rest of the pulled meat. The fad started in Kansas City and has spread.

WILD WHITE MOPPING SAUCE

The first time I had this sauce, I was confused. My eyes saw something that looked like ranch dressing, but my mouth tasted barbecue! This sauce makes smoked or grilled chicken come alive. Use a mop-type brush for slathering it on the meat.

YIELD: 2 CUPS

1 cup cider vinegar

1 cup mayonnaise

1 tablespoon lemon juice

1 tablespoon black pepper

$^1/_2$ teaspoon salt

$^1/_4$ teaspoon crushed red pepper

Place the vinegar, mayonnaise, lemon juice, black pepper, salt, and red pepper in a jar with a tight-fitting lid. Cover and shake well to emulsify. Refrigerate until ready to use. Brush on any grilled meat during the last 5 minutes of cooking or bring to room temperature and serve on the side
Note: Always store in the refrigerator and use within two weeks for best quality.

DEFINITION: While some people refer to "barbecue" as grilling, Southerners define "barbecue" as food that has been slow cooked and slathered in a highly seasoned sauce. The sauce can be used to baste the meat and/or to serve along with the meat. The usual Southern side dishes to accompany barbecue are deviled eggs, potato salad, coleslaw, and baked beans. Sometimes the coleslaw is served on the barbecue if it's in the form of a sandwich.

BEANS

(BAKED AND BLACK)

FOR YEARS, BEANS WERE CALLED THE "POOR MAN'S MEAT," AND IN MANY AREAS OF THE SOUTH, that rang very true. Today, the once humble bean is on the move and perhaps finally gaining the respect it so rightfully deserves.

Lately, I've become a bean counter. Years ago, I was content to find a selection of six or seven varieties of dried and canned beans at a well-stocked supermarket. That's not the case now. Routinely, I'm finding quite literally dozens of fresh, canned, and dried beans available all over the place. Bean shopping is becoming a lot more fun!

Where these nutritional powerhouses used to regularly pop up only in my simmering stockpot, I'm now noticing that they are moving to the forefront of many Southern restaurant menus. Where we used to sentence them to service as a measly side dish, they are now trekking toward the center of the plate. There's no doubt about it ... the little bean is big.

My Home Economics roots always kick in when it comes to using beans. You will be hard pressed to find a more economical food item anywhere. I often preach that everyone should have a stash in their pantry of both canned and dried beans. They literally cost pennies on the dollar, are incredibly versatile, a cinch to prepare, satisfying, and extremely nutritious. What else could you want?

I love it that even though we love to label them as oven baked, beans were originally baked in covered clay pots stuck in holes in the ground. Those holes were lined with hot rocks and stones to cook the beans. Perhaps that noble beginning is why Southerners still love to serve this American classic outside with barbecued meat. If you aren't in the habit already, it's time to spill some beans ... in your pots, saucepans, baking dishes, kettles, and of course, oven!

Nutrition: Beans are a good source of protein, iron, phosphorous, dietary fiber, and B vitamins. That makes them an excellent choice for meatless main dishes. Dry beans are naturally low in sodium. Canned beans can have the sodium content significantly reduced by rinsing the drained beans one minute with cold water and then draining again.

Soaking: Dried beans are incredibly cheap, but have to be soaked in water to replace the moisture lost in the drying process. The secret to successful cooking is to soften the outer skins and then slowly simmer them to the desired degree of tenderness.

Traditional Soak: It's easiest to soak dry beans overnight in the refrigerator, but that requires thinking and planning ahead. Add six cups of cold water to every pound of dry beans. Let stand at room temperature eight hours or overnight. Drain, rinse, and cook the beans in fresh water.

"A HILL OF BEANS" SALAD

I didn't know it until I moved to Tennessee, but we raise a lot of soybeans in the western area of our state. I had this salad one day for lunch at the home of a soybean producer, and it has been a favorite of mine ever since. The colors are simply beautiful and it's delicious.

YIELD: 8 SERVINGS

3 cups frozen soybeans (edamame)

1 (15-ounce) can kidney beans, drained and rinsed

1 (15-ounce) can garbanzo beans (chickpeas), drained and rinsed

1 purple onion, peeled and thinly sliced

$\frac{1}{2}$ cup chopped fresh cilantro

$\frac{1}{4}$ cup olive oil

1 teaspoon grated lime zest

$\frac{1}{4}$ cup fresh lime juice

$\frac{1}{2}$ teaspoon salt

Prepare the soybeans according to the package directions. Drain and rinse with cold water. In a large mixing bowl, combine the cooked soybeans, kidney beans, garbanzo beans, onions, and cilantro.

In a small bowl, whisk together the oil, lime zest, lime juice, and salt. Pour over the beans, tossing to evenly coat. Cover and refrigerate up to 24 hours. Stir again before serving cold or at room temperature.

Yields: One cup of dried beans equals three cups cooked. One pound will give you six cups of cooked beans.

Celebrations

July is National Baked Bean Month.
January 6 is National Bean Day.
July 13 is National Beans 'n Franks Day

APPALACHIAN BAKED BEANS

Sorghum gives these beans a tangy sweetness. It will make your house smell like a spring barbecue!

YIELD: 10 SERVINGS

1 tablespoon vegetable oil

1 large white onion, peeled and chopped

1 large green bell pepper, seeded and chopped

4 garlic cloves, minced

4 (14.5-ounce) cans diced tomatoes, drained

$1\frac{1}{2}$ cups chicken stock

1 cup sorghum

3 (15.5-ounce) cans Great Northern beans, drained and rinsed

1 teaspoon black pepper

Preheat the oven to 375°F.

Place the oil in a large Dutch oven over medium-high heat. Add the onion, pepper, and garlic. Sauté 4 minutes, stirring frequently, or until tender.

Add the tomatoes, stock, sorghum, beans, and black pepper, stirring well to blend. Bake, uncovered, for 3 hours, stirring occasionally. Serve warm.

Quick Soak: If you're pressed for time, the quick soak method is for you. It takes only an hour, and by that time, you've got everything else prepped and dinner on the way. Put the dry beans in a large saucepan and cover with cold water by two inches. Place over high heat and bring to a boil. Boil two minutes, remove from the heat, and let the beans soak, covered, for one hour. Drain and they are ready to use in your recipes.

BLACK BEAN BUSTER SOUP

Black beans are sometimes called turtle beans and have a sweet flavor. The black outer skin covers a cream-colored flesh. This is my favorite black bean soup. I always enjoyed it when visiting Florida, but had a similar soup that included smoked sausage in South Georgia one year on vacation. Add smoked sausage to this dish if you like.

YIELD: 6 SERVINGS

1 tablespoon canola or vegetable oil

1 white onion, peeled and diced

2 tablespoons brown sugar

1 tablespoon chili powder

1 tablespoon ground cumin

1 teaspoon ground coriander

2 garlic cloves, minced

1 (14-ounce) can roasted diced tomatoes

1 (8-ounce) can tomato sauce

$1\frac{1}{2}$ cups chicken stock

$\frac{1}{2}$ cup orange juice

$\frac{1}{4}$ cup tomato paste

1 pound chicken tenders,
  cut into $\frac{1}{2}$-inch pieces

2 (15-ounce) cans black beans,
  drained and rinsed

$\frac{1}{2}$ teaspoon seasoned salt

Chopped fresh cilantro

Place the oil in a large Dutch oven over medium heat. Add the onions and sauté 3 minutes. Add the brown sugar, chili powder, cumin, coriander, and garlic. Cook 1 minute longer.

Stir in the tomatoes, tomato sauce, stock, orange juice, tomato paste, and chicken. Cover, reduce heat to low, and cook 2 hours. Add the beans and the salt. Cook 10 minutes longer. Serve in warmed soup bowls with a garnish of fresh cilantro.
Note: Leftovers can be frozen up to 3 months.

CAJUN RED BEANS AND RICE

Bravo to Louisiana for giving us this incredible mixture of red kidney beans, salt pork, seasonings, and rice. It was so adored by jazz great Louis Armstrong that he used to sign his letters, "Red beans and ricely yours." Kidney beans are earthy reddish brown beans that take their name from the organ they resemble.

YIELD: 8 SERVINGS

1 pound dried kidney beans

1 (1-pound) ham hock or $\frac{1}{2}$ pound salt
  pork, cubed

3 quarts water

1 large white onion, peeled and chopped

$\frac{1}{2}$ cup Worcestershire sauce

$1\frac{1}{4}$ teaspoons garlic salt

$\frac{1}{2}$ teaspoon black pepper

$\frac{1}{2}$ teaspoon crushed red pepper

3 bay leaves

1 pound smoked sausage,
  cut into $\frac{1}{4}$-inch slices (optional)

6 cups hot cooked rice

$\frac{1}{4}$ cup chopped fresh parsley

Place the beans, ham hock, and water in a large Dutch oven over medium-high heat. Bring to a boil, cover, reduce the heat to low, and simmer 2 hours, stirring occasionally.

Remove and discard the ham hock. Mash half of the cooked beans against the side of the pot with the back of a wooden spoon. Add the onions, Worcestershire, garlic salt, black pepper, red pepper, and bay leaves. If using the sausage, brown in a large skillet over medium heat 5 minutes. Drain and add to the bean mixture.

Cover and increase the heat to high. Bring to a boil, reduce the heat to medium, and cook, uncovered, 1 hour, or to the desired degree of doneness, stirring frequently. Discard the bay leaves and serve over the rice. Garnish with the parsley.

GENUINE SOUTHERN BAKED BEANS

Great Northern beans are large and creamy white with a delicate flavor. This recipe is from my mother's notebook. I have used it over and over again when I want regular baked beans with nothing fancy to distract me. It is the best!

YIELD: 10 SERVINGS

1 pound dried Great Northern beans
1 (16-ounce) can diced tomatoes
$\frac{1}{2}$ cup vegetable or chicken stock
3 white onions, peeled and chopped
$\frac{1}{2}$ pound salt pork, cubed
1 cup sugar
1 tablespoon white vinegar
1 teaspoon prepared mustard
1 teaspoon salt
$\frac{1}{4}$ teaspoon black pepper

Place the beans in a large Dutch oven over high heat. Cover with 2 inches of water and bring to a boil. Cook 2 minutes. Remove from the heat, cover, and let soak 1 hour. Drain well.

Preheat the oven to 350°F. Lightly grease a 4-quart baking dish and set aside.

Return the beans to the Dutch oven and stir in the tomatoes, stock, onions, pork, sugar, vinegar, mustard, salt, and pepper. Blend well. Transfer to the prepared baking dish. Cover and bake 4 hours or until tender. Check after 2 hours and add more stock or water if necessary. Serve hot.

HAM AND BEAN BAG SOUP

This soup uses several beans. Cannellini beans look like white kidney beans. Navy beans are also white, but very small and sometimes called pearl haricots. I like to make this soup with leftover ham from the holidays and again with leftovers from Easter. When I make it during the spring, I throw in a handful of chopped fresh spinach from my garden at the last minute.

YIELD: 8 SERVINGS

2 tablespoons canola or vegetable oil
1 large white onion, peeled and diced
1 bunch green onions, chopped
2 large carrots, peeled and chopped
2 celery stalks, diced
1 garlic clove, minced
1 tablespoon ham soup base or bouillon
$\frac{1}{2}$ teaspoon black pepper
2 cups chopped cooked ham
2 (15-ounce) cans navy beans, drained and rinsed
2 (15-ounce) cans cannellini beans, drained and rinsed
1 (15-ounce) can black beans, drained and rinsed
4 Yukon Gold potatoes, peeled and diced

Place the oil in a large Dutch oven over medium-high heat. Add the onions, green onions, carrots, celery, garlic, ham base, and pepper. Sauté 5 minutes, or until the onions are tender. Stir in the ham, navy beans, cannellini beans, black beans, and potatoes. Add enough water to cover. Bring to a boil, cover, and reduce the heat to low. Cook 45 minutes, stirring occasionally. Serve warm.

HILL COUNTRY CIDER-BAKED BEANS

This recipe is old and undoubtedly has been used for years by mountain mothers for feeding many hungry mouths. I love how the cider and sorghum team up to sweeten these beans. Pinto beans are speckled and come in various shades of red and brown. Salt pork is similar to bacon, but not smoked and contains little if any lean meat. Look for it in the meat case.

YIELD: 8 SERVINGS

3 cups dried pinto beans

3 cups apple cider

$^1\!/_2$ pound salt pork, thinly sliced

1 large yellow onion, peeled and sliced

6 tablespoons sorghum

1 tablespoon dry mustard

$^1\!/_2$ teaspoon black pepper

Place the beans in a large Dutch oven and cover with cold water by 3 inches. Cover and let stand at room temperature 8 hours or overnight.

Drain and rinse the beans. Transfer to a large heavy saucepan. Add the cider and place over medium heat. Bring to a gentle boil and cook 30 minutes. Remove from the heat and drain, reserving the cider.

Meanwhile, preheat the oven to 300°F. Layer half of the salt pork and onion slices in the bottom of a 2-quart baking dish. Spoon the beans over the top and top with the remaining onions.

In a small saucepan, combine the sorghum, mustard, and pepper. Place over medium heat and stir just until the mixture barely heats and blends. Pour evenly over the onions and beans and top with the remaining salt pork slices. Pour the reserved cider over the top and enough water to cover the beans. Cover and bake 3 hours.

Uncover and add more water if the beans seem dry. Recover and continue baking until the beans are tender, about 1$^1\!/_2$ or 2 hours. Serve hot.

ROOT OF THE MATTER BAKED BEANS

Root beer gives these beans a subtle sweet flavor that replaces the brown sugar used in many recipes.

YIELD: 6 SERVINGS

4 bacon slices

1 white onion, peeled and diced

2 (16-ounce) cans pork and beans

$^1\!/_2$ cup root beer (not diet)

$^1\!/_4$ cup hickory smoked barbecue sauce

$^1\!/_2$ teaspoon dry mustard

$^1\!/_4$ teaspoon hot sauce

Preheat the oven to 400°F. Lightly grease a 1-quart baking dish and set aside.

In a large skillet over medium heat, cook the bacon until crisp, around 8 minutes. Drain on paper towels and crumble when cool enough to handle. Set aside.

Increase the heat to medium high and sauté the onions in the drippings about 5 minutes, or until tender.

In a mixing bowl, stir together the bacon, onions, pork and beans, root beer, barbecue sauce, mustard, and hot sauce. Blend well. Transfer to the prepared dish. Bake, uncovered, 55 minutes, or until the sauce is thick and bubbly. Serve warm.

SEASIDE
BLACK BEANS AND RICE

This is South Florida's version of Louisiana's Red Beans and Rice. Yellow rice is substituted for white and black beans for red. I like to serve this with pork or fish.

YIELD: 10 SERVINGS

3 tablespoons canola or vegetable oil

1 large white onion, peeled and chopped

1 green bell pepper, seeded and chopped

2 garlic cloves, minced

3 (15-ounce) cans black beans, drained and rinsed

1 (14.5-ounce) Cajun-style stewed tomatoes, undrained and chopped

1½ cups water

1 tablespoon red wine vinegar

1 teaspoon sugar

1 teaspoon black pepper

½ teaspoon sea salt

1 (8-ounce) can tomato sauce

6 cups hot cooked yellow rice

½ cup chopped green onions

Sour cream

Place the oil in a large Dutch oven and set over medium-high heat. Sauté the onions, bell peppers, and garlic 4 minutes, or until tender, stirring frequently. Add the beans, tomatoes, water, vinegar, sugar, pepper, salt, and tomato sauce. Stir well to blend. Bring to a boil, cover, reduce heat to low, and simmer 1 hour. Uncover and simmer 20 minutes longer, stirring occasionally.

Serve hot over yellow rice. Top each serving with green onions and a dollop of sour cream.

TENNESSEE
THREE-BEAN CASSEROLE

When our friend Tom Harper told us about this casserole, I thought it sounded dreadful. But thankfully, he simply insisted that we give it a try. We did and we love it! Leftovers freeze well.

YIELD: 8 SERVINGS

4 bacon slices

½ pound ground beef

½ white onion, peeled and chopped

1 (15-ounce) can pork and beans

1 (15-ounce) can kidney beans, drained and rinsed

1 (15-ounce) can baby lima beans, drained and rinsed

⅓ cup packed light brown sugar

⅓ cup ketchup

3 tablespoons barbecue sauce

Preheat oven to 350°F. Lightly grease a 2 quart baking dish and set aside.

In a large skillet over medium heat, fry the bacon until crisp, about 8 minutes. Drain on paper towels and crumble when cool enough to handle. Set aside.

Meanwhile, brown the beef and onions in the pan drippings. Cook until no pink remains in the beef, around 9 minutes. Drain well. In a large mixing bowl, combine the beef mixture, pork and beans, kidney beans, lima beans, brown sugar, ketchup, and barbecue sauce. Mix thoroughly but gently. Transfer to the prepared dish and top with the bacon. Bake 30 minutes, or until hot and bubbly. Serve warm.

BEEF

I LOVE IT THAT GRILLING HAS BECOME SUCH A POPULAR COOKING METHOD IN THE SOUTH. It wasn't always that way for us. Grilling was an activity once reserved for only part of the year because we had projects, homework, 4-H activities, and household chores to complete. It was something we enjoyed on an infrequent basis, such as hamburgers on Memorial Day and steaks on Father's Day. The rest of the time our beef was delivered in the form of chili and casseroles or from the oven, stove, or slow cooker.

While life is still hectic, my preference of cooking methods has grown up just as much as I have. A case in point is how I handle the beef family, a unique mixture of cuts that can turn the meat case into a work of art. The beauty of beef is that it has what I call "extremes and in-between." It can be enormously economical or only reserved for special occasions. It can be cooked in a flash or require hours of attention.

Beef frequently has the entire meal built around it and adores being center stage. Southerners like putting it there and have been doing so since the days when everyone had cows to give us all kinds of fresh beef cuts. In the South, beef is typically teamed with loads of garden vegetables.

To this day, I dearly love the smell of a roast simmering away in the kitchen. It makes me think of Sunday dinners and is cold-weather cooking at its finest. But let a daffodil pop its cute head out of the ground and I'm ready for the great outdoors. It only takes one sniff of a hamburger being grilled and I'm ravenously hungry.

While most Southerners are used to utilizing every part of the cow thanks to our farm backgrounds, I see many shoppers who only reach for one or two cuts. If you find yourself purchasing the same types of beef, start looking around. There are more than sixty cuts available that can satisfy your meat craving in lots of different ways.

Freezing: The shrink-wrapped tray that beef is originally packaged in is not freezer safe. In other words, throw it in the freezer as is and you'll surely experience freezer burn. Instead, place that original packaging in a freezer bag or wrap in freezer paper. Steaks and roasts can maintain good quality in the freezer for eight to twelve months. Ground beef should be frozen for no longer than six months.

Sear and Slide: If you are grilling steaks that are relatively thick, you'll need to cook them over two types of heat. First, sear the steaks on both sides over medium-high heat to seal in the juices. Then slide the steaks to the part of the grill that isn't so hot and finish cooking. The medium heat will cook it through without overcooking the outside.

Selection: Beef should be firm to the touch and moist looking with a bright red color and white fat. The most tender cuts will have marbling, or bits, pieces, or layers of fat, that is evenly distributed throughout the meat.

A SIMPLY MARVELOUS MEATLOAF

As much as I love meatloaf straight from the oven, it's even better the following day on a sandwich. This recipe makes plenty so that's always possible. Serve with Tomato Gravy (page 238).

YIELD: 6 SERVINGS

2 teaspoons olive oil

3 garlic cloves, minced

1 purple onion, peeled and chopped

2 to 3 pounds ground beef

2 eggs, lightly beaten

$1/4$ cup plain fresh breadcrumbs

1 teaspoon tomato paste

1 teaspoon Worcestershire sauce

1 teaspoon pepper sauce

1 teaspoon dried thyme

1 teaspoon dried basil

1 teaspoon dried parsley

1 teaspoon salt

1 teaspoon black pepper

Preheat the oven to 350°F. Lightly grease a loaf pan and set aside.

Place the oil in a large sauté pan over medium-high heat. Add the garlic and onion and sauté 4 minutes, or until tender. Set aside to cool.

In a large bowl, combine the beef, eggs, breadcrumbs, tomato paste, Worcestershire, pepper sauce, thyme, basil, parsley, salt, and pepper. Stir well. Add the onion mixture, stirring until well combined.

Transfer to the prepared pan. Bake 50 minutes, or until cooked through. Let cool in the pan at least 10 minutes before slicing and serving.

CHICKEN-FRIED STEAK WITH SAGE CREAM GRAVY

Created as a way to use inexpensive beef cuts, this has become a dish for everyone. It is always served with gravy … always!

YIELD: 6 SERVINGS

6 tablespoons unsalted butter

6 tablespoons plus $1/4$ cups all-purpose flour, divided

$2/2$ cups milk

2 teaspoons plus 1 tablespoon kosher salt

2 teaspoons chopped fresh sage

2 teaspoons hot sauce

1 tablespoon black pepper

2 eggs

$1/2$ cup buttermilk

Peanut oil for frying

6 beef cutlets

Melt the butter in a saucepan over low heat. Slowly add 6 tablespoons of the flour, whisking constantly until a roux forms and the flour browns, about 5 minutes. Add the milk, 2 teaspoons of the salt, the sage, and hot sauce, whisking constantly. Simmer until thickened, about 3 minutes longer. Cover and set aside.

Combine the remaining flour, the remaining tablespoon of salt, and the pepper in a shallow dish. In a separate bowl, whisk together the eggs and buttermilk. Heat 1 inch of the oil in a large heavy skillet over medium-high heat until it reaches 375°F.

Dredge the cutlets in the flour, coating them completely. Then dredge the cutlets in the egg mixture and again in the flour. Repeat until all the cutlets are thoroughly coated. Using a pair of tongs, carefully place as many cutlets as will fit in the skillet without overcrowding. Fry 4 to 5 minutes per side, or until the crust is crisp and brown. Drain on paper towels and repeat with the remaining cutlets. Serve hot with the gravy on the side.

··

DELTA COUNTRY BEEF TIPS AND RICE

It's hard to believe there are areas flatter than the Mississippi Delta. The topography is why the area has become famous for growing rice. Pair it with these beef tips simmered in their own pan gravy and you've got a Delta classic.

YIELD: 6 SERVINGS

1 (3-pound) sirloin tip roast, cut into 1-inch cubes

$\frac{1}{3}$ cup plus 3 tablespoons all-purpose flour, divided

5 tablespoons canola or vegetable oil, divided

1 large yellow onion, peeled and chopped

1 green bell pepper, seeded and chopped

$4\frac{1}{3}$ cups water, divided

$\frac{1}{4}$ cup soy sauce

$\frac{1}{4}$ cup Worcestershire sauce

1 teaspoon garlic salt

1 teaspoon black pepper

Hot cooked rice

Chopped fresh parsley for garnish

Toss the beef cubes with $\frac{1}{3}$ cup of the flour and set aside.

In a Dutch oven, heat 2 tablespoons of the oil over medium heat. Add the onions and bell peppers and cook 6 minutes, or until tender. Drain on paper towels.

Add the remaining oil to the pot. Add the beef and brown 10 minutes, stirring frequently. Return the onions and bell peppers to the pot. Add 4 cups of the water, the soy sauce, Worcestershire, garlic salt, and pepper. Bring to a boil. Partially cover and reduce the heat to low. Simmer 1 hour.

In a small bowl, combine the remaining flour with the remaining water. Stir until smooth. Add to the beef mixture. Cook until the sauce thickens, about 3 minutes. Serve over hot cooked rice and garnish with fresh parsley.

··

FIVE ONION BEEF TENDERLOIN

If you don't like onions, this is not the recipe for you. We grow lots of onions in the South, and the various types mellow in the oven to become a side dressing that resembles marmalade.

YIELD: 6 SERVINGS

1 ($3\frac{1}{2}$-pound) beef tenderloin

$1\frac{1}{2}$ teaspoons salt, divided

1 teaspoon black pepper, divided

2 tablespoons vegetable oil

3 tablespoons unsalted butter

1 large purple onion, peeled, sliced, and separated in rings

1 large yellow onion, peeled, sliced, and separated in rings

1 large white onion, peeled, sliced, and separated in rings

2 bunches green onions, sliced

6 shallots, peeled and chopped

5 garlic cloves, minced

$\frac{1}{2}$ cup cognac

$\frac{1}{2}$ cup beef broth

Sprinkle the beef with $\frac{1}{2}$ teaspoon of the salt and $\frac{1}{2}$ teaspoon of the pepper. Tie with kitchen twine to secure in 2-inch intervals.

Heat the oil in a large roasting pan over medium-high heat. Add the beef and brown on all sides around 5 minutes. Remove the beef and reserve the drippings. Add the butter to the drippings. When the butter is melted, add the purple, yellow, and white onion rings. Sauté 5 minutes.

Meanwhile, preheat the oven to 400°F.

Add the green onions, shallots, and garlic. Cook 10 minutes and stir in the cognac and broth. Increase the heat to high and stir constantly until the liquid evaporates, about 5 minutes. Place the beef on top of the onion mixture.

Bake 45 minutes, uncovered, or until a meat thermometer registers 150°F when inserted in the thickest portion. Transfer the beef to a cutting board and loosely cover with aluminum foil. Let rest 10 minutes.

Meanwhile, transfer the pan drippings and onion mixture to a medium saucepan. Place over medium heat and stir constantly until the liquid evaporates, about 5 minutes. Stir in the remaining salt and pepper. Thinly slice the tenderloin and serve warm with the onion mixture.

Storage: Fresh beef must be kept refrigerated. Place it on a plate so that any package leakage will not drip onto other foods. Use steaks and roasts within three days of purchase. Ground beef should be used within two days. Cooked leftovers should be used within three days.

Cuts: Beef cuts from the center of the animal are not exercised and will be naturally tender. These will come from the loin and rib sections. Chuck, rump, and round sections are heavily exercised and should be cooked with moist heat.

HERB GARDEN GRILLED HAMBURGERS

Nearly every Southern cook has an herb garden at her fingertips. So get your kitchen shears ready for snipping. The secret to these juicy burgers is the combination of ground sirloin and ground chuck.

YIELD: 8 SERVINGS

2 tablespoons fresh chopped thyme

2 tablespoons fresh chopped oregano

2 tablespoons fresh chopped parsley

2 tablespoons fresh chopped chives

$\frac{1}{2}$ teaspoon salt

$\frac{1}{2}$ teaspoon black pepper

$\frac{1}{2}$ teaspoon ground red pepper

$1\frac{1}{2}$ pounds ground chuck

1 pound ground sirloin

8 hamburger buns

Preheat the grill to medium-high heat. Meanwhile, combine the thyme, oregano, parsley, chives, salt, black pepper, and red pepper in a small bowl. Set aside.

Combine the ground chuck and ground sirloin in a medium bowl. Divide the beef into 8 patties. Sprinkle the herb mixture evenly on each patty and press gently into the meat.

Grill 6 minutes on each side, or until the beef is no longer pink in the center. Serve immediately on hamburger buns with your preferred condiments.

Celebrations

January is National Meat Month.

May is National Hamburger Month.

April 27 is National Prime Rib Day.

Memorial Day is National Cheeseburger Day.

August 13 is National Filet Mignon Day.

JUST BECAUSE HERBED BEEF ROAST

Surprise dinners don't have to be reserved for special occasions. Maybe you want to celebrate because it's March, or because the hummingbirds returned today, or because the mail contained no bills. This roast requires an oven, herbs, and about 5 minutes of your time. What a way to celebrate!

YIELD: 8 SERVINGS

1 (3½ to 4 pound) boneless beef rump roast
1 tablespoon canola oil
2 teaspoons garlic salt
2 teaspoons black pepper
2 teaspoons dried basil
2 teaspoons dried thyme
2 teaspoon dried parsley

Preheat the oven to 325°F. Lightly grease a roasting rack and place the beef on the rack in a shallow pan. Rub the oil over the outside of the roast.

In a small bowl, combine the garlic salt, pepper, basil, thyme, and parsley. Rub the herb mixture over the outside of the beef. Insert an ovenproof thermometer in the thickest portion of the roast.

Position the roast in the oven so you can view the thermometer dial from the oven window. Roast 2 hours, or until the roast reaches the desired doneness. Transfer to a cutting board and cover loosely with aluminum foil. Let rest 15 minutes. Carve into thin slices and serve warm.

"Beef is the soul of cooking."
—MARIE ANTOINE CAREME

MARINATED FLANK STEAK WITH BLUE CHEESE BUTTER

Flank steak became known as the "poor man's steak" in the South and was more affordable than other steak cuts. It requires marinating or it's not going to be tender at all. Sometimes you'll see flank steak labeled as London Broil. London Broil is actually a recipe, not a beef cut. For the best presentation, slice it against the grain.

YIELD: 8 SERVINGS

4 pounds flank steak
½ cup dry red wine
6 tablespoons vegetable oil
4 garlic cloves, minced
½ teaspoon black pepper
½ teaspoon dry mustard
4 ounces blue cheese, softened
4 tablespoons unsalted butter, softened
1 tablespoon chopped fresh chives

Place the flank steak in a heavy-duty zip-top plastic bag. Combine the wine, oil, garlic, pepper, and mustard in a jar with a tight-fitting lid. Shake to blend. Pour the marinade over the steak and refrigerate at least 8 hours or overnight.

Remove the steak from the marinade, discarding the marinade. Broil or grill 5 to 7 minutes on each side, or to the desired degree of doneness. Meanwhile, combine the blue cheese, butter, and chives. When the steak is done, place on a large piece of aluminum foil. Spread the cheese butter over the top, cover, and allow to rest 10 minutes. Slice very thin and serve warm.

MID-WEEK CAJUN SLOPPY JOES

Wednesday night dinners don't always get the respect they deserve. It's not quite time for something special during the weekend, but you've used up all the leftovers. That's when Sloppy Joes come to the rescue. Pull out plenty of paper napkins because they aren't called sloppy for nothing!

YIELD: 6 SERVINGS

1½ pounds ground beef
1 white onion, peeled and chopped
1 green bell pepper, seeded and chopped
1 (8-ounce) can tomato sauce
¾ cup ketchup
1 tablespoon Worcestershire sauce
1 teaspoon prepared mustard
1 teaspoon brown sugar
½ teaspoon Creole or Cajun seasoning
½ teaspoon garlic powder
½ teaspoon black pepper
6 hamburger buns, toasted

In a large skillet over medium heat, cook the beef, onions, and peppers until the meat crumbles and no pink remains. Drain and return to the skillet.

Add the tomato sauce, ketchup, Worcestershire, mustard, brown sugar, Creole seasoning, garlic powder, and pepper. Reduce the heat to low and simmer 20 minutes, stirring frequently. Serve warm on toasted buns.

"PULL OUT A SWEATER" POT ROAST

Winter comfort comes easy with this roast that bubbles away in the slow cooker while you accomplish other things. Use the tomatoes you canned over the summer to make it exceptional.

YIELD: 6 SERVINGS

3 tablespoons canola oil
3½ pounds trimmed rib-eye roast
1 sweet onion, peeled and finely chopped
4 garlic cloves, minced
2 celery stalks, sliced
2 large carrots, peeled and sliced
1 teaspoon black pepper
½ teaspoon salt
⅛ teaspoon ground cloves
1 cup dry red wine or beef stock
1 (28-ounce) can crushed tomatoes
Chopped fresh parsley for garnish

Heat the oil over medium-high heat in a large skillet. When hot, add the meat and cook about 12 to 15 minutes, or until browned on all sides. Transfer to a slow cooker.

Add the onions and cook 10 minutes, stirring frequently. Add the garlic, celery and carrots. Sauté 4 minutes. Add the pepper, salt, cloves, and wine. Cook 10 minutes more, or until the liquid is reduced by one-third.

Pour over the meat, adding the tomatoes. Cover and cook on low 8 hours or until the meat falls off the bone. Transfer to serving platter, garnish, and serve immediately.

TOWN DRUNK BEEF STEW

Southern vegetables are all over this glorious version of beef stew. The recipe uses a whole bottle of red wine. You'll be able to tell when it's so tender a fork will hardly hold it.

YIELD: 8 SERVINGS

3 pounds stew beef, cut into bite-size pieces

3 cups all-purpose flour

4 tablespoons olive oil

3 garlic cloves, minced

1 pound fresh baby carrots

1 pound fresh pearl onions, peeled

10 red potatoes, cut into quarters

3 cups beef stock

2 cups (16-ounces) crushed tomatoes

1 bottle dry red wine, divided

2 bay leaves

1 teaspoon dried basil

½ teaspoon salt

½ teaspoon black pepper

1 cup frozen English peas

Preheat the oven to 325°F. Dredge the beef in the flour until coated on all sides, shaking off the excess. Place a large Dutch oven over high heat and add the oil. When the oil is hot, add the meat a few pieces at a time.

Cook, turning several times with tongs, until the meat is crispy and brown on all sides. Remove to a large dish. Repeat until all the meat is cooked and set aside. Reduce the heat to medium high.

In the same pot, add the garlic, carrots, onions, and potatoes. Sauté 5 minutes. Add the browned meat, stock, tomatoes, 2 cups of the wine, bay leaves, basil, salt, and pepper. Cover and place in the oven. Bake 1 hour.

Add the remaining wine and bake, covered, 3 hours more, or until the stew is fork tender. Gently stir in the peas and adjust the seasonings if necessary. Remove the bay leaves and discard. Serve hot.

> "There may be things better than beef stew and baked potatoes and home-made bread— there may be."
>
> —DAVID GRAYSON

PERFECT STEAK GRILL MARKS: For diamond-shaped grill marks that look like the pros, think of the grill as a clock and the meat as the hands on the clock. Once the grill is hot, place the steaks on the rack so one end points toward ten o'clock. Leave in place a few minutes then rotate to two o'clock. Leave in place a few minutes longer. Turn the steaks over and repeat.

THERMOMETERS: Good instant read and ovenproof thermometers are the most important pieces of equipment for perfectly cooked beef. Always insert into the thickest portion of the meat. If the beef has bones, do not let the tip rest against it or your reading will be false. Medium-rare is 145°F, medium is 160°F, and well done is 170°F. While roasts and steaks can be cooked medium-rare and medium, all ground beef should be cooked well done.

TRIVIA: Beef Stroganoff was named for Russian diplomat Count Paul Stroganov.

BEETS

THERE'S A REALLY OLD JOKE AMONG THOSE OF US WHO ARE CONSIDERED "SISTERS OF THE Skillet" (aka Home Economics graduates) that asks, "What words have never been spoken in the English language?" The answer: "May I have your beets?"

Every time I hear that joke I laugh because for some people, it's unfortunately true. It illustrates perfectly that there are some vegetables that are destined never to be the darling of the produce bin. Beets are loved by some but certainly not by the masses. What a shame that many have not discovered one of nature's sweetest vegetables.

When I began to realize I actually liked beets, I was in college and strangely, not in a foods class, but in a textiles class. We were given an assignment of dying wool with natural products. Naturally, I went running to my grandmother's house for help. We used canned beet juice to dye my fabric and let it soak in the ink-looking juice for more than twenty-four hours. While it soaked, my grandmother coaxed me into trying the beets we drained, and I liked them, to my complete shock! When we finally rinsed my fabric, I expected it to be a beautiful burgundy color. Instead, it was the most gorgeous shade of pale yellow. From that moment on, I've been surprised by beets.

Like every other vegetable, I look forward to the fresh season every year beginning in the early summer. However, I have discovered that beets are one of the few vegetables that are equally good fresh or canned. So while I'll stock up on them all summer, I don't panic when the season comes to a close because those canned varieties are just as marvelous.

Old-timers still refer to beets as "garden beets." Even though there are loads of other colors to be found, Southerners like the common red variety that is the most inexpensive on the market. We like to cook the green tops like spinach. The roots can be pickled, steamed, boiled, baked, roasted, fried, and even grilled after precooking. Any way you cook them, they are "unbeetable!"

Nutrition: The green leafy tops are just as edible and nutritious as the roots. The greens are high in vitamin A and the roots are rich in potassium. A cooked one-half-cup serving of the greens has around twenty calories and the same portion of the root contains around thirty-four calories.

Preparation: Scrub the roots under cold running water before using. Never peel fresh beets before cooking or they will bleed to death. Cut off the stem an inch above the bulb and leave the roots attached. The skins slip off easily after the beets are tenderized through cooking. I usually wear plastic gloves for the peeling step to keep my hands from becoming stained. Remove any stains on your hands by rubbing with salt and then washing with soap and water.

BODACIOUS BEET GREENS

Southerners love greens of any kind. If you've never had the leafy tops of beets, you've been missing a treat. Discard any damaged or discolored leaves and wash thoroughly before using.

YIELD: 2 SERVINGS

1 pound beet greens
$^1/_2$ teaspoon salt
1$^1/_2$ tablespoons unsalted butter, softened
2 lemon wedges

Wash the greens well and place in a large Dutch oven with just the water clinging to the leaves. Sprinkle with the salt, cover, and place over medium heat. Cook 5 minutes, or until the leaves have just started to wilt. Turn once or twice with tongs so the top leaves fall to the bottom during cooking. If the water evaporates too fast and the leaves show signs of sticking to the pan, add a tiny bit of water to the pan.

Cook another 3 to 5 minutes. The cooking time will vary depending on the age and coarseness of the greens. Drain and either leave whole or chop. Transfer to a serving dish and add the butter, stirring until the butter coats the leaves and completely melts. Serve warm with lemon wedges.

Storage: Store fresh beets in the refrigerator crisper drawer. Use the tops as soon as possible. The beets themselves will keep for a couple of weeks in a loosely closed plastic bag with a tablespoon of water added to keep them hydrated. Do not wash until you are ready to use.

CAN-DO SWEET-AND-SOUR BEETS

What is it about sweet and sour that always grabs my attention? This recipe uses the convenience of canned beets, making it quick!

YIELD: 8 SERVINGS

3 (16-ounce) cans sliced beets, undrained
$^1/_2$ cup sugar
$^1/_2$ cup white wine vinegar
6 whole cloves
3 tablespoons ketchup
2 tablespoons cornstarch
1 teaspoon pure vanilla extract

Drain the beets, reserving 1$^1/_2$ cups of the liquid. Set the beets aside.

In a large saucepan over medium heat, whisk together the beet liquid, sugar, vinegar, cloves, ketchup, cornstarch, and extract. Stir constantly until the mixture comes to a boil. Boil 1 minute. Remove the cloves and stir in the beets. Serve warm or refrigerate and serve cold.

Selection: Fresh beets should come with the tops and roots still attached. The tops should look fresh and not wilted, and the roots should be smooth and round. Avoid those with growth cracks or that appear to be soft or shriveled. When you get them home, separate the tops from the beets, except for an inch at the top. The tops pull moisture from the beets and will decrease the shelf life. Leaving an inch of the stems will hold the color and prevent "bleeding" when cooked.

FRIED BEET CHIPS

Slip these chips into your family's lunch and they will quickly discover an improved beet attitude. These are not only delicious, but really pretty.

YIELD: 8 SERVINGS

Vegetable or canola oil
6 large beets, peeled, trimmed, and thinly sliced
$1/2$ teaspoon kosher salt

Pour the oil to a depth of 3 inches in a heavy skillet and place over medium-high heat. Bring to 375°F. Carefully lower small batches of the beet slices in the hot oil. Fry 10 minutes. Drain on paper towels and sprinkle with the salt. Repeat with the remaining beets. Serve warm or at room temperature.

HOT BEET RELISH

You will find yourself making roast beef simply to serve with this relish. It's creamy with a dash of heat and a great way to use canned beets.

YIELD: 4 CUPS

1 (8-ounce) container sour cream
$1/4$ cup prepared horseradish
2 tablespoons red wine vinegar
$2^1/2$ teaspoons sugar
$1/2$ teaspoon dry mustard
$1/4$ teaspoon salt
$1/8$ teaspoon white pepper
2 (15-ounce) cans cut beets, drained, rinsed, and diced

In a medium mixing bowl, whisk together the sour cream, horseradish, vinegar, sugar, mustard, salt, and pepper. When well blended, add the beets, stir-ring gently to combine. Cover and refrigerate at least 4 hours before serving.

INDIAN SUMMER BEET SALAD

Southerners label any days that should feel like fall but actually feel like summer an Indian summer day. These typically are in September or October, when you'll find plenty of apples, walnuts, honey, and late-season beets on hand.

YIELD: 12 SERVINGS

3 large beets
1 tablespoon olive oil
$1/4$ cup white wine vinegar
2 tablespoons honey
1 tablespoon Dijon mustard
$1/4$ teaspoon salt
$1/4$ teaspoon black pepper
$1/2$ cup canola or vegetable oil
2 tablespoons walnut oil
1 head iceberg lettuce, washed and torn
1 large Granny Smith apple, thinly sliced
$1/2$ cup walnuts halves, toasted
$1/4$ cup crumbled blue cheese

Preheat the oven to 350°F. Rub the beets with the olive oil and wrap in heavy-duty aluminum foil. Place on a baking sheet and bake 45 minutes. Cool, slip off the outer skins, and cut in julienned strips.

In a jar with a tight-fitting lid, combine the vinegar, honey, mustard, salt, pepper, canola oil, and walnut oil. Shake until well blended. Arrange lettuce leaves on individual salad plates. Top evenly with the apple slices and beets. Sprinkle the tops with walnuts and cheese. Drizzle with the dressing and serve immediately.

ORANGE-GLAZED BEETS

This dish will become Florida sunshine on your plate. The subtle orange flavor is just enough to make these beets addictive.

YIELD: 6 SERVINGS

1½ pounds beets
2 tablespoons unsalted butter
2 teaspoons cornstarch
1 teaspoon sugar
⅛ teaspoon salt
1 teaspoon cider vinegar
2 teaspoons grated orange zest
½ cup orange juice

Trim and discard the beet tops, leaving 1 inch of the stem and roots. Wash thoroughly and place in a large saucepan. Cover with water, place over medium-high heat, and bring to a boil. Cover and reduce the heat to low. Simmer 35 minutes, or until tender. Drain and discard the cooking liquid. Rinse the beets with cold water. When cool enough to handle, trim off the roots and stems and slip off the skins. Cut into ½-inch slices.

In a heavy saucepan over medium heat, melt the butter. Whisk in the cornstarch, sugar, salt, vinegar, zest, and juice, stirring constantly until smooth and thick, around 4 minutes. Add the beets, stirring gently to evenly coat. Cook an additional 4 minutes and serve warm.

PICKLED BEETS

Leaving an inch of the beet stems and roots will prevent color bleeding. These make great gifts.

YIELD: 8 PINTS

7 pounds beets
4 cups white vinegar
1½ teaspoons pickling salt
2 cups sugar
2 cups water
2 cinnamon sticks
12 whole cloves
4 onions, peeled and thinly sliced

Trim the beet tops, leaving 1 inch of the stem and roots. Wash thoroughly and sort according by size. Cover the similar sizes with boiling water and cook until tender, about 25 to 30 minutes. Drain and discard the cooking liquid. Set the beets aside to cool. When cool enough to handle, trim off the roots and stems and slip off the skins. Slice into ¼-inch slices.

In a large saucepan, combine the vinegar, salt, sugar, and water over medium-high heat. Tie the cinnamon and cloves in a cheesecloth bag and add to the vinegar mixture. Bring to a boil. Add the beets and onions. Simmer 5 minutes. Remove and discard the spice bag.

Fill hot canning jars with the beets and onions, leaving ½-inch headspace. Add the hot vinegar solution to within ½-inch of the rim. Remove any air bubbles, wipe the jar rims, and adjust the lids. Process in a boiling water bath 30 minutes. (See page 12 for detailed canning instructions.)

Place the jars on a wire rack so they don't touch each other. Make sure they are away from drafts. Let stand at room temperature until completely cool and sealed. Store at room temperature.
Note: To pickle whole beets, use sizes that are no

larger than 1 $\frac{1}{2}$ inches. Pack the beets whole into the hot jars and omit the onions. Follow the directions above for processing.

. . . .

THE BEET GOES ON

These beets are roasted, which concentrates the natural sugars and makes them a perfect topping for mixed salad greens.

YIELD: 8 SERVINGS

6 large beets
1 tablespoon olive oil
$\frac{1}{2}$ teaspoon salt
$\frac{1}{4}$ teaspoon black pepper

Preheat the oven to 400°F. Lightly grease a jelly-roll pan and set aside.

Slice and remove the tops and roots from the beets. With a sharp paring knife, peel the beets and cut into wedges. Place on the jelly-roll pan and drizzle with the olive oil, tossing to evenly coat. Sprinkle with the salt and pepper. Bake 35 to 40 minutes, or until tender, stirring occasionally. Serve warm.

BOTANY: Beets belong to the same family as Swiss Chard and are closely related to spinach and quinoa. Garnet red is the most common beet color on the market. There is a rainbow of other color options ranging from reddish orange to gold and even white. The Chioggia variety has rings of red and white, giving it the appearance of an odd piece of peppermint candy.

ORIGIN: Beets originated in the sandy soils of the Mediterranean area, where the tops were used as a vegetable long before the roots. The first directions for cooking the beet roots were in Roman writings of the third century.

EQUIVALENTS: One pound of fresh greens will yield nearly one-and-three-quarters cups cooked. A pound of beet roots will yield two cups of cooked, sliced beets.

TIP: If you use too much salt when seasoning beets, add a dash of either sugar or vinegar (or both) to the dish. It will counteract the salty flavor.

TRIVIA: Beets are the pagan symbol for love and beauty.

BISCUITS

WHEN I WAS GROWING UP, BISCUITS WERE FOR BREAKFAST, WITH THE OCCASIONAL LEFT-over making its way into the noon meal. Today they transition into every meal and include all kinds of embellishments from herbs to sweet potatoes.

Like many youngsters, biscuit making was one of my first baking experiences. I learned from experience not to overwork the dough or the outcome would be tough, not tender. I only twisted the cutter once before my grandmother showed me how to correctly cut them. Now, I could make them with my eyes closed.

I always bake biscuits on a round cast-iron griddle, known as a biscuit baker in the South. Like all cast iron, it promotes even baking and browning. If you don't have one, a regular baking pan will work.

Everything about biscuit making is therapeutic for me. I love the kneading that produces a dough that is pliable and easy to roll. I enjoy rolling out the dough and learned quickly to roll it evenly so I wouldn't end up with lopsided biscuits!

Certain areas are known for specific breads. These are the local specialties you expect to have when visiting there. The English have scones. Out West, you'll see a vast utilization of whole grains. Try to weave your way through the North and not experience a delicious bagel. Here in the South, we have biscuits.

So pull out your rolling pin and biscuit cutters. This bread is not only quick but marvelously satisfying to make any time of the day.

Fat: This is absolutely essential in making biscuits and can be in the form of butter, vegetable shortening, or lard. Shortening or lard will produce the lightest, fluffiest product because neither contains milk solids. Lard is rendered and clarified pork fat that, by far, produces the flakiest, most tender biscuits. If using butter in a biscuit recipe, make sure it is straight from the refrigerator. Cold butter is very easy to cut into the dry ingredient mixture in the recipe and forms small pockets of butter throughout the dough.

Baking Powder: Many biscuit recipes call for baking powder. This leavening ingredient has more than likely been sitting on your pantry shelf for a while. To test for freshness, drop a teaspoon of baking powder in a cup of warm water. It should fizzle and sizzle immediately. If not, replace it with a new container for best results. Double action baking powder is the most common on the market and what I use. That simply means it releases part of the carbon dioxide gas needed for bread to rise when it becomes wet and the rest when it gets hot in the oven.

Baking Soda: Frequently, baking soda is also used as a leavening agent in biscuit recipes. It is often called for in recipes that utilize buttermilk. The acid in buttermilk activates the carbon dioxide in baking soda, causing the biscuits to rise.

BACON BISCUIT CUPS

There's no kneading, rolling, or cutting with this satisfying version of biscuits.

YIELD: 10 SERVINGS

6 ounces cream cheese, softened
2 tablespoons milk
1 egg
$^1/_2$ cup shredded Swiss cheese
1 green onion, chopped
1 (10-ounce) can refrigerated flaky biscuits
5 bacon slices, cooked, crumbled, and divided

Preheat the oven to 375°F. Lightly grease 10 muffin cups and set aside.

In the bowl of an electric mixer, combine the cream cheese, milk, and egg at medium speed. When well blended, stir in the Swiss cheese and onion. Set aside.

Separate the refrigerated biscuits into 10 portions. Pat each biscuit into a 5-inch circle. Press into the bottom and up the sides of each muffin cup. Sprinkle evenly with half of the bacon.

Spoon the cream cheese mixture on top. Bake 22 minutes, or until set. Sprinkle with the remaining bacon and set the pan on a wire rack to cool 5 minutes. Remove the biscuits from the pan and serve warm.

BAKING POWDER BISCUITS

Some will call these "Sky-High Biscuits" because they have extra rising help from baking powder.

YIELD: 12 TO 14 BISCUITS

2 cups all-purpose flour
1 tablespoon baking powder
1 teaspoon salt
3 tablespoons vegetable shortening or lard
$^3/_4$ cup milk

Preheat the oven to 450°F. Lightly grease a cast-iron biscuit baker or baking pan and set aside. Place the flour, baking powder, and salt in a mixing bowl. With a pastry blender or 2 forks, cut in the shortening until it resembles coarse meal. Add the milk and stir until a soft dough is formed, about 25 strokes.

Transfer the dough to a lightly floured surface and knead until smooth, about 10 times. Roll to $^1/_2$-inch thickness. Cut with a 2-inch cutter and place on the prepared pan. Bake 13 to 15 minutes, or until golden brown. Serve hot.

BEATEN BISCUITS

If you are feeling stressed and need to take your frustrations out on something, this is the recipe to make. Don't expect the results to be light and fluffy because it's more like a cracker. Traditionally, these biscuits were beaten a hundred times for family and five hundred times for company. It's a fun recipe to make!

YIELD: 6 TO 8 SERVINGS

$2^1/_2$ cups all-purpose flour
1 teaspoon sugar
$^1/_3$ teaspoon salt
$^1/_2$ teaspoon baking powder
$^1/_3$ cup lard or vegetable shortening
$^1/_3$ to $^1/_2$ cup milk

Preheat the oven to 375°F. Lightly grease a cast-iron biscuit baker or baking pan and set aside.

In a large bowl, combine the flour, sugar, salt, and baking powder. With a pastry blender or 2 forks, cut in the lard until the mixture resembles coarse meal. Stir in $\frac{1}{3}$ cup of the milk, mixing well. If the dough is too dry or crumbly, add the remaining milk.

Transfer the dough to a lightly floured surface and knead 4 times or until it holds together. With a rolling pin, beat the dough until the dough blisters. Beat a minimum of 100 times, turning and folding the edges toward the center with every 10 whacks.

Roll the dough to $\frac{1}{4}$-inch thickness. Cut into rounds with a small cutter and prick the tops with a fork a couple of times. Bake 30 minutes, or until lightly browned. Serve warm or at room temperature.

BEST EVER BISCUITS

This is the recipe I use regularly for making biscuits. It's a good recipe for teaching young ones the art of biscuit making, thanks to there being only three ingredients.

YIELD: 8 BISCUITS

2 cups self-rising flour
$\frac{1}{4}$ pound (1 stick) unsalted butter, cubed
$\frac{2}{3}$ cup milk

Preheat the oven to 400°F.

Place the flour in a medium bowl. With a pastry blender or 2 forks, cut the butter into the flour until it resembles coarse meal. Make a well in the center and add the milk, mixing well.

Transfer the dough to a lightly floured surface and knead 12 times. Roll to $\frac{1}{2}$-inch thickness. Cut the biscuits with a 2-inch cutter and place on an ungreased cast-iron biscuit baker or baking sheet. Bake 10 to 12 minutes, or until golden brown. Serve hot.

BEER BISCUITS

These are marvelous with chicken. It only uses three-fourths cup of beer, so you'll have to find another use for the leftover brew!

YIELD: 10 BISCUITS

2 cups all-purpose flour
3 teaspoons baking powder
1 teaspoon salt
$\frac{1}{4}$ cup vegetable shortening or lard
$\frac{3}{4}$ cup beer, chilled

Preheat the oven to 450°F. Lightly grease a cast-iron biscuit baker or baking pan and set aside. Place the flour, baking powder, and salt in a mixing bowl. With a pastry blender or 2 forks, cut in the shortening until it resembles coarse meal. Add the beer and stir until a soft dough forms, about 15 strokes.

Transfer the dough to a lightly floured surface and knead until smooth, about 7 times. Roll to $\frac{1}{2}$-inch thickness. Cut with a 2-inch cutter and place on the prepared pan. Bake 11 to 13 minutes, or until golden brown. Serve hot.

BLUEBERRY BISCUITS

You only need to be the least bit hungry for these delightfully sweet biscuits to grab your attention. You can glaze them if you want, but the buttery cinnamon sugar topping is exceptional.

YIELD: 8 SERVINGS

2 cups all-purpose flour
2 teaspoons baking powder
$\frac{1}{4}$ teaspoon baking soda
1 teaspoon salt

½ cup plus 2 tablespoons sugar, divided

⅓ cup vegetable shortening or lard

1 egg

¾ cup buttermilk

½ cup fresh blueberries

3 tablespoons unsalted butter, melted

¼ teaspoon ground cinnamon

Preheat the oven to 400°F. Lightly grease a cast-iron biscuit baker or baking sheet and set aside.

In a large bowl, combine the flour, baking powder, baking soda, salt, and ½ cup of the sugar. Cut in the shortening with a pastry blender or 2 forks until crumbly.

In a separate bowl, whisk together the egg and buttermilk. Add to the flour mixture, stirring just until moistened. Gently fold in the blueberries.

Transfer the dough to a lightly floured surface and knead 4 times. Roll the dough to ¾-inch thickness and cut with a 2-inch cutter. Transfer to the prepared pan and bake 15 minutes, or until golden brown.

Meanwhile, in a small bowl, stir together the butter, remaining sugar, and cinnamon. Brush over the warm biscuits and serve immediately.

BUTTERMILK BISCUITS

These biscuits deliciously hold sausage patties as well as homemade jam and butter.

YIELD: 12 TO 14 BISCUITS

2 cups all-purpose flour

2½ teaspoons baking powder

½ teaspoon baking soda

1 teaspoon salt

2 tablespoons vegetable shortening or lard

1 cup buttermilk

Preheat the oven to 450°F. Lightly grease a cast-iron biscuit baker or baking pan and set aside.

Place the flour, baking powder, baking soda, and salt in a mixing bowl. Cut in the shortening with a pastry blender or 2 forks until the mixture resembles coarse meal. Add the buttermilk and stir until a soft dough is formed, about 25 strokes.

Transfer the dough to a lightly floured surface and knead until smooth, about 10 times. Roll to ½-inch thickness. Cut with a 2-inch cutter and transfer to the prepared pan. Bake 13 to 15 minutes, or until golden brown. Serve hot.

CINNAMON SUGAR BISCUITS

Serve these hot biscuits with homemade applesauce or apple butter.

YIELD: 8 SERVINGS

2 cups all-purpose flour

1 teaspoon baking powder

1 teaspoon baking soda

½ teaspoon salt

¼ pound (1 stick) unsalted butter

¾ cup buttermilk

2 teaspoons ground cinnamon, divided

1 tablespoon sugar

Preheat the oven to 400°F. Lightly grease a cast-iron biscuit baker or baking pan and set aside.

In a mixing bowl, combine the flour, baking powder, baking soda, and salt. With a pastry blender or 2 forks, cut the butter into the flour mixture until crumbly. Stir in the buttermilk.

Transfer the dough to a lightly floured surface sprinkled with 1 teaspoon of the cinnamon. Knead 4 times. Roll the dough to ½-inch thickness and cut with a 2-inch cutter.

Place on the prepared pan. In a small bowl, combine the remaining cinnamon and sugar. Sprinkle over the biscuits. Bake 12 to 14 minutes, or until golden brown. Serve warm.

COUNTRY HAM AND CHEESE BISCUITS

Have a bit of leftover country ham but not enough for everyone to have their own piece? Just chop it up and make these savory biscuits.

YIELD: 12 BISCUITS

$1^2/_3$ cups all-purpose flour

$1/_3$ cup plain cornmeal

1 tablespoon baking powder

1 tablespoon sugar

$1/_4$ teaspoon salt

Pinch of ground red pepper

4 tablespoons unsalted butter

$1/_2$ cup shredded Monterey Jack cheese

$1/_2$ cup chopped country ham

1 tablespoon chopped green onions, white part only

$3/_4$ cup milk

Preheat the oven to 425°F. Lightly grease a cast-iron biscuit baker or baking sheet and set aside.

In a large mixing bowl, combine the flour, cornmeal, baking powder, sugar, salt, and red pepper. Cut in the butter with a pastry blender or 2 forks until crumbly. Stir in the cheese, ham, and onion. Make a well in the center and add the milk, stirring just until moistened.

Transfer the dough to a lightly floured surface and knead 4 times. Roll the dough to $3/_4$-inch thickness and cut with a 2-inch cutter. Place on the prepared pan and bake 12 minutes, or until lightly browned. Serve hot.

DAISY BISCUITS

The dainty shape of these biscuits makes them perfect for serving at a brunch for your lady friends or for young girls.

YIELD: 20 BISCUITS

$2^1/_2$ cups self-rising flour

3 ounces cream cheese

6 tablespoons unsalted butter

1 cup milk

$1/_4$ cup orange marmalade or raspberry jam

Preheat the oven to 450°F.

Place the flour in a large mixing bowl. With a pastry blender or 2 forks, cut in the cheese and butter until the mixture is crumbly. Add the milk, stirring just until moistened.

Transfer the dough to a lightly floured surface and knead 4 times. Roll to $1/_2$-inch thickness and cut with a 2-inch cutter. Place on a large ungreased baking sheet. Make 6 slits through the dough around the edges of each biscuit to $1/_4$ inch from the center.

Press your thumb in the center of each biscuit to leave an indentation. Spoon $1/_2$ teaspoon of the marmalade into the indentation. Bake 9 to 10 minutes, or until golden brown. Serve warm.

Celebrations

September is National Biscuit Month.

May 14 is Buttermilk Biscuit Day.

The second week in September is Biscuit and Gravy Week.

FOOD PROCESSOR BISCUITS

Make sure you don't overmix the dough in the food processor or the biscuits will be tough.

YIELD: 12 BISCUITS

2½ cups self-rising flour
¼ pound (1 stick) cold unsalted butter, cut into 5 pieces
¾ cup buttermilk

Preheat the oven to 450°F. Lightly grease a cast-iron biscuit baker or baking sheet and set aside.

Position the knife blade in the food processor bowl. Add the flour. Drop the butter pieces over the flour. Pulse 6 or 7 times until the mixture resembles coarse meal.

With the processor running, add the buttermilk through the chute until the dough forms a ball, leaving the sides of the bowl.

Transfer the dough to a lightly floured surface and knead 4 times. Roll the dough to ½-inch thickness and cut with a 2-inch cutter. Transfer to the prepared pan. Bake 10 minutes, or until golden brown. Serve warm.

GLAZED RAISIN BISCUITS

These sweet biscuits are brushed with a vanilla glaze as soon as they come out of the oven.

YIELD: 16 BISCUITS

2½ cups biscuit mix
½ cup raisins
2 tablespoons granulated sugar
1 teaspoon ground cinnamon
1 egg, lightly beaten

⅔ cup milk
⅔ cup confectioners' sugar
1 tablespoon water
¼ teaspoon pure vanilla extract

Preheat the oven to 350°F. Lightly grease a baking sheet and set aside.

In a medium bowl, combine the biscuit mix, raisins, granulated sugar, and cinnamon. Add the egg and milk, stirring just until moistened.

Transfer the dough to a lightly floured surface and knead 5 times. Roll the dough to ½-inch thickness and cut with a 2-inch cutter. Place on the prepared sheet and bake 15 minutes, or until golden brown.

Meanwhile, in a small bowl, combine the confectioners' sugar, water, and extract. Stir until smooth. As soon as the biscuits are done, brush the tops with the glaze. Let stand 5 minutes before serving.

GREEN ONION AND BUTTERMILK BISCUITS

These are the biscuits I make as soon as I harvest the first green onions out of my vegetable garden. They are deliciously buttery and rich.

YIELD: 12 BISCUITS

2 cups all-purpose flour
2 garlic cloves, minced
8 green onions, chopped
1 tablespoon baking powder
1 teaspoon salt
½ pound (2 sticks) unsalted butter, cubed
¾ cup buttermilk

Preheat the oven to 350°F.

Place the flour, garlic, onions, baking powder,

and salt in a large mixing bowl, stirring to combine. Using a pastry blender or 2 forks, cut in the butter until the mixture resembles coarse meal.

Add the buttermilk and mix just until the dough comes together. Form the dough into a ball and transfer to a well-floured surface. Roll to $\frac{1}{2}$-inch thickness and cut with a 2-inch cutter. Place on an ungreased pan and bake 20 to 25 minutes, or until golden brown. Serve hot.

HERB GARDEN BISCUITS

My perennial herbs barely make it out of the winter ground before I'm ready to snip them for these biscuits. I love to serve them with baked ham during Easter.

YIELD: 18 BISCUITS

3 cups all-purpose flour
3 teaspoons baking powder
1 teaspoon salt
$\frac{1}{2}$ teaspoon baking soda
$\frac{1}{2}$ pound (1 stick) unsalted butter, cubed
1 tablespoon chopped fresh parsley
1 tablespoon chopped fresh chives
1 tablespoon chopped fresh thyme or oregano
$1\frac{1}{2}$ cups cream

Preheat the oven to 450°F. Lightly grease a cast-iron biscuit baker or baking sheet and set aside.

In a large bowl, combine the flour, baking powder, salt, and baking soda. Using a pastry blender or 2 forks, cut in the butter until the mixture resembles coarse meal.

Add the parsley, chives, thyme, and cream. Stir only until the dough begins to form.

Transfer the dough to a lightly floured surface and knead 4 times. Roll the dough to $\frac{3}{4}$-inch

thickness and cut with a 2-inch cutter. Transfer to the prepared pan and bake 12 to 15 minutes, or until golden brown. Serve warm.

HOT CHEESE DROP BISCUITS

You may see drop biscuits sometimes called "cathead biscuits," referring to the irregular shape of the baked product.

YIELD: 18 BISCUITS

2 cups all-purpose flour
2 teaspoons baking powder
$\frac{1}{2}$ teaspoon salt
$\frac{1}{2}$ teaspoon cayenne
1 cup (4 ounces) shredded extra-sharp Cheddar cheese
$\frac{1}{4}$ cup vegetable shortening or lard
1 cup buttermilk

Preheat the oven to 450°F. Lightly grease a cast-iron biscuit baker or baking sheet and set aside.

In a large bowl, combine the flour, baking powder, salt, cayenne, and cheese. Cut in the shortening with a pastry blender or 2 forks until the mixture is crumbly.

Add the buttermilk, stirring just until moistened. Drop by heaping tablespoons onto the prepared pan. Bake 9 minutes or until golden brown. Serve warm.

RASPBERRY-ALMOND BISCUITS

These sweet biscuits need no jam or jelly because the fruit is baked right in. Just have butter handy as soon as they come out of the oven.

YIELD: 18 BISCUITS

3 cups all-purpose flour
1/2 cup sugar
1 tablespoon baking powder
1/2 teaspoon baking soda
1/8 teaspoon salt
12 tablespoons unsalted butter, cubed
1 cup fresh raspberries (or frozen, but not thawed)
1/2 cup chopped almonds
1 teaspoon grated orange zest
3/4 cup milk
3/4 cup plain yogurt

Preheat the oven to 400°F. Lightly grease a cast-iron biscuit baker or baking sheet and set aside.

In a large bowl, combine the flour, sugar, baking powder, baking soda, and salt. With a pastry blender or 2 forks, cut in the butter until the mixture is crumbly.

Stir in the raspberries, almonds, and zest. Add the milk and yogurt, stirring just until moistened.

Transfer the dough to a lightly floured surface and knead 5 times. Roll to 3/4-inch thickness and cut with a 2-inch cutter. Place on the prepared pan and bake 20 to 25 minutes, or until golden brown. Serve warm.

POTATO BISCUITS

Leftover mashed potatoes have never gone to waste in a Southern kitchen. Here's proof!

YIELD: 10 TO 12 BISCUITS

1 cup all-purpose flour
3 teaspoons baking powder
1 teaspoon salt
2 tablespoons bacon drippings
1 cup mashed potatoes
1/2 cup milk

Preheat the oven to 400°F. Lightly grease a cast-iron biscuit baker or baking pan and set aside.

In a large mixing bowl, combine the flour, baking powder, and salt. Add the drippings and potatoes. Add just enough milk to make a soft dough. Stir until moistened.

Transfer the dough to a lightly floured surface and roll to 1/2-inch thickness. Cut with a 2-inch cutter and transfer to the prepared pan. Bake 12 to 15 minutes, or until golden brown. Serve hot.

WHIPPING CREAM BISCUITS

When I'm away from home and need to quickly whip up something for breakfast, this is the recipe I use. It can easily be remembered, and the ingredients are more than likely already on hand.

YIELD: 12 BISCUITS

2 cups self-rising flour
1 cup whipping cream

Preheat the oven to 450°F. Lightly grease a cast-iron biscuit baker or baking sheet and set aside.

In a mixing bowl, combine the flour and cream, stirring just until blended. (The dough will be a little stiff.)

Transfer the dough to a lightly floured surface and knead 10 times. Roll to ½-inch thickness and cut with a 2-inch cutter. Transfer to the prepared pan and bake 10 to 12 minutes, or until golden brown. Serve warm.

REFRIGERATOR BISCUITS

My husband calls these "Company's Coming Biscuits" because I always have them ready and in the refrigerator for the breakfast of overnight guests. They are also perfect for Christmas morning.

YIELD: 2 DOZEN BISCUITS

1 (¼-ounce) package active dried yeast
¼ cup hot water (110 to 115°F)
5 cups all-purpose flour
¼ cup sugar
1 tablespoon baking powder
1 teaspoon baking soda
1 teaspoon salt
1 cup vegetable shortening or lard
2 cups buttermilk

Place the yeast in a small bowl and cover with the water. Stir to dissolve the yeast and set aside.

In a large bowl, mix together the flour, sugar, baking powder, baking soda, and salt. Cut in the shortening with a pastry blender or 2 forks until the mixture resembles coarse meal. Make a well in the center and add the yeast mixture and buttermilk. Stir until moistened. Cover and refrigerate overnight.

Preheat the oven to 450°F. Lightly grease a cast-iron biscuit baker or baking sheet and set aside.

Transfer the dough to a lightly floured surface and knead 5 times. Roll the dough to ½-inch thickness and cut with a 2-inch cutter. Transfer to the prepared pan and bake 12 to 15 minutes, or until golden brown. Serve warm.

ROSEMARY CREAM BISCUITS

There's no need to cut in any fat with these biscuits because of the addition of cream. This is the perfect way to serve the season's first fresh strawberries.

YIELD: 8 SERVINGS

2 cups all-purpose flour
1 tablespoon baking powder
1 tablespoon sugar
½ teaspoon salt
¼ teaspoon finely chopped fresh rosemary
1¼ cups heavy cream
4 tablespoons unsalted butter, melted
Sliced strawberries, if desired

Preheat the oven to 425°F. Lightly grease a cast-iron biscuit baker or baking sheet and set aside.

Combine the flour, baking powder, sugar, salt, and rosemary in a large mixing bowl. Gradually pour in the cream, stirring constantly with a wooden spoon to moisten evenly.

Transfer the dough to a lightly floured surface and knead about 1 minute. Roll to ½-inch thickness and cut with a 2-inch fluted cutter dipped in flour. Transfer to the prepared pan and brush the tops with the butter. Bake 14 to 15 minutes, or until the edges are lightly browned. Cool on wire racks or serve warm with sliced fresh strawberries.

SNOWFLAKE BISCUITS

Do not confuse these feather-light biscuits with snowflake cookies. These rise on the baking pan.

YIELD: 24 BISCUITS

1 ($\frac{1}{2}$ -ounce) package active dried yeast

$\frac{1}{4}$ cup hot water (110°F to 115°F)

2 cups buttermilk

5 cups all-purpose flour

3 tablespoons sugar

1 tablespoon baking powder

2 teaspoons salt

1 teaspoon baking soda

$\frac{3}{4}$ cup vegetable shortening or lard

Lightly grease a large baking sheet and set aside.

In a medium bowl, combine the yeast and water. Let stand 5 minutes. Stir in the buttermilk and set aside.

In a separate bowl, combine the flour, sugar, baking powder, salt, and baking soda. With a pastry blender or 2 forks, cut in the shortening until the mixture resembles coarse meal. Add the buttermilk mixture, stirring until just moistened.

Transfer the dough to a lightly floured surface and knead 5 times. Roll the dough to $\frac{1}{2}$-inch thickness and cut with a 2-inch cutter. Place on the prepared pan. Cover and let rise 1 hour in a warm place free from drafts.

Preheat the oven to 425°F. Bake 10 minutes, or until golden brown. Serve warm.

KNEADING: Unless you are making drop biscuits, the dough will be kneaded. Don't overwork the dough by kneading or handling it too much. This is my favorite part of making biscuits.

SWEET POTATO BISCUITS

I first made these biscuits with two leftover baked sweet potatoes from a dinner party. Now I bake and mash the sweet potatoes just to have an excuse to make these. I especially like to serve them with slices of roasted turkey tucked inside.

YIELD: 7 SERVINGS

4 cups all-purpose flour

2 tablespoons baking powder

2 teaspoons salt

$\frac{1}{2}$ pound (2 sticks) unsalted butter

1 cup cooked mashed sweet potatoes

1 cup buttermilk

Preheat the oven to 425°F. Lightly grease a cast-iron biscuit baker or baking sheet and set aside.

In a large mixing bowl, combine the flour, baking powder, and salt. Cut in the butter with a pastry blender or 2 forks until the mixture is crumbly.

In a separate bowl, stir together the sweet potatoes and buttermilk. Add to the flour mixture, stirring just until moistened.

Transfer the dough to a lightly floured surface and knead 4 times. Roll the dough to $\frac{1}{2}$-inch thickness and cut with a 2-inch round cutter. Transfer to the prepared pan and bake 12 to 15 minutes, or until golden brown. Serve warm.

NAME: The word "biscuit" comes from a French term meaning "twice cooked." This name was given to sea biscuits that were often carried on ships. In order for the biscuits to remain crisp on the long journey, they had to be baked twice. This removed the excess moisture and kept spoilage at a minimum.

BLACKBERRIES

CHIGGERS ARE NASTY LITTLE BUGS THAT DEARLY LOVE TO BITE SOUTHERNERS YOUNG AND old. They seem to particularly enjoy being around when blackberries are ready to pick. They are a major concern at the very beginning of picking and right after you finish, but in between, I am always too busy munching on fruit to care!

As kids, we picked wild blackberries in the vacant lot next to our house. Did those nasty creatures ever stop us from heading over there to pick? No way! It was a difficult day to see that lot cleared of natural "debris" when a house was eventually built. Those blackberry canes were our summer friends.

When fresh blackberries burst on the local scene, my cooking quickly changes. Just pop one of these naturally sweet fruit bonbons in your mouth and you'll get an explosion of flavor that immediately turns addictive.

Although there are more than a thousand varieties worldwide, Southerners generally classify blackberries according to the plants they are coming from. In other words, do they have thorns or not? If you attempt to determine which are best, you'll quickly find there are fans on both sides.

I like them both, with my preference being determined by how I will be using the fruit. Thornless blackberries have a strong, tart flavor that is perfect for making jams and jellies. They are easier to pick, but should be harvested at the perfect stage of ripeness or you're in for a pucker!

The thorned varieties have a much smaller seed. They can be served whole in fruit salads and in yummy desserts without having to go to any trouble as far as removing the seeds.

Mother Nature is a curious creature. You would think that when temperatures soar in the summer, it would take a horrible toll on something as delicate as a fresh blackberry. But actually, it only serves to enhance the flavor and ripen them to perfection. If you ever wanted to know what summer tastes like, a ripe blackberry is it!

Nutrition: These jewels are high in vitamins B and C as well as dietary fiber. One cup of fresh fruit contains about sixty calories.

Selection: Good quality blackberries will be plump and look like they are so full of juice they could pop at any moment. The berries will also have a solid color that looks bright. Stem caps usually adhere only to immature fruit. You shouldn't have to tug very hard to separate the fruit from the cane. If you are purchasing picked fruit, there should be no sign of leakage on the container.

Storage: Blackberries are one of the most perishable fruits on the market. Use right away or you can freeze or can them for later use. Keep them refrigerated, preferably in a single layer to prevent bruising. Wash with a gentle spray of cold water just before using and drain on paper towels.

AFTER DINNER BLACKBERRY COBBLER

You might want to tell your family or guests what is on the menu for dessert before they begin eating the main course. They will want to save plenty of room! Add vanilla ice cream and you're in glory land!

YIELD: 6 SERVINGS

4 cups fresh blackberries
1 tablespoon lemon juice
1 egg
1 cup all-purpose flour
1 cup sugar
6 tablespoons unsalted butter, melted

Preheat the oven to 375°F. Lightly grease an 8-inch baking dish. Place the blackberries in the baking dish and sprinkle with the lemon juice.

In a medium bowl, combine the egg, flour, and sugar. Sprinkle evenly over the blackberries and drizzle with the melted butter.

Bake 35 minutes, or until lightly browned and bubbly. Let cool on a wire rack 10 minutes before serving.

BOTANY: Blackberries are the largest of all the wild berries grown in the United States. They are members of the rose family and are brambles that are closely related to boysenberries, raspberries, loganberries, and dewberries. The plants have roots that live for many years and tops that live only two years. They bear fruit on canes grown the previous year. Those canes die soon after fruiting.

FRESH BLACKBERRIES AND DUMPLINGS

Chicken shouldn't always get the dibs on dumplings. This dessert proves that dumplings can deliciously move to the end of the meal.

YIELD: 4 SERVINGS

$\frac{1}{2}$ cup all-purpose flour
$\frac{1}{4}$ cup sugar, divided
1 teaspoon baking powder
$\frac{1}{4}$ teaspoon salt
$\frac{1}{4}$ cup milk
2 cups blackberries
$\frac{2}{3}$ cup water
$\frac{1}{8}$ teaspoon ground nutmeg

In a mixing bowl, combine the flour, 2 tablespoons of the sugar, the baking powder, and salt. Stir well and make a well in the center. Add the milk and blend well. Set aside.

In a large saucepan, bring the blackberries, the remaining sugar, and the water to a boil over medium heat. Drop tablespoons of the batter in the boiling mixture and sprinkle the top with nutmeg.

Cover and cook 10 minutes, or until the dumplings are done. Serve warm.

ORIGIN: The wild blackberry is believed to have originated in North America. Other varieties are natives of Europe. The European and American species are believed to have been separated by the southern movement of glaciers in the ice age.

FAMILY REUNION BLACKBERRY SANGRIA

This recipe makes a boatload, but sometimes the gathering is large and a boat is necessary!

YIELD: 13 CUPS

4 cups fresh blackberries, divided
$^3/_4$ cup sugar
1$^1/_2$ cups water
Dash of salt
2 (750-mililiter) bottles rosé or blush wine
1 cup cognac
$^1/_4$ cup lime juice
1$^1/_2$ cups sliced nectarines
1$^1/_2$ cups sliced plums

In a medium saucepan over medium-high heat, combine 2 cups of the blackberries with the sugar, water, and salt. Bring to a boil and reduce the heat to medium low. Simmer 10 minutes, stirring occasionally. Cool and strain through a fine mesh strainer, pressing gently. Discard the solids.

In a gallon jar or large pitcher, combine the cooked syrup, wine, cognac, lime juice, nectarines, plums, and the remaining blackberries, stirring well to blend. Cover and refrigerate at least 4 hours and up to 24 hours. Serve over ice.

BLACKBERRY BARS

George and I sit on the front porch in our rockers when it rains. These treats make us sit there a little longer and enjoy the free water our lawn receives!

YIELD: 12 BARS

1 cup all-purpose flour
$^3/_4$ cup packed brown sugar
4 tablespoons unsalted butter
$^1/_2$ cup sour cream
1 egg, lightly beaten
1 teaspoon ground cinnamon
$^3/_4$ teaspoon baking soda
$^1/_2$ teaspoon pure vanilla extract
$^1/_4$ teaspoon salt
1 cup blackberries
Confectioners' sugar

Preheat the oven to 350°F.

In a mixing bowl, combine the flour and brown sugar, mixing well. Cut in the butter with a pastry blender or 2 forks until the mixture resembles coarse meal. Press 1$^1/_3$ cups in the bottom of an ungreased 8-inch square baking pan and set aside.

In the bowl of an electric mixer, combine the remaining crumbs with the sour cream, egg, cinnamon, baking soda, extract, and salt. Blend well. Fold in the berries and spoon over the crust, spreading evenly.

Bake 35 minutes. Cool completely on a wire rack. Sprinkle with confectioners' sugar before cutting into bars.

INDIVIDUAL FRESH BLACKBERRY TARTS

I always like individual servings because it looks like more time and effort was put into each guest. These tarts use prepackaged shells that are available in the frozen food section of the supermarket.

YIELD: 8 SERVINGS

1 (10-ounce) package frozen tart shells
2 quarts fresh blackberries
1 cup water
1³/₄ cups sugar, divided
¹/₂ cup self-rising flour
4 tablespoons unsalted butter
2¹/₈ teaspoons pure vanilla extract, divided
1 cup whipping cream

Bake the tarts according to the package directions and cool completely. Bring the blackberries and water to a boil over medium heat. Reduce the heat to low and simmer 5 minutes.

Mash the berries with the back of a wooden spoon in a fine mesh strainer into a liquid measure. You should have 2 cups of liquid.

Stir together 1¹/₂ cups of the sugar and the flour in a saucepan. Gradually add the blackberry juice, whisking constantly until smooth. Bring to a boil over medium heat, whisking constantly. Reduce the heat to low and simmer 3 minutes, or until the mixture is thickened. Remove from the heat and stir in the butter and 2 teaspoons of the extract.

Spoon the filling into the prepared tart shells and cool completely. Beat the cream at high speed of an electric mixer until foamy. Gradually add the remaining ¹/₂ cup sugar and the remaining ¹/₈ teaspoon extract. Beat until stiff peaks form. Dollop the whipped cream over the tarts just before serving.

ICEBOX BLACKBERRY SAUCE

Old-time Southerners call the refrigerator an icebox and I love the charm of that term. That's exactly where you'll keep this make-ahead sauce that can be spooned over everything from sponge cake to ice cream.

YIELD: 4 CUPS

5 cups fresh blackberries
1 cup plus 2 tablespoons water, divided
³/₄ cup sugar
1 tablespoon cornstarch
1 tablespoon lemon juice

In a large saucepan over medium-high heat, combine the blackberries, 1 cup of the water, and the sugar and bring to a boil.

Meanwhile in a small bowl, whisk together the remaining 2 tablespoons of water and the cornstarch. Stir into the blackberry mixture when it comes to a boil. Boil 1 minute, stirring constantly. Add the lemon juice and blend well. Cool to room temperature, cover, and refrigerate until ready to serve.

PRESERVING: Blackberries make excellent jams, jellies, and syrups. They can also be canned and frozen whole with good results. I freeze them in a single layer on a tray until they are hard. Then I pack them into freezer containers, seal, label, and freeze. There is no reason to thaw them before use. Throughout the South, blackberries are frequently used to make wine.

SEEDLESS BLACKBERRY FREEZER JAM

I adore the ease of making freezer jam. There's no specialized canning equipment necessary and you don't have to spend time over a hot stove.

YIELD: 7 HALF-PINTS

2 quarts blackberries
5$\frac{1}{2}$ cups sugar
1 (1.75-ounce) box powdered pectin
$\frac{3}{4}$ cup water

Place the blackberries in a large saucepan over medium heat. When soft, about 4 minutes, press through a sieve or food mill into a large mixing bowl. Discard the seeds. Toss the berries with the sugar and let stand 10 minutes, stirring occasionally.

Meanwhile, combine the pectin and water in a small saucepan over medium-high heat. Bring to a boil and boil 1 minute, stirring constantly. Add to the berry mixture and stir constantly 3 minutes.

Pour into freezer containers or canning jars, leaving $\frac{1}{2}$-inch headspace. Cover and let stand at room temperature up to 24 hours or until set. Freeze or refrigerate.

SUNDAY MORNING BLACKBERRY SYRUP

Pancakes and waffles never had it so lively! This is equally good over ice cream.

YIELD: 1$\frac{2}{3}$ CUPS

3 cups blackberries
1$\frac{1}{4}$ cups sugar

$\frac{1}{4}$ cup light corn syrup
1 teaspoon cornstarch

Place the berries in a blender and process until smooth. Pour through a fine mesh strainer into a medium saucepan. Discard the solids.

Add the sugar, corn syrup, and cornstarch and place over medium heat. Bring to a boil, stirring occasionally. Boil 1 minute. Cool to room temperature and serve.

SWEET GLORY BLACKBERRY SHERBET

This sherbet reminds me of blackberry cheesecake.

YIELD: 1 QUART

4 cups blackberries
2 cups sugar
2 cups buttermilk

Place the berries and sugar in a large bowl and toss gently. Let stand 30 minutes.

Transfer the berry mixture to a blender and process until smooth. Pour through a fine mesh strainer into a 9-inch square baking pan and discard the solids. Stir in the buttermilk, cover, and freeze 8 hours.

Break into chunks and place in the bowl of an electric mixer. Beat at medium speed until smooth. Return to the pan, cover, and freeze 3 hours or until firm. Serve in chilled serving glasses or bowls.

TENNESSEE BLACKBERRY JAM CAKE

Jam cakes can be made with any type of jam, but I'm partial to blackberry. It is just the right balance of tart with the caramel frosting.

YIELD: 12 SERVINGS

3 cups plus 1 tablespoon all-purpose flour

1^1/$_2$ teaspoons ground allspice

1^1/$_2$ teaspoons ground cloves

1^1/$_4$ teaspoons salt

^{1}/$_2$ teaspoon ground cinnamon

^{1}/$_2$ pound (2 sticks) unsalted butter, softened

2 cups sugar

5 eggs, lightly beaten

1 cup buttermilk

1 teaspoon baking soda

1 cup blackberry jam

1 cup chopped golden raisins

1 cup chopped pecans

Grandmother's Heavenly Caramel Frosting
(page 122)

Preheat the oven to 325°F. Grease and flour two 9-inch cake pans and set aside.

In a mixing bowl, combine 3 cups of the flour with the allspice, cloves, salt, and cinnamon. Set aside.

In the bowl of an electric mixer, beat the butter and sugar until light and fluffy, about 3 minutes. Add the eggs and beat until well combined.

In a small bowl, combine the buttermilk and baking soda. Alternately add the flour mixture and buttermilk mixture to the butter mixture, beating well after each addition. Stir in the jam.

In a small bowl, toss the raisins and pecans with the remaining tablespoon of flour. Add to the batter and stir until combined. Pour the batter evenly into the prepared pans.

Bake 42 to 45 minutes, or until a tester inserted in the center comes out clean. Cool in the pans on wire racks 15 minutes before cooling completely. Frost with the caramel frosting.

SHADE TREE BLACKBERRY SORBET

While most Southerners resort to cooling off under shade trees, this sorbet can accomplish the task anywhere. It's a frozen hot weather treat with a beautiful lavender color.

YIELD: 8 SERVINGS

2^1/$_2$ cups boiling water

1 regular tea bag

3 cups blackberries

1^1/$_4$ cups sugar

^{1}/$_4$ cup fresh lemon juice

Mint sprigs for garnish

Pour the boiling water over the tea bag and steep 10 minutes. Squeeze the tea bag and discard.

In a medium bowl, toss the blackberries with the sugar. With the back of a wooden spoon, crush the berries to release the juices. Pour the tea over the berries and completely cool.

Purée the blackberry mixture in a food processor. Strain through a fine sieve into a large bowl. Add the juice and stir well. Refrigerate 1 hour.

Transfer the sorbet mixture to an ice cream maker and freeze according to manufacturer's instructions. Garnish with mint sprigs and serve cold.

BLUEBERRIES

I **DID NOT GROW UP ANYWHERE NEAR FARMERS WHO GREW FRESH BLUEBERRIES AND, HENCE,** was seriously unfamiliar with this delicacy for years. We had canned and frozen blueberries that were used in pies, tarts, and cobblers, but farm-fresh blueberries were simply not around the area of Mississippi where I grew up.

As a result, it was one of those fruits that I thought was just okay in the taste department. Then I moved to Tennessee and met Dick Kleinau, who grew gorgeous blueberries. I finally had a taste of the real deal right off the plant. "My gracious!" was my initial reaction and I have looked for ways to use them ever since.

There was a time not long ago when blueberries were reserved for a fate of either muffins or pies. Getting creative with this tiny fruit usually meant you made a jam or jelly out of it, but nothing more than that. Well, those days are thankfully over.

Unlike many other fruits, the season for fresh blueberries is relatively long. That's good news because who can resist eating them by the handful? It's the perfect snack with no need for peeling, pitting, coring, or cutting.

Every summer when I head to local patches to "pick" blueberries, I have to nearly laugh because the berries will just about fall off the plant when fully ripe. I learned to harvest this fruit by "tickling them" and the ripe berries would literally pour themselves into my waiting bucket. It is about as easy as falling asleep after Easter dinner.

If you haven't located a farm near you for picking purposes, start investigating. It will be the easiest fruit you have ever harvested. These recipes will take care of the "What do I do with them now?" dilemma!

Nutrition: These berries have more to offer than good looks and good taste. They are loaded with dietary fiber and vitamin A, containing more than any other berry. A half-cup serving contains only 42 calories.

Storage: Refrigeration is essential to prolong the shelf life of blueberries. Store them unwashed because moisture will cause the berries to break down faster and mold. Just give them a quick, but gentle, rinse of cold water before using.

Allow them to dry on paper towels and blot the excess moisture. This will keep the bold color from bleeding into other ingredients with which they are mixed. Also, toss the berries with a small amount of flour before folding into baked goods and it will inhibit color bleeding as well.

ALABAMA BLUEBERRY CRUNCH

When I lived in Mobile, this recipe was in a leaflet I picked up from the Alabama Blueberry Association. It looked so easy, I just had to give it a try…year after year after year after year!

YIELD: 10 SERVINGS

1 (20-ounce) can crushed pineapple, undrained

1 (18.25-ounce) package yellow cake mix

3 cups fresh or frozen blueberries (if frozen, do not thaw)

1/2 cup sugar

1/4 pound (1 stick) unsalted butter, melted

1 cup chopped pecans

Preheat the oven to 350°F. Lightly grease a 13 x 9-inch baking dish. Spread the pineapple evenly in the bottom of the prepared dish. Sprinkle the cake mix, blueberries, and sugar on top, in that order. Drizzle with the butter and top with the pecans.

Bake 45 minutes, or until bubbly. Cool at least 10 minutes. Serve warm or at room temperature.

"BLUE" BLUEBERRY SAUCE

This sauce has literally dozens of uses. Spoon it over ice cream, frozen yogurt, toasted pound cake, pancakes, waffles, or cheesecake.

YIELD: 2 1/2 CUPS SAUCE

2 cups fresh blueberries

2/3 cup sugar

1 teaspoon lemon juice

1/2 teaspoon ground cinnamon

In a small saucepan set over high heat, combine the blueberries, sugar, lemon juice, and cinnamon. Cook 10 minutes, stirring occasionally.

Transfer to a blender or food processor and purée. Strain and serve warm, at room temperature, or cold.

BLUEBERRY-LEMON POUND CAKE

I have always loved to match up the colors blue and yellow. I dreamed of having a blue and yellow room with white wicker furniture as a kid. No wonder this cake is so gorgeous to me!

YIELD: 12 TO 16 SERVINGS

1 pound (4 sticks) unsalted butter, softened

3 cups sugar

6 eggs

4 cups all-purpose flour

1 tablespoon baking powder

1/2 teaspoon salt

1 cup milk

2 teaspoons pure lemon extract

1/4 cup fresh lemon juice

1 teaspoon freshly grated lemon zest

2 cups fresh blueberries

Preheat the oven to 350°F. Grease and flour the bottom and sides of a 10-inch tube or Bundt pan. Set aside.

In a large bowl, cream the butter and sugar together at medium speed until light and fluffy. Add the eggs, one at a time, beating well after each addition.

In a separate bowl, sift together the flour, baking powder, and salt. In another bowl, combine the milk, extract, juice, and zest. Add the dry and wet mixtures alternately to butter mixture, beginning and ending with the dry. Fold in the blueberries.

Transfer the batter into the prepared pan. Bake 50 to 60 minutes, or until a tester inserted in the center comes out clean. Cool 10 minutes in the pan, and then turn onto a wire rack and cool completely before slicing.

COUNTRY TIME BLUEBERRY COBBLER

The sweet, biscuit-like crust on this cobbler is the perfect host for fresh blueberries.

YIELD: 8 SERVINGS

$^1/_4$ pound (1 stick) unsalted butter
1 cup all-purpose flour
$1^1/_2$ teaspoons baking powder
$^1/_2$ teaspoon salt
$^3/_4$ cup sugar, divided
$^3/_4$ cup milk
2 cups fresh blueberries
$^1/_2$ cup water
Vanilla ice cream

Preheat the oven to 350°F. While the oven preheats, place the butter in a shallow $1^1/_2$-quart baking pan and place in the oven to melt.

Meanwhile, in a medium bowl, combine the flour, baking powder, salt, $^1/_2$ cup of the sugar, and milk. Pour evenly over the melted butter, but do not stir.

Combine the blueberries, the remaining $^1/_4$ cup sugar and the water. Distribute evenly over the flour mixture. Do not stir. Bake 40 to 45 minutes, or until golden brown. Serve warm with vanilla ice cream.

GLAZED BLUEBERRY-ORANGE BREAD

A glaze is a Southerner's version of a sauce that is barely seen. Sunny oranges are a nice accompaniment for the sweet blueberries.

YIELD: 1 LOAF

2 cups all-purpose flour
1 cup sugar
$^1/_4$ teaspoon baking soda
1 teaspoon baking powder
$^1/_2$ teaspoon salt
1 egg, well beaten
2 tablespoons unsalted butter, melted
1 tablespoon grated orange zest
$^3/_4$ cup plus 2 tablespoons orange juice
1 cup fresh blueberries
2 tablespoons honey

Preheat the oven to 350°F. Grease a loaf pan and set aside.

In a large bowl, sift together the flour, sugar, baking soda, baking powder, and salt. Make a well in the center of the dry ingredients. Set aside.

In a medium bowl, combine the egg, butter, zest, and $^3/_4$ cup of the juice. Add to the dry mixture all at once and stir just until moistened. Gently fold in the blueberries.

Spoon the batter into the prepared pan. Bake 50 to 60 minutes, or until a tester inserted in the center comes out clean. Cool in pan on a wire rack 10 minutes. Then remove and cool completely on wire rack.

In a small bowl, combine the honey and the remaining 2 tablespoons of the juice. Using a pastry brush, glaze the loaf with the honey mixture. Slice and serve.

"RISE AND SHINE" BLUEBERRY MUFFINS

This is the finest of all breakfast muffins. Pulling sleepyheads out of bed has never been easier.

YIELD: 12 MUFFINS

$3\frac{1}{2}$ cups all-purpose flour

$1\frac{1}{2}$ teaspoons baking powder

$\frac{1}{4}$ teaspoon baking soda

$\frac{3}{4}$ teaspoon salt

11 tablespoons unsalted butter, softened

$1\frac{1}{2}$ cups packed brown sugar

2 eggs

2 teaspoons pure vanilla extract

$1\frac{1}{4}$ cups buttermilk

3 cups fresh blueberries

Preheat the oven to 350°F. Grease the muffin cups or, if using paper liners, place liners in the cups and mist with cooking spray. Set aside.

Sift together the flour, baking powder, baking soda, and salt in a mixing bowl. Set aside. In a separate bowl, cream the butter and brown sugar until light and fluffy. Add the eggs, extract, and buttermilk, mixing well.

Gradually add the flour mixture, beating until just combined. Gently fold in the blueberries. Use an ice cream scoop to divide the batter among the muffin cups. Place the muffin tin on a baking sheet to catch any drips.

Bake 30 to 40 minutes, or until golden brown and springy to the tough. Cool in the pan 15 minutes. Serve warm.

SOUR CREAM BLUEBERRY PIE

I love this pie, I love this pie, I love this pie! You will too!

YIELD: 8 SERVINGS

1 recipe Single Pie Pastry (page 402)

1 cup sour cream

$\frac{3}{4}$ cup granulated sugar

1 egg

1 teaspoon pure vanilla extract

$2\frac{1}{2}$ cups fresh blueberries

2 tablespoons plus $\frac{1}{3}$ cup all-purpose flour, divided

$\frac{1}{8}$ teaspoon salt

$\frac{1}{3}$ cup packed light brown sugar

$\frac{1}{3}$ cup chopped pecans

3 tablespoons unsalted butter, melted

Preheat the oven to 400°F. Place the prepared crust in a 9-inch pie pan and set aside.

In a medium bowl, stir together the sour cream, granulated sugar, egg, and extract. In another bowl gently toss the blueberries with 2 tablespoons of the flour and the salt. Fold into the sour cream mixture and transfer to the prepared piecrust. Bake 25 minutes.

Meanwhile, combine the remaining $\frac{1}{3}$ cup of the flour, the brown sugar, pecans, and butter. During the last 10 minutes of baking, spread over the top of the pie. Cool on a wire rack completely before slicing and serving.

VODKA BLUEBERRY CORDIAL

I have always loved the word "cordial." It just sounded much more Southern and ladylike than a liqueur. This spirited concoction makes a terrific gift. You can also serve it with an equal amount of club soda or ginger ale over ice.

YIELD: 2½ CUPS

1²/₃ cups vodka

1 cup sugar

3 cups fresh or frozen blueberries
  (if frozen, do not thaw)

In a wide-mouthed 1-quart canning jar, combine the vodka and sugar. Cover and shake vigorously to dissolve the sugar. Add the blueberries, cover tightly, and shake again. Let stand in a cool, dark place 2 months.

Pour the mixture through a fine mesh strainer into a decorative jar. Discard the blueberries. Serve as a cordial. Store at room temperature.

ORIGIN: Blueberries are natives of North America, where 95 percent of the world's commercially produced fruits are grown.

BOTANY: This tiny little berry is huge in the eyes of fruit lovers. Blueberries are related to cranberries, huckleberries, mountain laurels, heather, rhododendrons, and azaleas. The plants are shrub-like and dependent on bees for pollination. They thrive in acid soils. The powdery gray, naturally occurring "bloom" on the skin surface helps retain moisture after harvest.

TEA ROOM FRESH BLUEBERRY SHORTCAKE

Step aside, strawberries. Blueberries are the star of this show! Serve as an afternoon pick-me-up with tea or anytime you are craving something luscious.

YIELD: 4 SERVINGS

1 pint fresh blueberries

2 tablespoons confectioners' sugar

1/3 cup plus 1 tablespoon all-purpose flour

1 teaspoon baking powder

1 tablespoon plus a pinch granulated sugar

Pinch of salt

2 tablespoons unsalted butter, cut into
  small pieces

2 tablespoons buttermilk

2 tablespoons almond slivers

1 cup vanilla yogurt

Preheat the oven to 375°F. Combine the blueberries and confectioners' sugar and set aside.

In a mixing bowl, sift together the flour, baking powder, a pinch of the granulated sugar, and the salt. With a pastry blender or 2 forks, cut in the butter until the mixture resembles coarse meal. Add the buttermilk and blend just until combined.

On a lightly floured surface, pat the dough into a 4-inch square about ½ inch thick. Cut into 4 biscuits with a 2-inch cutter. Place on a parchment paper-lined baking sheet and sprinkle evenly with the remaining 1 tablespoon of sugar. Top each with the almond slivers. Bake 15 minutes, or until golden brown.

Meanwhile add the yogurt to the blueberries. When the biscuits are done, cut in half. Place a fourth of the blueberry mixture on half of each biscuit. Top with the other half. Serve immediately.

BREAD BASKET

NOTHING COULD BE FINER THAN TO WALK IN A KITCHEN WHILE LOAVES OF HOMEMADE bread are baking in the oven. It is an instantly recognizable aroma that can cause even those with full bellies to salivate and suddenly feel a little hungry once more.

While most would rightfully place hot biscuits and cornbread in the Southern bread basket, many other breads are just as frequently made and served. And in the old South, cooks never had trouble finding a warm place for yeast bread to rise thanks to our weather!

For me, bread baking is nothing short of culinary therapy. When I feel even the least bit stressed, it's time to take those frustrations out in the kitchen. Bread making requires my complete attention for measuring, mixing, kneading, rising, punching down, rolling out, shaping, rising again, and finally baking.

All of that time and effort is worth it in the end when a hot-from-the-oven loaf is pulled out to enjoy. Suddenly any stress I was feeling is long gone, and I didn't even notice when it left the room.

While some bakers let bread machines do all the work for them, I find that doing it myself is much more satisfying. It returns me to my Southern baking roots and forces me to pay attention to details. And after five or ten minutes of kneading, you've given your arms and hands a great work-out!

So go ahead and pull the butter out of the refrigerator and let it soften. You'll need it as soon as that first loaf comes out of the oven and is cool enough to slice.

Yeast: Yeasts are actually tiny plants that can be found throughout nature. They are in everything from the nectar of flowers to the soil in our yards. It takes 20 billion yeast cells to weigh one gram or $1/28$ of an ounce. There are two types of yeast available commercially, which are **brewer's yeast** and **baker's yeast**. Brewer's yeast is used in beer making, but baker's yeast is what we use for bread making. It is available in three forms: Active dried, compressed fresh, and in yeast starters.

Yeast Starters: Yeast starters are homemade mixtures of flour, water, sugar, and yeast that are allowed to ferment. After a sufficient amount of time, you can use a portion of the "starter" as the leavening in certain recipes. Starters must be kept refrigerated and replenished every week with equal portions of additional flour and water. Two cups of starter is the equivalent of one (.25-ounce) package of active dried yeast.

Active Dried Yeast: The most commonly used yeast in the South is active dried yeast, which is dehydrated granules of yeast cells that are still alive but dormant thanks to the absence of moisture. Liquid that is heated to a temperature between 110°F and 115°F will cause the cells to become active again. It can also be mixed with flour and then activated with liquid that is between 120°F and 130°F. The flour serves as a protective barrier to keep the yeast safe from the hotter liquid.

BASIC WHITE BREAD

This recipe is bread baking at its finest. Since it makes two loaves, either freeze the extra or gift it to a friend.

YIELD: 2 LOAVES

1 (.25-ounce) package active dried yeast
2 cups hot milk (110°F to 115°F)
2 cups hot half-and-half (110°F to 115°F)
4 tablespoons unsalted butter, melted
1/4 cup confectioners' sugar
8 cups all-purpose flour
1 tablespoon plus 1 teaspoon salt
1 egg
2 tablespoons water

In a mixing bowl, combine the yeast, milk, and half-and-half, stirring until the yeast dissolves. Let stand 5 minutes. Whisk in the butter and confectioners' sugar. Mix well.

In a mixing bowl, combine the flour and salt. Slowly add the yeast mixture and mix well. Turn the dough onto a well-floured surface and knead 5 to 7 minutes.

Place the dough in a generously greased bowl, turning to grease the top. Cover and let rise in a warm place free from drafts 1 hour.

Grease two loaf pans and set aside. Punch the dough down with your fist and divide it into two equal portions. Shape into loaves and place in the prepared pans. Let it rise another 45 minutes in a warm place free from drafts.

Preheat the oven to 400°F. In a small bowl, whisk together the egg and water. Brush over the tops of the dough.

Bake 1 hour, or until golden brown and hollow sounding when tapped. Immediately remove from the pans and cool at least 1 hour on wire racks before slicing and serving.

BOURBON STREET BEIGNETS

Beignet is the French word for "fritter" and these yeast pastries are served all over New Orleans. The dough is refrigerated overnight, which slows down but does not stop the yeast activity.

YIELD: 2½ DOZEN

1 (.25-ounce) package active dried yeast
1 cup hot water (110°F to 115°F)
3/4 cup evaporated milk
1/4 cup granulated sugar
1 teaspoon salt
1 egg
4¼ cups all-purpose flour
Vegetable oil
Confectioners' sugar

In a small bowl, combine the yeast and water, stirring until the yeast dissolves. Let stand 5 minutes.

Meanwhile, whisk together the milk, granulated sugar, salt, and egg. Stir in the yeast mixture. Gradually add the flour to make a soft dough. Cover and refrigerate 8 hours or overnight.

Pour the oil to a depth of 4 inches in a Dutch oven. Place over medium-high heat and bring to 375°F.

Turn the dough onto a well-floured surface and knead six times. Roll the dough into a 15 x 12-inch rectangle and cut into 2½-inch squares.

Carefully lower a few dough squares into the hot oil and fry 1 minute on each side or until golden brown. Drain on paper towels and sprinkle with the confectioners' sugar. Repeat with the remaining dough. Serve warm.

FIRST TIMER'S FLATBREAD

This is the bread recipe to use when teaching young (or old!) ones how to make yeast bread for the first time. Since it's supposed to be flat, you don't have to worry about mile-high rising.

YIELD: 1 LOAF

1 (.25-ounce) envelope active dried yeast
1 cup hot water (110°F to 115°F)
3 cups all-purpose flour, divided
4 tablespoons unsalted butter, softened
$\frac{1}{2}$ teaspoon salt
4 tablespoons olive oil, divided
$\frac{1}{2}$ teaspoon onion or garlic salt
$\frac{1}{4}$ teaspoon black pepper

In a small bowl, combine the yeast and water, stirring until the yeast dissolves. Let stand 5 minutes.

Place 2 cups of the flour in a mixing bowl and make a well in the center. Add the yeast mixture and stir until a soft dough forms. Cover and let rise in a warm place free from drafts for 1 hour, or until doubled in size.

Sprinkle the remaining cup of flour on a flat surface. Turn the dough onto the surface and knead until the flour is incorporated to make a firm dough. Gradually knead in the butter and salt. Knead until the dough is smooth and elastic, around 5 minutes.

Brush a jelly-roll pan with 1 tablespoon of the oil and set aside.

Roll the dough into a 15 x 10-inch rectangle and place in the prepared pan. Using your fingertips, press small indentions in the top of the dough. Drizzle with the remaining 3 tablespoons of oil and sprinkle evenly with the onion salt and pepper.

Cover and let rise in a warm place away from drafts 40 to 45 minutes, or until almost doubled in size. Preheat the oven to 375°F.

Bake 25 to 30 minutes, or until the top is golden brown. Cut into squares and serve warm.

PARTY BUTTER MUFFINS

Use a miniature muffin pan for baking these melt-in-your-mouth muffin bites. This is a quick bread thanks to the leavening in self-rising flour.

YIELD: 2½ DOZEN MINI MUFFINS

2 cups self-rising flour
$\frac{1}{2}$ pound (2 sticks) unsalted butter, melted
1 (8-ounce) container sour cream

Preheat the oven to 350°F. Lightly grease a miniature muffin pan and set aside.

In a mixing bowl, combine the flour, butter, and sour cream. Stir just until blended. Spoon the batter into the prepared muffin cups, filling to the top.

Bake 25 minutes, or until lightly browned. Serve warm or cool to room temperature.

POPPY SEED TWISTED BREAD

This bread looks difficult to make, but isn't. You can substitute toasted sesame seeds for the poppy seeds if you wish.

YIELD: 1 LOAF

$2\frac{1}{2}$ cups all-purpose flour, divided
3 tablespoons sugar
1 (.25-ounce) package active dried yeast
1 teaspoon plus $\frac{1}{8}$ teaspoon salt, divided
$\frac{1}{2}$ cup milk
$\frac{1}{4}$ cup water

5 tablespoons unsalted butter, divided

2 eggs

1 cup chopped onion

1 1/2 tablespoons poppy seeds, divided

In a large bowl, combine 1 cup of the flour, the sugar, yeast, and 1 teaspoon of the salt.

In a heavy saucepan, combine the milk, water, and 3 tablespoons of the butter over medium-high heat. Stir until the butter melts and the temperature is between 120°F and 130°F. Gradually stir into the yeast mixture. Add 1 egg and the remaining 1 1/2 cups of flour. Blend well.

Turn the dough onto a well-floured surface and knead 6 minutes or until smooth and elastic. Place in a well-greased bowl, turning to evenly grease the top. Cover and let stand 10 minutes.

In a small bowl, melt the remaining 2 tablespoons of butter on low power in the microwave 1 minute. Add the onion, 1 tablespoon of the poppy seeds, and the remaining 1/8 teaspoon of salt. Set aside.

On a lightly floured surface, roll the dough into a 14 x 10-inch rectangle. Cut in half lengthwise. Spoon half of the onion mixture down the center of each rectangle. Bring the sides over the filling to make a loaf and pinch the seams to seal.

Place the loaves side by side on a lightly greased baking sheet, seam side down. Pinch the ends of each loaf together at one end to seal. Twist the loaves together and pinch the other ends together. Cover and let rise in a warm place away from drafts 30 minutes, or until doubled in size.

Preheat the oven to 350°F. Lightly beat the remaining egg and brush over the dough. Sprinkle with the remaining poppy seeds. Bake 35 minutes, shielding with aluminum foil after 25 minutes. Cool completely on a wire rack.

PULL APART MONKEY BREAD

Who can resist pulling these clumps of buttery bread apart? Not many! This recipe is neither sweet nor savory. You can make it either way by adding two teaspoons of cinnamon sugar or dried herbs to the mixture.

YIELD: 8 SERVINGS

3 1/4 cups bread flour, divided

1 (.25-ounce) package active dried yeast

1 egg

1 cup very hot water (120°F to 130°F)

2 tablespoons unsalted butter, melted, divided

1 tablespoon sugar

1/2 teaspoon salt

3 tablespoons unsalted butter, melted

Grease a 10-inch Bundt pan and set aside.

Place 1 1/2 cups of the flour, the yeast, egg, water, softened butter, sugar, and salt in the bowl of a food processor. Process 2 minutes. Add the remaining flour through the chute with the processor running to form a dough ball.

Turn the dough onto a lightly floured surface and knead 1 minute. Roll into a 15 x 12-inch rectangle and brush with 1 tablespoon of the melted butter. Cut into 1 1/2-inch squares and layer half of the pieces with the buttered side down in the prepared pan.

Brush what is now the top of the dough in the pan with the remaining tablespoon of the melted butter. Repeat with the remaining dough and butter. Cover and let rise in a warm place free from drafts 45 minutes, or until doubled in size.

Preheat the oven to 400°F. Bake 22 to 25 minutes, or until golden brown. Cool in the pan 2 minutes. Invert on a wire rack to cool at least 30 minutes before serving or cool completely and serve.

YEAST ROLLS

These go with nearly every food ever made!

YIELD: 24 ROLLS

1 (.25-ounce) package active dried yeast
$\frac{1}{4}$ cup hot water (110°F to 115°F)
1 teaspoon plus 2 tablespoons sugar, divided
2 tablespoons unsalted butter, softened
$1\frac{1}{4}$ teaspoons salt
1 egg
$1\frac{1}{4}$ cups milk
4 cups all-purpose flour

In small bowl, combine the yeast, hot water, and 1 teaspoon of the sugar. Let stand 5 minutes.

Meanwhile, in the bowl of an electric mixer, combine the remaining 2 tablespoons of sugar, the butter, and salt until creamy. Add the egg, milk, and yeast mixture, beating until well blended.

With the mixer on low speed, gradually add the flour, beating until smooth. Turn the dough out onto a well-floured surface and knead 3 minutes, or until smooth and elastic. Place in a well-greased bowl, turning to evenly coat all the dough. Cover and let rise in a warm place away from drafts 35 minutes, or until doubled in size.

Preheat the oven to 400°F. Lightly grease two 9-inch square baking pans and set aside.

Punch the dough down and turn onto a floured surface. Divide the dough into 24 pieces and shape into balls. Place in the prepared pans, cover, and let rise 15 minutes. Bake 15 minutes, or until golden brown on top. Serve warm.

YOGURT FREEZER BREAD

This is called freezer bread because it truly does freeze beautifully. Since it makes two loaves, you have one for now and another for later. To freeze, wrap in heavy-duty aluminum foil and seal in a zip-top freezer bag. Use within one month.

YIELD: 2 LOAVES

2 (.25-ounce) packages active dried yeast
$\frac{1}{2}$ cup hot water (110°F to 115°F)
2 tablespoons sugar
$4\frac{1}{4}$ cups all-purpose flour, divided
$1\frac{1}{2}$ cups plain yogurt
1 tablespoon unsalted butter, melted
1 teaspoon salt
1 egg

In a small bowl, combine the yeast, hot water, and sugar, stirring until the yeast and sugar dissolve. Let stand 5 minutes.

In a mixing bowl, combine 1 cup of the flour with the yogurt, butter, and salt. Stir in the yeast mixture and stir until well blended. Gradually add the remaining $3\frac{1}{4}$ cups of flour to make a stiff dough.

Turn the dough onto a well-floured surface and knead 5 minutes or until elastic and smooth. Place in a generously greased bowl and turn to grease the top. Cover and let rise in a warm place free from drafts 1 hour, or until doubled in size.

Punch the dough down and divide into two equal portions. Shape into loaves and place in two greased loaf pans. Cover and let rise in a warm place free from drafts 40 minutes, or until doubled in size.

Preheat the oven to 375°F. Beat the egg and brush over the tops of the dough. Bake 30 minutes, or until golden brown. Immediately remove from the pans and cool on wire racks at least 1 hour before slicing and serving.

BROCCOLI & CAULIFLOWER

I GREW UP WITH TWO OF THE FINEST FLOWER GROWERS IN MISSISSIPPI. MY MOTHER AND grandmother were the envy of everyone thanks to their talent for growing gorgeous blooms of every color, shape, and fragrance. In fact, they inspired my own love of flower gardening. All my life flowers have been enjoyed in the garden, cut for enjoying in the house, and the seeds and divided plants passed on to friends for their own flowerbeds.

To be honest, there was never a time when I thought I just wanted to pick one of those flowers and chow down on it. However, that's exactly what I do when I eat broccoli and cauliflower. Those beautiful green and cream florets are composed of tiny clusters of unopened flowers. In cauliflower, the florets are sometimes called curd. I never thought I would say this, but these flowers are absolutely delicious!

I believe most of those who continue to say they do not enjoy eating these vegetables have probably had it served to them either overcooked or raw with dip. After all, that seems to be common at every gathering no matter where you live.

But consider these two Mediterranean natives in a different light. They sing when roasted, barely sautéed, quickly steamed, or stir-fried. Casseroles love them, as do soups and salads that are served either warm or chilled.

If you are picturing the cheese-drenched concoction dished up on your school lunch tray, think again. These recipes are designed to put aside any preconceived notions of how you think these vegetables will forever and always taste. They would love a second chance and you'll be glad you gave them one!

Nutrition: Broccoli and cauliflower are quite literally nutritional powerhouses. Both are loaded with calcium, potassium, vitamin A, vitamin C, and dietary fiber. Broccoli only has forty calories per cup and cauliflower contains only thirty calories per cup.

Selection: Broccoli should have an allover deep, rich, green color and feel solid. Cauliflower heads should be white or cream colored. In both cases, the florets should be tightly closed and the stalks firm. Avoid any with yellow flowers or yellow spots. Definitely pass up any that have begun to bloom! Size is not an indicator of quality.

Storage: Remove any outer leaves before storing. Keep both broccoli and cauliflower unwashed until ready to use. Both prefer the vegetable crisper drawer or the bottom of your refrigerator. The plastic produce bag you place it in at the supermarket is fine for storage and will prevent the odors from being transferred to other foods. Use within one week for the best quality.

BROCCOLI WITH LEMON SAUCE

Sometimes the simplest recipes get the job done best. This recipe is done and on the table in 10 minutes.

YIELD: 6 SERVINGS

1½ pounds fresh broccoli, trimmed and cut into spears

2 tablespoons olive oil

1 tablespoon unsalted butter

1 garlic clove, minced

2 tablespoons lemon juice

½ teaspoon kosher salt

Place the broccoli in a large Dutch oven and add water to a depth of 2 inches. Place over high heat and bring to a boil. Boil 6 minutes or just until the broccoli is tender. Drain and place in a serving bowl.

While the broccoli is boiling, place the oil and butter in a small skillet over medium-high heat. Add the garlic and sauté 1 minute. Stir in the lemon juice and salt. Toss over the broccoli and serve warm.

BROWN BUTTER SEARED CAULIFLOWER

This is the recipe I use to change the thinking of those who say they don't like cauliflower. It is cooked and then pan seared so it's nice and brown. Toss it with butter that has been browned and then seasoned. This is an irresistible side dish for turkey or pork.

YIELD: 8 SERVINGS

1 head cauliflower, cut into 8 wedges

1 tablespoon canola oil

4 tablespoons unsalted butter

1 garlic clove, minced

1 tablespoon chopped fresh tarragon

1 teaspoon white wine vinegar

½ teaspoon kosher salt

½ teaspoon black pepper

Bring a large Dutch oven full of water to a boil over high heat. Add the cauliflower and cook 4 minutes. Drain and set aside.

Place the oil in a large skillet over medium-high heat. Add the cauliflower and sear 2 minutes on each side or until browned. Transfer to a serving platter and set aside.

In a small saucepan over medium-high heat, melt the butter. Cook about 2 minutes, or until golden brown. Add the garlic, tarragon, vinegar, salt, and pepper, mixing well. Pour over the cauliflower and serve hot.

CREAM CHEESE BROCCOLI SQUARES

Fresh broccoli slaw is located in the produce department next to the lettuce and coleslaw. It is beautiful, and these squares are great for picnics or potluck dinners because they are served cold.

YIELD: 12 SERVINGS

1 (8-ounce) package refrigerated crescent rolls

1 (8-ounce) package cream cheese, softened

½ cup mayonnaise

1 (4-ounce) envelope dry ranch salad dressing mix

1 cup broccoli slaw

1 cup finely shredded white Cheddar cheese

Preheat the oven to 350°F. Press the roll dough into the bottom of a lightly greased 13 x 9-inch baking pan. Press the perforations to seal. Bake 12 minutes, or until golden brown. Cool completely on a wire rack.

In a small bowl, stir together the cream cheese, mayonnaise, and dressing mix. Spread over the cooled crust. Sprinkle the slaw evenly over the cream cheese mixture. Top with the Cheddar cheese, pressing slightly. Cover and refrigerate at least 2 hours before cutting into squares and serving.

CRUNCH TIME BROCCOLI SALAD

This salad can be made with broccoli, cauliflower, or a mixture of both. Peanuts add an unexpected crunch.

YIELD: 6 TO 8 SERVINGS

1 pound broccoli florets, roughly chopped
3 green onions, chopped
1 (4-ounce) jar diced pimientos, drained
$\frac{1}{2}$ cup dry roasted peanuts
$\frac{1}{2}$ cup golden raisins
$\frac{1}{2}$ cup mayonnaise
2 tablespoons honey

In a large bowl, combine the broccoli, onions, pimientos, peanuts, and raisins. Toss gently to combine. In a small bowl, whisk together the mayonnaise and honey. Spoon over the broccoli mixture and toss gently to evenly coat. Cover and refrigerate at least 2 hours before serving.

HERBED BROCCOLI CASSEROLE

Casseroles are a great tool for getting kids interested in cooking. The dish can hardly be ruined and stimulates interest in cooking, measuring, and perhaps vegetables! This one is foolproof.

YIELD: 8 SERVINGS

3 cups broccoli florets, chopped
2 eggs, lightly beaten
1 garlic clove, minced
1 (10.75-ounce) can cream of mushroom soup
1 cup shredded mozzarella cheese
1 cup mayonnaise
4 slices bacon, cooked and crumbled
$\frac{1}{2}$ cup herb-seasoned stuffing mix

Preheat the oven to 350°F. Lightly grease a 2-quart shallow baking dish and set aside.

In a large mixing bowl, combine the broccoli, eggs, garlic, soup, cheese, and mayonnaise. Transfer to the prepared baking dish. Sprinkle the bacon over the top and then the stuffing mix. Bake 30 minutes, or until lightly browned. Serve warm.

BOTANY: Broccoli and cauliflower belong to the same large family as cabbage, Brussels sprouts, kale, collard greens, turnips, and mustard greens. Broccolini is a cross between broccoli and Chinese kale. It looks like broccoli that has been on a diet. Broccoli rabe or rapini is the skinny kid brother with a bitter-flavor edge.

NAME: The word broccoli comes from the Latin word "bracchium" and the Italian word "brocco," which both mean "branch." The name cauliflower actually means "cabbage flower."

MASON JAR CREAM OF BROCCOLI SOUP

This is the soup I like to pack in fall picnics. I heat it just before leaving and put individual servings in small mason jars. It's the perfect temperature by the time we arrive with blankets in tow. It's equally delicious in a thermos or served at your own table.

YIELD: 8 SERVINGS

7 cups vegetable or chicken stock
2 carrots, peeled and chopped
1 purple onion, peeled and chopped
1 celery stalk, chopped
1 russet potato, peeled and chopped
1 pound broccoli florets, chopped
2 cups milk
1 tablespoon sour cream
1 teaspoon lemon pepper
1 teaspoon kosher salt
$\frac{1}{2}$ teaspoon dried dill

Place the stock, carrots, onions, celery, and potatoes in a large Dutch oven and place over medium-high heat. Bring to a boil and reduce heat to medium. Cook 20 minutes, or until the vegetables are tender.

Add the broccoli and simmer 20 minutes longer. Remove half of the broccoli mixture and set aside. Using an immersion blender, purée the remaining mixture until smooth. Add the milk, sour cream, lemon pepper, salt, and dill. Stir until smooth.

Return the reserved broccoli mixture to the pot. Heat 10 minutes, or until thoroughly warm. Serve warm.

ROASTED CAULIFLOWER (OR BROCCOLI)

Roasting is my single favorite cooking method for vegetables of any kind. Take your pick of using either vegetable or a combination of the two.

YIELD: 6 SERVINGS

1 head cauliflower or broccoli
2 tablespoons olive oil
$\frac{1}{2}$ teaspoon salt
$\frac{1}{4}$ teaspoon black pepper

Preheat the oven to 375°F. Lightly grease a jelly-roll pan and set aside.

Cut the cauliflower vertically into $\frac{1}{4}$-inch slices. Arrange in a single layer on the prepared pan. Drizzle evenly with the oil and then sprinkle with the salt and pepper.

Bake 35 to 45 minutes, or until golden brown. Flip, if desired, halfway through the cooking time. Serve warm.

HISTORY: Broccoli came to the U.S. via Italian immigrants and really didn't develop a loyal following until the 1920s.

PRESERVING: Both cauliflower and broccoli can be frozen, but require blanching first. You can either water blanch them for three minutes or steam blanch them for five minutes. Use within one year for best quality.

BROWNIES

WHAT COULD BE MORE INTERESTING THAN A CROSS BETWEEN A CAKE AND A COOKIE? Enter the lowly brownie, the perfect dessert for a crowd. Brownies can be pulled together and baking in the oven in a snap and are practically foolproof. They are the "go to guys" of the Southern dessert world.

Trying to describe a brownie is like trying to describe happiness. It means different things to different people. You might call it a square of rich chocolate cake, but it's really a bar cookie and not always chocolate.

In the dictionary, it's described as "usually chocolate and often made with nuts." But that leaves out a whole list of other characteristics. Like, are they served frosted or plain? Are they supposed to be dense and chewy or fluffy and cake-like?

Is the recipe prepared in one bowl or in a double boiler, plus a bowl? Is the batter thin and pourable or thick, requiring a spoon? Are extras like fruit and mint flavors included or not? Should nuts, such as pecans, walnuts, or almonds, be added? And finally, do you cut it in squares or rectangles?

Try to find a single standard recipe and you'll get frustrated. There are quite literally hundreds of recipes that run the range of elegant to healthy. But as varied as they are, they all usually have a moist texture, which is a plus when storing and even cutting them. Although we usually think of chocolate brownies, they can be blonde, and even marbled.

My grandmother used to refrigerate the pan before cutting. She told me it was to "firm it up," and it certainly made the cutting process clean and neat. It also served to keep kids out of the pan until they were ready to be served!

So what's the definition of a brownie? It's a moist, usually chocolate bar cookie that's cut into either squares or rectangles that could contain nuts of some kind ... but not always!

Mixing: Take care not to overmix brownie batter or you could end up with a tough dessert. Sometimes overmixing will cause a thin crust to develop on the top when the brownies are baked. Mix brownie batter as you would muffin batter ... just until it combines and then it's ready to bake.

Cutting: Cool completely in the pan on a wire rack; then refrigerate for thirty minutes. Use a serrated knife that has been dipped in hot water and cut away. You may need to wipe the knife and dip it again after partially cutting some really fudge-like brownies.

Freezing: Freezer storage is great for brownie excess. You can wrap individually cut brownies or freeze the entire pan. Use heavy-duty aluminum foil or freezer bags to prevent freezer burn. They just need to thaw at room temperature. Use frozen brownies within six months for best quality.

BLONDIES

Not all brownies are chocolate based. Some call these butterscotch brownies because they are loaded with pecans, butter, and brown sugar.

YIELD: 24 BROWNIES

1 (1-pound) package brown sugar

12 tablespoons unsalted butter

3 eggs

2¾ cups all-purpose flour

2½ teaspoons baking powder

½ teaspoon salt

1 cup chopped pecans

1 teaspoon pure vanilla extract

1 teaspoon butter extract

Preheat the oven to 350°F. Lightly grease a 13 x 9-inch baking pan and set aside.

In a heavy saucepan over medium heat, combine the brown sugar and butter. Stir constantly until the butter melts and the mixture is smooth. Cool 5 minutes.

Add the eggs, one at a time, beating well after each addition. In a separate bowl, combine the flour, baking powder, and salt. Add to the sugar mixture, blending well. Stir in the pecans, vanilla extract, and butter extract.

Spread evenly in the prepared pan. Bake 25 to 28 minutes. Cool completely on a wire rack before cutting into squares.

BROWNIE MINT JULEP SOUFFLÉ

This dessert has all the elements of a great brownie flavor but is not presented in cut squares. Be careful not to over bake.

YIELD: 8 SERVINGS

1 (22-ounce) package brownie mix

½ cup water

½ cup vegetable oil

1 teaspoon peppermint extract

4 eggs, separated

Vanilla ice cream

Mint sprigs for garnish

Preheat the oven to 375°F. Lightly grease a 9- or 10-inch springform pan and set aside.

In a large mixing bowl, combine the brownie mix, water, oil, extract and egg yolks until well blended.

In a separate bowl, beat the egg whites until soft peaks form. Gradually fold into the brownie mixture.

Pour the batter into the prepared pan. Bake 35 to 38 minutes, or until the center is almost set. Cool 30 minutes in the pan (the center will sink slightly). Carefully remove the sides of the pan and cool completely or cut into wedges and serve warm. Top with a scoop of vanilla ice cream and garnish with the mint sprigs.

DOUBLE CHOCOLATE BROWNIES

You get to pick whether you want these brownies enhanced by white or semisweet chocolate. Either way is a crowd pleaser.

YIELD: 24 BROWNIES

½ pound (2 sticks) unsalted butter, softened

2 cups sugar

4 large eggs

1 cup unsweetened cocoa

1 teaspoon pure vanilla extract

1 cup all-purpose flour

1 cup chopped pecans

$^2/_3$ cup white chocolate or semisweet
   chocolate chips

Preheat the oven to 350°F. Lightly grease a 13 x 9-inch baking pan and set aside.

Beat the butter at medium speed with an electric mixer until creamy. Gradually add the sugar, beating well. Add the eggs, one at a time, beating until just blended. Add the cocoa and extract.

Beat on low speed 1 minute.

Gradually add the flour, beating well. Stir in the pecans and chips. Pour the batter into the prepared pan. Bake 30 to 35 minutes, or until done. Cool completely on a wire rack before cutting into squares.

FROSTED THREE LEVEL BROWNIES

There are times when regular brownies simply will not do. You want them with frosting because your sweet tooth demands it. That's the time to pull out this recipe.

YIELD: 16 BROWNIES

1 cup quick oats

$^1/_2$ cup plus $^2/_3$ cup all-purpose flour,
   divided

$^1/_2$ cup packed brown sugar

$^1/_4$ teaspoon baking soda

$^1/_2$ teaspoon salt, divided

12 tablespoons unsalted butter, divided

2 (1-ounce) squares unsweetened
   chocolate, divided

$^3/_4$ cup granulated sugar

1 egg

$^1/_4$ teaspoon baking powder

$^1/_4$ cup milk

$1^1/_2$ teaspoons pure vanilla extract, divided

$^1/_2$ cup chopped pecans

$1^1/_2$ cups confectioners' sugar

Preheat the oven to 350°F.

In a medium bowl, stir together the oats, $^1/_2$ cup of the flour, the brown sugar, baking soda, and $^1/_4$ teaspoon of the salt.

Place 6 tablespoons of the butter in a microwave-safe container and microwave on low power 20 seconds. Stir until completely melted. Add to the flour mixture and press in the bottom of an 11 x 7-inch baking pan. Bake 10 minutes.

Meanwhile, place 4 tablespoons of the butter and 1 square of the chocolate in the same microwave-safe container. Microwave on low power 15 seconds. Stir and continue microwaving in 10-second increments until the mixture is completely melted and smooth. Transfer to the bowl of an electric mixer. Add the granulated sugar and egg. Beat well.

In a separate bowl, combine the remaining $^2/_3$ cup of the flour, the baking powder, and the remaining $^1/_4$ teaspoon of the salt. Alternately add to the chocolate mixture with the milk. Fold in $^1/_2$ teaspoon of the extract and the pecans. Evenly spread over the baked crust. Continue baking 25 minutes longer. Cool completely on a wire rack.

Place the remaining square of the chocolate and the remaining 2 tablespoons of the butter over low heat in a medium saucepan. Stir until completely melted and smooth. Remove from the heat and stir in the confectioners' sugar and remaining teaspoon of the extract. Blend well. If the frosting is too thick, add up to 2 tablespoons of milk to thin. Spread over the cooled brownies before cutting into squares.

MERLOT BROWNIES

If you like dry red wine, you already know how well it pairs with chocolate. Now go a level deeper by reducing the wine before adding it to the brownies.

YIELD: 24 BROWNIES

1 cup merlot or dry red wine

12 tablespoons unsalted butter, softened

4 ounces unsweetened chocolate, coarsely chopped

2 cups sugar

3 eggs

1 teaspoon pure vanilla extract

1 cup all-purpose flour

1 cup chopped pecans, divided

Preheat the oven to 350°F. Lightly grease a 13 x 9-inch baking dish and set aside.

In a small saucepan, simmer the wine over medium heat until reduced to $1/4$ cup, about 20 minutes. Pour into a large bowl and add the butter and chocolate. Stir until the butter and chocolate melt and the mixture is smooth.

In the top of a double boiler, whisk together the sugar, eggs, and extract over simmering water until very light and thick, about 12 minutes. Pour into the chocolate mixture and whisk until smooth. Stir in the flour and half of the pecans.

Pour into the prepared baking dish and sprinkle the remaining pecans on top of batter. Bake 40 to 45 minutes, or until a tester inserted in the center comes out clean. Cool completely on a wire rack before cutting into squares.

PEANUT BUTTER CUP BROWNIES

Who doesn't love the combination of creamy peanut butter and milk chocolate? This is candy disguised as a brownie.

YIELD: 18 BROWNIES

$1/2$ cup creamy peanut butter

6 tablespoons unsalted butter, softened

1 cup packed brown sugar

2 eggs

1 teaspoon pure vanilla extract

1 cup all-purpose flour

1 teaspoon baking powder

$1/2$ teaspoon salt

1 cup milk chocolate chips

Preheat the oven to 350°F. Lightly grease a 9-inch baking pan and set aside.

In the bowl of an electric mixer, beat together the peanut butter, butter, and brown sugar until light and fluffy. Add the eggs, one at a time, beating well after each addition. Add the extract.

In a separate bowl, stir together the flour, baking powder, and salt. Gradually add the flour mixture to the batter, stirring just until combined. Fold in the chips.

Spread the batter evenly in the prepared pan. Bake 25 to 30 minutes, or until a tester inserted in the center comes out clean. Cool completely on a wire rack before cutting into squares.

TRIPLE CHOCOLATE BROWNIES

Chocolate, chocolate, and more chocolate equals yum, yummier, and the yummiest!

YIELD: 21 BROWNIES

12 tablespoons unsalted butter
6 ounces bittersweet chocolate
2 ounces unsweetened chocolate
1$^1\!/_2$ cups sugar
2 teaspoons pure vanilla extract
4 eggs
1 cup all-purpose flour
$^3\!/_4$ teaspoon salt
1 cup semisweet chocolate chips

Place the butter, bittersweet chocolate, and unsweetened chocolate in the top of a double boiler. Set over medium heat and bring the water to a simmer. Stir the chocolate mixture until melted and smooth. Cool 5 minutes.

Meanwhile, preheat the oven to 350°F. Lightly grease a 13 x 9-inch baking pan and set aside.

Add the sugar and extract to the chocolate mixture, blending well. Stir in the eggs, one at a time, mixing well after each addition.

Add the flour and salt, stirring just until combined. Fold in the chips. Transfer the batter to the prepared pan. Bake 25 to 28 minutes, or until the brownies are set. When a tester is inserted in the center, it should have some moist crumbs adhere. Cool completely on a wire rack before cutting into squares.

TUXEDO BROWNIES

These buttery bars combine the goodness of milk and white chocolate.

YIELD: 16 BROWNIES

1 cup semisweet chocolate chips
2 cups vanilla wafer crumbs
1 (14-ounce) can sweetened condensed milk
1 teaspoon pure vanilla extract
1 cup white chocolate chips

In a small saucepan over low heat, melt the semi-sweet chips until smooth, stirring frequently. Set aside to cool 15 minutes.

Meanwhile, preheat the oven to 350°F. Lightly grease a 9-inch square baking dish and set aside.

In a medium bowl, combine the crumbs, milk, and cooled melted chocolate. Stir in the extract and white chocolate chips. Spread the batter in the prepared pan.

Bake 25 to 30 minutes, or until a tester inserted in the center comes out clean. Cool completely on a wire rack before cutting into squares.

BUTTER BEANS

(AND LIMA BEANS)

SOME OF MY BEST CHILDHOOD MEMORIES REVOLVE AROUND SITTING ON MY GRANDMOTHER'S back patio in Mississippi shelling butter beans. Thanks to the heat, we waited until late in the afternoon to begin shelling. We always sat in old-fashioned chairs with a paper sack between us for shells and metal bowls that felt cold in our laps.

The most interesting conversations took place there while we were sitting and busy with our hands. By the time the job was finished, our thumbs and fingers would be sore, but we really didn't care.

In the South, the names lima beans and butter beans are used interchangeably, and they are one of my all-time favorite beans. I'm convinced the term "butter beans" was a very clever marketing ploy used by Southern mothers everywhere to get them into little mouths!

They have been called many names over the years. Just a few of them are Cape beans, Cape peas, Sieva beans, Sword beans, Jack beans, Madagascar beans and Chad beans. Somewhere along the line, the varieties that were whitish-green became known throughout the South as butter beans. The ones with purple flecks were not called Calico beans as they are in other areas, but Speckled Butter Beans.

Any time of the year, you can find them dried, canned, or frozen, but there is simply nothing like harvesting your own from a carefully tended garden. They take a while to develop, thanks to the size of the bean, but your patience will be rewarded. Only butter and a sprinkling of salt is necessary for a feast, but variety is the spice of life so keep a supply on hand in the freezer for the following recipes.

Nutrition: Butter beans are a good source of protein, phosphorus, potassium, iron, and dietary fiber.

Selection: Fresh lima beans are generally sold in their shells during the fresh season, which runs from June to September. Look for pods that are completely green in color with no pitting or dark areas. They should feel plump, firm, and full.

Storage: Dried lima or butter beans should be kept in an airtight container for up to one year. Never store them in the refrigerator. Fresh, on the other hand, loves the refrigerator. In fact, you can store the pods in a plastic bag for several days there. If possible, try not to shell them until you are ready to use.

B AND B SALAD

Some think "B and B" stands for Bed and Breakfast. Others think it is the famous mixture of benedictine and brandy. In the South, it's butter beans and bacon!

YIELD: 6 SERVINGS

4 slices bacon, chopped

1 white onion, peeled and finely chopped

1 green bell pepper, seeded and chopped

3 garlic cloves, minced

2 large tomatoes, seeded and chopped

4 cups chicken stock

4 cups fresh butter beans

2 tablespoons chopped fresh parsley

1 teaspoon salt

1 teaspoon black pepper

1 teaspoon Worcestershire sauce

$\frac{1}{2}$ teaspoon hot sauce

In a Dutch oven over medium heat, cook the bacon until crisp, around 8 minutes. Add the onions, bell peppers, and garlic. Sauté 2 minutes or until the vegetables are tender. Stir in the tomatoes and cook 3 minutes longer.

Add the stock and butter beans. Bring to a boil, cover, reduce the heat to low, and simmer 30 minutes, stirring occasionally.

Uncover and simmer 20 minutes longer, stirring frequently. Stir in the parsley, salt, pepper, Worcestershire, and hot sauce. Cook 5 minutes longer and serve warm.

"COME AND GET IT" BUTTER BEAN SOUP

A friend of mine gave me this recipe more than ten years ago. For that long, it's been a regular winter weekend dinner. Sometimes I throw in shrimp or Italian sausage, but most of the time, I leave it as is, which is so exceptional that you won't believe it until you try it.

YIELD: 8 SERVINGS

2 tablespoons canola oil

2 white onions, peeled and coarsely chopped

6 garlic cloves, minced

1 cup dry white wine

2 teaspoons saffron threads

6 cups chicken stock

1 red bell pepper, roasted, peeled, seeded, and coarsely chopped

1 (1-pound) package frozen butter or lima beans, thawed

1 teaspoon hot sauce

1 tablespoon Pernod or anisette

$\frac{1}{2}$ teaspoon salt

$\frac{1}{2}$ teaspoon black pepper

Chopped fresh parsley for garnish

Heat the oil in a large stockpot over medium-high heat. Add the onions and garlic and sauté about 2 minutes, or until tender.

Increase the heat to high and add the wine and saffron. Cook until the liquid is reduced by half, about 5 minutes. Add the stock, peppers and beans. Bring to a boil, reduce the heat to low, and simmer 45 minutes. Stir in the hot sauce, Pernod, salt, and pepper. Ladle into warm soup bowls and garnish with the parsley before serving.

CREOLE SPICED LIMA BEANS AND SAUSAGE

This is a dish that can easily become a warm winter entrée, a basis for soup, or a hearty side.

YIELD: 6 SERVINGS

4 cups fresh lima beans
2 tablespoons bacon drippings
2 cups sliced smoked sausage
3/4 cup finely chopped onion
1 teaspoon Creole seasoning
1/2 teaspoon black pepper

Place the beans in a large saucepan and cover with water. Bring to a boil over medium-high heat. Reduce heat to low and simmer, stirring occasionally until the beans are tender, around 30 minutes.

Meanwhile, melt the drippings in a large skillet over medium heat. Add the sausage and onions. Cook until light brown, around 15 minutes. Stir in the seasoning and pepper. Set aside.

When the beans are tender, add the sausage mixture, stirring well. Cook 10 minutes longer and serve warm.

DREAM BEAN CASSEROLE

I think this recipe has been around all my life. It is a delicious way to show off your butter bean harvest that is nestled underneath a crispy topping.

YIELD: 6 SERVINGS

4 cups fresh baby lima beans
4 slices bacon
2 tablespoons all-purpose flour
3 tablespoons brown sugar
1 teaspoon salt

1/2 teaspoon black pepper
1 tablespoon dry mustard
1 tablespoon lemon juice
1/2 cup dry plain breadcrumbs
2 tablespoons unsalted butter, melted

Place the beans in a medium saucepan and cover with water. Bring to a boil over medium-high heat. Reduce the heat to low and simmer 20 minutes, or until tender. Drain, reserving 1 cup of the cooking liquid. If there is less than 1 cup, add enough water to equal 1 cup. Transfer the beans to a lightly greased 8-inch square baking dish and set aside.

Preheat the oven to 350°F.

In a large skillet over medium heat, fry the bacon until crisp, around 8 minutes. Drain on paper towels and crumble when cool enough to handle. Set aside.

Add the flour to the hot drippings and stir constantly until smooth. Cook 1 minute. Gradually add the reserved bean liquid, stirring, about 2 minutes, or until the mixture thickens. Add the brown sugar, salt, pepper, mustard, and lemon juice, stirring well to blend. Pour over the beans.

In a small bowl, combine the breadcrumbs and butter. Sprinkle over the bean mixture. Bake 25 minutes. Sprinkle the bacon over the top and bake 5 minutes longer. Serve warm.

SUGARED LIMA BEANS

Sorghum syrup and brown sugar team up to turn ordinary dried lima beans into an unforgettable side dish. I like to serve this with roasted turkey, chicken, or pork.

YIELD: 8 SERVINGS

1 (1-pound) package large dried lima beans
11 cups water, divided

1 white onion, peeled and quartered

1 cup chopped country ham

$\frac{1}{2}$ cup sorghum syrup

3 tablespoons brown sugar

Combine the beans and 7 cups of the water in a large Dutch oven and place over medium-high heat. Bring to a boil and boil 1 minute. Remove from the heat, cover, and let stand 1 hour. Drain.

Preheat the oven to 350°F.

Spoon half of the beans into a large Dutch oven. Top evenly with the onions, ham, and the remaining beans. Pour the sorghum over the top layer of beans. Sprinkle evenly with the brown sugar. Pour the remaining water over the sugar.

Cover and bake 1$\frac{1}{2}$ hours. Remove the cover and bake 2 hours, or until the beans are tender. Serve warm.

"STRAIGHT FROM THE GARDEN" BUTTER BEANS

This is how I always cook the first butter beans I harvest from my garden. It is marvelous served as a country dinner with fresh sliced tomatoes, hot cornbread, and roasted okra.

YIELD: 4 SERVINGS

2 cups water

1 (6-inch) ham hock

3 cups fresh butter or lima beans

$\frac{1}{4}$ teaspoon black pepper

In a large saucepan, combine the water and ham hock. Place over medium-high heat and bring to a boil. Cook 5 minutes.

Add the beans and pepper. Return to a boil and reduce the heat to low. Cover and simmer 45 minutes, or until the beans are tender. Serve warm.

SUMMER SUCCOTASH

This mixture of cooked lima beans and corn is a Southern classic. The name "succotash" comes from a Narragansett Indian word "msickquatash," which means "boiled whole kernels of corn."

YIELD: 6 SERVINGS

2$\frac{1}{2}$ cups fresh lima beans

3 tablespoons olive oil

1 cup thinly sliced onions

2 cups fresh corn, cut from the cob

1 garlic clove, minced

12 ounces ripe cherry tomatoes, quartered

1 tablespoon chopped fresh basil

1 tablespoon chopped fresh thyme

1 teaspoon hot sauce

$\frac{1}{2}$ cup whipping cream

$\frac{1}{2}$ teaspoon salt

$\frac{1}{4}$ teaspoon black pepper

8 ounces bacon, cooked and crumbled

Cook the beans in boiling salted water approximately 10 minutes, or until tender. Drain and plunge into a bowl of ice water. After 4 minutes, drain and set aside.

In a large skillet, heat the oil over medium heat. When hot, add the onions. Cook 5 minutes and stir in the lima beans, corn, and garlic. Cook 2 minutes.

Stir in the tomatoes, basil, thyme, hot sauce, and whipping cream. Cook until the mixture is heated through. Season with the salt and pepper. Top with the crumbled bacon and serve.

BUTTERMILK

AS A CHILD, I THOUGHT BUTTERMILK WAS SOMETHING ONLY OLD PEOPLE LIKED. IT SEEMED too thick and smelly for my taste. I watched my daddy and grandparents pour it over crumbled cornbread and eat it out of a glass (never a bowl!) with a spoon.

Sometimes, they even had a giant glass of it with supper, while us kids secretly gagged. They always offered us a sip, which we immediately and vehemently declined, grabbing our throats as if we might die instantly should it touch our lips.

As a teenager, I saw it languishing in the dairy case: ignored, unloved, and misunderstood. I handled the carton only when I took my grandmother grocery shopping (a great opportunity to drive the car!) and she needed some. Then I started falling in love with cooking and that container of buttermilk took on a whole new meaning. Now I can't live without it.

Originally, buttermilk was the fluid remaining after butter was churned. It was named thanks to the flecks of butter that remained in the milk. Factory production of butter in this country began around 1860, however, most butter was still churned on Southern farms through the 1920s. The consistency and texture of buttermilk was pretty much left to chance. That changed as creameries began to produce cultured buttermilk in the 1940s.

Today, buttermilk is as much of a staple in my kitchen as eggs. It is a must for fried chicken, cornbread, biscuits, cakes, pies, candy, and dozens of other specialties. This tangy dairy product gives baked goods a bit of zip and zing that no other product can, but I still can't drink it out of a glass. Some things remain the same!

Nutrition: Buttermilk is more easily digested than any other form of milk. It is high in calcium and all eight essential amino acids. The calorie content is similar to those of the fluid milk from which it was made. So whether it was made with low-fat, skim, or whole milk will determine the calorie count.

Storage: The refrigerator is buttermilk's best friend. It has a longer shelf life than regular milk because of its acidity, which retards the growth of bacteria that cause spoilage. It will keep up to two weeks after purchase, but if you like to drink it straight, use it after one week for the best flavor. Freezing alters the taste and causes separation.

BEALE STREET BUTTERMILK BREAD PUDDING

Not long after I began working in Tennessee, I had to attend a meeting in Memphis and rediscovered the city that I hadn't visited in years. I had a fabulous bread pudding on Beale Street that I attempted to re-create when I returned home.

YIELD: 10 SERVINGS

4 tablespoons plus ¼ pound (1 stick) unsalted butter, divided

7½ cups cubed French bread

1 quart buttermilk

1 cup golden raisins

2 eggs, lightly beaten

1⅓ cups packed brown sugar

2 teaspoons pure vanilla extract

1 teaspoon rum extract

½ cup granulated sugar

1 egg yolk

¼ cup water

3 tablespoons rum

Preheat the oven to 350°F. Place 4 tablespoons of the butter in a 13 x 9-inch baking dish and place in the oven to melt.

Meanwhile, combine the bread cubes, buttermilk, and raisins in a large mixing bowl. In a separate bowl, whisk together the eggs, brown sugar, vanilla extract, and rum extract. Pour over the bread mixture and stir gently to combine.

Transfer to the prepared pan and pour over the melted butter. Bake 1 hour.

Meanwhile, combine the remaining butter, granulated sugar, egg yolk, and water in a small saucepan. Stir well and place over medium heat. Stir constantly until the sugar dissolves and the sauce begins to thicken, about 10 minutes. Add the rum.

To serve, cut the warm bread pudding in squares. Drizzle with the sauce and serve warm.

BUTTERMILK LAYER CAKE

I hope you've been practicing making Grandmother's Heavenly Caramel Frosting. These two are like Fred Astaire and Ginger Rogers dancing together. Marvelous!

YIELD: 16 SERVINGS

1¼ cups sugar

¼ pound (1 stick) unsalted butter, softened

2 eggs

1 egg white

2 teaspoons pure vanilla extract

2 cups all-purpose flour

½ teaspoon baking soda

½ teaspoon salt

1 cup buttermilk

Preheat the oven to 350°F. Grease and flour 2 (8-inch) round cake pans and set aside.

Combine the sugar and butter in a large mixing bowl. Beat at medium speed until well blended. Add the eggs and egg white, one at a time, making sure to beat well after each addition. Add the extract.

In a separate bowl, combine the flour, baking soda, and salt. Add the flour mixture to the sugar mixture alternately with the buttermilk, beginning and ending with the flour mixture. Beat well after each addition. Pour the batter into the prepared pans.

Bake 25 minutes, or until a tester inserted in the center comes out clean. Cool 10 minutes on a wire rack, and then remove from the pans. When completely cool, frost with Grandmother's Heavenly Caramel Frosting (page 122).

FRENCH QUARTER BUTTERMILK PRALINES

This version of traditional pralines will show you why the candy is so popular. It hardens quickly, so have a pair of extra hands around when it's time to drop them onto wax paper.

YIELD: 2½ DOZEN

2 cups sugar

1 teaspoon baking soda

⅛ teaspoon salt

1 cup buttermilk

2 tablespoons unsalted butter

1 tablespoon light corn syrup

2½ cups pecan halves

Line 3 baking sheets with wax paper and set aside.

In a heavy saucepan over medium-high heat, bring the sugar, baking soda, salt, and buttermilk to a boil, stirring constantly. Boil 5 minutes, or until a candy thermometer registers 210°F.

Add the butter, syrup, and pecans and return the mixture to a boil. Boil 5 minutes longer, stirring constantly, or until a candy thermometer registers 232°F.

Remove from the heat and beat with a wooden spoon 2 minutes, or until the mixture begins to thicken. Quickly drop tablespoons of the candy onto the prepared sheets. Let stand at room temperature until firm. Store in an airtight container between layers of wax paper.

GRADE A BUTTERMILK FUDGE

In a foods class in college, we were given the assignment of making fudge. It was an exercise in learning to use a candy thermometer and the stages of candy cooking. Everyone in the class made chocolate fudge, but at my grandmother's suggestion, I made her recipe using buttermilk instead. Mine was by far the best and earned me an "A!"

YIELD: 1¼ POUNDS

2 cups sugar

1 cup buttermilk

¼ pound (1 stick) unsalted butter

2 tablespoons light corn syrup

1 teaspoon baking soda

1 teaspoon pure vanilla extract

In a heavy saucepan over medium heat, combine the sugar, buttermilk, butter, and corn syrup. Stir constantly about 20 minutes, or until the mixture reaches 234°F on a candy thermometer (soft ball stage).

Stir in the baking soda. Let stand at room temperature about 10 minutes, or until the thermometer registers 180°F.

Meanwhile, lightly grease an 8-inch square baking pan and set aside. Stir in the extract and beat with a wooden spoon 2 minutes. Pour into the prepared pan, cool completely on a wire rack, and cut into squares.

Note: You can add ¾ cup of chopped pecans to the mixture when you add the extract, if desired. Store leftovers in the refrigerator.

PLANTATION BUTTERMILK POUND CAKE

Some of my favorite desserts are rich without being overly sweet. This is one of those recipes. The buttermilk keeps this cake moist, so no glaze is needed.

YIELD: 12 SERVINGS

$^{1}/_{2}$ pound (2 sticks) unsalted butter, softened

2 cups sugar

4 eggs

1 teaspoon pure lemon extract

1 teaspoon pure vanilla extract

3 cups all-purpose flour

$^{1}/_{2}$ teaspoon baking powder

$^{1}/_{2}$ teaspoon baking soda

$^{1}/_{4}$ teaspoon salt

1 cup buttermilk

Preheat the oven to 325°F. Lightly grease and flour a 12-cup Bundt pan and set aside.

In the bowl of an electric mixer, beat the butter at medium speed until creamy, around 2 minutes. Gradually add the sugar, beating 5 minutes.

Add the eggs, one at a time, beating just until the yellow disappears, Stir in the lemon extract and vanilla extract.

In a separate bowl, combine the flour, baking powder, baking soda, and salt. Add to the butter mixture alternately with the buttermilk, beginning and ending with the flour mixture. Beat on low speed just until blended. Transfer the batter to the prepared pan.

Bake 1 hour and 5 minutes, or until a tester inserted in the center comes out clean. Cool in the pan 10 minutes on a wire rack. Remove and cool completely on a wire rack before slicing and serving.

SHARP CHEDDAR BUTTERMILK BREAD

Buttermilk adds tenderness to this quick bread. This is not your usual passive dinner bread. The sharp cheese contributes character.

YIELD: 1 LOAF

2 cups all-purpose flour

$1^{1}/_{2}$ teaspoons baking powder

$^{1}/_{2}$ teaspoon baking soda

$^{1}/_{4}$ teaspoon salt

1 cup shredded sharp Cheddar cheese

2 eggs, lightly beaten

1 cup buttermilk

$^{1}/_{4}$ cup vegetable oil

Preheat the oven to 375°F. Lightly grease a loaf pan and set aside.

In a mixing bowl, combine the flour, baking powder, baking soda, salt, and cheese. Make a well in the center and set aside.

In a separate bowl, combine the eggs, buttermilk, and oil. Add to the flour mixture, stirring just until moistened. Transfer to the prepared pan, spreading evenly.

Bake 30 to 35 minutes, or until a tester inserted in the center comes out clean. Cool in the pan 10 minutes. Slice and serve or cool completely on a wire rack for later use.

SUNRISE BUTTERMILK CRUMB CAKE

Have a busy weekend ahead? This nutty breakfast cake bakes while you hit the shower before taking on the day. It is delicious served with country ham or bacon.

YIELD: 15 SERVINGS

3 cups all-purpose flour

2 cups packed brown sugar

$\frac{1}{4}$ pound (1 stick) unsalted butter, softened

2 teaspoons ground nutmeg

1 teaspoon ground cinnamon

2 eggs, lightly beaten

1 cup buttermilk

1 teaspoon baking powder

$\frac{1}{2}$ teaspoon baking soda

$\frac{1}{4}$ cup chopped pecans or walnuts

Preheat the oven to 350°F. Lightly grease a 13 x 9-inch baking dish and set aside.

In a mixing bowl, combine the flour, brown sugar, butter, nutmeg, and cinnamon. Stir until the mixture resembles crumbs. Reserve 1 cup of the mixture and set aside.

Make a well in the center of the remaining crumbs. Add the eggs, buttermilk, baking powder, and baking soda. Stir until well blended. Pour into the prepared baking pan. Sprinkle the top with the reserved crumbs and pecans.

Bake 45 minutes, or until a tester inserted in the center comes out clean. Cool 5 minutes before slicing and serving.

Note: This cake can also be served at room temperature.

WHITE LIE BUTTERMILK PIE

The first time I remember having this pie, my grandmother told me it was a new recipe for chess pie. Well, I love chess pie, so I dug in. It didn't taste a thing like chess pie! It was even better! Then she told me she had been making it forever, and it was made with buttermilk. Thank goodness for little white lies!

YIELD: 8 SERVINGS

1 recipe Single Pie Pastry (page 402)

8 tablespoons unsalted butter

1 cup sugar

3 tablespoons all-purpose flour

3 eggs

1 cup buttermilk

1 teaspoon pure vanilla extract

Preheat the oven to 450°F. Line a 9-inch pie pan with the pastry dough, and put a double layer of aluminium foil over the dough. Bake 8 minutes. Remove the foil and bake 5 to 6 minutes longer, or until the crust is lightly browned. Cool and reduce the oven temperature to 350°F.

In a medium saucepan, melt the butter over medium-low heat. Stir in the sugar and flour until smooth. Set aside.

In a mixing bowl, beat the eggs at medium speed of an electric mixer until fluffy, about 1 minute. Stir in the buttermilk and extract. Gradually whisk the buttermilk mixture into the butter mixture, stirring until the consistency is smooth.

Pour into the prebaked crust. Place the pie on the center oven rack. Carefully tent the whole pie with aluminum foil. Bake 50 to 55 minutes, or until center is set when gently shaken. Cool on a wire rack 1 hour. Cover and refrigerate 4 hours before serving.

CABBAGE & BRUSSELS SPROUTS

I LOVE GROWING MY OWN CABBAGE. FOR THOSE WHO HAVE NEVER TRIED IT, LET ME SAY IT'S ABOUT as easy as growing weeds. This unassuming vegetable is fine just taking care of itself in the back of the garden, not bothering anything else.

Fresh cabbage gets little, if any, respect except when the weather warms and Southerners head outside to enjoy barbecue or catfish dinners. The rest of the year, it could easily become forgotten, if not neglected.

That's not the case with me. I use it year-round, but especially love cutting the large ball-size heads from my garden. The first thing I usually make with my harvest is coleslaw, but I quickly move on to other dishes to showcase this nutritional powerhouse.

I've seen and been served cabbage that has suffered significant culinary abuse thanks to overcooking. When that happens, it gives homes a distinct "rooming house aroma" that seems to linger around for days on end. That's not how it has to be.

Try as it may, cabbage is like a great character actor in movies. You see it frequently on St. Patrick's Day served with corned beef, stuffed into eggrolls, and piled on Reuben sandwiches, but these are not typical Southern dishes.

No, we like it fried, stuffed, braised, rolled, and buttered. And don't forget the miniature version called Brussels sprouts. These Barbie-size cabbages are just as tasty as the humongous heads. So while cabbage may not be a star, it's certainly worth getting to know, whether you grow it yourself or not.

Nutrition: All cabbage is rich in dietary fiber, vitamins A and C, and iron. A cup of coarsely shredded raw cabbage only contains fifteen calories. A half-cup portion of Brussels sprouts contains only thirty calories.

Selection: Head cabbage should feel heavy for the size and be firm and unblemished. Avoid those with yellowing outer leaves, splits, or soft spots. Brussels sprouts should be selected on the basis of color. Grab only those that are vivid green. As the sprouts age, they lose that bright hue and take on a faded appearance.

Storage: Cold, humid conditions are best for storing cabbage. Room temperatures will cause it to wilt quickly. Place it in a loosely closed plastic bag and add a tablespoon of water to keep it hydrated. Store in the vegetable crisper or, if it won't fit, place in the next best place . . . the bottom of the refrigerator.

CABBAGE PATCH COLESLAW

It's the addition of buttermilk that gives this unique slaw an understated hint of tang. Serve it with any spicy barbecue.

YIELD: 10 SERVINGS

2 (10-ounce) packages finely shredded cabbage

1 carrot, peeled and shredded

1/2 cup sugar

1/2 cup mayonnaise

1/4 cup milk

1/4 cup buttermilk

2 1/2 tablespoons lemon juice

1 1/2 tablespoons white vinegar

1/2 teaspoon salt

1/8 teaspoon pepper

Place the cabbage and carrots in a large bowl and toss gently. In a separate bowl, whisk together the sugar, mayonnaise, milk, buttermilk, lemon juice, vinegar, salt, and pepper. Pour over the cabbage mixture, tossing to coat. Cover and refrigerate at least 2 hours before serving.

CREOLE CABBAGE

Creole seasoning should be on everyone's pantry shelf. It makes this cabbage dish refreshing and zippy. I like to serve it with grilled sausages.

YIELD: 8 TO 10 SERVINGS

2 thick bacon slices

1 large head green cabbage, cored and coarsely shredded

2 (28-ounce) cans chopped tomatoes with peppers and onions

1/3 cup white wine vinegar

2 teaspoons Creole seasoning

1/4 teaspoon cayenne

Cook the bacon in a Dutch oven over medium-high heat. When crisp, drain on paper towels. Crumble when cool. Reserve the drippings in the pan.

Stir the cabbage, tomatoes, vinegar, seasoning, and cayenne. Bring to a boil. Cover and reduce heat to low. Simmer 45 minutes. Transfer to a serving container and top with the bacon. Serve warm.

FRIED CABBAGE

As you have probably figured out, Southerners can think of a way to fry just about anything. Cabbage is no exception. In this case, it is fried in a pan.

YIELD: 6 TO 8 SERVINGS

1 head green cabbage, cored and cut into 8 wedges

2 teaspoons salt, divided

1 tablespoon unsalted butter

4 eggs

4 tablespoons milk

2 1/4 cups all-purpose flour

1/2 teaspoon black pepper

1/2 teaspoon cayenne

Bacon drippings or vegetable shortening for frying

Place the cabbage in a Dutch oven, cover with water and place over medium-high heat. Add 1 teaspoon of the salt and the butter. Boil 5 to 7 minutes. Drain in a large colander and set aside.

Whisk together the eggs and milk. Pour into a shallow dish. In a separate shallow dish, combine the flour, pepper, cayenne, and the remaining salt.

Heat the drippings in a large cast-iron pan or skillet over medium heat.

Dip the cabbage in the egg mixture and coat with the flour mixture. Fry 3 minutes on each side or until golden brown. Drain on paper towels and serve warm.

HOME-STYLE CABBAGE

The seasoning obtained from ham hocks is practically all green cabbage needs. This one-pot dish should be served with corned beef or pot roast.

YIELD: 4 TO 6 SERVINGS

2 pounds ham hocks
$1/4$ cup water
1 tablespoon red wine vinegar
$1/2$ teaspoon salt
$3/4$ teaspoon black pepper
1 head green cabbage, cored and shredded

Place the hocks and water in a large saucepan over medium heat. Bring to a simmer and add the vinegar, salt, pepper, and cabbage. Reduce heat to low and cover. Stir occasionally and continue to cook 25 minutes, or until the cabbage is tender. Add more water if necessary. Serve warm.

MAKING THE CUT RED CABBAGE

Red cabbage can become dull rather quickly when cooked. Vinegar tenderizes and brightens the appearance of this dish. You will love this with venison or any roast.

YIELD: 8 SERVINGS

3 tablespoons bacon drippings
1 yellow onion, peeled and chopped
1 Granny Smith apple, cored, peeled, and diced
1 cup plus 1 teaspoon water
$1/4$ cup dry red wine
$1/4$ cup red wine vinegar
$1/4$ cup grape jelly
2 tablespoons sugar
$1/2$ teaspoon ground cinnamon
$1/2$ teaspoon salt
$1/2$ teaspoon black pepper
1 head red cabbage, shredded
$1/2$ teaspoon cornstarch

Preheat the oven to 350°F.

Melt the drippings in a large ovenproof skillet over medium heat. Add the onions and apples. Cook 5 minutes. Add 1 cup of the water. Stir in the wine, vinegar, jelly, sugar, cinnamon, salt, and pepper. Bring to a boil.

Add the cabbage, cover tightly, and bake 1 hour. Return the skillet to the stove. In a small bowl, combine the cornstarch and the remaining water. Stir until smooth and add to the cabbage mixture. Bring to a boil and stir constantly 1 minute. Serve warm.

OLD-FASHIONED MAYONNAISE SLAW

I would hate to have to guess how long Southerners have been making this slaw. It is best served with fried catfish and white beans.

YIELD: 8 SERVINGS

6 cups finely chopped cabbage
1 tablespoon sugar
$1/2$ teaspoon salt

½ teaspoon black pepper
½ cup mayonnaise

Place the cabbage in a large bowl. In a small bowl, combine the sugar, salt, pepper, and mayonnaise, stirring well. Toss gently with the cabbage. Cover and refrigerate at least 2 hours before serving.

OLD SOUTH CABBAGE ROLLS

These were the original wraps. Before culinary experts began wrapping goodies in lettuce leaves, we were wrapping them in cabbage leaves. I see where they got the delicious idea!

YIELD: 6 SERVINGS

1 head green cabbage, cored
1 pound ground pork sausage, hot or mild
2 tablespoons chopped onions
1¼ cups cooked rice
2 eggs
½ teaspoon salt
½ teaspoon black pepper
3 pounds ham hocks
1¼ cups tomato sauce
1 cup water

Fill a large Dutch oven with water. Bring to a boil over medium-high heat. Add the whole cabbage head and boil 7 minutes. Drain in a large colander.

In a large bowl, combine the sausage, onions, rice, eggs, salt, and pepper. When cool enough to handle, remove the outer cabbage leaves from the head.

Place ¼ cup of the meat mixture in each leaf and roll, securing with a wooden pick. Repeat until all the meat mixture is used. Leftover cabbage can be reserved for another use.

Place the ham hocks in the bottom of a large cast-iron skillet with just enough water to cover the bottom of the skillet. Place the cabbage rolls over the ham hocks.

In a small bowl, combine the tomato sauce and the water. Pour over the cabbage rolls. Cover and cook over medium-low heat 1 hour. Serve warm.

PAN-FRIED COLESLAW

All coleslaw is not created equal, as you will see with this recipe. Instead of serving it cold, this one is served warm.

YIELD: 6 SERVINGS

2 slices thick-cut bacon
6 cups thinly sliced green cabbage
3 tablespoons cider vinegar
2 tablespoons water
1 tablespoon sugar
½ teaspoon salt
½ teaspoon celery seeds

In a large, deep skillet over medium-high heat, fry the bacon until crisp. Drain on paper towels and set aside.

Add the cabbage to the pan drippings. Cook 6 minutes, or until browned, stirring frequently. Add the vinegar, water, sugar, salt, and seeds. Cook 1 minute, stirring constantly. Crumble the bacon over the top and serve warm.

ROCKING CHAIR SAUERKRAUT

Although traditionally thought of as a German dish, sauerkraut became popular in the South thanks to good old-fashioned Home Economics. It was inexpensive to make, and everyone had a head or two of cabbage growing in their gardens. You'll have plenty of time to sit and rock while it ferments!

YIELD: 9 QUARTS OR 18 PINTS

1 quart water

1½ tablespoons kosher salt

25 pounds green cabbage, cored, shredded, and divided

¾ cup pickling salt, divided

Combine the water and the kosher salt and set aside.

Working with 5 pounds of cabbage at a time, toss well with 3 tablespoons of the pickling salt. Pack firmly in a large glass or stoneware crock. Repeat with the remaining cabbage and salt.

Pour enough of the kosher salt water over the cabbage to completely cover. Place a glass plate that is slightly smaller than the container top on the cabbage. Weigh it down by placing 2 or 3 canning jars filled with water on the top. Cover the top with a clean towel. Store where temperatures are between 70°F. and 75°F. Set aside to ferment at least 4 weeks. Fermentation is complete when the bubbling stops.

Transfer the sauerkraut and juice to a large Dutch oven. Bring to a boil over medium-low heat, stirring frequently. Pack into hot canning jars, leaving ½-inch headspace. Remove the bubbles and adjust the lids. Process quarts 15 minutes and pints 10 minutes in a boiling water bath. Cool on wire racks away from drafts. (See page 12 for detailed canning instructions.)

Note: Keep in mind that cabbage will not ferment at temperatures below 55°F, and may become soft and spoil above 75°F.

STUFFED CABBAGE

I'll be the first to admit this takes a bit of time to make, but the end result of this dish will melt in your mouth.

YIELD: 8 SERVINGS

1 large head green cabbage, cored

1 tablespoon unsalted butter

1 white onion, peeled and finely chopped

1 garlic clove, minced

1 celery stalk, finely chopped

1 carrot, peeled and chopped

¾ cup chopped peanuts

½ teaspoon salt

¼ teaspoon black pepper

2 cups ricotta cheese

3 tablespoons fresh lemon juice

2 tablespoons soy sauce

1 recipe Georgia Peanut Ginger Sauce (page 327)

Bring a large Dutch oven filled with water to a boil. Lower the cabbage head into the water. Reduce the heat to low and simmer 12 to 15 minutes. Drain and remove 12 outer leaves. Reserve the remaining cabbage for another use.

In a medium skillet over medium heat, melt the butter. Add the onion, garlic, celery, carrot, peanuts, salt, and pepper. Cook 10 minutes and remove from the heat. Stir in the ricotta, lemon juice, and soy sauce.

Preheat the oven to 325°F. Lightly grease a 13 x 9-inch baking dish and set aside.

Place 2 tablespoons of the ricotta mixture near the base of a cabbage leaf. Roll tightly and fold in the sides. Place in the prepared baking dish and repeat.

Prepare the sauce and pour over the rolls. Cover and bake 30 minutes. Let stand 5 minutes before serving warm.

CARAMEL

I HONESTLY BELIEVE THE MOST DIFFICULT THING I MAKE ON A REGULAR BASIS IS CARAMEL frosting. I don't think I fully appreciated the ease with which my grandmother prepared it until I began making it by myself.

Quite frankly, there is nothing finer when caramel frosting is made well and nothing worse when it is over or undercooked. If you rush the process, it's more than likely going to be too thin and lifeless. If you leave it thinking you have time to quickly do something else, you can have crunchy toffee before you know it. But when it's perfectly cooked, it's what I affectionately call "Grandmother Heaven."

In its simplest form, caramel is granulated sugar that has been slowly cooked until it melts. You want the color to change from clear to a deep golden brown. It demands stirring and your attention. I have a particular cast-iron skillet I use for the process and a long-handled wooden spoon. The wonderful heat conduction of cast iron makes the color of the caramel even and uniform.

You can enhance the caramel with things like cream and butter to make syrups, sauces, and frostings. Always use a large pot because when the caramelized sugar is combined with other ingredients because it tends to bubble vigorously.

My grandmother always said you couldn't make caramel frosting on a humid or rainy day, and I believe her after attempting it a couple of times. What a disaster! So turn the next clear, dry day into a golden opportunity and make something extraordinary. Make your friends and family some "Grandmother Heaven"…caramel frosting for a layer cake.

WHAT IS IT? Caramel is produced when you slowly heat sugar and remove any natural moisture. Depending on what you are making, the desired color can range from beige to dark brown.

CARAMEL VS. CARMEL: When you travel outside your norm, you begin to notice that others pronounce words funny. I mean, after all, the way you grew up saying something is always correct, right?! Enter the debate over whether it should be called "caramel" or "carmel." Quite frankly, Southerners use both and they mean exactly the same thing. It's just how we adapt with our language and is no different than the different ways people pronounce pecan, acorn, tomato or Caribbean.

CLEAN UP: Aren't those hardened bits of caramel fun to clean after caramel is made? The task becomes a bit easier when you soak your utensils in hot water. Make sure to cool the candy thermometer completely before washing it.

CRUSTLESS CARAMEL VELVET PIE

This is simply impossible to resist. It's creamy, rich, flavorful, and almost like pudding. The amber-colored caramel sauce is the only topping it needs.

YIELD: 8 SERVINGS

1½ cups sugar, divided
1½ cups milk
1½ cups cream
⅛ teaspoon salt
3 eggs
3 egg yolks
¾ teaspoon pure vanilla extract

Preheat the oven to 350°F.

Place a nonstick skillet over medium heat and add 1 cup of the sugar. Stir constantly until the sugar melts and turns golden brown, around 3 to 4 minutes. Pour into a pie plate and tilt to evenly coat the bottom. Set aside.

In a large heavy saucepan, combine the remaining ½ cup of sugar with the milk, cream, and salt. Place over medium-high heat. When the mixture just begins to simmer, remove from the heat and set aside.

In a medium bowl, whisk together the eggs, yolks, and extract. Slowly add to the cream mixture, whisking constantly. When well blended, pour through a fine mesh sieve into the pie plate on top of the caramel.

Place the pie plate into a baking pan and add enough water to reach halfway up the sides. Bake 42 to 45 minutes, or until the custard is set but still wiggles slightly. Remove from the water bath and cool completely on a wire rack.

Cover loosely with plastic wrap and refrigerate at least 2 hours and up to 1 day. To serve, run a knife around the edge of the pie plate. Invert on a serving plate and cut into wedges.

CHRISTMAS CARAMELS

Individual pieces of this candy should be wrapped in wax paper and tied with colorful ribbons. They make welcome hostess gifts or nice remembrances for everyone from the mailman to neighbors.

YIELD: 2 POUNDS

2 cups cream, divided
2 cups sugar
1⅓ cups light corn syrup
1 teaspoon pure vanilla extract
12 tablespoons unsalted butter, cubed

Lightly grease a 9-inch square pan and set aside.

In a heavy saucepan over low heat, combine 1 cup of the cream with the sugar and syrup. Stir constantly until the mixture boils. Slowly add the remaining cup of cream, vanilla, and the butter, one piece at a time.

Continue cooking and stirring until it reaches the firm ball stage, 260°F on a candy thermometer. Pour into the prepared pan. Cool 6 hours on a wire rack before cutting into squares.

GRANDMOTHER'S HEAVENLY CARAMEL FROSTING

Spread this billowy frosting over white or yellow cake layers. It could quite possibly be the most perfect way to end any evening meal.

YIELD: 4½ CUPS

3¾ cups sugar, divided
4 tablespoons unsalted butter
¼ teaspoon baking soda

1$^1/_2$ cups whipping cream

Bring 3 cups of the sugar, the butter, baking soda, and cream to a boil in a large heavy saucepan. Immediately remove from heat and keep warm.

Sprinkle the remaining $^3/_4$ cup sugar in a heavy saucepan. Cook over medium heat, stirring constantly, until the sugar melts and turns golden brown.

Gradually pour into the cream mixture and stir until smooth (the mixture will bubble as the cream and sugar combine). Cook over medium heat 10 to 12 minutes, or until a candy thermometer registers 240°F (soft ball stage). Stir frequently.

Remove from the heat and beat at high speed with an electric mixer until it has reached spreading consistency. (Have patience, it could take 10 minutes.) Spread on cooled Buttermilk Cake layers (page 112) or any pastry.

HOLIDAY CARAMEL FUDGE

Fudge was strictly a sweet we enjoyed over the holidays and rarely any other time of the year. Chocolate and peanut butter flavors need to move on over because caramel is incredible!

YIELD: 2$^1/_2$ POUNDS

5 cups sugar, divided
2 cups half-and-half
4 tablespoons unsalted butter
$^1/_2$ cup milk
2 cups miniature marshmallows
1 teaspoon pure vanilla extract
1 cup chopped pecans

In a Dutch oven over low heat, combine 4 cups of the sugar, the half-and-half, and butter, stirring gently until the sugar dissolves. Cover and

increase the heat to medium. Cook 3 minutes.

Meanwhile, sprinkle the remaining cup of sugar in a heavy skillet and place over medium heat. Stir constantly until the sugar turns golden brown, around 3 minutes.

Pour the caramelized sugar and milk into the half-and-half mixture. Reduce the heat to low and stir constantly until the caramelized sugar dissolves. Continue cooking until the mixture reaches 240°F. Cool to 160°F.

Grease a 9-inch square pan and set aside.

Stir in the marshmallows, vanilla, and pecans. Stir briskly until the marshmallows melt and the mixture thickens. Pour into the prepared pan and spread evenly. Cool completely on a wire rack before cutting into squares. Store in an airtight container between layers of wax paper.

SENTIMENTAL CARAMEL MERINGUE PIE

This pie brings forth all kinds of fond emotions from born-and-raised Southerners. It anchors the dessert menus of nearly every "meat and three" and instantly satisfies that sweet tooth you might not know you had. Take it to any gathering and you'll be a culinary hero.

YIELD: 8 SERVINGS

2$^1/_2$ cups sugar, divided
$^1/_3$ cup all-purpose flour
Pinch of salt
2 cups milk
5 eggs, separated
2 tablespoons unsalted butter
1$^1/_2$ teaspoons pure vanilla extract, divided
1 baked Single Crust Pie Pastry (page 402)
$^3/_4$ teaspoon cream of tartar

In a heavy saucepan, whisk together 1 cup of the sugar, the flour, salt, milk, and egg yolks. Place over medium heat and whisk constantly until the mixture is hot, around 4 minutes. Set aside.

Preheat the oven to 325°F.

Sprinkle 1 cup of the remaining sugar in a skillet and place over medium heat. Stir constantly until the sugar turns golden brown, around 3 minutes. Gradually add to the hot custard and place over medium heat.

Cook and stir constantly until the mixture thickens and comes to a boil. Immediately add the butter and 1 teaspoon of the extract. Blend well and pour into the pastry shell.

In the bowl of an electric mixer, beat the egg whites and cream of tartar at high speed until foamy. Gradually add the remaining $^1/_2$ cup of sugar, 1 tablespoon at a time, until stiff peaks form. Stir in the remaining $^1/_2$ teaspoon of extract and beat well.

Spread over the hot filling, sealing to the edge. Bake 25 to 27 minutes, or until golden brown. Cool completely on a wire rack before serving.

TRIVIA: Caramel is the most popular filling in boxed chocolates, followed by butter cream.

STICKY CARAMEL ROLLS

These breakfast rolls are appropriately named thanks to the glaze.

YIELD: 1 DOZEN ROLLS

2 cups biscuit mix
$^1/_2$ cup milk
6 tablespoons unsalted butter, softened
$^1/_2$ cup packed brown sugar, divided
1 teaspoon ground cinnamon
$^1/_2$ cup chopped pecans

Preheat the oven to 350°F. Lightly grease a 12-cup muffin pan and set aside.

In a medium bowl, stir together the biscuit mix and milk with a fork until blended. Turn on a floured surface and knead 5 times. Roll into a 15 x 9-inch rectangle. Spread the surface with 2 tablespoons of the butter.

In a small bowl, combine $^1/_4$ cup of the brown sugar and the cinnamon. Sprinkle evenly over the dough. Starting at the long side, roll the dough jelly-roll style. Cut into 12 slices.

In a microwave safe bowl, melt the remaining 4 tablespoons of butter on low power in the microwave for 10 seconds. Stir in the remaining $^1/_2$ cup of brown sugar and the pecans. Divide equally among the muffin cups. Place the slices cut side down on top of the pecan mixture. Bake 20 to 22 minutes, or until lightly browned.

Invert immediately onto a serving platter. Serve warm.

CARROTS

NAME THE VEGETABLES YOU PURCHASE EVERY WEEK AT THE SUPERMARKET. FOR ME, it's always lettuce, onions, and carrots. While the last one I named may not be a regular on many grocery lists, it has quietly become a craving at my house.

I used to love watching Bugs Bunny cartoons early every Saturday mornings as a child. His antics were always a bit on the crazy side, but his favorite snack sure wasn't. He was always the picture of Mr. Cool munching on a fresh carrot, and those of us who love this nutritious vegetable are accomplishing a lot more than looking cool.

Carrots routinely come to us here in the South from our friends who grow them in Florida. Bravo to those growers because they seem to have become much sweeter over the years. I can hardly resist nibbling on one raw as I prep them for dinner.

It's especially nice to see how we have much more carrot variety on the market than we used to have. There are wildly colorful types to choose from, as well as convenient cuts such as baby peeled, sticks, shredded, and medallions.

Cooking with these root vegetables has never been easier. That's the reason I like to use this beta-carotene winner over and over. While many still relegate this raw vegetable to a lifetime sentence of being stuck on a crudités platter, I like to take advantage of the many assets it lends to cakes, breads, slaws, salads, sides, soufflés, and casseroles. I sometimes even throw grated leftovers into meatloaf. So move over Bugs Bunny. We have a lot of things to do with those carrots of yours!

Nutrition: Carrots are an incredible source of beta-carotene or vitamin A. In fact, that orange color is what gives it the highest content of any vegetable. Eating one medium carrot will supply you with the recommended amount of vitamin A (good for your eyes!) for the whole day.

Selection: Sometimes, you'll see retailers leave the green tops attached to the carrots to emphasize freshness. That's a good indicator, actually, if the greens are brightly colored and fresh looking. The carrots themselves should be smooth and firm and not flex in the least when you bend them.

Storage: If you purchase carrots with the green tops still attached, cut those off immediately when you get them home. Why? The greens will pull moisture from the root in an effort to stay alive. This seriously reduces the shelf life of the carrots. Stored properly without the tops, carrots will last up to a whopping two weeks. Carrots like humidity and cool temperatures, so store them loosely wrapped in a plastic bag in the vegetable crisper drawer. Keep them away from such fruits as apples and peaches. These give off ethylene gas and can cause the carrots to become bitter quickly.

A TOAST TO CARROTS

This recipe is not like traditional roasting. Think of your toaster… it cooks at a higher temperature than roasting, and the pan is preheated in the oven. The result is perfect carrots to serve with duck, chicken, pork, or turkey.

YIELD: 6 SERVINGS

10 carrots, peeled and cut in large dice
6 garlic cloves, peeled and cut in half
2 tablespoons olive oil
$\frac{1}{2}$ teaspoon black pepper
$\frac{1}{4}$ teaspoon kosher salt

Preheat the oven to 425°F. Place a jelly-roll pan in the oven to preheat.

Meanwhile, combine the carrots, garlic, and oil, tossing to evenly coat. Place on the hot pan and roast 17 to 20 minutes, stirring once halfway through. Transfer to a serving dish and season with the salt and pepper. Serve warm.

IN A PICKLE WITH CARROTS

This is a great party dish for a buffet. It is equally yummy served cold or at room temperature. The fact that you make it ahead is another plus.

YIELD: 12 APPETIZER SERVINGS

$1\frac{1}{2}$ cups cider vinegar
$1\frac{1}{2}$ cups water
1 cup sugar
2 pounds carrots, peeled and cut into wedges
1 tablespoon dill seeds
4 garlic cloves, peeled

In a large saucepan over medium-high heat, combine the vinegar, water, and sugar. Bring to a boil, stirring until the sugar completely dissolves. Add the carrots, dill seeds, and garlic and return to a boil.

Cover and reduce the heat to low. Simmer 8 minutes. Cool completely, cover, and refrigerate at least 8 hours before serving. To serve, pour through a fine mesh strainer and discard the liquid and garlic cloves.

NO-FUSS CARROT-RAISIN SALAD

I believe one of the reasons this salad is so popular is because it's so incredibly easy to prepare. It complements baked chicken and pork chops well and can be doubled if necessary.

YIELD: 4 SERVINGS

$\frac{3}{4}$ pound carrots, peeled and shredded
$\frac{1}{4}$ cup plus 2 tablespoons golden raisins
$\frac{1}{4}$ cup plus 2 tablespoons chopped walnuts
$\frac{1}{2}$ cup mayonnaise
$1\frac{1}{2}$ tablespoons cider vinegar
1 tablespoon sugar
$\frac{1}{4}$ teaspoon lemon juice

In a large mixing bowl, toss together the carrots, raisins, and walnuts. In a separate bowl, whisk together the mayonnaise, vinegar, sugar, and lemon juice. Whisk until the sugar dissolves and the mixture is well blended.

Pour over the carrot mixture and toss gently to evenly coat. Cover and refrigerate at least 1 hour before serving. Serve cold or at room temperature.

PECAN-CARROT BREAD

Think of carrot cake that isn't as sweet and in the form of a bread. This recipe makes two loaves. One can be enjoyed immediately and the other can be given away or put in the freezer for another day.

YIELD: 2 LOAVES

3 cups all-purpose flour

2 cups sugar

1 cup chopped pecans

1 teaspoon ground cinnamon

1 teaspoon baking soda

$3/4$ teaspoon salt

3 eggs, lightly beaten

2 cups grated carrots

1 cup vegetable oil

1 (8-ounce) can crushed pineapple, drained

2 teaspoons pure vanilla extract

Preheat the oven to 350°F. Lightly grease and flour 2 loaf pans and set aside.

In a large mixing bowl, combine the flour, sugar, pecans, cinnamon, baking soda, and salt. Make a well in the center and set aside.

In a separate small bowl, combine the eggs, carrots, oil, pineapple, and extract. Add to the flour mixture, stirring just until moistened. Divide the batter evenly into the prepared pans.

Bake 1 hour, or until a tester inserted in the center comes out clean. Cool in the pans on wire racks 10 minutes. Remove and cool completely on wire racks before slicing and serving.

SUPREME CARROT CAKE WITH CREAM CHEESE FROSTING

This layered cake is spiced just right, moist, sweet, full of pecans, and topped off with mounds of cream cheese frosting. I like to make this cake the day before it will be served because it slices so much easier.

YIELD: 16 SERVINGS

2 cups all-purpose flour

2 teaspoons baking soda

2 teaspoons ground cinnamon

$1/2$ teaspoon salt

3 eggs

2 cups sugar

$3/4$ cup vegetable oil

$3/4$ cup buttermilk

2 teaspoons pure vanilla extract

2 cups grated carrots

1 (8-ounce) can crushed pineapple, drained

1 ($3^1/2$-ounce) can shredded coconut

1 cup chopped pecans

Cream Cheese Frosting (recipe follows)

Preheat the oven to 350°F. Lightly grease and flour 3 (9-inch) round cake pans and set aside.

In a medium bowl, stir together the flour, baking soda, cinnamon, and salt. Set aside.

In the bowl of an electric mixer, beat the eggs, sugar, oil, buttermilk, and extract at medium speed until smooth. Reduce the speed to low and add the flour mixture, beating until blended. Fold in the carrots, pineapple, coconut, and pecans.

Pour the batter evenly in the prepared pans. Bake 25 to 30 minutes, or until a tester inserted in the center comes out clean. Cool in the pans on wire racks 10 minutes. Remove and cool completely on wire racks before frosting between the layers, on the side, and on the top with the cream cheese frosting.

CREAM CHEESE FROSTING

Absolutely delicious on any cake or cupcake you make!

YIELD: 3½ CUPS

1 (8-ounce) plus 1 (3-ounce) package cream cheese, softened
12 tablespoons unsalted butter, softened
1 (16-ounce) package confectioners' sugar
1½ teaspoons pure vanilla extract

In the bowl of an electric mixer, combine the cream cheese and butter until smooth. Gradually add the confectioners' sugar, beating at low speed until light and fluffy. Stir in the extract. Spread on the cooled cake.

SWEET KISSED CARROTS

The ingredients are few and the results are huge. That's the sign of a recipe from my mother's notebook and a sign that it will be a regular of yours soon.

YIELD: 4 SERVINGS

4 cups sliced carrots
1½ cups water
¼ teaspoon salt
4 tablespoons unsalted butter, melted
¼ cup honey
1 tablespoon lemon juice

Preheat the oven to 375°F. Lightly grease a 1-quart baking dish and set aside.

Place the carrots, water, and salt in a medium saucepan over high heat. Bring to a boil and cook 7 minutes. Drain well. Place the carrots in the prepared baking dish and set aside.

In a small bowl, combine the butter, honey, and lemon juice. Stir until well combined. Drizzle over the carrots. Bake 30 minutes, stirring occasionally. Serve warm.

Botany: Carrots are members of the parsley family and are related to dill, parsnips, celery, caraway, fennel, anise, and coriander. They are also a relative of the common Southern wildflower Queen Anne's Lace. There are more than four hundred carrot varieties identified throughout the world, with colors that range from pale amber to almost red.

Origin: Carrots are believed to have originated in what is now present day Afghanistan. Like many foods, they were first used as medicine. The juice was a common remedy for snake bites, skin afflictions, and indigestion.

History: The common orange carrots we see today were not developed until the 1600s by the Dutch. They were developed to pay tribute to that nation's ruling House of Orange. Originally, carrots were white, yellow, green, red, and a purple that was so deep it was nearly black.

CATFISH

AS A MISSISSIPPI NATIVE, I KNOW A THING OR TWO ABOUT CATFISH. AFTER ALL, MY HOME STATE practically invented the industry, specializing in farming, processing, and shipping, not to mention preparation and consumption. I think that's why I love this unique fish so much ... it tastes like home.

If you've ever laid eyes on a catfish, you've probably been haunted with nightmares. It's not the most attractive fish you'll ever see. Catfish have no scales, but they have barbs on their fins. You'll know it if you ever grab one. Their eyes are very small and rather inefficient. For that reason, they rely on other senses to locate food. In come the barbels or what some describe as whiskers on the fish.

Catfish are bottom feeders, meaning they scavenge the bottom of the water for food. They inhabit mud-bottomed lakes, ponds, rivers, and creeks where seeing food is frequently difficult at best. External taste-buds are located in the barbels, which means the catfish can taste things just by touching it. It is estimated that catfish have around one hundred thousand taste receptors on just one "whisker."

There are thirty-seven different catfish families. Black bullheads are the smallest of all catfish, followed by yellow bullheads and brown bullheads. Farm-raised catfish are fed puffed food pellets that are high in protein. The pellets are a mixture of soybeans, corn, wheat, vitamins, and minerals—and one of the reasons catfish doesn't have a "fishy" odor like some other fish varieties.

Catfish are harvested around eighteen months with large weighted nets called seines. They are transported in aerated tanks and kept alive until they are processed. This makes catfish truly the freshest freshwater fish you can purchase on the market.

Cooking: For any fish, use the general rule of cooking it ten minutes for every inch of thickness, measured at the thickest part of the fillet. For fillets that are less than a half inch thick, there is no need to turn them during cooking. For fillets that are cooked in parchment, aluminum foil, or a sauce of any kind, add five minutes to the total cooking time. Catfish cooks quickly, so keep a timer on hand and don't overcook.

Nutrition: A four-ounce portion of broiled, grilled, steamed, or baked catfish contains only one hundred calories. It is rich in protein.

Selection: Catfish should always smell clean, with no fishy odor. It should have a firm flesh that is not separating, dry looking, or discolored. It should appear translucent and the packaging should keep it flat rather than bent. If the head of the catfish has not been removed, the eyes should be clear and protruding. If you are purchasing whole catfish, allow three-fourths of a pound per serving. If it's dressed, purchase one-half pound per person. Catfish fillets will demand one-third pound per serving.

DELTA BAKED CATFISH

I think of my daddy every time I make this recipe. He can tell you the exact moment he tasted corn flakes for the first time. When I crush them for this recipe, I think of him as a little boy sitting on his neighbor's front porch having his first bowl of corn flakes and it makes me smile. This recipe uses that crunch to make you think the fish was actually fried.

YIELD: 6 SERVINGS

3 cups corn flakes, finely crushed
$^2/_3$ cup shredded Parmesan cheese
1 teaspoon paprika
$^1/_2$ teaspoon salt
$^1/_2$ cup mayonnaise
1 teaspoon Worcestershire sauce
$1^1/_2$ teaspoons Cajun seasoning
6 (5 to 6-ounce) catfish fillets

Preheat the broiler. Line a baking sheet with aluminum foil. Lightly coat a wire rack with cooking spray and place over the baking sheet. Set aside.

In a shallow dish, combine the corn flakes, Parmesan, paprika, and salt. In a small bowl, whisk together the mayonnaise, Worcestershire, and Cajun seasoning.

Spread the mayonnaise mixture on both sides of each fillet. Dredge in the cornflake mixture and place on the wire rack. Broil 5 to 6 minutes on each side, or until golden brown. Serve immediately.

GRILLED CAJUN CATFISH

Because catfish has such a mild flavor, the Cajun spices really jazz it up. This recipe works equally well on tilapia fillets.

YIELD: 4 SERVINGS

4 (6-ounce) catfish fillets
2 tablespoons lemon juice
1 teaspoon lemon pepper
1 teaspoon white pepper
1 teaspoon Cajun seasoning
1 teaspoon dried parsley
$^1/_2$ teaspoon onion powder

Prepare the grill to medium heat.

Meanwhile, place the fillets in a single layer on a baking sheet. Sprinkle with the lemon juice and set aside. Combine the lemon pepper, white pepper, Cajun seasoning, parsley, and onion powder in a small bowl. Sprinkle evenly on both sides of the fish.

Spray a fish basket with cooking spray and transfer the fillets to the basket. Grill 7 to 9 minutes, or until the fish flakes easily with a fork. Serve hot.

HUSHPUPPY FRIED CATFISH

You will love how this batter makes the catfish puff up gloriously when fried.

YIELD: 4 SERVINGS

Vegetable or canola oil for frying
1 (8-ounce) package hushpuppy mix
$^1/_2$ cup milk
$^1/_2$ cup water
1 egg, lightly beaten
1 tablespoon hot sauce
$^1/_2$ teaspoon cayenne
$^1/_2$ teaspoon salt
4 (6 ounce) catfish fillets

Pour the oil to a depth of $^1/_2$ inch in a large skillet.

Place over medium-high heat and bring to 350°F.

Meanwhile, in a medium bowl, combine the hushpuppy mix, milk, water, egg, hot sauce, cayenne, and salt. Let stand 4 to 5 minutes.

Dredge the fillets in the hushpuppy mixture. Carefully place in hot oil and fry 4 to 5 minutes on each side, or until golden brown. Drain on paper towels and serve hot.

LOUISIANA BLACKENED CATFISH

Thanks will always go to New Orleans Chef Paul Prudhomme for making this cooking technique popular. Cheers to his genius!

YIELD: 4 SERVINGS

4 teaspoons paprika
1 teaspoon dried oregano
1 teaspoon dried thyme
1 teaspoon sugar
$\frac{1}{2}$ teaspoon cayenne
$\frac{1}{2}$ teaspoon salt
$\frac{1}{4}$ teaspoon black pepper
4 (6-ounce) catfish fillets
2 tablespoons canola oil
2 tablespoons unsalted butter

In a small bowl, combine the paprika, oregano, thyme, sugar, cayenne, salt, and pepper. Sprinkle the mixture evenly over each fillet, coating well. Set aside.

Heat the oil in a large skillet over medium-high heat. When hot, add the butter and stir until the foam subsides. Blacken 2 fillets at a time about 4 minutes on each side, turning once. Repeat with remaining fillets. Serve hot.

INSIDE/OUTSIDE FRIED CATFISH

Southerners typically fry catfish for a monster crowd. That demands for it to be fried outside, where the party is going on. Of course, you can also fry it inside for a smaller gathering. This recipe can be adapted for either crowd. Double it for more people or cut it in half for just a few. See notes below.

YIELD: 24 FILLETS

24 (6-ounce) catfish fillets
2 cups buttermilk
3 cups cornmeal
$\frac{1}{2}$ cup all-purpose flour
1 teaspoon salt
3 teaspoons red pepper
Vegetable oil

Place the fillets in a large zip-top plastic bag and add the buttermilk. Seal well and let marinate at room temperature 30 minutes.

Meanwhile, in a shallow dish, combine the cornmeal, flour, salt, and pepper, blending well.

Pour the oil to a depth of 2 inches in deep fryer over medium-high heat. Heat the oil to 350°F.

Drain the fillets from the buttermilk. Dredge in the cornmeal mixture, coating well. Carefully drop the fillets in the hot oil and fry until they float to the top and are golden brown, around 4 minutes. Drain on paper towels and repeat with the remaining fillets. Serve hot.

Note: For inside frying, heat the oil to a depth of 1 inch in a large cast-iron skillet and follow the same instructions as above. Cut the amount of everything in half.

PECAN CATFISH

Chopped pecans toast away in the batter for this cat-fish and add an almost buttery taste to the crunchy fish.

YIELD: 6 SERVINGS

3 cups chopped pecans
1 cup plain dry breadcrumbs
$1\frac{1}{2}$ teaspoons salt, divided
$1\frac{1}{2}$ teaspoons black pepper, divided
1 cup all-purpose flour
3 eggs
$\frac{1}{2}$ cup milk
4 tablespoons unsalted butter
$\frac{1}{4}$ cup canola or vegetable oil
6 (6-ounce) catfish fillets
1 tablespoon Creole or Cajun seasoning

In the bowl of a food processor, grind together the pecans, breadcrumbs, $\frac{1}{2}$ teaspoon of the salt, and $\frac{1}{2}$ teaspoon of the pepper. Transfer to a shallow dish.

In a separate shallow dish, combine the flour, $\frac{1}{2}$ teaspoon of the remaining salt, and $\frac{1}{2}$ teaspoon of the remaining pepper.

In a medium bowl, whisk together the eggs, milk, and the remaining $\frac{1}{2}$ teaspoon of the salt and the remaining $\frac{1}{2}$ teaspoon of the pepper.

Place the butter and oil in a large skillet over medium heat. Sprinkle the catfish with the Creole seasoning. Dredge in the flour mixture, dip in the egg mixture, and then dip in the pecan mixture. Fry 4 to 5 minutes on each side, or until completely done. Serve warm.

OVEN-FRIED CRACKER CATFISH

George loves saltine crackers. They are his favorites no matter what other types I purchase, so take a guess as to who loves this recipe!

YIELD: 4 SERVINGS

4 (6-ounce) catfish fillets
$\frac{1}{4}$ cup buttermilk or milk
$\frac{3}{4}$ cup crushed saltine crackers
$\frac{1}{4}$ teaspoon celery salt
$\frac{1}{4}$ teaspoon onion powder
$\frac{1}{4}$ teaspoon paprika
$\frac{1}{4}$ teaspoon white pepper

Preheat the oven to 350°F. Lightly grease a baking sheet and set aside.

Place the catfish in a single layer in a shallow dish and pour the buttermilk over the top. Set aside.

In a small bowl, combine the crackers, celery salt, onion powder, paprika, and white pepper. Remove the catfish from the buttermilk and place on the prepared sheet. Sprinkle the tops evenly with the cracker mixture.

Bake 25 to 30 minutes, or until the fish flakes easily with a fork. Serve hot.

Celebrations
August is National Catfish Month.
June 25 is National Catfish Day.

SPICY CORNMEAL-CRUSTED CATFISH

Don't let your family know the seasoning secret here of dry taco mix and they'll never guess it's what adds such a great flavor twist. This is also a great way to spice up potato wedges.

YIELD: 4 SERVINGS

1 (1.25-ounce) package dry taco seasoning mix
4 (5-ounce) catfish fillets
$\frac{1}{2}$ cup cornmeal
2 eggs, beaten
3 tablespoons vegetable or canola oil

Place the seasoning mix in a large zip-top bag. Add the fillets, shaking to evenly coat. Set aside 5 minutes.

Meanwhile, place the cornmeal in a shallow dish and the eggs in a separate shallow dish. Heat the oil in a large skillet over medium-high heat.

Dip the fillets in the eggs and dredge in the cornmeal. Add to the hot skillet and cook 4 to 5 minutes on each side, or until the fish flakes easily with a fork. Serve hot.

NAME: Catfish were named because of their long "whiskers," which are similar to those of a cat.

SUBSTITUTIONS: Catfish is a lean, firm fish with a mild flavor. You can substitute catfish in any recipe calling for mahi mahi or grouper.

TRIVIA: Belzoni, Mississippi, is the Catfish Capital of the World. Paris, Tennessee, is the home of the Largest Catfish Fry.

"UP IN SMOKE" CATFISH

I love smoked fish probably because it seems to soak up the hickory flavor more than any other food. This recipe will drive your neighbors crazy with the wonderful aroma!

YIELD: 10 TO 12 SERVINGS

7 pounds catfish fillets
2 cups water
$\frac{1}{2}$ cup packed brown sugar
$\frac{1}{4}$ cup salt
2 tablespoons concentrated liquid crab and shrimp boil
$\frac{1}{4}$ teaspoon dried dill
Hickory chips

Place the fish in a shallow dish. In a mixing bowl, combine the water, brown sugar, salt, crab boil, and dill. Cover and refrigerate 8 hours or overnight, turning occasionally.

Soak the hickory chips at least 2 hours in water. Prepare the smoker and place the drained chips on the lowest shelf.

Remove the fillets from the marinade and discard the marinade. Arrange the fillets on the rack. Smoke 3 hours, or until the fish is done and flakes easily with a fork. Serve hot.

Storage: Handle catfish as you would any perishable food. It is important to keep it refrigerated. Use within two days after purchasing or defrosting. Cooked leftovers should be used within two days as well. Use frozen catfish within six months and always thaw it in the refrigerator.

CHEESE

I **WAS PRACTICALLY RAISED ON CHEESE MADE AT THE MISSISSIPPI STATE DAIRY. A BIG RED-** waxed ball of Edam was a regular in our refrigerator. It was mellow, yet at the same time full of fantastic flavor. The Cheddar was incredible as well and equally at home in a grilled sandwich or topping macaroni.

When I first began cooking, I quickly discovered the cheese of my youth was difficult to find in the supermarket under any nationally recognized brand. For instance, if I was in need of Cheddar that had any flavor, I had to purchase those labeled sharp or extra sharp.

Then I discovered boutique cheese makers and the beauty of a really good deli. That's when I began experimenting with the loads of different cheeses available. It totally changed the way I cooked.

I believe many are still comfortable with only a few members of this vast family. While mozzarella, Swiss, Cheddar, and occasionally Monterey Jack are familiar, others remain exotic and unused. Boursin, for example, is one of my favorite appetizer cheeses because so few are familiar with it. I occasionally throw a bit in mashed potatoes or use it as a substitute for cream cheese.

To help you out of your cheese rut, I've included several different cheese suggestions in these recipes. Feel free to experiment on your own.

Serving: Other than soft cheese, allow all types to come to room temperature 30 minutes before serving. It allows you to truly taste the flavor of the cheese, as cold temperatures dull the tastebuds.

Storage: Keep all cheese cold, but not frozen, which changes the texture drastically. Hard and very hard cheeses should be wrapped in wax paper before placing in a plastic zip-top storage bag. This will keep the cheese from becoming slimy on the outside and extend the shelf life.

Varieties: Cheese is divided into categories depending on how hard they are when finished.
Soft Cheeses: Boursin, Brie, Camembert, cottage cheese, cream cheese, crème fraiche, feta, goat cheese, mascarpone, Montrachet, Neufchâtel, and ricotta.
Semi-Soft Cheeses: cream Havarti, fontina, Gouda, Monterey Jack, mozzarella, Muenster, pepper Jack, provolone, and Tilsit.
Hard Cheeses: Cheddar, colby, Edam, Emmentaler, Gruyère, Jarlsberg, longhorn, manchego, raclette, Swiss, and Tillamook.
Very Hard Cheeses: Parmesan, Parmigiano-Reggiano, and Romano.

BAKED PIMIENTO CHEESE

This version of the Southern classic is served hot as a dip, and it's perfect for cold-weather parties or tailgating.

YIELD: 6 SERVINGS

8 ounces extra-sharp Cheddar cheese, shredded
4 ounces chopped pimientos, drained
$1/4$ cup mayonnaise
1 tablespoon spicy brown mustard
$1^1/2$ teaspoons red wine vinegar
$1/8$ teaspoon celery salt
$1/8$ teaspoon black pepper
$1/8$ teaspoon garlic salt

Preheat the oven to 350°F. Lightly grease an 8-inch square baking dish and set aside.

In the bowl of an electric mixer, combine the Cheddar, pimientos, mayonnaise, mustard, vinegar, celery salt, pepper, and garlic salt.

Transfer to the prepared dish. Bake 10 minutes, or until the cheese is melted. Stir and serve warm with toasted pita chips, crackers, or vegetables.

"FOR JUST ABOUT ANYTHING" CHEDDAR CHEESE SAUCE

Dress up steamed vegetables, broiled chicken, or potatoes with this versatile sauce.

YIELD: $1^1/3$ CUPS

2 tablespoons unsalted butter
2 tablespoons all-purpose flour
1 cup milk
$1/2$ teaspoon salt
$1/8$ teaspoon white pepper
1 cup shredded white Cheddar cheese

In a heavy saucepan over low heat, melt the butter. Add the flour, stirring constantly until smooth. Cook 1 minute, stirring constantly.

Gradually add the milk and increase the heat to medium. Stir constantly until thick and bubbly, about 4 minutes. Stir in the salt and pepper. Add the cheese and continue stirring until the cheese is completely melted.
Note: You can substitute Swiss cheese or Monterey Jack for the Cheddar.

HEAVENLY PIMIENTO CHEESE

You'll find a recipe for this cold salad and sandwich spread in every Southern home. It's as common as chiggers.

YIELD: 3 CUPS

4 cups shredded sharp Cheddar cheese
1 (4-ounce) jar diced pimiento peppers, drained
$3/4$ cup mayonnaise
2 tablespoons Dijon or Durkee's mustard
1 garlic clove, minced
$1/2$ teaspoon white pepper
$1/8$ teaspoon cayenne
$1/4$ teaspoon sugar

In a medium bowl combine the cheese, pimientos, mayonnaise, mustard, garlic, white pepper, cayenne, and sugar, folding gently to mix.

Cover and refrigerate at least 2 hours. Before serving, bring to room temperature 10 minutes.
Note: This makes an excellent grilled sandwich!

OLD SOUTH CHEESE STRAWS

No party is complete without this Southern staple. Serve with Mint Juleps (page 264).

YIELD: 12 SERVINGS

1 sheet frozen puff pastry, thawed

1 egg

2 teaspoons water

1 cup finely grated Jarlsberg or sharp Cheddar cheese

$^1/_4$ teaspoon sea salt

Preheat the oven to 425°F. Lightly grease two baking sheets and set aside.

Roll out the pastry on a lightly floured surface to form a rectangle. With a sharp paring knife or a pastry wheel, cut in half crosswise to form two rectangles.

In a small bowl, whisk together the egg and water. Brush both rectangles with the egg wash. Sprinkle the cheese evenly over one rectangle. Top with the remaining rectangle, placing the egg washed side down. Press together firmly with a rolling pin to adhere the layers. Brush the top with the egg wash again and sprinkle evenly with the salt.

With a pastry wheel or paring knife, cut the pastry crosswise into 24 ($^1/_2$-inch) strips. Holding each end of the strip, twist 3 times and place on the prepared baking sheets. Press the ends to the baking sheets to keep them twisted. Place the strips 1 inch apart.

Bake 1 sheet in the middle of the oven 10 to 12 minutes. While the first sheet bakes, prepare the second sheet for baking. Immediately transfer to wire racks and cool. Serve warm or at room temperature.

Note: Before baking, the straws can be frozen up to two weeks. Place the baking sheet in the freezer. When solid, transfer to a freezer bag. Bake straight from the freezer.

MOTHER'S CHEDDAR CHEESE BREAD PUDDING

My mother gave me this recipe and it instantly became my cheese comfort food. It is a great side dish to serve with ham or turkey.

YIELD: 6 SERVINGS

9 slices loaf bread, crusts removed

9 slices Cheddar cheese

2 eggs

1 cup milk

$^1/_2$ teaspoon salt

$^1/_4$ teaspoon pepper

3 tablespoons unsalted butter, cubed

Lightly grease a 2-quart casserole dish. Cover the bottom with 3 slices of the bread, squeezing to fill in the gaps. Top with 3 slices of the cheese. Repeat twice and set aside.

In a medium mixing bowl, whisk together the eggs and milk. Pour over the layers of bread and cheese. Top with the salt and pepper. Cover and refrigerate 8 hours or overnight.

Preheat the oven to 350°F. Dot the top of the bread pudding with the butter. Bake, uncovered, 25 to 30 minutes. Serve immediately.

PRALINES AND CREAM CHEESECAKE

This recipe is so incredibly rich that I've increased the number of servings it provides. Cut small wedges and get ready for oohs and aahs! I use Lorna Doone cookies for the shortbread crumbs.

YIELD: 16 SERVINGS

2 cups crushed shortbread cookies

3 tablespoons unsalted butter, melted

1/2 cup chopped pecans

2 (8-ounce) packages cream cheese, softened

4 ounces cream cheese, softened

1 cup granulated sugar, divided

3/4 cup packed brown sugar

2 tablespoons all-purpose flour

1 1/2 teaspoons pure almond or vanilla extract

4 eggs

2 egg yolks

1/3 cup heavy cream

1/3 cup caramel dessert topping

Toasted pecan halves for garnish

Preheat the oven to 350°F. Grease a 10-inch spring-form pan and set aside. Cover a baking sheet with aluminum foil and set aside.

In a medium bowl, combine the crushed cookies and the butter. Press into the bottom and up the sides of the prepared springform pan. Bake 8 minutes. Immediately sprinkle the chopped pecans over the top of the crust. Cool on a wire rack.

Meanwhile, beat the cream cheese at medium speed of an electric mixer. Gradually add the granulated sugar, mixing well. Add the brown sugar, flour, and extract, blending until smooth. Add the eggs and yolks, one at a time. Stir in the cream.

Pour into the crust and place on the prepared baking sheet. Bake on the lowest oven rack 10 minutes. Reduce the oven temperature to 325°F and bake 1 hour and 20 minutes, or until set. Cool completely on a wire rack. Refrigerate overnight.

To serve, drizzle the caramel topping over the top and line the edges with toasted pecan halves.

Celebrations

January 20 is National Cheese Lover's Day.
May 18 is National Cheese Soufflé Day.
June 4 is National Cheese Day.
July 30 is National Cheesecake Day.

SOUTHERN TRINITY FONDUE

This is a dipper composed of what some would say is the second Southern trinity (beer, cheese, and sausage!).

YIELD: 6 CUPS

1/2 pound pork sausage, hot or mild

6 tablespoons unsalted butter

1 yellow onion, peeled and chopped

1 garlic clove, minced

6 tablespoons all-purpose flour

2 cups milk

4 cups shredded Edam or Cheddar cheese

1 cup beer

1 (4-ounce) can chopped green chiles

1/2 teaspoon salt

1/4 teaspoon ground red pepper

French bread, cubed

Cook the sausage in a large saucepan over medium heat, stirring until it crumbles and is completely done. Drain on paper towels and set aside.

Melt the butter in the same pan over medium heat. Add the onions and garlic and sauté until tender, around 3 minutes. Add the flour, stirring until smooth.

Cook 1 minute, stirring constantly. Gradually add the milk, stirring until thickened. Add the cheese, stirring until melted. Remove from the heat and stir in the sausage, beer, chiles, salt, and red pepper. Transfer to a fondue pot or slow cooker. Keep warm on a low setting and serve with cubed bread.

CHERRIES

I CAN BE EASILY DISTRACTED. MY ATTENTION IS PULLED IN MANY DIRECTIONS WHEN I VISIT local farm markets. At various times, I'll find myself totally in love with peaches, but then my affections will switch to berries and later I am totally dedicated to apples.

I'm constantly on the move with fruit, shifting my devotion from one to the next. But there are two times of year when I cannot live without luscious cherries: While celebrating George Washington's birthday in February and in the early summer when the home-grown crop arrives on the market.

The first time I picked cherries was one summer at my grandmother's house in Ecru, Mississippi. My twin sister and I ate nearly every one we plucked from the tree until she made us stop. I remember thinking they looked like small Christmas ornaments hanging from the branches. I had never seen anything more enchanting and lovely.

The two main types of cherries are sweet and sour. Sweet cherries have a familiar heart shape and are delicious right off the tree. The most popular varieties include Bing, Lambert, Rainier, and Royal Ann, which is used to make maraschino cherries. Sweet cherries are larger than the other type, which is unforgettably sour.

Yes, those sour cherries will certainly make you practice puckering. They are much too sour to enjoy raw, but are marvelous when mellowed out in pies and preserves. Early Richmond is my favorite sour cherry variety, probably because it hits the Southern market so early.

The U.S. grows more cherries than any other country in the world. Most of those grown here will end up in cherry pie filling, which is the most popular flavor on the market.

If you don't already own one, it's time to invest in a hand-held cherry pitter. It will make using these beautiful fruits much easier and you'll understand why they have such an avid following.

Nutrition: A cup of pitted cherries contains only seventy calories. Cherries are a good source of potassium, vitamins A and C, calcium, and phosphorus.

Preserving: Cherries must be pitted before they are frozen or the fruit turns bitter. Spread the pitted fruit on a baking sheet in a single layer and place in the freezer. When the fruit is frozen solid, transfer to a freezer container, label, and freeze. For best results, use within eight months. There is no need to thaw frozen cherries before using.

Selection: Fresh cherries should be plump, firm, and shiny. Look for a good color and fruit that is free from blemishes, shriveling, or any brown, sunken spots.

Storage: Don't remove the stems or wash fresh cherries until just before you are ready to use them. Store in a zip-top plastic bag with several holes punched in it. Keep in the crisper drawer of the refrigerator.

BE MINE
CHERRY-NUT BARK

This candy is a tradition on Valentine's Day. A tin of this makes an impressive gift for anyone you love.

YIELD: 3¼ POUNDS

1¼ cups dried cherries
2 tablespoons water
1 (24-ounce) package white chocolate morsels
6 (2-ounce) squares vanilla candy coating
1¼ cups chopped pistachios

Line a jelly-roll pan with wax paper and set aside. Place the cherries and water in a small glass bowl and microwave 2 minutes on high power. Drain and set aside.

In a heavy saucepan over low heat, melt the morsels and candy coating. When completely melted, stir in the cherries and nuts.

Spread evenly into the prepared pan. Refrigerate 1 hour or until firm. Cut with shaped cookie cutters or break into pieces. Store in an airtight container.

BIRTHDAY GIRL'S
CHERRY PINK FROSTING

Every year on our birthdays, Tina and I wanted a white cake with pink frosting. If this one isn't pink enough for you, add a few drops of red food coloring. Spread on cupcakes or double the recipe and use to frost a cake.

YIELD: 1¼ CUPS

2 cups confectioners' sugar
3 tablespoons unsalted butter, softened

3 tablespoons milk
1 tablespoon maraschino cherry juice
½ teaspoon pure almond extract

In the bowl of an electric mixer and on low speed, combine the sugar, butter, milk, juice, and extract. Blend well to spreading consistency.

CANDIED CHERRY
CROWN COOKIES

A childhood treat for us was to get these cookies from the Mississippi State bakery. Tina and I would eat all around the candied cherry center, saving it for last! To this day, I love them!

YIELD: ABOUT 5 DOZEN

½ pound (2 sticks) unsalted butter, softened
1 (3-ounce) package cream cheese, softened
1 cup sugar
1 egg yolk
1 teaspoon pure almond extract
2½ cups all-purpose flour
30 red candied cherries, halved

In the bowl of an electric mixer, cream the butter and cheese until creamy. Gradually add the sugar, beating well. Add the egg yolk and extract, mixing well. Gradually stir in the flour. Cover and refrigerate 1 hour.

Preheat the oven to 350°F. Lightly grease 2 cookie sheets and set aside.

Shape the dough into 1-inch balls (or extrude from a cookie press). Place 2-inches apart on the prepared sheets. Press a cherry half in the center of each cookie. Bake 15 minutes. Cool on wire racks. Store in an airtight container.

CHERRY CORNMEAL COOKIES

The addition of cornmeal gives these cookies an extra crunch and almost becomes the secret ingredient that no one will guess is included.

YIELD: 7 DOZEN COOKIES

12 tablespoons unsalted butter, softened

1$\frac{1}{2}$ cups sugar

2 tablespoons corn syrup

2 eggs

1 teaspoon pure almond extract

1 teaspoon pure vanilla extract

3 cups all-purpose flour

1 cup plain cornmeal

2 teaspoons baking powder

$\frac{1}{2}$ teaspoon salt

1$\frac{1}{2}$ cups chopped dried sweet cherries

Preheat the oven to 350°F. Lightly grease 2 cookie sheets and set aside.

In the bowl of an electric mixer, cream the butter and sugar 2 minutes. Add the syrup, eggs, almond extract, and vanilla extract. Beat 2 minutes longer.

In a separate bowl, combine the flour, cornmeal, baking powder, and salt. Gradually add to the butter mixture on low speed. Fold in the cherries.

Shape the dough into 1-inch balls and place 1-inch apart on the prepared sheets. Flatten slightly with the greased bottom of a glass.

Bake 10 to 13 minutes, or until the edges are lightly browned. Transfer to a wire rack and cool completely. Store in an airtight container.

CHERRY DIVINITY CANDY

This is the first candy I ever made. You need to work very quickly when dropping it onto the wax paper. An extra set of hands at that point will make things go a lot easier.

YIELD: 3 DOZEN PIECES

2$\frac{1}{2}$ cups sugar

$\frac{1}{2}$ cup light corn syrup

$\frac{1}{2}$ cup water

2 egg whites

1 teaspoon pure almond extract

1 cup finely chopped red candied cherries

In a large saucepan, combine the sugar, syrup, and water. Place over low heat, stirring constantly until the sugar dissolves. Cover and increase the heat to medium. Cook 3 minutes.

Uncover and continue to cook to the hard-ball stage or until a candy thermometer registers 260°F. Set aside.

In the bowl of an electric mixer, beat the egg whites at high speed until stiff peaks form. Carefully pour a heavy stream of the syrup over the egg whites while beating constantly at high speed.

Add the extract and continue beating just until the mixture holds its shape, about 4 minutes. Stir in the cherries. Drop by rounded teaspoons onto wax paper. Cool to room temperature and store in an airtight container.

> **"Happiness is a bowl of cherries and a book of poetry under a shade tree.**
>
> —ASTRID ALAUDA

FRESH CHERRY COBBLER

Juicy cherries are topped with a drop crust, so there's no rolling required. That's where the name originated, because the top is rough looking or cobbled. This has all the goodness of down-home cooking.

YIELD: 8 SERVINGS

2 pounds fresh cherries, pitted
1/4 cup honey
1/4 cup light brown sugar
1/4 teaspoon ground cinnamon
2 tablespoons lemon juice
2 tablespoons Kirsch or cherry brandy
1 tablespoon cornstarch
6 tablespoons unsalted butter, divided
1 1/2 cups biscuit mix
2 tablespoons granulated sugar
1 egg
1/4 cup milk
Vanilla ice cream

Preheat the oven to 400°F. Lightly grease a 2-quart baking dish and set aside.

In a medium bowl, stir together the cherries, honey, brown sugar, and cinnamon. Set aside.

In a small bowl, whisk together the juice and Kirsch. Add the cornstarch, whisking until smooth. Stir into the cherry mixture.

Spoon the cherry mixture into the prepared pan. Dot with 2 tablespoons of the chilled butter that is cut into pieces. Set aside.

In a mixing bowl, combine the biscuit mix and granulated sugar. Cut in the remaining butter with a pastry blender or 2 forks until the mixture is crumbly. Stir in the egg and milk. Drop spoonfuls of the dough over the cherry mixture.

Bake 20 to 25 minutes, or until the top is golden brown and the cobbler is bubbly. Let stand 5 minutes before serving with vanilla ice cream.

SOUR CHERRY LATTICE-TOPPED PIE

Tart cherries soften in texture and flavor in this gorgeous pie.

YIELD: 8 SERVINGS

1 cup plus 1 tablespoon sugar, divided
3 tablespoons cornstarch
1/4 teaspoon salt
5 cups sour cherries, pitted
1 teaspoon lemon juice
1/2 teaspoon pure almond extract
1 recipe Double Pie Pastry (page 400)
2 tablespoons unsalted butter, cut into cubes
1 tablespoon milk
Vanilla ice cream

Preheat the oven to 425°F. In a medium bowl, stir together 1 cup of the sugar and the cornstarch. Add the salt. Gently stir in the cherries, juice, and extract. Set aside.

Press 1 pastry in the bottom of a 9-inch pie pan. Trim any overhang to 1/2 inch. Place the second pastry on a lightly floured surface. Using a pastry wheel or a large knife, cut the dough into 3/4-inch strips.

Spoon the cherry filling into the pie pastry mounding slightly in the center. Dot the top with the butter. Arrange the pastry strips on top of the filling to form a lattice pattern. Fold the bottom pastry over the ends of the strips, pressing to seal.

Brush the top, but not the edges, with the milk. Sprinkle the remaining sugar evenly on the top. Place the pie on a jelly-roll pan and bake 15 minutes. Reduce the oven temperature to 375°F and bake 55 minutes longer. Cover the edges with foil if they are browning too quickly. Cool completely on a wire rack before serving with vanilla ice cream.

SWEET CHERRY HOMEMADE JAM

Making jam is much easier than jelly because there's no straining involved. This easy recipe provides an opportunity to preserve the harvest quickly.

YIELD: 4 HALF-PINTS

2$\frac{1}{2}$ cups chopped pitted sweet cherries
2 tablespoons lemon juice
4$\frac{1}{2}$ cups sugar
1 (3-ounce) package liquid pectin

Combine the cherries, juice, and sugar in a large saucepan over high heat. Bring to a rolling boil, stirring constantly. Add the pectin and stir constantly 1 minute.

Skim off any foam that develops. Immediately fill hot, sterilized canning jars, leaving $\frac{1}{4}$-inch headspace. Wipe the jar rims and adjust the lids. (See page 12 for detailed canning instructions.)

Process in a boiling water bath 5 minutes. Place on a wire rack away from drafts to cool completely

Celebrations
February is National Cherry Month.
February 22 is National Cherry Pie Day.
May 17 is National Cherry Cobbler Day.
June 18 is National Cherry Tart Day..

BOTANY: Cherries are known as "drupes," which are fleshy, one-seeded fruits. They are classified as indehiscent fruits, meaning they remain closed at maturity and have no natural way of splitting open.

Cherries are members of the rose family and relatives include apricots, nectarines, peaches, plums, and almonds. They are more closely related to plums than any other fruit in the family.

ORIGIN: It is unknown where cherries originated, but China frequently claims to be the homeland.

The earliest known reference to cherries is found in the "History of Plants" by Theophrastus, who wrote around 300 BC about cherries cultivation.

TREES: Cherry trees can become rather large. Trees in the wild can reach more than 40 feet tall. Orchard pruning practices keep those in commercial operations low-growing and wide for easy harvesting. The trees require a winter dormant period for proper fruit development. If not exposed to sufficient cold, the buds do not properly open in the spring.

THE PITS: A handheld cherry pitter is a great kitchen gadget that looks like a really strange single hole punch. You will sometimes see them called "stoners." Although it only pits one cherry at a time, it's incredibly efficient. You can also use it to pit olives.

PAIRING: For a cheese tray, pair cherries with Gorgonzola, Brie, Roquefort, or mascarpone.

CHICKEN

THERE IS HARDLY A MORE ECONOMICAL DINNER WINNER THAN CHICKEN. IT HAS BEEN gracing Southern tables for decades and shows no sign of losing any popularity. Versatility should be the synonym for chicken. It flies easily through both lunch and dinner, being coy and casual at one, while elegant and succulent at another. But if the South is famous for anything, it would be our knack for frying our favorite bird.

Although Southerners were not the first in history to fry chicken, we certainly act like we were. When I was growing up, it was an expected meal at some point during the week, and that was usually on Saturday. Some people express surprise at this because it was more traditional to have on Sunday after church, but who had time to fry chicken then? Those were usually leftovers from our Saturday night meal.

Today, some get ruffled feathers at the mention of chicken that is fried. However, an expertly fried food is incredibly efficient for keeping food moist on the inside, never greasy, and crispy on the outside.

I'll admit that these days, I roast chicken more often, but every now and then, my cast iron starts calling my name and there is nothing better to satisfy the need for comfort food more than Southern Fried Chicken.

Cooking: Cook chicken to an internal temperature of 180°F. Remember that the temperature continues to rise after you remove it from the grill, stove, or oven. There should be no pink left in the meat and the juices should run clear.

Preparation: As a general rule, use plastic cutting boards for raw meats and poultry. Then, after handling, scrub your hands, cutting board, knives, countertops, and other utensils with hot, soapy water to prevent the spread of potentially harmful bacteria.

Resting: Always let roasted chicken rest a minimum of ten minutes after cooking. This gives the juices a chance to soak back into the meat, giving you a moister product than if you carve it immediately after removing from the cooking surface.

Safety: Safety concerns shouldn't keep you from using chicken in family meals each week. Cross contamination in our own kitchen is the main culprit when it comes to any type of raw meat or poultry.

Splatter of chicken juices is one of the main reasons it is not recommended that you wash chicken before cooking. So unless you are willing to completely clean your sink, faucet, and surrounding area, just drain and use the chicken directly from the package.

A+ SOUTHERN FRIED CHICKEN

A+ is the grade you'll get from your family when this recipe is served. I could quite literally put hundreds of versions of this recipe in this chapter, but there's only one way to do it, and this is it! See the seasoning variations listed below.

YIELD: 6 SERVINGS

1 large whole chicken, cut into pieces
$\frac{1}{2}$ teaspoon salt
$\frac{1}{4}$ teaspoon black pepper
1 cup buttermilk
2 tablespoons water
2 eggs
1 cup bacon drippings
1 cup vegetable shortening or lard
1 tablespoon unsalted butter
2 cups all-purpose flour
$\frac{1}{2}$ teaspoon paprika

Place the chicken pieces in a 13 x 9-inch baking dish. Sprinkle evenly with the salt and pepper. Set aside 15 minutes.

Meanwhile, whisk together the buttermilk, water, and eggs. Pour the buttermilk mixture over the chicken. Cover and refrigerate 1 hour.

In a large cast-iron skillet or Dutch oven, heat the drippings, shortening, and butter to 350°F. Place the flour in a shallow dish and add the paprika. Roll the chicken in the flour mixture, shaking off the excess.

Fry in batches 10 to 15 minutes on each side, or until the chicken is completely done. Drain on paper towels and serve warm.

Note: Fried chicken can be changed in flavor just by switching the seasonings.

• Substitute garlic salt, onion salt, celery salt, or seasoned salt for the salt.

• Substitute red pepper, cayenne, Creole seasoning, or Cajun seasoning for the paprika.
• Substitute red pepper or cayenne for the black pepper.

BACON-WRAPPED GARLIC CHICKEN LIVERS

These appetizers are easy to prepare. The bacon may change the minds of those who think they don't like chicken livers.

YIELD: 8 SERVINGS

$\frac{1}{2}$ cup seasoned dry breadcrumbs
$\frac{1}{4}$ cup chopped fresh parsley
1 teaspoon paprika
1 teaspoon garlic salt
$\frac{1}{2}$ pound chicken livers
9 slices bacon, cut in half

Preheat the oven to 400°F. Place a wire rack over a jelly-roll pan and set aside.

In a shallow bowl, combine the breadcrumbs, parsley, paprika, and salt. Dredge the livers in the breadcrumb mixture. Wrap a piece of bacon around each piece and secure with a wooden pick. Place on the prepared pan. Bake 20 minutes, or until the bacon is crisp. Serve warm.

BARBECUED CHICKEN SALAD

This tangy salad is served in bite-size pieces in tortilla chips!

YIELD: 3$\frac{1}{2}$ CUPS

3 cups chopped cooked chicken

¾ cup black beans, drained and rinsed

¾ cup whole kernel corn with red and
    green peppers, drained

¼ cup finely chopped purple onion

½ cup hickory smoked barbecue sauce

¼ cup mayonnaise

¼ cup sour cream

¼ teaspoon salt

¼ teaspoon black pepper

Bowl-shaped tortilla chips

Fresh cilantro for garnish

In a medium bowl, gently combine the chicken, beans, corn, and onions. In a small bowl, mix together the barbecue sauce, mayonnaise, sour cream, salt, and pepper. Pour the dressing over the chicken mixture and toss to evenly coat. Cover and refrigerate at least 4 hours.

To serve, spoon into the tortilla chips and garnish with the fresh cilantro. Serve immediately.

BEER CAN CREOLE CHICKEN

An incredibly flavorful, yet tender, moist chicken is the result of this easy recipe. If you don't want to use beer, use a can of Coca-Cola instead.

YIELD: 6 SERVINGS

2 tablespoons Creole seasoning or
    barbecue dry rub, divided

1 (4 pound) whole chicken

1 tablespoon vegetable oil

1 (12-ounce) can full-flavored beer

Sprinkle 1 tablespoon of the seasoning into the cavity of the chicken. Rub the oil all over the outer skin. Pour ¾ cup of beer out of the can and reserve

for another use. With an ice pick, punch 2 additional holes in the top of the can.

With a small funnel, add the remaining seasoning to the beer can. Place the chicken upright onto the can, fitting the can into the cavity. Pull the legs forward to stand upright.

Prepare the grill to medium heat on one side only. Place a drip pan on the unlit side under the grate. Place the chicken on the grate over the drip pan. Cover and grill 1 hour, or until golden brown. Check with an instant-read meat thermometer to make sure the chicken is completely done (inserted in the thigh, not touching the bone, and it should register 180°F).

Let the chicken rest at least 5 minutes before carefully removing the can. Carve and serve warm.

BUFFALO RIVER HOT WINGS

No tailgate party is complete without these chicken hotties that look like miniature drumsticks. This recipe uses drummettes, which are the meatiest portion of the wing. Pressed for time? Dress up already fried drummettes with the sauce.

YIELD: 36 DRUMMETTES

Vegetable oil

½ cup all-purpose flour

1 teaspoon salt

¼ teaspoon black pepper

3 pounds chicken drummettes

¼ cup hot sauce

¼ cup water

4 tablespoons unsalted butter

1 tablespoon cider vinegar

Pour the oil to a depth of 2 inches in a large cast-iron skillet. Place over medium-high heat and bring to 350°F.

Preheat the oven to 350°F.

Meanwhile, combine the flour, salt, and pepper in a large zip-top plastic bag. Add the drummettes, a few at a time, shaking the bag to evenly coat. Fry 10 minutes, or until golden brown. Drain on paper towels. Arrange in a 13 x 9-inch baking dish.

In a small saucepan over low heat, combine the hot sauce, water, butter, and vinegar. Cook until the butter melts and the mixture is well blended. Pour over the chicken. Bake, uncovered, 12 to 15 minutes, or until hot. Serve warm.

BUTTERMILK BAKED CHICKEN

The acid in buttermilk works to tenderize the chicken as well as add some zip.

YIELD: 4 SERVINGS

4 tablespoons unsalted butter
4 bone-in, skinless chicken breasts
$1/2$ teaspoon salt
$1/2$ teaspoon black pepper
$1^1/2$ cups buttermilk, divided
$3/4$ cup all-purpose flour
1 (10.75 ounce) can cream of mushroom soup
Hot cooked rice

Preheat the oven to 425°F. Place the butter in a 13 x 9-inch baking dish and put in the preheating oven to melt.

Meanwhile, sprinkle the chicken with the salt and pepper. Pour $1/2$ cup of the buttermilk in a bowl and place the flour in a shallow dish. Dip the chicken in the buttermilk and dredge in the flour.

Arrange the chicken pieces in the baking dish

on top of the butter with the breast side down. Bake 25 minutes, and then turn the chicken over and bake 10 minutes more.

Meanwhile, whisk together the remaining buttermilk and soup. Pour over the chicken and bake 10 minutes longer. If necessary, cover to prevent excessive browning. Serve immediately over hot cooked rice.

CHICKEN AND BLUE CHEESE DUMPLINGS

Pull out the food processor to make this recipe preparation fast. It's a great way to change leftover cooked chicken into something no one will believe is leftover!

YIELD: 8 SERVINGS

2 tablespoons plus $1/4$ cup vegetable oil, divided
1 large white onion, peeled and diced
6 garlic cloves, minced
2 cups dry white wine
8 cups chicken stock
4 red potatoes, cut into large dice
3 carrots, peeled and sliced
3 celery stalks, diced
1 large red bell pepper, seeded and chopped
4 cups chopped cooked chicken
2 cups all-purpose flour
4 teaspoons baking powder
1 teaspoon salt
1 cup milk
1 tablespoon chopped fresh oregano
$1^1/2$ cups crumbled blue cheese
$1/2$ cup sliced mushrooms
1 large zucchini, halved lengthwise and sliced

Heat 2 tablespoons of the oil in a Dutch oven over medium-high heat. Add the onion and sauté 2 minutes. Add the garlic and sauté 1 minute longer. Stir in the wine and cook until reduced by half, about 10 minutes.

Add the stock and bring to a boil. Stir in the potatoes, carrots, celery, bell peppers, and chicken. Cover and cook 25 minutes, or until the potatoes are tender.

Meanwhile, make the dumplings by combining the flour, baking powder, and salt in a mixing bowl. In a separate bowl, whisk together the milk, the remaining $1/4$ cup oil, the oregano, and cheese. Gradually add to the flour mixture, stirring until moistened.

Add the mushrooms and zucchini to the stew. Drop tablespoons of the dumpling dough onto the surface of the stew. Cover and cook another 15 minutes. Serve hot.

CHICKEN-FRIED CHICKEN

This traditional beef dish shouldn't exclude chicken!

YIELD: 4 SERVINGS

Vegetable oil
4 (4-ounce) chicken cutlets
1 teaspoon salt, divided
1 teaspoon black pepper, divided
38 saltine crackers (1 sleeve), crushed
1 cup all-purpose flour
$1/2$ teaspoon baking powder
$1/2$ teaspoon red pepper
$3/4$ cup milk, divided
2 eggs

Pour the oil to a depth of $1/2$ inch in a large cast-iron skillet. Place over medium-high heat and bring to 350°F.

Meanwhile, sprinkle the chicken evenly with $1/2$ teaspoon of the salt and $1/2$ teaspoon of the black

pepper. Set aside.

In a shallow bowl, combine the cracker crumbs, flour, baking powder, red pepper, and the remaining salt and black pepper. In a separate bowl, whisk together the milk and eggs. Dredge the chicken in the crumb mixture, dip in the milk mixture, and dredge again in the crumbs. Repeat with the remaining chicken.

Place two of the cutlets in the hot oil. Fry 10 minutes. Turn and fry 4 minutes longer, or until golden brown. Drain on paper towels and repeat with the remaining cutlets. Serve warm.

CHICKEN LIVER PARTY SPREAD

Plan to make this recipe at least eight hours before serving so it will unmold properly.

YIELD: 1 CUP

$1/4$ pound (1 stick) unsalted butter, divided
1 white onion, peeled and chopped
1 garlic clove, minded
$1/2$ pound chicken livers
1 bay leaf
$1/4$ teaspoon salt
$1/4$ teaspoon black pepper
$1/4$ teaspoon dried thyme
1 tablespoon brandy

In a large skillet over medium heat, melt 4 tablespoons of the butter. Leave the remaining butter at room temperature to soften.

Sauté the onions and garlic in the butter until tender, around 4 minutes. Add the livers, bay leaf, salt, pepper, and thyme. Cook 7 minutes longer, stirring often. Cool to room temperature 30 minutes. Remove and discard the bay leaf.

Meanwhile, heavily grease a 1-cup mold and set aside. Place the remaining butter and brandy in the bowl of a blender or food processor. When the liver mixture has cooled, add to the blender and process until smooth.

Spoon into the prepared mold. Cover and refrigerate 8 hours or overnight. Unmold and serve with crackers.

CLASSIC CREAMED CHICKEN

Serve this creamy dish on Cornbread Waffles (page 190) or in crêpes.

YIELD: 8 SERVINGS

2 tablespoons unsalted butter

1 sweet onion, peeled and chopped

4 garlic cloves, minced

$1/4$ cup dry white wine

8 boneless, skinless chicken breasts, cut into large dice

1 teaspoon garlic salt

$3/4$ teaspoon black pepper

$1/2$ teaspoon paprika

1 (10.75 ounce) can cream of mushroom soup

1 (8-ounce) container sour cream

Melt the butter in a large saucepan over medium heat. Add the onion and garlic. Sauté 5 minutes, or until tender. Add the wine, chicken, salt, pepper, and paprika. Cook 10 minutes, stirring often until the chicken is done.

In a separate bowl, whisk together the soup and sour cream. Add to the chicken mixture, stirring well to combine. Cook 5 to 6 minutes longer, or until hot. Serve immediately.

"COMFORT WITH A CAPITAL C" CHICKEN POT PIE

There is just as much of a comfort making this dish as there is in eating it. It is a winter regular for me and a great way to use leftovers.

YIELD: 6 SERVINGS

6 tablespoons unsalted butter, divided

$1/4$ cup all-purpose flour

$1^1/2$ cups chicken stock

$1^1/2$ cups half-and-half

$1/4$ teaspoon salt

$1/2$ teaspoon black pepper

1 recipe Double Pie Pastry (page 400)

1 (8-ounce) package sliced fresh mushrooms

1 sweet onion, peeled and chopped

3 celery stalks, sliced

$3^1/2$ cups cooked chicken, chopped

2 hard-cooked eggs, chopped

Melt 4 tablespoons of the butter in a large heavy saucepan over low heat. Add the flour, stirring constantly until smooth. Cook 1 minute, stirring constantly. Gradually add the stock and half-and-half. Increase the heat to medium and stir until thick and bubbly, about 12 minutes. Stir in the salt and pepper and set aside.

Preheat the oven to 375°F. Place a single piecrust into a 9-inch deep-dish pan and set aside.

In a skillet over medium-high heat, melt the remaining butter. Add the mushrooms, onion, and celery, cooking until tender, about 5 minutes. Drain and stir into the sauce. Add the chicken and eggs, stirring well.

Spoon the filling into the prepared piecrust. Top with the remaining piecrust. Fold the edges under and flute. Cut 3 slits in the top for ventilation. Bake 35 to 40 minutes, or until the top is golden brown.

Cover the edges with strips of aluminum foil after 20 minutes to prevent excessive browning. Let rest 5 minutes before cutting and serving. Serve warm.

:::

CRUNCHY CHICKEN FINGERS WITH DOUBLE DIP SAUCE

These are simply a must-have dish at tailgating parties. Fry just before you leave for the big game. The aroma created in your car will be marvelous! The sauce is so good it makes you break the Southern hospitality rule of no double dipping, so have individual cups on hand!

YIELD: 4 SERVINGS

Vegetable oil
3 cups corn flakes
3/4 cup plain dry breadcrumbs
3/4 teaspoon garlic powder
3/4 teaspoon onion powder
3/4 teaspoon salt
3/4 teaspoon ground red pepper
1 cup milk
1 egg
2 pounds chicken tenderloins
3 tablespoons mayonnaise
2 tablespoons Dijon mustard
1 teaspoon prepared yellow mustard
1 1/2 teaspoons honey
1 teaspoon prepared horseradish

Pour the oil to a depth of 1 inch in a Dutch oven. Place over medium-high heat and bring to 350°F.

Meanwhile, combine the corn flakes, breadcrumbs, garlic powder, onion powder, salt, and pepper in the bowl of a food processor. Process

until smooth and transfer to a shallow container. In a small bowl, whisk together the milk and egg. Transfer to a shallow container.

Dip the chicken into the egg mixture, and then in the corn flake mixture. Fry the chicken in batches 5 to 6 minutes, or until golden brown. Drain on paper towels.

In a small bowl, whisk together the mayonnaise, Dijon mustard, yellow mustard, honey, and horseradish. Serve with the warm chicken.

:::

"CRUSH ON YOU" OVEN-FRIED CHICKEN

This alternative to traditional fried chicken is more enjoyable than you might think. It gets the crispy outer crust you would expect from "fried" chicken, thanks to crushed corn flakes and a hot oven.

YIELD: 4 SERVINGS

1 cup crushed corn flakes
1/3 cup grated Parmesan cheese
1/2 teaspoon salt
1/2 teaspoon garlic powder
1/4 teaspoon black pepper
1/4 pound (1 stick) unsalted butter, melted
1 tablespoon buttermilk or milk
1 whole chicken, cut into pieces or 1 (3-pound) package assorted chicken pieces

Preheat the oven to 400°F. Lightly grease a jelly-roll pan and set aside.

In a heavy-duty zip-top plastic bag, combine the corn flakes, cheese, salt, garlic powder, and pepper.

In shallow bowl, combine the butter and buttermilk, whisking to blend. Dip the chicken into the butter mixture and add to the corn flake mixture, shaking to completely coat.

Place the chicken on the prepared pan and repeat with the remaining pieces. Bake 45 minutes, or until the chicken is completely done and the juices run clear. Serve immediately.

DIRTY-FRIED CHICKEN

The mixture of dark spices is where this fried chicken gets its name.

YIELD: 4 TO 6 SERVINGS

Vegetable oil
1 cup all-purpose flour
1 teaspoon paprika
1 teaspoon dry mustard
$\frac{1}{2}$ teaspoon garlic powder
$\frac{1}{2}$ teaspoon black pepper
$\frac{1}{2}$ teaspoon ground nutmeg
3 pounds skinless chicken pieces
$\frac{1}{2}$ teaspoon salt

Pour the oil to a depth of 1 inch in a large cast-iron skillet. Place over medium-high heat and bring to 350°F.

Meanwhile, in a large zip-top plastic bag, combine the flour, paprika, dry mustard, garlic powder, black pepper, and nutmeg. Shake to mix and set aside.

Sprinkle the chicken evenly with the salt. Place 2 or 3 pieces in the bag and shake to evenly coat. Repeat with the remaining chicken.

Fry the chicken 15 minutes on each side, or until completely done. Drain on paper towels and serve warm.

FRIED CHICKEN GIZZARDS

Gizzards can be awful if they are just fried. That's why this recipe parboils them before frying. It gives you perfectly tender gizzards every time.

YIELD: 6 SERVINGS

$1\frac{1}{2}$ pounds chicken gizzards, washed and trimmed of excess fat
Vegetable oil
$\frac{1}{2}$ cup all-purpose flour
1 tablespoon salt
1 teaspoon black pepper

Place the gizzards in a large saucepan. Fill with water, place over medium-high heat, and bring to a boil. Boil 15 minutes.

Meanwhile, pour the oil to a depth of 2 inches in a large cast-iron skillet. Place over medium-high heat and bring to 350°F. Place the flour, salt, and pepper in a large zip-top plastic bag and set aside.

Pour the gizzards through a strainer and immediately rinse with cold water. Place in the flour mixture, shaking well to evenly coat. Add to the hot oil and cook until browned, around 4 minutes, turning as needed.

Reduce heat to medium. Cover and cook 10 minutes longer. Drain on paper towels and serve warm.

FRIED CHICKEN LIVERS FOR CHICKEN LIVER LOVERS

This is one of those dishes that people either love or hate. Done correctly, it should be crispy on the outside with a moist, pink center.

YIELD: 4 SERVINGS

Vegetable oil

1 pound chicken livers

2 cups all-purpose flour

1½ teaspoons seasoned salt

1 teaspoon black pepper

1 cup buttermilk

Pour the oil to a depth of 2 inches in a Dutch oven and place over medium-high heat. Bring to 360°F.

Meanwhile, pierce the livers several times with a fork. In a shallow bowl, combine the flour, seasoned salt, and pepper. Pour the buttermilk in a separate shallow bowl.

Dredge the livers in the flour mixture, dip in the buttermilk, and dredge again in the flour mixture. Carefully lower into the hot oil and fry 4 to 5 minutes, or until golden brown. Drain on paper towels and serve warm.

GRILLED GEORGIA PEANUT CHICKEN

I love the flavor explosion you get with this chicken. It is sweet and spicy at the same time.

YIELD: 6 SERVINGS

½ cup creamy peanut butter

⅓ cup honey

¼ cup soy sauce

2 tablespoons curry powder

2 garlic cloves, minced

6 bone-in chicken breasts (not skinless)

In a mixing bowl, whisk together the peanut butter, honey, soy sauce, curry powder, and garlic. Place the chicken in a 13 x 9-inch baking dish. Pour the peanut marinade over the chicken. Cover and refrigerate 8 hours or overnight.

Remove the chicken from the marinade, discard-

ing the marinade. Grill the chicken, covered, over medium-high heat (375°F) 15 to 20 minutes on each side, or until completely done. Serve warm.

HERB-ROASTED CHICKEN

Roasting is a dry heat cooking method that is done uncovered. The skin on the chicken serves as a baster so the meat will not dry out.

YIELD: 6 SERVINGS

4 tablespoons unsalted butter, softened

2 tablespoons minced fresh chives

3 garlic cloves, minced

2 tablespoons minced fresh oregano

1 (4-pound) whole chicken

8 fresh parsley sprigs

8 fresh oregano sprigs

½ teaspoon salt

¼ teaspoon black pepper

Preheat the oven to 425°F. In a small bowl, stir together the butter, chives, garlic, and minced oregano. Loosen the skin from the chicken without detaching it. Carefully rub the butter mixture under the chicken skin. Rub 1 tablespoon on the outside of the chicken.

Insert the parsley and oregano sprigs in the chicken cavity. Sprinkle the outside with the salt and pepper. Place the chicken breast side up in a roasting pan. Bake 20 minutes and reduce the oven temperature to 325°F. Bake 45 minutes more, or until the chicken is completely done. Cover lightly with aluminum foil and rest 10 minutes before carving and serving.

HOMEMADE CHICKEN NOODLE SOUP

Cheers to the best medicine in the world. Serve hot on a bed tray to someone who is sick or with a loaf of crusty bread for those who are just in need of the comfort it provides.

YIELD: 6 TO 8 SERVINGS

1 (3-pound) whole chicken, skinned

6 cups water

4 fresh celery leaves

$1/4$ teaspoon dried thyme

$1/2$ cup sliced celery

$1/2$ cup sliced carrots

1 cup thin egg noodles, uncooked

$1/3$ cup sliced green onions

2 tablespoons chopped fresh parsley

1 teaspoon chicken bouillon granules

$1/2$ teaspoon salt

$1/2$ teaspoon black pepper

1 bay leaf

In a large Dutch oven, combine the chicken, water, celery leaves, and thyme. Bring to a boil, cover, reduce heat to low, and simmer 45 minutes. Remove the chicken from the stock and set aside to cool.

Strain the stock, discarding any solids. Return the stock to the Dutch oven. Stir in the celery, carrots, noodles, green onions, parsley, bouillon granules, salt, pepper, and bay leaf. Cover and simmer 20 minutes.

Meanwhile, remove the chicken from the bones. Discard the bones and chop the chicken. Add to the stock and cook 5 minutes longer. Remove and discard the bay leaf. Serve in warmed soup bowls.

SPICY FRIED CHICKEN

This is my rendition of the absolutely delicious hot chicken served at Prince's in Nashville. If you ever find yourself in Nashville, you must go there. It has all the goodness of traditional fried chicken, but is really spicy. I like the medium, but everyone else I know can't get past the mild!

YIELD: 4 SERVINGS

1 (3-pound) whole fryer, cut into pieces

2 cups buttermilk

2 tablespoons cayenne, divided

Vegetable oil

2 cups all-purpose flour

1 tablespoon white pepper

1 tablespoon black pepper

1 tablespoon red pepper

1 tablespoon dry mustard

1 tablespoon seasoned salt

Place the chicken in a shallow dish. In a separate bowl, combine the buttermilk and 1 tablespoon of the cayenne. Pour over the chicken, cover and refrigerate 8 hours or overnight.

In a large skillet pour the oil to a depth of 1 inch. Place over medium-high heat and bring to 325°F. Meanwhile, remove the chicken from the marinade, discarding the marinade.

In a heavy-duty zip-top plastic bag, combine the remaining cayenne, the flour, white pepper, black pepper, red pepper, dry mustard, and salt. Shake well to blend. Add the chicken and shake to evenly coat. Add to the hot oil with the skin side down.

Fry 18 to 20 minutes, or until golden brown, turning halfway through. Make sure the chicken is completely done. Drain on paper towels and repeat with the remaining chicken. Serve warm.

KENTUCKY BURGOO

This thick stew is popular at any large gathering in the South. It contains a minimum of two meats and a garden full of fresh vegetables. Early burgoos were made with a combination of rabbit and squirrel. You'll need a very large stockpot.

YIELD: 24 SERVINGS

1 (4 to 5-pound) whole chicken

2 pounds beef stew meat

2 pounds beef bones

1 celery stalk with leaves, cut into large pieces

1 carrot, peeled and cut into large pieces

1 white onion, peeled and quartered

1 (6-ounce) can tomato paste

3 quarts water

1 cayenne pepper pod

2 tablespoons lemon juice

1 tablespoon Worcestershire sauce

1 tablespoon salt

2 teaspoons black pepper

$1/2$ teaspoon red pepper

9 tomatoes, peeled and chopped

6 yellow onions, peeled and finely chopped

2 green bell peppers, seeded and finely chopped

1 turnip, peeled and finely chopped

2 cups fresh lima or butter beans

2 cups fresh corn

2 cups thinly sliced celery

2 cups finely chopped green cabbage

2 cups sliced fresh okra

Place the chicken, beef, beef bones, celery pieces, carrots, white onion, tomato paste, water, pepper pod, salt, black pepper, red pepper, juice, and Worcestershire in a large stockpot. Place over medium-high heat and bring to a boil. Reduce heat to low and simmer 1 hour. Cool.

Strain the mixture, reserving the meat and liquid. Discard the vegetables and beef bones. Remove the skin, gristle, and meat from the chicken. Finely chop the meat and return the meat and liquid to the pot. Discard the skin, gristle, and bones. Cover and refrigerate 8 hours.

Discard the fat layer that forms on top of the meat mixture. Add the tomatoes, yellow onion, bell peppers, turnip, beans, corn, sliced celery, cabbage, and okra. Bring to a boil over medium-high heat. Reduce the heat to low and simmer, uncovered, 3 hours, stirring frequently. Serve warm.

Note: Leftovers can be frozen. Use within six months.

LADIES' LUNCH OLD-FASHIONED CHICKEN SALAD

Nothing screams "The ladies are coming" more than homemade chicken salad. It can be served on fresh white bread, with crackers, or on a bed of lettuce leaves.

YIELD: 6 SERVINGS

$1/4$ cup mayonnaise

$1/4$ cup sour cream

$1/2$ teaspoon salt

$1/2$ teaspoon white pepper

1 celery stalk, diced

2 scallions, peeled and chopped

1 cup coarsely chopped pecans, toasted

3 cups chopped cooked chicken

12 seedless red grapes, halved

In a large bowl, stir together the mayonnaise, sour cream, salt, and pepper. Gently stir in the celery, scallions, pecans, and chicken. Fold in the grapes. Cover and refrigerate at least 2 hours before serving.

LEMON FRIED CHICKEN

Lemon juice, lemon pepper, and lemon zest perk up this fried version of the South's favorite bird.

YIELD: 4 TO 6 SERVINGS

1 (3-pound) package assorted chicken pieces
$1/2$ teaspoon salt
$1/4$ teaspoon black pepper
$1/4$ cup vegetable shortening or lard
$1/3$ cup fresh lemon juice
$1/4$ cup vegetable oil
$1/2$ teaspoon sugar
$1/2$ teaspoon seasoned salt
$1/2$ teaspoon lemon pepper
$1/2$ teaspoon grated lemon zest
$1/4$ teaspoon prepared mustard
$1/4$ teaspoon paprika

Sprinkle the chicken evenly with the salt and pepper. Set aside.

Melt the shortening in a very large cast-iron skillet over medium-high heat. Add the chicken and fry 15 minutes on each side.

In a jar with a tight-fitting lid, combine the juice, oil, sugar, seasoned salt, lemon pepper, zest, mustard, and paprika. Shake well to emulsify. Pour over the chicken, cover, and reduce heat to low. Simmer 45 to 50 minutes, or until tender. Serve warm.

MAMA'S CHICKEN AND DUMPLINGS

This Southern classic has chunks of cooked chicken that simmer in a tasty sauce and dumplings are added at the end. The simplicity of the dish and inexpensive ingredients make it a star economically too.

YIELD: 6 TO 8 SERVINGS

1 (3-pound) whole chicken
4 tablespoons chicken bouillon granules
1 teaspoon black pepper
2 cups all-purpose flour
1 tablespoon baking powder
$1/2$ teaspoon salt
$1/4$ cup vegetable shortening
$3/4$ cup milk
4 hard-cooked eggs, chopped
Chopped fresh parsley for garnish

Place the chicken in a large Dutch oven and cover with water. Bring to a boil, reduce heat to low, and simmer 1 hour or until done. Remove the chicken from the stock and cool.

Pour the stock through a wire mesh strainer into a large saucepan. Discard the solids and return the stock to the Dutch oven.

When the chicken is cool enough to handle, remove and discard the skin and bones. Coarsely chop the chicken. Add the chicken, bouillon, and pepper to the stock. (At this point, you can proceed or refrigerate up to 3 days or freeze up to 2 months.)

Combine the flour, baking powder, and salt in a mixing bowl. Cut in the shortening with a pastry blender or 2 forks until crumbly. Add the milk, $1/4$ cup at a time, stirring until moist.

Turn the dough out onto a lightly floured surface and knead 4 times. Roll the dough to a thickness of $1/8$ inch. With a sharp knife, cut the dough into 2-inch strips.

Bring the stock mixture to a boil over medium-high heat. Drop the strips, one at a time, into the boiling stock, stirring very gently. Reduce heat to low and simmer 20 minutes, stirring often. Stir in the eggs and sprinkle with the parsley just before serving.

1960s MARINATED FRIED CHICKEN

The first "marinade" we ever had was a bottle of Italian dressing. It adds zing to this fried specialty.

YIELD: 6 SERVINGS

6 (6-ounce) bone-in chicken breast halves, skinned

1 (8-ounce) bottle Italian salad dressing

Vegetable oil

2 eggs

$\frac{1}{4}$ cup water

$1\frac{1}{2}$ cups all-purpose flour

$1\frac{1}{2}$ tablespoons paprika

$1\frac{1}{2}$ teaspoons curry powder

$\frac{1}{2}$ teaspoon salt

$\frac{1}{2}$ teaspoon black pepper

Place the chicken in a single layer in a large shallow baking dish. Pour the dressing over the chicken. Cover and refrigerate 8 hours.

Bring the chicken to room temperature 10 minutes. In a large cast-iron skillet, pour the oil to a depth of 1 inch. Place over medium-high heat and bring to 350°F.

In a shallow bowl, whisk together the eggs and water. In a large zip-top plastic bag, combine the flour, paprika, curry powder, salt, and pepper.

Drain the chicken and discard the marinade. Place 2 pieces of the chicken in the bag and shake to evenly coat. Dip in the egg mixture and dredge again in the flour mixture.

Fry 20 to 25 minutes, or until golden brown, turning to evenly brown. Drain on paper towels and repeat with the remaining chicken. Serve warm.

PECAN "FRIED" CHICKEN

If the chicken isn't fried in a skillet, Southerners like it to be fried in the oven. This chicken gets a hefty crunch from chopped pecans.

YIELD: 4 SERVINGS

1 cup biscuit mix

2 teaspoons paprika

$\frac{1}{2}$ teaspoon salt

$\frac{1}{2}$ teaspoon black pepper

$\frac{1}{2}$ teaspoon rubbed sage

$\frac{1}{3}$ cup finely chopped pecans

$\frac{1}{2}$ cup evaporated milk

1 (3-pound) package assorted chicken pieces

6 tablespoons unsalted butter, melted

Preheat the oven to 350°F. Lightly grease a 13 x 9-inch baking dish and set aside.

In a shallow bowl, combine the biscuit mix, paprika, salt, pepper, sage, and pecans. Place the milk in a medium bowl.

Dip the chicken pieces in the milk and dredge in the pecan mixture. Place in the prepared pan. Drizzle the butter over the chicken. Bake 1 hour, or until the chicken is completely done. Serve warm.

"PREACHER'S COMING" CHICKEN AND DRESSING

There is something about baking chicken on top of dressing that enhances the flavor of both.

YIELD: 4 SERVINGS

2 tablespoons vegetable oil, divided

1 white onion, peeled and diced

3 celery stalks, diced

1 large garlic clove, minced

1 cup uncooked long-grain rice

3½ cups chicken stock

1 recipe Buttermilk Cornbread (page 188), cooked and crumbled

2 slices white bread, torn

1 teaspoon rubbed sage

1 teaspoon black pepper

½ teaspoon poultry seasoning

4 bone-in chicken breast halves (with skin)

Preheat the oven to 350°F. Lightly grease a 13 x 9-inch baking dish and set aside.

Heat 1 tablespoon of the oil in a large skillet over medium-high heat. Add the onion, celery, and garlic. Sauté 2 minutes, or until tender. Add the rice and sauté 1 minute. Stir in the stock and bring to a boil. Cover, reduce heat to low, and simmer 20 minutes.

Meanwhile, in a large mixing bowl, combine the crumbled cornbread, white bread, sage, pepper, and poultry seasoning. After the rice is done, add the contents of the skillet to the mixing bowl. Stir well and spoon into the prepared pan.

Heat the remaining oil in the same skillet over medium-high heat. Brown each chicken breast 2 minutes on each side. Place the chicken over the dressing and cover. Bake 45 minutes, or until the chicken is completely done. Serve warm.

ROASTED LEMON CHICKEN

Leaving the chicken unwrapped in the refrigerator overnight makes the skin crisp up nicely!

YIELD: 6 SERVINGS

1 (4-pound) whole chicken

¾ teaspoon salt

¾ teaspoon black pepper

2 whole lemons

Sprinkle the chicken all over (inside and out) with the salt and pepper. Refrigerate, uncovered, overnight.

Preheat the oven to 350°F. Place the chicken breast side down on the greased rack in a roasting pan.

Soften the lemons in the microwave 15 seconds. Pierce all over several times with an ice pick. Insert both lemons in the cavity of the chicken.

Roast 30 minutes and turn the chicken over so the breast side is up. Insert an ovenproof meat thermometer into the breast without touching any bone and roast another 30 minutes.

Increase the oven temperature to 400°F and continue roasting until the meat thermometer registers at least 175°F. Rest 10 minutes before slicing and serving.

SPICED MILK FRIED CHICKEN

This is the recipe my grandmother used when she didn't have buttermilk in the refrigerator. It calls for spiced up evaporated milk for marinating the chicken overnight.

YIELD: 4 TO 6 SERVINGS

1 (13-ounce) can evaporated milk

1 tablespoon Worcestershire sauce

1 teaspoon cayenne

1 (3-pound) package assorted chicken pieces

Vegetable oil

¾ cup all-purpose flour

¾ cup plain cornmeal

¾ teaspoon salt

¼ teaspoon black pepper

In a medium bowl, whisk together the milk, Worcestershire, and cayenne. Place the chicken in a shallow baking dish in a single layer. Pour the milk mixture over the chicken. Cover and refrigerate at least 4 hours or overnight.

Pour the oil to a depth of $1/2$ inch in a large cast-iron skillet. Place over medium-high heat and bring to 350°F.

Meanwhile, drain the chicken from the marinade, discarding the marinade. In a shallow dish, combine the flour, cornmeal, salt, and pepper. Dredge the chicken in the flour mixture and let stand 5 minutes.

Fry in batches, 10 to 15 minutes on each side, or until done. Drain on paper towels and serve warm.

SOUTHERN CHICKEN CORDON BLEU

I tried this dish after my friend Bryan told me it was one of his all-time favorite chicken recipes. I can see why. It is so flavorful, with the wine giving it such a nice, flirty wink.

YIELD: 6 SERVINGS

6 boneless, skinless chicken breasts

$1/2$ teaspoon salt

6 slices Swiss cheese

6 thin slices ham

$1/4$ cup plus 2 tablespoons all-purpose flour, divided

6 tablespoons unsalted butter

1 cup water, divided

2 tablespoons instant chicken bouillon

1 (3-ounce) can sliced mushrooms, drained

$1/3$ cup sweet or dry red wine

$1/4$ cup slivered almonds, toasted

Preheat the oven to 350°F. Lightly grease an 11 x 7-inch baking pan and set aside.

Place the chicken breasts between layers of plastic wrap. With a meat mallet, pound each to a thickness of $1/4$ inch, working from the center to the edges.

Sprinkle evenly with the salt. Place a cheese slice and a ham slice on each piece of chicken. Roll tightly and tuck in the ends. Place $1/4$ cup of the flour in a shallow dish and dredge each roll to evenly coat.

Place the butter in a large skillet over medium-high heat. Add the chicken rolls and cook 5 minutes, rolling to evenly brown. Transfer to the prepared pan and set aside.

In the same skillet, add $1/2$ cup of the water, the bouillon, mushrooms, and wine. Cook 2 minutes, scraping any browned bits that may be stuck to the bottom of the skillet. Pour over the chicken. Cover and bake 1 hour, or until tender. Transfer to a serving platter.

Blend the remaining flour with the remaining water. Stir into the juices remaining in the baking pan. Place over medium heat. Cook and stir 4 minutes or until thickened. Pour half of the gravy over the chicken and garnish with the almonds. Pour the remaining gravy in a gravy boat and serve on the side.

> "Only a Southerner knows how to fry a chicken. Period!"
>
> —ANONYMOUS

CHILI

THERE'S A REASON I LIVE IN THE SOUTH. I DON'T LIKE TO BE COLD, EXCEPT FOR AROUND Christmas. But unfortunately, the South does experience cold weather and when it does, I want to warm up from the inside out. That's when a good bowl of chili comes to the rescue. I like it both temperature hot and spicy hot.

If you want to start a debate among nearly everyone who cooks, ask them what's in the best chili recipe. The answers will be as diverse as anyone can imagine. Some contain beans, others don't. Some have meat, others don't. Some are mildly spiced and others are blistering hot infernos. Some are white, others are red, and still others are in between. There's nothing like a good culinary argument to get your heart racing!

About the only thing you can get people to agree on is that it's a hearty stew that contains tomatoes, chiles, and/or chili powder. They will also agree that it tends to improve with age and taste better the longer it cooks. Like meatloaf, chili leftovers are even tastier than the original dish.

In my travels throughout the South, I have come to appreciate the different slants each area puts on this incredible warm concoction. In fact, the differences make it all wonderfully interesting and have shown me that each is uniquely delicious. And while there are some I prefer over others, I have yet to find one that I truly didn't like.

I love it that everyone thinks their chili cooking traditions are simply the best. How boring it would be if everyone made chili the same way! So in true Southern Belle fashion, I've learned to keep my opinions about what spices chili needs, how it should be served, and the cooking techniques I enjoy most to myself. My motto when enjoying a bowl of chili outside of my own home is "I'll have what they're having!"

Chili Powder: Chili powder is a mixture of dried and ground chiles, cloves, coriander, cumin, garlic, and oregano.

Chili Sauce: Chili sauce is a condiment made of a mixture of mainly tomatoes, with onions, green bell peppers, sugar, vinegar, and either chiles, chili powder, or both. If you make your own chili sauce, it must be processed in a boiling water bath fifteen minutes.

Origin: Chili originated in Texas, but there is much debate as to exactly where the birthplace is located. In the Lone Star State, chili is called a "bowl of red." Texas chili does not contain beans.

Name: Sometimes you may see "Chili Con Carne" listed on a menu. That is Spanish for "chili with meat."

CHILLY NIGHT CHILI

I love to make a big pot of this chili all winter. It is perfect for Halloween night when you have lots of goblins and ghosts dropping by for treats. Their parents could always use a bowl of this to keep them going!

YIELD: 6 SERVINGS

1 pound ground beef
2 medium yellow onions, peeled and chopped
1 green bell pepper, seeded and chopped
1 (24 ounce) can diced tomatoes, undrained
1 (8-ounce) can tomato sauce
2 teaspoons chili powder
1 teaspoon salt
$1/4$ teaspoon cayenne
$1/8$ teaspoon paprika
1 (15-$1/2$ ounce) can kidney beans, drained

Cook the beef in a heavy stockpot over medium heat until brown. Add the onions and bell pepper. Cook 5 minutes longer, or until vegetables are tender.

Stir in the tomatoes, tomato sauce, chili powder, salt, cayenne, and paprika. Bring to a boil. Reduce heat to low, cover, and simmer 2 hours, stirring occasionally. Stir in the beans during the last hour of cooking. Serve hot.

FIRESTARTER HOT CHILI

For those of us who can't seem to get enough heat, this is the chili to beat all those other wimpy versions. Have a glass of milk handy to kill the fire in your mouth, if necessary.

YIELD: 6 SERVINGS

$1/4$ cup vegetable oil
3 pounds lean beef chuck, well-trimmed and cut into 1-inch cubes
1 cup chopped purple onion
3 garlic cloves, minced
3 tablespoons chili powder
2 teaspoons ground cumin
2 teaspoons salt
2 tablespoons hot sauce (or 2 teaspoons if you want it to be milder)
$1/4$ teaspoon black pepper
3 cups water
1 (4-ounce) can chopped green chiles, drained
6 jalapeño peppers, seeded and chopped

In a Dutch oven, heat the oil over medium-high heat. In three batches, brown the beef well, removing each batch with a slotted spoon. Drain on paper towels and set aside.

Add the onions and garlic to the Dutch oven. Cook 5 minutes, stirring frequently. Stir in the chili powder, cumin, salt, hot sauce, and pepper. Blend well and cook 1 minute.

Add the water, chiles, and jalapeños. Bring to a boil and return the beef to the pot. Stir well to combine. Reduce heat to low and simmer, uncovered, $1\frac{1}{2}$ hours. Serve warm with additional hot sauce.

GREEN CHILI

There are times when I want to give meat a rest and concentrate on meals that focus on vegetables. This chili uses green chiles as a base, and it's just perfect to serve with hot cornbread.

YIELD: 8 SERVINGS

6 cups mild or medium green chiles, chopped
1 garlic clove, minced
1 medium-size sweet onion, peeled and coarsely chopped
$1/8$ teaspoon ground coriander

½ tablespoon chili powder

½ teaspoon ground white pepper

½ teaspoon cumin powder

1 tablespoon salt

1½ cups water, divided

2 tablespoons cornstarch

In a large stockpot, combine the chiles, garlic, onions, coriander, chili powder, pepper, cumin, salt, and 10 cups of the water. Bring to a boil and cook, uncovered, 1 hour.

In a small bowl, combine the cornstarch and the remaining 1½ cups of the water. Mix thoroughly. Add to the chili mixture and cook 20 minutes longer. Serve hot.

MILD OR WILD PINTO CHILI

How you handle the flavor of this chili is completely up to you. If you have adventuresome eaters, use hot sausage and cayenne. If you're not in the mood for fire, use mild sausage and eliminate the cayenne. It's delicious either way.

YIELD: 12 SERVINGS

2 pounds dry pinto beans, soaked according to package instructions

1 teaspoon dry mustard

10 cups water

1 (28-ounce) can diced tomatoes, undrained

1 pound mild or hot pork sausage

1 pound lean ground beef

2 large purple onions, peeled and chopped

2 tablespoons chili powder

1 teaspoon cayenne (optional)

¼ teaspoon black pepper

In a large stockpot, cook the soaked beans and mustard in 10 cups water 1 hour over medium heat.

Stir in the tomatoes and cook 15 minutes.

Meanwhile, in a heavy skillet over medium heat, cook the sausage and beef until brown. Remove with a slotted spoon and drain on paper towels. Set aside.

Cook the onions in the pan drippings until tender, about 8 minutes. Stir the meat and onions into the cooked beans. Add the chili powder, cayenne (if using), and pepper. Simmer 2 hours, or until the mixture is thickened and the beans are tender. Serve hot.

NO-BEAN BRISKET CHILI

Beans are considered a side dish for those who really love chili. I love to make this chili at least a day ahead of when I'll serve it. The flavors come alive!

YIELD: 8 TO 10 SERVINGS

6 dried ancho chiles, stemmed, seeded, and coarsely torn

6 bacon slices, diced

2 large sweet onions, peeled and chopped

1 (5 pound) flat cut beef brisket, cut into 2-inch cubes

3 teaspoons kosher salt, divided

6 garlic cloves, peeled

2 tablespoons chili powder

2 teaspoons cumin seeds

1 teaspoon dried oregano

1 teaspoon ground coriander

2 (10-ounce) cans diced tomatoes with green chiles

1 (12-ounce) bottle dark beer

¼ cup finely chopped fresh cilantro

1 (3 pound) butternut squash, peeled, seeded, and cut into 2-inch dice

½ teaspoon black pepper

Cover the chiles with boiling water and soak at least 1 hour and up to 3 hours.

Preheat the oven to 350°F. In a large ovenproof pot over medium-high heat, Sauté the bacon and onions 1 minute. Reduce the heat to medium and cover. Cook 5 minutes, or until the onions are tender.

Meanwhile, sprinkle the beef with half of the salt. Add to the onion mixture and reduce the heat to low.

Drain the chiles, reserving the soaking liquid. Purée in a blender or food processor, along with 1 cup of the soaking liquid. Add the garlic, chili powder, cumin, oregano, coriander, and remaining salt. Purée until smooth, adding more soaking liquid if too thick.

Transfer the purée to the brisket pot and add the tomatoes, beer, and cilantro. Cover and cook in the oven 2 hours. Uncover and cook 1 hour longer.

Stir in the squash and cook 45 minutes longer, uncovered. If necessary, add more soaking liquid. Add the pepper and serve hot.

Note: For serving later, let the chili cool, and then refrigerate and gently reheat the following day.

"TIME FOR THE GAME" BEER CHILI

The addition of beer to this chili adds a layer of flavor that no other ingredient can accomplish. You are ready to spend an afternoon with friends watching football with this dish that serves plenty.

YIELD: 10 SERVINGS

2 pounds ground beef

1 medium yellow onion, peeled and chopped

4 garlic cloves, minced

2 (15-ounce) cans pinto beans, drained and rinsed

3 (8-ounce) cans tomato sauce

1 (12-ounce) bottle dark beer

1 (6-ounce) can tomato paste

1 (4.5-ounce) can chopped green chiles

1 1/2 cups beef stock

2 tablespoons chili powder

1 tablespoon Worcestershire sauce

2 teaspoons ground cumin

2 teaspoons ground red pepper

1 teaspoon paprika

1 teaspoon hot sauce

Place a large Dutch oven over medium heat. Add the beef, onion, and garlic. Cook until the meat crumbles and is no longer pink. Drain.

Add the beans, tomato sauce, beer, tomato paste, chiles, stock, chili powder, Worcestershire, cumin, red pepper, paprika, and hot sauce to the meat mixture. Bring to a boil and then reduce the heat to low. Simmer 3 hours, or until thickened. Serve hot.

VEGETARIAN BEAN CHILI

This is the chili I carry to potluck dinners or any occasion when you are likely to have a wide range of likes and dislikes. This recipe appeals to all and is a good way to use cooked bean leftovers.

YIELD: 8 SERVINGS

1/2 cup white beans, cooked

1/2 cup kidney beans, cooked

1/2 cup pinto beans, cooked

1/2 cup black beans, cooked

3 cups bean cooking liquid

2 cups diced white onions

5 carrots, peeled and diced

1/2 bunch celery, diced

2 tablespoons canola oil

2 garlic cloves, minced

2 tablespoons chili powder

1 tablespoon toasted ground cumin

9 large plum tomatoes, diced

3 cups corn kernels

1 cup tomato purée

1/2 cup puréed chipotle peppers

1 tablespoon cracked black peppercorns

Salt

Freshly squeezed lime juice

2 tablespoons minced fresh cilantro

Cook the beans and save the cooking water (except from the black beans) to make 3 cups. Sauté the onions, carrots, and celery in canola oil in a large stockpot over low heat about 8 minutes. Add the garlic, chili powder, and cumin. Cook 2 minutes.

Add the tomatoes and the bean cooking liquid. Simmer until the tomatoes are soft, about 15 minutes. Add the beans, corn, tomato purée, chipotles, and peppercorns. Simmer 30 minutes. If the chili seems too dry, add warm water a little at a time. Finish with the salt and lime juice to taste. Garnish with cilantro and serve warm.

===

> ## "Wish I had time for just one more bowl of chili."
> **—ALLEGED DYING WORDS OF KIT CARSON**

===

WHITE LIGHTNING CHICKEN CHILI

This recipe is ready lightning fast if using leftover cooked chicken.

YIELD: 6 SERVINGS

2 tablespoons olive oil

1 cup chopped onions

1 green bell pepper, seeded and chopped

1 cup chopped celery

4 pickled jalapeño peppers, chopped (2 tablespoons)

4 garlic cloves, minced

2 tablespoons chili powder

2 teaspoons ground cumin

2 cups chicken stock

2 (15-ounce) cans Great Northern beans, drained

2 cups cooked chicken, chopped

1/2 cup half-and-half

1/2 teaspoon salt

1/4 teaspoon white pepper

Fresh cilantro for garnish

Heat the oil in a large saucepan over medium-high heat. Add the onions, bell pepper, celery, and jalapeños. Sauté the vegetables 4 minutes, or until they begin to soften.

Stir in the garlic, chili powder, and cumin. Cook 1 minute. Add the stock and bring to a boil. Reduce the heat to medium and simmer 5 minutes.

Add the beans, chicken, and half-and-half. Cook 10 minutes, stirring occasionally. Stir in the salt and pepper just before serving. Garnish with fresh chopped cilantro. Serve hot.

CHOCOLATE

ALTHOUGH I'VE COME ACROSS A FEW PEOPLE THROUGHOUT MY LIFE WHO CLAIM NOT TO LIKE chocolate, most Southerners consider it one of life's greatest treats. As my daddy says, any month with a name that contains the letters a, e, or u is the proper time for having chocolate! My daddy is a smart man!

Some reserve their chocolate baking extravagance for a certain day in mid-February. But I can personally tell you that chocolate deliciously and magically enhances moods any time of the day, week, month, or year. It doesn't take a red, heart-shaped box to do the trick when it comes to ending a meal with indulgence.

While chocolate is a pure joy to use in cooking, it can be a temperamental little diva when melting it to use in baked items or frostings. If overheated, it may scorch and turn coarse and grainy. If water gets in it, the mixture will seize up into a hard mass.

When I was in Home Economics in college, I quickly learned that melting chocolate was perhaps the sole reason to own a double boiler. I saw that it required a low, gentle heat, not to mention time and patience, which few of us had.

While that tried-and-true method still works like a charm, the microwave comes racing to the rescue to those pressed for time. I usually melt it on low power because the words of Dr. Stickler still ring in my head from college, "Low and slow is the way to go!"

Make a piece of artwork this week and let it be based in chocolate. You'll see faces light up, smiles appear from nowhere, and hugs spontaneously occur for giving your family a culinary "I love you!"

Equivalents: One square of baking chocolate is equal to one ounce. Any sweet chocolate pieces can be substituted for semisweet chocolate. For best results, use the type of chocolate called for in the recipe since each has its own special properties. One cup of melted chocolate is equal to twelve ounces or two cups of morsels or chips.

Nutrition: It's like a dream come true. Research consistently shows that controlled consumption of dark chocolate can contribute to improved health. It turns out that dark chocolate contains the same natural antioxidants found in green tea and blueberries. In fact, dark chocolate is now considered a super food when consumed in moderation.

Since chocolate in its original form comes from a plant, it contains no cholesterol. It does contain saturated fat, however, along with around 200 calories per average sized milk or dark chocolate bar. The carbohydrates in a 1.4 ounce serving of dark chocolate (5.2 grams) compared to the same size serving of milk chocolate (23.8 grams) is dramatic. You also have 2.4 grams of fiber in dark chocolate and 1.4 in milk chocolate. So come on over to the dark side as far as chocolate consumption is concerned. Your heart will thank you!

CHOCOLATE FUDGE MERINGUE PIE

Pie ranks high on the South's list of favorite desserts. This chocolate pie with fluffy meringue will show you why.

YIELD: 8 SERVINGS

1 cup plus 6 tablespoons sugar, divided

3 tablespoons cornstarch

$^1/_8$ teaspoon salt

2 cups milk

3 eggs, separated

1 (1-ounce) square unsweetened chocolate, coarsely chopped

1 tablespoon unsalted butter

1 teaspoon pure vanilla extract

1 recipe Single Crust Pie Pastry, baked (page 402)

$^1/_2$ teaspoon cream of tartar

Preheat the oven to 350°F.

In a heavy saucepan, combine 1 cup of the sugar with the cornstarch and salt. Mix well. In a medium bowl, whisk together the milk and egg yolks. Whisk 1 minute, or until frothy. Gradually stir into the sugar mixture, blending well.

Place over medium heat, stirring constantly until thick and bubbly, around 5 minutes. Remove from the heat and stir in the chocolate, butter, and extract. Stir until the chocolate and butter melt and the mixture is smooth. Spoon into the prepared pastry and set aside.

In the bowl of an electric mixer, beat the egg whites 2 minutes. Add the cream of tartar. Add the remaining sugar, one tablespoon at a time, beating until stiff peaks form. Spread over the filling, sealing to the edge of the pastry.

Bake 10 to 12 minutes, or until golden brown. Cool completely on a wire rack before serving.

EASY CHOCOLATE TRUFFLES

These are one of the first chocolate candies I ever made, and I was amazed at how easy it was to do. Now I make them around the holidays when I don't have a lot of time to spend on something that needs to look like I spent a lot of time on it!

YIELD: 24 TRUFFLES

12 ounces bittersweet chocolate, finely ground

$^3/_4$ cup cream

4 tablespoons unsalted butter, softened

$^1/_4$ cup Amaretto or almond liqueur

$^1/_3$ cup chopped pecans

$^1/_4$ cup unsweetened cocoa

Line an 8-inch square baking pan with plastic wrap or wax paper and set aside. Place the chocolate in a medium mixing bowl and set aside.

In a small saucepan heat the cream to boiling over high heat. Immediately remove from the heat and add the butter, stirring constantly until it melts and combines.

Pour over the chocolate and continue stirring until all the chocolate melts. Add the liqueur and blend well. Pour into the prepared pan and spread evenly. Refrigerate at least 4 hours.

Place the pecans and cocoa on separate sheets of wax paper. Invert the cold chocolate block onto a cutting board and peel away the plastic. Cut into 8 strips and cut each strip into 8 squares. Dip half of the squares in the nuts and the remaining squares in the cocoa. Store in a tightly covered container in the refrigerator up to two weeks.

HOLIDAY RED VELVET CAKE

No Southerner can make it through the holidays with-out this cake at some point. Yes, it's a stunningly beauti-ful red cake, but look past the coloring and it's actually a chocolate cake. This is my grandmother's recipe.

YIELD: 12 SERVINGS

$^{1}/_{2}$ cup vegetable shortening
$1^{1}/_{2}$ cups sugar
2 eggs
2 (1-ounce) bottles red food coloring
1 teaspoon pure vanilla extract
$2^{1}/_{2}$ cups cake flour
$^{1}/_{2}$ teaspoon salt
2 teaspoons unsweetened cocoa
1 cup buttermilk
1 tablespoon white vinegar
1 teaspoon baking soda
Cream Cheese Frosting (page 128)

Preheat the oven to 350°F. Grease and flour 3 (8-inch) round cake pans and set aside.

In the bowl of an electric mixer, beat the short-ening at medium speed until fluffy, about 2 min-utes. Gradually add the sugar, beating well. Add the eggs, one at a time, and stir in the food color-ing and extract. Mix well.

In a separate bowl, combine the flour, salt, and cocoa and set aside. In a large liquid measuring cup, combine the buttermilk, vinegar, and baking soda.

At low speed, add the flour mixture to the short-ening mixture alternately with the buttermilk mix-ture. Begin and end with the flour mixture. Increase the mixer speed to medium and beat 2 minutes.

Evenly distribute the batter among the prepared cake pans. Bake 25 minutes. Cool in the pans on wire racks 10 minutes. Remove and cool com-pletely on wire racks before spreading with Cream Cheese Frosting.

CHILDHOOD CHOCOLATE PUDDING

Maybe it's the funny word, but what child doesn't squeal with delight when it's time for pudding? I still do!

YIELD: 4 SERVINGS

$^{1}/_{4}$ cup sugar
$^{1}/_{4}$ cup unsweetened cocoa
2 tablespoons cornstarch
Pinch of salt
2 cups whole milk
1 egg
4 ounces semisweet chocolate, finely chopped

In a heavy saucepan, whisk together the sugar, cocoa, cornstarch, and salt. Gradually whisk in the milk and place over medium-high heat. Bring to a boil, whisking constantly. Whisk 3 to 5 minutes, or until the mixture is thick. Remove from the heat.

Beat the egg in a heatproof bowl. Very gradually, add the hot pudding in a steady stream to the egg, whisking constantly. Continue to whisk until all the pudding is incorporated into the egg. Stir in the semisweet chocolate until it is melted and the mixture is smooth.

Pour the pudding into 4 ramekins or custard cups. Cover the surface with plastic wrap to pre-vent a skin from forming. Refrigerate, covered, at least 2 hours or until chilled. Serve cold.

> **COCOA:** Natural cocoa is unsweetened. Instant cocoa is a combination of cocoa, sugar, starches, and dry milk. Three tablespoons of cocoa plus one tablespoon of vegetable short-ening equals one square or one ounce of bak-ing chocolate.

LATE-NIGHT CHOCOLATE CHIP COOKIES

All you need is a frosty mug of cold milk and your midnight snack just turned gourmet!

YIELD: 5 DOZEN COOKIES

12 tablespoons unsalted butter, softened
$^3/_4$ cup granulated sugar
$^3/_4$ cup packed brown sugar
2 eggs
$1^1/_2$ teaspoons pure vanilla extract
$2^1/_4$ cups plus 2 tablespoons all-purpose flour
1 teaspoon baking soda
$^3/_4$ teaspoon salt
1 (12-ounce) package semisweet chocolate chips

Preheat the oven to 350°F. Lightly grease two baking sheets and set aside.

In the bowl of an electric mixer, beat the butter, granulated sugar, and brown sugar until creamy, about 2 minutes. Add the eggs and extract, beating until well blended.

In a separate small bowl, combine the flour, baking soda, and salt. Gradually add to the butter mixture, beating well. Stir in the chips.

Drop by tablespoons onto the prepared baking sheets. Bake 8 to 12 minutes, or until the desired degree of doneness. Immediately transfer to wire racks to cool.

MARBLED CHOCOLATE FUDGE

This recipe works every time, so fear not that you'll have fudge that doesn't "fudge!"

YIELD: 2$^1/_3$ POUNDS

1 (18-ounce) package semisweet chocolate chips (3 cups)
1 (14-ounce) can sweetened condensed milk
Dash of salt
$1^1/_2$ teaspoons pure vanilla extract
1 (10-ounce) package white chocolate chips

Line an 8-inch square baking dish with wax paper and set aside.

In a heavy saucepan over low heat, melt the semisweet chips with the milk and salt. When the mixture is smooth, remove from the heat and stir in the extract. Add the white chocolate chips and stir just until blended.

Spread evenly in the prepared pan. Refrigerate 2 hours, or until firm. Turn fudge out onto a cutting board and remove the wax paper. Cut into squares. Store leftovers in an airtight container between layers of wax paper.

MAKING CHOCOLATE: Chocolate begins with cacao, the beans of a tropical plant. These beans are found in pods that are harvested, allowed to ferment, dry, and finally roast. After roasting, the beans are cracked open, leaving only the pure essence of chocolate, which is known as nibs.

The nibs are ground and heated, making a thick substance known as chocolate liquor. From here, various forms of chocolate begin to take shape. It can be finely ground and turned into cocoa powder or mixed with other ingredients to give us any number of chocolate products.

MISSISSIPPI MUD CAKE

This is the perfect Southern sheet cake, which makes it easy to transport. It's loaded with pecans, marshmallows, and chocolate! Don't you love the name? Mud never looked so good!

YIELD: 15 SERVINGS

12 tablespoons unsalted butter, softened and divided

2 cups granulated sugar

$^1/_2$ cup plus $^1/_3$ cup unsweetened cocoa, divided

$^1/_8$ teaspoon salt

4 eggs, lightly beaten

1 teaspoon pure vanilla extract

$1^1/_2$ cups all-purpose flour

$1^1/_2$ cups coarsely chopped pecans, toasted

$^1/_3$ cup unsweetened cocoa

1 (16-ounce) package confectioners' sugar

$^1/_2$ cup milk

1 (10.5-ounce) bag miniature marshmallows

Preheat the oven to 350°F. Lightly grease and flour a 15 x 10-inch jelly-roll pan and set aside.

Melt 8 tablespoons of the butter in a small saucepan over low heat. Transfer to a large mixing bowl. Whisk in the granulated sugar, $^1/_2$ cup of the cocoa, the salt, eggs, and extract. Stir in the flour and pecans.

Transfer the batter to the prepared pan. Bake 20 to 25 minutes, or until a tester inserted in the center comes out clean.

Meanwhile, in the bowl of an electric mixer, combine the confectioners' sugar, milk, the remaining 4 tablespoons of the butter, and the remaining $^1/_3$ cup of the cocoa at low speed. Increase the speed to medium and beat until smooth. Set aside.

When the cake tester comes out clean, immediately top the cake with the marshmallows. Return to the oven 5 minutes. Remove from the oven. Drizzle the chocolate frosting over the warm cake and cool completely on a wire rack.

VELVETY CHOCOLATE FUDGE PIE

This age-old Southern pie tastes like a cross between fudge and pie.

YIELD: 8 SERVINGS

1 recipe Single Crust Pie Pastry (page 402)

2 eggs

1 cup sugar

$^1/_4$ pound (1 stick) unsalted butter, melted

$^1/_4$ cup unsweetened cocoa

$^1/_4$ cup all-purpose flour

1 teaspoon pure vanilla extract

$^1/_8$ teaspoon salt

Preheat the oven to 350°F. Place the pastry in a 9-inch pie pan and set aside.

In a mixing bowl, whisk together the eggs and sugar until well blended. Stir in the butter, cocoa, flour, extract, and salt, whisking until smooth. Transfer into the prepared pastry.

Bake 25 to 30 minutes. Cool completely on a wire rack. The pie will rise while baking and fall as it cools. Serve at room temperature.

BOTANY: Evergreen cacao trees are delicate and sensitive. They grow best if cultivated in the shade, especially for the first two to four years of growth. The quality and taste of the beans come from the rich soil in which the trees are grown.

CITRUS

(ORANGES, LEMONS, LIMES, AND GRAPEFRUITS)

I WAS NEVER ONE TO GET OVERLY EXCITED ABOUT RECEIVING AN ORANGE IN THE BOTTOM OF my Christmas stocking, but my parents thought it was great. They could tell endless stories about how wonderful it was in "their day" to have such an extravagance.

The stories of "my day" would include yummy remembrances of creamy lemon meringue pies, citrus-enhanced cookies, and the lemon drop ice cream sold at our local "superette" or convenience mart. It's all perspective, right?

Juicy oranges, sunny lemons, blushing grapefruits, and cool green limes each impart an individual goodness. These are the citrus fruits of my youth and still the ones I run to today. Every now and then, I'll purchase a kumquat, tangelo, citron, ugli fruit, or pomelo, but they are not regulars in my refrigerator. Instead, I prefer citrus fruits that remind me most of trips to Florida, our Southernmost state.

The best part about purchasing any type of citrus fruit is that nearly every part can be utilized with virtually no waste. Yes, we all probably discard the seeds we come across and we all know about the juicy pulp that lies inside the peel. But what about the outside?

The colorful outer rind of all citrus has tiny oil sacs that are full of intense flavor. When the rind is grated, it's appropriately called "zest" because that's exactly what it adds to any recipe. Zest is a marvelous way to add a citrus aroma and flavor without adding excess liquid. Think of it as citrus concentrate.

It is so nice to have a good supply of citrus products available in the market all year long. However, I particularly enjoy citrus fruits during the winter months. It's Southern sunshine for my tastebuds.

Nutrition: All citrus fruits are high in vitamin C. A medium orange equals sixty calories, and a medium grapefruit comes in around ninety calories.

Selection: Look for citrus skins that are free from any soft spots or cuts. Lift, but don't squeeze the fruit. It should feel heavy and firm. Brown markings on the outer rind are caused by the wind and do not negatively influence taste in any way.

Storage: Room temperature storage is fine. In fact, room temperature fruit yields the most juice, especially when it is rolled on the countertop just before squeezing. However, like most fresh fruits, you significantly increase the shelf life by keeping citrus products in the refrigerator. Place in the crisper drawer or in the bottom of your refrigerator. Then allow the fruit to come to room temperature thirty minutes prior to using.

LEMON CHESS PIE

The South made this particular pie famous thanks to the addition of cornmeal!

YIELD: 8 SERVINGS

1 recipe Single Pie Pastry (page 402)
4 tablespoons unsalted butter, melted
1¼ cups sugar
4 eggs
1 tablespoon lemon zest
¼ cup fresh lemon juice
¼ cup milk
2 tablespoons self-rising cornmeal
1 tablespoon self-rising flour

Preheat the oven to 375°F. Press the pie pastry into a 9-inch pie pan and crimp the edges.

In the bowl of an electric mixer, combine the butter, sugar, eggs, zest, juice, milk, cornmeal, and flour. Mix well. Pour into the prepared crust.

Bake 35 to 40 minutes, or until set in the center. Cool 1 hour on a wire rack before slicing and serving.

Celebrations
February is National Grapefruit Month.
March 31 is National Oranges and Lemons Day.
August 15 is Lemon Meringue Pie Day.
August 20 is Lemonade Day.

CREAMSICLE ORANGE SHERBET

This reminds me of the Orange Push-Ups we used to have as kids.

YIELD: 1 QUART

3 cups half-and-half or whole milk
⅔ cup fresh orange juice
1¼ cups sugar
1½ teaspoons finely grated orange zest

In a large mixing bowl, combine the half-and-half, juice, sugar, and zest, stirring until the sugar dissolves. Cover and refrigerate 1 hour. Transfer to an ice cream maker and freeze according to the manufacturer's directions.

HOME-SQUEEZED LEMONADE

You can increase or decrease the amount of sugar used according to your taste.

YIELD: 8 CUPS

1½ cups sugar
½ cup boiling water
2 teaspoons grated lemon zest
1½ cups fresh lemon juice
5 cups cold water
Lemon slices for garnish

Stir together the sugar, boiling water, and zest. Stir until the sugar dissolves. Cool 15 minutes. Pour through a fine mesh strainer into a pitcher.

Stir in the juice and cold water. Refrigerate 8 hours. Pour over ice and garnish with fresh lemon slices.

"ARRRRR-RANGE" RUM CAKE

Bring out the Southern pirate in your family. Make sure to glaze the cake while it is still warm so the glaze will absorb into the cake.

YIELD: 10 SERVINGS

$1\frac{1}{2}$ cups all-purpose flour

$\frac{3}{4}$ plus $\frac{1}{3}$ cup sugar, divided

$\frac{3}{4}$ teaspoon baking powder

13 tablespoons unsalted butter

3 eggs

2 tablespoons half-and-half

1 tablespoon rum

1 tablespoon finely grated orange zest

1 teaspoon rum extract

$\frac{1}{3}$ cup fresh orange juice

Preheat the oven to 350°F. Grease and flour a loaf pan and set aside.

In the bowl of an electric mixer, combine the flour, $\frac{3}{4}$ cup of the sugar, and the baking powder. With the mixer on medium speed, add the butter, 1 tablespoon at a time.

In a separate bowl, whisk together the eggs, half-and-half, rum, zest, and rum extract. Add to the flour mixture, mixing until just combined. Transfer the batter to the prepared pan. Bake 55 to 60 minutes, or until a tester inserted in the center of the cake comes out clean. Cool in the pan 5 minutes and transfer to a wire rack.

While the cake bakes, combine the remaining sugar and orange juice over medium-high heat in a small saucepan. Stir until sugar dissolves and bring to a boil. Cook until reduced by half, about 4 minutes. Cool slightly.

With a skewer, poke several holes in the top of the cake. Brush the top of the cake with the glaze, making sure it is completely absorbed before applying more. Cool completely before slicing and serving.

LEMON MERINGUE WAFER PIE

This pie pulls me right back to childhood. It's the first pie I ever made!

YIELD: 8 SERVINGS

7 whole graham crackers, finely crushed

4 tablespoons unsalted butter, melted

18 vanilla wafer cookies

1 (14-ounce) can sweetened condensed milk

$\frac{1}{2}$ cup lemon juice

3 eggs, separated

$\frac{1}{4}$ teaspoon cream of tartar

$\frac{1}{2}$ cup sugar

Combine the crushed graham crackers and melted butter until moist crumbs form. Press into the bottom of a 9-inch pie pan. Arrange the cookies with the rounded side out around the sides of the dish to form the outer crust. Set aside.

Preheat the oven to 350°F. Whisk together the milk, juice, and egg yolks in a medium bowl. Pour into the crust and set aside.

Beat the egg whites at high speed of an electric mixer until soft peaks form. Add the cream of tartar. Gradually add the sugar, one tablespoon at a time. Continue beating until the meringue forms glossy peaks around 3 minutes.

Spoon the meringue over the filling, spreading all the way to the edges. Bake until the meringue is golden brown in spots, about 15 minutes. Cool completely on a wire rack, and then cover, and refrigerate before serving.

Note: Refrigerate leftovers.

"NOT A CLOUD IN THE SKY" LIME CUPCAKES

If you want, use a couple of drops of green food coloring in the frosting of these cupcakes.

YIELD: 12 CUPCAKES

1 cup all-purpose flour
$3/4$ cup self-rising flour
$1/2$ pound (2 sticks) unsalted butter, softened and divided
$1^1/4$ cups granulated sugar
2 eggs
$2^1/2$ tablespoons fresh lime juice
2 tablespoons lime zest, divided
$3/4$ cup buttermilk
1 (8-ounce) package cream cheese, softened
$1^1/2$ cups confectioners' sugar
$1/2$ teaspoon pure vanilla extract

Preheat the oven to 350°F. Line a muffin pan with 12 paper liners. In a small bowl, combine the all-purpose flour and self-rising flour and set aside.

In the bowl of an electric mixer, beat 1 stick of the butter at medium speed until fluffy, about 1 minute. Add the granulated sugar and mix well. Add the eggs, one at a time, mixing well after each addition.

Stir in the juice and 1 tablespoon of the zest. Add the flour mixture alternately with the buttermilk, beginning and ending with the flour. Spoon the batter evenly into each liner.

Bake 20 to 25 minutes, or until a tester inserted in the center comes out clean. Cool 10 minutes in the pan, and then transfer to a wire rack to cool completely.

While the cupcakes are cooling, combine the cream cheese, confectioners' sugar, the remaining stick of butter, the remaining zest, and the extract. Beat at medium speed until smooth. Spread over the cooled cupcakes.

SOUTHERN SUNSHINE GRAPEFRUIT FREEZE

There's something incredibly refreshing about this sweet, tangy, frozen slush.

YIELD: ABOUT 2 QUARTS

$1^1/2$ cups sugar
1 cup water
1 (46-ounce) can unsweetened grapefruit juice
Fresh mint sprigs for garnish

In a large saucepan, combine the sugar and water over medium-high heat. Bring to a boil and remove from heat.

Pour the juice into an 8-cup container. Add the sugar syrup, mixing well. Cover and refrigerate at least 1 hour.

Pour the mixture into two 1-quart freezer containers. Cover and freeze. Remove from the freezer 1 hour before serving. Spoon the slushy mixture into chilled custard cups, garnish with mint, and serve.

ORIGIN: Citrus fruits are natives of Southeast Asia and have been cultivated for around four thousand years.

BOTANY: The cultivated lemon trees we are used to seeing today are believed to be a cross between limes and citron. The average lemon tree is harvested of fruit about six times a year and yields fifteen hundred lemons annually. Key limes are the most widely used limes in the world. They are often confused with lemons because they are yellow when fully ripe. They grow on thorny trees that are very sensitive to cold weather.

COCA-COLA

OH, THE GLORY OF REACHING SATURDAY EVERY WEEK AS A CHILD. NOT ONLY WAS THERE no school, but that was the day we got to have an ice cold Coca-Cola if we were good and got our chores done. There were no large two-liter plastic bottles where no one really knew how much you drank. No, ours were small glass bottles and we were only allowed to have one.

Here in the South, we were recycling before going green became cool. Every other week, we lugged six-packs of those empty glass bottles back to the grocery store for a refund. The six-packs were only sold at room temperature, but once again, if we were extra helpful, we might be rewarded with one straight from the chest-type icebox in the store that kept the drinks frosty cold.

Woe be unto children who didn't have a Coca-Cola to leave out on Christmas Eve for Santa. Oh sure, he didn't mind milk, but more than likely, that went to Rudolph and the other reindeer. All kids knew that he was sure to give you extra goodies if you left him a nice, cold bottle of Coke (and didn't forget the opener).

How appropriate that Coca-Cola was invented in Atlanta, Georgia, by John Pemberton, a local pharmacist. His bookkeeper, Frank Robinson named the beverage and wrote it out in the same script that is still used today. I love that! History shows us that Pemberton sold only nine glasses a day of his new product during the first year. If I had to guess, I would say it probably slowly gained popularity as a way to combat the stifling and oppressive Southern heat. Now, it's as much a part of the cooking scene as any other beverage and still popular with Santa!

Origin: Coca-Cola was invented in Atlanta, Georgia, in 1886 by Dr. John Styth Pemberton. It was originally made with extracts of coca leaves and kola nuts, which is where the name Coca-Cola came from.

Beginning: The first Coca-Cola was sold in the Jacob's Pharmacy soda fountain in Atlanta on May 8, 1886, for five cents per glass. It was a caramel-colored syrup mixed with carbonated water and served over ice. The term "Coke" wasn't used until 1941, when it was introduced in magazine ads.

Bottles: To combat those who were trying to copy Coca-Cola's success, the company developed the still recognizable contour bottle. It began bottling six-and-one-half ounces in 1916. Bell-shaped glasses were the official glass used for serving Coca-Cola in soda fountains as of 1929.

Polar Bears: The world was introduced to the Coca-Cola Polar Bear family in 1993 and the slogan "Always Coca-Cola" became the holiday theme.

COCA-COLA CAKE

For as long as I can remember, this cake has been carried to church picnics, family gatherings, and office parties. It is one of my favorite sheet cakes.

YIELD: 12 SERVINGS (IF YOU'RE LUCKY!)

1 cup Coca-Cola
$\frac{1}{2}$ cup buttermilk
$\frac{1}{2}$ pound (2 sticks) unsalted butter, softened
$1\frac{3}{4}$ cups sugar
2 eggs
2 teaspoons pure vanilla extract
2 cups all-purpose flour
$\frac{1}{4}$ cup unsweetened cocoa
1 teaspoon baking powder
$1\frac{1}{2}$ cups miniature marshmallows
Coca-Cola Frosting (recipe follows)

Preheat the oven to 350°F. Lightly grease a 13 x 9-inch baking dish and set aside.

In a medium bowl, combine the cola and buttermilk. Set aside.

In an electric mixer, beat the butter at medium-low speed until light and fluffy, about 2 minutes. Gradually add the sugar and beat 1 minute longer, or until well blended. Add the eggs, one at a time, beating well after each addition. Fold in the extract.

In a separate bowl, combine the flour, cocoa, and baking powder. Reduce the mixer speed to low and alternately add the flour mixture and the cola mixture to the batter. Begin and end with the flour mixture, blending well so the batter is smooth. Fold in the marshmallows.

Transfer the batter to the prepared pan. Bake 30 to 35 minutes, or until a tester inserted in the center comes out clean. Cool 10 minutes in the pan on a wire rack. Pour the Coca-Cola Frosting over the warm cake. Cool completely on a wire rack before slicing and serving.

COCA-COLA FROSTING

This delicious frosting is excellent over any chocolate sheet cake. Don't make it too far ahead of time. It's best when it's still warm and poured over the warm cake.

YIELD: $2\frac{1}{4}$ CUPS

$\frac{1}{4}$ pound (1 stick) unsalted butter
$\frac{1}{3}$ cup Coca-Cola
3 tablespoons unsweetened cocoa
1 (16-ounce) package confectioners' sugar
1 tablespoon pure vanilla extract

In a large saucepan over medium heat, combine the butter, cola, and cocoa. Whisk until the butter completely melts and the mixture is smooth. Remove from the heat and whisk in the confectioners' sugar and extract. Stir until smooth.

CHERRY COKE BARBECUE SAUCE

You will love the sweet flavor Cherry Coke adds to this sauce. Make it hotter if you like by using more hot sauce. This is especially good on chicken and ribs.

YIELD: 4 CUPS

1 tablespoon canola or vegetable oil
1 large white onion, peeled and chopped
2 garlic cloves, minced
1 (12-ounce) bottles chili sauce
1 (12-ounce) jar cherry jam or preserves
1 cup cherry Coke (not diet)
$\frac{1}{2}$ cup packed brown sugar
$\frac{1}{4}$ cup balsamic vinegar
$1\frac{1}{2}$ teaspoons hot sauce

¼ teaspoon salt
¼ teaspoon black pepper

Place the oil in a heavy saucepan over medium heat. Add the onion and sauté 6 minutes. Add the garlic and stir 1 minute. Stir in the chili sauce, jam, cherry Coke, brown sugar, and vinegar. Bring to a simmer, stirring frequently. Reduce the heat to medium-low and simmer, uncovered, about 50 minutes, stirring frequently to prevent scorching. Stir in the hot sauce, salt, and pepper. Cool completely.
Note: The sauce can be made up to two weeks ahead and kept refrigerated.

SEASONED GREETINGS COCA-COLA HAM

You can use either regular or cherry Coca-Cola for this recipe, just not diet. It ends up making a syrup and keeps the ham incredibly moist.

YIELD: 16 SERVINGS

1 (6 to 7 pound) fresh ham
15 whole cloves
1 cup packed brown sugar, divided
2 cups Coca-Cola

Preheat the oven to 325°F.

Score the fat on the ham in a diamond design and stud the center of the diamonds with the cloves. Place the ham with the fat side up in a roasting pan. Press ½ cup of the brown sugar onto the top of the ham. Pour the cola over the top of the ham so some of the brown sugar washes to the bottom of the pan. Pat the remaining ½ cup of the brown sugar on top of the ham.

Bake, uncovered, 3 hours, or until a meat thermometer inserted in the thickest part registers 160°F. Baste the ham with the cola drippings every hour. If the ham becomes too dry, add ½ cup more of cola. If the ham browns too quickly, cover loosely with aluminum foil. Let rest 15 minutes before slicing and serving. Serve warm, room temperature, or cold.

"SOAKIN' AND SMOKIN'" COLA CHICKEN

Liquid smoke and Coca-Cola give this chicken crowing rights among the best chicken recipes!

YIELD: 8 SERVINGS

1 (4-pound) package assorted chicken pieces
4 cups Coca-Cola
3 tablespoons salt
2 tablespoons black pepper
2 tablespoons Worcestershire sauce
1 tablespoon hot sauce
1 teaspoon liquid smoke
Vegetable oil for frying
2 cups all-purpose flour
1 teaspoon garlic salt
1 teaspoon cayenne

Place the chicken in a single layer in a large shallow dish. In a large mixing bowl, combine the cola, salt, pepper, Worcestershire, hot sauce, and liquid smoke. Stir well and pour over the chicken. Cover and refrigerate overnight or at least 6 hours.

Pour oil to a depth of 2 inches in a large cast-iron skillet. Place over medium-high heat and bring to 350°F. Meanwhile, drain the chicken and discard the marinade. Combine the flour, garlic salt, and cayenne in a shallow bowl. Dredge the chicken in the flour mixture and carefully place in the hot oil. Fry in batches 10 to 15 minutes on each side, or until the chicken is completely done. Drain on paper towels and serve warm.

"SWEET ON YOU" BING CHERRY SALAD

Gelatin salads are a fixture on the Southern tablescape. This salad was a favorite of mine growing up and I didn't realize for years that it actually had Coca-Cola in it. Some serve it as a side dish.

YIELD: 12 SERVINGS

2$\frac{1}{2}$ cups water

3 (3-ounce) packages cherry-flavored gelatin (select black cherry if it is available)

2 cups Coca-Cola

1 (16-ounce) can whole-berry cranberry sauce

1 (15-ounce) can pitted Bing cherries, drained and quartered

2 cups chopped pecans, toasted

Lightly grease a 12-cup ring mold and set aside.

Bring the water to a boil in a large saucepan over high heat. Remove from the heat and add the gelatin, stirring 2 minutes, or until the gelatin completely dissolves. Stir in the cola, cranberry sauce, cherries, and pecans.

Transfer to the prepared mold. Cover and refrigerate at least 8 hours, or until firm. Unmold onto a serving plate and serve cold.

UNDERCOVER COLA POT ROAST

Let the oven work its magic with this roast and you'll be rewarded with lots of yummy gravy!

YIELD: 8 SERVINGS

2 tablespoons vegetable oil

1 (3 to 4 pound) beef roast

4 cups Coca-Cola

2 (10.5-ounce) cans cream of mushroom soup

1 teaspoon dried chives

$\frac{1}{2}$ teaspoon black pepper

Preheat the oven to 325°F.

Heat the oil in a large Dutch oven over medium-high heat. Add the roast and brown 2 minutes on each side. Remove from the heat and set aside.

In a mixing bowl, combine the cola, soup, chives, and pepper, stirring until smooth. Pour over the roast. Cover and bake 2 to 3 hours, or to the desired degree of doneness. Rest 15 minutes before slicing and serving with the pan gravy.

GEORGIA COCA-COLA MARINADE

Named in honor of Coca-Cola's birthplace, use this marinade on flank steak or any beef cut of your choice.

YIELD: 1 QUART

1 quart Coca-Cola

1 cup vegetable oil

1 cup white vinegar

3 garlic cloves, minced

1 teaspoon salt

1 teaspoon black pepper

In a large bowl, stir together the cola, oil, vinegar, garlic, salt, and pepper. Blend well. Pour over the beef cut of your choice and marinate overnight or 8 hours. Discard marinade and prepare the meat as you desire.

COCONUT

TRADITIONS WITH FOOD ARE TYPICALLY TIED TO HOLIDAYS OR SPECIAL OCCASIONS. EVERY year at Christmas, my grandmother would make a coconut cake. It would be all my daddy talked about for days leading up to the cutting. He could hardly wait for dessert time. I remember she kept it cold and it was incredibly moist and delicious.

For some reason, I like to make something with coconut around Easter. It varies greatly as to what that coconut concoction will be according to schedules and the amount of company we have. But I always want it to lead me into spring.

Like many items we label as "nuts," the coconut is botanically classified as a fruit and specifically classified as a drupe. The coconut, with its fibrous husk, is actually a giant seed. In fact, it's one of the largest seeds known in the world. These huge "seeds" develop between the fronds of the coconut palm at the top or crown.

Perhaps you are just not in the mood to attempt to crack fresh coconuts at home. It can be a real test of patience, to say the very least.

Most cooks I know use pre-shredded coconut because it's relatively inexpensive, quick, convenient, and easy to use. I especially like it toasted, which brings out the best flavor.

Obviously, fresh coconuts are not grown in the South. However, it became a holiday tradition because shredded coconut was a treat frequently brought to Southern homes by traveling friends and family. It remains a Christmas favorite to this day.

Whether you crack your own or just crack open a bag or can, coconut in all its forms is a fun ingredient to use . . . any time of the year!

Nutrition: Coconut is a good source of potassium but is high in saturated fat.

Cracking: Locate the seam that runs between the eyes. The drain opening of your kitchen sink is the perfect place to cradle the coconut while you open it. Using a screwdriver and hammer, forcefully and firmly tap around the equator of the coconut. Keep rotating and tapping until the coconut splits open. For a stubborn one, crack it open on concrete! The easiest way to remove the coconut meat is to place it in a 350°F oven. After fifteen to twenty minutes, it should be soft enough to remove from the shell. A potato peeler works great for peeling off the inner husk.

Selection: Only purchase fresh coconuts that are heavy. If you can't hear the liquid moving when you shake it, don't buy it.

COCONUT CREAM CHEESE FROSTING

I love spreading this on Coconut Milk Cupcakes (recipe follows) or on any white cake or cupcake.

YIELD: 2½ CUPS

1 (8-ounce) package cream cheese, softened
¼ pound (1 stick) butter, cut into pieces and softened
1 cup confectioners' sugar
1 teaspoon coconut extract

Combine the cream cheese and butter in a medium bowl with the electric mixer on medium speed. Decrease the speed to low and add the sugar and extract. Mix well. Spread on cooled cupcakes or cake.

COCONUT MERINGUE PIE

Meringue is a mixture of stiffly beaten egg whites and slowly added sugar. This pie has shredded coconut sprinkled on the top.

YIELD: 8 SERVINGS

6 tablespoons plus ¾ cup sugar
¼ cup cornstarch
2 cups milk
5 eggs, separated
4 tablespoons unsalted butter
1 teaspoon coconut extract
1 teaspoon pure vanilla extract
1 cup shredded coconut, divided
1 baked Single Pie Pastry (page 402)
¼ teaspoon cream of tartar

In a heavy saucepan over medium heat, combine 6 tablespoons of the sugar and the cornstarch. Whisk in the milk, egg yolks, and butter, stirring constantly until the custard begins to boil around the edge of the saucepan, around 8 minutes.

Remove from the heat and stir in the coconut extract and vanilla extract. Fold in ¾ cup of the flaked coconut. Pour into a medium bowl and press plastic wrap directly onto the surface to prevent skin from forming. Refrigerate 4 hours.

Preheat the oven to 425°F. Spoon the filling into the baked piecrust and set aside.

Beat the egg whites and cream of tartar in the bowl of an electric mixer until soft peaks form. Add the remaining sugar, one tablespoon at a time, beating until stiff peaks form. Spread the meringue over the pie filling, sealing all the way to the edge.

Sprinkle the remaining flaked coconut on top of the meringue. Bake 12 minutes, or until the top is golden brown. Cool completely on a wire rack.

Note: Pie can be made ahead and refrigerated up to four hours before serving.

COCONUT MILK CUPCAKES

This recipe is enhanced with coconut milk, which is made of equal parts of fresh coconut and water.

YIELD: ABOUT 2 DOZEN CUPCAKES

2¼ cups all-purpose flour
1 teaspoon baking powder
1 teaspoon baking soda
1 teaspoon salt
12 tablespoons unsalted butter, softened
1¼ cups sugar
3 eggs
1 teaspoon coconut extract
1 cup coconut milk

½ cup shredded coconut

Coconut Cream Cheese Frosting (page 177)

Toasted coconut for garnish

Preheat the oven to 350°F. Lightly grease a cupcake pan or add paper liners and set aside.

In a medium bowl, combine the flour, baking powder, baking soda, and salt. Set aside.

In the bowl of an electric mixer, cream the butter and sugar on medium speed until light and fluffy. Add the eggs, one at a time, mixing well after each addition. Stir in the extract.

Reduce the mixer speed to low and add the flour mixture alternately with the coconut milk, beginning and ending with the dry ingredients. Fold in the shredded coconut.

Spoon the batter evenly into the cups, filling two-thirds full. Bake 25 to 30 minutes, or until a tester inserted in the center comes out clean. Transfer the cupcakes to wire racks and completely cool. Spread with Coconut Cream Cheese Frosting and garnish with toasted coconut.

COMPANY AMBROSIA

I felt incredibly grown up when I had this fruit salad for the first time. It's still a favorite.

YIELD: 8 SERVINGS

9 oranges, peeled, seeded and sectioned

2 (20-ounce) cans crushed pineapple, drained

1 cup shredded coconut

1 cup honey

2 teaspoons pure almond extract

In a large bowl, stir together the oranges, pineapple, and coconut. Drizzle the honey and extract over the top, tossing gently to coat. Cover and refrigerate at least 8 hours before serving cold.

COCONUT MILK FROSTING

Use this frosting when making a Four-Layer Coconut Cake (page 179).

YIELD: 9 CUPS

¾ pound (3 sticks) unsalted butter, softened

¼ teaspoon salt

2 teaspoons pure vanilla extract

½ teaspoon coconut extract

3 (16-ounce) packages confectioners' sugar

1 cup canned coconut milk

Beat the butter, salt, vanilla extract, and coconut extract at medium speed of an electric mixer until fluffy. Reduce the speed to low and add the confectioners' sugar alternately with the coconut milk. Beat until smooth and then spread between the layers, on the top, and on the sides of the cooled cake.

COCONUT SORBET

Believe it or not, this sorbet is great served with a dry red wine.

YIELD: 1 QUART

4 cups coconut milk

1⅓ cups sugar

¼ cup heavy whipping cream

Toasted coconut

Place the coconut milk and sugar in a heavy saucepan over medium heat and bring to a boil. Boil about 3 minutes, or until the sugar dissolves. Stir in the cream, mixing well. Refrigerate 2 hours.

To freeze, follow the manufacturer's directions for your ice cream maker. Transfer the sorbet to a covered container and place in the freezer until completely frozen. Serve in chilled serving bowls and top with toasted coconut.

TOASTED COCONUT CREAM PIE

Toasted coconut is folded in the pie and sprinkled on top to add an intense coconut flavor.

YIELD: 8 SERVINGS

1 recipe Single Pie Pastry (page 402)

2 eggs

1 cup half-and-half

$^3/_4$ cup sugar

2 tablespoons all-purpose flour

$^1/_4$ cup cornstarch

1 tablespoon unsalted butter, melted

1 cup plus 1 tablespoon shredded coconut, toasted

Preheat the oven to 425°F. Press the pastry into a 9-inch pie pan, crimping the edges. Set aside.

In a large bowl, beat the eggs. Add the half-and-half and sugar, stirring until sugar dissolves.

In a small bowl, stir together the flour, cornstarch, and butter until smooth. Add to the egg mixture, blending well. Fold in 1 cup of the toasted coconut.

Pour into the prepared pastry and sprinkle the top with the remaining coconut. Bake 25 minutes. Cool completely on a wire rack before serving.

Celebration
May 31 is National Macaroon Day.

FOUR-LAYER COCONUT CAKE

This is it … my daddy's favorite cake. It is my grandmother's recipe.

YIELD: 12 SERVINGS

3 cups all-purpose flour

1 teaspoon baking powder

$^1/_2$ teaspoon salt

$2^2/_3$ cups sugar

1 cup vegetable shortening

$^1/_4$ pound (1 stick) unsalted butter, softened

1 cup milk

2 teaspoons coconut extract

1 teaspoon pure vanilla extract

5 eggs

1 (6-ounce) package shredded coconut

Coconut Milk Frosting (page 178)

Preheat the oven to 400°F. Lightly grease and flour 4 (9-inch) round cake pans and set aside.

In the bowl of an electric mixer, combine the flour, baking powder, salt, sugar, shortening, and butter. Mix well.

Add the milk, coconut extract, and vanilla extract. Add the eggs, one at a time, beating until well blended after each addition. Stir in the coconut.

Pour the batter evenly into the prepared pans. Bake 20 minutes, or until a tester inserted in the center comes out clean. Cool in the pans 10 minutes and transfer to wire racks to cool completely. When cool, spread with the Coconut Milk Frosting.

CORN

THERE IS A CERTAIN TIME OF YEAR WHEN "AW SHUCKS!" MEANS SOMETHING DELICIOUSLY wonderful, and that's during the summer. Everything about fresh corn screams that hot, humid weather has arrived in the South. Look at the sunshine yellow kernels and the bright green husks. There is nothing more beautiful than bushels of freshly picked corn.

As kids, we would sit on the back porch in aluminum chairs with nylon webbing that scratched our legs to help silk corn. We knew that if we didn't help, we didn't eat! That chore was bearable because we loved to feel the butter drip off our chins as we ate it "boiled and buttered," as my daddy used to say.

Even today, fresh corn is one of those summer produce goodies that I never seem to get tired of eating. The joy of serving it is worth every moment spent shucking and silking the ears and I've graduated to a much better chair!

Most will buy their fresh corn from farm stands or on farm markets. I grow my own every year and battle raccoons for the harvest. They seem to know exactly when I plan to pick the bounty and try to beat me to the ears. Some years, they win, but most of the time I am able to outsmart them to harvest my favorite variety, which is perfectly named "Incredible."

Maybe you don't have all that drama associated with your pickings. If not, you probably buy it, shuck it, boil it, butter it, and eat it! Always buy extra to stock in your freezer or can for your pantry. Preserving will take a bit of time now, but what a happy camper you'll be when the season is over and you still have plenty of the good stuff on hand!

Nutrition: A medium-size ear of boiled corn contains only seventy calories. That same ear provides about the same amount of vitamin B as two slices of enriched bread.

Preparation: Never add salt to the cooking water of corn because it tends to toughen the kernels. You can, however, add a pinch of sugar to the pot to enhance corn's natural sweetness.

Selection: Look for just-picked ears that have bright green husks and fresh silks. Pull the husks back and examine the kernels. They should be even, plump, and well-filled. There is no need to puncture any kernels. You can tell by looking if it's fresh.

Storage: When corn is picked, it is full of natural sugar. After harvest, those sugars begin to convert to starch. The speed of this conversion depends on temperature, so keeping it cold will slow the process down.

A-MAIZE-ING CORN AND EGG PIE

Sweet corn and unassuming eggs get just enough heat from jalapeño peppers to keep things interesting.

YIELD: 8 SERVINGS

1 recipe Single Pie Pastry (page 402)
3 slices bacon
$\frac{1}{2}$ cup chopped onion
1 (17-ounce) can cream-style corn
2 jalapeño peppers, seeded and finely chopped
2 eggs, lightly beaten
$\frac{1}{4}$ cup half-and-half
$\frac{1}{2}$ cup shredded Cheddar cheese
1 tablespoon all-purpose flour
$\frac{1}{4}$ teaspoon salt
$\frac{1}{4}$ teaspoon black pepper

Preheat the oven to 400°F. Place the pastry in a 9-inch pie plate. Prick the bottom and sides with a fork. Bake 8 minutes and set aside on a wire rack to cool.

Decrease the oven temperature to 375°F.

In a large skillet over medium-high heat, cook the bacon until crisp. Drain on paper towels and reserve 1 tablespoon of the drippings. Crumble the bacon and set aside. Sauté the onions in the drippings until tender, about 4 minutes. Drain well on a paper towel.

In a mixing bowl, combine the onions, corn, jalapeño, eggs, half-and-half, cheese, flour, salt, and pepper. Mix well and pour into the pastry. Sprinkle the bacon on top and bake 45 minutes, or until set. Serve warm.

BROWN BUTTERED CORN

Watch the butter so it doesn't burn, but just browns. Sauté the corn in the browned butter for an unforgettable side dish.

YIELD: 4 SERVINGS

2 tablespoons unsalted butter
3 cups fresh corn kernels
$\frac{1}{4}$ teaspoon salt
$\frac{1}{8}$ teaspoon white pepper

In a large skillet over medium-high heat, melt the butter. Let it foam and brown in the skillet without stirring, about 4 to 5 minutes. When the butter is brown, add the corn, salt, and pepper. Cook 4 minutes longer, stirring constantly until the corn is tender. Serve warm.

BUTTERMILK FRIED CORN

These crispy niblets are delicious sprinkled on top of salads, soups, or by themselves. I like to use field corn for this recipe, but if sweet corn is all you can find, it will work just fine.

YIELD: 3 CUPS

3 cups whole kernel corn
2 cups buttermilk
1 cup all-purpose flour
1 cup cornmeal
1 teaspoon salt
1 teaspoon black pepper
Vegetable or canola oil

Stir together the corn and buttermilk. Let stand 30 minutes. Drain.

Meanwhile, combine the flour, cornmeal, salt, and pepper in a large zip-top plastic bag. Add the corn a bit at a time and shake to coat.

Pour the oil to a depth of $^1/_2$ inch in a large skillet and heat to 375°F. Fry the corn in small batches until golden, about 2 minutes per batch. Drain on paper towels and serve warm.

··

COVERED DISH BAKED CORN

This is a great way to use leftover cooked corn and it transports well.

YIELD: 6 SERVINGS

3 tablespoons unsalted butter

1 tablespoon chopped onion

1 tablespoon chopped green bell pepper

2 tablespoons all-purpose flour

$^3/_4$ cup milk

3 eggs, separated

2 cups cooked corn

$^1/_2$ teaspoon white wine vinegar

1 teaspoon salt

$^1/_2$ teaspoon black pepper

4 tablespoons plain dry breadcrumbs

Preheat the oven to 400°F. In an ovenproof skillet, melt the butter over medium heat. Add the onions and bell peppers, stirring to wilt, about 3 minutes.

Gradually add the flour and milk. Stir and cook 5 minutes, or until thick and smooth. Add the egg yolks, corn, vinegar, salt, and pepper. Set aside.

Beat the egg whites on high speed of an electric mixer 4 minutes, or until soft peaks form. Gently fold into the corn mixture and top with the breadcrumbs. Bake 25 to 30 minutes, or until golden brown. Serve warm.

FRESH CORN BISQUE

The ingredient list is long, but it all goes into one pot and this dish is really easy to make.

YIELD: 8 SERVINGS

1 tablespoon vegetable oil

1 yellow onion, peeled and diced

3 garlic cloves, minced

1 cup dry red wine

4 cups fresh corn

2 Yukon Gold potatoes, peeled and diced

4 poblano peppers, roasted, peeled, seeded, and diced

2 red bell peppers, roasted, peeled, seeded, and diced

4 cups chicken stock

2 cups whipping cream

Juice of $^1/_2$ lime

2 teaspoons ground cumin, toasted

1 teaspoon chopped fresh cilantro

$^1/_2$ teaspoon salt

$^1/_4$ teaspoon black pepper

$^1/_2$ cup sour cream for garnish

Cilantro sprigs for garnish

Heat the oil in a stockpot over medium-high heat. When hot, add the onion and garlic. Sauté 2 minutes. Add the wine and reduce until $^1/_4$ cup remains, around 10 minutes.

Add the corn, potatoes, poblanos, bell peppers, and stock. Simmer until the potatoes are tender, about 10 minutes.

Use an immersion blender to purée (or cool slightly and purée in a regular blender). Add the cream and simmer about 15 minutes. Add the juice, cumin, and cilantro. Mix well and season with the salt and pepper. Serve with a dollop of sour cream and cilantro sprigs on top.

FRIED CORN CAKES

*These fried cakes are loaded with melted moz-
zarella, but feel free to substitute another cheese of
your choice. Sometimes I give them a squeeze of
fresh lime juice just before serving to counter the
sweet corn flavor.*

YIELD: 3 DOZEN

$2^1/_2$ cups fresh corn kernels

3 eggs

$^3/_4$ cup milk

3 tablespoons unsalted butter, melted

$^3/_4$ cup all-purpose flour

$^3/_4$ cup plain cornmeal

1 cup shredded mozzarella

2 tablespoons chopped fresh chives

1 teaspoon black pepper

$^3/_4$ teaspoon salt

In a large mixing bowl, combine the corn, eggs,
milk, and butter. Whisk briskly until well mixed.
Add the flour and cornmeal, and then add the
cheese, chives, pepper, and salt, stirring just until
moistened.

Place a lightly oiled griddle over medium-high
heat. When hot, spoon $^1/_8$ cup of the batter onto
the hot griddle. Cook 3 to 4 minutes, or until the
tops are covered with bubbles. Turn and cook 2 to
3 minutes more. Repeat with the remaining batter.
Serve warm.

GARDEN CORN CUSTARD

*This is similar to corn pudding, but utilizes other
goodies from your garden for extra color and flavor.*

YIELD: 8 SERVINGS

2 cups fresh corn kernels

3 eggs, lightly beaten

1 cup shredded sharp Cheddar cheese

2 tablespoons chopped banana peppers

$^1/_4$ cup all-purpose flour

1 tablespoon sugar

$^1/_2$ teaspoon salt

$^1/_4$ teaspoon black pepper

2 cups half-and-half

2 tablespoons unsalted butter, melted

2 tomatoes, seeded and chopped

1 green bell pepper, seeded and chopped

Preheat the oven to 325°F. Lightly grease a $1^1/_2$-
quart baking dish and set aside.

In a mixing bowl, combine the corn, eggs,
cheese, and banana peppers. In a separate bowl,
mix together the flour, sugar, salt, and pepper. Add
to the corn mixture, blending well. Stir in the half-
and-half and butter. Pour into the prepared dish.

Combine the tomatoes and bell peppers. Sprinkle around the edge of the corn mixture. Carefully
place the casserole in a 13 x 9-inch baking pan.
Add hot water to the depth of 1 inch.

Bake 1 hour and 10 minutes, or until a knife
inserted in the center comes out clean. Serve warm.

GRILLED CORN WITH
MAPLE VINAIGRETTE

*This is so simple and so good. Soak the corn and husks
in water to prevent the husks from burning on the grill.*

YIELD: 6 SERVINGS

6 ears sweet corn, silk removed but with
   husks still intact

$^1/_4$ cup unsweetened brewed tea

$^1/_4$ cup olive oil

3 tablespoons balsamic vinegar

2 tablespoons maple syrup

1 garlic clove, minced

1/4 teaspoon salt

1/4 teaspoon black pepper

Place the corn in water and soak 30 minutes. Drain and pat dry. Pull the husks over the corn. Preheat the grill to medium (350°F). Place the corn on the grate and grill 15 minutes, turning occasionally.

Meanwhile, place the tea, oil, vinegar, syrup, garlic, salt, and pepper in a jar with a tight fitting lid. Shake to blend. With tongs, carefully pull back the husks and remove from the corn. Place in a 13 x 9-inch baking dish. Pour the maple vinaigrette over the corn, turning to coat evenly. Serve warm with corn handles.

ROASTIN' EARS

Every vegetable is delicious roasted, including corn! This is the essence of what fresh corn should taste like.

YIELD: 6 SERVINGS

6 ears sweet corn, husked and silk removed

1/4 pound (1 stick) unsalted butter, softened

1 tablespoon milk

1/2 teaspoon salt

1/2 teaspoon paprika

1/2 teaspoon black pepper

Preheat the oven to 400°F. Place the corn in a 13 x 9-inch baking dish. In a small mixing bowl, combine the butter, milk, salt, paprika, and pepper. Spread over the ears and cover. Bake 30 minutes or until the corn is tender. Serve warm.

HOW SWEET IT IS CORN PUDDING

This Southern side dish is at home with any meal. It is beautifully uncomplicated and savory with a hint of sweetness.

YIELD: 8 SERVINGS

6 tablespoons unsalted butter, divided

1 sweet onion, peeled and chopped

1/3 cup all-purpose flour

3/4 teaspoon salt

1/2 teaspoon black pepper

6 cups fresh corn kernels

2 1/2 cups half-and-half

6 eggs, lightly beaten

1 1/2 cups shredded Cheddar cheese

1 cup seasoned dry breadcrumbs

Preheat the oven to 350°F. Lightly grease a 3-quart baking dish and set aside.

In a large skillet over medium heat, melt 4 tablespoons of the butter. When hot, add the onion and cook 5 minutes or until softened. Stir in the flour, salt, and pepper. Cook 3 minutes, stirring constantly. Stir in the corn and set aside.

In a large bowl, whisk together the half-and-half and eggs. Stir in the cheese and gently fold in the corn mixture. Pour into the prepared baking dish.

In a small bowl, melt the remaining butter. Add the breadcrumbs, stirring to evenly coat. Sprinkle over the corn mixture. Bake 1 hour and 10 minutes, or until a tester inserted in the center comes out clean. Serve warm.

Note: You can substitute frozen whole kernel corn or canned shoepeg corn for fresh.

IN PERFECT HOMINY CASSEROLE

My good friend Sonja gave me this recipe and it is now a regular side dish on my dinner table. I sometimes substitute chopped country ham for the bacon.

YIELD: 6 TO 8 SERVINGS

4 slices bacon
1 large purple onion, peeled and chopped
1 green bell pepper, seeded and chopped
1 (29-ounce) can hominy, drained
1 (10-ounce) can tomatoes with green chiles
1 (4-ounce) can sliced mushrooms, drained
1 teaspoon Worcestershire sauce
1 teaspoon salt
$\frac{1}{4}$ teaspoon black pepper
1 cup sharp shredded Cheddar cheese, divided

In a large skillet over medium heat, cook the bacon until crisp. Drain on paper towels and reserve the drippings. When the bacon is cool enough to handle, crumble and set aside.

Add the onion and bell pepper to the hot drippings and cook until tender, about 4 minutes. Stir in the hominy, tomatoes, mushrooms, Worcestershire, salt, and pepper. Cook 20 minutes, stirring occasionally.

Meanwhile, preheat the oven to 350°F. Lightly grease a 2-quart casserole dish and set aside. Stir the bacon into the hominy mixture. Place half of the hominy mixture in the prepared pan. Sprinkle with half of the cheese. Repeat the layering and bake 20 minutes. Serve warm.

SMOKED CORN-ON-THE-COB

This recipe requires a smoker. If you don't have one, use the grill instead. Make sure to soak the wood chips a minimum of thirty minutes before using. Although I like hickory chips, you can use mesquite, apple, cherry, or pecan if you wish.

YIELD: 8 SERVINGS

Hickory wood chips, soaked
8 ears sweet corn
$\frac{1}{4}$ pound (1 stick) unsalted butter, softened
2 tablespoons chopped fresh thyme

Place the chips in the smoker water pan and fill with water. Preheat the smoker.

Peel back the corn husks, leaving them attached. Carefully remove the silk. Stir together the butter and thyme. Rub over the corn kernels and pull the husks back over the corn.

Place the corn on the upper rack. Smoke 30 to 35 minutes. Let stand 10 minutes. Pull back the husks and serve warm with corn picks.

TIP: Do kernels scatter everywhere when you cut them from the cob? After years of scraping super-glued corn splatter off everything, I've finally found a foolproof trick to cut down on that work. Position the ear in the center hole of a tube pan (an Angel Food or Bundt pan). Cut downward with a sharp knife and scrape the cob to get the "milk." The tube pan serves as an anchor and will catch that nasty splatter!

SOUTHERN SWEETHEART CORN PUPPIES

These are a cross between fritters and hushpuppies. They are marvelous served with baked or roasted chicken or for breakfast with sorghum syrup.

YIELD: 12 TO 15 SERVINGS

2 cups all-purpose flour
$1/8$ teaspoon salt
2 cups water
$1/4$ cup olive oil
1 egg, separated
Vegetable oil for frying
$3^1/4$ cups corn

In a large bowl, combine the flour and salt. Gradually add the water and olive oil, stirring constantly. Add the egg yolk and stir until smooth.

Beat the egg white at high speed with an electric mixer until stiff peaks form. Fold gently into the batter. Cover the batter and leave at room temperature 1 hour.

Heat the vegetable oil in a large pot over medium-high heat and bring to 375°F. Meanwhile, stir the corn into the batter. Carefully drop rounded tablespoons into the hot oil. Fry until golden brown, 4 to 5 minutes. Remove with a slotted spoon and drain on paper towels. Repeat with the remaining batter. Serve warm.

HISTORY: Most food historians believe "flint corn," which is what most think of as Indian corn, progressed through the area that is now the Southwestern United States around 1000 BC.

SPICED CORN RELISH

Warning: If you plan on making this for gifts, it will be difficult to give away. Hide at least one pint in the back of the pantry for yourself.

YIELD: 4 PINTS

4 cups fresh corn kernels
3 green bell peppers, seeded and chopped
1 cup chopped sweet onions
1 cup chopped cucumbers
$1/4$ cup chopped celery
1 (28-ounce) can whole tomatoes, undrained and chopped
1 cup sugar
2 teaspoons salt
1 teaspoon whole mustard seeds
$3/4$ teaspoon ground turmeric
$1/4$ teaspoon dry mustard
$1^1/2$ cups distilled white vinegar

In a large Dutch oven over medium heat, combine the corn, bell peppers, onions, cucumbers, celery, tomatoes, sugar, salt, seeds, turmeric, dry mustard, and vinegar. Bring to a boil.

Pack into hot canning jars, leaving $1/2$-inch headspace. Remove any air bubbles, wipe the jar rims, and adjust the lids. Process in a boiling water bath 15 minutes. (See page 12 for detailed canning instructions.) Cool completely on a wire rack away from drafts. Store at room temperature.

SHELF LIFE: The old saying of having the water boiling before you head to harvest sweet corn has some truth in it. Cooking fresh corn as soon as possible is imperative to having it remain sweet. Cooked leftovers should be used within a couple of days.

CORNBREAD

CORNBREAD IS THE ORIGINAL SOUTHERN QUICK BREAD. A STRAIGHT-FROM-THE-OVEN SKILLET of hot cornbread could qualify as the perfect comfort food. It immediately evokes memories of home with an aroma that can't be beat and a taste that is indescribably good.

Let's face it: The best cornbread is baked in a cast-iron skillet. It's the first nonstick cooking vessel because when seasoned correctly, everything slips out with ease. I have my grandmother's cast-iron cornbread skillet and the inside of it looks like glass. I only use it for cornbread and nothing else.

For years I watched my grandmother make cornbread by using a coffee cup with a broken handle as a cup measure and her palm as a teaspoon measure. Even though there was no one secret ingredient, she seemed to have a knack for making cornbread that was especially delicious and steamy. You know the type!

Cornbread has a primary ingredient of cornmeal. Cornmeal is dried corn kernels that have been ground into either a fine, medium, or coarse texture. Some cooks prefer white cornmeal, which is made from white corn and has a mild flavor. The slightly stronger flavored yellow cornmeal is my personal preference. Both have been pantry staples in Southern kitchens for decades.

The process for making good cornbread is very simple. Just preheat your seasoned cast-iron skillet in the oven, mix the ingredients, pour into the skillet, and bake. Nothing could be easier and nothing could taste as marvelous!

CAST IRON

There are lots of cookware options on the market. The reason to select cast iron (particularly for cornbread baking and chicken frying) is because of its enormous heat retention. In addition, properly cared for and seasoned cast iron is practically indestructible, so you will not have to replace it, but can pass it on instead.

Seasoning: The purpose of seasoning cast-iron cookware is to prevent rust from forming and to create a nonstick cooking surface. This is sometimes called "curing." It is accomplished by using oil to fill in the microscopic pores that you can't see or feel in the surface of the cookware.

To season a cast-iron skillet, preheat the oven to 350°F. Place a large jelly-roll pan on the bottom rack of your oven. Wash the cast iron in hot, soapy water, and then rinse and dry it well. Apply a very thin, even coating of vegetable oil or melted vegetable shortening to the inside of the cast iron. Do not use any flavored oil, such as olive, sunflower, peanut etc. or you will "flavor" the cast iron! Place the cast iron upside down on the center rack directly above the jelly-roll pan. After one hour, turn the oven off and allow the cast iron to cool in the oven. Repeat twice more beginning with the thin coating of oil step.

Don't forget the lid! One reason you season cast iron is to create a moisture barrier so rust cannot form. So while you are seasoning the cookware, season the lid as well. Seasoning is an on-going process. The more you use cast iron, the more it is seasoned.

Removing Rust: My grandmother used to tell me she removed rust by putting the cast iron in a fire to burn it off. You can remove it by using a fine grade of steel wool and old-fashioned elbow grease. Once the rust is removed, season the cookware immediately.

Cleaning cast iron: Forget the dishwasher. After cooking, wipe out the cookware with a paper towel or clean it with a stiff nylon brush and hot water if necessary. Do not use soap or any harsh detergent because these strip away oils and will remove the seasoning.

BACON CORNBREAD MUFFINS

I love cornbread muffins because you have plenty of the crispy outer crust to enjoy.

YIELD: 12 MUFFINS

12 slices bacon
1 cup plain cornmeal
2 tablespoons sugar
3 teaspoons baking powder
$^1/_2$ teaspoon salt
3 eggs
1 cup milk
2 tablespoons bacon drippings

Preheat the oven to 425°F. Grease a 12-cup muffin pan (cast iron preferred) and set aside. In a large skillet over medium heat, fry the bacon until crisp. Drain on paper towels and set aside. When cool enough to handle, crumble the bacon.

In a small mixing bowl, combine the cornmeal, sugar, baking powder, and salt. Set aside.

In a mixing bowl, lightly beat the eggs. Add the milk and drippings from the bacon skillet, whisking until well combined. Add the cornmeal mixture to the egg mixture, stirring well. Fold in the crumbled bacon.

Spoon the batter into the prepared muffin cups, filling two-thirds full. Bake 20 minutes, or until the tops are golden brown. Transfer immediately to a wire rack. Serve warm.

BASIC SOUTHERN CORNBREAD

This is the recipe I use on a monthly basis. It is perfect every time and any leftover wedges can be individually wrapped and frozen for later use.

YIELD: 8 SERVINGS

2 cups plain cornmeal
1 tablespoon baking powder
1 teaspoon salt
$1^3/_4$ cups buttermilk
1 egg, beaten
$^1/_4$ cup vegetable oil or melted shortening

Preheat the oven to 450°F. Place a greased 9-inch cast-iron skillet in the oven to heat while the desired temperature is reached.

Meanwhile, in a large bowl combine the cornmeal, baking powder, and salt. Make a well in the center and add the buttermilk, egg, and oil, blending well. Pour the batter into the preheated skillet.

Bake 25 minutes, or until golden brown. Transfer to a serving plate and cool 5 minutes. Cut into slices and serve warm.

BUTTERMILK CORNBREAD

This is the cornbread I love to have with soup in the winter.

YIELD: 8 SERVINGS

2 cups self-rising cornmeal mix
$1^3/_4$ cups buttermilk
1 egg, beaten
$^1/_4$ cup vegetable oil or melted shortening

Preheat the oven to 450°F. Place a greased 9-inch cast-iron skillet in the oven to heat while the desired temperature is reached.

Meanwhile, in a large bowl, combine the cornmeal mix, buttermilk, egg, and oil, blending well. Pour the batter into the preheated skillet. Bake 25 minutes. Transfer to a serving plate and cool 5 minutes. Cut into slices and serve warm.

BAKED HOT WATER CORNBREAD

This version of hot-water cornbread isn't fried in a skillet like the traditional one.

YIELD: 8 SERVINGS

$^1/_3$ cup plus 1 tablespoon vegetable oil, divided
2 cups plain cornmeal
$1^1/_4$ teaspoons salt
1 teaspoon sugar
$^1/_4$ teaspoon baking powder
$^1/_4$ cup half-and-half
$^3/_4$ cup boiling water

Preheat the oven to 475°F. Place $^1/_3$ cup of the oil in a jelly-roll pan, tilting to evenly distribute. Set aside.

In a mixing bowl, combine the cornmeal, salt, sugar, and baking powder. Make a well in the center and stir in the half-and-half and the remaining 1 tablespoon vegetable oil. Gradually add the boiling water, stirring until the batter is the consistency of cooked grits.

With a $^1/_4$-cup measure, place scoops of the batter onto the prepared pan. Bake 13 to 15 minutes. Turn the patties over and bake 5 minutes longer, or until golden brown. Serve hot.

CORNBREAD SALAD

There are oodles of recipes for this delightful salad. This is the one I've been making for years and it's beautiful served in a trifle dish.

YIELD: 10 SERVINGS

1 pan-cooked cornbread (use Old-Fashioned Cornbread recipe, page 195), cooled
2 (16-ounce) cans pinto beans, drained (not rinsed)
1 cup chopped red bell peppers
1 cup chopped tomatoes
$^1/_2$ cup chopped green onions, green parts only
2 jalapeño peppers, seeded and finely chopped
2 cups shredded Cheddar cheese, divided
1 (15-ounce) can whole kernel corn, drained and divided
6 slices bacon, cooked, crumbled, and divided
3 tablespoons dry ranch dressing mix
1 (8-ounce) container sour cream
1 cup mayonnaise

Crumble half of the cooked cornbread in the bottom of a trifle dish or a large serving bowl. Top with one can of the beans.

In a separate bowl, combine the bell peppers, tomatoes, onions, and jalapeños. Spoon half of the mixture on top of the beans. Top with half of the cheese, half of the corn, and half of the bacon. Repeat the layering.

In a small bowl, combine the dressing mix, sour cream, and mayonnaise. Spread evenly over the top of the salad. Cover and refrigerate at least 4 hours before serving.

CORNBREAD WAFFLES

Serve these nontraditional waffles with Classic Creamed Chicken (page 148) or as an accompaniment to soup.

YIELD: 12 SERVINGS

1½ cups plain cornmeal
½ cup all-purpose flour
2½ teaspoons baking powder
¾ teaspoon salt
2 tablespoons sugar
1 egg
1½ cups milk
4 tablespoons unsalted butter, melted
1½ cups frozen shoepeg corn, thawed

Preheat the waffle iron after greasing lightly.

In a medium bowl, combine the cornmeal, flour, baking powder, salt, and sugar. In a separate bowl, combine the egg, milk, butter, and corn. Add to the cornmeal mixture, stirring until moistened.

Pour ½-cup measures into the waffle iron and cook until crisp. Repeat with the remaining batter. Serve warm.

CORN DOG NIBLETS

These bite-size appetizers are perfect for kids of all ages. Use wooden picks to make dipping into the batter easier.

YIELD: 10 SERVINGS

Vegetable or canola oil
1 cup all-purpose flour
⅔ cup plain cornmeal
1 tablespoon sugar
1½ teaspoons baking powder
1 teaspoon salt
2 tablespoons melted bacon drippings
1 egg
1 cup buttermilk
½ teaspoon baking soda
1 pound frankfurters

Pour the oil to a depth of 4 inches in a Dutch oven. Place over medium-high heat and bring to 375°F.

Meanwhile, in a mixing bowl, combine the flour, cornmeal, sugar, baking powder, and salt. Make a well in the center and set aside.

In a separate bowl, whisk together the bacon drippings, egg, buttermilk, and baking soda. Stir into the cornmeal mixture, blending well. Set aside.

Cut each frankfurter into 8 pieces. Dip into the batter and carefully drop into the hot oil. Do not overcrowd the pan. Fry 3 to 4 minutes, or until golden brown, turning as necessary. Drain on paper towels and repeat with the remaining pieces. Serve warm with prepared mustard and ketchup.

Note: For whole corn dogs, insert wooden sticks or skewers into the frankfurters and fry about 10 minutes, or until golden.

CORN LIGHT BREAD

This cornbread will not have the crispy crust of traditional recipes. Instead, it has more of a cake-like texture. Serve it with barbecue.

YIELD: 1 LOAF

2 cups plus 1 tablespoon self-rising cornmeal, divided

1 cup self-rising flour

$^1/_3$ cup sugar

$^1/_4$ teaspoon baking soda

2 cups buttermilk

$^1/_4$ pound (1 stick) unsalted butter, melted

1 egg, lightly beaten

Preheat the oven to 400°F. Lightly grease a loaf pan. Sprinkle 1 tablespoon of the cornmeal on the bottom of the pan and set aside.

In a large mixing bowl, combine the remaining 2 cups cornmeal, the flour, sugar, and baking soda. In a separate bowl, combine the buttermilk, butter, and egg. Add the buttermilk mixture to the cornmeal mixture, stirring until blended. Pour the batter into the prepared pan.

Bake 40 minutes, or until lightly browned. Cool in the pan on a wire rack 5 minutes before transferring to a wire rack to cool completely.

CORNMEAL MUSH

Think of this as a hot cooked cereal. In the South, it is typically served for breakfast with syrup.

YIELD: 6 SERVINGS

2 tablespoons bacon drippings

$2^1/_4$ cups plain cornmeal

$1^1/_2$ teaspoons salt

1 teaspoon baking powder

1 cup heavy cream

$^1/_2$ cup water

Place the bacon drippings in a large cast-iron skillet over medium heat.

Combine the cornmeal, salt, and baking powder in a mixing bowl. Add the cream and water, stirring well. Pour the batter into the hot skillet. Lower the heat and cook 15 minutes, stirring occasionally. Serve warm.

CORN PONES

This is cornbread made without eggs that is hand shaped into ovals and baked.

YIELD: 10 TO 12 SERVINGS

2 cups plain cornmeal

1 teaspoon baking powder

$^1/_2$ teaspoon salt

1 tablespoon melted vegetable shortening

$^1/_2$ cup milk

Preheat the oven to 425°F. Lightly grease a baking sheet and set aside.

In a large mixing bowl, combine the cornmeal, baking powder, and salt. Make a well in the center and add the shortening and milk, stirring to form a stiff dough.

Form into four oval cakes and place on the prepared baking sheet. Bake 30 minutes, or until golden brown. Serve warm.

CRACKLING CORNBREAD

Cracklings are crunchy pieces of rendered pork fat that are crispy and brown. They are sold in specialty markets and in some supermarkets. They add a delicious and unmatched texture to this cornbread.

YIELD: 10 SERVINGS

1½ cups plain cornmeal

¼ cup all-purpose flour

1 teaspoon salt

1 teaspoon baking soda

1 egg, lightly beaten

2 cups buttermilk

1 cup cracklings

Preheat the oven to 450°F. Place a greased 10-inch cast-iron skillet in the oven to heat while the desired temperature is reached.

Meanwhile, in a large bowl, mix together the cornmeal, flour, salt, and baking soda. Add the egg and buttermilk, stirring just until moistened. Fold in the cracklings.

Pour the batter into the preheated skillet. Bake 25 minutes, or until golden brown. Serve warm.

CREAMY CORNBREAD

If for no other use, make it a point to save bacon drippings for this recipe. Just refrigerate the drippings until you are ready to use.

YIELD: 4 TO 6 SERVINGS

3 cups plain cornmeal

2 teaspoons salt

1 teaspoon bacon drippings or melted shortening

1¼ cups boiling water

2 eggs

1 cup heavy cream, at room temperature

2 teaspoons baking powder

In a mixing bowl, combine the cornmeal, salt, and drippings. Add the boiling water and stir until well mixed. Set aside to cool 1 hour.

Preheat the oven to 400°F. Place a greased 10-inch cast-iron skillet in the oven to heat while the desired temperature is reached.

Add the eggs, cream, and baking powder to the cornmeal mixture. Beat well and pour into the preheated skillet. Bake 30 to 35 minutes, or until golden brown. Transfer to a serving plate and cut into wedges. Serve hot.

CRISPY SOUTHERN HUSHPUPPIES

This unique name originated when hunters would gather around the fire at the end of the day. The hunting dogs would start barking and begging for food. The cook would drop bits of cornbread batter in the oil and throw them to the hungry dogs, with the admonition, "Hush puppy!" Brilliant!

YIELD: 12 SERVINGS

Vegetable or canola oil for frying

3⅓ cups plain cornmeal

1¼ cups all-purpose flour

2 tablespoons baking powder

2 teaspoons salt

¾ teaspoon black pepper

3 eggs

1¼ cups milk

⅓ cup finely chopped onion

½ cup vegetable oil

Pour the oil 4 inches deep in a cast-iron skillet.

Place over medium-high heat and bring to 350°F.

Meanwhile, in a large mixing bowl, combine the cornmeal, flour, baking powder, salt, and pepper.

Make a well in the center and add the eggs, milk, onion, and oil. Stir until blended.

With an ice cream scoop, carefully transfer balls of dough to the hot oil. Fry 5 minutes, or until golden brown. Drain on paper towels. Serve hot.

HOE CAKES

These unique cakes were named by field workers who cooked small, flat pieces of cornbread on a hoe held over an open fire.

YIELD: 6 SERVINGS

4 tablespoons bacon drippings, divided
2 cups plain cornmeal
1 cup all-purpose flour
2 teaspoons baking powder
1 teaspoon salt
2 tablespoons sugar
1 cup milk

In a large skillet over medium heat, melt 3 tablespoons of the drippings. In a mixing bowl, combine the cornmeal, flour, baking powder, salt, and sugar. Add the remaining tablespoon of drippings and milk. Mix well (the batter will be stiff).

Drop spoonfuls of the batter into the hot skillet and brown on one side 2 to 3 minutes before turning. Turn only once. Drain on paper towels and repeat with the remaining batter. Serve warm or at room temperature.

GARLIC CHIVE CORN STICKS

If you don't have a cornstick pan, it's time to go shopping. It's a cast-iron pan with divided, corn-shaped sections or sticks. Season the individual sticks like you would an entire pan. This cooks in a flash.

YIELD: 18 STICKS

1¼ cups plain cornmeal
¾ cup all-purpose flour
1 tablespoon plus 1 teaspoon baking powder
1 tablespoon sugar
¾ teaspoon garlic salt
¾ teaspoon garlic powder
1 tablespoon chopped fresh chives
2 eggs, lightly beaten
1 cup milk
¼ cup vegetable oil

stick pan in the oven while the desired temperature is reached.

Meanwhile, in a large bowl, combine the cornmeal, flour, baking powder, sugar, garlic salt, garlic powder, and chives. In a separate bowl, combine the eggs, milk, and oil.

Add the egg mixture to the cornmeal mixture, stirring just until moistened. Spoon the batter into the preheated pan, filling two-thirds full. Bake 12 minutes, or until golden brown. Serve warm.

HOT PEPPER CORNBREAD

Serrano chiles are hot, so if you can't handle the heat, omit them from this dish completely or cut in half the amount called for in the recipe.

YIELD: 8 TO 10 SERVINGS

$1\frac{1}{4}$ cups plain cornmeal
1 cup all-purpose flour
1 tablespoon sugar
1 tablespoon baking powder
1 teaspoon salt
$\frac{1}{4}$ teaspoon baking soda
1 tablespoon vegetable oil
4 serrano chiles, seeded and finely chopped
3 garlic cloves, minced
1 red bell pepper, seeded and finely chopped
1 green bell pepper, seeded and finely chopped
1 egg, lightly beaten
1 cup buttermilk
$\frac{1}{3}$ cup vegetable shortening or lard, melted
5 tablespoons unsalted butter, melted
2 tablespoons plain yogurt
1 (11-ounce) can white shoepeg corn, drained
2 tablespoons chopped fresh cilantro

Preheat the oven to 450°F. Place a greased 10-inch cast-iron skillet in the oven to heat while the desired temperature is reached.

Meanwhile, in a mixing bowl, stir together the cornmeal, flour, sugar, baking powder, salt, and baking soda. Make a well in the center and set aside.

Place the oil in a large skillet over medium heat. When hot, add the chiles, garlic, red and green bell peppers. Cook 3 minutes and set aside.

In a separate bowl, whisk together the eggs, buttermilk, shortening, butter, and yogurt. Stir in the corn and cilantro. Add to the flour mixture, along with the pepper mixture. Stir until moistened and transfer to the prepared pan.

Bake 25 minutes, or until golden brown. Let cool 5 minutes in the pan. Transfer to a serving plate and serve warm.

LOADED HUSHPUPPIES

These "puppies" are practically a salad, with just a hint of spice. Catfish, here's your buddy!

YIELD: 5½ DOZEN

Vegetable oil for frying
5 cups self-rising cornmeal
1 (14.75-ounce) can cream-style corn
1 (10-ounce) can diced tomatoes and green chiles
2 large white onions, peeled and chopped
1 banana pepper, seeded and chopped
1 green bell pepper, seeded and chopped
2 cups buttermilk
2 eggs, lightly beaten
1 teaspoon Creole seasoning

Pour the oil to a depth of 2 inches in a large skillet. Place over medium-high heat and bring to 375°F.

Meanwhile, stir together the cornmeal, corn, and tomatoes and green chiles. Add the onions, banana pepper, and bell pepper. Stir in the buttermilk, eggs, and seasoning.

Carefully drop tablespoons of the batter into the hot oil. Fry 2 minutes, or until golden brown, turning if necessary. Serve hot.

NO-EGG CORNBREAD

When I first experimented with this recipe, I didn't think it would work, but it's nice and light thanks to the combination of cornmeal and flour.

YIELD: 8 SERVINGS

2 cups plain cornmeal

6 tablespoons all-purpose flour

1 tablespoon baking powder

$^1\!/_2$ teaspoon salt

$^1\!/_4$ teaspoon baking soda

$1^1\!/_2$ cups buttermilk

6 tablespoons unsalted butter, melted

Preheat the oven to 400°F. Place a greased 9-inch cast-iron skillet in the oven to heat while the desired temperature is reached.

Meanwhile, in a large bowl, stir together the cornmeal, flour, baking powder, salt, and baking soda. Make a well in the center and add the buttermilk and butter. Stir until evenly moistened.

Pour the batter into the preheated skillet. Bake 25 minutes, and then cool 5 minutes in the skillet. Transfer to a serving plate and cut into wedges.

OLD-FASHIONED CORNBREAD

This is the recipe my grandmother always made, so naturally, it is my "special" cornbread!

YIELD: 8 SERVINGS

2 cups plain cornmeal

$^1\!/_4$ cup all-purpose flour

$1^1\!/_2$ teaspoons baking powder

1 teaspoon salt

$1^1\!/_2$ cups buttermilk

2 eggs, beaten

2 tablespoons bacon drippings

Preheat the oven to 400°F. Place a greased 9-inch cast-iron skillet in the oven to heat while the desired temperature is reached.

Meanwhile, in a mixing bowl, combine the cornmeal, flour, baking powder, and salt. Add the buttermilk, eggs, and drippings. Stir only until all ingredients are mixed well.

Pour the batter into the preheated skillet. Bake 25 to 28 minutes, or until golden brown on top. Cool 5 minutes in the skillet. Transfer to a serving plate and cut into wedges. Serve hot.

PIMIENTO CHEESE CORNBREAD

This cornbread could be a meal for me. I love the change in texture it has with the cheese and the dots of pimiento throughout the slices.

YIELD: 12 SERVINGS

1 cup plain cornmeal

1 cup all-purpose flour

$^1\!/_4$ cup sugar

2 teaspoons baking powder

$^1\!/_2$ teaspoon salt

2 cups shredded Cheddar cheese

1 (4-ounce) jar diced pimiento peppers, drained

1 cup milk

1 egg, beaten

$^1\!/_4$ cup vegetable or canola oil

Preheat the oven to 400°F. Place a greased 10-inch cast-iron skillet in the oven to heat while the desired temperature is reached.

Meanwhile, in a large bowl, combine the cornmeal, flour, sugar, baking powder, and salt. Add the cheese, pimientos, milk, egg, and oil, stirring until moist.

Pour the batter into the preheated skillet. Bake 45 minutes, or until the top is golden brown. Immediately transfer to a serving plate and cool 5 minutes before slicing.

* * *

SAUSAGE-CORNBREAD CASSEROLE

One dish and one meal that can be served for breakfast, brunch, lunch, or dinner.

YIELD: 6 SERVINGS

1 pound pork sausage, hot or mild

1 cup chopped onions

1 garlic clove, minced

1 (28-ounce) can whole tomatoes, undrained

1 (4-ounce) can chopped green chiles

1 cup whole kernel corn

1 teaspoon chili powder

1 cup plain cornmeal

$^2/_3$ cup all-purpose flour

2 teaspoons baking powder

1 teaspoon sugar

$^1/_2$ teaspoon salt

1 egg beaten

$^2/_3$ cup milk

$^1/_4$ cup vegetable oil

In a large skillet over medium heat, cook the sausage until it crumbles and is no longer pink. Drain and return the pork to the skillet. Add the onions, garlic, tomatoes, chiles, corn, and chili powder. Simmer 20 minutes.

Meanwhile, preheat the oven to 375°F. Lightly grease an 8-inch square baking dish and set aside.

In a mixing bowl, stir together the cornmeal, flour, baking powder, sugar, and salt. Make a well in the center. Add the egg, milk, and oil and stir just until moistened.

Layer the sausage and vegetable mixture in the bottom of the prepared baking dish. Spread the cornbread batter on top of the vegetables. Bake 40 minutes, or until golden brown. Serve warm.

* * *

SOUR CREAM CORN STICKS

Just add soup, stew, or a green salad and the meal is done!

YIELD: 16 CORN STICKS

3 eggs, lightly beaten

1 cup self-rising cornmeal

1 (8-$^3/_4$ ounce can) cream-style corn

1 (8 ounce) container sour cream

$^1/_4$ cup vegetable oil

Preheat the oven to 400°F. Heat a lightly greased cornstick pan in the oven while the desired temperature is reached.

Meanwhile, in a large bowl, combine the eggs, cornmeal, corn, sour cream, and oil. Stir just until the dry ingredients are moistened.

Spoon the batter into the preheated sticks. Bake 16 to 18 minutes, or until golden brown. Serve warm.

FESTIVALS: South Pittsburg, Tennessee, is the home of the National Cornbread Festival.

DO YOU HAVE LEFTOVER CORNBREAD? Use it to make the ultimate Southern snack! Crumble it into a tall glass (never a bowl!) and pour milk or buttermilk to the top of the glass. Enjoy with a long-handled iced-tea spoon.

SQUASH PUPPIES

You can make these hushpuppies with any type of winter squash. I like to serve these with potato or mushroom soup.

YIELD: 24 HUSHPUPPIES

1 acorn squash, cut in half and seeded
Vegetable oil
2 cups self-rising cornmeal
$1/4$ cup all-purpose flour
1 egg, lightly beaten
$1/2$ cup milk
$1/2$ cup finely chopped onion

Preheat the oven to 375°F. Place the squash cut side down in a shallow baking dish. Add water to a depth of $1/2$ inch. Bake 45 minutes, or until the squash is tender. Drain and cool.

Pour the oil to a depth of 2 inches in a large cast-iron skillet. Bring to 350°F.

Meanwhile, remove the pulp from the squash and discard the shells. Purée in a food processor until smooth. Measure $1^1/4$ cups of purée and set aside. Reserve any remaining purée for another use.

In a mixing bowl, combine the cornmeal and flour. Make a well in the center and add the purée, egg, milk, and onions. Stir just until moistened.

Carefully drop tablespoons of batter in the hot oil. Fry 2 minutes, or until golden, turning once. Drain on paper towels and serve warm.

THANKSGIVING DRESSING

This is the recipe my mother made every year at Thanksgiving. It was my favorite part of the meal and quite frankly, is the best dressing in the world!

YIELD: 12 TO 14 SERVINGS

4 to 5 cups chicken or turkey stock, divided
2 large white onions, peeled and chopped
6 celery stalks, chopped
1 recipe Buttermilk Cornbread (page 188), cooked, cooled and crumbled
$1/2$ loaf sliced white bread, crumbled
$1^1/4$ tablespoons dried sage
$1^1/4$ tablespoons black pepper
$1/4$ pound (1 stick) unsalted butter
4 eggs

Lightly grease a large roasting pan and set aside.

In a large saucepan over medium heat, combine 1 cup of the stock with the onions and celery. Cook until tender, about 7 minutes.

Meanwhile, place the crumbled cornbread, white bread, sage, pepper, and butter in a very large mixing bowl. Add the cooked onion mixture and all but 1 cup of the remaining stock. Stir well to combine, using the remaining stock if necessary.

When the mixture is the consistency of thick raw cornbread batter, add the eggs. Pour into the prepared pan and cover tightly with aluminum foil. Refrigerate overnight.

Preheat the oven to 375°F. Bake 1 hour, or until firm but not hard. Let rest 10 minutes before serving. Serve warm with Giblet Gravy (page 235).

CRAWFISH

WANT TO IMMEDIATELY KNOW IF YOU ARE TALKING TO A TRUE SOUTHERNER? ASK THEM TO pronounce the name of the small, freshwater crustacean that looks like a miniature version of lobster. An imposter will say "crayfish" and you'll know they "aren't from around here." A Southerner will say either "crawfish" or "crawdad." Either of the latter terms is acceptable in polite conversation. Every now and then, you'll hear them referred to as "mudbugs," but that doesn't sound as nice.

Thanks to the mighty waters of the Mississippi basin, crawfish has inched its way into Cajun and Creole cuisines like no other competitor. This tiny crustacean has a huge following, particularly in Louisiana. That's the original home of the crawfish boil, which is a major dinner food reserved for family reunions, company, or any kind of special occasion we can dream of creating. If you've never experienced one, we Southerners can only say one thing: "You poor thing!"

In the event of a crawfish boil, there is no need to worry about pulling out the nice dishes or even silverware for setting the table. Forget a centerpiece too because frequently, the entire cooked batch is dumped right in the middle of the table . . . on a clean plastic table covering or layers of newspaper, of course. We weren't raised in a barn!

It is a delicacy that requires plenty of paper napkins or rolls of paper towels when served. That's because there hasn't been a food utensil invented that works on boiled crawfish better than human fingers. The sweet meat has to be picked or sucked out of the small shells. It's fine eating. Fine!

Cooking: Soaking the crawfish in salted water before cooking reduces the size of the black vein that runs down the back of the tail. A short cooking period and low temperatures prevents toughening of the meat and safe guards against moisture loss. If cooked too long or at too high a temperature, the crawfish meat will be shrunken and tough. Like lobster, crawfish turns bright red when cooked.

Peeling: Peeling the cooked crawfish is easier than you might think. Holding the body firmly in one hand, gently twist the crawfish tail from the body. Unwrap two or three sections of the tail shell then pinch the end of the tail while pulling out the meat.

Selection: Crawfish can be purchased live or cooked, whole or peeled, fresh or frozen. It takes approximately ten pounds of live crawfish to yield one pound of peeled tails. Crawfish fat can also be purchased and is the key to flavoring most crawfish dishes.

Storage: Store live crawfish in the container in which they come. Keep it in the refrigerator and use within one day. When buying cooked crawfish, make sure they have curled tails. This means they were alive until cooked and will be the freshest.

BAYOU BOILED CRAWFISH

Get your paper napkins and cold beer ready. This is best served straight from the cooking pot. The recipe can easily be doubled or tripled.

YIELD: 4 SERVINGS

7 cups water

1 white onion, peeled and quartered

1 lemon, quartered

1 bay leaf

2 large garlic cloves, peeled and halved

1 tablespoon salt

3 pounds whole crawfish

Place the water in a large Dutch oven over medium-high heat and bring to a boil.

Meanwhile, tie the onion, lemon, bay leaf, and garlic together in a large piece of cheesecloth. Add to the boiling water, along with the salt. Boil 5 minutes.

Add the crawfish and cook 5 minutes longer or until the shells turn bright red. Drain and discard the cheesecloth bag. Serve immediately.

"BEYOND THE BAYOU" CRAWFISH REMOULADE

The French influence in this appetizer is clearly seen and deliciously tasted.

YIELD: 12 SERVINGS

$\frac{1}{2}$ cup tarragon vinegar

$\frac{1}{4}$ cup prepared horseradish

2 tablespoons ketchup

1 tablespoon paprika

1 teaspoon salt

$\frac{1}{2}$ teaspoon cayenne

1 garlic clove, minced

1 cup canola or vegetable oil

$\frac{1}{2}$ cup finely minced green onions

$\frac{1}{2}$ cup finely minced celery

3 pounds cooked crawfish

Fresh parsley for garnish

In a large bowl, whisk together the vinegar, horseradish, ketchup, paprika, salt, cayenne, and garlic. Pouring in a slow, steady stream, whisk in the oil until well blended. Stir in the onions and celery. Gently stir in the crawfish, tossing evenly to coat.

Cover and refrigerate at least 4 hours before serving. When ready to serve, garnish with fresh-snipped parsley. Serve with crackers.

CHILL CHASIN' CRAWFISH STEW

This gumbo-style stew is hearty, spicy, and full of tender crawfish.

YIELD: 6 SERVINGS

4 tablespoons unsalted butter

$\frac{1}{3}$ cup all-purpose flour

1 cup chopped onions

1 cup chopped celery

1 jalapeño pepper, seeded and minced

2 cups water

1 (14.5-ounce) can crushed or diced tomatoes

$1\frac{1}{2}$ teaspoons salt

$\frac{1}{4}$ teaspoon black pepper

3 cups crawfish tails

1 (10-ounce) package frozen sliced okra

1 medium green bell pepper, seeded and chopped

$\frac{1}{4}$ cup chopped fresh parsley

2 teaspoons gumbo filé powder

3 cups hot cooked rice

In a large Dutch oven over medium heat, melt the butter. Whisk in the flour and stir constantly until the roux is the color of chocolate, 10 to 12 minutes. Stir in the onions, celery, and jalapeño pepper. Cook 3 minutes longer.

Stir in the water, tomatoes, salt, and pepper. Cook 15 minutes. Add the crawfish, okra, bell pepper, and parsley. Simmer 10 minutes, stirring frequently. Stir in the filé powder. Ladle the rice into warm soup bowls. Top with the stew and serve warm.

CRAWFISH CAKES

Not your usual cornmeal cakes! I patterned these after enjoying them at a restaurant named Pearl's on the mountain in Sewanee, Tennessee.

YIELD: 8 SERVINGS

2 cups corn oil

3 pounds crawfish

$^1/_2$ pound trimmed white bread, cut in $^1/_2$-inch cubes

2 tablespoons Old Bay seasoning

$^1/_2$ teaspoon ground white pepper

$^3/_4$ cup chopped pimientos

2 tablespoons chopped fresh parsley

1 egg

$1^1/_2$ cups mayonnaise

1 teaspoon prepared mustard

1 teaspoon lemon juice

1 teaspoon Worcestershire sauce

Pour the oil in a large skillet and place over medium-high heat. Bring to 350°F.

Meanwhile, mix together the crawfish, bread cubes, seasoning, white pepper, pimientos, and parsley. In a separate bowl, beat the egg and stir in the mayonnaise, mustard, juice, and Worcestershire.

Stir into the crawfish mixture and combine to a meat loaf-like texture. The mixture should not be too dry or too wet. Adjust accordingly with more bread.

Divide the mixture into 16 equal portions (about 4 ounces each) and shape into patties. Carefully place a few patties at a time into the hot oil and cook each side 4 to 5 minutes, or until golden brown. Drain on paper towels and repeat with the remaining patties. Serve immediately.

CRAWFISH ÉTOUFFÉE

This popular Cajun dish is a wonderfully spicy stew served over rice. The word comes from the French term etouffer *which means "to smother."*

YIELD: 6 SERVINGS

2 pounds crawfish tails with fat

2 teaspoons hot sauce

$^1/_2$ teaspoon red pepper, divided

$^1/_4$ cup canola or vegetable oil

$^1/_4$ cup all-purpose flour

2 celery stalks, chopped

2 white onions, peeled and chopped

2 large green bell peppers, seeded and chopped

$^1/_2$ cup chopped green onions

$^1/_4$ cup water

$^1/_2$ teaspoon salt

$^1/_4$ teaspoon black pepper

$^1/_4$ cup chopped fresh parsley

3 cups hot cooked rice

Remove the fat packet from the crawfish tails and set aside. Place the crawfish in a medium bowl and sprinkle with the hot sauce and $^1/_4$ teaspoon of the red pepper. Set aside.

In a large Dutch oven over medium heat, combine the oil and flour. Cook, stirring constantly, 10 to 12 minutes, or until the roux resembles the color of chocolate.

Stir in the celery, onions, bell peppers, and green onions. Cook, stirring frequently, until tender, about 5 minutes. Add the crawfish and water and reduce the heat to low. Cook 15 minutes, stirring occasionally.

Stir in 2 tablespoons of the crawfish fat. If there is more in the packet, refrigerate or freeze for a later use. Add the salt, black pepper, and the remaining ¼ teaspoon of the red pepper. Simmer 5 minutes and stir in the parsley. Serve hot over the cooked rice.

CREOLE CRAWFISH JAMBALAYA

This dish varies widely from cook to cook, but I've never had one that wasn't divine. The name is believed to be derived from the French word jambon *meaning "ham," which was a main ingredient in early jambalayas.*

YIELD: 10 SERVINGS

1 pound Italian sausage, sliced
1 green bell pepper, seeded and chopped
1 cup chopped celery
1 cup chopped onions
½ cup chopped green onions
2 garlic cloves, minced
1 cup uncooked rice
2 cups water
1 (14.5-ounce) can diced tomatoes
½ cup diced tomatoes with green chiles
2 teaspoons Creole seasoning
1 pound crawfish tails

In a large skillet over medium heat, cook the sausage, pepper, celery, onions, green onions, and garlic until tender but not brown, around 4 minutes. Stir in the rice, water, tomatoes, tomatoes and green chiles, and Creole seasoning. Simmer 10 minutes, stirring frequently. Stir in the crawfish and simmer 10 minutes longer, or until the crawfish is done. Serve warm.

FRIED CRAWFISH TAILS

Evaporated milk adds another layer of sweetness to these fried delicacies. Don't worry about ever having to store leftovers of this dish.

YIELD: 6 APPETIZER SERVINGS

Vegetable oil for frying
1 egg, lightly beaten
¼ cup evaporated milk
½ teaspoon prepared mustard
¾ teaspoon garlic salt
¼ teaspoon black pepper
1 cup all-purpose flour
½ cup plain cornmeal
½ teaspoon baking powder
2 pounds large crawfish tails

Pour the oil to a depth of 2 inches in a large cast iron skillet. Place over medium-high heat and bring to 375°F.

Meanwhile, in a medium bowl, whisk together the egg, milk, mustard, garlic salt, and pepper. Blend well and set aside. In a shallow bowl, combine the flour, cornmeal, and baking powder, stirring well.

Dip the crawfish tails in the egg mixture and dredge in the flour mixture. Place on a wax paper–lined plate until half the tails are ready to fry. Carefully drop in the hot oil and cook until golden brown, about 2 minutes. Drain on paper towels and repeat with the remaining crawfish. Serve warm with cocktail sauce or lemon butter.

····································

CRAWFISH DRESSING

Cornbread is still there, but this dressing is enhanced with succulent crawfish for an unforgettable reason to give thanks.

YIELD: 12 SERVINGS

10 tablespoons unsalted butter

1 large white onion, peeled and chopped

1 large green bell pepper, seeded and chopped

1 recipe Basic Southern Cornbread (page 188), crumbled

1 pound cooked crawfish tails

2 cups chicken stock

2 eggs, lightly beaten

$1/4$ cup chopped fresh parsley

1 teaspoon black pepper

1 teaspoon red pepper

1 teaspoon white pepper

$1/4$ teaspoon garlic salt

Preheat the oven to 350°F. Lightly grease a 13 x 9-inch baking dish and set aside.

In a large skillet over medium-high heat, melt the butter. Add the onion and bell pepper. Cook 5 minutes, or until tender.

In a large mixing bowl, combine the onion mixture with the cornbread. Stir in the crawfish, stock, eggs, parsley, black pepper, red pepper, white pepper, and garlic salt. When all the ingredients are moistened, transfer to the prepared baking dish.

Bake 1 hour, or until firm and golden brown. Let stand 10 minutes before serving. Serve warm.

"SAVOR THE FLAVOR" CRAWFISH CREOLE

You can always recognize Creole cooking by the tomatoes. Cajun cooking utilizes more spices. This dish freezes well.

YIELD: 10 SERVINGS

1 cup vegetable oil

1 cup all-purpose flour

2 cups chopped onions

1 cup chopped celery

$1/2$ cup chopped green bell pepper

3 garlic cloves, minced

2 teaspoons salt

1 teaspoon Worcestershire sauce

$1/2$ teaspoon red pepper

$1/2$ teaspoon black pepper

1 (14.5-ounce) can chopped tomatoes

1 (6-ounce) can tomato paste

6 cups water

3 pounds peeled crawfish tails

Hot cooked rice

2 tablespoons chopped fresh parsley

2 tablespoons chopped green onions

In a large Dutch oven over medium heat, combine the oil and flour. Cook, stirring constantly, 10 to 12 minutes, or until the roux resembles chocolate.

Stir in the onions, celery, bell peppers, garlic, salt, Worcestershire, red pepper, and black pepper. Cook 4 minutes. Add the tomatoes and tomato paste, stirring well, and cook 5 minutes.

Stir in the water and bring to a boil. Reduce the heat to low and simmer 1 hour. Add the crawfish and simmer 10 minutes, or until the crawfish are done. Spoon over hot rice and garnish the tops with the parsley and green onions. Serve hot.

CUCUMBERS

THERE ARE DAYS IN THE SOUTH THAT START OUT HOT AND ONLY GET HOTTER. THE GOAL IS TO somehow get your work done outside, but stay as cool as possible. You don't even want to eat warm food, so chilled dishes are practically a necessity. Luckily those steamy days just happen to match the peak of fresh cucumber season.

This prolific member of the gourd family has been multiplying to extremes in Southern gardens for centuries. If you've ever planted cucumbers, you know what I mean. The relationship between gardener and produce can quickly progress from love to not-so-much-love. Why? The plant seems to try to produce enough to feed multitudes. In that respect, cucumber plants are a lot like zucchini and yellow squash.

But unlike those other vegetables, cucumbers do not have their versatility when it comes to preservation. While zucchini and summer squash varieties freeze beautifully, cucumbers do not. They become soggy and almost seem to become instantly water-logged. They are also not suitable for drying. That's why you have many a Southern gardener saying, "Prolific is not always terrific."

The old standby is to toss the raw, crisp rounds into salads. However the overabundance can go beyond the salad bowl into dips, sauces, soups, and sandwiches. Oh, and don't forget the lowly pickle. Who would guess that something preserved in vinegar could taste so marvelous? It has the kind of sour power that I truly relish! Get it?

Nutrition: Cucumbers are great sources of vitamin C and dietary fiber. Cucumbers are very low in calories with fair amounts of vitamin A, potassium, iron, and calcium. Six slices with the peel still intact has only five calories because it's so full of water.

Selection: Pick solid green cucumbers with no signs of yellow streaks at the base, which is a sign of overmaturity. Cucumbers should feel firm and have no water-soaked spots or pitting. Unless purchasing hothouse types (sometimes marketed as Burpless or English and are virtually seedless), avoid any exceptionally large cucumbers. Although the seeds are edible when it is mature, if allowed to age too much, those seeds become hard and any cucumber crispness flies out the window.

Storage: Keep cucumbers in the crisper drawer of the refrigerator. Adequate humidity is important so that shriveling doesn't occur due to moisture loss. They will keep up to a week or longer if kept refrigerated.

DILL PICKLES

Pickles are high acid products that are brined, which means they must be processed in a boiling water bath, which vacuum seals the jars and destroys yeasts, molds, and bacteria that may cause the products to spoil.

YIELD: 6 PINTS

3 cups white vinegar

3 cups water

6 tablespoons pickling salt

12 sprigs fresh dill sprigs

6 garlic cloves, peeled

3 teaspoons mustard seeds

30 (4-inch-long) cucumbers, trimmed

In a medium saucepan, bring the vinegar, water, and pickling salt to a boil over medium-high heat. Meanwhile place one sprig of dill, 1 garlic clove, and $\frac{1}{2}$ teaspoon of the mustard seeds in the bottom of each pint canning jar. Pack the cucumbers into the jars.

When the jars are half filled with cucumbers, add one more dill sprig and complete packing with cucumbers. Fill with the brine solution and leave $\frac{1}{2}$-inch headspace. Remove any air bubbles, wipe the jar rims, and adjust the lids. Process 10 minutes in a boiling water bath. (See page 12 for detailed canning instructions.)

Place on a wire rack away from drafts to cool completely. Store at room temperature.

ICE WATER PICKLES

The name of these crispy pickles comes from the ice water soak they receive prior to being packed into hot canning jars.

YIELD: 6 QUARTS

6 pounds medium cucumbers

Ice

3 quarts white vinegar

1 cup pickling salt

3 cups sugar

36 small pickling onions, peeled

6 (2-inch-long) slices celery

2 tablespoons mustard seeds

Cut each cucumber into 4 to 8 spears. Place in a large bowl and soak in ice water 3 hours. Replace the ice as needed.

Bring the vinegar, pickling salt, and sugar to a boil over medium-high heat.

Meanwhile, drain the cucumbers and pack into hot canning jars. Add 6 onions, 1 celery slice, and 1 teaspoon of mustard seeds to each quart jar. Pour the hot brine in each jar, leaving $\frac{1}{2}$-inch headspace.

Remove any air bubbles, wipe the rims, and adjust the lids. Process 10 minutes in a boiling water bath. (See page 12 for detailed canning instructions.)

Place on a wire rack away from drafts to cool completely. Store at room temperature.

QUICK SOUR PICKLES

These pickles are easy to prepare and have a tart flavor. They develop a better flavor if you allow them to stand at room temperature three weeks before using.

YIELD: 8 PINTS

$\frac{1}{2}$ gallon cider vinegar

2 cups water

$\frac{1}{2}$ cup pickling salt

½ cup sugar

¼ cup mustard seeds

25 medium cucumbers, sliced lengthwise

Place the vinegar, water, pickling salt, sugar, and mustard seeds in a large stockpot and bring to a boil. Meanwhile, pack the cucumber slices into hot canning jars. Fill the jars with the hot liquid, leaving ½-inch headspace. Remove any air bubbles, wipe the jar rims, and adjust the lids. Process 10 minutes in a boiling water bath. (See page 12 for detailed canning instructions.)

Place on a wire rack away from drafts to cool completely. Store at room temperature.

SWEET PICKLE CHIPS

This is a marvelous blend of spices, sugar, and vinegar. The pickles have a firm, crisp texture and pungent flavor.

YIELD: 5 PINTS

4 pounds pickling cucumbers (3 to 4 inches long), cut into ¼-inch slices

5⅔ cups white vinegar, divided

3 tablespoons pickling salt

1 tablespoon mustard seeds

3½ cups sugar, divided

1 tablespoon whole allspice

2¼ teaspoons celery seeds

In a large stockpot, combine the cucumbers with 4 cups of the vinegar, the pickling salt, mustard seeds, and ½ cup of the sugar. Cover and simmer over medium-high heat, about 7 minutes, or until the cucumbers change color from bright to dull green.

Meanwhile in a medium saucepan, combine the remaining 1⅔ cups of the vinegar and the remaining 3 cups of the sugar with the allspice and celery seeds over medium-high heat. Bring to a boil.

Drain the cucumber slices and pack while still hot into canning jars. Cover with the hot syrup, leaving ½-inch headspace. Remove any air bubbles, wipe the jar rims, and adjust the lids. Process 10 minutes in a boiling water bath. (See page 12 for detailed canning instructions.)

Place on a wire rack away from drafts to cool completely. Store at room temperature.

SWEET PICKLE RELISH

This is the relish to use on grilled hot dogs or add to tuna or chicken salad.

YIELD: 4½ PINTS

4 cups chopped cucumbers

2 cups chopped sweet onions

1 green bell pepper, seeded and chopped

1 red bell pepper, seeded and chopped

½ cup pickling salt

1¾ cups sugar

1 cup cider vinegar

1½ teaspoons celery seeds

1½ teaspoon mustard seeds

In a large bowl, combine the cucumbers, onions, green bell pepper, and red bell pepper. Sprinkle evenly with the pickling salt. Cover with cold water and let stand 2 hours. Drain well.

Combine the sugar, vinegar, celery seeds, and mustard seeds in a large Dutch oven. Bring to a boil and add the vegetables. Return to a boil and reduce the heat to low. Simmer 10 minutes.

Pack the relish into hot canning jars, leaving ½-inch headspace. Remove any air bubbles, wipe the jar rims, and adjust the lids. Process 10 minutes in a boiling water bath. (See page 12 for detailed canning instructions.)

Place on a wire rack away from drafts to cool completely. Store at room temperature.

* * *

TREASURED TRADITION CUCUMBER SANDWICHES

They are cool when the weather is hot. They say welcome in the most Southern way when guests arrive. They are something you've heard of, but maybe never tried. It's time!

YIELD: 8 SERVINGS

1 large cucumber, peeled, seeded, and grated
1 (8-ounce) package cream cheese, softened
1 tablespoon mayonnaise
1 shallot, peeled and minced
$1/4$ teaspoon seasoned salt
1 (16-ounce) loaf white sandwich bread

Press the grated cucumbers between layers of paper towels to reduce excess moisture. Transfer to a medium bowl and add the cream cheese, mayonnaise, shallot, and seasoned salt. Blend well and set aside.

Remove the crusts from the bread. Using a 2-inch round cutter, cut the bread into rounds. Spread the cucumber filling evenly over half of the bread rounds. Top with the remaining rounds. Serve immediately or refrigerate in an airtight container up to 2 hours.

Celebration
November 14 is National Pickle Day.

"YA'LL COME" CUCUMBER SOUP

No heat required for this creamy soup that takes the edge off a midday meal or a sultry evening.

YIELD: 8 SERVINGS

2 large cucumbers, peeled, seeded, and coarsely chopped
1 green onion, coarsely chopped
1 tablespoon lemon juice
1 (8-ounce) container sour cream
1 cup half-and-half
1 tablespoon minced fresh dill
1 teaspoon salt
$1/2$ teaspoon white pepper
$1/8$ teaspoon hot sauce
Fresh dill sprigs for garnish

Process the cucumbers, onion, and lemon juice in a food processor until smooth. Transfer to a large mixing bowl. Add the sour cream, half-and-half, dill, salt, pepper, and hot sauce, stirring well to blend. Cover and refrigerate at least 2 hours. Serve in chilled soup bowls and garnish with fresh dill.

BOTANY: Cucumbers are members of the gourd family that include melons, pumpkins, zucchini, and lots of other items we call squash. You can easily see the family resemblance in the plants. Cucumbers are annual trailing or climbing vines with flowers of both sexes on the same plant. Botanically, cucumbers are fruits that we use as a vegetable. They depend on bees for pollination and can grow satisfactorily in a wide range of soil types.

EGGS

BEFORE I WAS EVER LET LOOSE IN THE KITCHEN TO ACTUALLY COOK ON MY OWN, I WAS allowed to peel cooled hard-cooked eggs. My mother loved to have the slices for lunch along with pieces of cheese and lettuce leaves. I liked them too, but preferred mine stuffed with billowy yolk mixtures.

From there, I had to learn how to separate eggs for making pies. Oh, the frustration I would feel if the least bit of egg yolk ended up in the whites. I knew I would have to start over because the meringue would never whip.

And speaking of meringue, Tina and I had to take turns with a hand beater when it came time to whip those whites because we didn't have an electric hand mixer. We would turn that beater until it quite literally felt like our arms were going to fall off. Thanks to that experience, I still believe the mixer is my favorite electric appliance!

Eventually, we became members of the 4-H Poultry Judging Team under the teaching of Mrs. McCluskey. I loved the part where we got to judge eggs that were broken out onto clear plates, ready for our eyes to evaluate. It was serious stuff to check the thickness of the whites and the stand of the yolks! Our competition never stood a chance!

Those childhood experiences showed me the marvelous versatility of a product that I would have a hard time cooking without. I love them scrambled, fried, baked, pickled, hard-cooked, stuffed, and poached. I adore the leavening they provide for cakes and breads, the thickening they give sauces and custards, the way they make coating adhere to battered or breaded foods, and the base they provide for the South's most beloved sandwich spread: mayonnaise! In short, they are hard to beat (pun intended!).

Peeling: Have you ever tried to peel hard-cooked eggs, only to have the shell come off in a million little pieces? The fresher the eggs, the harder it will be to peel. Older eggs peel in a snap!

Safety: Make it a rule never to consume raw or undercooked eggs. They pose a real danger of salmonella poisoning and should never be served. Don't purchase eggs with cracked shells.

Separating: Eggs separate best when the task is done straight from the refrigerator. I have an egg separator, but I rarely use it. Instead, I sharply tap the egg in the middle and gently pull the two halves apart. Then pass the yolk back and forth between the two shell halves letting the whites fall into a bowl.

Storage: Eggs should be stored with the large end up because it keeps the yolk centered, which is very important if you want to serve them stuffed. Store eggs in the refrigerator away from foods with strong odors. That's because the egg shell is porous and can easily absorb aromas from other foods. Eggs will age more in one day out of the refrigerator than they will if refrigerated one week.

BOILED CUSTARD

This is my grandmother's recipe that she made every year for the holidays. You'll never buy this in a carton again! It's a perfect holiday dessert.

YIELD: 10 SERVINGS

1 quart milk
5 eggs, separated
$1\frac{1}{3}$ cups sugar, divided
$5\frac{1}{4}$ tablespoons all-purpose flour
Pinch of salt

Place the milk in a large saucepan over medium heat. Bring to barely a simmer, around 7 minutes. Meanwhile, beat the egg yolks. Gradually add 1 cup of the sugar, the flour, and the salt. Mix well.

In a separate bowl, beat the egg whites until frothy. Increase the mixer speed to high and slowly add the remaining sugar, one tablespoon at a time. Set aside.

When the milk is hot, add $\frac{1}{4}$ cup to the beaten egg yolk mixture, stirring well. Add the remaining egg yolks and cook, stirring constantly until thick, about 10 minutes. Beat the custard at low speed into the egg whites. Cover and refrigerate overnight. Serve cold with a few drops of whiskey or pure vanilla extract.

CAMPFIRE CASSEROLE

Everything in this easy dish cooks in the same skillet. Whether you are preparing it over a fire outside or on your stove inside, it's done in a jiffy so you can grab the fishing pole and go!

YIELD: 6 SERVINGS

$\frac{1}{2}$ pound bacon

2 pounds red potatoes, diced
1 white onion, peeled and diced
1 teaspoon kosher salt, divided
$\frac{1}{2}$ teaspoon black pepper, divided
12 eggs
$1\frac{1}{2}$ cups shredded sharp Cheddar cheese

In a large skillet over medium heat, cook the bacon. Drain on paper towels and crumble when cool enough to handle.

Sauté the potatoes and onion in the pan drippings. Sprinkle with $\frac{1}{2}$ teaspoon of the salt and $\frac{1}{4}$ teaspoon of the pepper. Stir occasionally and cook about 20 minutes or until browned.

Meanwhile, whisk together the eggs and the remaining $\frac{1}{2}$ teaspoon of the salt and $\frac{1}{4}$ teaspoon of the pepper. Pour over the potato mixture and cook 4 to 5 minutes, or until the eggs are set, stirring if necessary. Sprinkle the top with the cheese and the crumbled bacon. Serve warm with ketchup, if desired.

FESTIVE BRUNCH EGGS

If there was ever a place for eggs to star, it's during brunch. This recipe uses a whole dozen and is layered, giving it a beautiful presentation.

YIELD: 10 SERVINGS

2 cups shredded sharp Cheddar cheese
4 tablespoons unsalted butter, divided
2 cups sliced fresh mushrooms
8 ounces sour cream
2 teaspoons Worcestershire sauce
1 cup half-and-half
2 tablespoons Dijon mustard
$\frac{1}{4}$ teaspoon salt
$\frac{1}{4}$ teaspoon black pepper
12 eggs, beaten

1 (2-ounce) jar diced pimientos, drained

2 tablespoons shredded Parmesan cheese

Preheat the oven to 325°F. Lightly grease a 13 x 9-inch baking dish and evenly distribute the cheese over the bottom of the dish. Dot randomly with 2 tablespoons of the butter and set aside.

In a medium skillet, melt the remaining 2 tablespoons of the butter over medium heat. Add the mushrooms and sauté 7 minutes. Remove from the heat and add the sour cream and Worcestershire, stirring well to combine. Spoon over the cheese and set aside.

Place the half-and-half, mustard, salt, and pepper in a mixing bowl and stir well. Pour half of this mixture over the mushrooms. Combine the eggs and the pimientos, stirring well. Pour over the mustard mixture. Pour the remaining mustard mixture over the eggs. Sprinkle with the Parmesan cheese. Bake 45 minutes, or until set. Serve warm.

MERINGUE KISSES

Serve these feather-light confections with fresh fruit.

YIELD: 4 DOZEN

3 egg whites

$\frac{1}{2}$ teaspoon cream of tartar

1 cup confectioners' sugar

1 teaspoon pure vanilla or almond extract

Preheat the oven to 275°F. Line 3 baking sheets with parchment paper and set aside.

Beat the egg whites until foamy and add the cream of tartar. Beat until the whites are fluffy and just beginning to hold their shape when the beater is lifted.

Gradually add the sugar, one tablespoon at a time. Add the extract when half of the sugar has been added. Continue beating until the whites are smooth, glossy, and stand in stiff peaks.

Place teaspoons of meringue on the prepared sheets and space at least 1 inch apart. Bake 30 minutes and turn off the oven. Leave the meringues in the oven overnight to crisp. Store in an airtight container between sheets of wax paper.

MILLION DOLLAR POUND CAKE

Pound cakes were so named because the original recipe called for a pound each of butter, sugar, flour, and eggs.

YIELD: 12 SERVINGS

1 pound (4 sticks) unsalted butter, softened

3 cups sugar

6 eggs

4 cups all-purpose flour

$\frac{3}{4}$ cup milk

1 teaspoon pure almond extract

1 teaspoon pure vanilla extract

Preheat the oven to 300°F. Grease and flour a 10-inch tube pan and set aside.

Beat the butter at the medium speed of an electric mixer until creamy. Gradually add the sugar, beating until light and fluffy.

Add the eggs, one at a time, beating well after each addition. Add the flour, alternating with the milk, beginning and ending with the flour. Stir in the almond and vanilla extracts.

Pour into the prepared pan and bake 1 hour and 30 minutes, or until a tester inserted in the center comes out clean. Cool in the pan on a wire rack 10 minutes. Remove and cool completely on a wire rack.

Note: Cut cake slices can be freezer wrapped and frozen up to one month.

PUFFED CAJUN EGGS

This is similar to individual soufflés but has a kick from hot sauce and Cajun seasoning.

YIELD: 4 SERVINGS

$\frac{1}{2}$ cup sour cream

$\frac{1}{2}$ cup milk

6 eggs

6 dashes hot sauce

$\frac{1}{4}$ teaspoon Cajun seasoning

$\frac{1}{8}$ teaspoon dry mustard

1 cup shredded sharp Cheddar cheese

Preheat the oven to 325°F. Grease 4 (8-ounce) ramekins with cooking spray and set aside.

In a medium bowl, whisk together the sour cream, milk, eggs, hot sauce, Cajun seasoning, and mustard. Stir in the cheese. Pour into the prepared ramekins. Bake 35 minutes and serve immediately.

SPICY BAKED EGGS WITH DILL CHEESE SAUCE

Southerners love cheese sauce, and this one is perfect served on the side of these eggs. Don't be the last to grab the gravy boat or you'll be sorry!

YIELD: 6 SERVINGS

5 tablespoons unsalted butter, divided

$\frac{1}{4}$ cup all-purpose flour

$\frac{1}{2}$ teaspoon baking powder

$\frac{1}{4}$ teaspoon salt

5 eggs, beaten

2 tablespoons diced green chiles

1 cup cottage cheese

2 cups shredded Monterey Jack cheese

$\frac{1}{2}$ cup milk

$\frac{1}{2}$ cup heavy cream

$\frac{1}{2}$ teaspoon salt

$\frac{1}{4}$ cup shredded sharp Cheddar cheese

1 tablespoon freshly chopped dill

Preheat the oven to 350°F. Lightly grease an 8-inch square baking dish and set aside.

In a large saucepan, melt 4 tablespoons of the butter over medium heat. Add the flour, baking powder, and salt, stirring constantly until slightly thickened, around 2 minutes. Remove from the heat and add the eggs, chiles, cottage cheese, and Monterey Jack, stirring well. Pour into the prepared pan and bake 45 minutes to 1 hour, or until the center is firm.

Meanwhile, heat the remaining tablespoon of the butter in a small saucepan over medium heat. Add the milk and cream. Bring to a slow boil and reduce the heat to low. Add the salt, Cheddar, and dill, stirring until the cheese completely melts. Serve the warm cheese sauce in a gravy boat with the baked eggs.

SUNDAY MORNING SCRAMBLE

Sunday mornings take on a hectic feel that Saturdays rarely have. I suppose it's the dash to church and then on to a fall football game or a summer date with your hammock and the newspaper! In either case, this easy, but filling, breakfast will keep you going until lunch!

YIELD: 2 SERVINGS

5 eggs

1 tablespoon milk

1 tablespoon chopped fresh chives

1 tablespoon chopped fresh parsley

$\frac{1}{4}$ teaspoon salt

$^{1}/_{4}$ teaspoon black pepper
3 tablespoons unsalted butter

In a medium bowl, whisk together the eggs, milk, chives, parsley, salt, and pepper. Place the butter in a large skillet over medium-high heat. Allow it to melt and bubble, but not brown. Add the egg mixture, whisking gently into the butter. Allow the eggs to almost set, and then whisk again and cook to the desired degree of doneness. Serve immediately.

"THE DEVIL IS IN THE DETAILS" STUFFED EGGS

Every true born-and-raised Southern woman owns a deviled egg plate. I have several and can't imagine trying to nestle egg halves without the conveniently placed scoops. Some plates hold a dozen halves, while others are larger. That's why you need more than one!

YIELD: 8 TO 10 SERVINGS

8 eggs
$^{1}/_{2}$ teaspoon salt
$^{1}/_{8}$ teaspoon black pepper
Filling variations (see below)
Paprika for garnish

Place the eggs in a single layer in the bottom of a large saucepan. Add enough water so the eggs are covered at least 1 inch. Place over high heat. As soon as the water comes to a boil, remove from the heat, cover, and let stand 15 minutes.

Drain and immediately cover with cold water. Let stand 5 minutes or until cool enough to handle. Gently tap the eggs all over and hold under cold running water as you remove the shells. Discard the shells and cut the eggs in half lengthwise.

Carefully remove the yolks, place in a small bowl, and mash with a fork. Add the salt, pepper, and desired filling ingredients and stir until well blended. Spoon or pipe the yolk mixture into the egg whites. Refrigerate until ready to serve. Sprinkle the tops with paprika and serve.

Filling Variations:
Traditional: add to the egg yolks $^{1}/_{4}$ cup mayonnaise, $1^{1}/_{2}$ tablespoons sweet pickle relish, and 1 teaspoon prepared mustard.
Easy Traditional: add to the egg yolks $^{1}/_{3}$ cup tartar sauce
Herb: add to the egg yolks $^{1}/_{3}$ cup sour cream, 2 tablespoons chopped fresh chives, and 2 teaspoons white wine vinegar.
Hot Deviled: add to the egg yolks 3 ounces softened cream cheese, 2 tablespoons milk, and 1 teaspoon hot sauce.

SHELL COLOR: The breed of the chicken determines the color of the shell, which can range from snow white to deep brown. There is no difference in flavor, performance, or nutritional value between eggs that come from shells of different colors.

WHITES AND YOLKS: Albumen is the actual name of egg whites and it makes up 60 percent of the egg weight. Fresh eggs have a thick portion of egg white as well as a thin portion. As the egg ages, the thin portion will increase and the thick will decrease.

The type of food consumed by the chicken will largely determine the color of the yolk. Egg yolks are one of the few foods that naturally contain vitamin D.

EGGPLANT

THERE ARE SOME FAMILIES WHO INSTANTLY ESTABLISH THEMSELVES AS BEING MORE LIKABLE than others. Relationships with them are easy, comfortable, and you never find yourself at a loss of what to do with them. They blend in with any crowd and never dominate.

I find myself feeling that way with the "nightshade" family—a group of diverse relations that includes potatoes, peppers, tomatoes, eggplant, and even tobacco and petunias. Eggplant especially grabs the spotlight for me because it's at home anywhere it's placed.

Eggplant is a chunky, funky vegetable that tends to be a sleeping giant in the produce world. In addition to the versatile flavor, I like the color and texture of this late-season home garden favorite. It commands attention and fits in well with many other foods.

In the South, we prefer the common large, pear-shaped variety with that unmistakable dark purple skin. It takes a while for local supplies to hit the market, but beginning in August, we've got plenty of eggplant to last us through the first frost.

All varieties have edible skins, but the thickness and tenderness will differ. If I am using a young, small eggplant, I don't usually peel it. One that is more mature with a thicker skin is more palatable when peeled before cooking.

If I have one complaint about eggplant, it's that annoying tendency to discolor when cut. This natural oxidation process happens rapidly, so don't cut or peel it until just before using. Have the citrus juice ready to combat the problem.

Look past serving it just in lasagna. Eggplant is wonderful roasted, grilled, in dips, casseroles, and in just about anything with tomatoes, onions, garlic, and peppers.

Nutrition: Eggplant is a good source of dietary fiber, potassium, iron, niacin, and thiamine. It is very low in calories. A three-ounce steamed or boiled portion contains only twenty-five calories.

Selection: Choose firm, smooth-skinned fruits that are shiny with a uniform color. The common purple variety should feel heavy for its size. Avoid purchasing any that are soft, wrinkled, and shriveled or that have large brown spots, cuts, or skin scars. Size is not an indication of quality.

Storage: Refrigerator storage is best. Eggplant should be placed in the crisper or vegetable drawer and used within three days of purchase. Although eggplant is firm in texture, it's more lightweight for the size than other produce items and doesn't withstand heavy pressure. Make sure you don't pile heavier vegetables on top of it while storing.

CRISP SAUTÉED EGGPLANT

What a contrast! The eggplant is crispy on the out-side and almost like custard on the inside.

YIELD: 8 SERVINGS

1 cup corn flake crumbs

$\frac{1}{2}$ teaspoon salt

$\frac{1}{4}$ teaspoon white pepper

1 egg, beaten

2 tablespoons vegetable oil

1 tablespoon unsalted butter

2 pounds eggplant, peeled and cut into
$\frac{1}{2}$-inch slices

Grated Parmesan cheese for garnish

Preheat the oven to the lowest setting or 200°F.

In a pie plate or other shallow dish, combine the crumbs, salt, and pepper. Place the egg in a separate flat dish. In a large skillet, heat the oil and butter over medium heat. Tilt the skillet to evenly distribute.

Dip the eggplant slices in the egg, covering both sides. Dredge both sides in the crumb mixture. Sauté 4 minutes on each side, placing a single layer in the skillet.

When golden brown, arrange the cooked slices in a single layer on a baking dish and place in the oven to keep warm. Repeat with the remaining slices. Serve warm with a sprinkling of Parmesan cheese.

ORIGIN: Two areas claim to be the original home of eggplant—tropical India and China. The oldest record is in a Chinese book written in the fifth century.

EGGPLANT AND GREEN TOMATO KEBABS

This unlikely combination is unbeatable!

YIELD: 6 SERVINGS

2 garlic cloves, minced

2 tablespoons soy sauce

2 tablespoons vegetable or canola oil

2 tablespoons dry white wine

1 tablespoon rice wine vinegar

1 tablespoon honey

Zest of 1 lime

Juice of 1 lime

1 large eggplant, peeled and cut into
1-inch cubes

2 large green tomatoes, cut into 1-inch cubes

2 to 3 yellow squash, cut into chunks

1 purple onion, peeled and cut into chunks

In a jar with a tight fitting lid, combine the garlic, soy sauce, oil, wine, vinegar, honey, zest, and juice. Shake to emulsify and set aside.

Place the eggplant, tomatoes, squash, and onion in a 13 x 9-inch baking dish. Pour the marinade over the vegetables, cover, and refrigerate 1 hour.

Prepare the grill to medium heat (350°F). Remove the vegetables from the marinade, shaking off the excess, and thread alternately onto skewers. Place the skewers onto the hot grate and, turning frequently, grill about 4 minutes on each side, or until tender. Baste with the remaining marinade. Serve warm.

EGGPLANT CAVIAR

This vegetarian classic can be made ahead or served on the spot. If desired, tinker with the seasonings to fit the tastes of your guests.

YIELD: 3 CUPS

1 large eggplant
$\frac{1}{3}$ cup chopped tomato
3 tablespoons finely chopped onion
2 tablespoons chopped fresh parsley
2 tablespoons olive oil
2 tablespoons lemon juice
1 tablespoon chopped fresh basil
1 garlic clove, minced
$\frac{1}{4}$ teaspoon kosher salt
$\frac{1}{4}$ teaspoon black pepper

Preheat the oven to 450°F. Pierce the eggplant several times with a sharp paring knife. Place on a baking sheet and bake 22 minutes, or until the pulp feels soft. Set aside to cool.

Peel the eggplant and finely chop. Transfer to a serving bowl and add the tomatoes, onion, parsley, oil, juice, basil, garlic, salt, and pepper. Stir to blend and serve with crackers or raw vegetables.

FREEZING: Eggplant slices can be successfully frozen, but the eggplant needs to be harvested before the seeds harden and mature. Make sure you use eggplant that has just developed a complete color for best results. Wash, peel, and cut the eggplant into one-third-inch slices.

Blanch the slices four minutes in a gallon of water containing a half cup of lemon juice. Drain, cool, and package into freezer containers with freezer paper between the slices.

GRILLED EGGPLANT AND COUNTRY HAM SANDWICHES

The smoky flavor of eggplant comes to the surface when it is grilled and simply seasoned. If you don't want to serve this as a sandwich, serve it as a side item.

YIELD: 4 SERVINGS

1 pound eggplant, peeled and thickly sliced
$\frac{1}{4}$ cup olive oil, divided
$\frac{1}{2}$ teaspoon salt
$\frac{1}{2}$ teaspoon black pepper
8 slices good quality bread
2 cups shredded Monterey Jack cheese
4 ounces thinly shaved country ham

Preheat the grill to medium heat (350°F). Place the eggplant slices in a 13 x 9-inch baking dish. Sprinkle with 2 tablespoons of the oil and the salt and pepper, tossing well to evenly coat. Transfer to a grilling basket and grill 12 minutes, turning once halfway through.

Place 4 slices of bread on a baking sheet. Top with the grilled eggplant slices. Divide the cheese and ham between the sandwiches and top with the remaining bread slices.

Brush the outside of the bread with the remaining oil. Grill 2 minutes, turning once halfway through. Serve immediately.

HERB-CRUSTED BAKED EGGPLANT

The spring-like flavor of this dish is highlighted by a mixture of fresh herbs and salty cheese.

YIELD: 4 SERVINGS

1 large eggplant, peeled and sliced
$\frac{1}{4}$ teaspoon kosher salt
$\frac{1}{4}$ teaspoon black pepper
$\frac{1}{3}$ cup seasoned dry breadcrumbs
2 tablespoons grated Romano cheese
3 tablespoons chopped fresh basil
2 tablespoons chopped fresh parsley
2 garlic cloves, minced
1 tablespoon unsalted butter

Preheat the oven to 400°F. Lightly grease a pie pan and set aside.

Season the eggplant slices with the salt and pepper. Arrange, overlapping, in the prepared pan.

In a small bowl, combine the breadcrumbs, cheese, basil, parsley, and garlic. Sprinkle evenly over the eggplant slices. Dot the top with the butter.

Bake, uncovered, 30 to 40 minutes, or until the top is golden brown. Serve warm.

PRODUCERS: Florida produces over half of the commercially grown eggplant in the United States. In fact, the other Southern states receive this vegetable from Florida every month of the year, except during August and September, when local supplies are on the market. Supplies are typically lightest in February.

HARVESTING: Eggplant can be harvested from the time it is about one-third grown until it reaches full size. The best maturity is when it is nearly 85 percent grown.

SOUTHERN-FRIED EGGPLANT

Rather than fried monster slices, these are strips that make serving it as an appetizer or finger food easy.

YIELD: 4 SERVINGS

1 large eggplant
4 cups water
1 teaspoon kosher salt, divided
$\frac{1}{2}$ teaspoon black pepper
2 eggs
$\frac{1}{2}$ cup milk
$\frac{3}{4}$ cup all-purpose flour
Vegetable oil for frying

Peel and slice the eggplant into thin strips. Soak 30 minutes in the water and $\frac{1}{2}$ teaspoon of the salt. Drain and sprinkle with the remaining salt and pepper. Let stand 10 minutes.

Meanwhile, mix together the eggs and milk. Place in a shallow dish. Place the flour in a separate shallow dish.

Pour the oil to a depth of 1 inch in a large skillet and place over medium-high heat. Dip the eggplant strips in the egg mixture and dredge in the flour, shaking off the excess. Fry 3 to 5 minutes, or until golden brown. Drain on paper towels and serve warm.

TYPES: Varieties of eggplant can range from the size of an English pea to twelve inches in length. Shapes can be anything from oblong to pear-shaped to round. Color can run the gamut from white to deep purple. The name "eggplant" was originally given to a white skinned variety.

FIGS

THERE IS A STREET IN NASHVILLE, TENNESSEE, NAMED HILLSBORO ROAD THAT GIVES DRIVERS plenty of time to look around and notice their surroundings. On this particular road, drivers are always engulfed by loads of cars no matter what time of the day and encounter traffic lights that can't quite seem to be synchronized.

But Hillsboro Road is loaded with fig trees all along the route, and each fall, I find myself hungry for them every time I make that drive. Maybe constant stop-and-go traffic isn't so horrible after all.

The first time I really enjoyed a truly fresh fig was nearly twenty years ago at a farm in Adams, Tennessee, that has a Cedar Hill address (you have to love the post office!). My friend Don Hall plucked a Brown Turkey fig from one of his trees and told me to dig in. I wasn't quite sure what to do, so I just took a bite. Heaven met me that day on his farm. It was a taste of the good life unlike anything I had ever known.

I have enjoyed many fresh figs with equally interesting names since that delightful day. It began a culinary quest to make all kinds of delicacies with my newfound friends. Preserves are a "must make" every year because I love using them during the rest of the year when fresh local supplies are a memory.

I find myself wondering if the Hillsboro Road commuters even know what they are looking at as they inch their way to and from downtown. I hope they do and that it enhances their daily drive just as much as it does mine.

Nutrition: Figs are a powerhouse of dietary fiber. They contain modest sources of iron, calcium, phosphorus, and vitamins A and C. One medium fig contains around forty calories.

Selection: Choose figs that are as soft and ripe as possible. Avoid bruised fruit, but those shriveled by the sun will be especially sweet. Figs do not need to be peeled before use.

Storage: Until the figs are ripe, you can store them at room temperature. Once ripe, bruises easily occur with fresh figs, so if possible, store them in a single layer in a shallow dish lined with paper towels in the refrigerator. For the best flavor, use them as quickly as possible.

Botany: Figs are members of the mulberry family and grow on small trees that can sometimes look like large bushes. Although we call them fruit, figs are actually syconiums, which are heads of flowers that are turned inside out. They are closely related to ficus trees.

Origin: Figs are believed to have originated in Asia. We know they were grown in the Middle East thousands of years before Christ. They grew in the Hanging Gardens of Babylon and were well known as Cleopatra's favorite fruit.

ALL MINE FIG PRESERVES

These are my second favorite fruit preserves (after pear) and with only one taste, you'll understand the allure. Make the first batch for yourself. A second batch can be made for neighbors and friends.

YIELD: 9 HALF-PINTS

4½ quarts water, divided
3 quarts fresh figs
4 cups sugar

In a large Dutch oven over high heat, bring 3 quarts of the water to a boil. Add the figs, remove from the heat, cover, and let stand 15 minutes. Drain the figs in a colander and discard the soaking liquid. Rinse the figs with cold water, remove the stems, and drain well.

In the same Dutch oven, combine the remaining water and sugar and bring to a boil over high heat. Boil rapidly 10 minutes. Skim and discard any foam that develops.

Drop the figs into the syrup a few at a time. Continue to cook until the figs are transparent, around 50 to 55 minutes. Remove the figs with a slotted spoon and place in a shallow pan. Boil the leftover syrup until thick, around 15 minutes. Pour over the figs and let stand 6 to 8 hours in the refrigerator.

Reheat the figs and syrup to boiling. Pour the preserves into hot, sterilized half pint canning jars, leaving ¼-inch headspace. Remove any air bubbles, wipe the jar rims, and adjust the lids. Process 5 minutes in a boiling water bath. Let cool completely on a wire rack away from drafts.

COUNTRY HAM–WRAPPED FIGS

Salty ham and sweet figs get crunch from pecans and elegance from a pooled cream sauce. Or you can eliminate the cream sauce and serve larger amounts of these as appetizers.

YIELD: 6 TO 8 SERVINGS

¾ cup cream
2 tablespoons lemon juice
24 pecan or walnut halves
12 fresh figs, stemmed and cut in half lengthwise
24 very thin slices (around 6 to 8 inches long) cooked country ham

In a small bowl, whisk together the cream and juice. Set aside.

Preheat the broiler and lightly grease a broiler pan. Set aside.

Place a pecan half in the center of each fig. Wrap with the ham and place on the prepared pan with the cut side up. Repeat with the remaining figs.

Broil 3 minutes. Serve 3 to 4 fig halves on each serving plate in a pool of the cream mixture.

FALL FIG MUFFINS

I am so stingy with my fig preserves that it was difficult for me to use them in experimenting with this muffin recipe. I'm so glad I gave it a try, because these are excellent and worth the sacrifice of those preserves!

YIELD 20 MUFFINS

¼ pound (1 stick) unsalted butter, softened
½ cup sugar
2 eggs

1½ cups all-purpose flour

2 teaspoons baking powder

½ teaspoon ground cinnamon

¼ teaspoon ground cloves

½ cup milk

½ cup fig preserves

½ cup chopped pecans

Preheat the oven to 350°F. Lightly grease 20 muffin cups and set aside.

In the bowl of an electric mixer, cream the butter and sugar until light and fluffy, around 4 minutes. Add the eggs, one at a time, beating well after each addition.

In a separate bowl, combine the flour, baking powder, cinnamon, and cloves. Add to the creamed mixture, alternately with the milk, stirring just until moistened. Fold in the preserves and pecans, blending well.

Spoon the batter evenly into the prepared muffin cups, filling each two-thirds full. Bake 20 minutes, or until a tester inserted in the center comes out clean. Cool 5 minutes in the pan, and then transfer to wire racks to finish cooling or serve warm.

FRESH FIG SAUCE

Use this delightful sauce as a topping for pancakes, waffles, ice cream, or pound cake.

YIELD: 3½ CUPS

15 fresh figs, stemmed

1 cup water

½ cup sugar

1 tablespoon unsalted butter

3 tablespoons lemon juice

1 tablespoon cornstarch

In a large saucepan over medium-high heat, bring the figs, water, sugar, and butter to a boil, stirring frequently. Reduce the heat to medium low and simmer 7 to 8 minutes, or just until the figs are tender.

In a small bowl, whisk together the juice and cornstarch until smooth. Stir into the fig mixture and reduce the heat to low. Cook around 5 minutes, stirring constantly until thick and bubbly. Serve warm or cool to room temperature.

LATTICE-TOPPED FIG PIE

What is it about a lattice topping that draws such attention? Perhaps it's because we realize that it required a bit of extra effort. That effort is certainly worth it for this dessert.

YIELD: 6 SERVINGS

6 cups fresh figs, stemmed and halved

¾ cup sugar

3 tablespoons all-purpose flour

2 tablespoons unsalted butter

1 recipe Single Pie Pastry (page 402)

Preheat the oven to 375°F. Lightly grease an 8-inch square baking dish and set aside.

In a medium bowl, combine the figs, sugar, and flour, mixing well. Transfer to the prepared baking dish and dot with the butter. Set aside.

Roll the pastry to ¼-inch thickness on a lightly floured surface. With a pastry wheel or a sharp knife, cut into 9 x ½-inch strips. Arrange the strips in a lattice fashion over the fig mixture. If necessary, trim the edges.

Bake 45 minutes, or until golden brown and bubbly. Let stand on a wire rack 10 minutes before serving. Serve warm or cool completely and serve at room temperature.

"SWEET SENSATION" FIG PRESERVES CAKE

Now you understand why I say you must make an entire batch of fig preserves for yourself. You can use them in so many delicious desserts. This cake is fantastically old-fashioned and moist.

YIELD: 15 SERVINGS

2 cups all-purpose flour

1 teaspoon ground cinnamon

1 teaspoon salt

1 teaspoon baking soda

$\frac{1}{2}$ teaspoon ground cloves

$\frac{1}{4}$ teaspoon ground nutmeg

3 eggs

1 cup vegetable oil

1 cup sugar

$\frac{1}{2}$ cup buttermilk

1 teaspoon pure vanilla extract

$1\frac{1}{2}$ cups fig preserves

$\frac{1}{2}$ cup applesauce

1 cup chopped walnuts, toasted

Cream Cheese Frosting (page 128)

Preheat the oven to 350°F. Lightly grease and flour 2 (8-inch) round cake pans and set aside.

In a medium bowl, combine the flour, cinnamon, salt, baking soda, cloves, and nutmeg. Stir to blend and set aside.

In the bowl of an electric mixer, combine the eggs, oil, and sugar until well blended. Add the buttermilk and extract. Stir in the flour mixture until smooth. Fold in the preserves, applesauce, and walnuts.

Evenly pour the batter into the prepared pans. Bake 35 to 40 minutes, or until a tester inserted in the center comes out clean. Cool in the pans 10 minutes on wire racks. Remove and cool completely before frosting with the Cream Cheese Frosting. Store in the refrigerator.

"RISE TO THE TOP" FIG COBBLER

It seems counter-intuitive to place the crust batter in the bottom of the pan, and the fruit on top, but magic happens when it hits the oven.

YIELD: 8 SERVINGS

4 tablespoons unsalted butter

1 cup all-purpose flour

1 cup sugar

2 teaspoons baking powder

1 egg

1 cup milk

1 teaspoon pure vanilla extract

2 (11-ounce) jars fig preserves

Preheat the oven to 375°F. Place the butter in a 2-quart baking dish and place in the preheating oven to melt.

Meanwhile, in a mixing bowl, combine the flour, sugar, and baking powder. Make a well in the center and set aside. In a separate bowl, whisk together the egg, milk, and extract. Add to the flour mixture and blend until smooth.

Pour the batter over the melted butter. Spoon the preserves over the batter. Bake 20 minutes. Cover with aluminum foil and bake 20 minutes longer. Let stand 5 minutes before serving warm.

Celebrations
January 16 is National Fig Newton Day.

FISH

THERE IS A LAKE THAT RUNS FAIRLY CLOSE TO OUR HOUSE WHERE FISHERMEN GATHER TO spend a good part of the day on the water. I find myself wanting to high-five these individuals that I don't know because they are clearly dedicated to a hobby they love. They somehow manage to get the word spread quickly when something is biting, because you'll see droves of them when the "reeling is real."

While I don't particularly enjoy fishing, I simply love the harvest they manage to pull from the waters, whether it's fresh or salt water. And the techniques and tricks they use to outsmart their prey are signs that these are masters of their craft.

Many picture Southerners with a cane pole and bucket of worms walking barefoot down to the local creek on a Sunday afternoon when they imagine us fishing. While that is certainly done all across the area, there are also plenty of those who do this activity as a means of making a fairly good living. From the smallest brim (called "bream" up north) to the largest tuna, Southern waters have been providing a varied and versatile harvest for decades.

From the kitchen end, I have hardly found an easier, faster, more fulfilling dinner than any type of fish. Thanks to already cleaned and prepared steaks, fillets, and pan-dressed fish, you rarely need more than 30 minutes from the beginning of preparation to the minute you sit down and place a napkin in your lap.

That's why I always smile as I pass fishermen pulling a plethora of gear from their vehicles. I know that with any luck, dinner will be worth the day spent outdoors.

Doneness: Properly cooked fish will be opaque and will not cling to the bones. It should flake easily when a fork or knife is inserted in the thickest part. The timing can be tricky. Undercooked fish will be translucent and watery. Overcooked fish will be dry.

Selection: If purchasing frozen fish, do not select packages that are misshapen or that appear to have interior ice. These have more than likely been allowed to thaw and then refrozen. Truly fresh fish should not smell fishy. It should have a firm, elastic flesh that tends to spring back when pressed.

Storage: There is an easy rule to remember when storing fish: The colder the storage temperature, the longer the fish will keep. Lean fish has a longer shelf life than oily fish. Large fish keep longer than small ones, as do whole fish over fillets or steaks. Never refreeze fish that has been frozen and thawed. You can, however, cook the thawed raw fish and freeze the leftovers.

Thawing: Never thaw frozen fish at room temperature or in a pan of warm water. It will quickly lose flavor as well as moisture. Head to the refrigerator instead. Allow from eighteen to twenty-four hours to thaw a one-pound package in the refrigerator.

"AFTER THE FRY" FISH LOAF

If there is one thing that most will not reheat, it is left-over fish. However, this is the one dish I have found that tastes fantastic with the excess. If the fish has been fried, remove the breading. Fish that has been broiled or grilled with just a bit of lemon juice, salt, and pepper works very well with this recipe.

YIELD: 6 SERVINGS

2 cups flaked cooked fish
1 1/2 cups soft breadcrumbs
1 cup milk
2/3 cup chopped celery
1/3 cup chopped onion
2 tablespoons chopped green bell pepper
1 tablespoon lemon juice
1 tablespoon diced pimientos
1 1/4 teaspoon Cajun or Creole seasoning
1/2 teaspoon salt
1/2 teaspoon hot sauce
1/4 teaspoon black pepper

Preheat the oven to 350°F. Lightly grease a loaf pan and set aside.

In a mixing bowl, combine the fish, breadcrumbs, milk, celery, onion, bell pepper, lemon juice, pimientos, Cajun seasoning, salt, hot sauce, and black pepper. Blend well and transfer to the prepared pan.

Bake 30 minutes. Let stand 5 minutes in the pan before slicing and serving.

CREAM SHERRY BAKED FISH

This classic Cajun fish entrée is enhanced with cream sherry, which is aged longer and is more expensive than regular sherry. It makes a big difference in the taste, so don't scrimp.

YIELD: 4 SERVINGS

1 pound fresh fish fillets (carp, cod, sole, sea bass or snapper)
1/2 cup chopped onion
2 tablespoons chopped celery
8 button mushrooms, sliced
1/2 cup cream sherry
2 garlic cloves, minced
1 tablespoon lemon juice
1/2 teaspoon hot sauce
1/2 teaspoon salt
1/2 teaspoon black pepper
1 teaspoon olive oil

Preheat the oven to 350°F. Lightly greased a 13 x 9-inch baking dish.

Place the fillets in the prepared dish. Cover the fish with the onion, celery, and mushrooms. In a small bowl, whisk together the sherry, garlic, lemon juice, and hot sauce. Pour over the fillets. Sprinkle with the salt and pepper, and then drizzle with the oil. Bake 30 minutes, or until the fish flakes easily with a fork. Serve immediately.

HOOKED ON GRILLED FISH

Grouper or snapper fillets get some spice with this practically instant dinner recipe.

YIELD: 4 SERVINGS

4 (4- to 5-ounce) grouper or snapper fillets
$\frac{1}{4}$ cup lemon juice
2 tablespoons unsalted butter, melted
2 tablespoons hot sauce
1 tablespoon vegetable oil
$\frac{1}{2}$ teaspoon salt
$\frac{1}{4}$ teaspoon black pepper
1 tablespoon chopped fresh parsley

Place the fillets in a 13 x 9-inch baking dish and set aside.

In a small bowl, combine the lemon juice, butter, hot sauce, oil, salt, and pepper. Whisk until smooth. Divide the mixture in half. Cover and refrigerate half of the mixture.

Pour the remaining mixture over the fish, turning once to evenly coat. Cover and refrigerate 1 hour, turning occasionally.

Preheat the grill to hot heat (400°F to 450°F). Meanwhile, remove the remaining marinade from the refrigerator and heat 30 seconds on low power in the microwave. Whisk until smooth and set aside.

Remove the fillets from the marinade and discard the marinade. Place on a grilling basket coated with cooking spray. Cook 5 minutes on each side or until the fish flakes easily with a fork. Baste the fish with the reserved marinade. Sprinkle with the parsley and serve hot.

FRESH CATCH SWORDFISH WITH WALNUT CRUST

This easy, quick dinner is excellent with hot grits and fresh green beans. Tuna steaks make a good substitution for the swordfish.

YIELD: 4 SERVINGS

$1\frac{1}{2}$ cups walnuts
1 tablespoon black pepper
4 (6- to 8-ounce) swordfish or tuna steaks
2 tablespoons vegetable oil

Place the walnuts in the bowl of a food processor and process until ground. In a shallow bowl, mix the ground walnuts with the pepper. Coat both sides of the steaks with the walnut mixture and set aside.

Pour the oil in a large skillet and place over medium heat. Add the steaks and cook 10 minutes on each side or until the fish flakes easily when tested with a fork. Serve immediately.

PRESERVING: Fresh fish can be frozen a couple of different ways. I prefer wrapping it in freezer paper rather than aluminum foil. I wrap the fish like a package with wax paper between the fillets in order to keep them from freezing together. Some like to freeze fish in blocks of ice. This is done by placing the fish in a shallow pan and covering it with water. Freeze the entire pan. When frozen solid, remove from the pan and wrap in freezer paper or heavy-duty aluminum foil. In either case, make sure you label the outside with the type of fish and the date it was frozen.

LAGNIAPPE FISH

Lagniappe means "something extra" and that's exactly what this fish dish has in store for you. It is not a dish to make ahead, but it only takes a minute to get it into the oven. In half an hour, you have dinner ready.

YIELD: 4 SERVINGS

1 teaspoon Cajun or Creole seasoning

4 (8-ounce) fish fillets (amberjack, mullet, whitefish, trout, butterfish, or carp)

1 white onion, peeled and sliced

1 cup sour cream

¼ cup dry white wine

1 tablespoon all-purpose flour

1 teaspoon paprika

1 teaspoon lemon juice

¼ teaspoon hot sauce

Preheat the oven to 350°F. Lightly grease a 13 x 9-inch baking dish and set aside.

Sprinkle the seasoning over the fish and place in a shallow baking dish. Arrange the onion slices on top of the fillets. Set aside.

In a small bowl, whisk together the sour cream, wine, flour, paprika, lemon juice, and hot sauce. Evenly spread over the onions. Bake 30 minutes, or until the fish flakes easily when tested with a fork. Serve immediately.

CUTS: Fillets are large pieces of boneless fish cut from the sides and are terrific fried. Use any frying technique from the chapter on catfish to fry fish fillets, or substitute another fish for catfish in any recipe. Steaks are a cross section cut from a whole fish. Pan-dressed fish has had the head, fins, and tail removed. A whole fish is exactly that.

"LURE OF THE GRILL" FRESH FISH

Fish from the grill is a dream for any busy cook because it's ready and on the table in a flash. This will taste best if served immediately.

YIELD: 4 SERVINGS

¼ cup vegetable oil

¼ cup chopped fresh tarragon, basil, or chives

¼ cup fresh lemon juice

½ teaspoon salt

¼ teaspoon black pepper

2 (2-pound) pan-dressed trout or other freshwater fish

1 lemon

2 sprigs fresh tarragon, basil or chives

In a small saucepan over medium-low heat, combine the oil and chopped tarragon. Cook 20 minutes, stirring occasionally. Pour through a fine-mesh strainer and discard the solids. Add the lemon juice, salt, and pepper to the infused oil, whisking to blend.

Brush half of the mixture inside each trout. Trim the ends off the lemon and slice the remainder into 4 large slices. Place 2 fresh herb sprigs and 2 of the lemon slices inside each trout. Place in a 13 x 9-inch baking dish. Pour the remaining oil mixture over the trout. Cover and refrigerate 2 hours, turning occasionally.

Prepare the grill to hot heat (400°F to 450°F). Meanwhile, remove the trout from the marinade and discard the marinade. Place the trout in a grilling basket that has been coated with cooking spray.

Grill, covered, 5 minutes on each side, or until the fish flakes easily with a fork. Let stand 2 minutes before serving hot.

Note: To bake the trout, preheat the oven to 350°F. Place on a lightly greased broiler pan and bake 30 minutes, or until the fish flakes easily with a fork. Do not turn during cooking.

∙∙∙

REELED IN BLACKENED FISH

The process of blackening fish was created by Paul Prudhomme specifically for Louisiana redfish, but don't limit yourself to only that type of fish. Just make sure you have a good cast-iron skillet and an even better exhaust fan because quite a bit of smoke is given off in the cooking process.

YIELD: 4 SERVINGS

$1/4$ pound (1 stick) unsalted butter, melted

4 tablespoons vegetable oil

1 teaspoon salt

1 teaspoon cayenne

$1/2$ teaspoon black pepper

$1/2$ teaspoon paprika

$1/2$ teaspoon dried thyme

4 ($1/2$-inch thick) fish fillets (redfish, mackerel, monkfish, grouper, or swordfish)

Place a large cast-iron skillet over high heat for 10 minutes.

Meanwhile, in a shallow bowl, combine the butter and oil. In a separate small bowl, mix together the salt, cayenne, black pepper, paprika, and thyme.

Dip each fillet in the butter mixture, and then sprinkle evenly with about 1 teaspoon of the seasoning mixture.

Place the fillets in the hot skillet 2 minutes. Turn and cook 2 minutes longer. Serve immediately.

MOUNTAIN TROUT AMANDINE

Amandine means garnished with almonds and the golden crunchy slivers are a terrific contrast to the delicate flavor of trout. You can substitute bass, pike, or even perch for the trout in this recipe if desired.

YIELD: 6 SERVINGS

6 trout fillets

1 cup milk

4 tablespoons unsalted butter

$1/2$ cup slivered almonds

2 tablespoons vegetable oil

$1/2$ cup all-purpose flour

$1/2$ teaspoon salt

$1/4$ teaspoon black pepper

$1/2$ teaspoon paprika

Place the fillets in a single layer in a shallow dish. Pour the milk over the fillets. Cover and refrigerate 2 hours.

Place the butter in a small skillet over medium heat. Add the almonds and brown slowly, stirring frequently.

Remove the fillets from the milk marinade. Discard the marinade. Heat the oil in a large skillet over medium-high heat. Meanwhile, place the flour, salt, pepper, and paprika in a shallow dish and stir to evenly blend.

Dredge the fillets in the flour mixture. Brown in the hot oil 3 to 4 minutes on each side, turning to evenly brown. Transfer the fillets to a serving dish. Pour the almond butter over the fillets and serve immediately.

GAME

(PHEASANT, DUCK, QUAIL, DOVE, VENISON, ETC.)

I LIKE TO SHOOT GUNS, BUT I AM NOT A HUNTER. A PAPER BULLS-EYE IS MY TARGET. LUCKILY, I know plenty of people who relish this activity, mainly my nephew Brad. I honestly believe he could successfully bag any animal he stalks. It takes more patience than I have, and remember, I don't like being cold.

My grandfather was a hunter and a fisherman as well. I remember my grandmother cooking squirrel, rabbit, quail, and doves. We knew better than to be anywhere near when the meat was being cleaned, so Tina and I filled that time inside with our paper dolls.

Southern wild game is nothing less than a gift. It provides us with some of the most flavorful meat available. To me, it is meat with an exclamation point. Your tastebuds will explode from the impact.

It pays to know people who hunt wild game; otherwise you have to purchase farm-raised game from the supermarket or directly from the owners of the farm. I can safely say that hunters are generous to a fault and are willing to share their bounty with those of us who depend on them for the feast.

If you aren't used to enjoying this kind of meat, ease yourself into it slowly. Keep an open mind and follow the recipe closely. Also, realize that our Southern ancestors survived and thrived on this kind of food. It has nourished us for centuries and is just as delicious today as it was when my grandfather and yours traipsed through the woods to bring home a mighty fine dinner.

Selection: Most of the game you will find on the market will be sold in the frozen state. It is likely that you don't know how long it has been frozen, so use within six months is recommended for the best flavor. Thaw in the refrigerator overnight.

Pheasant: Pheasant is a great example of how farm-raised doesn't compare to those we hunt in the wild. The flavor difference is extremely noticeable, with the wild winning at the end of the day. As is usual with birds, the male is more brilliantly colored than the female. However, you will find that the meat of the female is more tender and juicier than that of the male . . . a trade-off, but in the kitchen, only the meat matters!

Game Birds: You'll find a large group of birds in the game bird category. These can range from the wild turkey, goose, and duck to the dove, partridge, pigeon, and quail. You will have to look hard to find these on the mass market, and when you do, they will more than likely be frozen. Wild birds have much leaner meat than domesticated birds.

Duck: If you like to hunt for ducks, you have to learn to call them. Credit is given to the Chinese for being the first to raise ducks for food. All ducks are descendants of either the mallard or the muscovy duck. On the market, you'll see them labeled as either broilers, fryers, or roasters. Broilers and fryers are less than eight weeks old. Roasters are no more than twice that age. As you would expect, older ducks are generally larger in size. Usually, they are sold with giblets. If that is the case, remove the giblets from the cavity and store separately.

Quail: The familiar "bob-white" whistle is commonly heard in the South during the early spring especially. It is an indication that the males and females are beginning their courtship. The two will usually pair off for the entire nesting season.

Rabbits: Rabbits are interesting animals to hunt. They usually don't flush until you stop walking, so you must be ready to fire as you walk. A mature rabbit will weigh between three and five pounds. The best and most tender flesh, however, will be on those that register the scales from two to two-and-a-half pounds. The meat is tender and mildly flavored. Older rabbits benefit from any moist heat cooking method, such as braising.

Turtle: I've heard the word "terrapin" all my life, but never really knew what that meant. It actually refers to a small turtle that is eight inches or less. These turtles have incredible meat and it is sometimes pounded and served like you would steak.

WILD GAME GUMBO

Anyone who really makes gumbo will tell you it's an all-day event but worth every second. This one is proof of that and an exceptional way to feed the entire neighborhood.

YIELD: 4 QUARTS, 8 TO 10 SERVINGS

2 quarts water

1 (3-pound) whole chicken

1½ teaspoons plus 1 tablespoon salt, divided

8 dove breasts

1 pound venison roast, cut into 1-inch cubes

2 quail, dressed

1 white onion, peeled and cut in half

1 stalk celery

1 bay leaf

¾ teaspoon red pepper, divided

1½ pounds smoked sausage, cut into ½-inch slices

¼ cup bacon drippings

½ cup all-purpose flour

1 cup chopped onion

1 cup chopped celery

1 cup chopped green bell pepper

2 teaspoons black pepper

1 teaspoon hot sauce

1 teaspoon Worcestershire sauce

Hot cooked rice

Place the water in a large Dutch oven over medium-high heat. Add the chicken and 1½ teaspoons of the salt. Bring to a boil, cover, and reduce the heat to low. Simmer 1 hour, or until the chicken is done. Remove the chicken from the stock.

Cover and refrigerate the stock. When the chicken is cool enough to handle, remove from the bones and chop into bite-size pieces. Discard the skin and bones. Refrigerate the meat.

In the same Dutch oven, combine the dove breasts, venison, quail, halved onion, celery stalk, bay leaf, the remaining 1 tablespoon of the salt, and $\frac{1}{4}$ teaspoon of the red pepper. Add enough water to cover and place over medium-high heat. Bring to a boil, cover, and reduce the heat to low. Simmer 2 hours. With tongs and a slotted spoon, remove all the meat from the stock. Strain the stock, discarding the solids. When the dove and quail are cool enough to handle, remove from the bones and chop into bite-size pieces. Set aside.

In a heavy skillet over medium heat, brown the sausage, 5 to 7 minutes. Drain on paper towels and set aside. Add the bacon drippings to the skillet. When hot, stir in the flour and cook, stirring constantly, until the roux is dark brown, around 18 minutes.

Add the chopped onions, chopped celery, bell peppers, and black pepper. Cook 10 minutes.

In the large Dutch oven, combine the roux and reserved chicken stock. Place over medium heat and simmer, covered, 30 minutes.

Add the reserved chicken, game, sausage, the remaining red pepper, hot sauce, and Worcestershire. Simmer, uncovered, 2 hours. If more liquid is needed, add the reserved game stock. Serve over hot cooked rice.

BAKED DOVE BREASTS WITH SHERRY GRAVY

If you have a large cast-iron skillet with a lid, you have the perfect utensil for making this dish. If not, use a Dutch oven.

YIELD: 5 SERVINGS

4 tablespoons unsalted butter
10 dove breasts
$\frac{1}{2}$ teaspoon salt
$\frac{1}{4}$ teaspoon black pepper
2 cups sherry
2 tablespoons cornstarch
$\frac{1}{4}$ cup water
Hot cooked rice

Preheat the oven to 400°F. Place the butter in a large cast-iron skillet and put in the preheating oven to melt.

Meanwhile, sprinkle the dove breasts with the salt and pepper. Add the breasts to the skillet, along with the sherry.

Cover and bake 40 minutes. Remove the breasts and cover with aluminum foil to keep warm. Place the skillet with the pan drippings over medium heat. In a small bowl, whisk together the cornstarch and water until smooth. Add to the pan drippings and whisk constantly 1 minute, or until thick and bubbly. Place the dove breasts over hot cooked rice. Serve the warm gravy on the side.

CREOLE TURTLE SOUP

Leave it to those creative Louisiana people to make this exceptional soup that is worthy of the finest restaurant.

YIELD: 6 SERVINGS

4 quarts water
$1\frac{1}{2}$ to 2 pounds turtle meat, cut in bite-size pieces
2 tablespoons vegetable shortening
3 tablespoons all-purpose flour
2 medium white onions, peeled and chopped
3 celery stalks, chopped
1 large green bell pepper, seeded and chopped
6 garlic cloves, minced
2 lemons, thinly sliced
4 tablespoons Worcestershire sauce

½ teaspoon Creole seasoned salt

3 tablespoons whole allspice

½ cup sherry

Chopped fresh parsley

In a large Dutch oven, bring the water to a boil over medium-high heat. Add the turtle meat and reduce the heat to medium-low. Cover and simmer 3 hours, or until the meat is tender. Strain the stock and return to the pot, along with the meat. Set aside.

In a heavy skillet over medium heat, melt the shortening. When hot, stir in the flour and cook, stirring constantly, until the roux is dark brown, around 15 minutes. Add the onions, celery, bell pepper, and garlic. Cook 10 minutes.

Add the roux to the stock, along with the lemons, Worcestershire, and seasoned salt. Tie the allspice in cheesecloth bag and add to the soup. Simmer over medium heat 1 hour. Remove and discard the allspice bag. Stir in the sherry. Serve hot with a garnish of chopped fresh parsley.

ONION-ROASTED VENISON

I hope you like onions, because this recipe mellows them out beautifully. The venison benefits from long, slow cooking that makes this roast tender and flavorful.

YIELD: 8 TO 10 SERVINGS

¼ cup bacon drippings

1 (4-pound) venison rump or shoulder roast

1 teaspoon onion salt

1 teaspoon black pepper

1 (1-ounce) envelope dry onion soup mix

1 yellow onion, peeled and cut into 4 wedges

½ cup water

Preheat the oven to 300°F.

In a medium, oven-proof Dutch oven, heat the bacon drippings over medium-high heat. Add the venison and brown on all sides, turning as necessary, around 9 minutes.

Sprinkle with the salt, pepper, and soup mix. Place the onion wedges around the edges. Add the water, cover, and roast 2½ to 3 hours, or until tender. Let stand 10 minutes before serving.

ORANGE-GLAZED DUCK BREASTS

Although this recipe calls for duck breasts, you can substitute a whole quartered duck if desired.

YIELD: 4 SERVINGS

¼ cup vegetable shortening

4 duck breasts, skinned

½ cup all-purpose flour

1 small white or yellow onion, peeled and chopped

1⅓ cups fresh orange juice

1½ teaspoons salt

1 teaspoon grated orange zest

¼ teaspoon ground ginger

1 tablespoon cornstarch

1 tablespoon water

Hot cooked wild rice

Preheat the oven to 350°F. Lightly grease a 13 x 9-inch baking pan and set aside.

In a large skillet over medium-high heat, melt the shortening. Meanwhile, coat the duck breasts with the flour, shaking off the excess. Brown on all sides, turning as needed, around 5 minutes total. Transfer the breasts to the prepared baking pan.

Remove the skillet from the heat, and stir in the onion, letting it wilt in the already hot grease.

After 1 minute, add the juice, salt, zest, and ginger, stirring well to combine. Pour around the duck breasts, cover, and bake 1½ hours, or until the duck is tender.

Remove the breasts to a serving platter. Pour the pan drippings back into the skillet and place over medium-high heat. In a small bowl, stir together the cornstarch and water until smooth. Add to the drippings and stir constantly until thick and bubbly, around 3 minutes. Serve on the side with the duck over hot cooked wild rice.

OVEN-BAKED PHEASANT

Let the oven take care of this dish while you handle the rest of dinner. It smells marvelous, so get ready for mouths to water and everyone to be hungry.

YIELD: 4 SERVINGS

1 pheasant, cut into 8 serving pieces
1 teaspoon salt
½ teaspoon white pepper
½ cup all-purpose flour
1 tablespoon unsalted butter
1 cup chicken stock

Preheat the oven to 375°F. Lightly grease a roasting pan and set aside.

Sprinkle the pheasant pieces with the salt and pepper. Dredge in the flour and place on the prepared pan. Dot with the butter and bake 30 minutes. Add the stock, cover, and reduce the oven temperature to 300°F. Bake 1 to 1½ hours, or until tender. Serve warm.

PAN-ROASTED QUAIL WITH GRAVY

Quail has such a marvelous, delicate flavor, you don't want to add any strong ingredients that will distract. Make sure you have a large skillet with a lid for this recipe.

YIELD: 4 SERVINGS

8 quail, dressed
¾ teaspoon kosher salt
½ teaspoon black pepper
4 tablespoons unsalted butter
1 cup chicken stock
2 tablespoons all-purpose flour
2 tablespoons water

Sprinkle the quail all over with the salt and pepper. Set aside.

In a large skillet over medium heat, melt the butter. Add the quail and brown on both sides, around 5 minutes. Add the stock, cover, and reduce the heat to low. Simmer 40 minutes, or until tender. Remove the quail from the skillet and cover with heavy-duty aluminum foil to keep warm.

In a small bowl, combine the flour and water, whisking until smooth. Add to the pan drippings and cook, stirring constantly, until the gravy is thick and bubbly. Depending on the amount of pan drippings, this will take from 4 to 8 minutes. Serve on the side with the quail.

GRAPES

(AND RAISINS)

ENJOYING RIPE GRAPES STRAIGHT FROM THE VINE HAS ALWAYS BEEN AN ACTIVITY MEANT TO be done outside in the sun. In the late summer, Southern grapevines are loaded with fruit that literally drips with flavor. If you've never tasted one that fresh, you will need a quick lesson to get you through the experience successfully.

Pull the grape from the vine and plop it in your mouth. You will then need to press it against the roof of your mouth with your tongue. The juicy pulp will fly out of the skin and you'll have a burst of flavor as you munch away. Spit out the seeds and if you don't want the skin, spit it out too. Then do it again. It's totally addictive. And you thought Southerners were only good at spitting out watermelon seeds! We recycle grape seeds the same way!

Every time I hear the saying "Eat, drink, and be merry" I think about grapes. They seem to fulfill that command beautifully between the luscious fruit we enjoy and the wine and juice we receive after squeezing.

Traditionally, the South has been famous for growing sweet grapes like muscadines and scuppernongs. However, the ever-expanding Southern wine industry has transformed the land into showcasing vines of increasing variety. But, don't get the wrong idea! We continue to grow quite a lot of sweet grapes and transform them into loads of delicious goodies.

Still, don't be surprised to see plenty of us home folks milling around the vines throughout August and September, just having a little snack!

Nutrition: Regardless of the variety, grapes are great sources of potassium and vitamin A. They are good sources of calcium, phosphorus, vitamin C, dietary fiber, and magnesium. The exact calorie count will depend on the variety you select, but will average around one hundred calories per cup.

Selection: Be choosy when shopping for grapes. All varieties should be purchased in bunches with well-colored berries that are firmly attached to pliable green stems. Grapes don't continue to ripen after harvesting, so make sure they are firm and wrinkle-free. The color of the variety should be consistent throughout the bunch.

Storage: Place grapes in a ventilated plastic bag and store in the crisper drawer of the refrigerator. Store them unwashed and they will keep up to a week. Wash with a gentle spray of cold water just before using. Allow the grapes to drain in a colander or pat them dry. Don't remove them from the stems until ready to use.

BREAKFAST IN BREAD

Chunks of chopped apples keep this bread moist. You also have a lovely mosaic of apples, raisins, and pecans dotted throughout the bread.

YIELD: 1 LOAF

3 cups all-purpose flour
1 tablespoon baking powder
1 teaspoon salt
$^3/_4$ cup sugar
2 teaspoons ground cinnamon
3 eggs, lightly beaten
$1^1/_2$ cups milk
1 cup chopped pecans
$1^1/_4$ cups golden raisins
1 cup peeled and chopped Golden Delicious
    apples

Preheat the oven to 375°F. Grease and flour a loaf pan and set aside.

In mixing bowl, combine the flour, baking powder, salt, sugar, and cinnamon. In the bowl of an electric mixer, combine the eggs and milk, beating well. Gradually add the flour mixture. Fold in the pecans, raisins, and apples.

Spoon the batter into the prepared pan. Bake 1 hour, or until a tester inserted in the center comes out clean. Immediately remove from the pan and cool completely on a wire rack before slicing and serving.

FRUITCAKE COOKIES

My grandmother made these delicious cookies on years that she didn't make a fruitcake. They are filled with lots of raisins and have enormous keeping qualities.

YIELD: 9 DOZEN

4 tablespoons unsalted butter, softened
$^1/_2$ cup packed brown sugar
2 eggs, separated
$1^1/_2$ tablespoons milk
$1^1/_2$ teaspoons baking soda
2 tablespoons orange juice
$1^1/_2$ cups all-purpose flour
$^1/_2$ teaspoon ground cinnamon
$^1/_2$ teaspoon ground cloves
$^1/_2$ teaspoon ground allspice
$^1/_2$ teaspoon ground nutmeg
1 (8-ounce) package chopped dates
$^1/_2$ pound red candied cherries, quartered
$^1/_3$ pound candied pineapple, chopped
1 (15-ounce) package golden raisins
3 cups chopped pecans

Preheat the oven to 300°F. Lightly grease 2 baking sheets and set aside.

In the bowl of an electric mixer, cream the butter and brown sugar until light and fluffy. Add the egg yolks, beating just until blended.

In a separate bowl, combine the milk and baking soda, stirring until the baking soda completely dissolves. Add the orange juice and set aside.

In a separate bowl, combine the flour, cinnamon, cloves, allspice, and nutmeg. Remove $^1/_2$ cup of the flour mixture and toss with the dates, cherries, pineapple, raisins, and pecans. Set aside.

Alternately add the remaining flour mixture and milk mixture to the egg mixture, beginning and ending with the flour. Gradually stir in the fruit mixture.

Beat the egg whites at high speed of an electric mixer until stiff peaks form. Fold into the batter. Drop tablespoons of the dough onto the prepared baking sheets. Bake 15 to 18 minutes, or until light golden brown. Cool on wire racks. Store in an airtight container between layers of wax paper. Or you can freeze the cookies up to three months.

GOLDEN RAISIN PIE

This recipe of my grandmother's reluctantly became a craving. I believe she made it a couple of times before I tried it, for some reason. As soon as I did, I loved it and wondered why I had been so stubborn!

YIELD: 8 SERVINGS

1 recipe Single Pie Pastry (page 402)
3 eggs, lightly beaten
$1/4$ pound (1 stick) unsalted butter, melted
2 tablespoons white vinegar
$1^1/_2$ cups sugar
$1/2$ teaspoon ground cinnamon
1 cup golden raisins
1 teaspoon pure vanilla extract

Preheat the oven to 450°F. Place the pastry in a 9-inch pie plate and flute as desired. Prick the bottom and sides with a fork. Bake 4 minutes. Remove from the oven and cool completely on a wire rack.

Meanwhile, decrease the oven temperature to 350°F.

In a mixing bowl, combine the eggs, butter, vinegar, sugar, and cinnamon, blending well. Stir in the raisins and extract. Pour into the prepared pastry. Bake 30 minutes, or until the pie is set. Cool completely on a wire rack before slicing and serving.

GRAPE EXPECTATIONS JELLY

Spread your bread with peanut butter and get ready to top it with a homemade jelly that will knock your socks off!

YIELD: 4 HALF-PINTS

4 cups grape juice
3 cups sugar

In a large heavy saucepan over high heat, combine the grape juice and sugar, stirring well. Boil, stirring frequently, until a thermometer reaches 220°F. Remove from the heat and quickly skim off the foam. Pour into hot sterilized canning jars, leaving $1/4$-inch headspace. Remove any air bubbles, wipe the rims, and adjust the lids. Process 5 minutes in a boiling water bath. Cool completely on wire racks away from drafts.

MUSCADINE SAUCE

This will look like grape jelly that hasn't jelled, but it's supposed to look that way. It's a sauce that is marvelous with roasted turkey. Do not overcook!

YIELD: 5 PINTS

5 pounds muscadine grapes
9 cups sugar
2 cups cider vinegar
1 tablespoon ground cinnamon
1 tablespoon ground allspice
1 teaspoon ground cloves

Squeeze the pulp from the grapes into a bowl. Place the skins in a large saucepan and place over medium-high heat. Bring to a boil, cover, and reduce the heat to medium. Cook 15 minutes, stirring occasionally.

Place the pulp in a saucepan over medium heat and cook 20 minutes. Pour through a fine mesh strainer into the saucepan containing the skins. Discard the solids. Add the sugar and, stirring occasionally, cook over medium heat 1 hour, or until thickened.

Stir in the vinegar, cinnamon, allspice, and cloves.

Cook exactly 10 minutes longer. Ladle into hot, sterilized canning jars, leaving $\frac{1}{2}$-inch headspace. Remove any air bubbles, wipe the rims, and adjust the lids. Set aside to cool completely on a wire rack. Refrigerate until ready to use.

RUM RAISIN ICE CREAM

You might as well get yourself prepared for brain freeze. You will find this ice cream so luscious, you won't be able to keep from eating it quickly.

YIELD: 2 QUARTS

$1\frac{1}{4}$ cups golden raisins
$\frac{1}{3}$ cup dark rum
3 cups milk
1 cup sugar
9 egg yolks
2 cups cream

Place the raisins in a small bowl and mix with the rum. Cover and let stand 8 hours at room temperature.

In a heavy saucepan over medium heat, bring the milk just to a simmer. Meanwhile, whisk together the sugar and egg yolks until thick. Gradually whisk in the hot milk. When thoroughly mixed, return to the saucepan.

Reduce the heat to medium-low. Cook around 7 minutes, whisking constantly until the custard thickens and coats a spoon. Place the saucepan over a pan of ice and whisk until the mixture cools. Around 8 minutes.

Pour the raisin mixture through a fine mesh strainer and discard the rum. Stir the raisins and cream into the cooled custard, blending well.

Transfer the custard to a 5-quart ice cream freezer and freeze according to the manufacturer's directions.

SNACK ATTACK OATMEAL RAISIN COOKIES

Childhood memories will come rushing back with one bite of these tasty cookies.

YIELD: 2 DOZEN COOKIES

$\frac{1}{2}$ pound (2 sticks) unsalted butter, softened
1 cup granulated sugar
1 cup packed brown sugar
2 eggs
2 cups self-rising flour
2 teaspoons ground cinnamon
3 cups uncooked regular oats
1 cup golden or dark raisins
1 cup chopped pecans

Preheat the oven to 400°F.

In the bowl of an electric mixer, cream the butter, granulated sugar, and brown sugar until light and fluffy, around 3 minutes. Add the eggs, beating until well blended.

Reduce the mixer speed to low and gradually add the flour and cinnamon. Stir in the oats, raisins, and pecans. Drop tablespoons of batter onto ungreased baking sheets. Bake 10 to 12 minutes, or until golden brown. Cool on wire racks. Store in an airtight container between layers of wax paper.

GRAVY

I REMEMBER THE FIRST TIME I MADE GRAVY. IT WAS PART OF A MEAL MANAGEMENT CLASS at Mississippi State University. Like anyone who has ever been assigned the task, I was a nervous wreck wondering if the finished product would be lump free. I had watched my grandmother make it for years and just tried to imitate her actions. It ended up being, quite simply, perfection.

After that successful experience, I realized the truth of learning through watching others and practicing. But making gravy continues to be a source of frustration for many cooks who can normally whip out a dish without even thinking. I would venture to say that failed gravy is very likely one of the most discarded of all homemade recipes.

Yet, gravy is so tied with traditional Southern cooking that it sometimes becomes more important than the item it is ladled over. Gravy isn't just something made for company, but enhances suppers and dinners on a regular basis. In many areas of the South, it is practically considered a beverage! Honestly, the gravy boat has a rightful place during any meal and can transform even the most ordinary foods.

Gravy begins with pan drippings, the natural juice leftover after cooking meat. That is where it differs from a sauce, which may have nothing in common ingredient-wise with the food item it is accompanying. The only exception is chocolate gravy. Technically, it is a sauce, but don't tell Southern cooks that!

Gravy is usually, but not always, thickened with flour. Occasionally, cornstarch will sneak in, while at other times, you don't use a thickener at all (such as with red-eye gravy). Gravy is able to be poured thanks to the addition of liquids, such as stock, milk, wine, or juice. The secret to success is stirring, so pull out that wooden spoon and start practicing. These recipes will make a gravy professional out of you!

Thin: Is your gravy too thin? The best thickening agent is time. As gravy cooks, liquid evaporates, but not the other ingredients. This will work in your favor, but resist the temptation to rush the process. Don't go higher than medium heat or you'll scorch the gravy rather than thicken it.

Lumpy: If you find yourself with lumpy gravy in spite of your best effort, it is salvageable. Place a large wire mesh strainer over a bowl. Pour the gravy into the strainer, mashing it through with the back of a wooden spoon. Return the strained gravy to your skillet to gently reheat. Discard those nasty lumps!

Fatty: If your gravy ends up with too much fat on the top, you have a couple of options. You can either skim it off or sop it up with a piece of loaf bread. Discard the loaf bread and serve.

Too Salty: If you have over-salted the gravy, add a pinch or two of light brown sugar to counteract the saltiness. Stir until the sugar dissolves and serve.

Not Smooth: A tablespoon of butter stirred into cream gravy will give it a satiny texture.

BROWN GRAVY

I love this gravy with roast beef of any kind.

YIELD: 1½ CUPS

2 tablespoons pan drippings, bacon grease,
    or unsalted butter
3 tablespoons all-purpose flour
¼ teaspoon salt
⅛ teaspoon black pepper
1½ cups cold water

In a heavy skillet over medium heat, melt the drippings. Stir in the flour, salt, and pepper, blending well. Continue to stir about 1 minute, or until the mixture is dark brown. Add the water and reduce heat to low. Simmer 5 minutes. Adjust the seasonings if necessary. Serve warm.

CHICKEN GRAVY

You've already fried the chicken. Now it's time to make the gravy for those mashed potatoes you'll be serving with it!

YIELD: 2¼ CUPS

¼ cup pan drippings from frying chicken
¼ cup all-purpose flour
½ teaspoon salt
¼ teaspoon black pepper
2 cups milk

In a heavy skillet over medium heat, combine the drippings, flour, salt, and pepper. Cook 1 minute, stirring constantly. Gradually add the milk and bring to a boil, stirring constantly. Reduce heat to low and cook 3 minutes, stirring constantly. Adjust the seasonings if necessary. Serve warm with fried chicken.

CHOCOLATE GRAVY

This is a Southern dessert served with leftover biscuits. Put a small pat of butter on the hot biscuit and cover with chocolate gravy for an end-of-the-meal delight!

YIELD: 1½ CUPS

1½ cups milk
1 cup sugar
3 tablespoons unsweetened cocoa powder
2 tablespoons all-purpose flour
1 tablespoon unsalted butter

Place the milk in a heavy saucepan over medium heat. Add the sugar, cocoa powder, and flour, whisking until smooth. Bring to a boil, stirring constantly. Cook 7 minutes, or until thick and bubbly. Stir in the butter, blending well. Serve warm.

GIBLET GRAVY

This is better known as Thanksgiving gravy.

YIELD: 1¼ CUPS

3 cups turkey stock
Giblets
4 tablespoons pan drippings from roasted
    turkey or bacon grease
3 tablespoons all-purpose flour
½ teaspoon salt
½ teaspoon black pepper
½ teaspoon poultry seasoning
2 hard-cooked eggs, chopped

In a large saucepan, bring the stock to a boil. Add the giblets and cook until tender, about 1 hour. Remove the giblets from the stock and cool. When cool enough to handle, remove the meat from the neck and finely chop.

In a large saucepan, heat the drippings over medium heat until hot. Add the flour, salt, pepper, and poultry seasoning and stir about 1 minute, or until brown. Add the stock (around 1 cup) from the boiled giblets, and cook, stirring constantly, until smooth and thick, about 2 minutes.

Add the chopped giblets and reduce heat to low. Simmer 5 minutes. Stir in the eggs and adjust the seasonings if necessary. Serve warm.

MUSHROOM GRAVY

Go ahead and spoon this over anything, but it is particularly excellent with quail or beef.

YIELD: 2 CUPS

2 tablespoons pan drippings or vegetable shortening
1 cup sliced mushrooms
2 tablespoons all-purpose flour
1 cup vegetable or beef stock
$1/2$ teaspoon Worcestershire sauce
$1/2$ teaspoon salt
$1/4$ teaspoon black pepper

In a heavy skillet over medium heat, melt the pan drippings. Stir in the mushrooms and cook 3 to 4 minutes. Add the flour and continue stirring until brown, about 1 minute.

Add the stock, Worcestershire, salt, and pepper, stirring until well blended. Reduce heat to low and simmer 5 minutes. Adjust the seasonings if necessary and serve warm.

MUSTARD GRAVY

This unique gravy makes any type of grilled or roasted pork come alive!

YIELD: 1 CUP

1 tablespoon pan drippings or unsalted butter
1 tablespoon all-purpose flour
$1/2$ teaspoon salt
$1/4$ teaspoon black pepper
1 cup milk
3 tablespoons prepared mustard
1 tablespoon prepared horseradish

In a heavy saucepan over medium heat, melt the drippings. Whisk in the flour, salt, and pepper. Cook about 1 minute, stirring constantly until the mixture is smooth.

Gradually stir in the milk and bring to a boil. Boil and stir 1 minute. Add the mustard and horseradish, stirring until heated through. Adjust the seasonings if necessary. Serve warm.

ORANGE GRAVY

Match this gravy with roasted duck and you'll suddenly love roasted duck! It's also divine with grilled chicken.

YIELD: ¾ CUP

1 tablespoon pan drippings or unsalted butter
1 large scallion, sliced
1 cup chicken stock
4 (2-inch-long) strips orange zest
$1/4$ cup dry white wine
2 tablespoons fresh orange juice
$1/8$ teaspoon salt

¹⁄₈ teaspoon black pepper
¹⁄₈ teaspoon red pepper
2 teaspoons cornstarch
1 tablespoon water

Melt the drippings in a heavy saucepan over medium heat. Add the scallion and sauté until tender, about 2 minutes. Add the stock and zest. Bring to a boil and reduce heat to low. Simmer 10 minutes. Strain the stock and discard the solids.

Return the stock to the saucepan and add the wine, juice, salt, black pepper, and red pepper, mixing well. Increase the heat to medium. In a separate bowl, combine the cornstarch and water. Stir into the stock mixture.

Cook, stirring constantly, until the gravy comes to a boil. Boil 1 minute. Serve warm.

RED-EYE GRAVY

The story goes that Andrew Jackson asked his cook to prepare lunch. The cook had been on a drinking binge the night before and looked the part. General Jackson told him to fix some country ham and gravy as red as the cook's eyes. It was overheard by others and became known as red-eye gravy from then on. This gravy can only be made with the fat left in the skillet after country ham has been fried. Darkening the gravy with instant coffee is optional.

YIELD: ¹⁄₃ CUP

2 tablespoons drippings from country ham
  that has been pan-fried
1 teaspoon sugar
¹⁄₄ cup cold water
1 tablespoon instant coffee granules (optional)

After the country ham has been fried, add the sugar to the liquid leftover in skillet. Place over medium-high heat and allow the sugar to brown about 1 minute while scraping the leftover pan residue. Add the water and simmer 1 minute, or until well blended. If desired, add the coffee. Serve warm.

SAUSAGE GRAVY

Meet the best friend of a hot biscuit!

YIELD: 3 CUPS

¹⁄₄ pound ground pork sausage, hot or mild
4 tablespoons unsalted butter
¹⁄₃ cup all-purpose flour
3¹⁄₄ cups milk
¹⁄₂ teaspoon salt
¹⁄₂ teaspoon black pepper

Brown the sausage in a large skillet over medium heat, stirring until it crumbles. Drain on paper towels and set aside.

Reduce the heat to low and reserve 1 tablespoon of the drippings in the skillet. Add the butter, stirring until it melts. Add the flour, stirring until smooth. Cook 1 minute, stirring constantly.

Gradually add the milk and increase the heat to medium. Stir constantly until thick and bubbly, about 4 minutes. Add the reserved sausage, salt, and pepper. Cook 2 minutes more, stirring constantly. Serve warm.

SAWMILL GRAVY

This is a wonderful white gravy that is served with Chicken-Fried Steak (page 61) or Chicken-Fried Chicken (page 147).

YIELD: 1 CUP

2 tablespoons pan drippings or unsalted butter
2 tablespoons all-purpose flour
$\frac{1}{2}$ teaspoon salt
$\frac{1}{4}$ teaspoon white pepper
1 cup milk

In a heavy saucepan over medium heat, melt the drippings. Stir in the flour, salt, and pepper until well blended. Gradually add the milk, blending well.

Reduce the heat to low and simmer 4 to 5 minutes, or until thick and bubbly, stirring constantly. Adjust the seasonings if necessary. Serve warm.

SOUR CREAM GRAVY

The perfect accompaniment to fried pork chops.

YIELD: 1 $\frac{1}{3}$ CUPS

2 tablespoons all-purpose flour
$\frac{1}{3}$ cup water
2 tablespoons pan drippings from frying pork chops
1 (8-ounce) container sour cream
$\frac{1}{2}$ teaspoon salt
$\frac{1}{4}$ teaspoon white pepper

Combine the flour and water, stirring until smooth. Add to the pan drippings in the pork chop skillet and cook over low heat, stirring constantly until thick and bubbly, around 2 minutes.

Stir in the sour cream, salt, and pepper. Cook until thoroughly heated, about 4 minutes. Serve warm.

TASSO GRAVY

Tasso is cured pork or beef that has been seasoned with Cajun spices and smoked. This gravy transforms Shrimp and Grits.

YIELD: 3$\frac{3}{4}$ CUPS

4 tablespoons pan drippings or unsalted butter
$\frac{1}{2}$ cup all-purpose flour
4 cups chicken stock
$\frac{3}{4}$ cup chopped tasso

Melt the drippings over medium-low heat in a heavy saucepan. Add the flour, whisking until smooth. Cook 4 minutes or until light brown, stirring constantly.

Gradually add the stock. Increase heat to medium and stir constantly until the mixture has thickened, around 3 minutes. Bring to a boil and reduce heat to low. Simmer 12 to 15 minutes, stirring occasionally. Stir in the tasso just before serving.

TOMATO GRAVY

Forget serving ketchup with meatloaf. This gravy is easy to make and enhances the meatloaf flavor without being overpowering.

YIELD: 1$\frac{1}{2}$ CUPS

2 tablespoons pan drippings or bacon grease
3 tablespoons all-purpose flour
$\frac{1}{2}$ teaspoon salt
$\frac{1}{4}$ teaspoon black pepper
$\frac{1}{2}$ cup tomato juice
1 cup cold water

In a heavy skillet over medium heat, melt the drippings. Stir in the flour, salt, and pepper, blending well. Continue to stir until it turns brown, around 2 minutes.

Add the juice and water, stirring until well blended. Reduce the heat to low and simmer 5 minutes. Serve warm.

WHITE WINE GRAVY

I've served this gravy with everything from grilled turkey tenderloins to fish to steamed vegetables. It is incredibly versatile.

YIELD: 2 CUPS

4 tablespoons pan drippings or unsalted butter
$1/2$ dry white wine
$1^1/4$ cups chicken stock
$1/2$ teaspoon salt
$1/2$ teaspoon black pepper
2 tablespoons cornstarch
$1/4$ cup water

In a heavy saucepan over medium heat, melt the drippings. Whisk in the wine, stock, salt, and pepper, stirring well to combine.

In a separate bowl, mix together the cornstarch and water. Add to the wine mixture, stirring well. Bring to a boil and continue to boil 1 minute, stirring constantly. Serve warm.

BOATS: A great invention is a gravy boat where the spout goes to the bottom of the boat. This allows you to use the warmest gravy that is on the bottom. It has an additional benefit if you have gravy that seems a bit fatty. You'll be pouring from the bottom and not the fatty top.

NAME: Gravy boats get their name from the boat shape of the pitcher. It usually has a matching plate that is attached to the boat in some cases. This plate protects your table linens by catching drips.

"Getting the nomination is like gravy. Winning would be like whatever is better than gravy."

—BILLY BOB THORNTON

GREEN BEANS

THINK ABOUT THE VEGETABLES MOST FREQUENTLY GROWN IN THE SOUTH. YOU PROBABLY immediately think of large quantities of tomatoes, corn, and squash, and you would be right . . . but only partially right. The South is green bean country.

Until I moved to Tennessee, I didn't realize what an important agricultural crop green beans were to the South. We grow thousands of acres of this unique bean with fields covering the Southern landscape in every state.

Some Southerners refer to green beans as snap beans or string beans. This goes back to our heritage and the old-time varieties that used to be grown by our ancestors. They were often called snap beans because that's how you prepared them for cooking, by snapping the freshly harvested beans into bite-size pieces.

The term "string bean" came into play because you had to string the beans you snapped in a couple of ways. First of all, in older varieties, there was a string that ran along the edge of the bean pod that had to be pulled off and discarded. You certainly didn't want that tough string making its way into your cooking pot.

Then, green beans were often strung with a needle and fishing line just as many would commonly today string hot peppers. These were hung to dry so Southerners could have green beans long after the fresh season was over.

Many Southern cooks still belong to the "cook them to death" club when it comes to preparing green beans. I love green beans cooked that way. But I also venture out occasionally to enjoy these beans in a more recognizable state and find they are just as delicious.

Nutrition: Green beans that are cooked in a small amount of water for a short time contain only twenty-seven calories per cup. They are good sources of vitamins A, B1, and C and also contain moderate amounts of dietary fiber and trace elements.

Preparation: Fresh green beans should snap easily when broken. The entire pod is edible, with only the ends needing to be trimmed away before using.

Selection: When purchasing green beans, select those that are well shaped and slender. The beans should appear crisp and brightly colored with no skin blemishes. Wilted, dull colored beans have been stored too long.

Storage: Although they appear sturdy, green beans are very perishable. They should be stored for only a few days before using. Keep them cold and humid, which means they need to be in the vegetable crisper drawer. Because of the high rate of respiration, store green beans in a loosely closed plastic bag to prevent moisture loss and wilting.

ALMOND-COATED GREEN BEANS

You'll find yourself going back to this recipe over and over. The beans are coated with ground almonds that have been toasted in garlic butter.

YIELD: 4 SERVINGS

1 pound fresh green beans, trimmed
$\frac{1}{2}$ cup whole almonds
2 tablespoons unsalted butter
1 garlic clove, minced
$\frac{1}{2}$ teaspoon salt
$\frac{1}{4}$ teaspoon black pepper

Place the green beans in a large pot of boiling water and cook 10 minutes. While the beans are cooking, place the almonds in the bowl of a food processor and grind. Set aside. Drain the beans and set aside.

Melt the butter in a large skillet over medium heat. Add the garlic and cook, stirring constantly, 1 minute. Stir in the ground almonds and cook 2 minutes.

Add the beans and cook 2 minutes longer, or until the beans are heated through. Sprinkle evenly with the salt and pepper. Serve warm.

"COME ALIVE" BLANCHED GREEN BEANS

You will be amazed at how the color comes alive when green beans are blanched. It is remarkable. Use this recipe if you have extra beans to freeze.

YIELD: 8 SERVINGS

$1\frac{1}{2}$ pounds green beans, trimmed
$\frac{1}{2}$ teaspoon salt

Place a Dutch oven filled with water over medium-high heat. Bring to a boil. Add the beans and salt. Cover and boil 4 to 5 minutes. Drain and plunge into ice water 4 minutes. Drain again. Package into freezer containers and freeze or refrigerate and use within two days.

BROWN BUTTER GREEN BEANS

Butter is browned in a skillet until it becomes nutty and incredibly aromatic. Then it's tossed over fresh cooked green beans. It's simple and divine!

YIELD: 4 SERVINGS

2 cups water
$\frac{1}{4}$ teaspoon salt
1 pound green beans, trimmed
$\frac{1}{4}$ pound (1 stick) unsalted butter

Place the water and salt over medium-high heat and bring to a boil. Add the beans and cook 10 minutes, or to the desired degree of tenderness, and drain.

Meanwhile, place the butter in a small skillet over medium heat. Cook 6 minutes or until the butter turns a dark amber color. Drizzle the hot beans with the butter. Serve warm.

Note: If you want "cooked to death" green beans, cook the beans at least 30 minutes or to the desired degree of doneness.

HOLIDAY TRADITION GREEN BEAN CASSEROLE

Who hasn't made this? Who doesn't love it?

YIELD: 6 TO 8 SERVINGS

1 (10.75-ounce) can condensed cream of mushroom soup

$^3/_4$ cup milk

$^1/_8$ teaspoon black pepper

2 (14.5-ounce) cans green beans, drained and rinsed

1 cup fried onion bits, divided

Preheat the oven to 350°F. Lightly grease a 1$^1/_2$-quart baking dish and set aside.

In a large bowl, combine the soup, milk, and pepper, mixing well. Stir in the green beans and $^1/_2$ cup of the onion bits. Pour into the prepared baking dish.

Bake 30 minutes. Stir the casserole and sprinkle with the remaining onion bits. Bake 5 minutes longer. Let stand 5 minutes before serving.

LAKESIDE GREEN BEAN SALAD

This cold salad can be made the day ahead and is perfect for carrying to a picnic beside the lake. It is surprisingly simple and great with fried chicken. It utilizes green beans you've frozen from the garden or bought frozen.

YIELD: 4 SERVINGS

1$^1/_2$ pounds small red potatoes

1 (9-ounce) package frozen whole green beans

$^1/_2$ cup mayonnaise

$^1/_4$ cup sour cream

2 tablespoons white wine vinegar

2 tablespoons chopped onion

1 tablespoon sugar

1$^1/_2$ teaspoons chopped fresh dill

$^1/_2$ teaspoon white pepper

Place a large stockpot of water over medium-high heat and bring to a boil. Add the potatoes and cover. Cook 10 minutes or until tender. Drain. When cool enough to handle, cut in wedges, place in a serving bowl, and set aside.

Cook the beans according to the package directions. Drain, rinse with cold water, and add to the potatoes. Gently toss.

In a small bowl, whisk together the mayonnaise, sour cream, vinegar, onion, sugar, dill, and pepper. Add to the potato and green bean mixture and gently toss to evenly coat. Cover and refrigerate at least 4 hours before serving.

LEATHER BRITCHES

In the South, dried green beans are called Leather Britches. It is an age-old process of blanching the beans first to destroy bacteria, drying the beans, and then stringing them as you would hot peppers. They can be rehydrated in water or stock and used in any recipe calling for green beans.

YIELD: 1 STRING

2 pounds fresh green beans, trimmed

Bring a pot of water to a boil over medium-high heat. Place the beans in a steamer and steam 2$^1/_2$ minutes. Run cold water over the steamed beans and place in a single layer on a jelly-roll pan. Place in the freezer 30 minutes.

Lay the beans on the racks of a food dehydrator. Dry 8 to 10 hours or follow the instructions on your dehydrator. When the beans are completely dry, string, and hang in a dry, dark place until ready to use.

Note: You can also place the dried beans in a canning jar or any tightly closed container.

....

"PIMENA" GREEN BEANS

Southerners are known for shortening words on occasion. Hardly anyone in the South properly says the word "pimiento," so you'll really fit in by pronouncing it the way we do! The addition of bright red pimientos accents this green bean dish with flair.

YIELD: 6 TO 8 SERVINGS

1½ pounds fresh green beans, trimmed

3 bacon slices

1 large yellow onion, peeled and chopped

3 garlic cloves, minced

1 (2-ounce) jar diced pimientos, drained

¼ cup red wine vinegar

1 teaspoon sugar

½ teaspoon salt

½ teaspoon black pepper

½ teaspoon cumin seeds

Cover the green beans in boiling water and cook 15 minutes. Drain and set aside.

Meanwhile, cook the bacon in a large skillet over medium heat until crisp, around 8 minutes. Drain on paper towels and reserve the drippings in the skillet. When the bacon has cooled enough to handle, crumble and set aside.

Sauté the onions and garlic in the hot drippings over medium-high heat until tender, about 7 minutes. Stir in the pimientos, vinegar, sugar, salt, pepper, and cumin seeds. Stir in the green beans, cover, and reduce heat to medium. Simmer 5 minutes. Sprinkle with the bacon just before serving.

ROASTED GREEN BEANS WITH MUSHROOMS

Easy, easy, easy! This recipe lets the oven do all the work and you just have to dish it up.

YIELD: 6 TO 8 SERVINGS

1½ pounds fresh green beans, trimmed

1 (8-ounce) package button or cremini mushrooms

2 tablespoons olive oil

1 teaspoon kosher salt

½ teaspoon black pepper

Preheat the oven to 350°F. Line a jelly-roll pan with aluminum foil and lightly grease with cooking spray. Lay the green beans on the pan.

Wash and slice the mushrooms. Scatter over the green beans. Drizzle with the oil and toss gently. Sprinkle with the salt and pepper. Bake 25 to 30 minutes, shaking the pan halfway through to evenly roast. Serve warm.

ORIGIN: Green beans are American natives. We know Indians cultivated varieties of green beans here for centuries, and they eventually spread to the Caribbean Islands. In the 1500s they spread through Europe, but were not common. In fact, they were known as a rich man's dish until early in the 1600s.

DIFFERENCES: Green beans differ from other beans thanks to a pod that has a thick wall. Unlike other beans, such as kidney, lima, or pinto, the green bean pod is edible. The strings of some older varieties have been removed through refined breeding techniques, so there are now no strings attached!

GREENS

(COLLARDS, MUSTARD, TURNIP, POKE SALLET, AND KALE)

IF YOU GREW UP IN THE SOUTH, YOU PROBABLY HAVE THE WORDS OF TONY JOE WHITE'S "POKE Salad Annie" memorized. It's a song about a girl who had to pick wild greens just to have something to eat.

While Tony Joe wrote and sang wonderfully, his spelling left a bit to be desired. The actual spelling for this Southern roadside green is "poke sallet." If you only sing about it and never taste it, you've missed a huge part of Southern culture.

Unfortunately, that's the way it is with lots of young, tender leaves we lump into the family just known as "greens." Although greens are quite popular in the South, they don't enjoy that same level of enthusiasm in other parts of the country.

Greens have been a basic part of Southern cooking for generations. All the varieties taste slightly different and have a different texture. Generally, when you hear of a side dish of greens, it means the leaves and more tender stems of turnips, collards, or mustard greens.

Greens do something very few other foods can pull off. They make bitterness a virtue. When very young, it's not as noticeable, but as they age a bit, the tang comes to the forefront. Many believe that a nip of frost, especially on turnip greens, improves the flavor. I tend to agree after growing my own and experimenting.

If you don't speak "greenology," let me give you a crash course. A "mess" is any measured amount necessary to serve a certain amount of people. It is usually the amount that can be picked and carried in a brown paper grocery sack and it serves the number of people it serves.

Cooked greens are always served with a slotted spoon. The leftover cooking liquid is commonly referred to as "pot liquor" (sometimes spelled "pot likker") and is delicious. Pour it off in a gravy boat and serve it on the side with cornbread. That is what Southerners call supper!

Nutrition: Greens are a pharmacy of vitamins and minerals. They are high in dietary fiber and loaded with vitamins A, C, and B. In addition, they contain calcium, folic acid, and are high in essential minerals.

Preparation: Wash, wash, and wash the leaves, and then wash them again. For good measure, you might consider washing them once more. Drain them in a large colander. Some squeeze the leaves dry, but I usually don't.

Selection: Select leaves with a good, even color that show no signs of wilting or yellowing. They should always look crisp and fresh.

BRAISED KALE

Cooked kale is quickly browned in fat and cooked on the stove. A tight-fitting lid is a must for this cooking technique.

YIELD: 4 SERVINGS

$3/4$ pound fresh kale
$1^1/2$ teaspoons bacon drippings
$1/4$ cup purple onion, diced
2 garlic cloves, minced
2 tomatoes, peeled and roughly chopped
$1/4$ teaspoon dried basil
$1/8$ teaspoon dried oregano
$1/8$ teaspoon salt
1 teaspoon balsamic vinegar
$1/4$ teaspoon black pepper

Remove the stems from the kale and wash thoroughly. Drain but do not pat dry. Place in a large Dutch oven. Cover and cook over medium heat 7 to 8 minutes, or until tender. Drain well, reserving 2 tablespoons of the cooking liquid. Squeeze the kale between paper towels until barely moist. Coarsely chop and set aside.

Heat the drippings in a large skillet over medium-high heat. Add the onion and garlic and sauté 4 minutes. Add the chopped kale, tomatoes, the reserved cooking liquid, basil, oregano, and salt. Stir to combine, cover, and cook 5 minutes. Remove from the heat and stir in the vinegar and pepper. Serve immediately.

COUNTRY COLLARDS

This is my grandmother's recipe for collards. It is marvelous and seasoned just right. You can use the same recipe for any type of green.

YIELD: 6 SERVINGS

2 pounds collard greens
1 pound ham hocks
4 cups water
$1^1/2$ teaspoons sugar
1 teaspoon salt
$1/4$ teaspoon black pepper

Wash the greens thoroughly and drain. Coarsely chop and place in a large Dutch oven that has been coated with cooking spray. Add the ham hocks, water, sugar, salt, and pepper. Bring to a boil and reduce the heat to low. Cover and simmer 30 to 40 minutes, or until tender. Serve warm.

DOWN-HOME TURNIP GREEN CASSEROLE

Although this calls for cooked turnip greens, you can use any leftover cooked greens for this recipe. It's got the cornbread that is traditionally served on the side with greens, crumbled over the top.

YIELD: 12 SERVINGS

3 cups cooked turnip greens
1 white onion, peeled and chopped
1 tablespoon hot sauce
2 (10.75-ounce) cans cream of mushroom soup
$1/2$ teaspoon white pepper
3 cups crumbled cornbread
$1/4$ pound (1 stick) unsalted butter, melted

Preheat the oven to 350°F. Lightly grease a 13 x 9-inch baking dish. Spread the turnip greens evenly in the dish. Layer with the onion and sprinkle with the hot sauce.

Spread the soup over the top and sprinkle with the pepper. Top with the cornbread and drizzle with the melted butter. Bake 30 minutes, or until golden brown. Serve warm.

•••

GOOD LUCK SOUP

Eating greens on New Year's Day is rumored to bring lots of "folding green" money in the upcoming year. But don't just save this delectable blend of ham, peas, and collards for one day of the year. It's a great one-pot meal any day.

YIELD: 4 TO 6 SERVINGS

$1/4$ cup bacon grease or pan drippings

2 medium white onions, peeled and finely chopped

3 garlic cloves, minced

$1/2$ pound cooked chopped ham

1 pound collard or turnip greens, finely chopped

4 cups vegetable or chicken stock

4 cups water

2 (16-ounce) cans black-eyed peas, drained and rinsed

$3/4$ teaspoon seasoned salt

$1/2$ teaspoon black pepper

2 teaspoons cider vinegar

Place the drippings in a large stockpot over medium heat. Add the onions, garlic, and ham. Cook, stirring frequently, until the onions are soft, about 12 minutes.

Add the collards, stock, and water and bring to a boil. Reduce the heat to low and simmer, uncovered, 20 minutes. Mash one can of the peas with a fork. Stir in the mashed peas and whole peas. Simmer another 5 minutes. Stir in the seasoned salt, pepper, and vinegar. Cook another 2 minutes and serve hot.

GREEN PASTA SALAD

This Southern pasta salad is loaded with greens and then topped off with parsley from the garden and crumbled bacon. Serve it with pork chops or ham.

YIELD: 6 SERVINGS

1 pound greens (mustard, kale, or collards), washed

12 ounces macaroni

2 tablespoons bacon drippings

$1/2$ cup crumbled feta cheese

$1/4$ cup coarsely chopped toasted walnuts

$1/2$ teaspoon seasoned salt

$1/4$ teaspoon black pepper

2 tablespoons chopped fresh parsley

4 bacon slices, cooked and crumbled

Bring 6 cups of water to a boil over medium-high heat in a large stockpot. Remove and discard the thick stems and cut the greens into 1-inch strips. Add to the boiling water and cook 6 minutes. Using a skimmer or slotted spoon, transfer the greens to a colander to drain. Chop when cool enough to handle.

Return the water to a boil and add the macaroni. Cook just until tender, but still firm to the bite, around 8 minutes. Drain, reserving $3/4$ cup of the cooking liquid. Return the macaroni and greens to the pot, along with the drippings.

Toss to coat and stir in feta, walnuts, salt, and pepper. Add enough reserved cooking liquid to moisten, at least $1/4$ cup. Transfer to serving bowl and sprinkle with parsley and bacon. Serve warm.

"GREEN WITH ENVY" BEANS

These greens are terrific with grilled chicken or turkey. The leftovers are just as tasty as the original version.

YIELD: 6 SERVINGS

3 tablespoons bacon drippings

3 garlic cloves, thinly sliced

$\frac{1}{4}$ teaspoon dried crushed red pepper

1 pound greens (mustard, kale, turnip, or collards) washed, stemmed, and cut into strips

1 cup vegetable stock

1 (15-ounce) can white kidney beans (cannellini beans), drained and rinsed

1 teaspoon red wine vinegar

$\frac{1}{4}$ teaspoon salt

$\frac{1}{4}$ teaspoon black pepper

Place the drippings in a large skillet over medium heat. Add the garlic and crushed pepper. Stir-fry 1 minute. Add the greens by handfuls and allow each to wilt before adding more, tossing to coat.

Add the stock. Simmer, covered, until the greens are tender, around 8 to 10 minutes. Stir in the beans and simmer uncovered until nearly all the liquid has evaporated, about 3 minutes. Add the vinegar, salt, and pepper. Transfer to a serving bowl and serve hot.

MIXED GREENS AND BACON

I love this mixture of turnip and mustard greens. Each lends the dish a terrific depth of flavor that is distinctly Southern and welcome on any dinner table.

YIELD: 10 SERVINGS

5 bacon slices, chopped

2 large white onions, peeled and chopped

4 quarts chicken stock

1 pound turnip greens, washed and chopped

8 ounces mustard greens, washed and chopped

Place the bacon in a large Dutch oven over medium heat. Cook 2 minutes and add the onions. Cook 4 minutes longer, stirring frequently.

Stir in the stock. Add the turnip greens and mustard greens, one handful at a time until all the greens are in the pot. Cook, uncovered, 1 hour or until the greens are tender. Stir occasionally. Serve warm.

MUSTARD GREENS WITH HAM

Mustard greens are so named thanks to the mustard-like, almost peppery flavor of the dark green leaves. Sorghum gives these greens just a hint of sweetness.

YIELD: 6 SERVINGS

1 tablespoon vegetable oil

1 pound country ham, chopped

2 cups water

2 pounds fresh mustard greens

1 teaspoon salt

$\frac{1}{2}$ teaspoon black pepper

1 tablespoon sorghum syrup

Wash the greens thoroughly and drain.

Heat the oil in a large Dutch oven over medium-low heat. Add the ham and cook 4 minutes. Stir in the water and greens. Cover and cook 30 minutes, stirring occasionally.

Add the salt, pepper, and syrup, mixing well. Cover and cook another 15 minutes. Serve warm.

SOUTHERN COOKED COLLARDS

You can also use this recipe for making poke sallet, but substitute ham hock for the bacon. Start with a large pot, but the collards will cook down quickly.

YIELD: 8 TO 10 SERVINGS

2 bunches collard greens, washed
   and trimmed
1 pound bacon, chopped
4 tablespoons unsalted butter
2 white onions, peeled and diced
3 cups chicken stock
$^1/_2$ cup cider vinegar
1 teaspoon salt
$^1/_2$ teaspoon black pepper

Coarsely chop the collards and set aside. Cook the bacon in a large stockpot over medium heat. When crisp, remove with a slotted spoon and drain on paper towels. Add the butter to the drippings. Add the onions and sauté 8 to 10 minutes, or until wilted and translucent.

Stir in the collards, stock, vinegar, salt, pepper, and all but $^1/_4$ cup of the bacon. Bring to a boil and reduce heat to low. Cook, stirring occasionally, 20 minutes, or to the desired degree of tenderness.

Drain in a colander over a measuring cup. Transfer the collards to a serving dish. Add $^1/_4$ cup of the cooking liquid and stir. Top with reserved bacon and serve hot.

TURNIP GREENS WITH POT LIQUOR

Pot liquor is the liquid left over after greens have been cooked. You must *serve cornbread with these greens to soak up the extra liquor. Never discard pot liquor. True Southerners will keep making cornbread until it is gone!*

YIELD: 10 SERVINGS

2 bunches turnip greens
$^1/_2$ pound ham, diced
6 cups water
Pepper Sauce (page 346)

Remove the stems from the turnip greens and wash thoroughly. Drain in colander.

Meanwhile, place the ham and water in a large stockpot over medium-high heat. Just as the water comes to a boil, add the greens. Reduce the heat to medium-low and cook 30 minutes.

Remove the greens with a large slotted spoon to a serving dish. Pour the cooking liquid into a gravy boat. Serve hot in bowls with the extra cooking liquid and pepper sauce.

Collard greens are a variety of cabbage that doesn't form a head but instead a loose form of a head at the top of a tall stem. Many confuse collards with kale, but they have a unique flavor all their own. Some have described the flavor as a cross between kale and cabbage.
Kale doesn't form a head either and has a mild cabbage flavor. The leaves are green and sometimes tinged with purple. This green is a near twin of collards, which handles the hot weather much better than kale.
Mustard greens have very deep, dark green leaves and a pungent mustard-like flavor.
Turnip greens are the leafy tops of the turnip root vegetable. They are slightly sweet when young, with a stronger taste as they age.

GRITS

IF YOU HAVEN'T NOTICED, SOUTHERNERS HAVE THEIR OWN WAY OF DEFINING THINGS. I HAVE A particular friend who is "not from around here," as we say of anyone who was not born and raised in the South. For some reason, we were talking about grits one day at lunch and she told me she just loved grits made from oats.

Although technically, she is correct (grits can even be made out of rice), in the South, when we say "grits" we are always talking about ground corn. Some call them hominy grits, but we generally keep our grits separate from our hominy, which is puffed corn thanks to the addition of lye.

I'm fairly certain I have adored grits since birth. I really don't remember the first time I ate them. I suppose, like most Southerners, it was around the time I learned to walk, if not before. Don't you love it that whether it is used as a plural or singular, the spelling and pronunciation of the word is the same?

I can eat grits plain or lavishly enhanced. I enjoy them during any meal of the day but particularly at breakfast. My husband, on the other hand, is the only Southerner I know who doesn't like them. It's the only thing I can find that's wrong with him!

So, in order to satisfy my deep-rooted desire for grits, I serve them regularly when others are headed to my house for any type of meal. I routinely make grits during cooking classes and on television. I like to take side dishes based on grits to holiday dinners, brunches, and to potlucks ... anything to take care of my need for this truly Southern sidekick that is made from ground *corn*!

Quick and Regular Grits: I use quick and regular grits in cooking and like them both. You'll find the difference is in the grind. Quick grits have a fine texture and regular grits have a medium grind. Another major difference is in the cooking time required, with quick living up to the name. Always follow the cooking directions on the package for the best results.

Instant Grits: I'm not a big fan of individually packaged instant grits. These are fine-textured grits that have already been cooked and then dehydrated, much the same as instant rice. They only need to have boiling water added to be quickly reconstituted.

Definition: Grits are made by grinding dried whole corn kernels. Whether it is labeled white or yellow depends on the corn from which it was ground.

Grinds: You will quickly discover that grits are available in several different grinds. Coarse grinds are typically labeled as stone ground. You can also find medium and fine, which is usually sold in supermarkets. Grind a little too fine and you have cornmeal.

ANDOUILLE GRILLED GRITS

This is a great side dish for catfish or with a green salad. If you don't have good weather for grilling, broil them in the oven for a couple of minutes on each side.

YIELD: 6 SERVINGS

2 tablespoons vegetable oil

$^1/_2$ cup chopped andouille or spicy smoked sausage

$^1/_2$ cup chopped sweet onion

1 (14.5-ounce) can chicken stock

$^3/_4$ cup half-and-half

1 cup quick grits, uncooked

$^1/_2$ teaspoon salt

$^1/_4$ teaspoon black pepper

2 tablespoons unsalted butter, melted

Place the oil in a large saucepan over medium-high heat. Add the sausage and onions and sauté until tender, around 4 minutes. Stir in the stock and half-and-half. Bring to a boil and gradually stir in the grits, salt, and pepper.

Cover, reduce the heat to low, and simmer 10 minutes, stirring occasionally until thickened. Lightly grease a small jelly-roll pan. Pour the grits mixture in the prepared pan. Cover and refrigerate overnight or 8 hours.

Prepare the grill to medium heat (325°F to 350°F). Meanwhile, invert the grits on a flat surface and cut into squares. Brush both sides of each square with the melted butter. Grill, uncovered, 3 to 4 minutes on each side. Serve warm.

FOOTHILLS GRITS CUSTARDS

I love these individual servings of cheesy herbed grits because they can be made ahead of time. They look marvelous on the plate and pair well with turkey, pork, or beef.

YIELD: 6 SERVINGS

3 cups water

$^3/_4$ cup regular grits, uncooked

1 teaspoon salt

2 garlic cloves, minced

$^3/_4$ cup shredded sharp Cheddar cheese

2 tablespoons snipped fresh chives

1 tablespoon chopped fresh parsley

1 egg yolk

Preheat the oven to 350°F. Lightly grease 6 (4-ounce) ramekins and set aside.

Place the water in a heavy saucepan over medium-high heat and bring to a boil. Gradually add the grits and salt. Cook according to the package directions.

Remove the grits from the heat and stir in the garlic, cheese, chives, and parsley. Beat the egg yolk in a medium bowl and add about one-fourth of the hot grits to the egg. Mix well and add back into the grits pot, stirring constantly to blend.

Spoon the grits into the prepared ramekins. Place the ramekins in a 13 x 9-inch baking dish and pour hot water around the ramekins to a depth of 1 inch in the pan. Cover with aluminum foil and bake 30 minutes.

Remove the ramekins from the water bath and cool on a wire rack. When ready to serve, preheat the oven to 300°F. Invert onto a lightly greased baking sheet and remove the ramekins. Bake 7 minutes, or until thoroughly heated. Transfer to individual plates and serve warm.

GREENS AND GRITS

This dish is a great marriage between collards and cheese-enhanced grits. It's one of my favorite ways to showcase both and is perfect with turkey or veal.

YIELD: 8 SERVINGS

4 cups chicken stock, divided

1 cup cream

1 cup regular grits, uncooked

$\frac{1}{2}$ cup milk

1 pound fresh collard greens, washed, drained, and cut into $\frac{1}{2}$-inch strips

4 tablespoons unsalted butter

$1\frac{1}{2}$ cups shredded Parmesan cheese

$\frac{1}{2}$ teaspoon black pepper

In a large saucepan over medium-high heat, combine 3 cups of the stock with the cream. Bring to a boil and gradually stir in the grits. Reduce the heat to medium and stir until the mixture returns to a boil. Reduce the heat to low, cover, and simmer 25 to 30 minutes, stirring frequently. Gradually add the milk if the grits seem too dry.

Meanwhile, place the greens and the remaining cup of stock in a large saucepan over medium-high heat. Bring to a boil and reduce the heat to low. Cover and simmer 5 minutes or until the greens are tender.

Drain and plunge the greens into ice water. Drain well and set aside.

When the grits are done, add the milk if you have not already done so. Stir in the butter, cheese and pepper. Stir until the butter and cheese melt. Stir in the greens. Cook 3 to 4 minutes longer, stirring constantly until thoroughly heated. Serve warm.

HERITAGE GRITS SOUFFLÉ

This light, fluffy side dish is as impressive looking as it is tasty. It's very easy to prepare, so don't be intimidated by the word "soufflé."

YIELD: 6 SERVINGS

2 tablespoon unsalted butter

2 garlic cloves, minced

4 cups water

$\frac{3}{4}$ teaspoon salt

$\frac{1}{2}$ teaspoon black pepper

$\frac{1}{4}$ teaspoon dry mustard

1 cup regular grits, uncooked

4 eggs, separated

2 cups shredded sharp Cheddar cheese

$\frac{1}{8}$ teaspoon hot sauce

$\frac{1}{4}$ teaspoon cream of tartar

1 teaspoon paprika

Place the butter in a heavy saucepan over medium heat. Add the garlic and sauté 2 minutes. Stir in the water, salt, pepper, and mustard. Gradually stir in the grits. Reduce the heat to low and simmer 15 to 20 minutes, stirring occasionally until thickened.

Meanwhile, preheat the oven to 400°F. Lightly grease and flour a 2-quart soufflé dish and set aside.

Remove the grits from the heat and stir in the egg yolks, cheese, and hot sauce. Set aside.

Beat the egg whites and cream of tartar at high speed with an electric mixer until stiff peaks form. Fold half of the egg whites into the grits mixture. Gently fold the remaining whites into the grits. Transfer to the prepared soufflé dish and sprinkle with the paprika.

Bake 45 minutes or until puffed and lightly browned. Serve immediately.

PASS THE GRITS DRESSING

At Thanksgiving, cornbread dressing reigns supreme. But any other time of the year is perfect to pass the grits dressing instead. It pairs well with beef, pork, or chicken.

YIELD: 10 SERVINGS

3 cups regular grits, uncooked
1 cup all-purpose flour
2 teaspoons baking powder, divided
$1/4$ teaspoon baking soda
4 eggs, divided
4 cups buttermilk
2 tablespoons vegetable oil
1 white onion, peeled and chopped
1 cup chopped celery
2 tablespoons dried sage
1 (12-ounce) can evaporated milk
2 (14.5-ounce) cans chicken stock

Preheat the oven to 325°F. Place a well-greased 10-inch cast-iron skillet in the oven to preheat while the oven reaches the desired temperature.

Meanwhile, in a mixing bowl, combine the grits, flour, 1 teaspoon of the baking powder, and the baking soda. Make a well in the center and set aside.

In a separate bowl, whisk together 2 of the eggs, the buttermilk, and the oil. Add to the well in the grits mixture, stirring just until moistened.

Pour the batter into the hot skillet. Bake 1 hour, or until firm in the center but not browned. Cool on a wire rack. Crumble into a mixing bowl when cool enough to handle. Stir in the onion, celery, sage, milk, stock, the remaining teaspoon of the baking powder, and the remaining 2 eggs.

Transfer to a greased 13 x 9-inch baking dish. Bake 50 minutes, or until the dressing is firm and set in the center. Serve hot.

HOT TOMATO GRITS

These are served hot and thanks to cayenne, taste hot. Adjust the amount to fit the tastebuds of your family.

YIELD: 6 SERVINGS

3 bacon slices, chopped
2 (14.5-ounce) cans chicken stock
$1/2$ teaspoon black pepper
1 cup quick grits, uncooked
2 tomatoes, peeled and chopped
2 tablespoons canned chopped green chiles
$1/2$ teaspoon cayenne
1 cup shredded sharp Cheddar cheese

Cook the bacon in a large saucepan over medium-high heat until crisp, around 6 to 7 minutes. Gradually add the stock and pepper and bring to a boil.

Stir in the grits, tomatoes, and chiles. Return to a boil, stirring frequently. Reduce the heat to low and simmer 20 minutes, stirring frequently.

Stir in the cayenne and cheese. Cover and let stand 5 minutes. Stir again and serve warm.

PINEAPPLE CHESS GRITS PIE

You would never know grits play a role in the making of this creamy pie! Take one to the office or a neighbor and keep one for yourself.

YIELD: 2 (9-INCH) PIES

2 cups water
$1/2$ cup quick grits, uncooked
$1/4$ teaspoon salt
1 (8-ounce) can crushed pineapple, drained
4 ounces cream cheese, softened

3 eggs

1 cup sugar

1/2 cup milk

1/4 teaspoon coconut or rum extract

2 (9-inch) graham cracker crusts

Preheat the oven to 300°F.

Place the water in a saucepan over medium-high heat. Bring to a boil. Gradually add the grits and salt. Return to a boil, cover, and reduce the heat to low. Cook 5 minutes, stirring frequently.

Remove from the heat and stir in the pineapple and cream cheese.

Transfer to the container of an electric blender and process until smooth. With the blender running on low, add the eggs, one at a time. Blend well. Add the sugar, milk, and extract and process until smooth.

Evenly pour the mixture into the crusts. Bake 1 hour, or until the pies are set. Cool completely on wire racks before slicing and serving.

SOUTHERN HOSPITALITY CHEESE GRITS

Don't associate grits as only a breakfast food. Serve this Southern staple any time of the day. Play with the cheese variety to change the taste and texture.

YIELD: 4 TO 6 SERVINGS

2 cups half-and-half

1/4 teaspoon salt

1/8 teaspoon garlic powder

1/8 teaspoon black pepper

1/2 cup quick grits, uncooked

2 ounces cream cheese, softened and cubed

3/4 cup shredded Jarlsberg or sharp Cheddar cheese

1/4 teaspoon hot sauce

In a large saucepan over medium-high heat, combine the half-and-half, salt, garlic powder, and pepper. Just as the mixture comes to a boil, gradually stir in the grits. Return to a boil, cover, and reduce the heat to low. Simmer 5 to 7 minutes, or until thick.

Remove from the heat and add the cream cheese, Jarlsberg, and hot sauce, stirring until the cheeses melt. Serve immediately.

"TAKE IT EASY" BAKED CHEESE GRITS

Use either yellow or white grits for this dish, or a mixture of the two. The oven takes care of things while you attend to other brunch details.

YIELD: 12 SERVINGS

5 cups water

1 garlic clove, minced

1 teaspoon onion salt

1/2 teaspoon white pepper

1 1/3 cups quick grits, uncooked

1/4 pound (1 stick) unsalted butter, softened

2 cups shredded sharp Cheddar cheese

1/2 cup grated Parmesan cheese

Place the water, garlic, salt, and pepper in a heavy saucepan over medium-high heat. Bring to a boil and gradually add the grits. Return to a boil and reduce the heat to medium low. Simmer 4 to 5 minutes, stirring occasionally.

Meanwhile, preheat the oven to 350°F. Lightly grease a 13 x 9-inch baking dish and set aside.

Remove the grits from the heat. Stir in butter and Cheddar cheese, blending well. Transfer to the pan and spread evenly. Sprinkle with the Parmesan.

Bake 45 minutes or until set and lightly browned. Let stand 5 minutes before serving warm.

SUNDAY BRUNCH GRILLADES AND GRITS

This incredible recipe is Louisiana in the morning. Grillades, pronounced "gree-Yahds," are thinly pounded rounds of beef. They are served on top of hot grits.

YIELD: 4 SERVINGS

1$\frac{1}{2}$ pounds top round steak

1$\frac{1}{2}$ teaspoons salt

$\frac{3}{4}$ teaspoon black pepper

$\frac{1}{2}$ teaspoon dried thyme

$\frac{1}{8}$ teaspoon cayenne

4 garlic cloves, minced

2 tablespoons all-purpose flour

2 tablespoons vegetable oil

1 cup chopped onion

$\frac{1}{2}$ cup chopped celery

$\frac{1}{2}$ cup chopped green bell pepper

1 (16-ounce) can stewed tomatoes, undrained

1 cup water

2 cups regular grits, uncooked

With a meat mallet or a rolling pin, pound the steak to $\frac{1}{4}$-inch thickness. Cut into 2-inch squares and set aside.

In a small bowl, combine the salt, pepper, thyme, cayenne, and garlic. Rub into the meat and sprinkle with the flour.

Place the oil in a large Dutch oven over medium-high heat. In batches, brown the meat on both sides, around 2 minutes. Drain the meat on paper towels and set aside.

Add the onions, celery, and pepper to the pot and reduce the heat to medium. Cook 5 minutes, stirring frequently or until the vegetables are tender. Add the tomatoes, water, and the reserved meat. Cover, reduce the heat to low and simmer 30 minutes. Turn the meat and cook, covered, an additional 15 minutes, or until the meat is tender.

Cook the grits according to the package directions. Spoon the grillades over the grits and serve warm.

HAM

I **LOVE HOLIDAY TRADITIONS WHEN IT COMES TO FOOD. TURKEY BELONGS TO THANKSGIVING,** steak is under the spotlight for Father's Day, burgers and hot dogs get July Fourth and Memorial Day. Easter means ham. It couldn't be a more perfect time for this meat. It seems to be made for all the other side dishes that signal spring, one of my favorite seasons of the year. Pair it with fresh asparagus and early peas and you have a feast.

For Southerners of old, ham was an economic necessity. While many could not afford the expense of owning beef cattle, nearly everyone owned some hogs. For many, it was one of the only regularly served meats they had to enjoy. Every Southern house had a smokehouse on the property, and the hams that hung from the rafters would tempt royalty. The first frost meant that hog-killing time was near.

There are vast differences in flavor between fresh ham and country ham, and Southerners love them both. Fresh ham is exactly what the name says . . . fresh, with no curing taking place, and a shelf life that is no longer than any other fresh meat product.

Country ham, on the other hand, is dry cured and smoked. It is a Southern delicacy that involves time, patience, and a well-protected family recipe. The curing mixture mainly consists of salt, along with sugar and other seasonings. This mix effectively pulls moisture from the meat, and the amount of time it takes depends on the size of the ham.

After the salt solution is rinsed off, the ham is smoked and aged, and like good wine and vanilla extract, the time process only serves to improve the flavor. The South wrote the book on country ham, and if you haven't had one from Kentucky, Virginia, Georgia, or Tennessee, you really haven't had country ham.

Purchasing: Always plan on purchasing enough ham to have for the main meal, with plenty of leftovers to enjoy afterward. Allow two generous or three more conservative servings per pound, but don't forget the bone! If I'm serving eight people, I usually purchase a seven-pound ham so I'll have plenty of leftovers for ham sandwiches and recipes calling for cooked ham.

Slicing: Remember the old electric knife with twin serrated blades that your parents used to have? Well now is the perfect time to plug it back in because it does a remarkable job of slicing baked ham. After the ham has rested, start carving by cutting a few thin slices from the side of the ham that is round and protruding. That makes a flat base with the meatiest part on top. Baked ham is usually sliced straight down and in quarter-inch intervals.

Storage: Vacuum-sealed is the ideal way to store ham because air and moisture are kept at bay. Cooked leftover ham should be tightly wrapped in aluminum foil and refrigerated. Plastic wrap tends to hold in too much moisture and can speed up the spoilage of the ham.

COUNTRY HAM AND GRUYÈRE THUMBPRINTS

Lots of Southern cheese shops make Gruyère, which has a great nutty flavor. You can also substitute Vallagret. My favorite is made at the Mississippi State Cheese Shop.

YIELD: 3 DOZEN

1/4 pound (1 stick) unsalted butter, cut into large pieces

1/2 teaspoon salt

1 cup water

1 cup all-purpose flour

4 large eggs

1/2 teaspoon black pepper

1/2 cup finely chopped country ham

1 cup finely shredded Gruyère cheese

36 (1/2-inch) cubes Gruyère (8 ounces total)

Preheat the oven to 400°F. Line 2 baking sheets with parchment paper and set aside.

Bring the butter, salt, and water to a boil in a heavy saucepan over medium heat. Stir until the butter is melted.

Add the flour and stir vigorously until incorporated. Continue to cook, stirring until the mixture pulls away from sides of pan, about 2 minutes. Remove from the heat and let cool 2 minutes.

Transfer the dough to a large bowl and add the eggs, one at a time, beating well after each addition. Stir in the pepper, ham, and shredded cheese. Spoon the dough into a pastry bag.

On the prepared sheets, pipe 1 1/2-inch-wide rosettes 1 inch apart. Make a deep indentation in the center of each with your water-dampened thumb.

Bake until crisp, about 25 to 30 minutes. Transfer to a wire rack and press a cheese cube into each indentation. Serve warm or cool completely.

Note: This appetizer can easily be frozen for later use. Place on baking sheets and freeze uncovered until firm, about 1 hour. Transfer to an airtight container and freeze up to 6 weeks. To serve, preheat the oven to 425°F and bake until the cheese is melted, 12 to 14 minutes.

BREAKFAST COUNTRY HAM PUFF

This breakfast favorite is so named because it puffs up beautifully in the oven. It's best to let it sit a few minutes after baking before serving…that's a hard few minutes to wait!

YIELD: 8 SERVINGS

4 slices white bread, torn

2 cups milk

3 eggs, beaten

1/2 teaspoon spicy mustard

1/8 teaspoon paprika

Dash of garlic powder

2 cups shredded sharp Cheddar cheese

1 1/2 cups diced country ham

1/2 cup chopped onion

4 bacon slices, cooked and crumbled

2 tablespoons chopped fresh parsley

Preheat the oven to 375°F. Lightly grease a 13 x 9-inch baking dish and set aside.

Combine the bread, milk, eggs, mustard, paprika, and garlic powder in a large mixing bowl. Beat at medium speed of an electric mixer 1 minute or until smooth.

Stir in the cheese, ham, onions, bacon, and parsley. Pour into the prepared pan and bake 25 minutes, or until center is set. Let stand 10 minutes before serving.

COUNTRY HAM LOAF

Think meatloaf, but with a ham twist.

YIELD 8 SERVINGS

1 tablespoon unsalted butter

1 medium white onion, peeled and chopped

1½ pounds ground pork

1½ pounds ground country ham

1 egg

¾ cup buttermilk

3 tablespoons Dijon mustard

2 tablespoons chopped fresh parsley

½ teaspoon black pepper

½ cup fresh breadcrumbs

Preheat the oven to 375°F. Line a jelly-roll pan with parchment paper and set aside.

In a medium skillet over medium heat, melt the butter. Add the onion and cook 5 minutes or until soft. Cool slightly.

Meanwhile, in a large bowl, combine the pork and ham. In a separate bowl, whisk together the egg, buttermilk, mustard, parsley, and pepper. Add the egg mixture, onions, and breadcrumbs to the pork mixture, stirring only until combined. Do not over mix.

Form the meat into a loaf and place on the prepared pan. Bake 1 hour, or until a meat thermometer registers 170°F. Let rest 15 minutes before slicing and serving.

DEEP-FRIED HAM AND CHEESE BALLS

Start the party! Whether it's tailgating, the holidays, or an impromptu gathering of friends, this appetizer gets things off to a great start. It's a delicious way to use leftover cooked ham.

YIELD: 4 DOZEN APPETIZERS

2 cups plain dry breadcrumbs, divided

2 cups ground cooked ham

1 cup shredded Parmesan cheese

4 eggs, lightly beaten

½ cup finely chopped onion

¼ cup finely chopped fresh parsley

Vegetable oil

Place ½ cup of the breadcrumbs in a shallow dish and set aside.

In a large mixing bowl, combine the remaining breadcrumbs with the ham, cheese, eggs, onion, and parsley. Mix well and shape into 1-inch balls. Roll in the reserved breadcrumbs and place on a jelly-roll pan. Refrigerate 30 minutes.

Meanwhile, pour the oil to a depth of 2 inches in a large cast-iron skillet. Place over medium-high heat and bring to 375°F. Cook the ham balls 3 minutes in the hot oil, or until golden brown. Drain on paper towels and serve warm.

Note: These appetizers are great served with honey-mustard dressing.

FRIED COUNTRY HAM

Go ahead and turn to the recipe for Red-Eye Gravy (page 237) and Buttermilk Biscuits (page 75) because if you are going to do this, you must do it right.

YIELD: 4 SERVINGS

4 country ham slices, cut in ¼-inch slices

Place the ham slices in a heavy skillet over medium heat. Do not trim excess fat from the slices until after frying. However, you need to score the edges to prevent buckling. Fry 2 or 3 minutes. Turn only once and cook until both sides are light brown. Drain on paper towels and serve warm. **Note:** Leftovers should be wrapped tightly in aluminum foil and refrigerated. Do not use plastic wrap because it holds in too much moisture and speeds up spoilage.

NEIGHBORLY COUNTRY HAM BREAD

Use this lovely bread to welcome new neighbors to the area or to thank them for gathering your mail and newspapers while you were out of town. It makes two loaves, so you'll still have one for yourself.

YIELD: 2 LOAVES

1 ($^1/_4$-ounce) envelope active dried yeast
$^1/_2$ cup warm water (100°F to 110°F)
1 cup plus 2 teaspoons plain cornmeal, divided
3 tablespoons sugar
2 cups buttermilk
1 egg, lightly beaten
3 tablespoons unsalted butter, melted
2 teaspoons black pepper
$^1/_2$ teaspoon ground red pepper
5 to 6 cups all-purpose flour
2$^1/_2$ cups cooked ground country ham

Combine the yeast and warm water in a large bowl and let stand 5 minutes. Stir in 1 cup of the cornmeal, the sugar, buttermilk, egg, butter, black pepper, and red pepper. Stir in just enough of the flour to make a stiff dough. Turn the dough out onto a lightly floured surface.

Knead in the ham until the dough is smooth and elastic, about 8 minutes. Place in a well-greased bowl, turning to grease the top. Cover and let rise in a warm place free from drafts 2 hours or until doubled in bulk.

Grease 2 (9-inch) round cake pans and sprinkle evenly with the remaining cornmeal. Punch the dough down and divide in half. Shape each half into a round loaf and place in the prepared pans. Brush the tops with water. Cover and let rise 30 to 40 minutes, or until doubled in size.

Preheat the oven to 375°F. Bake 30 to 40 minutes, or until loaves sound hollow when tapped. Remove from the pans immediately and cool at least 10 minutes on wire racks. Serve warm with butter.

JAZZED UP COUNTRY HAM SPREAD

This is a great way to use leftover country ham and is a terrific appetizer!

YIELD: 2 CUPS

1$^1/_2$ cups cooked country ham, ground
1 (3-ounce) package cream cheese, softened
$^1/_4$ cup chopped yellow sweet onion
$^1/_4$ cup chopped pecans, toasted
2 tablespoons chopped fresh parsley
1 scant tablespoon spicy brown mustard
Toasted pecan halves for garnish

In a medium bowl, mix together the ham, cream cheese, and onions. If using a hand mixer, use the lowest speed to blend. Add the chopped pecans, parsley, and mustard. Cover and refrigerate at least 2 hours or overnight to allow the flavors to meld.

When ready to serve, bring to room temperature 30 minutes. Transfer to a serving bowl and garnish with pecan halves. Serve with whole-wheat crackers.

MESQUITE GRILLED SMOKED HAM

Although this ham is fully cooked, you get extra flavor by grilling and basting it with a brown sugar and mustard glaze.

YIELD: 14 SERVINGS

Mesquite wood chips
1 (7-pound) smoked, fully cooked ham half
$\frac{1}{2}$ cup packed light brown sugar
$\frac{1}{2}$ cup water
$\frac{1}{3}$ cup dry mustard

Soak the wood chips in water at least 2 hours and up to 24 hours before grilling.

Loosen the bone from the ham, but do not remove.

In a small mixing bowl, combine the brown sugar, water, and mustard. Whisk until smooth. Brush some of the sugar mixture over the ham.

Prepare a charcoal grill to low heat (300°F) and place the soaked chips around the edge of the grill. Place the ham on the rack at least 8 inches from the heat source. Cover and grill 1 hour, turning and brushing with the glaze often. Cook until a meat thermometer registers 140°F, continuing to brush with the glaze. Let rest 10 minutes.

Remove the bone and slice. Serve warm.

Note: You can bake the ham if desired. Preheat the oven to 325°F and bake $2\frac{1}{2}$ to 3 hours or until a meat thermometer registers 140°F.

LOUISIANA PRALINE HAM

A warm combination of maple syrup, sugar, butter, and pecans makes this ham taste like candy.

YIELD: 12 SERVINGS

1 (8-pound) fully cooked ham
$1\frac{1}{2}$ cups maple syrup
$\frac{1}{2}$ cup packed light brown sugar
2 tablespoons unsalted butter
1 cup chopped pecans

Preheat the oven to 325°F.

Score the outside of the ham in a diamond design. Place the ham in a large shallow baking dish or roasting pan with the fat side up. Insert an oven-safe meat thermometer in the center so the thermometer face can be seen from the oven window. Make sure the tip of the thermometer does not touch any bone.

Bake the ham $1\frac{1}{2}$ hours, uncovered. Meanwhile, combine the syrup, sugar, and butter in a small saucepan over medium heat. Bring to a simmer and stir until the sugar dissolves and the butter melts. Stir in the pecans.

Baste the ham with the glaze every 15 minutes until the thermometer registers 140°F. Let rest at least 10 minutes before slicing.

OVEN-BRAISED SOUTHERN COUNTRY HAM

This recipe is your best friend when you have other recipes or items that require your attention. Plus, it makes its own gravy.

YIELD: 6 SERVINGS

6 (4-ounce) slices country ham
2 tablespoons brown sugar
$\frac{1}{4}$ cup water

Preheat the oven to 350°F. Place the ham slices in a lightly greased 13 x 9-inch baking dish. Sprinkle with the brown sugar and pour the water around ham. Cover tightly with aluminum foil and bake 30 minutes. Serve immediately.

HERBS

FOR YEARS, I WAS IN AN HERB RUT. I ONLY USED PARSLEY, BASIL, CHIVES, AND OREGANO, WITH a bit of sage every now and then. Oh, I grew lots of other things and for the record, growing herbs in the South is as easy as breathing. But it was the use that baffled me.

I did not grow up around fresh herbs. My mother and grandmother would rather have grown flowers or vegetables, which they did with flare. Herbs did not find a way into my life until after college when I was on my own. A friend gave me a dill plant and I thought, "Okay, what am I supposed to do with this?"

That gift changed my cooking life. From there, I slowly began to expand my herb horizons. Now, I am an herb maniac. I make daily trips to my herb garden to snip on something that simply must be added to a dish. Even when I'm not snipping from it, I'll find a reason to wander through the plants.

From nature's standpoint, herb gardening is the original aromatherapy. Every time a Southern wind blows, I get the benefit of the fragrance. Even weeding is a pleasure because your sleeves and hands carry the smell long after the chore is complete.

I have managed to convert my husband to an herb lover on most levels. At first, George would whine that there was grass in his food. With the exception of rosemary, which he can pick up in even the smallest amounts, he's now on the herb bandwagon.

It's time for you to get on board too. If you don't grow your own, there are good supplies available year-round in the produce department of your local supermarket and at farmers' markets. Start experimenting with different flavors and forms of the more common ones. You'll be glad you did.

Flavors:
Strong Flavors: Use herbs with the strongest flavor sparingly. Just a little goes a long way! The strongest-flavored herbs are cilantro, oregano, rosemary, sage, and thyme.
Medium Flavors: Use medium-flavored herbs more generously than those with a strong flavor. These include basil, dill, fennel, and mint.
Delicate Flavors: Chives and parsley have soft flavors and can be used in abundance. Parsley is a hardy biennial plant and is the most widely used herb in the U.S.

Snipping: Harvest fresh herbs early in the morning just after the dew has dried. Give them a gentle spray of cool water and pat dry. Want real flavor? The pungency of any herb will be strongest just before it flowers. That's when the flavor oils are most concentrated.

Storage: Place fresh herbs that you purchase already cut or that you over-cut from the garden in a vase with the stems in an inch or two of water. Cover the foliage loosely with a plastic bag and refrigerate. You can keep several types in the same vase.

COUNTRY HERB FLATBREAD

I experimented with this recipe for my friend John Gordon's surprise birthday party. When guests gobbled it up as soon as I put it out, I knew it was a hit.

YIELD: 20 APPETIZER SERVINGS

1 (6-ounce) package pizza crust mix (or refrigerated pizza dough)

4 teaspoons olive oil, divided

2 teaspoons herbes de Provence, divided

$1/2$ cup sun-dried tomatoes, chopped

$1/3$ cup goat cheese, softened

2 eggs

Freshly cracked pepper

Preheat the oven to 400°F. Lightly grease a 13 x 9-inch baking pan and set aside.

Prepare the pizza dough according to the package directions. Place in center of the prepared pan and starting at the center, press out evenly. With your fingers, make indentations over the surface of the dough.

Brush with 3 teaspoons of the oil, and then sprinkle with 1 teaspoon of the herbes de Provence. Top with the tomatoes.

In a medium bowl, combine the cheese, eggs, the remaining oil, and the remaining herbes de Provence. Pour evenly over the tomatoes. Bake 15 to 20 minutes, or until the edges are golden brown. Sprinkle with freshly cracked black pepper before cutting into squares. Serve warm.

Note: Herbes de Provence is a mixture of basil, fennel seed, lavender, marjoram, rosemary, sage, summer savory, and thyme. Look for it in specialty stores.

FANCY HERB BUTTERS

Use this as a way to become a creative culinary artist. Any herbs you like or have on hand will work, except for strong rosemary. In that case, halve the amount used.

YIELD: ¾ CUP

$1/4$ pound (1 stick) unsalted butter, softened

$1/4$ cup chopped fresh herbs (basil, oregano, chives, parsley, tarragon, or a mixture)

In a medium bowl, mix the herbs and butter until well blended. Cover and refrigerate at least 4 hours before serving. Use within 1 week, or freeze and use within 1 month.

FLAVORED HERB VINEGARS

My pantry has a variety of herb vinegars in use. They are terrific for adding a flavor impact to salads or sauces and make excellent gifts.

YIELD: 1 PINT

2 cups distilled vinegar

$1/2$ cup crushed herbs (basil, oregano, chives, tarragon, thyme, or rosemary)

Place the vinegar in a saucepan over medium-high heat. Bring to a slight simmer, but do not boil.

Meanwhile, place the herbs in a plastic jug or container. Pour the hot vinegar over the herbs. Cool to room temperature.

Cover and store in a dark, cool place four to six weeks. Strain through a fine mesh sieve, discarding the solids. Add several sprigs of fresh herbs to decorative bottles. With a funnel, add the flavored vinegar. Add more distilled vinegar if the vinegar is too strong. Seal and store at room temperature.

FRESH HERB YEAST ROLLS

Don't feel married to the herbs called for in this recipe. Change them up according to what you have available or that needs to be snipped in the garden.

YIELD: 18 ROLLS

$^1/_4$ pound (1 stick) unsalted butter
$^3/_4$ cup milk
$^3/_4$ cup water
$^1/_2$ cup sugar
2 tablespoons chopped fresh chives
2 tablespoons chopped fresh parsley
1 tablespoon chopped fresh thyme
1 teaspoon salt
2 ($^1/_4$-ounce) packages active dried yeast
2 eggs
$7^1/_4$ cups bread flour, divided

In a medium saucepan over medium heat, combine the butter, milk, water, sugar, chives, parsley, thyme, and salt. When the butter is melted and the mixture is blended, remove from the heat. Stir in the yeast and eggs. Set aside.

In a large bowl, stir together 5 cups of the flour and the yeast mixture. Cover and let rise 30 minutes in a warm place away from drafts.

Stir in another $1^1/_2$ cups of the flour. Mix well and cover. Let rise another 30 minutes in a warm place away from drafts.

Place the remaining flour on a hard surface or board. Transfer the dough to the board and knead in the flour 3 minutes. Divide the dough into 18 equal pieces and shape into balls. Place on a lightly greased baking sheet. Cover with greased wax paper and let rise an additional 30 minutes.

Preheat the oven to 400°F. Bake 13 to 15 minutes, or until golden brown. Serve warm.

GARLIC-HERB PUFF PASTRY ROLLS

These puffy, tender pastries are irresistible and very transportable for tailgate parties or holiday events away from home.

YIELD: 5 DOZEN

1 (17 ounce) package frozen puff pastry, thawed
3 tablespoons unsalted butter, melted
2 garlic cloves, minced
$^1/_2$ teaspoon seasoned salt
2 tablespoons minced fresh chives, divided
2 tablespoons minced fresh parsley, divided
1 egg, lightly beaten

Preheat the oven to 375°F. Lightly grease 2 baking sheets and set aside.

Roll 1 pastry sheet into a large rectangle. Stir together the butter, garlic, and salt. Brush half of the butter mixture over the pastry. Sprinkle with half of the chives and parsley. Roll jelly-roll style, starting with each short side and ending at the middle of the pastry.

Repeat with the remaining pastry. Cut rolls crosswise into $^1/_3$-inch slices. Place on the prepared sheets. Brush with the egg. Bake 10 to 15 minutes, or until golden brown. Serve warm or at room temperature.

GREEN MINT JELLY

Whether you like lamb or not (a really good marriage partner), you will love the fresh flavor of this jelly any time of year. It is nice spooned over a block of cream cheese. The few drops of food coloring will keep the color from being dull.

1 cup finely chopped fresh mint
1³⁄₄ cups cold water
3¹⁄₂ cups sugar
2 tablespoons lemon juice
2 drops green food coloring
1 (3-ounce) package liquid pectin

Combine the mint and water in a covered saucepan over medium heat. Bring to a boil, cover, and let stand 15 minutes.

Pour through a cheesecloth-lined sieve into a large pot. Squeeze the cheesecloth to extract as much juice as possible from the mint. Discard the mint.

Place over medium-high heat and add the sugar, lemon juice, and food coloring, stirring well to blend. Bring to a rolling boil, stirring constantly. Add the pectin and boil 1 minute longer. Skim any foam from the surface.

Ladle into hot, sterilized canning jars, leaving ¹⁄₄-inch headspace. Wipe the rims and adjust the lids. Process in a boiling water bath 5 minutes. (See page 12 for detailed canning instructions.) Transfer to a wire rack to cool, away from drafts. Let stand at least 1 day to set before using.

HERB AND FRESH VEGETABLE STOCK

I like to poach fish in this stock, as well as use it for the base of soups and stews.

YIELD: 6 CUPS

3 carrots, cut in 1-inch pieces
3 celery stalks, cut in 1-inch pieces
  (including leaves)

1 white onion, peeled and quartered
1 head garlic, outside skin and ¹⁄₄ inch of the
  top removed
2 (1-inch) strips lemon zest
2 bay leaves
4 sprigs fresh parsley
2 sprigs fresh thyme
2 sprigs fresh oregano
1 whole dried red chili
10 peppercorns
1 clove
¹⁄₄ teaspoon salt

In a large stockpot, combine the carrots, celery, onion, garlic, zest, bay leaves, parsley, thyme, oregano, chili, peppercorns, clove, and salt. Add at least 2 quarts of water and up to 3 if the stockpot is large enough.

Place over medium-high heat and bring to a boil. Reduce heat to low and simmer gently 1 hour. Cool to room temperature and strain through a fine mesh sieve, pushing on the solids with the back of a spoon. Discard the solids. Use immediately or store in the refrigerator up to one week or the freezer up to one month.

HERBED CREAM CHEESE

The first time I had this incredible mixture of herbs and cheese, I was living on the coast of Alabama. I have been making it ever since for an appetizer or to add to mashed potatoes or hot pasta.

YIELD: 8 SERVINGS

1 (8-ounce) package cream cheese, softened
2 tablespoons half-and-half
2 garlic cloves, minced
¹⁄₄ teaspoon herbes de Provence
¹⁄₄ teaspoon dried basil

¼ teaspoon dried thyme
¼ teaspoon dried chives
¼ teaspoon dried parsley
¼ teaspoon black pepper
Fresh herbs for garnish

In the bowl of a food processor, combine the cheese, half-and-half, garlic, herbes de Provence, basil, thyme, chives, parsley, and pepper. Process until evenly blended.

Transfer to a serving bowl and cover with plastic wrap. Refrigerate at least 8 hours and up to 24 hours before serving.

When ready to serve, bring to room temperature at least 20 minutes. Garnish with fresh herbs and serve with crackers.

LEMON BASIL MAYONNAISE

Spread on a turkey sandwich or use instead of tartar sauce when serving fish of any kind.

YIELD: 2 CUPS

1 garlic clove, peeled
½ cup firmly packed basil leaves
1 tablespoon grated lemon zest
2 cups mayonnaise

In the bowl of a food processor, pulse the garlic, basil, and zest several times until the basil is finely chopped. Stir into the mayonnaise. Cover and refrigerate at least 1 hour before serving.
Note: This mayonnaise can be kept refrigerated up to one week.

THE SOUTH'S FINEST MINT JULEPS

There are thirty species of mint and nearly five hundred varieties of juleps that range from chocolate to ginger. This cocktail uses the common variety and is the South's favorite elixir. It is famously served at the Kentucky Derby, and all spring and summer long!

YIELD: 6 SERVINGS

Crushed ice
1½ cups sugar
¾ cup water
½ cup mint sprigs
12 ounces 100-proof bourbon
6 mint sprigs for garnish

Fill 10-ounce silver julep cups with crushed ice and place in the freezer overnight.

Bring the sugar and water to boil in a medium saucepan over medium-high heat. Reduce the heat to medium-low. Simmer 8 to 10 minutes, or until the syrup becomes clear and thick. Set aside to cool slightly.

Crushed the mint sprigs in your hand and stir in the syrup. Cool to room temperature. Strain into a small pitcher, discarding the solids.

Remove the cups from the freezer. Pour 2 ounces of the bourbon and 2 ounces of the syrup into each cup. Garnish with the mint sprigs and let stand 2 minutes while frost forms on the cups. Serve cold.

> "Parsley is the jewel of herbs,
> both in the pot and on the plate."
>
> —ALBERT STOCKLI

HONEY

IN THE SOUTH, WE LOVE TO SPOON HONEY ON A HOT BUTTERED BISCUIT OR BRUSH IT OVER A baking ham. We drizzle it over sticky buns, add it in any kind of batter, and cannot resist licking our fingers when the leftovers drip onto our plates.

One of my favorite Mae West lines is, "Honey, chances are you'll love me once you get to know me." It was true with her, and it is also true with the honey there in your pantry. That jar of amber liquid is a truly amazing product.

I am passionate about honey because of the enormous versatility it has in cooking. And since I work with farmers, I also appreciate the critical role bees play in agriculture. It is estimated that at least one-third of the world's food crops are pollinated by bees. Without them, we would be in a mess.

Our bee friends have produced honey for us in their highly efficient factories known as hives for eons. They busily go about collecting nectar from clover fields, wildflowers, gardens, and orchards while we go about our daily lives. Then they present us with nothing short of culinary magic. Honey is nature's masterpiece.

Both my mother and grandmother always had honey in the house and used it regularly. Now I know why. It doesn't spoil, requires no refrigeration, and can be used as a spread, topping, or baking ingredient. Honey is hygroscopic, meaning it attracts and holds moisture, so baked goods do not dry out as quickly and the shelf life is extended.

But the main reason I use it is because it tastes good. It is a supreme sweetener that adds a distinctive flavor to anything it touches. So pull that jar out of the pantry. It's time to get "busy as a bee" in the kitchen with honey!

Storage: Honey is best stored tightly closed at room temperature in a dry place, such as a pantry shelf. There is no need to refrigerate honey.

Types: Liquid honey is most popular in the South, but honey is available in several different forms. Cut comb honey has chunks or pieces of the beeswax comb in the honey. The comb is completely edible and you will notice that every honeycomb cell has six sides. **Cream or spun honey** is crystallized honey that is spun so that the crystals are extremely fine. This gives you a honey that can be spread like butter with no drips.

Making Honey: Honey is only processed by bees. Man has not figured out how to duplicate it, which makes the end product even more wonderful. Nectar is minute drops of liquid found in flower blossoms that the plant actually secretes. An average worker bee will visit anywhere from fifty to one hundred flowers on each nectar collection trip. Yet during its lifetime, each bee will only gather enough nectar to make one-twelfth of a teaspoon of honey.

CHERRY HONEY BALLS

I love anything rolled in confectioners' sugar. It sometimes makes me cough when I inhale at the wrong time, but I can't resist the temptation!

YIELD: 2 DOZEN

$1/4$ pound (1 stick) unsalted butter, softened

3 tablespoons honey

1 cup all-purpose flour

$1/2$ teaspoon salt

2 teaspoons pure vanilla extract

1 teaspoon pure almond extract

1 cup finely chopped pecans, toasted

$1/2$ cup dried tart cherries

$3/4$ cup confectioners' sugar

In the bowl of an electric mixer, cream the butter and honey until light and fluffy, about 2 minutes. Add the flour, salt, vanilla extract, and almond extract. Fold in the pecans and cherries. Wrap the dough in plastic and refrigerate 1 hour.

Preheat the oven to 300°F. Roll the dough into 1-inch balls and place 2 inches apart on an ungreased baking sheet. Bake 35 to 40 minutes, or until golden brown.

Meanwhile, place the confectioners' sugar in a shallow dish. While still warm, roll the cookies in the sugar. When the cookies have cooled completely, roll in the sugar again. Store in an airtight container between layers of wax paper.

BEE-MINE HONEY SAUCE

This is my "go to" sauce for any meat I grill or roast. It is done by the time the meat is ready and doesn't require any exotic ingredients.

YIELD: 6 SERVINGS

$1/4$ cup honey

1 (2-inch) sprig fresh thyme

$1/2$ cup red wine vinegar

$1/2$ cup chicken stock

$1/2$ teaspoon salt

$1/2$ teaspoon black pepper

Combine the honey and thyme in a heavy saucepan over low heat. Bring to a boil and cook about 10 minutes. Watch carefully and stir often to avoid scorching. Remove from the heat and add the vinegar, stock, salt, and pepper. Stir well to combine. Return to medium heat and cook until thickened, about 15 minutes, stirring frequently. Serve warm.

COOKIE JAR HONEY COOKIES

I love these lusciously big cookies that have excellent keeping qualities thanks to the honey. If there ever was a cookie jar cookie, this is it!

YIELD: 4 DOZEN COOKIES

4 cups all-purpose flour

2 teaspoons ground cinnamon

2 teaspoons ground ginger

$1^{1}/_{2}$ teaspoons salt

1 teaspoon baking powder

1 teaspoon baking soda

$1/2$ teaspoon ground cloves

$1/2$ pound (2 sticks) unsalted butter

$1^{1}/_{4}$ cups honey

$1/4$ cup sugar

1 egg

In a medium bowl, combine the flour, cinnamon, ginger, salt, baking powder, baking soda, and cloves. Set aside.

In a large saucepan over low heat, combine the butter, honey, and sugar, stirring until the sugar and butter melt completely. Set aside to cool 15 minutes. Beat in the egg. Add the flour mixture in several additions, beating until the dough is well mixed. Refrigerate 10 minutes.

Meanwhile, preheat the oven to 350°F. Lightly grease 2 baking sheets and set aside.

Roll the dough into 1½-inch balls and place on the prepared sheets 2 inches apart. Bake 15 minutes, or until lightly browned. Immediately transfer to wire racks to cool.

HONEY OF A WHEAT BREAD

This beautiful brown bread transforms a turkey sandwich into a masterpiece. It is equally perfect toasted and smeared with butter for breakfast.

YIELD: 2 LOAVES

3 cups whole-wheat flour, divided

2 cups bread flour, divided

2 teaspoons salt

1½ cups water

1 cup milk

½ cup honey

4 tablespoons unsalted butter

2 (¼-ounce) packages active dried yeast

1 egg, room temperature

In a large bowl, combine 2 cups of the whole-wheat flour, 1 cup of the bread flour, and the salt. Set aside.

In a medium saucepan, heat the water, milk, honey, and butter to 115°F. Remove from the heat and add the yeast. Stir about 3 minutes to dissolve the yeast and add the egg, stirring well. Pour the yeast mixture into the flour mixture and stir 2 minutes. Add the remaining 1 cup of the bread flour and

then the remaining 1 cup of the whole-wheat flour.

Turn out onto a floured surface and knead 6 times, adding more bread flour if needed. Place the dough in a lightly greased bowl and cover. Let stand in a warm place until doubled in size, about 1 hour. Punch down and divide the dough in half to form 2 loaves.

Place each loaf in a lightly greased loaf pan. Let stand in a warm place until doubled in size, about 1 hour. Preheat the oven to 325°F oven and bake 40 minutes. Turn out immediately onto wire racks to cool completely before serving.

MAKE-AHEAD HONEY SQUARES

The flavor of these cookies greatly improves with age. Make them at least the day before you plan on serving them.

YIELD: 16 COOKIES

1 cup all-purpose flour

½ cup sugar

⅛ teaspoon baking soda

Pinch of salt

2 egg whites

¾ cup shredded coconut

¼ cup honey

4 tablespoons unsalted butter, melted

1 tablespoon milk or cream

½ teaspoon ground nutmeg

Preheat the oven to 350°F. Lightly grease an 8-inch square baking pan and line the bottom of the pan with parchment paper. Lightly grease the parchment paper and set aside.

In a mixing bowl, combine the flour, sugar, baking soda, and salt. Make a well in the center and add the egg whites, coconut, honey, butter, milk, and nutmeg. Mix just until the ingredients are moistened. Transfer to the prepared pan.

Bake 35 minutes, or until golden brown. Immediately remove from the pan and remove the parchment paper. Place on a wire rack to cool completely. Cut into squares and store at least one day in an airtight container before serving.

NUT AND HONEY CRISPS

These crispy cookies are just the thing for an after-school snack. They are not overly sweet and easy to make.

YIELD: 2½ DOZEN COOKIES

1 cup all-purpose flour
½ teaspoon baking soda
½ teaspoon salt
6 tablespoons unsalted butter, melted
⅓ cup honey
½ teaspoon pure almond extract
1 egg
1 cup chopped almonds

Preheat the oven to 375°F.

In a mixing bowl, combine the flour, baking soda, and salt. Set aside.

In the bowl of an electric mixer, combine the butter, honey, and extract. Add the flour mixture, the egg, and almonds, mixing until the batter is well combined.

Drop teaspoons of the dough onto ungreased cookie sheets. Bake 9 to 10 minutes or until lightly browned. Immediately transfer to wire racks to cool completely. Store in airtight containers between layers of wax paper.

SPICED HONEY PECAN FINGERS

These bars remind me of autumn. They have all the spices that make me think of falling leaves, changing colors, and cooler weather.

YIELD: 36 COOKIES

2 cups all-purpose flour
½ teaspoon baking powder
½ teaspoon baking soda
¼ teaspoon salt
1 teaspoon ground cinnamon
¼ teaspoon ground cloves
12 tablespoons unsalted butter, softened
¾ cup sugar
2 egg yolks
¾ cup honey
¾ cup chopped pecans

Preheat the oven to 325°F. Lightly grease a 13 x 9-inch baking pan and set aside.

In a medium bowl, combine the flour, baking powder, baking soda, salt, cinnamon, and cloves. Set aside.

In the bowl of an electric mixer, cream the butter and sugar until light and fluffy, around 4 minutes. Add the egg yolks and then the honey, beating until well combined.

Reduce the mixer speed to low and add the flour mixture. When just blended, fold in the pecans. Spoon the batter into the prepared pan and spread evenly.

Bake 40 minutes, or until the top is lightly browned. Cool completely on a wire rack. Cut into strips and leave in the baking pan. Cover tightly with foil until ready to serve.

WAKE-UP-CALL CRUMB CAKE

Honey and pecans combine to make this old-fashioned crumb cake divine and perfect for breakfast or brunch. It can be served warm directly from the pan. In the rare event you have leftovers, wrap in aluminum foil and reheat in a 325°F oven.

YIELD: 10 TO 12 SERVINGS

12 tablespoons unsalted butter, softened

1 cup packed light brown sugar

2$\frac{1}{4}$ cups all-purpose flour

$\frac{1}{2}$ teaspoon salt

$\frac{1}{2}$ teaspoon ground cinnamon

$\frac{1}{2}$ teaspoon ground nutmeg

$\frac{3}{4}$ cup chopped pecans

1 teaspoon baking soda

$\frac{1}{2}$ teaspoon baking powder

1 cup buttermilk

$\frac{3}{4}$ cup honey

1 egg

Preheat the oven to 350°F. Lightly grease a 13 x 9-inch baking pan and set aside.

In the bowl of an electric mixer, cream the butter and brown sugar until smooth, around 2 minutes. Reduce the mixer speed to low and add the flour, salt, cinnamon, and nutmeg. Blend until the mixture forms coarse crumbs.

Set aside $\frac{1}{2}$ cup of the crumb mixture in a small mixing bowl. Add the pecans and stir until well combined. Set aside.

Add the baking soda and baking powder to the remaining crumb mixture. In a separate bowl, combine the buttermilk, honey, and egg. Stir into the crumb mixture until all the ingredients are moist. Transfer to the prepared pan and sprinkle the reserved crumb mixture evenly over the top, pressing in gently.

Bake 25 to 30 minutes or until the cake begins to pull away from the sides of the pan and the top springs back when gently pressed. Serve warm.

FLAVOR: If you think all honey tastes and looks the same, you've been purchasing mass produced honey too long. The flavor of honey is determined solely by the nectar source. That means that some flavors will be stronger than others. As a general rule, the lighter the honey, the milder the flavor.

CRYSTALLIZATION: All honey will naturally crystallize over time. Some crystallize faster than others. It doesn't mean the honey has gone bad. It can be used in the crystallized form, particularly if it's going to be melted. Or, you can warm it slightly in the microwave or dip the jar in hot water until the crystals dissolve. I prefer the warm bath. If you microwave it, remove the lid and stir every thirty seconds, being careful not to overheat.

BUSY AS A BEE: It is estimated that bees will visit nearly two million blossoms to make a pound of honey. It would take about one ounce of honey to fuel a bee's flight around the world. A honey bee flies about fifteen miles per hour.

> "If you want to gather honey, don't kick over the beehive."
> —ABRAHAM LINCOLN

LAMB

MARCH CAME IN LIKE A LION AND WENT OUT LIKE A LAMB . . . I CAN RELATE TO THAT STATE-ment. There was a time in my life when lamb was just a yearly treat. Every Easter, you could count on it to be served for dinner surrounded by fresh asparagus and decorations of tulips and daffodils. Then I started wondering why I was limiting myself to enjoying a meat I love only one time a year. The answer? I was stuck in the past.

In early farming days, the term "spring lamb" was a label for the highest quality product. It referred to lambs slaughtered early in life because their meat was particularly tender and greatly prized. This was in direct contrast to tougher, older animals that were used for meat. Today, it's different and the term is merely used as a marketing tool. All lambs are now slaughtered between five and seven months, so nearly every lamb cut you purchase is tender and delicious.

Lamb became common for Southerners with small family farms, particularly those who didn't have vast amounts of pasture land. During hard times, it was the meat that pulled families through the hardship. Lamb didn't have the expense of beef or dairy cattle.

Lamb is a wonderfully delicate-flavored meat that has a slight sweet, almost earthy undertone. It can easily handle strong-flavored seasonings, like rosemary, mint, garlic, citrus, and even hot peppers.

Thankfully in my house, the days are gone of only serving it at Easter. So when those spring bulbs begin to fade and make way for summer bloomers, remember that the season for lamb has only begun.

Nutrition: Since lamb comes from a less than one-year-old animal, the meat is lean. A three-ounce cooked portion, which is about the size of a deck of cards, contains about one hundred seventy-five calories. It is a great source of protein, iron, and B vitamins (niacin, thiamin, and riboflavin).

Selection: Let the color of the meat be your guide when purchasing lamb. As a general rule, the darker the meat, the older the animal when slaughtered. Go for the lighter colored meat and you'll have a more tender end product.

Storage: Fresh lamb is best if used within a couple of days of purchase. Freeze it if you can't use the meat within four days. Ground lamb can be frozen up to six months. The shelf life for all other cuts is around one year. Always thaw in the refrigerator and allow five hours per pound of thawing time.

EARLY SEASON LAMB STEW

A Southern garden planted with vegetables that are harvested early will come in handy for this dish. It's perfect for dinner when there's still a nip in the air at night.

YIELD: 8 SERVINGS

Juice of 2 lemons

3 pounds boneless lamb shoulder, cubed

12 cups water, divided

4 medium Russet potatoes, peeled and quartered

2 large yellow onions, peeled and sliced

4 garlic cloves, minced

3 chicken bouillon cubes

$\frac{1}{2}$ teaspoon salt

$\frac{1}{2}$ teaspoon black pepper

12 pearl onions

8 small new potatoes, peeled and quartered

8 baby carrots, peeled and cut in half

$1\frac{1}{2}$ teaspoons fresh thyme

Sprinkle the lemon juice over the lamb and set aside 10 minutes.

Meanwhile, bring 6 cups of the water to a boil in a Dutch oven over medium-high heat. Add the lamb and boil 5 minutes. Drain in a colander and discard the liquid.

Return the lamb to the Dutch oven and add the Russet potatoes, sliced onions, garlic, bouillon cubes, salt, pepper, and the remaining 6 cups of the water. Bring to a boil, reduce the heat to low and simmer, uncovered, $1\frac{1}{2}$ hours.

Remove the potatoes and onions with a slotted spoon. Place in the container of a food processor or blender and add $\frac{1}{4}$ cup of the cooking liquid. Process until smooth and return to the Dutch oven.

Add the pearl onions, new potatoes, carrots, and thyme. Cover and simmer 45 minutes. Serve warm.

APRICOT-BRAISED LAMB SHANKS

Shanks are the front legs of the animal and are wonderfully flavorful. They require long, slow cooking, which is accomplished here by braising. To braise, the meat is browned and then covered and cooked over low heat for a lengthy period of time.

YIELD: 4 SERVINGS

$\frac{1}{4}$ cup olive oil

6 pounds lamb shanks

$\frac{1}{2}$ cup all-purpose flour

2 (12-ounce) bottles dark, stout beer

2 (11.5-ounce) cans apricot nectar

4 garlic cloves, minced

2 fresh rosemary sprigs

$1\frac{1}{2}$ teaspoons salt

$\frac{1}{2}$ teaspoon black pepper

Preheat the oven to 375°F.

Heat the oil in a large skillet over medium-high heat. Dredge the lamb in the flour. Brown on all sides in the skillet, around 5 minutes.

Transfer the lamb to a large roasting pan or Dutch oven. Add the beer, nectar, garlic, rosemary, salt, and pepper. Cover and bake 2 hours. Uncover and bake 1 hour longer. Let rest 10 minutes before serving warm with the pan drippings.

HICKORY LAMB BURGERS

This is a great recipe to try if you've never experimented with using lamb. It will ease you into the flavor.

YIELD: 4 SERVINGS

Hickory or mesquite smoking chips

1 pound ground lamb

1 garlic clove, minced

1 jalapeño pepper, seeded and chopped

½ cup chopped onion

½ teaspoon salt

¼ teaspoon black pepper

3 tablespoons mayonnaise

4 hamburger buns

1 tomato, sliced

4 lettuce leaves

Soak the smoking chips in water at least 1 hour before starting the grill. Drain and place over the coals of a medium-high grill.

Meanwhile, in a mixing bowl, combine the lamb, garlic, jalapeño, onion, salt, and pepper. Blend well and shape the mixture into 4 patties. Grill 15 to 25 minutes or until completely done, turning only once.

Smear the mayonnaise on the buns. Add the grilled patties, tomatoes, and lettuce. Serve warm.

GRILLED LEG OF LAMB

Nearly everyone in the South owns a grill and this outdoor appliance makes leg of lamb incredible. This is my friend Karen's favorite food. After just a taste, it could become yours too. Tenderness comes from an entire bottle of red wine used for the marinade.

YIELD: 8 SERVINGS

1 garlic bulb

1 (7-pound) leg of lamb, trimmed

1 bottle dry red wine

½ cup olive oil

1 tablespoon dried rosemary

1 tablespoon dried oregano

2 teaspoons paprika

¼ teaspoon black pepper

Peel all the garlic cloves. Cut the 5 largest cloves

into thin slices. Mince the remaining cloves and set aside.

Make 1-inch cuts in the lamb with a sharp knife. Insert a garlic slice into each cut. Place the lamb in a large shallow dish and set aside.

In a large bowl, combine the minced garlic, wine, oil, rosemary, oregano, paprika, and pepper. Blend well. Reserve 1 cup of the wine mixture and refrigerate. Pour the remaining mixture over the lamb. Cover and refrigerate 8 hours or overnight, turning occasionally.

Prepare the grill to low heat (just under 300°F). Remove the lamb from the marinade and discard the marinade. Grill the lamb 1½ hours or until a meat thermometer inserted in the thickest portion registers 145°F (make sure the thermometer does not touch the bone). Turn and baste with the reserved wine mixture every 15 minutes.

Remove from the grill, cover, and let stand 30 minutes, or until the meat thermometer registers 150°F (medium rare) or to the desired degree of doneness. Carve and serve warm.

LEMON-HERB LAMB CHOPS

Sunny Florida lemon juice, herbs, and wine elevate this dish to the extraordinary. It's a great special occasion dish.

YIELD: 4 SERVINGS

4 (½-inch-thick) lamb chops

¼ cup lemon juice

3 tablespoons olive oil, divided

3 garlic cloves, minced

½ teaspoon dried oregano

½ teaspoon salt

¼ teaspoon black pepper

¼ cup dry white wine

Place the lamb chops in a shallow baking dish. In a small bowl, whisk together the lemon juice, 1½ tablespoons of the oil, the garlic, oregano, salt, and pepper. Pour over the chops and marinate in the refrigerator at least 1 hour and up to 3 hours, turning occasionally.

Remove the lamb from the refrigerator and bring to room temperature 20 minutes. Meanwhile, heat the remaining 1½ tablespoons of the oil in a large skillet over medium-high heat. Add the lamb chops to the skillet and cook 4 to 6 minutes per side or to the desired degree of doneness. Discard the marinade.

Add the wine to the skillet and deglaze 1 minute, scraping any brown bits. Pour the pan sauce over the warm chops and serve immediately.

PAN-FRIED MUSTARD LAMB CHOPS

These lamb chops are not quickly fried like pork chops. Instead, they are browned and then covered to finish cooking on a slower note.

YIELD: 6 SERVINGS

6 (½-inch thick) lamb chops
¼ cup Dijon mustard
1 tablespoon chopped fresh thyme or rosemary
¼ cup all-purpose flour
2 tablespoons olive oil
¾ cup dry white wine
½ cup cream
½ teaspoon kosher salt
¼ teaspoon black pepper

Place the lamb chops in a shallow baking dish. Lightly spread the mustard over both sides of the chops. Sprinkle the tops with the thyme and let stand at room temperature 10 minutes.

Meanwhile, place the flour in a shallow dish. Heat the oil in a large skillet over medium-high heat. Dredge the chops in the flour and add to the hot skillet. Fry the chops 2 minutes on each side. Reduce the heat to medium, cover, and cook 10 minutes.

Remove from the skillet and keep warm. Add the wine to the pan, stirring to loosen any brown bits. Cook 10 minutes, stirring frequently. Add the cream, salt, and pepper. Simmer 2 minutes. Serve the sauce on the side with the lamb.

ROSEMARY-CRUSTED LEG OF LAMB

If you don't grow fresh rosemary, you really need to start. It is such a hardy, aromatic herb and is made for this dish.

YIELD: 4 SERVINGS

¼ cup chopped fresh rosemary
4 garlic cloves
3 tablespoons olive oil
3 tablespoons lemon juice
1 teaspoon kosher salt
1 teaspoon black pepper
1 (6-pound) leg of lamb, trimmed

Preheat the oven to 450°F. Lightly grease a roasting pan and set aside.

Place the rosemary, garlic, oil, lemon juice, salt, and pepper in the bowl of a food processor. Process until smooth. Spread evenly on the lamb and place on the prepared pan. Insert a meat thermometer into the thickest portion, making sure it doesn't touch the bone. Position so the thermometer face can be seen through the oven window.

Bake 45 minutes or until the thermometer registers 160°F. Let stand 10 minutes before slicing and serving warm.

LETTUCE

DEEP IN THE HEART OF THE SOUTH, WE HAVE A MAY TRADITION THAT GOES BACK TO NEARLY our beginning. No, I'm not talking about the Kentucky Derby, Mother's Day, graduations, strawberry festivals, or field days at school. It's the wonderful custom of having a wilted salad.

Every spring in our household, as in countless others, this salad is served as soon as the leaf lettuce is about as tall as your hand. There's no recipe really. The lettuce is harvested and washed, along with a few of your spring onions. Then bacon is fried and crumbled. Everything is assembled on individual serving plates.

At that point, the hot bacon drippings are drizzled over the crisp lettuce, making it quickly wilt. It's served with hot cornbread and is a once yearly feast. Rumor has it that without this meal, the garden will not be successful. I'm not willing to take that chance!

Most of us expect lettuce to do exactly what it does best: To serve as a vehicle for other ingredients and provide a brief break in the flavor action during a meal. It doesn't have a speck of star quality, but is the world's best back-up singer. I have a friend who says it's as close to chewing on nothing as you can get . . . and that's exactly why I love it.

In many ways, I'm a purist when it comes to lettuce. I still love a crisp wedge of iceberg lettuce served with really good Thousand Island dressing. Hamburgers are never made without it in my house, and I'm sure all Southerners would agree that a BLT just isn't the same without the L.

There are lots of fancy lettuce varieties on the market. I usually find myself going back to Bibb and iceberg, the lettuce types that are plentiful throughout the year thanks to growers from the far South. They are dependable and wonderfully forgettable when I want them to be, and your basic essential the rest of the time.

Preparation: All lettuce types should be washed thoroughly and promptly drained in a colander. Soaking lettuce in water will soften the leaves and hasten decay. If you are in a rush, a salad spinner is perfect for removing excess moisture in a snap.

Storage: Refrigeration is a must, even though it tends to pull moisture from the leaves. Make sure you have just a touch of water in your storage container to keep the lettuce hydrated and only very slightly moist. Freezer storage is never recommended because it destroys the cell structure and will be a mess once it is thawed. Since lettuce is mostly water, drying is out of the question.

BABY LETTUCE SALAD WITH MUSTARD VINAIGRETTE

George gets onto me every year because as soon as our lettuce begins to poke out of the ground, I'm out there snipping. I just can't resist baby greens! They are terrific with this mustard dressing.

YIELD: 4 SERVINGS

¹/₂ cup rice wine vinegar

1 tablespoon Dijon mustard

1 tablespoon dry white wine

2 teaspoons Worcestershire sauce

¹/₂ teaspoon sugar

¹/₄ teaspoon lemon juice

¹/₄ teaspoon white pepper

¹/₈ teaspoon hot sauce

4 cups baby lettuce leaves

In a jar with a tight fitting lid, combine the vinegar, mustard, wine, Worcestershire, sugar, lemon juice, pepper, and hot sauce. Shake well to emulsify.

Place the lettuce in a large serving bowl. Drizzle with the dressing, tossing well to coat. Serve on chilled salad plates.

"DO-IT-YOUR-WAY" CHOPPED SALAD

I love chopped salads because they are whatever you want them to be. Use this recipe as your guide, but feel free to utilize any vegetables in your crisper drawer. It's a great way to clean out the fridge at the end of the week. This simple dressing doesn't interfere with the vegetables.

YIELD: 6 SERVINGS

¹/₃ cup olive oil

2 tablespoons lemon juice

1 garlic clove, minced

1 teaspoon sugar

¹/₂ teaspoon salt

¹/₄ teaspoon black pepper

1 head lettuce, cored and chopped

2 tomatoes, seeded and chopped

1 yellow or orange bell pepper, seeded and chopped

1 cucumber, chopped

1 small purple onion, peeled and chopped

¹/₂ cup chopped fresh parsley

In a jar with a tight fitting lid, combine the oil, lemon juice, garlic, sugar, salt, and pepper. Shake to emulsify and set aside.

Combine the lettuce, tomatoes, pepper, cucumber, onion, and parsley in a large salad bowl. Drizzle with the dressing and toss to evenly coat. Serve on chilled salad plates.

ICEBERG AHEAD! (WITH PARMESAN PECANS)

This salad is so simple and sensational with beef. It will ignite a renewed love for iceberg lettuce.

YIELD: 6 SERVINGS

2 tablespoons unsalted butter

1 cup chopped pecans

3 tablespoons shredded Parmesan cheese

¹/₄ teaspoon onion salt

4 cups iceberg lettuce leaves

¹/₂ cup canola oil

¹/₄ cup balsamic vinegar

Preheat the oven to 350°F. Place the butter in an 8-inch square pan and melt while the oven preheats.

When completely melted, add the pecans and stir to evenly coat. Bake 5 minutes. Sprinkle with the cheese, tossing to coat, and onion salt. Bake 5 minutes longer or until the cheese is light golden brown. Cool completely.

When ready to serve, place the lettuce in a large serving bowl. In a jar with a tight-fitting lid, combine the oil and vinegar. Shake well to emulsify. Drizzle over the lettuce, tossing to gently coat. Top with the pecans and serve immediately.

"LET-US" HEAD SOUTH SALAD

If anything will remind you of the sunny South, it's this perky salad. Serve as a side with turkey, pork, chicken, or fish.

YIELD: 6 SERVINGS

3 cups mixed lettuce leaves
2 navel oranges, peeled and sectioned
1 large grapefruit, peeled and sectioned
$\frac{1}{2}$ cup coarsely chopped pecans, toasted
$\frac{3}{4}$ cup olive oil
$\frac{1}{4}$ cup white wine vinegar
3 tablespoons fresh orange juice
1 tablespoon sugar
2 teaspoons grated orange zest
$\frac{1}{2}$ teaspoon kosher salt
$\frac{1}{2}$ teaspoon white pepper

Evenly divide the lettuce, orange sections, grapefruit sections, and pecans onto chilled serving plates. In a jar with a tight-fitting lid, combine the oil, vinegar, orange juice, sugar, orange zest, salt, and pepper.

Shake to emulsify and drizzle over the prepared salads. Serve immediately.

MOONLIGHT PEANUT-APPLE SALAD

After you've spent the day picking apples at the local orchard, come home, build a fire outside, and throw together this salad. The rest of the apples can wait on a pie the next day! Any apple variety will work.

YIELD: 6 SERVINGS

2 apples (select the variety of your choice)
1 tablespoon plus 2 teaspoons lime juice, divided
6 cups mixed lettuce leaves
$\frac{1}{4}$ cup plain yogurt
2 tablespoons creamy peanut butter
1 tablespoon water
$\frac{1}{4}$ teaspoon salt

Core the apples and cut into thin matchsticks. Toss with 1 tablespoon of the lime juice in a large bowl to prevent discoloration. Add the lettuce, tossing gently and set aside.

In a small bowl, whisk together the remaining 2 teaspoons of the lime juice, the yogurt, peanut butter, water, and salt. Whisk until smooth. Drizzle over the salad, tossing gently to evenly coat. Serve immediately.

NO-RECIPE WILTED SALAD

Southerners have no recipe for this spring essential, but for those who have never tried it, here is the way it works!

YIELD: 4 SERVINGS

6 cups torn lettuce leaves
2 green onions, sliced
8 bacon slices, cut in pieces

Evenly divide the lettuce between 4 salad plates. Top with the onions and set aside.

In a large skillet over medium heat, fry the bacon until crisp, around 6 minutes. Remove with a slotted spoon and evenly distribute over the onions. Pour the hot drippings over the salad. Let stand 3 minutes and serve immediately.

SEVEN-LAYER SALAD

You won't attend many potluck dinners in the South without seeing this salad on the table. Getting the first serving is the hardest because it's nearly too pretty to eat!

YIELD: 10 SERVINGS

1 head lettuce, cored and torn into small pieces
1 (10-ounce) bag frozen peas, uncooked
1 purple onion, peeled and thinly sliced
6 hard-cooked eggs, sliced
1 pound bacon, cooked and crumbled
2 tablespoons sugar
1 cup mayonnaise or salad dressing
4 cups shredded sharp Cheddar cheese

In this order, layer the lettuce, peas, onion, eggs, and all except ¼ cup of crumbled bacon in a 13 x 9-inch baking dish or glass bowl. Sprinkle the sugar over the top and cover with the mayonnaise. Top with the cheese and remaining ¼ cup of the bacon. Cover and refrigerate overnight before serving.

TYPES:

Butterhead: Butterhead lettuces have small, but loosely formed heads. They were named for the buttery hearts even though the leaves are very soft and quite tender. Gentle washing is a must. They have just a hint of sweetness and color can range from maroon to yellow-green. Boston and Bibb are both butterhead types.

Crisphead: Crisphead varieties include the ever-popular iceberg, the most commonly sold lettuce in the U.S. These lettuce types have a neutral flavor and are known for being close to wilt-resistant when stored correctly. They are larger than butterhead types and have tighter packed leaves.

Leaf: You can't help but love leaf lettuce, so called because the leaves branch out from a single stalk. This forms more of a loose bunch rather than a single tight head. This is the type of lettuce I grow in my garden because you can harvest it early, leaf by leaf, or later by cutting the rosettes just above the ground. What you gain in garden convenience, you lose in shelf life because these are more perishable than head lettuce types.

Romaine: If you like Caesar salads, you like Romaine lettuce. Because it is believed to have originated on the Aegean island of Cos, it is sometimes called Cos lettuce. The elongated head has dark green outer leaves that lighten considerably as you move to the center. Crunch comes from the thick midribs and the leaves are slightly bitter.

MACARONI AND CHEESE

THERE ARE FEW DISHES THAT EVOKE AS MUCH PASSION AS MACARONI AND CHEESE. IN THE South, it is practically sacred, with cooks staking their entire reputations on this dish. In this area of the country, you are well known in the community for macaroni and cheese just as much as fried chicken.

I am one of the lucky ones who cannot remember not having a piping hot dish of macaroni with perfectly melted cheese on the dinner table. It was, and still is, one of my favorite comfort foods. I serve it in the baking dish my grandmother always used, which she bought for ten cents at the local hardware store.

Southerners certainly did not concoct this heavenly dish, but we have loved and embraced it as one of our own for years. I would go out on a limb and say it is always a part of family reunion, potluck, and special occasion dinners. It is economical, soothing, delicious, and loved by one and all.

When it comes to macaroni and cheese, I can be quite a snob. I cannot endorse the orange powdered boxed imposter that lurks from every supermarket and convenience store shelf in the country. Every good Southern cook will tell you that it cannot hold even the dimmest candle to any homemade version.

Instead, I want to see superbly cooked elbow macaroni swimming away in what is a close equivalent to milk gravy. I want to have real cheese melted with the macaroni, which elevates the dish to a culinary masterpiece. I want it to be pulled out of the oven, not the microwave. And most of all, I want it served in my grandmother's clear glass baking dish that has love etched all over it.

Cooking: Macaroni will double in size when cooked. Just like any pasta, it needs plenty of water so it can cook evenly. Too little water will result in macaroni that clumps together and is not sufficiently cooked. Drain it well in a large colander because the elbow shape can trap extra water. If in spite of this, you have macaroni that is stuck together, plunge it back into boiling water and immediately pull back out.

Boiling Over: The starch content in macaroni will cause it to frequently boil over if not carefully watched while it cooks. To prevent this, coat the inside of the cooking pot with cooking spray before adding the water, particularly the top inch inside the pot. If you forget, blow on the surface, which will give you around 10 seconds to locate a pot holder or turn down the heat.

FIRST-FROST MACARONI AND CHEESE SOUP

You'll find yourself craving and making this soup over and over. It's cold weather comfort from the first frost through the early spring.

YIELD: 6 SERVINGS

1 cup elbow macaroni

4 tablespoons unsalted butter

$1/2$ cup diced carrots

$1/2$ cup diced celery

1 small white onion, peeled and diced

4 cups milk

$1^1/2$ cups shredded American cheese

2 tablespoons chicken bouillon granules

$1/2$ teaspoon black pepper

$1/8$ teaspoon red pepper

2 tablespoons cornstarch

2 tablespoons water

1 (8-ounce) can whole kernel corn, drained

$1/2$ cup frozen English peas

Cook the macaroni according to the package directions. Drain and set aside.

Place the butter in a medium skillet over medium-high heat. Add the carrots, celery, and onion. Sauté 6 minutes, stirring constantly. Set aside to cool slightly.

In a Dutch oven over medium heat, combine the milk and cheese. Stir frequently until the cheese melts and the mixture is well blended. Add the bouillon, black pepper, and red pepper.

In a small bowl, whisk together the cornstarch and water until smooth. Stir into the milk mixture. Stir constantly until the mixture comes to a boil. Boil 1 minute, stirring constantly. Add the macaroni, vegetable mixture, corn, and peas. Reduce the heat to low and cook 7 minutes, stirring frequently. Serve in warm soup bowls.

GORGONZOLA MACARONI

The slightly pungent flavor of Gorgonzola is memorable in this macaroni. Pull out a hearty dry red wine and some crusty bread to complete the meal.

YIELD: 6 SERVINGS

1 (8-ounce) package elbow macaroni

1 cup milk

$3/4$ cup crumbled Gorgonzola cheese

1 (8-ounce) container sour cream

$1/2$ teaspoon white pepper

$1/2$ cup plain dry breadcrumbs

2 tablespoons shredded Parmesan cheese

2 tablespoons unsalted butter, melted

Preheat the oven to 350°F. Lightly grease a shallow $1^1/2$-quart baking dish and set aside.

Cook the macaroni according to the package directions. Drain and set aside.

In a large saucepan over medium heat, combine the milk and Gorgonzola. Cook and stir occasionally until the cheese melts. Remove from the heat and stir in the sour cream and pepper. Add the macaroni, stirring well.

Pour into the prepared baking dish. In a small bowl, combine the breadcrumbs, Parmesan, and butter. Sprinkle over the macaroni and bake 30 minutes. Let stand 5 minutes before serving warm.

JACK AND MAC

The melting quality of Monterey Jack cheese is perfect for this dish. I like to use varieties that are loaded with jalapeño peppers to give it a swift kick!

YIELD: 6 SERVINGS

1 (8-ounce) package elbow macaroni

2 tablespoons unsalted butter

¼ cup chopped onions

¼ cup chopped red bell pepper

2 cups shredded Monterey Jack cheese

1 (10.75-ounce) can cream of celery soup, undiluted

½ cup sour cream

1 teaspoon chili powder

Preheat the oven to 350°F. Lightly grease a shallow 2-quart baking dish and set aside.

Cook the macaroni according to the package directions. Drain and set aside.

In a Dutch oven, melt the butter over medium heat. Add the onion and pepper. Sauté 3 minutes, stirring constantly. Remove from the heat and stir in the cheese, soup, and sour cream, blending well.

Add the macaroni and gently stir to evenly coat. Transfer to the prepared baking dish. Sprinkle the chili powder evenly over the top.

Bake 30 minutes, or until the macaroni is bubbly. Let stand 5 minutes before serving warm.

MACARONI AND CHEESE WITH THYME BACON CRUMBS

This dish is beautiful and a people magnet thanks to the bacon crumbles that enhance the topping.

YIELD: 8 SERVINGS

1 (8-ounce) package elbow macaroni

8 ounces bacon, cut into ¼-inch pieces

1 cup plain dry breadcrumbs

1 teaspoon minced fresh thyme

3 tablespoons unsalted butter

3 tablespoons all-purpose flour

½ teaspoon ground nutmeg

1 tablespoon dry mustard

3½ cups milk

2 shallots, peeled and minced

3 cups shredded sharp white Cheddar cheese

1 teaspoon salt

½ teaspoon black pepper

Preheat the oven to 350°F. Cook the macaroni in boiling salted water as directed on the package. Drain and set aside.

Meanwhile, in a large skillet over medium heat, sauté the bacon until crisp, around 7 minutes. Drain on paper towels.

Reserve the drippings and reduce the heat to low. Add the breadcrumbs and thyme and toss to evenly coat. Stir in the bacon and set aside.

In a 4-quart saucepan, melt the butter over medium-low heat. Add the flour, nutmeg, and dry mustard. Stir vigorously with a wooden spoon to work the dry ingredients into the butter. Cook 3 minutes, stirring frequently.

Whisk in the milk in ½ cup increments, making sure to stir until smooth each time before adding more milk. Whisk in the shallots and simmer about 10 minutes, stirring frequently. Remove from the heat and whisk in the cheese until completely melted. Season with the salt and pepper.

Stir in macaroni and pour into a greased 2-quart baking dish. Top with the breadcrumb mixture and bake, uncovered, 45 minutes, or until golden brown. Let stand 5 minutes before serving.

LUNCHBOX MAGIC MACARONI AND CHEESE SALAD

Macaroni doesn't always have to be served hot straight from the oven. This recipe takes care of your craving for our favorite comfort food during lunch.

YIELD: 6 SERVINGS

2 cups elbow macaroni

2 tablespoons olive oil

$\frac{1}{2}$ cup mayonnaise

$\frac{1}{4}$ cup sour cream

$\frac{1}{2}$ teaspoon salt

$\frac{1}{4}$ teaspoon garlic powder

$\frac{1}{4}$ teaspoon black pepper

$\frac{1}{8}$ teaspoon red pepper

1 cup shredded sharp Cheddar cheese

$\frac{1}{2}$ cup cooked chopped chicken or ham

$\frac{1}{2}$ cup frozen English peas, thawed

$\frac{1}{4}$ cup sliced green onions

2 tablespoons chopped fresh parsley

Cook the macaroni according to the package directions. Drain and transfer to a large mixing bowl. Toss with the oil and set aside.

In a mixing bowl, whisk together the mayonnaise, sour cream, salt, garlic powder, black pepper, and red pepper. Blend well. Stir in the cheese, chicken, peas, onions, and parsley. Add to the macaroni and stir gently to blend. Cover and refrigerate at least 1 hour before serving at room temperature or cold.

MACARONI AND GOAT CHEESE

The distinctive tang of goat cheese really wakes up your tastebuds with this dish. It's perfect to serve with a simple roasted chicken or turkey.

YIELD: 8 SERVINGS

1 (1-pound) package elbow macaroni

3 tablespoons unsalted butter, divided

1 tablespoon olive oil

4 slices bacon, cooked and crumbled

1 cup dry plain breadcrumbs

2 tablespoons chopped fresh parsley

1 teaspoon crushed red pepper

1 tablespoon minced shallot

1 large garlic clove, minced

$1\frac{1}{4}$ cups half-and-half, at room temperature

1 cup shredded Parmesan cheese

$\frac{1}{3}$ cup goat cheese, crumbled

1 tablespoon minced fresh chives

$\frac{3}{4}$ teaspoon salt

$\frac{1}{2}$ teaspoon black pepper

Cook the macaroni in boiling salted water according to the package directions. Drain and transfer to a large serving bowl. Cover and set aside.

Meanwhile, in a medium saucepan, melt 1 tablespoon of the butter in the olive oil. Add the bacon, breadcrumbs, parsley, and crushed pepper. Toss well and set aside.

Melt the remaining butter in a heavy saucepan over medium heat. Stir in the shallot and garlic, cooking 1 minute. Add the half-and-half and simmer 5 minutes, stirring constantly. Remove from the heat and stir in the Parmesan, goat cheese, and chives. Season with the salt and pepper.

Add the cheese mixture to the macaroni and stir well. Sprinkle the breadcrumb mixture on top and serve immediately.

MEAT-AND-THREE MACARONI AND CHEESE

This dish has it all...meat, vegetables, macaroni, and cheese. It's the perfect one-dish meal.

YIELD: 8 SERVINGS

1 (8-ounce) package elbow macaroni

1 tablespoon unsalted butter

2 shallots, peeled and chopped

2 cups sliced mushrooms

2 garlic cloves, minced

1 pound cooked spicy smoked sausage, sliced

2 cups baby spinach leaves

1 (10-ounce) package frozen chopped broccoli, thawed

1 cup milk

1 tablespoon all-purpose flour

$^1/_2$ teaspoon salt

$^1/_4$ teaspoon black pepper

$1^1/_2$ cups shredded Monterey Jack cheese, divided

Cook the macaroni according to the package directions and drain. Transfer to a mixing bowl, cover, and set aside.

Place the butter in a heavy saucepan over medium heat. Add the shallots, mushrooms, and garlic. Sauté 4 minutes, or until the vegetables are tender. Stir in the sausage, spinach, and broccoli. Cover and cook 2 minutes. Add to the macaroni and set aside.

Meanwhile preheat the oven to 350°F. Lightly grease a 13 x 9-inch baking dish and set aside.

In a medium saucepan, whisk together the milk, flour, salt, and pepper and place over medium heat. Cook, whisking constantly, 10 minutes. Add 1 cup of the cheese, continuing to stir until the cheese is completely melted.

Pour over the macaroni mixture, tossing gently to evenly coat. Transfer to the prepared baking dish and sprinkle evenly with the remaining $^1/_2$ cup of the cheese. Bake 35 minutes, or until the macaroni is bubbly. Let stand 5 minutes before serving warm.

MUSHROOM MACARONI AND CHEESE

This is one of the easiest ways to add vegetables to your kid's diet…hide it in the macaroni!

YIELD: 8 SERVINGS

1 (8-ounce) package elbow macaroni

1 tablespoon olive oil

1 cup sliced mushrooms

2 shallots, peeled and chopped

1 (10.75-ounce) can cream of mushroom soup, undiluted

1 cup mayonnaise

2 cups shredded sharp Cheddar cheese

1 (2-ounce) jar diced pimientos, drained

$^1/_4$ teaspoon black pepper

$^3/_4$ cup crushed round butter crackers

2 tablespoons unsalted butter, melted

Preheat the oven to 325°F. Lightly grease a 2-quart casserole dish and set aside. Cook the macaroni according to the package directions, drain into a large mixing bowl, cover, and set aside.

Place the oil in a large skillet over medium-high heat. Add the mushrooms and sauté 3 minutes. Stir in the shallots and sauté 2 minutes longer. Stir into the macaroni.

Stir in the soup, mayonnaise, cheese, pimientos, and pepper, gently mixing to thoroughly combine.

Transfer to the prepared baking dish. Evenly sprinkle the cracker crumbs over the top. Drizzle with the butter. Bake 30 minutes, or until golden brown and bubbly. Let stand 5 minutes before serving warm.

ROASTED PEPPER MACARONI AND CHEESE

Rich, earthy poblano peppers lend character to this double-cheese macaroni.

YIELD: 8 SERVINGS

4 poblano peppers

1 (1-pound) package elbow macaroni

$1/4$ pound (1 stick) unsalted butter

$1/2$ cup all-purpose flour

2 cups cream

1 cup milk

$2^3/4$ cups shredded Monterey Jack cheese

1 (4-ounce) package plain goat cheese, crumbled

1 teaspoon salt

$1/4$ teaspoon black pepper

$1/4$ cup dry seasoned breadcrumbs

$1/2$ cup shredded Parmesan cheese

Preheat the broiler and place the peppers on an aluminum foil–lined baking sheet. Broil 5 minutes on each side or until the peppers look blistered. Transfer to a heavy-duty zip-top plastic bag. Seal and let stand 10 minutes. Remove the peel, discard the seeds, and cut the peppers into strips. Set aside.

Meanwhile, cook the macaroni according to the package directions. Drain, cover, and set aside. Preheat the oven to 375°F. Lightly grease a 13 x 9-inch baking dish and set aside.

Melt the butter in a Dutch oven over low heat. Whisk in the flour until smooth. Cook, 1 minute, whisking constantly. Gradually whisk in the cream and milk. Increase the heat to medium and whisk constantly 5 minutes, or until the mixture is thick and bubbly.

Stir in the Monterey Jack cheese, stirring until melted. Add the goat cheese, salt, and pepper, stirring until smooth. Stir in the peppers and maca-roni. Transfer to the prepared baking dish. Top evenly with the breadcrumbs and Parmesan.

Bake 40 minutes, or until the macaroni is bubbly and golden brown. Let stand 5 minutes before serving warm.

SUMMER VEGETABLE MACARONI AND CHEESE

Why serve vegetables on the side when they can become part of the dish itself? This dish is a full meal and takes advantage of the delicious summer veg-etable abundance.

YIELD: 8 SERVINGS

1 (8-ounce) package elbow macaroni

1 tablespoon vegetable oil

1 tablespoon unsalted butter

1 cup chopped fresh broccoli

1 cup chopped yellow squash

$1/2$ cup chopped carrots

1 small purple onion, peeled and chopped

1 red bell pepper, seeded and chopped

2 garlic cloves, minced

1 (16-ounce) container ricotta cheese

1 (12-ounce) can evaporated milk

1 tablespoon Dijon mustard

1 teaspoon salt

1 teaspoon black pepper

2 eggs, lightly beaten

3 Roma tomatoes, sliced

$1/3$ cup dry seasoned breadcrumbs

$1/2$ cup shredded Parmesan cheese

Cook the macaroni according to the package directions. Drain, cover, and set aside.

Preheat the oven to 350°F. Lightly grease a

13 x 9-inch baking dish and set aside.

Place the oil and butter in a Dutch oven over medium heat. Add the broccoli, squash, carrots, onion, pepper, and garlic. Sauté 4 to 5 minutes, or until the vegetables are tender. Remove from the heat and stir in the macaroni. Set aside.

In a mixing bowl, combine the ricotta, milk, mustard, salt, pepper, and eggs. Stir well to blend. Pour over the macaroni mixture and gently stir to evenly coat. Transfer to the prepared baking dish. Top with the tomatoes. Sprinkle the breadcrumbs and Parmesan evenly over the top.

Bake, covered, 15 minutes. Uncover and bake 20 minutes longer, or until golden brown. Let stand 5 minutes before serving warm.

ANCIENT HISTORY: Many believe that macaroni was first made in China and brought to Italy by Marco Polo. But macaroni is made from hard wheat, which was not typical of the region, so the exact origin is unknown. We do know that Europeans for centuries served a dish baked in a mixture of cream and cheese.

U.S. HISTORY: Thomas Jefferson made macaroni and cheese popular after returning to America from his tour as minister to France. He purchased a pasta machine while there and was fascinated with making the machine better. The first documentation of it being served in the White House was in 1802 by Thomas Jefferson.

DEFINITION: Macaroni traditionally does not contain eggs but only semolina wheat and water. The shape is in the form of a tube. Although Southerners use short, curved, elbow macaroni for the dish most often, there are many other types of pasta that are technically classified as macaroni, such as penne, rigatoni, and ditalini.

"THE REAL DEAL" MACARONI AND CHEESE

After you've played around with all the variations of this Southern classic, it's time to make it the old-fashioned way. This recipe inspired all the other versions.

YIELD: 6 SERVINGS

1 (8-ounce) package elbow macaroni
2 tablespoons unsalted butter, softened
1$\frac{1}{2}$ cups milk
$\frac{3}{4}$ teaspoon salt
$\frac{1}{4}$ teaspoon white pepper
8 ($\frac{1}{4}$- to $\frac{1}{2}$-inch thick) slices sharp Cheddar cheese

Preheat the oven to 350°F. Lightly grease a 2-quart baking dish and set aside.

Prepare the macaroni according to the package directions. Drain and transfer to a mixing bowl. Add the butter and gently stir until the butter melts. Stir in the milk, salt, and pepper. Transfer to the prepared baking dish.

Place the cheese slices evenly on the top. Bake 20 to 25 minutes, or until the cheese has melted and the macaroni is bubbly. Let stand 5 minutes before serving warm.

> "It's diamonds in your pockets one week, macaroni and cheese the next."
>
> —JOLENE BLALOCK

MELONS

(CANTALOUPE AND HONEYDEW)

THERE IS AN OLD CLAUDE MERMET SAYING THAT WE USED TO CHANT IN MY MISSISSIPPI STATE home economics classes. It says: Friends are like melons. Shall I tell you why? To find one good, you must a hundred try!

Now I know why our instructors used to laugh at us for saying that. We obviously didn't know the first thing about picking out a fresh ripe melon and had a lot in common with good old Claude! I still see many with the same affliction and it's not just Southern college home ec students.

For some reason, I regularly witness consumers mashing the stem end of cantaloupes and honeydews with their thumbs. I really don't know what they think they are doing or accomplishing as far as selection is concerned. But I do know they are successfully bruising the melons in that area.

That particular area is sometimes called the "thumbprint" for that very reason, I suppose. It's where the melon came off the vine and will be slightly sunken. If you are one of those mashers, stop that! Instead, smell it when picking up a cantaloupe or honeydew. If it's a good one that's ready to eat, it should have a faint aroma of the fruit at the stem end.

So, it's your nose that knows a good melon, not your thumb. No odor? No sale! When you select one correctly, you are going to suddenly realize that you've been harboring a madness for melons you didn't know you had. These recipes could very well push you over the edge!

Preparation: Cut whole cantaloupes and honeydews in half with a large chef's knife and scrape out the center seeds and stringy flesh with a spoon. Then cut the halves into wedges and peel. You can leave it in the wedge form, cut into smaller bite-size chunks, or use a melon baller.

Selection: Sniff the melon! It should have a melon aroma when you sniff the dime-size spot where the stem used to be. Also, pick it up. The melon should feel heavy for the size. If it is lightweight, don't buy it. There should be no cracks or soft spots on the outer skin.

Storage: Mistakenly, many head straight to the refrigerator with freshly harvested melons, thinking of the old fruit/fridge rule. However, if it's really fresh from the farm, it will benefit from being held at room temperature to mellow out and enhance the flavor.

If the melons are overripe, keep them in the refrigerator and certainly any that have been cut. Cut leftovers can easily absorb odors from other foods, so keep it tightly covered. If you are only using half of a melon, do not remove the seeds of the unused half until ready to enjoy.

IN A PICKLE WITH CANTALOUPE

With one taste, you'll quickly find the time invested in making these pickles was totally worth it. They are excellent on a summer appetizer tray and a great way to use excess melons.

YIELD: 2 QUARTS

2 medium cantaloupes, seeded, peeled, and cut in 1-inch cubes

1 teaspoon crushed red pepper

1 cinnamon stick

2 teaspoons ground cloves

1 teaspoon ground ginger

$4^1/_2$ cups cider vinegar

2 cups water

$1^1/_2$ cups granulated sugar

$1^1/_2$ cups packed light brown sugar

Place the cantaloupe cubes in a large bowl. Tie the pepper, cinnamon, cloves, and ginger in a spice bag.

In a large stockpot, combine the vinegar and water. Place over high heat and bring to a boil. Add the spice bag and remove from the heat. Allow to steep 5 minutes, stirring occasionally. Pour the entire mixture over the cantaloupe. Cover and refrigerate 18 hours.

Carefully pour off the vinegar solution into a large stockpot and bring to a boil. Add the granulated sugar and brown sugar and stir until completely dissolved. Add the cantaloupe and return to a boil.

Reduce the heat to low and simmer 1 hour, or until the cantaloupe is translucent. With a slotted spoon, remove the cantaloupe to a bowl, cover, and set aside.

Increase the heat to medium high and bring the remaining liquid to a boil. Boil 5 minutes. Return the cantaloupe to the syrup and return to a boil.

With a slotted spoon, pack the cantaloupe pieces into hot, sterilized canning jars, leaving 1 inch of headspace. Pour the hot syrup over the cantaloupe. Remove any air bubbles, wipe the rims, and adjust the lids.

Process in a boiling-water bath 15 minutes. Place on a wire rack away from drafts to completely cool.

FRIGIDAIRE MELON SORBET

George's Aunt Lorene has stayed with us with several times over the years. She called the refrigerator a "Frigidaire" and I loved the term. We always made this sorbet together in the hopes of serving it to the rest of the family when they came later in the week, but it was long gone before they arrived!

YIELD: 1 QUART

3 cups water

$1^1/_2$ cups sugar

1 large cantaloupe or honeydew melon

1 tablespoon lemon juice

In a heavy saucepan bring the water and sugar to a boil over medium-high heat. Boil 5 minutes and cool completely.

Meanwhile, peel and seed the melon. Cut in cubes and purée in a food processor. Stir in the cooled syrup mixture and juice. Transfer to an ice cream maker and freeze according to the manufacturer's directions. Scoop into chilled sherbet glasses to serve.

MARINATED MELON WEDGES

I love everything about this dish. I knew it was a hit when I served it and I caught a guest pouring the left-over marinade in her glass! It is a perfect breakfast or brunch side dish, or even a light dessert.

YIELD: 8 SERVINGS

$^1/_2$ cup sugar

1 cup sweet white wine

$^1/_4$ cup banana liqueur

1 ($^1/_2$ -inch) slice fresh ginger, peeled

1 cinnamon stick

1 teaspoon frozen orange juice concentrate, thawed

$^1/_8$ teaspoon pure vanilla extract

1 large cantaloupe

In a heavy saucepan over medium high heat, combine the sugar, wine, liqueur, ginger, cinnamon, juice concentrate, and extract. Bring the mixture to a boil and cook 5 minutes, stirring constantly. Let cool completely.

Meanwhile, cut the cantaloupe in half and remove the seeds. Cut into wedges and peel. Place in a 13 x 9-inch baking dish and set aside. When the syrup has cooled, pour over the melon wedges.

Cover and refrigerate at least 2 hours and up to 24 hours. To serve, place the wedges on serving plates and drizzle with the extra syrup.

MELLOWED OUT CHUTNEY

Nearly anything you pull off the grill can be served with this tangy chutney. I especially like it with chicken, fish, turkey, and pork.

YIELD: 3 CUPS

$^1/_2$ cup sugar

$^1/_4$ cup white wine vinegar

$^1/_4$ cup chopped onions

$^1/_4$ cup golden raisins

$^1/_2$ teaspoon crushed red pepper

$^1/_4$ teaspoon salt

$^1/_4$ teaspoon ground cumin

2 cups diced cantaloupe

2 tablespoons lime juice

$^1/_4$ cup chopped fresh cilantro

In a large saucepan over medium-high heat, combine the sugar, vinegar, onions, raisins, pepper, salt, and cumin. Bring to a boil, stirring constantly. Boil 5 minutes, continuing to stir and reduce the heat to medium-low.

Simmer, stirring frequently until thick and bubbly, around 10 minutes. Set aside to cool 15 minutes.

Stir in the cantaloupe, lime juice, and cilantro. Cool completely, cover, and refrigerate at least 2 hours. Bring to room temperature before topping grilled meat.

MELON PATCH SALAD

Serve this rainbow of fruits refrigerator cold on any hot day.

YIELD: 8 SERVINGS

1 large cantaloupe, peeled, seeded, and cubed

1 large honeydew, peeled, seeded, and cubed

$^1/_2$ small seedless watermelon, cubed

1 cup red seedless grapes

1 cup fresh blueberries

2 freestone peaches, peeled and sliced

2 firm bananas, sliced

1 Golden Delicious or Granny Smith
apple, cored and cubed

1 (12-ounce) can frozen limeade or
lemonade concentrate, thawed

1 (3.4-ounce) package instant vanilla
pudding mix

In a large bowl, combine the cantaloupe, honey-dew, watermelon, grapes, and blueberries. Cover and refrigerate 1 to 2 hours.

Gently toss in the peaches, bananas, and apple. In a small bowl, whisk together the limeade concentrate and pudding mix. Pour over the fruit, tossing to evenly coat. Serve immediately.

MELON PORT MINGLE

How can something so simple be so divine? Use a really good port for this dish, since you'll be showcasing the flavor.

YIELD: 8 TO 10 SERVINGS

1 cantaloupe

1 honeydew melon

1 cup port wine

Cut melons in half, remove the seeds, and peel. Make 3 or 4 gashes in the flesh of each half with a spoon. Add 2 ounces of port to each half and let stand 30 minutes to mellow at room temperature. When ready to serve, cut into slices and place in a large serving bowl. Serve with any excess juice.

SUNDOWN CANTALOUPE PUNCH

Why not watch the sun go down with a drink that matches the color? This can be made for adults only or for everyone.

YIELD: 8 CUPS

$2\frac{1}{2}$ cups water

$\frac{2}{3}$ cup fresh lime juice

$\frac{2}{3}$ cup sugar

1 cantaloupe, seeded, peeled, and diced

2 cups orange juice

1 cup vodka (optional)

Lime wedges for garnish

Bring the water, lime juice, and sugar to a boil in a large saucepan over medium-high heat. Boil 3 minutes and cool completely.

Meanwhile, process the cantaloupe in a blender until smooth. Pour through a wire-mesh strainer into a bowl, reserving 3 cups of the juice. Discard the pulp.

When the lime juice mixture has cooled, stir into the cantaloupe juice and add the orange juice and vodka, if using. Chill thoroughly. Serve over crushed ice and garnish with lime wedges.

ORIGIN: It is believed that cantaloupes and honeydew originated in the Middle East. They both are descendants of the squash and cucumber families.

NUTRITION: Half of a medium-size melon (or five ounces of fruit) contains around fifty calories. Melons are a great source of vitamins A and C, dietary fiber, and potassium. They also contain respectable amounts of beta-carotene, calcium, and phosphorus.

VERANDA CANTALOUPE SALAD

This is not your typical ladies' lunch salad, but it should be. It is a lovely substitution for a main dish. Just serve it with a great bread or a light soup.

YIELD: 8 SERVINGS

$\frac{1}{2}$ cup white wine or red wine vinegar

$\frac{1}{3}$ cup sugar

1 teaspoon salt

1 teaspoon dry mustard

1 teaspoon grated onion

1 cup vegetable oil

1 tablespoon poppy seeds

Lettuce leaves

1 large or 2 small cantaloupes, peeled and cut into bite-size pieces

1 large white onion, peeled, thinly sliced, and separated into rings

$\frac{1}{2}$ pound bacon, cooked and crumbled

Process the wine, sugar, salt, mustard, and grated onion in a food processor 20 seconds. Gradually add the oil in a slow, steady stream. Stir in the poppy seeds and refrigerate until ready to use.

Arrange the lettuce leaves on chilled individual salad plates. Layer with the cantaloupe, onion slices, and the crumbled bacon. Drizzle with the poppy seed dressing and serve immediately.

TYPES OF MELONS:

Muskmelons: The muskmelon group includes honeydew, cantaloupe, Crenshaw, and casaba melons. "Musk" is a Persian word for a kind of perfume, and since the ripe melons are quite fragrant, the name stuck.

Cantaloupes: Cantaloupes have a coarse, corky netting on the outer rind. If you are picking your own and the melon doesn't easily separate from the vine, it's not ready to harvest. For that same reason, never purchase cantaloupes that have any portion of the stem attached.

Honeydew Melons: Honeydew melons are large, ranging from four to eight pounds and around eight to ten inches in diameter. When perfectly ripe, they are sweeter than cantaloupes. The outer rind is waxy and will change color several times as it matures. In the end, it will range from creamy white with a green to yellow cast. The flesh is a light green color.

> "He who fills his stomach with melons is like him who fills it with light—there is a blessing in it."
>
> —ARAB PROVERB

MUSHROOMS

MY HUSBAND THINKS HE DOESN'T LIKE MUSHROOMS. ACTUALLY, HE EATS THEM ALL THE time, but I "forget" to tell him I've chopped them up and thrown them into some of his favorite recipes. One of these days, I'm going to tell him that he really does like them, but for right now, I think I'll let him go on believing otherwise. It's sneaky, but effective!

I think the reason he believes he doesn't like them is because he knows what they are. Quite honestly, "fungus" is such an unappetizing word. I hate to connect it with those delicious rooty nuggets that add depth to practically any dish. But mushrooms truly are an edible fungus and a gift to us from the forest.

A fungus is a plant that has no seeds or flowers. It propagates through spores and generally needs dark, moist areas to grow. You'll often see mushrooms popping up after periods of rain, but do not harvest these for eating.

Although you might not think of mushrooms as a typical Southern food, it became a regular item on our tables thanks to Creole cooking. In the beginning of the eighteenth century, French colonists began settling in the area known as the Delta (the area that surrounds the Mississippi River). Shortly before that, Spanish colonists settled in the same area. The combination of the two brought us Creole cooking and mushrooms were an important part of the blended cuisine.

All types of mushrooms are fabulously healthy and seem to transform a recipe to elegant instantly. As a general rule, the darker the mushrooms are in color, the stronger the flavor will be. There are plenty of varieties available both fresh and dry. Interchange them in these recipes and you'll see how different they really are.

Nutrition: Even though mushrooms have a meaty texture, an entire pound contains only one hundred twenty-five calories. All varieties have a healthy dose of dietary fiber and potassium. They contain fair amounts of B vitamins, phosphorus, and calcium.

Preparation: I like to brush fresh mushrooms free of any debris with a vegetable brush or a damp paper towel. Some people, however, prefer to wash them. If the latter is your method, just do so very quickly and immediately drain in a colander. Mushrooms act like little sponges and you don't want to waterlog them before use.

Selection: Firm, fresh looking mushrooms that have not begun to shrivel or change color are best. You do not want to purchase any that appear slimy. Within varieties, size is no indication of quality. Buy only the amount you will be able to use within a few days.

Storage: Keep fresh mushrooms refrigerated and unwashed until you are ready to use. If they come in an original container that is plastic, transfer them to a paper bag so they don't get slimy.

"CAP OFF THE PARTY" STUFFED MUSHROOMS

This dish is a little labor-intensive, but worth the effort. Pair it with champagne as a first course for Christmas Eve dinner or let it help you ring in the New Year. But don't limit it only to holiday celebrations. It's equally at home with a green salad for Sunday night dinner.

YIELD: 24 APPETIZERS

48 large cremini or button mushrooms

$^1/_2$ pound hot or mild pork sausage

$^1/_4$ cup diced onion

3 ounces Monterey Jack cheese, thinly sliced and julienned

Preheat the oven to 350°F. Remove the stems from the mushrooms and place the caps in a 13 x 9-inch baking dish. Set aside.

In a large skillet over medium heat, brown the sausage, adding the onion after 2 minutes. Chop the mushroom stems and add to the sausage mixture. When the sausage is done, drain and blot dry on paper towels.

Stuff the caps with the sausage mixture. Top with 2 strips of cheese in an X formation. Bake 15 minutes, or until the cheese is melted and the mushrooms are tender. Transfer to a serving platter and serve warm.

DEEP-FRIED BUTTONS

All of us have a particular mushroom we rely on most. For me, it's the common button mushrooms you see everywhere. They are inexpensive, unassuming, and versatile. I like to serve these with horseradish or cocktail sauce.

YIELD: 6 SERVINGS

Peanut or vegetable oil

$^3/_4$ cup cornmeal

$^1/_4$ cup all-purpose flour

$^1/_2$ teaspoon seasoned salt

1 egg, beaten

1 tablespoon milk

1 pound whole button or cremini mushrooms, cleaned

In a Dutch oven, pour the oil to a depth of 4 inches. Place over medium-high heat and bring to 350°F.

Meanwhile, in a shallow bowl combine the cornmeal, flour, and salt. Combine the egg and milk and place in a separate shallow bowl. Dip the mushrooms in the egg mixture. Dredge in the cornmeal mixture, making sure the entire mushroom is coated.

Drop carefully in the hot oil and fry 3 to 4 minutes, or until golden brown. Drain on paper towels and serve warm with cocktail sauce or horseradish sauce.

FIRST-FROST CREAM OF MUSHROOM SOUP

Southerners are known for being practical. The popularity of this soup underlines that fact because it uses very little of any one thing. A loaf of hearty bread is all you need to have a complete meal.

YIELD: 8 TO 10 SERVINGS

4 tablespoons unsalted butter

1 tablespoon olive oil

2 cups chopped onions

1 cup chopped celery

2 garlic cloves, minced

$1^1/_2$ teaspoons chopped fresh thyme

1 pound sliced morel or button mushrooms

$^1/_3$ cup all-purpose flour

¹/₂ teaspoon kosher salt

¹/₂ teaspoon black pepper

6 cups vegetable stock

1 cup heavy cream, at room temperature

2 tablespoons dry red wine

In a large stockpot, combine the butter and oil over medium heat. When the butter is completely melted, add the onions and celery. Cook 5 minutes, stirring frequently.

Add the garlic and thyme, cooking 2 minutes more. Add the mushrooms and cook 15 minutes, stirring often. Add the flour, salt, and pepper. Cook 2 more minutes, stirring constantly. Gradually add the vegetable stock, whisking until smooth.

Bring to a simmer and cook 20 minutes, uncovered, stirring occasionally. Gradually add the cream and wine. Return to a simmer and cook 15 minutes more. Serve hot.

MIXED MUSHROOM TART

I love the elegance of this tart. It is earthy and has all the elements of an ordinary comfort food that is dressed in its Sunday best. Serve with a glass of dry red wine and a simple green salad.

YIELD: 8 SERVINGS

1 recipe Single Pie Pastry (page 402)

4 tablespoons olive oil

2 garlic cloves, minced

¹/₄ cup minced onion

3 cups mixed mushrooms, sliced (button, morel, chanterelle, shiitake, or baby portobello)

2 cups shredded Monterey Jack cheese

2 eggs, beaten

³/₄ cup half-and-half

¹/₄ teaspoon seasoned salt

¹/₄ teaspoon black pepper

Preheat the oven to 350°F. Place the pastry in a 9-inch tart pan with a removable bottom. Use a fork to generously prick the bottom and fill with pie weights. Bake 12 minutes. Remove the pie weights and bake an additional 6 minutes. Cool completely on a wire rack.

Increase the oven temperature to 375°F. In a large skillet, heat the oil over medium heat. Add the garlic, onion, and mushrooms. Cook 8 minutes, stirring frequently.

Meanwhile, combine the cheese, eggs, half-and-half, salt, and pepper in a medium bowl. Add the mushroom mixture and blend well. Pour into the prepared crust. Bake 25 to 30 minutes, or until the tart is set. Cool on a wire rack at least 5 minutes before slicing and serving.

MUSHROOM CAVIAR

Chopped mushrooms are enhanced with balsamic vinegar, so use a good one. The tiny pieces make this appetizer easy to serve on crackers or toast points. Leftovers make a great topping for pasta.

YIELD: 1 CUP

1 tablespoon olive oil

4 green onions, sliced

¹/₂ pound button mushrooms, chopped

4 garlic cloves, minced

¹/₂ teaspoon chopped fresh thyme

2 teaspoons lemon juice

4 teaspoons balsamic vinegar

¹/₄ teaspoon black pepper

Place the oil in a large saucepan over medium heat. Add the onions, mushrooms, and garlic. Sauté 10 minutes. Cool 5 minutes. Transfer to a food processor and pulse until coarsely chopped.

Do not overprocess.

Return to the saucepan and add the thyme, lemon juice, vinegar, and pepper. Sauté over medium-high heat until the liquid has evaporated. Serve warm with crackers or cool to room temperature, and then refrigerate until ready to use. If chilled, bring to room temperature 30 minutes before serving.

PUFFED MUSHROOM CRISPS

The beauty of puff pastry is that it adds a wow factor to the end result. These little pastries are tender on the inside and crispy on the outside.

YIELD: 9 APPETIZER SERVINGS

1 pound button mushrooms

2 tablespoons unsalted butter

2 tablespoons minced shallots

2 garlic cloves, minced

$\frac{1}{4}$ cup dry red wine

$\frac{1}{2}$ teaspoon chopped fresh tarragon

$\frac{1}{2}$ teaspoon kosher salt

$\frac{1}{4}$ teaspoon black pepper

1 (17.3-ounce) package puff pastry, thawed

1 egg, beaten

1 (4-ounce) jar prepared horseradish

1 cup sour cream

Remove all stems from the mushroom caps and chop the stems. Set 18 whole mushrooms aside and chop any remaining mushrooms.

Melt the butter in a medium skillet over medium heat. Add the chopped mushrooms, shallots, and garlic. Cook 10 minutes, stirring frequently. Stir in the wine and tarragon. Cook until the liquid has evaporated, about 8 minutes. Season with the salt

and pepper and set aside.

Preheat the oven to 450°F. Lightly grease a baking sheet and set aside.

Roll each puff pastry sheet into an 11-inch square on a lightly floured surface. Cut each sheet into 9 equal squares. Distribute the cooked mushroom mixture evenly among the squares. Top with a mushroom cap. Brush the pastry edges with the beaten egg.

Fold the pastry to enclose and pinch to seal. Place the seam side down on the prepared sheet. Brush the tops with the egg. Bake about 12 minutes, or until golden brown.

Meanwhile, combine the horseradish and sour cream in a small bowl. Serve with the warm mushrooms, 2 per serving.

SKILLET-POACHED MUSHROOMS

I have been making this cold appetizer since college. It's incredibly easy to prepare with no exotic ingredients to find. It's a sturdy dish that can be made ahead, making it an excellent party food.

YIELD: 6 APPETIZER SERVINGS

24 button mushroom caps

$\frac{1}{2}$ cup olive oil

$\frac{1}{3}$ cup white wine vinegar

$\frac{1}{3}$ cup dry white wine

2 garlic cloves, peeled

1 bay leaf

1 tablespoon chopped fresh tarragon or oregano

1 teaspoon kosher salt

$\frac{1}{2}$ teaspoon black pepper

Place the mushrooms in a deep skillet. Add enough water to barely cover the mushrooms. Add the oil, vinegar, wine, garlic, bay leaf, tarragon, salt, and pepper. Do not stir.

Place the skillet over medium heat and slowly bring to a boil. Reduce heat to low and poach 10 minutes or until the mushrooms are tender when pierced with a fork.

Cool in the liquid and transfer to a covered dish. Refrigerate at least 8 hours or overnight. When ready to serve, strain from the poaching liquid.

Note: The poaching liquid can be refrigerated up to one week and reused.

SOUTHERN-FRIED MORELS

This recipe has a very different end result than Deep-Fried Buttons (page 291). In fact, you'll think they are hardly related. The spongy texture and honeycomb crevices of these unique mushrooms quite literally grab the batter, making no sauce necessary for serving.

YIELD: 4 SERVINGS

1 cup peanut or canola oil

2 eggs

$^3/_4$ cup milk

$^1/_2$ cup finely crushed saltine crackers or corn flakes

1 pound morel mushrooms

$^1/_2$ teaspoon kosher salt

$^1/_2$ teaspoon black pepper

Place the oil in a large cast-iron skillet over medium-high heat.

Meanwhile, whisk together the eggs and milk in a small bowl. Place the crackers in a shallow bowl. Dip the mushrooms in the egg mixture and dredge in the crackers.

Carefully add to the hot oil. Fry 2 to 3 minutes, or until golden brown. Turn to evenly brown and don't overcrowd the pan. Drain on paper towels. Sprinkle with the salt and pepper and serve warm.

BOTANY: There are more than forty thousand varieties of mushrooms in the world. Mushrooms are commercially produced in nearly every state in the U.S.

HISTORY: Evidence shows that as early as 3000 BC, mushrooms were being used. However, the primary use was medicinal. They did not become popular in the U.S. until the late 1800s.

PICKING YOUR OWN: This is one of the few produce items that I'll never suggest harvesting from nature. The risk of it being a poisonous type or contaminated is simply too great. So, depend on the supermarket or gourmet market for your mushrooms rather than your own backyard.

REHYDRATING: Dried mushrooms are incredibly convenient and don't take up any refrigerator space. To prepare them for throwing on pizza or pasta, soak in warm water at least thirty minutes. Drain and remove the tough stems.

YIELDS: One pound of fresh mushrooms will give you four to six servings. Frequently, fresh mushrooms are sold in eight-ounce containers, which is the equivalent of three cups sliced.

OKRA

LIKE MOST KIDS, I WAS TRICKED INTO EATING OKRA BECAUSE IT WAS FRIED. IF IT GOT THE LEAST bit cold, I would pick off the fried batter and leave the sad looking naked okra on the plate. As I got older and ventured out of my Mississippi food world, okra worked its way into my gumbo, stew, and soup pots. But that movement took a while.

I missed about a week of college thanks to appendicitis. When I returned to my favorite cooking class, I had missed the basics of Creole cooking. When my instructor kept talking about "smothered okra," I knew I had some catching up to do because I was totally lost. I could not imagine how you would smother this vegetable and wasn't sure I wanted to try. By the way, that's a common term for stewed okra!

Okra is as essential to Creole cooking as a large pot and a good knife. The vegetable was a staple of cooking on Southern plantations and believed to have been brought here on some of the very earliest slave ships. As a result, okra found a way to slip into every form of Southern regional cooking.

As I began to use okra in different ways other than fried, I soon discovered the taste was similar to unseasoned fresh green beans and quite delicious. In my quest to use this vegetable constantly through the growing season, I saw the remarkable versatility of this Southern aristocrat. I now love to throw the cut pods in muffins and fritter batter, and stew them with tomatoes.

There is only one way I buy okra: fresh. I've seen the pre-breaded and frozen stuff as well as the commercially canned, but I just can't bring myself to pick any of it up. Luckily, the fresh market has plenty in produce bins most of the year. Okra is also grown in my garden and it won't let you neglect it. Even in dry weather, it continues to produce and demands to be harvested regularly. I don't mind because there are plenty of ways to enjoy this formerly only-fried favorite.

Nutrition: Okra is a good source of calcium, phosphorus, vitamins A and C, and iron. Raw okra is nearly 90 percent water, which accounts for the low-calorie content. Eight cooked pods contain only twenty-five calories.

Selection: Look for firm, crisp, brightly colored pods that show no signs of blemishes or yellowing. Avoid any that are shriveled, dull in appearance, limp, blemished, or blackened.

Those that are four inches in length or shorter are the most tender and the best as far as quality is concerned. Long, large pods are more than likely tough and fibrous. You can tell as soon as you start to cut the pods into slices. Overmature pods have the texture of sugarcane.

Storage: Although it looks tough, okra bruises easily and should be handled with care. Keep it refrigerated in the crisper or vegetable drawer and use quickly. It can be stored for up to four days, depending on the quality purchased. Do not wash until you are ready to use it. For longer storage, okra can be frozen, but must be blanched first.

EASY STREET OVEN-FRIED OKRA

Let's face it … sometimes you don't have time to stand over the stove frying loads of okra. No fear! The oven is here!

YIELD: 6 SERVINGS

1 egg
$\frac{1}{4}$ cup buttermilk
1 pound fresh okra, trimmed and sliced
$\frac{2}{3}$ cup plain cornmeal
$\frac{1}{3}$ cup all-purpose flour
1 teaspoon baking powder
$\frac{1}{2}$ teaspoon salt
Vegetable cooking spray

Preheat the oven to 450°F. Lightly grease a jelly-roll pan and set aside.In a medium bowl, whisk together the egg and buttermilk. Add the okra, stirring well to evenly coat. Set aside 10 minutes.

In a heavy zip-top bag, combine the cornmeal, flour, baking powder, and salt. In small batches, drain the okra from the egg mixture with a slotted spoon. Place in the zip-top bag and shake gently to coat. Place okra in a single layer on the prepared pan. Repeat with the remaining okra.

Coat the okra with cooking spray. Bake 8 minutes, stir, and coat with cooking spray again. Bake another 8 minutes. Set the broiler on high and broil 5 minutes or until lightly browned. Serve warm.

ORIGIN: Okra is a native of Africa in the area now known as Ethiopia. It spread north from there, but the dates and methods of distribution are largely unknown. The earliest recorded history is around 12 BC.

BLUE PLATE SPECIAL OKRA AND TOMATOES

Blue Plate Specials are low-priced meals usually served at diners. The special changes daily depending on what foods are in abundance. That's why this dish is so popular. Okra and tomatoes are in abundance all summer long.

YIELD: 6 SERVINGS

2 tablespoons vegetable oil
$\frac{3}{4}$ cup chopped onion
$\frac{1}{4}$ cup chopped green bell pepper
2 garlic cloves, minced
1 pound fresh okra, trimmed
2 tomatoes, peeled and coarsely chopped
$\frac{1}{2}$ teaspoon salt
$\frac{1}{2}$ teaspoon black pepper
$\frac{1}{4}$ cup water
Dash of hot sauce

Place the oil in a large skillet over medium-high heat. Add the onions, pepper, and garlic. Sauté 3 minutes, stirring constantly. Add the okra, tomatoes, salt, pepper, water, and hot sauce. Bring to a boil and reduce the heat to low. Cover and simmer 25 minutes, stirring occasionally. Serve warm.

FABULOUS FRIED OKRA

No matter how many times you double or triple this recipe, there is never enough.

YIELD: 4 TO 6 SERVINGS

12 okra pods, sliced into $\frac{1}{4}$-inch slices
1 tablespoon water
1 cup plain cornmeal
1 tablespoon all-purpose flour

1 teaspoon salt

½ teaspoon black pepper

Vegetable oil

Sprinkle the okra with the water and set aside. In a medium bowl, mix together the cornmeal, flour, salt, and pepper. Pour the oil to the depth of 1 inch in a large cast-iron skillet and place over medium-high heat. Bring to 350°F.

Coat the okra in the cornmeal mixture and carefully drop in the hot oil. Fry until golden brown, about 4 minutes. Drain on paper towels and serve.

FEED THE MASSES OKRA GUMBO

Everyone knows that gumbo is made by the boatload. It is meant to be enjoyed by everyone you know and even those you might not know so well. The leftovers can be easily frozen for later use if necessary.

YIELD: 16 SERVINGS

7 cups sliced okra

2 cups chopped onion

⅔ cup chopped green bell pepper

½ cup chopped celery

⅔ cup tomato sauce

2 teaspoons salt

1 teaspoon black pepper

2 bay leaves

4 cups water

2 (16-ounce) cans whole tomatoes, undrained

2 pounds medium shrimp, peeled and deveined

1 teaspoon seasoned salt

Hot cooked rice

Preheat the oven to 300°F. Lightly grease a 13 x 9-inch baking pan and set aside.

In a large mixing bowl, combine the okra, onions, peppers, celery, tomato sauce, salt, pepper, and bay leaves. Transfer to the prepared pan. Bake 2 hours, stirring after 1 hour.

Transfer to a very large Dutch oven. Stir in the water and tomatoes and place over medium-high heat. Bring to a boil, reduce the heat to low, cover, and simmer 1 hour. Add the shrimp and seasoned salt. Simmer 20 minutes longer.

Remove the bay leaves. Serve hot over cooked rice.

GARDEN GOODIE OKRA CREOLE

This recipe blends all the fabulous Southern summer vegetables. Tomatoes, corn, green peppers, and okra combine for a great meal when served over cooked rice.

YIELD: 6 SERVINGS

2 tablespoons unsalted butter

1 cup chopped green bell pepper

½ cup chopped onion

1½ cups corn, cut from the cob

½ cup water

2 tomatoes, peeled, seeded, and chopped

1½ tablespoons tomato paste

½ teaspoon seasoned salt

¼ teaspoon black pepper

¼ teaspoon dried thyme

¼ teaspoon paprika

1½ cups sliced okra

In a large skillet over medium heat, melt the butter. Add the peppers and onions and sauté until tender, about 4 minutes. Stir in the corn and water, cover, and cook 10 minutes, stirring occasionally.

Add the tomatoes, tomato paste, salt, pepper, thyme, and paprika. Cover and simmer 10 minutes, stirring occasionally. Add the okra, cover, and simmer 7 minutes longer, or until the okra is done. Serve warm.

....

HARD TIMES OKRA SOUP

This recipe was in my grandmother's recipe drawer, which I was going through one day while still in college. She told me it was the soup commonly made when you didn't have very much to eat because it was filling and tasty, better yet, delicious! When I make it now, I always think of the numerous people this has beautifully nourished.

YIELD: 6 SERVINGS

4 tablespoons bacon drippings

1 cup chopped celery

1 small green bell pepper, seeded and chopped

1 white onion, peeled and chopped

6 cups water

1 ham hock

4 cups sliced okra

4 tomatoes, cut in wedges

1 teaspoon salt

1 teaspoon brown sugar

$^1/_2$ cup uncooked rice

Heat the drippings in a large Dutch oven over medium heat. Add the celery, pepper, and onion and sauté 5 minutes.

Stir in the water and add the ham hock. Boil 20 minutes. Remove the ham hock and set aside until cool enough to handle. Cover the pot and reduce the heat to medium low.

Remove the meat from the bone. Chop the meat and return it to the pot. Discard the bone.

Stir in the okra, tomatoes, salt, brown sugar, and rice. Simmer, covered, about 1 hour. Serve hot.

OVEN OKRA ÉTOUFFÉE

This version of the Louisiana classic omits the crayfish, and instead of stirring a pot on the stove, you let it bubble away in the oven. It is a great vegetable-only dinner.

YIELD: 6 SERVINGS

3 cups sliced okra

$^1/_4$ cup canola or vegetable oil

1 (10-ounce) can diced tomatoes and green chiles, undrained

1 white onion, peeled and chopped

1 green bell pepper, seeded and chopped

$^3/_4$ teaspoon salt

$^1/_4$ teaspoon black pepper

Hot cooked rice

Preheat the oven to 400°F. Lightly grease a $1^1/_2$ -quart baking dish and scatter the okra over the bottom. Drizzle with the oil.

Top evenly with the tomatoes, onion, and bell pepper. Sprinkle with the salt and pepper. Cover and bake 1 hour, stirring occasionally. Uncover and bake 15 minutes longer. Serve warm over hot cooked rice.

....

"PODS OF PLENTY" OKRA PILAU

Pilau is pronounced "pih-LOW" in the South and has been a regular on Carolina and Florida coastal tables for years. Add cooked salad shrimp to this dish at the last minute if you want to use it as a one-pot meal.

YIELD: 4 SERVINGS

8 bacon slices, diced

$1^1/_2$ cups sliced fresh okra

1 large white onion, peeled and chopped

1 green bell pepper, seeded and chopped

2 cups water

1½ cups uncooked long-grain rice

½ teaspoon salt

¼ teaspoon black pepper

In a large skillet over medium heat, fry the bacon until crisp, around 6 minutes. Remove with a slotted spoon and drain on paper towels. Set aside.

Add the okra, onion, and pepper to the pan drippings and sauté 5 minutes or until tender. Stir in the water, rice, salt, and pepper and bring to a boil. Cover and reduce the heat to low. Simmer 20 minutes or until the water is absorbed and the rice is tender.

Remove from the heat and add the bacon. Let stand 5 minutes uncovered. Stir again and serve warm.

"TASTE OF HOME" OKRA FRITTERS

Fritters are fried cakes or patties. In this case, they are savory and full of color.

YIELD: 6 SERVINGS

Vegetable oil

2 cups sliced fresh okra

¼ cup plain cornmeal

¼ cup all-purpose flour

½ cup finely chopped onion

3 tablespoons chopped fresh parsley

2 tablespoons shredded Parmesan cheese

½ teaspoon seasoned salt

¼ teaspoon red pepper

½ cup evaporated milk

1 egg, lightly beaten

Pour the oil to a depth of 2 inches in a large cast-iron skillet. Place over medium-high heat and bring to 350°F.

Meanwhile, in a mixing bowl, combine the okra, cornmeal, flour, onions, parsley, cheese, salt, and pepper. Make a well in the center.

In a small bowl, combine the milk and egg. Pour into the dry mixture and stir to blend. Drop tablespoons of the dough into the hot oil. Fry 3 to 4 minutes, or until golden brown. Drain on paper towels and serve warm.

BOTANY: Okra is a tropical plant and a member of the mallow family. It is considered to be an edible hibiscus and relatives include ornamental flowering hibiscus plants, hollyhocks, and cotton. Okra plants love warm temperatures and humid climates, so no wonder it is welcomed in the South. The plants are easily injured by frost, so the homegrown season comes to a screeching halt at that time.

GROWING: Dwarf okra varieties are perfect for home gardeners and only reach heights of around three feet. Other older varieties can grow to heights that are difficult to harvest unless you play for the NBA or have a stepladder handy. Once the plant starts producing, cut the pods regularly, which is about every other day. Overmature pods that are left on the plant will reduce future yields, so if you miss a couple of days, pull those off and discard them immediately.

ONIONS

IF YOU'VE NEVER TRAVELED MUCH IN THE GREAT SOUTHERN STATE OF GEORGIA, YOU NEED TO put some gas in the car and head in that direction. It is the historical home of many Southern traditions, belles, and exceptional fruits and vegetables. But the most notorious of those would be the Vidalia onion, Georgia's culinary gift to the world.

Vidalias are sweet onions that were first grown in Vidalia, Georgia, in the early 1930s. They were discovered by a man named Mose Coleman. Well, let me tell you … those Georgia folks are quite smart. They eventually realized that the unmatched sweetness of that particular onion was present thanks to the low amounts of sulfur in the soil.

Only certain counties had the soil it took for maximum sweetness. So, in the 1980s, they trademarked the Vidalia onion, saying that only those particular areas could market onions as Vidalias. Marketing history got a shot in the arm from that point forward. It revolutionized the industry there and forever made Georgia the undisputed home of the Vidalia onion.

While sweet Vidalia onions are not the only onions grown in the South, they are certainly the most popular. Don't ignore the others. We still grow loads of white, yellow, purple, and green.

My daddy used to get so excited when he harvested green onions from our family garden. He would eat a couple of them that very evening just washed and trimmed. Although as a child, I never shared that same enthusiasm, I did think it looked nice on his plate.

Then I started growing my own and quickly developed a passion of my own for the entire family.

Whether using it as a seasoning or as a vegetable side dish, onions are far from a tear-starter in any Southern kitchen.

Nutrition: Onions are good sources of phosphorus, potassium, calcium, and vitamin A. One medium onion contains only forty-nine calories.

Selection: When buying onions classified as "dry," look for those with short necks and papery outer skins. They should be firm and free of bruises. Moisture at the neck, soft spots, and spongy bulbs with fresh sprouts are signs of decay.

Storage: Onions like temperatures around 35°F, which means the refrigerator is ideal, but space is usually limited there. It can make it just as well, but not as long in a cool, dry, well-ventilated place. Avoid placing them in direct sunlight, which can cause green sun spots on the flesh. Also avoid storing them with potatoes. Each gives off a gas that causes the other to decay more quickly.

FLASH-IN-THE-PAN BARBECUED ONIONS

This recipe is quick and cooks the onions just enough to tame their bite. Serve over grilled chicken or pork or as a side dressing for beans.

YIELD: 6 TO 8 SERVINGS

1 cup ketchup
³/₄ cup water
¹/₄ cup cider vinegar
2 garlic cloves, minced
1 tablespoon sugar
1 tablespoon Worcestershire sauce
1 teaspoon salt
1 teaspoon celery seeds
¹/₄ teaspoon hot sauce
¹/₄ teaspoon black pepper
2 large yellow onions, peeled and sliced

In a large saucepan over medium-high heat, combine the ketchup, water, vinegar, garlic, sugar, Worcestershire, salt, celery seeds, hot sauce, and pepper. Stir to blend and bring to a boil, stirring frequently. Cover, reduce heat to low, and simmer 5 minutes. Add the onions, stirring to blend. Cover and simmer 4 to 6 minutes longer. Serve warm or cool completely and serve at room temperature.

FOUR-CHEESE GREEN ONION BREAD

This bread smells so nice while baking and is loaded with speckles of green onion bits. It is a good accompaniment to ham.

YIELD: 1 LOAF

2¹/₂ cups all-purpose flour

1 tablespoon sugar
2 teaspoons black pepper
1 teaspoon baking powder
³/₄ teaspoon salt
¹/₂ teaspoon baking soda
2 eggs, lightly beaten
8 ounces plain yogurt
¹/₄ cup shredded sharp Cheddar cheese
¹/₄ cup shredded Swiss cheese
¹/₄ cup shredded Monterey Jack cheese
¹/₄ cup shredded Emmentaler or Gruyère
¹/₂ cup vegetable oil
10 to 12 green onions, thinly sliced
¹/₄ cup milk

Preheat the oven to 350°F. Lightly grease a loaf pan and set aside.

In a large mixing bowl, combine the flour, sugar, pepper, baking powder, salt, and baking soda. In a separate bowl, combine the eggs, yogurt, Cheddar, Swiss, Monterey Jack, Emmentaler, oil, onions, and milk.

Add the egg mixture to the flour mixture, stirring just until moist. Transfer the batter to the prepared pan. Bake 45 to 50 minutes, or until a tester inserted in the center comes out clean.

Cool in the pan 10 minutes. Remove and cool completely on a wire rack before slicing and serving.

FRESH ONION MARMALADE

Marmalade is normally a preserve we associate with Florida oranges. Put that notion aside. This onion-based delicacy is exceptional on any menu, and I mean that. I've serve it with everything from veal to fish. It's superb.

YIELD: 5 CUPS

3 tablespoons olive oil

2 large purple onions, peeled and julienned

2 large yellow onions, peeled and julienned

2 cups sliced green onions, green parts only

$1^{1}/_{2}$ cups balsamic vinegar

$^{1}/_{4}$ cup packed brown sugar

$^{1}/_{2}$ teaspoon salt

$^{1}/_{4}$ teaspoon black pepper

Heat the oil in a large skillet over medium heat. Add the purple and yellow onions. Sauté 5 minutes, or until the onions begin to soften. Add the green onions, cover, and cook 8 minutes longer.

Increase the heat to high and add the vinegar. Cook, stirring occasionally, until the liquid is reduced by half, about 8 minutes. Add the brown sugar, salt, and pepper. Reduce the heat to low and continue cooking until the liquid is almost absorbed and the marmalade is thick, about 10 minutes. Serve warm.

"HOT OFF THE GRILL" STUFFED ONIONS

Summer suppers are complete with these aromatic sweet onions. Serve them with grilled or smoked turkey tenderloins, sliced tomatoes, and fresh corn. Don't have the right weather for the grill? Bake them in a 350°F oven for an hour, or until tender.

YIELD: 6 SERVINGS

$1^{1}/_{2}$ cups herb-seasoned dry stuffing mix

1 cup shredded sharp Cheddar or Swiss cheese

6 tablespoons unsalted butter, melted

$^{1}/_{3}$ cup vegetable stock

1 teaspoon poultry seasoning

6 medium sweet onions, peeled

Preheat the grill to medium heat (350°F). Cut 6 (12-inch) pieces of heavy-duty aluminum foil and coat

one side of each with cooking spray. Set aside.

Meanwhile, in a mixing bowl, combine the stuffing mix, cheese, butter, stock, and poultry seasoning. Blend well and set aside.

Cut each onion into 3 horizontal slices. Spread 2 tablespoons of the stuffing mixture between the slices and reassemble. Place each onion on the prepared foil square. Bring the opposite corners together and twist to seal.

Cook, covered, 27 to 30 minutes, or until the onions are tender. Serve warm.

ODE TO ONION PIE

This breakfast pie is a meal in itself. Just add some fruit and milk and you've got everyone ready to take on the day.

YIELD: 8 SERVINGS

1 recipe Single Crust Pie Pastry (page 402)

6 bacon slices

2 sweet onions, peeled and chopped

2 small garlic cloves, minced

1 cup shredded sharp Cheddar cheese

4 eggs

1 (12-ounce) can evaporated milk

1 teaspoon dry mustard

1 teaspoon Worcestershire sauce

$^{1}/_{2}$ teaspoon salt

$^{1}/_{2}$ teaspoon paprika

$^{1}/_{4}$ teaspoon black pepper

Dash of hot sauce

Preheat the oven to 400°F. Line a 9-inch pie pan with the pastry. Prick the bottom and sides with a fork. Bake 3 minutes, prick with a fork again, and bake 5 minutes longer. Cool on a wire rack and reduce the oven temperature to 325°F.

Meanwhile, cook the bacon in a large skillet over medium heat until crisp, around 6 to 7 minutes. Drain on paper towels and crumble when cool enough to handle.

Sauté the onions and garlic in the bacon drippings until tender, about 5 to 6 minutes, stirring frequently. Drain and spoon into the pastry shell. Sprinkle the bacon and cheese evenly over the top.

In a mixing bowl, beat the eggs until light and fluffy. Stir in the milk, mustard, Worcestershire, salt, paprika, pepper, and hot sauce until well blended. Pour into the pastry shell. Bake 1 hour, or until set. Let stand 10 minutes before slicing and serving.

SPICY SWEET ONION RINGS

I cannot resist good fried onion rings. This is my favorite recipe for making them at home. George prefers them without the peppers, but I like the mixture of hot and sweet. Try them both ways and see which you like best.

YIELD: 6 SERVINGS

Vegetable oil
2 medium yellow or white onions, peeled
1 cup self-rising flour
$1/3$ cup self-rising cornmeal
1 egg, lightly beaten
$1/2$ cup sweetened condensed milk
$1/4$ cup club soda
$1/2$ cup finely minced jalapeño pepper
Kosher salt

Pour the oil to depth of 3 inches in a Dutch oven and place over medium-high heat. Bring to 375°F.

Cut the onions into $1/4$-inch slices and separate into rings. In a medium bowl, combine the flour and cornmeal. In a separate bowl, combine the egg, milk, and club soda. Add to dry ingredients and stir until smooth. Stir in the jalapeños.

Dip the onion rings into the batter, coating well. Fry a few at a time until golden brown, around 3 to 4 minutes. Drain on paper towels and sprinkle with the salt. Serve immediately.

THREE ONION SOUP

This smooth, creamy soup is enhanced with plain yogurt rather than sour cream. If you don't own an immersion blender, this is the reason to buy one!

YIELD: 6 SERVINGS

4 tablespoons unsalted butter
1 tablespoon olive oil
1 yellow onion, peeled and chopped
1 purple onion, peeled and chopped
4 shallots, peeled and chopped
4 cups chicken stock
1 teaspoon dried oregano
$1/2$ teaspoon dried thyme
$1/2$ teaspoon ground cumin
$1/4$ teaspoon white pepper
3 tablespoons dry white wine
1 (8-ounce) carton plain yogurt
Chopped fresh parsley

Place the butter and oil in a large Dutch oven over medium heat. Add the yellow onion, purple onion, shallots, stock, oregano, thyme, cumin, and pepper. Bring to a boil and reduce heat to low. Simmer 20 minutes, stirring frequently.

Add the wine and simmer 20 minutes longer, stirring frequently. Use an immersion blender to purée the soup until smooth (or cool and purée in a blender or food processor). Stir in the yogurt and heat another 15 minutes. Serve hot with a garnish of chopped parsley.

....

VIDALIA ONION RELISH

This easy to make relish is so good on black-eyed peas or cooked white beans.

YIELD: 1¾ CUPS

1 tablespoon canola or vegetable oil
2 large sweet onions, peeled and chopped
¼ cup apple jelly
1½ teaspoons salt
½ teaspoon crushed red pepper

Place the oil in a large skillet over medium-high heat. Add the onions and sauté 10 minutes, stirring frequently. Add the jelly, salt, and pepper. Stir constantly until the jelly completely melts. Serve warm or cool to room temperature. The relish can also be refrigerated until ready to use.

BOTANY: Onions are members of the lily family and the Allium genus. There are more than four hundred fifty species of Allium grown in the world, with the majority being grown in North America.

ORIGIN: Onions are believed to have originated along the shores of the Mediterranean more than five thousand years ago. The earliest traces of onions were found in Egyptian tombs dating to thirty five hundred years ago, but paintings of onions were found on the inner walls of pyramids dating to 2423 BC.

NAME: In the South, we simply refer to Vidalia onions as sweet onions . . . that's how it will be listed in the recipes. You will see them marketed under both names throughout the South.

CLASSIFICATIONS: Onions are classified as either dry or green. The green category includes scallions, leeks, chives, and green onions. These are harvested before the bulbs are fully developed. They have a sweeter, milder, and more delicate flavor than dry onions and are frequently sold by the bunch.

Dry onions are more fully developed and are easy to identify because of their brittle, papery outer thin skins. Dry onions are further divided into fresh and storage onions. Fresh onions hit the market during the spring and summer months and have a higher water and sugar content than storage onions. That translates into a shorter shelf life.

Storage onions hit the market around Labor Day and continue through March. They are firm, compact, and less susceptible to bruising and shipping damage.

FREEZING: Onions are one of only two vegetables that do not need blanching before freezing. The other is bell pepper. Simply chop and place in a freezer container. They will not hold their texture very well, but are fine for using in cooked dishes.

TEARS: The tear-inducing characteristics of onions come primarily from sulfuric compounds in the vegetable. When onions are peeled and cut, these chemicals are let loose and dissolve in the small quantities of water in our eyes. This produces a mild form of sulfuric acid that is an irritant and causes tears to flow.

OYSTERS

GROWING UP IN A LAND-LOCKED AREA, I DIDN'T FULLY APPRECIATE OYSTERS UNTIL I MOVED to the Gulf Coast for a while. I first began to nibble on them during summer beach vacations after I graduated from college. I didn't just dive into oysters. Instead, they pulled me into liking them bit by bit.

The southern Gulf Coast is quite lovely and a common getaway for sunshine-starved people from all over the country. It has been one of my favorite places of escape for years. It is also the home of a huge commercial fishing industry, and oysters from the Gulf make sure we have a consistently good product year-round.

However, there is a really old adage that says you should only eat oysters in months containing the letter *R*. Thanks to improved oyster farming and cold storage techniques, that rule no longer applies and is thankfully merely folklore.

Oysters could be described as the Southerners in the seafood family. They survive and thrive in climates that range from mild to warm, where they settle on the floor of shallow coastal waters. The Southern Gulf Coast region routinely supplies around 40 percent of all the oysters consumed in the U.S.

Even though I now love oysters prepared dozens of ways, those that are Southern fried are nearly impossible for me—and countless others—to resist. Crisp brown oyster nuggets that are still warm from the hot oil need nothing other than my time to sit and enjoy them … during any month of the year!

Cooking: Oysters have a high water content, so overcooking is easy to do and will cause loss of moisture and shrinkage. For that reason, follow your recipe closely and cook just until the edges begin to curl.

Nutrition: Oysters are an excellent source of vitamins A, B1, B2, B3, C, and D. Oysters are one of nature's richest sources of iron. In fact, five medium oysters will supply the recommended daily allowance of iron, as well as copper, iodine, magnesium, calcium, zinc, manganese, and phosphorus.

Shucking: An oyster knife is a really sturdy, short knife that is invaluable when shucking oysters. So is a sturdy glove to protect your hand. Scrub the oysters under cold, running water with a stiff brush to remove any grit that might be clinging to the outer shell. Hold the oyster with the flat side up and insert the knife into the narrow hinged end. With quite a bit of force, twist the knife until the shell pops open.

Storage: Frozen oysters should be used within four months for the best quality. They should be allowed to thaw in the refrigerator for one day before use. Never refreeze thawed oysters and use them within two days of thawing. Canned and smoked oysters are best if used within one year.

FAMILY DINNER OYSTER BISQUE

This creamy soup only needs to be paired with a green salad and plenty of hot cornbread. Southerners love to feed a crowd, but if your family is not as big as this recipe will feed, freeze the leftovers. Use within two months for the best quality.

YIELD: 2 QUARTS

1 quart oysters, undrained
$\frac{1}{4}$ pound (1 stick) unsalted butter
1 shallot, peeled and chopped
1 garlic clove, minced
2 cups cream
2 cups half-and-half
$\frac{1}{2}$ teaspoon kosher salt
$\frac{1}{4}$ teaspoon white pepper
2 tablespoons dry sherry

Drain the oysters, reserving the liquid. Place the oysters in the bowl of a food processor and process just until coarsely chopped. Set aside.

In a large Dutch oven, melt the butter over medium heat. Add the shallot and garlic. Sauté 4 minutes or until tender. Stir in the cream, half-and-half, salt, pepper, and the reserved oyster liquid.

Cook 8 minutes, stirring frequently. Do not allow to boil. Stir in the oysters and simmer 8 minutes longer. Add the sherry and heat 1 minute longer. Ladle into warm soup bowls.

MELTING-POT OYSTER GUMBO

This hearty gumbo contains a melting pot of seafood. It has shrimp, crab, but most importantly, oysters. It commands respect, and a second helping!

YIELD: 12 SERVINGS

$1\frac{1}{2}$ pounds small in-shell shrimp
1 purple onion, peeled and cut in half
1 carrot, cut in half
4 parsley sprigs
1 teaspoon black peppercorns
1 bay leaf
2 teaspoons salt, divided
3 quarts water
$\frac{1}{3}$ cup vegetable oil
$\frac{1}{2}$ cup all-purpose flour
1 large white onion, peeled and chopped
1 green bell pepper, seeded and chopped
2 celery stalks, chopped
$\frac{1}{2}$ pound lump crabmeat
1 (12-ounce) container oysters, undrained
1 cup sliced green onion tops
$\frac{1}{4}$ teaspoon hot sauce
Hot cooked rice

Peel the shrimp and reserve the shells. Refrigerate the shrimp, covered.

In a large Dutch oven, combine the shrimp shells, onion halves, carrot, parsley, peppercorns, bay leaf, $1\frac{1}{2}$ teaspoons of the salt, and the water. Place over high heat and bring to a boil. Reduce heat to medium-low and simmer, uncovered, 45 minutes.

Pour the stock through a fine-mesh strainer into a large bowl. Discard the solids. Return the stock to the Dutch oven and set aside, uncovered.

In a large skillet over medium heat, combine the oil and flour. Cook 30 minutes, or until the roux is dark brown, stirring constantly. Add the chopped onion, pepper, and celery. Cook around 15 minutes, or until softened, stirring occasionally.

Meanwhile, reheat the stock over medium-high heat. Add the roux mixture a spoonful at a time to the stock, stirring well after each addition. Bring to a boil, stirring frequently. Reduce the heat to medium and simmer 15 minutes, stirring occasionally.

Stir in the shrimp, crabmeat, and oysters with their liquid. Simmer, stirring occasionally until the edges of the oysters begin to curl, around 7 minutes. Add the green onions, hot sauce, and the remaining $\frac{1}{2}$ teaspoon of the salt. Cook 1 minute longer. Ladle over hot cooked rice and serve with extra hot sauce.

FRIED OYSTERS

If you have those in your midst who think they don't like oysters, start them out on this Southern dish to change their minds. Use a thermometer to make sure the oil is heated to the proper level before you begin.

YIELD: 6 SERVINGS

Vegetable oil
1 cup self-rising flour
1 cup self-rising cornmeal
$\frac{1}{2}$ teaspoon red pepper
2 eggs
2 tablespoon milk
2 (12-ounce) containers oysters, drained

Pour the oil to a depth of 3 inches in a large Dutch oven or skillet. Place over medium-high heat and bring to 375°F.

Meanwhile, in a medium bowl, combine the flour, cornmeal, and red pepper. In a separate bowl, whisk together the egg and milk. Dip the oysters in the egg mixture and dredge in the flour mixture.

Fry until golden brown in the oil, $1\frac{1}{2}$ to 2 minutes. Drain on paper towels and serve warm.

OYSTERS BIENVILLE

This dish is named in honor of Jean Baptise Le Moyne, Sieur de Bienville, the founder of New Orleans. It was created in the late 1930s at Antoine's restaurant and is baked on a bed of rock salt.

YIELD: 3 DOZEN APPETIZERS

3 pounds rock salt
36 oysters in the shell, scrubbed with top shells discarded
6 tablespoons unsalted butter
$\frac{2}{3}$ cup chopped green onions
3 tablespoons chopped fresh parsley
2 garlic cloves, minced
$\frac{1}{3}$ cup all-purpose flour
$1\frac{1}{4}$ cups milk
$\frac{1}{3}$ cup half-and-half
2 egg yolks, lightly beaten
3 tablespoons sherry
1 teaspoon salt
$\frac{1}{2}$ teaspoon white pepper
$\frac{1}{4}$ teaspoon cayenne
$\frac{2}{3}$ cup chopped fresh mushrooms
$\frac{1}{2}$ pound cooked shrimp, chopped
$\frac{1}{4}$ cup shredded Parmesan cheese
$\frac{1}{4}$ cup soft breadcrumbs

Sprinkle the rock salt in 2 large jelly-roll pans. Arrange the oyster shells (containing the oysters) over the rock salt and set aside. Preheat the oven to 350°F.

Place the butter in a large skillet over medium-high heat. Add the onions, parsley, and garlic. Sauté 2 minutes, stirring constantly.

Add the flour and stir until smooth. Gradually add the milk and half-and-half. Reduce the heat to medium and cook, stirring constantly, until thick and bubbly, around 6 minutes.

Slowly stir about one-fourth of the milk mixture

into the egg yolks, whisking constantly. Add back into the milk mixture. Stir in the sherry, salt, pepper, cayenne, and mushrooms. Cook 2 minutes, stirring constantly. Add the shrimp.

Spoon the shrimp mixture evenly over the oysters. In a small bowl, combine the Parmesan and breadcrumbs. Sprinkle over the oysters. Bake 17 to 20 minutes, or until the tops are lightly browned. Serve warm.

OYSTER PO'BOYS

Two brothers, Benny and Clovis Martin, owned a sandwich shop in New Orleans in 1929. When the streetcar workers' union went on strike, they fed the striking workers sandwiches. A greeting of "Here comes another poor boy" worked its way into the name of this popular sandwich.

YIELD: 4 SERVINGS

$^1/_2$ cup mayonnaise
1 tablespoon hot sauce
1 (24-inch) loaf French bread
1 recipe Fried Oysters (page 307)
Juice of 1 lemon
4 cups shredded iceberg lettuce

In a small bowl, whisk together the mayonnaise and hot sauce. Split the bread in half lengthwise. Smear the mayonnaise mixture on the inside of the top and bottom.

Fry the oysters as directed in the recipe. After draining on paper towels, drizzle with lemon juice.

Place the oysters on the bottom slice and top with the lettuce. Place the top bread slice on the lettuce and press down gently. Cut the entire loaf into 4 sandwiches and serve immediately.

"PEARLS OF FLAVOR" OYSTER PUPPIES

Oysters are folded into a hushpuppy-type batter and fried crisp. They make a fabulous appetizer or can accompany soup and salad.

YIELD: 2 $^1/_2$ DOZEN

Vegetable oil
1 cup plain cornmeal
1 cup all-purpose flour
2 teaspoons baking powder
1 teaspoon salt
$^1/_2$ teaspoon red pepper
2 eggs
2 tablespoons sour cream
$^1/_2$ cup buttermilk
2 (12-ounce) containers oysters, drained and cut into fourths

Pour the oil to a depth of 3 inches in a large Dutch oven or skillet. Place over medium-high heat and bring to 375°F.

Meanwhile, in a mixing bowl, combine the cornmeal, flour, baking powder, salt, and red pepper. Make a well in the center and set aside.

In a separate bowl, whisk together the eggs, sour cream, and buttermilk. Add to the cornmeal mixture and stir until moistened. Fold in the oysters, blending well.

Drop tablespoons of the batter into the hot oil. Fry until golden brown, turning as necessary, around 3 to 4 minutes. Drain on paper towels and serve warm.

OYSTERS ROCKEFELLER

At a restaurant in New Orleans called Antoine's in 1899, this legendary dish was born. Jules Alciatore named it "Rockefeller" after John D. Rockefeller because the dish is extremely rich. The original recipe has never been released, so we are left to guess. We do know that it does not contain spinach, which many versions include in the dish. Here's my rendition.

YIELD: 36 APPETIZERS

36 large fresh oysters, scrubbed and shucked
1/4 pound (1 stick) unsalted butter
2 cups finely chopped Boston lettuce
1 cup loosely packed fresh watercress leaves
1/2 cup sliced green onion tops
1/4 cup chopped fresh parsley
1 1/4 plain dry breadcrumbs, divided
1 1/2 tablespoons minced celery
1 garlic clove, minced
1 tablespoon Pernod or licorice-flavored liqueur
1 1/2 teaspoons anchovy paste
1/4 teaspoon salt
1/4 teaspoon black pepper
1/8 teaspoon cayenne
6 bacon slices
3 cups kosher salt

Reserve the bottom shells of the oysters and scrub thoroughly. Set aside to dry. Reserve 1/4 cup of the oyster liquor and refrigerate. In a separate container, refrigerate the oysters.

In a large skillet over medium heat, melt the butter. Meanwhile, in a mixing bowl, combine the lettuce, watercress, green onions, parsley, 1/4 cup of the breadcrumbs, the celery, and garlic. Add the lettuce mixture to the skillet and cook 2 minutes, or until the greens are wilted.

Stir in the Pernod, anchovy paste, salt, pepper, and cayenne. Spread the mixture in a shallow dish to cool to room temperature. Refrigerate, covered, 45 minutes.

Preheat the oven to 450°F. In a large skillet over medium heat, fry the bacon until crisp, around 6 minutes. Drain on paper towels and crumble when cool enough to handle.

Spread the kosher salt on two large jelly-roll pans. Place an oyster in each shell and moisten slightly with some of the reserved liquor. Place a heaping tablespoon of the vegetables on each oyster and top with the bacon. Sprinkle each with the remaining cup of the breadcrumbs.

Nestle the oysters in the salt. Bake until the oyster edges begin to curl and the tops are golden brown, around 17 minutes. To serve, transfer the salt to a serving plate and nestle the baked oysters in the salt.

FAMILY: Oysters are members of the Ostreidae family that includes a number of different types of mollusks. They are odd little creatures that breathe much like fish, using both gills and mantle, with the gills acting as a filter for plankton.

BEST AVAILABILITY: Although oysters are available year-round, there are peaks in that availability. The best-quality ones are found during the fall and winter months. That's because oysters spawn during the summer months and become succulent and soft.

SIZE: As a general rule, the smaller the oyster is, the younger and more tender it will be.

PANCAKES AND WAFFLES

I **HAVE A THEORY AS TO WHY THOSE AWFUL COMMERCIALLY FROZEN PANCAKES AND WAFFLES** ever became popular on the market. I believe they were catapulted into a common weekend breakfast item thanks to mothers who never got to enjoy one hot.

At least my mother never seemed to be able to eat one with us on pancake mornings. She was always too busy at the griddle in her futile attempt to keep up with our family's hungry demands. That may be the only positive thing about those flash frozen versions. They certainly don't compare in taste, tenderness, or crispness.

Everyone knows you have to "eat 'em while they're hot." The Southern etiquette that dictates waiting until everyone has their food before you begin eating is thrown out the window on pancake and waffle mornings. Hospitality is gone too because you are constantly pushing to get the next batch.

I think that's one of the reasons why homemade ones are especially fabulous. You get to eat a nice, solitary meal with just you and your plate of hot, steamy treats. In our house, the only table conversation tends to be a request to pass the syrup or sausages.

At one point, waffle irons were expected gifts for every engaged couple in the South. Then it would find a nice resting place in the back of some cabinet where you piled teak salad bowls on top of it. There have been many neighborhood garage sales that had waffle irons for a steal.

Thanks to my husband's request for one, our focus on the weekend now regularly includes both pancakes and waffles. As we entertain more at home, we are realizing how versatile, easy to prepare, and inexpensive these truly are. Plus, you can change them from sweet to savory, taking it from Saturday morning to Sunday dinner in a flash. Do you hear it? Your griddle and waffle irons are calling!

Pancake Essentials: I use a flat griddle when making pancakes. If you don't have one, you'll need a skillet that is at least 12 inches in diameter. A friend of mine uses her electric skillet and likes the results.

Waffle Essentials: Waffle makers are still available that heat over the stove. They are not as convenient as electric models, nor as predictable. Electric versions are incredible and come in a variety of shapes and sizes. You can find round, square, rectangular, heart-shaped, and even in the shapes of cartoon characters. Those labeled for making Belgian waffles produce a thick waffle with deep grids.

Toppings: Experiment with different toppings and flavored syrups as a change from your normal routine. There are dozens of flavored syrups on the market or you can make your own (see Syrups chapter, page 433). In addition, you can offer fresh fruit, whipped cream, and preserves.

BUTTERMILK PANCAKES

This is the standard for which all pancakes are judged. It's classic and can be served with any topping your heart desires.

YIELD: 8 PANCAKES

1¼ cups all-purpose flour

1½ teaspoons baking powder

½ teaspoon baking soda

½ teaspoon salt

1 tablespoon sugar

1 egg

1 tablespoon plus 2 teaspoons vegetable oil

1½ cups buttermilk

Lightly grease a griddle or skillet and place over medium-high heat.

In a large mixing bowl, combine the flour, baking powder, baking soda, salt, and sugar. Make a well in the center. In a small bowl, combine the egg, oil, and buttermilk, whisking until well blended. Add to the flour mixture and stir to combine.

Using a ¼ cup measure, pour the batter on the griddle. Cook until the tops are covered with bubbles and the edges look dry, about 2 minutes. Flip and cook until golden brown, about 1 minute longer. Repeat with the remaining batter. Serve warm with butter and syrup.

BUTTERMILK WAFFLES

Beating the egg whites separately and folding them into the batter makes these waffles light and airy.

YIELD: 8 WAFFLES

3 cups all-purpose flour

1 teaspoon salt

2½ teaspoons baking powder

1 teaspoon baking soda

4 eggs, separated

2½ cups buttermilk

7 tablespoons melted vegetable shortening

Lightly grease and preheat a waffle iron.

In a medium mixing bowl, combine the flour, salt, baking powder, and baking soda. Set aside.

In the bowl of an electric mixer, beat the egg whites at high speed until stiff and set aside. In a separate large bowl, mix together the egg yolks, buttermilk, and shortening. Add the dry ingredients and beat until creamy.

Gently fold in the egg whites. Pour ½ cup of the batter onto the hot waffle iron and cook until golden brown. Repeat with the remaining batter. Serve hot with butter and syrup.

CLUB SODA WAFFLES

You'll love the ease of preparing this batter. The club soda gives it a spark that guests will have trouble naming.

YIELD: 4 TO 6 SERVINGS

2¼ cups biscuit mix

3 tablespoons vegetable oil

1 egg

1 (10-ounce) bottle club soda

Lightly grease and preheat a waffle iron.

In the bowl of an electric mixer, combine the biscuit mix, oil, and egg at medium speed until smooth. Lower the mixer speed to low and gradually add the club soda until well blended.

Pour no more than ½ cup of the batter in the hot iron and cook until golden brown. Repeat with the remaining batter. Serve warm with any syrup.

NECTARINE JOHNNYCAKES

The term "johnnycakes" goes back to the 1700s and is derived from "journey cakes." It is still used today in the South. This recipe is great for breakfast or to serve as a nontraditional dessert.

YIELD: 14 SMALL PANCAKES

2 cups biscuit mix
2 tablespoons sugar
2 teaspoons baking powder
$\frac{1}{2}$ teaspoon ground cinnamon
$1\frac{1}{2}$ cups buttermilk
1 egg, lightly beaten
$1\frac{1}{2}$ cups peeled and diced nectarines
Sweetened whipped cream for garnish
Nectarine slices for garnish

Lightly grease a griddle or skillet and place over medium-high heat.

Meanwhile, in a large bowl, combine the biscuit mix, sugar, baking powder, and cinnamon. Stir in the buttermilk and egg. Gently fold in the nectarines.

Using a $\frac{1}{4}$ cup measure, pour batter on the griddle. Cook until the tops are covered with bubbles and the edges look dry, about 2 minutes. Flip and cook until golden brown, about 1 minute longer. Repeat with the remaining batter. Serve warm with whipped cream and garnish with fresh nectarine slices.

Note: You can substitute fresh peaches for the nectarines, if desired.

GINGERBREAD HOTCAKES

Fall mornings just got a facelift. These are great topped with applesauce.

YIELD: 6 TO 8 SERVINGS

$1\frac{1}{2}$ cups all-purpose flour
$1\frac{1}{2}$ tablespoons baking powder
$1\frac{1}{2}$ teaspoons cocoa
$\frac{1}{2}$ teaspoon ground cloves
$\frac{1}{2}$ teaspoon ground cinnamon
$\frac{1}{2}$ teaspoon ground ginger
2 tablespoons ground pecans
3 egg whites, lightly beaten
$1\frac{1}{2}$ cups milk
$2\frac{1}{2}$ tablespoons sorghum syrup
$2\frac{1}{2}$ teaspoon vegetable oil

Lightly grease a griddle or skillet and place over medium-high heat.

Meanwhile, in a large mixing bowl, combine the flour, baking powder, cocoa, cloves, cinnamon, ginger, and pecans. Make a well in the center and set aside.

In a separate bowl, whisk together the egg whites, milk, syrup, and oil. Add to the dry ingredients, stirring just until moistened.

Using a $\frac{1}{4}$-cup measure, pour the batter on the griddle. Cook until the tops are covered with bubbles and the edges look dry, about 2 minutes. Flip and cook until golden brown, about 1 minute longer. Repeat with the remaining batter. Serve warm with butter pecan syrup.

OLD-FASHIONED WAFFLES

These are the waffles I make for my husband every month. I change the syrup depending on the season.

YIELD: 6 WAFFLES

2 cups all-purpose flour
1 tablespoon baking powder
$\frac{1}{2}$ teaspoon salt
1 tablespoon plus 1 teaspoon sugar

3 eggs, at room temperature and separated

1 2/3 cups milk

6 tablespoons unsalted butter, melted and cooled slightly

Lightly grease and preheat a waffle iron.

Combine the flour, baking powder, salt, and sugar in a bowl. Make a well in the center.

In a small bowl, whisk together the egg yolks, milk, and butter, mixing well. In a separate bowl, beat the egg whites until stiff but still moist and glossy.

Pour the egg yolk mixture in the center of the well and stir only until combined (the batter will be lumpy). Add the egg whites and fold in quickly, leaving marble-size bits of egg white in the batter.

Pour 1/2 cup batter on the hot iron. Cook until golden brown and repeat. Serve warm.

PECAN WAFFLES

Amazing how a good handful of chopped pecans will totally change the way waffles taste.

YIELD: 8 SERVINGS

1 3/4 cups all-purpose flour

2 teaspoons baking powder

1/2 teaspoon salt

2 eggs, separated

1 1/4 cups milk

1/2 cup vegetable oil

1/2 cup chopped pecans

Lightly grease and preheat a waffle iron.

Combine the flour, baking powder, and salt in a bowl. Make a well in the center.

In a separate bowl, whisk together the egg yolks, milk, and oil, mixing well. Stir into the dry ingredients just until moistened. Set aside.

In the bowl of an electric mixer, beat the egg

whites on high speed until stiff peaks form. Gently fold into the batter.

Pour 1/2 cup batter on the hot iron and sprinkle 1 tablespoon pecans on top. Cook until golden. Repeat with the remaining batter and pecans.

PUFFED FRUIT PANCAKES

Puffed pancakes have been cradling fruit in the South for years.

YIELD: 8 SERVINGS

4 tablespoons unsalted butter

2 Golden Delicious apples or ripe pears, peeled, cored, and thinly sliced

4 eggs

1 cup milk

3 tablespoons granulated sugar

1 teaspoon pure vanilla extract

1/2 teaspoon salt

1 teaspoon ground cinnamon

2/3 cup all-purpose flour

3 tablespoons packed light brown sugar

Preheat the oven to 425°F. Place the butter in a 13 x 9-inch baking dish and melt while the oven preheats.

Place the fruit slices in overlapping rows over the butter. Return to the oven and bake 9 minutes.

In a large bowl, whisk together the eggs, milk, granulated sugar, extract, salt, and cinnamon. Add the flour and whisk until smooth. Pour the batter over the softened fruit and sprinkle with the brown sugar. Bake 20 minutes more, or until puffed and golden brown. Serve immediately.

PARSNIPS

DO YOU EVER HAVE THAT ANCIENT SOUTHERN FEAR THAT YOU'LL SHOW UP AT A BLACK-TIE event in your work clothes? Well, that's practically the story of the life of a vegetable we too often neglect, but grow by the truckload.

Parsnips are certainly not sexy, well-dressed vegetables, but Southerners have been depending on this inexpensive, versatile root for decades. Their Southern roots go back to the Civil War era, when hungry foragers pulled up anything they could find to cook and eat. It progressed from those desperate days to a time now where parsnips can be used for adding a level of sweetness to any root worthy side dish.

Parsnips can be a little persnickety. They are not fans of overly hot, wet, tropical areas, so South Florida is not the ideal place for them to grow. Instead, they prefer soils that are well-drained and climates that are moderate. They don't grow well in pots and, instead, prefer the good old earth. But in spite of that, as my favorite Extension agent says, if you can grow carrots, you can grow parsnips.

While they may not be the best-dressed items in the produce department, they are downright work horses when brought to the kitchen. They have an unbelievably long shelf life in the refrigerator of up to two weeks. Then they can be baked, boiled, roasted, fried, steamed, mashed, whipped, and even stir-fried.

Southerners sometimes call parsnips "mock sweet potatoes" just to encourage consumption. We can be quite sneaky like that, but who doesn't like to pull for an underdog?

Origin: Parsnips originated in Europe and are believed to be natives of the Mediterranean area. They were brought to the U.S. in the early 1600s and are now grown practically all over North America.

Nutrition: Parsnips are sources of potassium, iron, calcium, and some protein and vitamin C. There are one hundred and two calories in a cup of cooked, diced parsnips.

Selection: Select smooth, firm, clean, well-shaped parsnips that are fairly uniform in size. There should be no obvious outer skin blemishes on the root. Generally, plan on allowing two parsnips per serving. Small to medium roots usually have the best flavor and texture, so avoid those that are overly large. Also avoid purchasing any that appear withered or have the appearance of an uneven color.

Preparation: Parsnips must always be peeled before using. This is easily accomplished with a vegetable peeler. Although they resemble carrots, you wouldn't want to use them in the same way. Parsnips shouldn't be eaten raw, for instance, because they are very fibrous, starchy, and almost woody tasting until they are cooked. They are most frequently boiled, baked, roasted, steamed, sautéed, or stir-fried.

CARROT AND PARSNIP SLAW

Not only is this slaw visually appealing, but its sweet flavor marries well with fish or a salty ham.

YIELD: 8 SERVINGS

1 cup water

1 pound parsnips, peeled and shredded

1 pound carrots, peeled and shredded

2 tablespoons unsalted butter, softened

1 tablespoon sorghum syrup or honey

1 teaspoon dried tarragon

$\frac{1}{2}$ teaspoon kosher salt

$\frac{1}{4}$ teaspoon black pepper

Place the water in a heavy saucepan over medium-high heat and bring to a boil. Add the parsnips and carrots. Cover and cook 6 to 7 minutes or until crisp, yet tender.

Meanwhile, in a small mixing bowl, combine the butter, syrup, tarragon, salt, and pepper. Mix well.

Drain the parsnips and carrots. Immediately drizzle with the syrup mixture, tossing evenly to coat. Serve immediately.

DEEP-FRIED PARSNIPS

Want a unique substitute for French fries? Here it is!

YIELD: 4 SERVINGS

4 cups water

12 parsnips, peeled

Vegetable oil

$\frac{3}{4}$ cup plain dry breadcrumbs

1 teaspoon black pepper

$\frac{3}{4}$ teaspoon salt

Place the water in a large saucepan over medium-high heat. Bring to a boil and add the parsnips. Cover and cook 20 minutes, or until tender. Drain and when cool enough to handle, cut into 3 x $\frac{1}{2}$ - inch strips. Pour the oil to a depth of 3 inches in a large Dutch oven or deep skillet. Place over medium-high heat and bring to 375°F.

Meanwhile, in a heavy-duty zip-top bag, combine the breadcrumbs, pepper, and salt. Add the parsnips, a few at a time, and shake to evenly coat.

Carefully lower into the hot oil. Fry the parsnips in batches, 1 minute. Drain on paper towels and serve immediately.

HAND-MASHED PARSNIPS

This is not a puréed mashed dish that is done with an electric mixer, but is hand mashed so you have bits and chunks of the root vegetables still apparent. It sings alongside roasted duck.

YIELD: 6 SERVINGS

2 cups water

2 pounds parsnips, peeled and cut into 1-inch pieces

$1\frac{1}{2}$ teaspoons kosher salt, divided

$1\frac{1}{2}$ pounds baking potatoes, peeled and cut into 1-inch cubes

4 tablespoons unsalted butter, softened

$\frac{1}{2}$ teaspoon black pepper

Place the water in a large saucepan and bring to a boil over medium-high heat. Add the parsnips and 1 teaspoon of the salt. Cover and boil 5 minutes.

Add the potatoes and boil 10 to 12 minutes longer, or until tender. Drain and with a hand masher, crush the vegetables. Stir in the butter, the remaining $\frac{1}{2}$ teaspoon salt, and pepper. Serve warm.

HONEY-GLAZED PARSNIPS

This dish is practically candy. It is so good with turkey that has been prepared in any way.

YIELD: 8 SERVINGS

2 cups water

2 pounds parsnips, peeled and cut into 2-inch strips

$1/2$ teaspoon salt

4 tablespoons unsalted butter

$1/4$ cup honey

$1/4$ cup packed light brown sugar

Bring the water to a boil in a heavy saucepan over medium-high heat. Add the parsnips and salt. Cover and reduce the heat to medium. Simmer 8 minutes, or until the parsnips are crisp yet tender. Drain and set aside.

Melt the butter in the same saucepan over medium heat. Add the honey, sugar, and parsnips. Cook 5 minutes, stirring occasionally to make sure the parsnips are glazed. Serve warm.

NO PRESSURE PARSNIP SOUFFLÉ

The only pressure here is to have the rest of dinner ready and on the table as soon as this golden soufflé comes out of the oven.

YIELD: 6 SERVINGS

2 cups water

4 cups diced parsnips

2 tablespoons unsalted butter, softened

2 tablespoons chopped green onions

1 tablespoon brown sugar

$1/2$ teaspoon grated lemon zest

$1/4$ teaspoon salt

$1/8$ teaspoon ground nutmeg

3 eggs, separated

Place the water in a large saucepan over medium-high heat and bring to a boil. Add the parsnips, cover, and cook 15 to 20 minutes, or until tender.

Meanwhile, preheat the oven to 350°F. Lightly grease a $1/2$-quart soufflé dish and set aside.

Drain the parsnips and transfer to the bowl of a food processor. Process the parsnips until smooth. Add the butter, onions, brown sugar, zest, salt, and nutmeg. Process until smooth and well blended. Transfer to a mixing bowl.

Beat the egg whites at high speed of an electric mixer until stiff peaks form. Set aside.

Beat the egg yolks until thick, about 1 minute. Add to the parsnip mixture, blending well. Gently fold in the egg whites and transfer to the prepared soufflé dish.

Bake 30 to 35 minutes, or until the soufflé is puffed and golden brown. Serve immediately.

OVEN-ROASTED PARSNIPS

This is my favorite way to serve parsnips. It's easy and a gloriously simple side dish.

YIELD: 4 SERVINGS

2 cups diced parsnips

1 tablespoon olive oil

$1/2$ teaspoon kosher salt

$1/4$ teaspoon black pepper

Preheat the oven to 300°F. Lightly grease a 1-quart shallow baking dish and add the parsnips. Toss gently with the oil. Sprinkle evenly with the salt and pepper. Roast 1 hour or until tender. Serve warm.

"THE ROOT OF THE MATTER" CASSEROLE

A mixture of potatoes, onions, sweet potatoes, and parsnips gives this hearty side dish depth. It is excellent with baked ham or roast beef. Cooking in an oven roasting bag means cleanup is a breeze.

YIELD: 8 SERVINGS

¹⁄₄ cup all-purpose flour

2 Russet potatoes, peeled and cut into ¹⁄₄-inch slices

2 sweet potatoes, peeled and cut into ¹⁄₄-inch slices

4 parsnips, peeled and cut into ¹⁄₄-inch slices

1 small yellow onion, peeled and chopped

1 teaspoon salt

1 teaspoon black pepper

3 cups cream

Preheat the oven to 350°F.

Place a large oven-roasting bag in a 13 x 9-inch baking dish. Add the flour, twist the end of the bag to close, and shake to coat the inside of the bag.

Add the Russet potatoes, sweet potatoes, parsnips, onion, salt, and pepper. Twist the end again and close the bag. Shake to evenly coat. Add the cream and massage the bag to blend. Close the bag and cut 6 (¹⁄₂-inch) slits in the top.

Bake 1 hour. Let stand 5 minutes before transferring to a serving bowl. Serve warm.

AVAILABILITY: Although we receive parsnips from other parts of the world year-round, they are most plentifully available during the late fall and winter months. The tops are usually already removed when they hit the market because, like carrots, they tend to pull moisture from the root and decrease the shelf life.

BOTANY: One look and you can see that parsnips rightfully belong to the carrot family. It has the familiar carrot shape but, depending on the variety, is anywhere from light tan to creamy white on the outside. The inside color will always be white. Parsnips will typically range from five to ten inches in length. Their naturally sweet flavor is enhanced greatly by the first snap of cold temperatures.

NAME: You will sometimes see parsnips marketed as "white carrots."

PEACHES

PEACHES MEAN IT IS SUMMER IN THE SOUTH! FRESH PEACHES ARE AS COMMON AS SWING SETS, bicycles with baskets, and front porches with rockers. As a child, the beginning of the school year didn't bring apples; instead, the last remaining crop of fresh peaches were our treats. It was tucked into my U.S. Mail lunch box as a reminder of summer for the first month of school.

Those memories are probably why fresh peaches are still my choice fruit and why I will turn the world over to find them as soon as the local growing season gets underway. Luckily, I don't have to travel far because peach orchards are frequent dots on the Southern landscape.

That's where you'll find the finest … at local orchards where you can pick your own. I challenge you to try and make it through the orchard without taking a bite. In my experience, it can't be done!

Most growers plant several varieties, but that has never mattered much to me when I'm on the hunt for peaches. Why? Because I've never found a variety that isn't delicious. The mammoth-size prizes can have flesh the color of marigolds or vanilla ice cream and my tastebuds react the same … they dance.

Although the flesh is a bit more firm, nectarines can be used in any recipe calling for peaches. Think of it as a peach without the fuzz. They are picked, stored, and used the same as a peach. And while you'll certainly find nectarines throughout the South, peaches will forever reign supreme.

Warning! Do not wear anything with sleeves when you take that first bite of a fresh peach, and have a napkin or paper towel ready. Juice will run down your arm and drip off your elbow. There is nothing like it and you'll know summer has officially arrived.

Nutrition: Peaches are a good source of potassium and dietary fiber as well as vitamins A and C. One medium peach contains around forty calories.

Selection: Don't squeeze the peaches! This fragile fruit bruises easily. To test for ripeness, look for a creamy or golden undertone. If it has a green undertone, don't pick it from the tree or purchase it at the market because it is immature. Hold the peach in the palm of your hand and see if you can feel the softness or if it feels hard. I repeat: Do not squeeze!

Storage: Keep fresh peaches at room temperature unless you have too many ripe ones at once. Then refrigerate only completely ripe peaches and use them as quickly as possible. Bring them back to room temperature when ready to serve or use.

ALL-TIME BEST PEACH PIE

This is the peach pie I make every year with my first armload of fresh peaches. The flavor is enhanced with brandy and jam. Add a scoop of vanilla ice cream for a real treat!

YIELD: 8 SERVINGS

1 recipe Double Pie Pastry (page 400)
5 cups fresh peaches, peeled, pitted, and sliced
1 teaspoon peach brandy
$\frac{1}{4}$ cup peach jam
$\frac{3}{4}$ cup packed brown sugar
$\frac{1}{4}$ cup all-purpose flour
$\frac{1}{4}$ teaspoon ground cinnamon
2 tablespoons unsalted butter
1 tablespoon milk

Preheat the oven to 425°F. Line a 9-inch pie pan with half of the pastry.

In a large bowl, combine the peaches, brandy, and jam. In a small bowl, combine the brown sugar, flour, and cinnamon. Stir into the peaches and gently mix. Place in the piecrust and dot with the butter.

Cover with the top crust and make several slits for steam to escape. Seal and flute the edges. Brush the top with the milk. Bake 35 to 45 minutes, or until the crust is golden brown. Cool at least 10 minutes before serving.

Tip: Place a baking sheet on the rack underneath your pie to catch any fruit juices that might bubble over the edge of the pie pan.

AWARD-WINNING PEACH COFFEE CAKE

I won my first cooking award with this cake while I was in college. It was just a competition within my class, but I was thrilled with the honor and think of it every time I bake this cake.

YIELD: 8 SERVINGS

2 cups chopped pecans
$\frac{1}{3}$ cup firmly packed brown sugar
3 tablespoons plus 1 cup granulated sugar, divided
1 teaspoon ground cinnamon
$\frac{1}{2}$ cup vegetable shortening
2 eggs
2 cups all-purpose flour
$1\frac{1}{2}$ teaspoons baking powder
$\frac{1}{2}$ teaspoon baking soda
$\frac{1}{2}$ teaspoon salt
1 cup sour cream
1 teaspoon pure almond extract
2 cups fresh peaches, peeled, pitted, and sliced

Preheat the oven to 350°F. Lightly grease a 9-inch springform pan and set aside.

In a small bowl, combine the pecans, brown sugar, 3 tablespoons of the granulated sugar, and the cinnamon. Set aside.

In a large mixing bowl, cream the shortening and the remaining granulated sugar until light and fluffy. Add the eggs, mixing well.

In a separate bowl, combine the flour, baking powder, baking soda, and salt. Add alternately to the shortening mixture with the sour cream, beating until smooth. Add the extract and mix well.

Pour half the batter into the prepared pan. Sprinkle with 1 cup of the pecan mixture. Top with the remaining batter and $\frac{1}{2}$ cup of the pecan mixture.

Bake 30 minutes. Arrange the peaches evenly

over the cake and sprinkle with the remaining pecan mixture. Bake an additional 30 to 40 minutes, or until a tester inserted in the center comes out clean. Cool on a wire rack 10 minutes before removing the sides of the pan. Serve warm or at room temperature.

BALSAMIC GRILLED PEACHES

This recipe can be easily doubled and with one taste, you'll wish you had.

YIELD: 4 SERVINGS

³/₄ cup balsamic vinegar
3 tablespoons sugar
1 teaspoon black pepper
2 fresh peaches, peeled, pitted, and halved
2 ounces blue cheese, crumbled and softened

In a small saucepan, combine the vinegar, sugar, and pepper over medium heat. Simmer until the liquid is reduced by half, about 12 minutes. Set aside to cool slightly.

Preheat the grill to medium. Place the peaches, cut side down, on the grate. Grill about 5 minutes, or until the flesh is caramelized.

Flip the peaches over and brush with the glaze. Grill another 2 minutes. Transfer to a serving dish and drizzle with any remaining glaze. Sprinkle with the cheese and serve warm.

> "An apple is an excellent thing—until you have a peach!"
> —GEORGE DU MAURIER

"CHEERS TO THE SOUTH" BELLINI

This drink was created in the 1930s in Venice, Italy, in honor of painter Giovanni Bellini. It has become a regular at Southern weddings, anniversary parties, and holiday celebrations.

YIELD: 8 SERVINGS

1 (750 milliliter) bottle champagne, chilled
2 (11.5-ounce) cans peach nectar, chilled
? cup peach schnapps

In a large pitcher, combine the champagne, nectar, and schnapps, stirring until blended. Serve immediately in champagne flutes.

CARAMELIZED SKILLET PEACHES

I always prepare this dish in an old cast-iron skillet and the even heat conduction makes it perfect every time.

YIELD: 8 TO 10 SERVINGS

1 cup packed brown sugar
4 tablespoons water
4 tablespoons unsalted butter
4 to 6 large peaches, peeled, pitted, and halved
Vanilla ice cream
Chopped toasted pecans for garnish

In a large skillet over medium heat, combine the sugar, water, and butter. Stir until the butter and sugar melt. Reduce heat to low and add the peaches with the cut side down. Simmer gently until the peaches just begin to soften, about 5 minutes. Baste every minute with the sauce.

To serve, place the peach halves in individual

bowls. Place a scoop of ice cream beside each peach half. Drizzle with the caramel sauce and sprinkle with the pecans. Serve immediately.

PECAN-CRUSTED PEACH PIE

This pie is great, but the crust sends it into the realm of heavenly.

YIELD: 8 SERVINGS

1 cup all-purpose flour
$1/3$ cup packed brown sugar
$1/2$ cup chopped pecans
$1/4$ pound (1 stick) unsalted butter, melted
1 (8-ounce) package cream cheese, softened
$1/2$ cup confectioners' sugar
2 cups sliced peaches
3 cups crushed peaches
$1/3$ cup cornstarch
1 cup granulated sugar

Preheat the oven to 375°F. Grease a 10-inch spring-form pan and set aside.

Combine the flour, brown sugar, pecans, and butter in a medium bowl. Press into the prepared pan. Bake 12 minutes, or until lightly browned. Cool completely.

Meanwhile, combine the cream cheese and sugar in a mixing bowl until smooth. Spread over the cooled crust. Evenly arrange the sliced peaches on the top and refrigerate.

In a medium saucepan, cook the crushed peaches, cornstarch, and granulated sugar over medium heat, stirring constantly until thick, about 5 minutes. Set aside to cool completely. Pour over the top of the pie. Remove the sides of the pan, slice, and serve.

COLD PEACH SOUP

Serve in teacups with shortbread cookies or alone as a light meal starter.

YIELD: 6 TO 8 SERVINGS

2 pounds fresh peaches, peeled, pitted, and halved
1 cup orange juice
1 cup plain yogurt
2 tablespoon honey
2 tablespoons lime juice
$1/2$ teaspoon ground cinnamon

Place the peaches in a blender and process until smooth. Transfer to a large bowl and add the orange juice, yogurt, honey, lime juice, and cinnamon. Adjust the thickness with more lime juice if necessary. Cover and refrigerate at least 1 hour or up to 8 hours before serving.

"DO THE RIPE THING" PEACH BUTTER

This fruit butter actually contains no butter, but is used like butter as a spread for bread.

YIELD: 3 HALF-PINTS

$3^1/2$ cups sliced peaches
$1^1/2$ cups sugar
1 tablespoon lemon juice

Purée the peaches in a food processor or blender until smooth. Transfer to a medium saucepan and add the sugar and juice. Bring to a boil over medium heat, stirring constantly. Continue boiling, stirring occasionally until it has the consistency of thick applesauce, about 15 minutes.

Cool and refrigerate or pour immediately into hot sterilized canning jars. Remove any air bubbles, wipe the rims, and adjust the lids. Process in a boiling water bath 5 minutes. (See page 12 for detailed canning instructions.)

GRILLED BUTTERED RUM PEACHES

The grill mellows out the peaches and the topping jazzes them back up.

YIELD: 4 SERVINGS

4 large fresh peaches, peeled, pitted, and halved
3 tablespoons brown sugar
$1/2$ teaspoon ground cinnamon
3 teaspoons rum
1 tablespoon unsalted butter
Vanilla ice cream

Preheat the grill to medium heat.

Place 4 peach halves on a large sheet of heavy-duty aluminum foil with the cut side up. Repeat with the remaining peaches.

In a small bowl, combine the brown sugar and cinnamon. Spoon evenly into the center of each peach half. Sprinkle with the rum and dot with the butter. Fold the foil over the peaches and loosely seal.

Place the peach bundles on the grill rack. Cook 15 minutes, or until the peaches are thoroughly heated.

To serve, place 2 peach halves on each dessert plate. Place a small scoop of vanilla ice cream in the center. Drizzle with the drippings and serve immediately.

"LOVE AT FIRST BITE" PEACH CAKE

What makes this a great summertime dessert is that it is prepared and in the oven in a snap. I don't always have a lot of time to spend in the kitchen in the summer, but this recipe makes it look like I have.

YIELD: 8 TO 10 SERVINGS

2 cups chopped fresh peaches
$1^3/4$ cups sugar
3 eggs, beaten
1 cup vegetable oil
2 cups all-purpose flour
1 teaspoon salt
1 teaspoon baking soda
1 teaspoon ground cinnamon
$1/2$ cup chopped pecans
Whipped cream
Fresh peach slices for garnish

Preheat the oven to 375°F. Lightly grease a 13 x 9-inch baking pan and set aside.

Place the peaches in a large mixing bowl and sprinkle with the sugar. Add the eggs and oil, mixing gently.

In a separate bowl, combine the flour, salt, baking soda, cinnamon, and pecans. Add to the peach mixture and mix well. Transfer to the prepared pan and bake 50 minutes. Cool completely on a wire rack.

To serve, cut into individual servings, top with the whipped cream, and garnish with fresh peach slices.

Cheese Pairings: Fresh peaches pair especially well with Edam, blue cheese, and Monterey Jack.

OLD-FASHIONED PEACH COBBLER

This recipe allows the batter to rise to the top during baking. It's easy and delicious!

YIELD: 8 SERVINGS

2 cups fresh peaches, peeled, pitted, and sliced
2 cups sugar, divided
$1/4$ pound (1 stick) unsalted butter
$3/4$ cup all-purpose flour
2 teaspoons baking powder
Pinch of salt
$3/4$ cup milk

Preheat the oven to 350°F. Mix the peaches with 1 cup of the sugar. Set aside. Place the butter in a 2-quart square baking dish and place in the oven to melt.

Meanwhile, in a medium bowl, combine the remaining sugar, the flour, baking powder, salt, and milk. Pour over the melted butter and do not stir. Place the peaches evenly on the top. Bake 1 hour, or until golden brown. Cool at least 10 minutes before serving.

ORCHARD-FRESH PEACH ICE CREAM

Vanilla is good, but peach is great! Knowing it's only a treat for a short time makes it even sweeter.

YIELD: 1 QUART

2 cups heavy cream
1 cup whole milk
$2/3$ cup plus 1 tablespoon sugar, divided
4 large peaches, peeled, pitted, and halved
$1/4$ teaspoon ground cinnamon

Place the cream, milk, and $2/3$ cup of the sugar in a heavy saucepan over medium heat. Cook, stirring constantly, about 3 minutes, or until the sugar dissolves. Set aside to cool slightly.

Place the peaches in a blender with the remaining tablespoon of sugar and the cinnamon. Purée until smooth and blend with the milk mixture. Cover and refrigerate at least 1 hour. Freeze in an ice cream maker according to the manufacturer's instructions.

PEACH BEIGNETS

Beignets are the official pastry of New Orleans. The name comes from the French word for "fritter."

YIELD: 8 TO 10 SERVINGS

6 large peaches, peeled, pitted, and halved
2 tablespoons granulated sugar
2 tablespoons Kirsch or cherry brandy
Vegetable oil
$1 1/2$ cups buttermilk pancake mix
1 cup water
Confectioners' sugar

Place the peaches in a large bowl and sprinkle with the granulated sugar and Kirsch. Let stand 30 minutes at room temperature.

Meanwhile, pour the oil 2 inches deep in a Dutch oven and heat to 375°F. In a mixing bowl blend the pancake mix and water just until smooth. Dip the peaches in the batter, covering completely. Fry 2 to 3 minutes on each side. Drain on paper towels and serve hot with a dusting of confectioners' sugar.

"PRETTY AS A PEACH" MUFFINS

I love the little speckles of chopped peaches and raisins in these muffins. However, the real flavor punch comes from the puréed peaches added to the batter.

YIELD: 12 MUFFINS

3 fresh peaches, peeled, pitted, and halved
1 egg, beaten
$^{1}/_{4}$ cup vegetable oil
1 teaspoon pure vanilla extract
$^{1}/_{4}$ teaspoon pure almond extract
1 teaspoon grated orange zest
1 cup all-purpose flour
2 teaspoons baking powder
1 teaspoon ground cinnamon
1 cup old-fashioned oats
$^{3}/_{4}$ cup packed brown sugar
$^{1}/_{2}$ cup golden raisins

Preheat the oven to 350°F. Grease 12 muffin cups and set aside.

Chop $^{1}/_{4}$ cup of the peaches and set aside. Purée the remaining peaches in a food processor or blender. Transfer to a medium bowl and add the egg, oil, vanilla extract, almond extract, and zest.

In a separate bowl, combine the flour, baking powder, and cinnamon. Stir in the oats and brown sugar. Make a well in the center and add the peach mixture, stirring just until moistened. Gently fold in the reserved chopped peaches and raisins.

Spoon the batter evenly into the muffin cups, filling two-thirds full. Bake 16 to 18 minutes, or until a tester inserted in the center comes out clean. Cool in the muffin tin on a wire rack 5 minutes. Serve warm or at room temperature.

SOUTHERN-FRIED PIES

I cannot say enough about how the South uses dried fruit so beautifully. Fried right, these are never greasy and filled with the taste of summer.

YIELD: 12 PIES

1 pound dried peaches
$^{1}/_{4}$ cup water
$^{3}/_{4}$ cup sugar
2 tablespoons unsalted butter
1 teaspoon ground cinnamon
$2^{1}/_{2}$ cups all-purpose flour
$1^{1}/_{2}$ teaspoons salt
$1^{1}/_{2}$ teaspoons sugar
$^{1}/_{2}$ cup vegetable shortening
$^{3}/_{4}$ cup evaporated milk
Vegetable oil

Cover the peaches in water and soak overnight. Drain and transfer to a large saucepan. Add the water and cook over medium heat until the fruit is tender, about 20 minutes. Mash the fruit and add the sugar, butter, and cinnamon. Stir well and cool.

Meanwhile, in a mixing bowl, stir together the flour, salt, and sugar. Cut in the shortening with a pastry blender or 2 forks until the mixture is the consistency of coarse meal. Add the milk and stir until moistened. Gather the dough into a ball and flatten into a thick disk. Refrigerate 30 minutes.

Divide the dough in half. On a lightly floured surface, roll half of the dough to $^{1}/_{8}$-inch thickness and cut into 6-inch rounds. Place 2 tablespoons of the fruit in the center of each round. Dampen the edges and fold over. Seal the edges with the tines of a fork. Repeat with the remaining dough.

Pour the oil $^{1}/_{2}$ inch deep in a large cast-iron skillet over medium-high heat. Gently place no more than 2 pies in the hot oil. Fry until lightly browned on each side, about 3 to 4 minutes per side. Drain on paper towels. Repeat with the remaining pies. **Note:** Pies can also be baked in a preheated 400°F oven until golden brown. Brush the pastry with a beaten egg before baking.

SWEET-AND-SIMPLE PEACH MELBA

This is a beautiful, classic way to serve Southern peaches, and since summer raspberries ripen at the same time, you've got a double yummy!

YIELD: 8 SERVINGS

2 cups fresh raspberries, divided
$\frac{1}{2}$ cup light corn syrup
$\frac{1}{4}$ cup sugar
8 fresh peaches, peeled, pitted, and halved
1 pint fresh raspberries
Fresh mint leaves for garnish

In a small saucepan, combine 1 cup of the raspberries with the corn syrup and sugar. Bring to a boil, stirring frequently. Reduce the heat to low and simmer 10 minutes. Press through a fine mesh sieve, discarding the solids. Set aside to cool.

To serve, place 2 peach halves in each serving dish. Top evenly with the remaining raspberries and drizzle with the syrup. Garnish with fresh mint and serve immediately.

SWEET WITH HEAT PEACH SALSA

Luscious peaches and the heat from chipotles make this salsa a treat for everyone. Chipotles are dried, *smoked jalapeños but can also be found pickled. Use the dried for this dish and serve with blue corn chips.*

YIELD: 4 SERVINGS

3 fresh peaches, peeled, pitted, and coarsely chopped
1 purple onion, peeled and chopped
Juice of 1 lime
2 teaspoons chopped chipotle peppers
$\frac{1}{2}$ teaspoon salt

Mix together the peaches, onion, lime juice, peppers, and salt in a medium bowl. Cover and refrigerate at least 1 hour before serving. Serve at room temperature.

WHITE PEACH SANGRIA

The influence of Creole and Cajun cooking in the South made sangria a natural for cooling off after long, steamy days. Let the fruit macerate in the liquid mixture, and then serve over ice cream or eat as is.

YIELD: 1$\frac{1}{2}$ QUARTS

1 (750 ml) bottle dry white wine
$\frac{3}{4}$ cup peach schnapps
1 (11.5 ounce) can peach nectar
$\frac{1}{2}$ cup frozen pink lemonade concentrate, thawed
$\frac{1}{4}$ cup sugar
1 cup frozen sliced peaches

In a large pitcher, combine the wine, schnapps, nectar, lemonade concentrate, and sugar. Stir until the sugar dissolves. Cover and refrigerate at least 1 hour. Add the peaches 30 minutes before serving.

PEANUTS

(AND PEANUT BUTTER)

I DON'T KNOW A SOUTHERNER MY AGE OR OLDER WHO DIDN'T GROW UP POURING DRY ROASTED peanuts into a Coke that had about two sips out of it. Then you would happily consume the remainder of your Coke while munching on the peanuts that made it down the neck of the bottle to your mouth. The mixture of salt on the peanuts and the Coke was "swallow your tongue" good and the epitome of a great afternoon snack.

For years, peanuts were regarded as nothing more than nifty nibbles. Growing up, we also enjoyed them oven roasted, which my daddy always called "parched peanuts," a term I still use to this day. We used peanuts mainly as a snack and the puréed concoction of peanut butter in our school lunch boxes or to make cookies, candies, and pies. It never occurred to us to throw peanuts in salads, soup, or pasta dishes.

That, however, was Mississippi. Drive east to Georgia and then up to Virginia and you'll find yourself smack dab in the middle of peanut country. Then turn around and head to Texas and you'll find the same thing. That's when you'll find out how much of a peanut lover you really are.

That area of the South showcases peanuts all over the place. You'll see sale signs for boiled, roasted, and fried (some called it oil roasted, for those who worry about such things) peanuts all along the roadside. In addition, you'll see the smoke stacks and smell the marvelous aroma of really fresh peanuts being cooked. It's quite simply impossible to resist and enough to make nearly everyone who likes them, love them, crave them, and gobble them up like there was no tomorrow. Don't be surprised to find yourself buying peanuts by the armload. If you haven't been, head in any of those directions, buy yourself a Coke and let snack heaven begin!

Nutrition: Peanuts aren't called "Nutrition in a Nutshell" for nothing. They are great sources of protein, niacin, thiamin, vitamin E, magnesium, potassium, and phosphorus. They contain no cholesterol.

Storage: Raw peanuts should be refrigerated. Shelled roasted peanuts can be stored in a cool, dry place for about three months, or you can double that time by placing them in the refrigerator. You can triple the refrigerator shelf life when you store them in the freezer in a moisture-proof container. They can be used straight from the freezer with no need to thaw beforehand.

Types: The four peanut varieties that are commercially popular are **Virginia, Runners, Valencia**, and **Spanish**. Each develops remarkably similar leafy plants that will grow to about eighteen inches tall. Once the pale yellow flowers have bloomed, faded, and lost their petals, a fertilized ovary, or peg, develops. This will grow away from the plant, drop to the ground, and enter the soil. At the tip of each peg is an embryo that develops into peanuts.

BOILED SOUTHERN PEANUTS

In the fall, you'll see lots of boiled peanut stands dotting the roadway. They are delicious. If you want to put a bit of spice in this recipe, add one-fourth cup of dry shrimp/crab boil to the water. Leftover boiled peanuts can be frozen for later use.

YIELD: 8 SERVINGS

1½ pounds raw shelled peanuts

4 tablespoons salt, divided

Place the peanuts in a slow cooker. Cover with water. Soak 8 hours or overnight. Add more water and half of the salt. Cook, covered, on low 8 hours. Add the remaining salt during the last hour of cooking. Drain and serve warm.

Note: To boil freshly harvested peanuts that are still in the shell, wash thoroughly. Place in a large stockpot and cover with a gallon of water. Add 10 ounces of salt. Boil, covered, 45 minutes, or until the kernels are tender. Drain and serve warm.

GEORGIA PEANUT GINGER SAUCE

I love this sauce! It adds just the right punch to steamed vegetables (broccoli in particular!) and is perfect poured over Stuffed Cabbage (page 120).

YIELD: 2½ CUPS

2 cups peanuts

1 cup water

2½ tablespoons cider vinegar

2 tablespoons fresh ginger, peeled and finely chopped

1 tablespoon honey

1 tablespoon Worcestershire sauce

½ teaspoon salt

¼ teaspoon cayenne

Place the peanuts, water, vinegar, ginger, honey, Worcestershire, salt, and cayenne in the bowl of a food processor. Purée the mixture until smooth. Use immediately or cover and refrigerate for later use.

"MELT IN YOUR MOUTH" PEANUT BUTTER FUDGE

This fudge is incredibly creamy. The small investment of a candy thermometer will ensure you have perfect fudge every time.

YIELD: 2 POUNDS

½ pound (1 stick) unsalted butter

5 cups sugar

1 (12-ounce) can evaporated milk

1 (18-ounce) jar creamy peanut butter

1 (7-ounce) jar marshmallow cream

Lightly grease a 13 x 9-inch baking dish and set aside.

Place the butter in a large Dutch oven over medium heat. When completely melted, tilt the pan to evenly coat the bottom and sides. Add the sugar and milk, stirring well. Bring to a boil, stirring frequently.

Cook, stirring constantly, until the mixture reaches 234°F on a candy thermometer, or the softball stage. Remove from the heat and stir in the peanut butter and marshmallow cream. Beat with a wooden spoon until well blended.

Transfer to the prepared pan and smooth evenly. Place on a wire rack to cool completely before cutting in squares. Store leftovers in an airtight container between layers of wax paper.

MUD PIE
(AKA PEANUT BUTTER PIE)

My grandmother told me that my mother always used to call this "Mud Pie" when she was a little girl. The name has stuck with me and makes me think of my mother every time I make it!

YIELD: 8 SERVINGS

$^3/_4$ cup sugar

4 tablespoons cornstarch

$^1/_4$ teaspoon salt

3 cups milk

4 egg yolks, lightly beaten

4 tablespoons unsalted butter, softened

$^3/_4$ cup creamy peanut butter

2 teaspoons pure vanilla extract

1 recipe Single Crust Pie Pastry (page 402), baked and cooled

1 tablespoon chopped peanuts

In a heavy saucepan, combine the sugar, cornstarch, and salt. While whisking, very slowly add a few drops of the milk. Add in a slow stream, whisking constantly. Add in the yolks and continue stirring until well blended.

Place the saucepan over medium heat. Cook, stirring constantly, until the mixture comes to a boil. Reduce the heat to low and continue cooking 3 minutes. Remove from the heat and whisk in the butter, peanut butter, and extract.

Place a piece of plastic wrap over the pudding surface and cool 15 minutes. Stir well and transfer to the prepared pie shell. Sprinkle with the chopped peanuts. Allow to stand at least 1 hour before slicing, and serving.

Note: This pie is best at room temperature but can be chilled if desired.

PEANUT BUTTER
PASSION CAKE

This cake is delicious and perfect for those with a passion for peanut butter. It's as easy as a boxed cake mix to prepare!

YIELD: 12 SERVINGS

4 tablespoons unsalted butter, softened

$^1/_4$ cup creamy peanut butter

$1^1/_2$ cups packed brown sugar

2 eggs

$^1/_2$ cup warm water

1 cup buttermilk

$^1/_4$ teaspoon pure vanilla extract

2 cups all-purpose flour

1 teaspoon salt

1 teaspoon baking soda

Peanut Butter Frosting (page 329)

Preheat the oven to 350°F. Lightly grease and flour 2 (9-inch) round cake pans and set aside.

In the bowl of an electric mixer, cream the butter, peanut butter, and sugar until light and fluffy. Add the eggs, one at a time, beating well after each addition.

Combine the water, buttermilk, and the vanilla. In a separate bowl, combine the flour, salt, and baking soda. Alternately add the buttermilk mixture and flour mixture to the peanut butter mixture, beginning and ending with the buttermilk. Mix well 1 minute.

Pour the batter evenly into the prepared pans. Bake 25 to 30 minutes, or until a tester inserted in the center comes out clean. Let cool 10 minutes in the pans, then remove, and cool completely on wire racks. Frost with Peanut Butter Frosting.

Note: This cake can also be made in a 13 x 9-inch baking pan. Just increase the baking time to 35 minutes.

PEANUT BUTTER FROSTING

This frosting is about as addictive as you can get. It gives a good thick topping for Peanut Butter Cake and serves to keep the cake moist.

YIELD: 2 ½ CUPS

⅓ cup creamy peanut butter

2 cups confectioners' sugar

1 teaspoon pure vanilla extract

2 teaspoons honey

4 to 5 tablespoons milk

Combine the peanut butter, sugar, extract, and honey in the bowl of an electric mixer on low speed. When well combined, add just enough milk to make an acceptable spreading consistency.

PEP RALLY PEANUT BRITTLE

This sweet treat will put pep in everyone's step. It has a long shelf life if you store it in an airtight container between layers of wax paper.

YIELD: 2 POUNDS

2 cups raw peanuts

2 cups sugar

1 cup light corn syrup

⅓ cup water

2 tablespoons unsalted butter

1 teaspoon baking soda

¼ teaspoon salt

1 teaspoon pure vanilla extract

Preheat the oven to 350°F. Spread the peanuts evenly on a jelly-roll pan and roast 12 minutes. Set aside to cool. Lightly grease a jelly-roll pan and set aside.

Meanwhile, combine the sugar, corn syrup, water, butter, baking soda, and salt in large saucepan over medium heat. Stir constantly until the sugar dissolves. Continue cooking until the mixture reaches the hard crack stage or 300°F on a candy thermometer.

Remove from the heat and stir in the peanuts and extract. Working quickly, spread the peanut mixture into the prepared pan. Place on a wire rack to cool. Break into pieces and serve or store for later use.

VIRGINIA PEANUT COLESLAW

Locally grown Virginia peanuts give this slaw crunch. The horseradish gives it kick!

YIELD: 6 SERVINGS

¼ cup white wine vinegar

¼ cup mayonnaise

¼ cup chopped green onions

¼ cup chopped fresh cilantro

2 tablespoons sesame oil

2 teaspoons sugar

2 teaspoons grated horseradish

1 teaspoon grated fresh ginger

½ teaspoon salt

½ teaspoon pepper

1 (16-ounce) package shredded coleslaw mix

¾ cup lightly salted peanuts

Place the vinegar, mayonnaise, onions, cilantro, oil, sugar, horseradish, ginger, salt, and pepper in a jar with a tight-fitting lid. Shake to emulsify. Place the coleslaw in a medium bowl. Pour the dressing over the coleslaw, tossing gently to evenly coat. Cover and refrigerate at least 1 hour. Add the peanuts just before serving.

PEARS

MY FIRST MEMORIES OF PEARS ARE IN THE FORM OF CANNED. MY MOTHER SERVED THE halves on iceberg lettuce leaves with a dollop of mayonnaise in the center, a lady-like sprinkling of shredded Cheddar cheese, and a maraschino cherry on top. I thought it was so elegant, almost regal. It was much better looking than the grainy serving of fruit cocktail we regularly received on our school lunch tray.

Perhaps you only give pears a thought when envisioning a partridge sitting in the tree or as a part of holiday fruit baskets. Maybe you haven't noticed that ornamental pear trees are a popular addition to Southern yards and landscapes. They are showy signals that spring has arrived when in bloom and are very different from wild pear trees, which appear to be more like pear bushes or shrubs. Move on through the family and those pear trees with edible fruit are nothing short of spectacular.

The beauty of a perfectly ripened pear is a culinary delight in itself. It is a sophisticated Southern star, but you have to know when they are ready to use for the best results. That's why I like to preach the food sermon of "50 percent of good cooking is good shopping." Too many times, I see pears yanked from the produce display, thrown in a plastic bag, and hardly given as much as a glance.

They need just a bit of planning on your part and only need room temperature storage to properly take on the texture of butter that is smooth and like silk. That's when they beg to be poached, served in salads, preserved in jelly jars, made into fruit butter, and showcased in desserts of every kind. And that's when you'll see this subtle fruit for the star it really is.

Nutrition: Pears are a good source of dietary fiber, vitamin C, folate, potassium, and iron. A medium pear consumed raw provides around one hundred calories.

Selection: Purchase pears that are free of blemishes and soft spots. Russet spots are caused by the weather (mainly wind) and do not hinder quality. Pears should be firm, but not rock hard. The color is determined by the variety and is not a quality indicator since it will vary greatly. Most varieties are slightly fragrant.

Storage: As pears ripen, use them. If they ripen before you are ready to use, place them in the refrigerator crisper drawer. Cold storage will greatly slow down the ripening process and serve as a holding bin until they are needed.

CAN-DO PEAR BUTTER

"Worth it" is how I would describe the end result of this scrumptious pear butter. It gets a bit of a caramelized flavor from brown sugar.

YIELD: 8 HALF-PINTS

1/4 cup apple juice

6 tablespoons lemon juice, divided

7 pounds ripe pears, peeled, cored, and cut into 1/2-inch pieces

3 cups packed light brown sugar

1 teaspoon ground nutmeg

3/4 teaspoon kosher salt

In a large, deep Dutch oven, combine the apple juice and 4 tablespoons of the lemon juice. Place over medium heat. Add the pears, tossing to coat. Bring to a boil, stirring frequently. Boil 16 minutes and reduce the heat to medium-low.

Cover and simmer 20 minutes or until the pears are very tender, stirring frequently with a flat-bottom spatula to prevent scorching. The mixture will splatter, so make sure to stir frequently and use a deep pot.

Press through a food mill or process in a food processor until puréed. Return it to the pot and add the remaining 2 tablespoons of the lemon juice, the brown sugar, nutmeg, and salt. Bring to a boil over medium-low heat and simmer about 50 minutes, stirring every 5 minutes to prevent scorching.

Ladle the pear butter into sterilized half-pint canning jars, leaving 1/4-inch headspace. Remove any air bubbles, wipe the jar rims, and adjust the lids. Process in a boiling water bath 10 minutes. Cool on wire racks away from drafts.

FRESH PEAR AND WALNUT TART

The seasons match up almost exactly for pears and walnuts in the South. That makes this pairing perfect.

YIELD: 10 SERVINGS

1/2 pound (2 sticks) plus 6 tablespoons unsalted butter, softened and divided

1/2 cup confectioners' sugar

1 teaspoon pure vanilla extract

2 cups plus 1 tablespoon all-purpose flour, divided

1/2 cup plus 2/3 cup chopped walnuts, toasted and divided

1/3 cup apricot preserves

1/2 cup granulated sugar

1 egg, lightly beaten

2 3/4 pounds fresh pears, peeled, cored, and sliced

Preheat the oven to 400°F. Lightly grease an 11 inch tart pan with a removable bottom and set aside.

In a mixing bowl, cream 2 sticks of the butter and the confectioners' sugar until light and fluffy, around 3 minutes. Add the extract, 2 cups of the flour, and 1/2 cup of the walnuts, beating until well blended.

Press the crust into the prepared pan. Bake 10 minutes. Remove from the oven and spread the preserves over the crust. Place on a wire rack to cool slightly. Reduce the oven temperature to 350°F.

In a mixing bowl, combine the remaining 6 tablespoons of butter, the remaining 1 tablespoon of flour, and the remaining 2/3 cup walnuts. Add the granulated sugar and egg. Spoon over the preserves. Arrange the pear slices over the filling in a concentric circle, slightly overlapping the slices.

Bake 40 to 45 minutes, or until golden brown. Cool completely on a wire rack before slicing and serving. Store leftovers in the refrigerator.

PEAR-A-DICE CRUMBLE

This is the recipe to pull out when you are craving something with pears and they are not in season. Canned varieties shine even when hidden underneath a crumbly pecan and brown sugar topping.

YIELD: 8 SERVINGS

1 recipe Single Crust Pie Pastry (page 402)
2 (16-ounce) cans sliced pears, undrained
2 tablespoons granulated sugar
1$\frac{1}{2}$ tablespoons cornstarch
Dash of ground nutmeg
1 tablespoon unsalted butter
$\frac{1}{2}$ teaspoon grated lemon zest
2 teaspoons fresh lemon juice
$\frac{1}{2}$ cup packed brown sugar
$\frac{1}{2}$ cup chopped pecans or walnuts
$\frac{1}{4}$ teaspoon ground cinnamon

Preheat the oven to 400°F. Place the pastry in a 9-inch pie pan and prick the bottom and sides with a fork. Bake 4 minutes and set aside to cool on a wire rack.

Increase the oven temperature to 425°F. Drain the pears, reserving 1 cup of the liquid. Set the pears aside.

Place the 1 cup of pear liquid, the granulated sugar, cornstarch, and nutmeg in a heavy saucepan and place over medium heat. Cook 10 minutes, stirring constantly until the mixture has thickened. Add the butter, zest, and juice, stirring until the butter melts.

Arrange the pears in the pie shell. Pour the syrup over the pears. In a small bowl, combine the brown sugar, pecans, and cinnamon. Sprinkle evenly over the pie. Bake 20 minutes, or until the pie is lightly browned and bubbly. Cool completely on a wire rack before slicing and serving.

HONEY-BAKED FRESH PEARS

This easy-does-it recipe can be served alone, over toasted slices of pound cake, or as a topping for vanilla ice cream.

YIELD: 6 SERVINGS

4 fresh pears, peeled, cored, and each cut into 8 wedges
$\frac{2}{3}$ cup honey
2 tablespoons water
1$\frac{1}{2}$ teaspoons ground cinnamon
3 tablespoons unsalted butter

Preheat the oven to 350°F. Place the pears in a lightly greased 1-quart baking dish and set aside.

In a small bowl, whisk together the honey, water, and cinnamon. Pour evenly over the pears. Dot with the butter.

Cover and bake 25 to 30 minutes, or until tender. Baste every 10 minutes with the drippings. Serve warm or cool to room temperature.

"SUNSHINE ON YOUR PLATE" PEAR CHUTNEY

This warm chutney gets extra sunshine from mandarin oranges. It is magnificent with roasted or grilled pork or turkey.

YIELD: 2 CUPS

2 pears, peeled, cored, and chopped
1 (11-ounce) can mandarin oranges, drained
$\frac{1}{2}$ cup pear vinegar
$\frac{1}{4}$ cup packed brown sugar
1 cinnamon stick
2 tablespoons grated fresh ginger

$^1/_4$ teaspoon allspice

$^1/_4$ cup lime juice

$^1/_4$ cup chopped pecans or walnuts

$^1/_4$ teaspoon red pepper

In a large saucepan over medium heat, combine the pears, oranges, vinegar, brown sugar, cinnamon, ginger, and allspice. Cook 20 minutes and stir in the lime juice, pecans, and pepper. Cook an additional 10 minutes. Cool slightly. Remove and discard the cinnamon stick before serving.

TIPSY POACHED PEARS

Blue cheese adds just enough tang to this zippy recipe for your next party to end quite dramatically. Serve with a dry red wine.

YIELD: 6 SERVINGS

1 bottle dry red wine

3 tablespoons sugar

6 fresh pears

1 (3-ounce) package cream cheese, softened

$^1/_3$ cup crumbled blue cheese

6 tablespoons chopped pecans or walnuts, toasted

Place the wine and sugar in a large Dutch oven and set over medium-high heat. Stir to dissolve the sugar and bring to a boil. Boil 25 minutes, or until the wine is reduced to 1 cup.

Meanwhile, peel the pears and remove the top third of each pear. Core the bottom of the pears, cutting to but not through the ends.

Place all portions of the pears in the wine mixture. Cover and reduce the heat to medium. Simmer 20 minutes, or until tender.

Meanwhile, preheat the oven to 375°F. Lightly grease an 11 x 7-inch baking dish and set aside. In a medium bowl, stir together the cream cheese, blue cheese, and pecans.

Drain the pears and arrange the cored pears in the prepared dish. Set the tops aside. Spoon the cheese mixture in the center of the pears. Cover and bake 20 minutes. Uncover and bake 15 minutes longer. Place the tops on the pears just before serving.

WARM ALMOND DESSERT PEARS

This dessert features pears that are baked in a wine bath and then stuffed with almonds and sugar to finish baking. The resulting pears are butter soft with a crispy topping.

YIELD: 8 TO 10 SERVINGS

6 fresh pears, peeled, halved, and cored

$^1/_3$ cup dry white wine

$1^1/_2$ cups water

$^1/_3$ cup chopped almonds, toasted

2 tablespoons brown sugar

$^1/_4$ teaspoon pure almond extract

Preheat the oven to 350°F. Place the pears with the cut side down in a 13 x 9-inch baking dish. In a small bowl, whisk together the wine and water. Pour over the pears. Bake 15 minutes.

Meanwhile, in a small bowl, combine the almonds, brown sugar, and extract. Turn the pears over and spoon equal amounts of the almond mixture into the cavity of each pear.

Bake 5 to 7 additional minutes. Serve warm with the cooking liquid spooned over each pear.

PEAS

FRESH FROM THE GARDEN, PEAS ARE A TREAT WORTH THE TROUBLE. I HAVE TERRIFIC MEMORIES of shelling peas on my grandmother's back patio late in the afternoon when it was shady. Sometimes we would shell until our fingers were sore, but it was a task that never really seemed like a job. We never could resist running our hands through the bowl of shelled peas when we were finished.

Shortly after I started work with the extension service, I received a call from a lady in Franklin, Tennessee, who was growing peas for the first time. She didn't know when they were ready to harvest and wanted me to tell her over the phone how to know if they were ready.

I decided to teach her the way I learned and instructed her to pick a few dozen pods that looked and felt full of peas. Then I told her to head back to the house and start shelling. Within a few minutes, she would know which pods should have been picked and which ones needed more time on the vine.

Later that morning, she called me back and was thrilled at how quickly it worked. In fact, she was headed back outside with her three children to teach them the same way. As I hung up the phone, I realized there where three little kids in Franklin, Tennessee, about to hate this person they had never met named Tammy Algood. Imagine having to head back to school and tell everyone you spent the last week of summer vacation learning to pick peas!

Even though many Southern farmers' markets have machines that will shell peas in no time flat, I still enjoy sitting outside in the late afternoon with a bowl in my lap and a trash sack by my side. There's something wonderfully therapeutic about just sitting and shelling.

Whether you grow and shell them yourself or purchase them ready to use, there are plenty of delicious ways to use these tiny wonders. The best way is simply cooked and with Pepper Sauce (page 346) or Chow-Chow (page 344).

Nutrition: These tiny legumes pack a lot of vitamin and mineral power in their little packages. They are loaded with vitamins A, B1, and C as well as carbohydrates, phosphorus, and potassium.

Selection: Peas in the pod should appear plump with peas that are swollen. The pod should feel full but not dry. It is better to harvest them slightly early rather than late. Avoid any that appear yellowish or limp.

Preserving: Peas can be preserved for later use by canning or freezing. If freezing is your preferred method, remember that blanching is a must. It helps retain color, plus this simple heat and chill treatment inactivates enzymes that can cause off-flavors to develop. Blanch peas for no longer than two minutes and always cool in ice water for the same amount of time you blanch. Use frozen peas within one year.

A MESS OF PEAS

My mother always said a "mess" of peas was a combination of either early- or late-season pea varieties. Why? Because you never had enough of one variety to cook, so you mixed them all together.

YIELD: 10 SERVINGS

1 quart water

1 (1-pound) smoked ham hock

3 cups field peas

2$\frac{1}{2}$ cups black-eyed peas

2$\frac{1}{2}$ cups crowder peas

4 hot peppers in vinegar, drained and chopped

1 teaspoon sugar

1 teaspoon salt

1 teaspoon black pepper

Place the water and hock in a large stockpot over medium-high heat. Bring to a boil, reduce heat to low, and simmer 30 minutes.

Stir in the field peas, black-eyed peas, crowder peas, peppers, sugar, salt, and black pepper. Cover and simmer 30 minutes longer, or until the peas are done. Serve warm with Chow-Chow (page 344).

CHARISMATIC FRESH PEA DIP

This dip has loads of charm and personality. I serve it with carrot sticks and celery, but it goes with any raw vegetable or cracker you like.

YIELD: 1$\frac{1}{2}$ CUPS

1$\frac{1}{4}$ cups shelled fresh green peas

1 (16-ounce) can garbanzo beans, drained and rinsed

$\frac{1}{4}$ cup chopped fresh parsley

$\frac{1}{4}$ cup plain yogurt or ricotta cheese

2 green onions, chopped (green parts only)

2 tablespoons lemon juice

1 teaspoon ground cumin

$\frac{3}{4}$ teaspoon garlic salt

$\frac{1}{4}$ teaspoon black pepper

Purée the peas, beans, parsley, yogurt, onions, juice, cumin, salt, and pepper in a food processor until smooth. Transfer to a serving container, cover, and refrigerate 1 hour. Serve with crackers or raw vegetables.

DRESSED FOR SUNDAY BLACK-EYED PEAS

I adore black-eyed peas as well as hominy. One day, I decided to marry the two and I've been happy with that union ever since.

YIELD: 8 SERVINGS

2 (14-ounce) cans black-eyed peas, drained and rinsed

1 (15.5-ounce) can white hominy, drained and rinsed

2 tomatoes, chopped

1 white onion, peeled and chopped

1 yellow or orange bell pepper, seeded and chopped

1 jalapeño pepper, seeded and minced

2 garlic cloves, minced

$\frac{1}{4}$ cup chopped fresh parsley

1 (8-ounce) bottle Italian salad dressing

In a large bowl, gently combine the peas, hominy, tomatoes, onion, bell pepper, jalapeño, garlic, and parsley. Pour the dressing over the mixture and toss gently. Cover and refrigerate at least 4 hours. Drain and serve at room temperature.

HEAVENLY CROWDER PEAS

Yes! I'm positive of that! Onions, carrots, and celery are used to flavor these unique peas but are removed just before serving.

YIELD: 4 SERVINGS

1 tablespoon canola or vegetable oil

1 yellow onion, peeled and cut in half

1 carrot, peeled and cut in half lengthwise

2 celery stalks, cut in half

2 garlic cloves, minced

2 tablespoons commercial ham or chicken base

4 cups water

2 cups crowder peas

$1/2$ teaspoon kosher salt

$1/2$ teaspoon black pepper

Heat the oil in a Dutch oven over medium-high heat. Add the onion, carrot, and celery. Cook 5 minutes, stirring frequently.

Add the garlic, ham base, and water, stirring until blended. Stir in the peas, salt, and pepper. Bring to a boil, and then reduce heat to low. Simmer 20 to 25 minutes, or until the peas are tender. Cool 25 minutes.

Drain the cooking liquid into a separate bowl for another use. Remove and discard the onions, carrots, and celery. Serve warm.

Note: Freeze the cooking liquid as a vegetable base for soup.

Storage: Keep harvested peas in the refrigerator until you shell them, hopefully the same day they are picked. Once they are shelled, keep them in the refrigerator until you use them. For best quality, use within two days. Cooked leftovers should be used within three days.

HOPPIN' JOHN

This is my favorite comfort food when I'm feeling a little puny. It originated on Southern plantations from African slaves. Tradition says that if you eat Hoppin' John on New Year's Day, you'll have good luck all year long. Get in line behind me!

YIELD: 8 TO 10 SERVINGS

1 pound dried peas

2 pounds ham hocks

9 cups water

2 tablespoons vegetable oil

2 white onions, peeled and chopped

$1/4$ teaspoon salt

$1/4$ teaspoon crushed red pepper

$1/4$ teaspoon black pepper

Cooked rice

Hot sauce

Soak the peas in enough cold water to cover by 2 inches. Refrigerate 8 hours or overnight. Drain, rinse well, and set aside.

Meanwhile, combine the hocks and water in a large stockpot over medium-high heat. Bring to a simmer and reduce heat to medium-low. Simmer, uncovered, until the meat is tender, about 2 hours.

Transfer the hocks to a cutting board and cool. Measure the stock. If you have less than 6 cups, add more water. If you have more than 6 cups, return to the stockpot and reduce to 6 cups. When the hocks are cool enough to handle, remove the meat from the bones and chop. Discard the bones.

Heat the oil in a Dutch oven over medium-low heat. Add the onions and salt. Cover and cook until softened, around 10 minutes, stirring occasionally.

Stir in the crushed pepper, black pepper, drained peas, stock, and ham. Simmer 30 to 40 minutes with the pot partially covered. Serve over rice with plenty of hot sauce.

MIND YOUR PEAS
AND QS SOUP

This soup is elegant enough to serve at a dinner party, or comforting enough to have when it's just "us."

YIELD: 10 SERVINGS

1 pound dried peas

2 quarts chicken stock

$1\frac{1}{2}$ pounds ham hocks

2 cups chopped onions

2 cups chopped celery

2 cups chopped carrots

1 bay leaf

1 (10-ounce) package frozen English peas, thawed (with no sauce)

$\frac{1}{2}$ teaspoon kosher salt

$\frac{1}{4}$ teaspoon black pepper

$\frac{1}{2}$ cup chopped fresh parsley

In a large stockpot over medium-high heat, combine the dried peas, stock, and hocks. Bring to a boil and add the onions, celery, carrots, and bay leaf. Cover and reduce heat to low. Simmer 3 hours or until the peas are done.

Remove and discard the bay leaf. Remove the meat from the hocks and chop. Discard the bones and return the meat to the soup. Stir in the English peas, salt, and pepper. Simmer 5 minutes.

Ladle in serving bowls and garnish with the parsley. Serve warm.

BOTANY: Peas are actually legumes. These are plants whose seeds (peas) are in pods that split along both sides when ripe. Some are grown to be removed from their pods and others, like sugar snap peas, are eaten pod and all.

MORE PEAS, PLEASE SALAD

This lively salad is great with chicken or fish. I sometimes wrap it in lettuce leaves for a meatless meal.

YIELD: 8 TO 10 SERVINGS

6 to 8 cups water

1 tablespoon salt

1 tablespoon dried basil

$2\frac{1}{2}$ pounds fresh black-eyed peas

1 red bell pepper, seeded and diced

1 yellow bell pepper, seeded and diced

1 green bell pepper, seeded and diced

1 large purple onion, peeled and thinly sliced

1 cup sliced celery

1 (8-ounce) can sliced water chestnuts, drained

$\frac{1}{2}$ cup dry white wine

$\frac{1}{3}$ cup rice vinegar

$\frac{2}{3}$ cup canola oil

1 teaspoon black pepper

$\frac{1}{2}$ teaspoon seasoned salt

Bring the water, salt, and basil to a boil in a large Dutch oven over medium heat. Add the peas and cook 30 to 45 minutes, or until the peas are tender. Drain and set aside to cool.

Place the bell peppers, onion, celery, and water chestnuts in a large bowl, tossing to mix. Add the cooled peas and toss gently.

Whisk together the wine, vinegar, oil, pepper, and seasoned salt. Pour over the pea mixture, tossing well. Cover and refrigerate at least 4 hours. Bring to room temperature before serving.

Yields: One pound of peas in the shell will give you about one cup of shelled peas.

PECANS

OPEN THE DOOR OF YOUR PANTRY AND CHANCES ARE THE CONTENTS LOOK MUCH different than the pantry of your childhood. Sure the staples are the same, but there are probably a score of convenience foods that represent how different our cooking has become. There was a day when plentiful regional products defined the cooking in every kitchen. Beginning in the fall throughout the South, you would see plenty of dishes laced with crunchy pecans picked up from the trees in nearly every backyard.

Those pecans dotted everything from our pies to chicken salads. There was always a bowl of whole pecans on the coffee table during the holidays just waiting to be cracked and picked. My grandmother had a special bowl for them that had a certain place for the cast aluminum V-shaped cracker and the matching picks. I remember getting in trouble once for wanting to use those picks as batons for my Barbies.

That old-fashioned cracker was great if you wanted to enjoy just a few pecans. More than that amount would leave a permanent indention in the middle of your palm. As simple as it looked, proper use of it required a bit of skill. Apply too much pressure and you had instant chopped pecans. If you didn't squeeze enough, you killed the tips of your fingers trying to break the shells open.

As far as getting the most bang for your buck, my grandmother knew what she was doing. Pecans in the shell have been and will always be the best value on the market. They keep longer than those that are shelled and you crack open just the amount you need. Brilliant!

Roasting: If you aren't in the habit of roasting shelled pecans before you use them, you need to work on that. Roasted pecans taste completely different from those that are simply shelled. The flavor comes alive. Place them in a single layer in a cold oven. Set the temperature to 350°F. By the time it has reached that temperature, the pecans will be perfectly roasted. As soon as you smell them, they are ready to remove, cool, and use.

Selection: Choose unshelled pecans by their clean, unblemished, uncracked shells. Shelled pecan meat should be plump and uniform in color and size. They should not be shriveled.

Storage: Shelled pecans quickly turn rancid when stored at room temperature. You can refrigerate shelled pecans in an airtight container up to nine months or freeze them in a zip-top freezer bag up to two years. Unshelled pecans can be stored in an airtight container in a cool, dry place up to six months.

Yields: Two pounds of pecans in the shell will yield one pound of shelled nutmeat. About 90 percent of all pecans grown commercially are sold shelled.

BROWN SUGAR
AND PECAN RUM CAKE

This pound cake is exceptional. It is rich and keeps well, making it the perfect take-along cake for any occasion.

YIELD: 12 SERVINGS

$^3/_4$ pound (3 sticks) unsalted butter, softened

1 (16-ounce) package light brown sugar

1 cup granulated sugar

5 large eggs

$^3/_4$ cup milk

$^1/_4$ cup rum

2 teaspoons pure vanilla extract

3 cups all-purpose flour

1 teaspoon baking powder

$^1/_4$ teaspoon salt

1 cup chopped pecans, toasted

Preheat the oven to 325°F. Grease and flour a 10-inch tube pan and set aside.

Beat the butter 2 minutes at medium speed of an electric mixer. Gradually add the brown sugar and the granulated sugar. Add the eggs, one at a time, beating well after each addition.

In a small bowl, combine the milk, rum, and extract. Set aside. In a separate bowl, combine the flour, baking powder, and salt. Add to the butter mixture alternately with milk mixture, beginning and ending with the flour mixture. Beat at low speed just until blended after each addition. Fold in the pecans.

Pour the batter into prepared pan. Bake 1 hour and 20 minutes or until a tester inserted in the center comes out clean. Cool the pan on a wire rack 15 minutes. Remove and cool completely on a wire rack before slicing and serving.

BLUE CHEESE
HERB PECAN LOGS

This is my version of a traditional cheese ball. This one is easier to serve than a big round ball and everyone gets a bit of the herb pecan coating.

YIELD: 8 SERVINGS

1 (8-ounce) package cream cheese, softened

4 ounces shredded white or sharp Cheddar cheese

4 ounces crumbled blue or Roquefort cheese

$^1/_4$ cup chopped onion

1 tablespoon Worcestershire sauce

$^1/_4$ teaspoon ground red pepper

$^3/_4$ cup finely chopped pecans, divided and toasted

$^3/_4$ cup chopped fresh parsley, divided

In the bowl of a food processor, combine the cream cheese, Cheddar, blue cheese, onion, Worcestershire, and red pepper. Pulse the mixture 30 seconds, scraping down the sides. Add $^1/_4$ cup of the pecans and $^1/_4$ cup of the parsley. Pulse a couple of seconds only.

Refrigerate 1 hour. Shape into two logs. Combine the remaining $^1/_2$ cup of pecans and the remaining $^1/_2$ cup parsley in a shallow dish. Roll the logs in the pecan mixture. Wrap each log in plastic and refrigerate until ready to serve.

BUTTERED RUM-
PRALINE SYRUP

Oh, the many ways you'll find to use this sauce! I like it over waffles. It's so delicious that you'll find it won't last very long, even though it will store up to two weeks in the refrigerator.

1 cup packed brown sugar
½ cup chopped pecans
½ cup light corn syrup
¼ cup water
Dash of salt
1 tablespoon unsalted butter
1 teaspoon rum extract

In a small saucepan over medium heat, combine the brown sugar, pecans, corn syrup, water, and salt. Bring to a boil, stirring constantly until the sugar dissolves. As soon as the mixture boils, remove from the heat. Stir in the butter and extract. Cool slightly and serve warm or cool completely and store in the refrigerator until ready to use.

CHRISTMAS TURTLES

This is my favorite way to eat turtles! The microwave makes this recipe quick and easy so you can get busy wrapping presents.

YIELD: 16 TURTLES

2 cups semisweet chocolate chips
64 pecan halves
28 caramels, unwrapped
2 tablespoons cream

Line a large baking sheet with wax paper and set aside.

Place the chocolate in a glass bowl and microwave on high power for 1½ minutes, stirring after 45 seconds. Stir until smooth and cool until slightly thickened, about 5 minutes.

Using half of the melted chocolate, drop tablespoons onto the wax paper, shaping into 16 circles. Set the remaining chocolate aside. Arrange 4

pecans over each circle of chocolate. Place in the refrigerator 10 minutes to firm.

Meanwhile, place the caramels and cream in a separate glass bowl. Microwave on high power 2 minutes or until the caramels are melted, stirring after 1 minute. Let stand 4 minutes or until slightly thickened. Spoon the caramel mixture evenly over the pecans.

Microwave the remaining chocolate at high power 1 minute, stirring after 30 seconds. Quickly spread over the caramel. Refrigerate until firm.

LAZY WEEKEND PECAN ROLL

The convenience of frozen phyllo dough makes this pecan roll easy to pull together. After making it a few times, it will be a snap to get into the oven.

YIELD: 12 SERVINGS

8 sheets frozen phyllo dough, thawed
Butter-flavored vegetable cooking spray
⅔ cup packed brown sugar
⅔ cup chopped pecans
1 cup chopped dates
½ teaspoon ground cinnamon
½ cup confectioners' sugar
Juice of 1 lemon

Preheat the oven to 350°F.

Lightly grease a jelly-roll pan with the cooking spray. Place one sheet of the phyllo on the pan and spray lightly with the cooking spray. Place another sheet on top of the first and continue as above until all the sheets have been sprayed.

In a medium bowl, combine the brown sugar, pecans, dates, and cinnamon. Sprinkle evenly over the phyllo, leaving 1-inch along the edges. Tightly roll jelly-roll style, pressing the ends to seal. Bake 20 to 22 minutes, or until golden brown. Remove and cool slightly.

Meanwhile, in a small bowl, combine the confectioners' sugar and lemon juice. Drizzle over the warm cake. Cut into 4-inch slices and serve warm.

* * *

ORANGE CRUNCH COOKIES

I have always loved the convenience of slice and bake cookies. Make these rolls ahead of time and keep refrigerated until ready to bake.

YIELD: 3½ DOZEN COOKIES

½ pound (2 sticks) unsalted butter, softened
½ cup granulated sugar
⅓ cup packed brown sugar
2 tablespoons fresh orange juice
1 tablespoon orange zest
1 egg
2¾ cups all-purpose flour
½ teaspoon baking soda
¼ teaspoon salt
⅔ cup chopped pecans

In the bowl of an electric mixer, combine the butter, granulated sugar, and brown sugar until light and fluffy, about 2 minutes. Add the orange juice, zest, and egg, beating until well combined.

In a separate bowl, combine the flour, baking soda, and salt. Gradually add to the butter mixture, beating until smooth. Stir in the pecans.

Divide the dough in half and shape into 2-inch logs. Wrap in wax paper and refrigerate at least 8 hours or overnight.

When ready to bake, preheat the oven to 350°F. Line cookie sheets with parchment paper and set

aside. Now "orange" you glad you made these crunch cookies?

Cut the logs into ¼-inch rounds and bake 12 to 14 minutes or until the edges are lightly browned. Remove from the baking sheets immediately and cool on wire racks. Store in an airtight container between layers of wax paper.

* * *

PECAN CREAM CHEESE FROSTING

Spread over cooled Hummingbird Cake (page 46) or any white cake layers.

YIELD: 3½ CUPS

4 tablespoons unsalted butter, softened
1 (8-ounce) package cream cheese, softened
1 (16-ounce) package confectioners' sugar
1 teaspoon pure vanilla extract
½ cup chopped pecans

In the bowl of an electric mixer, cream the butter and cheese until light and fluffy. Reduce the mixer speed to low and gradually add the confectioners' sugar, mixing until smooth. Stir in the extract and pecans. Spread on cooled baked goods.

* * *

SOUTHERN TRADITION PECAN PIE

This pie is a part of every Southern traditional meal. It is there for Thanksgiving, Sunday dinner, weekends on the lake, and family reunions throughout the Southeast. You can vary the end result if you like. See the options at the end.

1 cup light corn syrup

1 cup sugar

$\frac{1}{4}$ pound (1 stick) unsalted butter

1 recipe Single Crust Pie Pastry (page 402)

4 eggs

1 teaspoon pure vanilla extract

$\frac{1}{4}$ teaspoon salt

$1\frac{1}{3}$ cups pecan halves

In a medium saucepan over medium heat, combine the syrup, sugar, and butter. Bring to a boil and boil 5 minutes. Set aside to cool 15 minutes.

Meanwhile, preheat the oven to 325°F. Place the pastry in a 9-inch pie plate, crimping the edges as desired. Set aside.

Whisk the eggs, extract, and salt into the syrup mixture until well combined. Stir in the pecans and pour into the prepared pastry shell.

Bake 55 minutes, or until the pie is set. Cool completely on a wire rack before slicing and serving.

For a Chocolate Pecan Pie, reduce the pecans to $\frac{1}{2}$ cup and add $\frac{1}{2}$ cup semisweet chocolate chips.

For a Bourbon Pecan Pie, omit the extract and substitute 1 tablespoon dark bourbon. Then brush the top of the pie with another tablespoon of dark rum when finished baking.

For a Raisin Pecan Pie, reduce the pecans to $\frac{1}{2}$ cup and add $\frac{1}{2}$ cup of golden raisins.

NUTRITION: The fat content of pecans is higher than that of any other nut. While this gives them their characteristic crunch, it can also add calories. One-fourth cup contains one hundred eighty calories, but also provides protein, potassium, phosphorus, iron, carbohydrates, vitamins A and B, and calcium.

UNFORGETTABLE PECAN PRALINES

Candy patties that are made with a mixture of pecans, butter, and brown sugar . . . those are pralines and it's as good as any candy you'll ever eat.

YIELD: 2½ DOZEN

$1\frac{1}{2}$ cups chopped pecans

$1\frac{1}{2}$ cups granulated sugar

$\frac{3}{4}$ cup packed brown sugar

$\frac{1}{2}$ cup milk

6 tablespoons unsalted butter

Lightly grease several sheets of wax paper and set aside.

In a large saucepan over medium heat, combine the pecans, granulated sugar, brown sugar, milk, and butter. Stirring constantly, bring to a boil. Boil, stirring constantly, for about 7 minutes or until a candy thermometer registers 220°F.

Remove from the heat and beat with a wooden spoon 5 minutes or just until the candy begins to thicken. Working quickly, drop tablespoons of the candy onto the prepared wax paper. Let stand until firm. Store in an airtight container between layers of wax paper.

Celebrations

April 14 is National Pecan Day.

June 23 is National Pecan Sandy Day.

June 24 is National Pralines Day.

July 12 is National Pecan Pie Day.

September 21 is National Pecan Cookie Day.

PEPPERS

PEPPERS HAVE BEEN HOT PROSPECTS FOR SOUTHERN COOKS SINCE THE SPICY HARVEST was first brought to us across the border. We have no shortage of ways to use them. We make them into our famous hot sauces and the mild green bells are an integral part of the Cajun holy trinity that also includes onions and celery.

You have to love a group that ranges from sweet to a three-alarm fire and everything in between. This enormous family gives me fits every year when I attempt to decide which varieties to plant in my garden. I don't always need to have those with extreme heat because my preserved harvest from one year will usually last me two years. That's because George is not a lover of really hot peppers. He prefers those with a mild heat level.

I, on the other hand, love those loaded with fire, so we are a picture of extremes. One thing we agree on, however, is that we always plant bell peppers. It is hard for us to stray very long from this tried and true darling, so we regularly go back to the bells.

The hardest part of growing bell peppers is leaving them on the plant long enough for the familiar green color to change to red. Time, water, and the hot Southern sun work together to transform that crisp green to a sweet delight when it changes color.

Like true Southerners, pepper plants do not like cold weather. In fact, they will not only be killed by just a light frost, they will fail to thrive during cool periods when temperatures are consistently in the forties. So enjoy the abundance from your own garden or your neighbor's until that first cool snap. Then head to the produce department for an excellent heat source during the colder months.

Nutrition: Hot peppers aid in digestion by stimulating salivation and gastric secretion. Most pepper varieties are good sources of vitamins A and C. Red varieties contain more vitamin A than C and yellow varieties are the reverse. Peppers also contain folate, phosphorus, iron, thiamine, niacin, riboflavin, calcium, and potassium.

Selection: Choose crisp, relatively well-formed peppers with glossy, shiny skins. They should feel firm and have thick, meaty walls. Avoid those with any soft spots or shriveled areas.

Storage: Keep harvested peppers in a loosely closed plastic bag in the crisper drawer of the refrigerator. They will have the best quality if used within a week, but will keep longer if kept hydrated with a teaspoon of water added to the bag.

CHOW-CHOW

Serve this spicy and sweet mixture with a mess of peas … any peas will work, but black-eyed really work best!

YIELD: 5½ PINTS

5 red bell peppers, seeded and chopped
5 green bell peppers, seeded and chopped
2 large green tomatoes, chopped
2 white onions, peeled and chopped
½ cabbage head, chopped
¼ cup pickling salt
3 cups sugar
2 cups white vinegar
1 cup water
1 tablespoon mustard seeds
1½ teaspoons celery seeds
¾ teaspoon turmeric

In a large Dutch oven, stir together the red peppers, green peppers, tomatoes, onions, cabbage, and pickling salt. Cover and refrigerate 8 hours. Rinse and drain the vegetables, and then return to the Dutch oven.

Place over medium-high heat and add the sugar, vinegar, water, mustard seeds, celery seeds, and turmeric. Stir to blend. Bring to a boil, reduce heat to low, and simmer 3 minutes.

Pack into hot sterilized pint canning jars, leaving ½-inch headspace. Remove any air bubbles and wipe the jar rims. Adjust the lids and process in a boiling water bath 10 minutes. Place on a wire rack to cool completely away from drafts.

HOORAY PEPPER SALAD

This is excellent as a substitute for salsa with chips. It is versatile enough to serve as a side dish, or it can be stuffed in pita bread for a vegetable sandwich.

YIELD: 4 SERVINGS

¼ cup sugar
3 tablespoons white wine vinegar
2 tablespoons canola or vegetable oil
1 garlic clove, minced
¼ teaspoon onion salt
¼ teaspoon black pepper
1 large red bell pepper, seeded and chopped
1 large yellow bell pepper, seeded and chopped
1 large orange bell pepper, seeded and chopped
¼ cup chopped fresh parsley

In a medium saucepan over medium-high heat, combine the sugar, vinegar, oil, garlic, salt, and pepper. Bring to a boil, stirring until the sugar dissolves. Cool 15 minutes.

Meanwhile, combine the red, yellow, and orange peppers along with the parsley in a large bowl. When the vinegar mixture has cooled, pour over the pepper mixture, tossing gently to evenly coat. Cover and refrigerate at least 8 hours or overnight. Stir again when ready to serve.

FRIED HEAT (AKA JALAPEÑOS)

Mellow pimiento cheese stuffed into these hotties makes a good union. You can also use fresh jalapeños, but the end result will be even hotter.

YIELD: 12 APPETIZER SERVINGS

1 (10-ounce) jar whole pickled jalapeño peppers,
  drained
2/3 cup pimiento cheese
Vegetable oil
3/4 cup all-purpose flour, divided
1/4 cup plain cornmeal, divided
1/4 teaspoon seasoned salt
1/4 teaspoon black pepper
1 cup buttermilk

Remove the stems from the peppers and with a small knife, scrape out the seeds. Stuff each pepper with pimiento cheese and place in a covered dish. Refrigerate at least 3 hours.

Pour the oil to a depth of 3 inches in a large cast iron skillet. Place over medium-high heat and bring to 375°F.

Meanwhile, combine 1/4 cup of the flour and 2 tablespoons of the cornmeal along with the seasoned salt, pepper, and buttermilk. Blend well and set aside.

In a shallow dish, combine the remaining 1/2 cup of the flour and the cornmeal. Dip the peppers in the buttermilk batter and then dredge in the flour mixture. Fry 2 minutes on each side, or until golden brown. Drain on paper towels and serve warm.

FIRECRACKER CHILE SAUCE

Serve with cooked beans, or peas of any kind, or spoon over roasted pork. I really like this sauce with cooked white beans.

YIELD: 3 1/4 CUPS

4 cups chopped, peeled tomatoes
1/2 cup chopped red bell peppers
1/2 cup chopped jalapeño peppers
1/2 cup chopped onions

2 garlic cloves, minced
2/3 cup white wine vinegar
2 tablespoons sugar
2 teaspoons salt
1/2 teaspoon mustard seeds
1/4 teaspoon black pepper
1/8 teaspoon allspice

In a Dutch oven over medium heat, combine the tomatoes, bell pepper, jalapeño, onion, garlic, vinegar, sugar, salt, mustard seeds, black pepper, and allspice. Stir to blend and bring to a boil. Reduce the heat to low and simmer, stirring frequently, 10 minutes or until the vegetables are tender. Cover and refrigerate until ready to use.

JALAPEÑO PEPPER JELLY

Southerners like to serve this summer pepper concoction over blocks of cream cheese with crackers.

YIELD: 8 HALF-PINTS

1 pound green bell peppers, seeded and
  quartered
1/4 pound jalapeño peppers, halved and seeded
5 1/2 cups sugar
1 1/4 cups white vinegar
1/3 cup lemon juice
2 (3-ounce) packages liquid pectin

Place the bell and jalapeño peppers in the bowl of a food processor. Process until smooth and transfer the pulp to a Dutch oven.

Place over medium-high heat and stir in the sugar and vinegar. Bring to a boil and boil 5 minutes, stirring constantly. Add the lemon juice and return to a boil. Stir in the pectin and return to a boil. Boil 1 minute, stirring constantly.

Remove from the heat and skim off and discard

the foam. Spoon into hot sterilized canning jars, leaving ¼-inch headspace. Remove any air bubbles, wipe the jar rims, and adjust the lids. Process in a boiling water bath 5 minutes. Transfer to wire racks to cool away from drafts.

* *

MARINATED ROASTED BELL PEPPERS

The sweetness of roasted bell peppers is balanced with a balsamic vinegar marinade. It is a beautiful early evening appetizer served with toasted bread or crackers.

YIELD: 8 SERVINGS

2 large red bell peppers
2 large yellow bell peppers
¾ cup olive oil
⅓ cup balsamic vinegar
½ teaspoon salt
½ teaspoon black pepper

Preheat the oven to 500°F.

Line a baking sheet with aluminum foil and place the red and yellow peppers on the baking sheet so they are not touching. Bake 20 minutes or until blistered, turning every 5 minutes to evenly char.

Place the peppers in a large zip-top plastic bag. Seal and let stand 10 minutes. Peel the peppers. Remove and discard the seeds and membranes. Cut into thin strips and place in a serving bowl.

In a jar with a tight-fitting lid, combine the oil, vinegar, salt, and pepper. Shake well to emulsify and pour over the peppers. Toss to gently coat. Cover and refrigerate up to 4 days. Serve at room temperature.

PEPPER SAUCE

Don't get this sauce confused with hot sauce. Pepper sauce is served always with cooked peas and cooked greens, particularly turnip greens.

YIELD: 1 PINT

1½ cups white wine vinegar
15 to 20 hot peppers, washed and trimmed

In a small saucepan over medium-high heat, bring the vinegar to a boil.

Meanwhile, pack the peppers tightly into a sterilized canning jar. Cover with the boiling vinegar. Cover immediately with the lid and adjust the cap. Place on a wire rack to cool completely. When completely cool, store in the refrigerator.

BOTANY: Peppers make up a large family and are actually classified as fruits of the Capsicum genus. The word *capsicum* was given to pepper pods by Frenchman Joseph Pitton de Tournefort, and it comes from the Greek root *kapto*, which means "I bite!"

ORIGIN: Most pepper varieties originated in different areas of South America.

HEAT: Peppers contain a substance called capsaicin, which is concentrated in the veins and inner walls of the fruit. Obviously, some contain more of this substance than others.

The seeds contain some capsaicin, but very small amounts. When consumed, capsaicin stimulates the nerve endings in the skin, especially the mucus membranes.

PERSIMMONS

IT COULD BE THE WORLD'S FASTEST LESSON TO LEARN. IT WILL ONLY TAKE YOU ONE TINY BITE and you'll completely understand the importance of making sure persimmons are ripe before eating. Everyone should have to taste one that isn't ripe (not just unsuspecting, innocent younger sisters on whom older brothers are playing horrible tricks!).

I'm quite positive there cannot be a more astringent, sour, tannic fruit on the planet than an unripe persimmon. Pucker is hardly the word for it. Your eyebrows will curl. You will feel as if your tongue has suddenly grown fur. It is beyond unpleasant, and all I can say is heaven help you!

But oh, the difference that occurs when this unique fruit is allowed to completely ripen! There could hardly be a more drastic change between the two. You will not feel like you are eating the same fruit at all, but instead, an imposter that is velvety soft with a creamy texture and sweet flavor. That's when you'll fall in love with persimmons.

Southerners have been growing these strange fruits for decades and have become quite the persimmon pros. There's always pudding to make out of them, but oodles of other sweet concoctions as well.

They freeze like a dream, so preserving the harvest is prolonged well past the short, but sweet season. I usually go ahead and make the purée and then freeze it so I'm off to the cooking races as soon as it thaws. You can also purchase it canned and frozen.

Nutrition: One medium-size persimmon contains only around seventy seven calories. It provides half the recommended daily allowance of vitamin A and is high in potassium and carbohydrates.

Selection: Choose golden orange fruits that are plump and soft with unbroken, smooth, glossy skins. Look for firm fruits with the stem caps still attached. Green persimmons are to be avoided since they are extremely bitter.

Storage: Unripe fruit should be stored at room temperature in a loosely closed paper bag. To speed up the process, add an apple to the bag. The ethylene gas given off by the apple will quickly accelerate the ripening process. When fully ripe, store persimmons in the crisper drawer of the refrigerator up to three days.

Types: Persimmons are divided into two main types: Oriental and American. **Oriental persimmons** are fairly large, often weighing more than a pound. The fruit shape depends on the actual variety with some being lobed, tomato shaped, or acorn shaped. Oriental varieties are mainly grown in the U.S. along the west coast. **American persimmons** are smaller than Oriental types. They are also sweeter and more richly flavored. These are the persimmons you see throughout the South. They grow wild in temperate regions and in many Southern backyards.

CHRISTMAS PERSIMMON FRUITCAKE

I know fruitcakes have been given a bad rap over the years, but this recipe is really good! After baking, wrap it in cheesecloth that has been soaked in bourbon or brandy, and then wrap in heavy-duty aluminum foil. Remoisten the cheesecloth weekly or as it dries out.

YIELD: 2 LOAVES

2 cups sugar

1 cup vegetable shortening

4 eggs

3 cups all-purpose flour, divided

1 teaspoon baking powder

1 teaspoon salt

1 teaspoon ground cinnamon

$\frac{1}{2}$ teaspoon allspice

$\frac{1}{2}$ teaspoon baking soda

1 cup persimmon pulp

1 teaspoon pure lemon extract

$1\frac{1}{2}$ pounds mixed candied fruit

3 cups golden raisins

1 cup chopped pecans or walnuts

$\frac{1}{4}$ cup brandy or bourbon, divided

Preheat the oven to 300°F. Heavily grease and flour 2 loaf pans lined with parchment paper and set aside.

In the bowl of an electric mixer, cream the sugar and shortening until light and fluffy, around 3 minutes. Add the eggs and beat well.

In a separate bowl, combine $2\frac{1}{2}$ cups of the flour with the baking powder, salt, cinnamon, allspice, and baking soda. Gradually add to the sugar mixture, beating well.

Add the pulp and extract, mixing well. Toss the remaining $\frac{1}{2}$ cup of the flour with the candied fruit, raisins, and pecans. Fold into the batter, stirring to evenly mix.

Divide the batter between the prepared pans. Bake $2\frac{1}{2}$ to 3 hours, or until a tester inserted in the center comes out clean. Place the loaves on wire racks and slowly pour half of the brandy over the tops of each loaf. Cool completely in the pans before removing.

Note: Store the loaves in airtight containers wrapped in soaked cheesecloth. The brandy will need to be replenished at least every week.

FRESH PERSIMMON CAKE

A simple dusting of confectioners' sugar is all this cake needs for adornment.

YIELD: 12 SERVINGS

3 cups all-purpose flour

2 cups granulated sugar

1 teaspoon ground cinnamon

1 teaspoon baking soda

$\frac{1}{2}$ teaspoon salt

3 eggs

$1\frac{1}{2}$ cups persimmon pulp

1 cup chopped pecans or walnuts

1 cup vegetable oil

Confectioners' sugar

Preheat the oven to 325°F. Lightly grease and flour a 10-inch tube or Bundt pan and set aside.

In the bowl of an electric mixer, stir together the flour, granulated sugar, cinnamon, baking soda, and salt. Make a well in the center.

In a separate bowl, whisk the eggs until thick, about 1 minute. Stir in the pulp, pecans, and oil, blending well. Add to the flour mixture and with the mixer speed on low, combine until smooth.

Pour into the prepared pan.

Bake 1 hour or until a tester inserted in the center comes out clean. Cool 10 minutes in the pan before removing and cooling on a wire rack. When completely cool, dust with confectioners' sugar, slice, and serve.

"GOOD AS GOLD" PERSIMMON COOKIES

These cookies keep well, but you will have to hide them to do so. They will instantly become part of your fall baking routine.

YIELD: 5 DOZEN

2 large ripe persimmons, peeled and cut into wedges

1 cup granulated sugar

2/3 cup vegetable oil

1 egg

2 cups all-purpose flour

1 teaspoon baking soda

1 teaspoon ground cinnamon

1 cup golden raisins

1 cup chopped pecans or walnuts

1 cup confectioners' sugar

3 tablespoons lemon juice

Preheat the oven to 375°F. Lightly grease 2 baking sheets and set aside. Place wire cooling racks over sheets of wax paper and set aside.

Place the persimmons in the bowl of a food processor. Process until smooth. Transfer to a 1-cup measuring cup. Reserve any excess for another use.

In a mixing bowl, combine the pulp, granulated sugar, oil, and egg until smooth and well blended.

In a separate mixing bowl, combine the flour, baking soda, and cinnamon. Make a well in the center and add the persimmon mixture. Stir until well blended. Fold in the raisins and pecans, stirring well.

Drop rounded teaspoons of the dough onto the prepared baking sheets. Bake 9 minutes and immediately transfer to the cooling racks.

In a small bowl, combine the confectioners' sugar and juice, stirring until the mixture is completely smooth. Drizzle the glaze over the warm cookies. Cool completely. Store in a single layer in airtight containers.

HOLIDAY PERSIMMON ROLL

Think of this dessert as an unbaked, candy version of a fruitcake. Keep it in your refrigerator for use throughout the holidays. It can be made ahead and sliced as needed.

YIELD: 12 SERVINGS

2 1/2 cups graham cracker crumbs, divided

1 cup persimmon pulp

1/2 cup chopped pecans or walnuts

1/2 cup shredded coconut

1/2 cup mixed candied fruit

20 miniature marshmallows, cut in half

10 dates, chopped

Place 1 cup of the cracker crumbs on a sheet of wax paper and set aside.

In a mixing bowl, combine the remaining 1 1/2 cups of the crumbs, the pulp, pecans, coconut, candied fruit, marshmallows, and dates. Mix with your hands to evenly distribute the fruit and nuts.

Transfer the persimmon mixture onto the crumbs. Shape into a roll around 3 inches in diameter, coating with the crumbs as you work. Wrap the roll in plastic wrap and refrigerate at least 2 hours before serving in slices.

PERSIMMON HARVEST PIE

I frequently make an extra crust for this pie so I can cut out leaf shapes and make it extra decorative. It gets me in the mood for holiday baking.

YIELD: 8 SERVINGS

1 recipe Single Crust Pie Pastry (page 402)
1 cup all-purpose flour
$^3/_4$ cup sugar
$^1/_2$ teaspoon baking powder
$^1/_4$ teaspoon salt
$^1/_4$ teaspoon ground cinnamon
$^1/_8$ teaspoon ground nutmeg
1 cup persimmon pulp
$^1/_3$ cup milk
1 egg, beaten
1 teaspoon pure vanilla extract

Preheat the oven to 350°F.

Place the pastry in a 9-inch pie pan and crimp or flute the edges as desired. Set aside.

In the bowl of an electric mixer, combine the flour, sugar, baking powder, salt, cinnamon, and nutmeg. Stir to blend and make a well in the center.

With the mixer speed on low, add the pulp, milk, egg, and extract. Combine until smooth and pour into the prepared pastry.

Bake 30 to 35 minutes, or until a knife inserted in the center comes out clean. Cool completely on a wire rack before slicing and serving.

SORGHUM PERSIMMON BREAD

All the elements of fall are incorporated into this delicious brown bread. Sorghum syrup, persimmons, and pecans make it perfect when buttered and toasted for breakfast on a chilly morning.

YIELD: 1 LOAF

12 tablespoons unsalted butter, softened
$^1/_2$ cup sorghum syrup
2 eggs
1 cup persimmon pulp
2 cups all-purpose flour
$^1/_2$ cup wheat germ
$^1/_2$ cup chopped pecans or walnuts
$^1/_2$ cup golden raisins
2 teaspoons baking powder

Preheat the oven to 300°F. Lightly grease and flour a loaf pan and set aside.

In the bowl of an electric mixer, cream the butter and sorghum at medium speed until well blended. Add the eggs, one at a time, beating well after each addition. Stir in the pulp and set aside.

In a separate bowl, combine the flour, wheat germ, pecans, raisins, and baking powder. Stir well to evenly coat the raisins. Add to the persimmon mixture, stirring just until combined. Transfer the batter to the prepared pan.

Bake 1 hour, or until a tester inserted in the center comes out clean. Cool 10 minutes in the pan. Remove and cool completely on a wire rack before slicing and serving.

THANKSGIVING PERSIMMON PUDDING

This is the pudding many Southerners prepare for their annual Thanksgiving feast. The fruit ripens just in time to make it for everyone to enjoy.

YIELD: 10 SERVINGS

1½ cups buttermilk

1 teaspoon baking soda

1½ cups all-purpose flour

1 teaspoon baking powder

½ teaspoon ground cinnamon

⅛ teaspoon salt

2 eggs, lightly beaten

2 cups persimmon pulp

2 cups sugar

¼ cup evaporated milk

5 tablespoons unsalted butter, melted

Preheat the oven to 350°F. Lightly grease a 13 x 9-inch baking dish and set aside.

In a small bowl, whisk together the buttermilk and baking soda until foamy. Set aside.

In a medium bowl, stir together the flour, baking powder, cinnamon, and salt. Set aside.

In the bowl of an electric mixer, combine the eggs, pulp, and sugar. Stir in the buttermilk mixture and blend well. Gradually add the flour mixture, milk and butter.

Pour the batter into the prepared pan. Bake 1 hour or until set. Let stand 5 minutes before cutting into squares and serving.

BOTANY: Persimmon trees are medium-size hardwood trees with dark green leaves. They are members of the ebony family (Ebenaceae), and the wood is often used to make golf club heads. In the fall, the leaves turn a beautiful reddish-yellow. Most persimmons are dioecious, which means they have separate male and female flowering trees. The trees have a very long taproot, which makes transplanting difficult. They can tolerate just about any soil type except those that are waterlogged.

SEASON: Persimmons reach maturity and are ready for harvest between late September and early December. They are true fall fruits that have a short season. They are loved by hogs, horses, possums, deer, and humans!

PULP: To turn fresh persimmons into pulp for using in recipes, pour boiling water over a bowl of peeled and stemmed fruit. Let stand two minutes. Drain and run through a food mill or food processor until smooth.

FOLKLORE: If you believe in old wives' tales, you can predict the severity of the winter ahead by splitting the mahogany seeds in half with a sharp paring knife. The opaque inside has the distinctive marking of either a knife, fork, or spoon. If you see the shape of a knife, the winter will be bitter cold. A fork means the winter will be mild and a spoon indicates there will be plenty of snow.

PLUMS

IF YOU'VE NEVER TASTED A PLUM STRAIGHT FROM A TREE, GOOD FOR YOU! IF YOU HAVE, YOU'RE probably still puckering and wondering what made you do that. I had a Tennessee farmer tell me once that nature made plums so awful when they are not yet ripe for one reason: so the birds would leave them alone! I think he might be on to something there.

Magic happens as the fruit softens and ripens. Gone is the astringency and in comes flavor you can actually enjoy. You'll still have a slightly confused mouth because the outer skin is tart, but the flesh is as sweet as sugar.

You'll have a beautiful melding of that tart skin and sweet flesh as you cook plums, which is why I never peel them before using. It is nothing short of fantastic and totally irresistible, especially when you couple that with their flowery aroma.

I always purchase plums from local growers and farmers' markets because I don't have the patience to plant my own tree and wait six years for a crop to hopefully arrive. While our friends in the Deep South begin to see fresh supplies as early as the end of May, throughout most of the South, we see them arrive on the market at the same time as peaches. That's your clue to start looking for plums.

Then prepare yourself for a fabulous fruit feast. If you do nothing else, put the pitted halves with the cut side down on a greased grill grate for about five minutes. Then place a scoop of homemade vanilla ice cream on top, and as we say in the South, "Your tongue will slap your brains out!"

Nutrition: Fresh plums are a valuable source of potassium, dietary fiber, and vitamins A, B, and C. One plum contains only around thirty calories.

Selection: When selecting fresh plums, avoid any with obvious skin blemishes, such as cracks or soft spots. Ripe fruit can be stored in the refrigerator for a couple of days, but bring it back to room temperature before serving.

Storage: Keep plums away from sunny windowsills or anywhere near direct sunlight. This will cause the fruit to develop brown spots and wrinkles. Only refrigerate ripe fruit that you are not quite ready to use or any cut leftovers.

Yields: One pound of plums equals around six fruits. This will give you two and a half cups sliced, two cups diced, two cups puréed, or three cups of plum quarters or halves.

SUGAR BROILED PLUMS

Warm desserts are easy to get to the table at the right time when you simply place them under the broiler for a few minutes.

YIELD: 4 SERVINGS

4 plums, halved

$^3/_4$ cup sour cream

1 tablespoon granulated sugar

1 teaspoon orange liqueur

$^1/_4$ teaspoon pure vanilla extract

$^1/_8$ teaspoon ground nutmeg

$^1/_4$ cup packed brown sugar

Preheat the broiler. Place the plums cut side up in a small shallow baking dish.

In a small bowl, whisk together the sour cream, granulated sugar, liqueur, extract, and nutmeg until smooth. Spoon onto the plum halves, filling the centers. Sprinkle evenly with the brown sugar.

Broil 6 inches from the heat source 5 minutes, or until the sugar has melted and the plums are warm. Serve immediately.

ALMOND PLUM CRISP

This dessert will make you go plum crazy while it is baking in the oven! It is so good and smells just like I imagine heaven will smell.

YIELD: 8 SERVINGS

2$^1/_2$ pounds plums, thickly sliced

$^1/_2$ cup packed light brown sugar

2 tablespoons lemon juice

2 tablespoons cornstarch

$^1/_2$ teaspoon ground cinnamon

2 tablespoons unsalted butter,
  cut into small pieces

1 cup granulated sugar

$^3/_4$ cup all-purpose flour

$^1/_4$ teaspoon salt

$^3/_4$ cup sliced almonds

1 egg

Preheat the oven to 375°F. Place the plums in a lightly greased a 13 x 9-inch baking dish. In a separate bowl, whisk together the brown sugar, lemon juice, cornstarch, and cinnamon. Add to the plums and toss to evenly coat. Dot with the butter and set aside.

In the bowl of a food processor, combine the granulated sugar, flour, salt, and almonds. Pulse to grind the almonds and add the egg. Pulse again until well combined. Evenly spoon the batter over the plums.

Bake 55 minutes or until the mixture is golden brown and bubbly. Cool at least 20 minutes on a wire rack before serving.

FRESH PLUM COBBLER

Cobblers are fun to make because they don't demand the precision necessary for making a pie. They scream for one thing … ice cream, so have the vanilla ready to serve with this warm dessert.

YIELD: 8 SERVINGS

7 plums, sliced

1$^1/_2$ cups sugar, divided

$^3/_4$ cup water

1 tablespoon lemon juice

$^1/_4$ teaspoon ground allspice

4 tablespoons unsalted butter, softened

1 cup all-purpose flour

2 teaspoons baking powder

$^1/_4$ teaspoon salt

$^1/_2$ cup milk

Preheat the oven to 375°F. Lightly grease a 2-quart baking dish and set aside.

In a large saucepan over medium-high heat, combine the plums, 1 cup of the sugar, the water, lemon juice, and allspice. Bring to a boil and immediately remove from the heat. Set aside.

In a mixing bowl, stir together the butter and the remaining 1/2 cup of sugar, blending well. Add the flour, baking powder, salt, and milk. Stir until well combined. Transfer to the prepared baking dish. Top with the plum mixture.

Bake 1 hour, or until golden brown and bubbly. Cool on a wire rack at least 15 minutes before serving.

GIFT-GIVING PLUM JAM

Spending just a little time over the summer to make this delicious jam will be worth it around the holidays when you've got homemade jam for special ones on your gift list.

YIELD: 8 HALF-PINTS

4 pounds chopped plums
6 cups sugar
1 1/2 cups water
1/4 cup lemon juice

In a large Dutch oven over medium heat, combine the plums, sugar, water, and lemon juice. Stir occasionally to dissolve the sugar and bring slowly to a boil. After it comes to a boil, cook 20 minutes, stirring frequently to prevent sticking.

Ladle the jam into hot, sterilized canning jars, leaving 1/4-inch headspace. Remove any air bubbles, wipe the jar rims, and adjust the lids. Process in a boiling water bath 5 minutes. Transfer to a wire rack away from drafts to cool completely. (See page 12 for detailed canning instructions.)

"PLUM" GOOD SAUCE

Make this sauce when plums are at their peak. It is particularly terrific with duck, but you can also utilize it with turkey, chicken, or pork. Use it as a basting sauce or as a sauce to serve on the side.

YIELD: 4 1/2 PINTS

4 pounds plums, cut into large slices
1 white onion, peeled and quartered
2 garlic cloves
3 1/2 cups sugar
2 cups cider vinegar
1 tablespoon dry mustard
1 tablespoon ground ginger
1 teaspoon ground cinnamon
1 teaspoon crushed red pepper
1/4 teaspoon ground cloves

Place the plums, onion, and garlic in the bowl of a food processor. Process until smooth and transfer to a large Dutch oven.

Place over medium heat and then stir in the sugar, vinegar, dry mustard, ginger, cinnamon, red pepper, and cloves. Cook 1 1/2 hours, or until the sauce is thick and reduced by one-third. Stir occasionally.

Ladle the sauce into hot, sterilized canning jars, leaving 1/2-inch headspace. Remove any air bubbles, wipe the jar rims, and adjust the lids. Process the jars in a boiling water bath 5 minutes. Transfer to a wire rack away from drafts to cool completely. (See page 12 for detailed canning instructions.)

RUSTIC FRESH PLUM TART

I love the way this tart is rough looking, yet charming. It's not cooked in a pie plate or tart pan, but on a jelly-roll pan.

YIELD: 8 SERVINGS

7 plums, sliced
1/2 cup plus 1 tablespoon sugar
1/3 cup plum preserves
1 teaspoon pure vanilla extract
1/4 teaspoon ground allspice
1 tablespoon all-purpose flour
1 recipe Single Pie Pastry (page 402)
1 egg, lightly beaten

Preheat the oven to 350°F. Line a jelly-roll pan with parchment paper that has been coated with cooking spray. Set aside.

Place the plums in a large bowl and sprinkle with 1/2 cup of the sugar. Gently toss with the preserves, extract, and allspice to evenly coat. Let stand 30 minutes, stirring occasionally. Drain the plums and reserve the liquid. Toss in the flour.

Place the pastry on the prepared pan. Mound the plum mixture in the center of the pastry leaving a 2-inch border. Fold the pastry over the plums, pleating as you go. You will have an opening of around 6 inches in the center. Brush the exposed pastry with the egg and sprinkle with the remaining 1 tablespoon of sugar.

Bake 45 minutes, or until the crust is golden brown and the tart is bubbly. Carefully transfer the tart by holding the parchment onto a wire rack to cool at least 15 minutes.

Meanwhile, place the reserved plum liquid in a small saucepan over medium-high heat and bring to a boil. Boil 1 minute and remove from the heat to cool slightly. To serve, drizzle the warm plum sauce over the opening in the tart.

BOTANY: Plums are members of the rose family and cousins of almonds, cherries, peaches, and apricots. Of the literally thousands of varieties grown worldwide, only around two hundred have any commercial significance. Some plum varieties are grown specifically to be dried as prunes, but the majority are grown for fresh consumption.

TREES: Bees are vital to a good plum crop because the trees are not self-fertile. They bloom in the spring and out of every one hundred blossoms, only around four will set fruit. The nickname for a plum tree that is in full bloom is a popcorn tree. The full, white blossoms resemble popped corn.

VARIETIES: Plums can range from marble-size to the equivalent of a mango; however, the average size is around three inches in diameter. The shape can go from oval to round depending on the variety. The outer skin color can be green, yellow, red, purple, and even a strange shade of blue. I like red-skinned plums for cooking and making jam and others for enjoying fresh. Usually purple-skinned varieties are made into prunes. The pale dusty "coating" on the outer skin is natural and called "bloom." It doesn't hurt quality or flavor but is nature's way of protecting the fruit.

PEELING: When I use plums, I never peel the fruit. I just give it a good wash in cold water before pitting and slicing. The contrast you'll find between the tartness of the skin and the sweetness of the fruit is what makes plums unforgettable.

PORK

BEING A CREATIVE COOK IS A LITTLE LIKE BEING A JUGGLER. YOU HAVE TO THINK ABOUT many things at the same time and concentrate on the other things you already have in the works. For years, Southern cooks have relied on pork to keep everyday meals from becoming ordinarily ho-hum and lackluster.

In the days of old, pigs were an ordinary sight on Southern farms. They were relatively easy to raise and, at slaughter, provided the family with much needed meat that was often cured and smoked. A plus was that pigs did not require the constant work or equipment of something like a dairy herd, nor as much land.

Today, Southern cooks turn to pork for very different reasons than our ancestors did. Most of us love to prepare meals fit for a king, but we don't want to pay the proverbial "king's ransom" to do so.

You've probably heard the old cliché that reminds us "you can't make a silk purse out of a sow's ear." That saying was meant to drive home the point that some things you're just stuck with and you can't change no matter how hard you try. That's certainly not the case with pork when it comes to the kitchen.

While a lovely pork roast, tenderloin, or loin instantly elevates dinner to elegant, even inexpensive cuts of pork can be transformed into a delectable meal that is extremely friendly to your food budget. That's the beauty of pork... it isn't stuck in the rut from which you bought it. With just a bit of effort on your part, you'll have your family eating high on the hog in no time flat!

Nutrition: Today's pork is much leaner than the pork of our grandparent's day. It is an important source of protein and iron. It is unexcelled in thiamine content (a B vitamin) and a good source of the mineral, zinc. Varying cuts have varying calorie counts. That is also influenced by how the meat was cooked. A three-ounce grilled portion has around one hundred ninety eight calories.

Purchasing: As a general rule, remember that boneless cuts have little waste and provide a great value for your dollar. For a one-pound boneless cut, you can feed four. Cuts with some bone provide from two or three servings per pound. Those with a large amount of bone provide a little over one serving per pound.

Storage: Fresh pork should be stored in the bottom of your refrigerator at all times. Use within a couple of days for the best quality, or freeze it for longer storage. Larger pieces have the longest shelf life in the freezer. A pork roast will keep up to one year, but cut chops should be used within six months of freezing.

GRILLED HERB-CRUSTED PORK ROAST

This is the recipe I pull out every year when the weather just begins to turn cool. It allows me to snip the remainder of my herb garden for the full-flavored crust.

YIELD: 8 SERVINGS

1 (4- to 4½-pound) pork loin roast, trimmed

2 teaspoons kosher salt

1 teaspoon black pepper

4 garlic cloves, minced

2 tablespoons olive oil

1 tablespoon chopped fresh thyme

1 tablespoon chopped fresh parsley

1 tablespoon chopped fresh rosemary or oregano

Soak four (10-inch) pieces of kitchen twine in water for at least 1 hour before grilling. Tie the pork in 3-inch intervals with the soaked twine. Sprinkle all over with the salt and pepper.

In a small bowl, mash together the garlic, oil, thyme, parsley, and rosemary with a pestle about 1 minute to release the herb flavor. Rub over the pork and set aside.

Bring one side of the grill to medium-high heat, around 375°F. Place the pork on the hot side, cover, and grill 9 minutes on each side. Move the pork to the unlit side of the grill. Cover and grill 45 minutes, or until a meat thermometer inserted in the center registers 155°F.

Cover and let stand 15 minutes before slicing. Serve warm.

MAPLE-CURED PORK LOIN

This might be the juiciest pork loin you'll ever enjoy. A maple syrup and balsamic vinegar mixture is injected into the meat prior to roasting. The result is a slightly sweet, tangy-flavored pork that is worthy for any guests.

YIELD: 10 TO 12 SERVINGS

½ cup packed brown sugar

¼ cup kosher salt

¼ cup black pepper

1 (4-pound) pork loin

½ cup balsamic vinegar

1 cup maple syrup

In a medium bowl, mix together the brown sugar, salt, and pepper. Rub all over the pork. Cover and refrigerate overnight.

Bring the pork to room temperature 15 minutes and place in a shallow roasting pan. Preheat the oven to 325°F.

In a small bowl, whisk together the vinegar and syrup. Inject into the pork. Roast 90 minutes, uncovered, or until a meat thermometer registers 160°F (medium) when inserted in the thickest part. Let stand 10 minutes before slicing and serving.

PERFECT ROASTED PORK LOIN

Slices of bacon wrapped around the pork serve as an automatic baster for the meat.

YIELD: 8 SERVINGS

2 teaspoons sugar

1 teaspoon coarsely ground black pepper

1 teaspoon sea salt

½ teaspoon ground coriander

½ teaspoon ground cumin

1 (2-pound) pork tenderloin

4 slices bacon

1 tablespoon vegetable oil

1 tablespoon balsamic vinegar

In a small bowl, combine the sugar, pepper, salt, coriander, and cumin. Rub on all sides of the pork, and then wrap tightly with plastic wrap. Refrigerate at least 4 hours or overnight.

Soak four pieces of 10-inch kitchen twine in water at least 1 hour before roasting. Preheat the oven to 375°F. Lightly grease a 13 x 9-inch baking dish.

Tie the pork with the twine every 4 inches. Tuck the thinner tail ends underneath for uniform thickness. Wrap the bacon slices around the pork between the string and tuck underneath. Place on the prepared dish.

In a small bowl, combine the oil and vinegar. Brush on the pork. Roast 1 hour, or until the pork reaches the desired doneness (around 160°F for medium). Let stand 10 minutes before slicing. Serve warm.

TERMS: The pork industry has specific production terminology. For instance, a boar is a male hog. A gilt is a young female that has not had its first litter. A sow is a young female that has had at least one litter. Gestation is the amount between breeding and pregnancy, which is known as farrowing. Gestation runs around 114 days in hogs. A feeder pig is a young, weaned pig that weighs between 30 and 90 pounds. As a general rule, the terms hog and pig are used interchangeably.

PORK MEDALLIONS WITH MUSHROOM SAUCE

This fancy-looking dish is actually ready in a jiffy. Serve with mashed potatoes and fresh green beans.

YIELD: 4 SERVINGS

1 pound pork tenderloin

¾ teaspoon black pepper

2 cups sliced fresh mushrooms

1 cup beef stock

4 teaspoons lemon juice

2 teaspoons brown sugar

2 teaspoons Dijon mustard

⅛ teaspoon salt

2 tablespoons water

1 tablespoon cornstarch

Slice the pork crosswise into eight medallions. Place each slice between two pieces of plastic wrap and pound lightly with a meat mallet to flatten to ½ inch thick. Remove the plastic wrap and season with the pepper.

Lightly grease a large nonstick skillet and place over medium heat.

Add the medallions and cook 3 minutes on each side. Drain on paper towels and cover with aluminum foil to keep warm.

In the same skillet, cook the mushrooms 3 minutes, stirring occasionally. Add the stock, lemon juice, brown sugar, mustard, and salt. Scrape up any remaining meat bits with the back of a wooden spoon. Bring the mixture to a boil and then reduce the heat to low. Simmer, uncovered, 5 minutes.

In a small bowl, combine the water and cornstarch. Stir into the mushroom mixture. Cook 2 minutes longer, stirring constantly until thick and bubbly. Add the medallions and heat through. Serve warm.

PORK SANDWICHES WITH ROSEMARY MAYONNAISE

Pull out the slow cooker for this pulled pork recipe. If rosemary is a bit too pungent for your liking, use oregano.

YIELD: 8 SERVINGS

2 cups canned chopped tomatoes, drained

1 tablespoon brown sugar

1 tablespoon chili powder

3 tablespoons red wine vinegar

3 tablespoons adobo sauce (purée of chile peppers, herbs, and vinegar)

1 tablespoon honey

4 garlic cloves, peeled and divided

4$\frac{1}{2}$ pounds pork shoulder

$\frac{1}{2}$ cup mayonnaise

1 tablespoon fresh rosemary

1 tablespoon lemon juice

$\frac{1}{8}$ teaspoon salt

8 sandwich buns

Place the tomatoes, brown sugar, chili powder, vinegar, adobo, honey and 2 of the garlic cloves in a blender or the bowl of a food processor. Process until the mixture is smooth.

Cut the pork in half and place in a 5-quart slow cooker. Pour the tomato mixture over the pork. Cook on high 8 hours.

Meanwhile, mince the remaining 2 garlic cloves. Add the mayonnaise, rosemary, lemon juice, and salt. Blend well and then cover and refrigerate until ready to use.

Shred the pork in the slow cooker. Smear the buns with the rosemary mayonnaise. Top with the warm pork and serve.

SKILLET FRIED PORK CHOPS

Serve this Saturday night classic with green beans, sliced tomatoes, and mashed potatoes with gravy. Leftovers make a great surprise addition for breakfast.

YIELD: 6 SERVINGS

6 pork chops

$\frac{1}{2}$ teaspoon salt

$\frac{1}{4}$ teaspoon black pepper

$\frac{1}{4}$ cup vegetable shortening or bacon drippings

1 cup milk

1 egg

1 cup all-purpose flour

Rub the pork chops all over with the salt and pepper. Let stand 10 minutes.

Meanwhile, melt the shortening in a large skillet over medium-high heat.

Whisk together the milk and egg. Transfer to a shallow bowl. Place the flour in a separate shallow bowl. Dip the chops in the milk mixture and dredge in the flour. For a thick crust, repeat dipping in the milk and flour.

Add to the hot skillet. Fry until golden brown on one side, around 4 minutes. Turn only once and fry on the remaining side until golden brown, around 3 minutes. Drain on paper towels and serve hot.

ORIGIN: Most food historians believe that hogs came to us from Europe and Asia. We know that by 4900 BC, hogs were domesticated in China and were being raised in Europe by 1500 BC. Today there are more than one hundred eighty species of pigs found on every continent except Antarctica.

POTATOES

IF YOU'VE GOT A SOUTHERN GARDEN, YOU PROBABLY ARE GROWING POTATOES OF SOME KIND. Potatoes like it here because our temperatures are so mild . . . okay, hot! Plus, who can have a Sunday dinner without them on the table?

I'm not sure I could name a more universally loved and utilized food than potatoes. Spuds have been a renowned comfort food for decades. Add the fact that they are inexpensive and wonderfully versatile and the ranking moves even higher.

There is a common misconception running amuck that all potatoes are created equal. That's simply not true. All potatoes are not all purpose.

Starch content determines how a particular potato should be used. A tried-and-true rule of thumb is "the more starch, the less moisture." Less moisture results in a potato that is fluffier in texture when cooked.

High starch varieties include the common Idaho baking potato or russets and the blue-skinned Caribe. These make great feather light mashed potatoes, but don't count on them to hold any kind of shape in dishes like gratins. They collapse well and are best when showcased baked, mashed, or in French fries.

Medium starch potatoes are good for roasting, boiling, and pan-frying. These include long whites (known as fingerlings), Yukon Gold, and Finnish Butter.

In addition to new potatoes, other low starch/high moisture potatoes are round reds, round whites, Purple Peruvian, All Blues, and Yellow Crescents. They are the ideal choice for steaming, throwing in soups and chowders, and using in potato salads.

I've offered a potato suggestion for each recipe, but feel free to experiment and find your favorites. And by all means, grow your own!

Nutrition: Potatoes are a great source of carbohydrates, potassium, and vitamin C. They are a good source of B vitamins and have only one hundred ten calories per medium potato.

Selection: Look for potatoes that are firm and clean, but not washed. They should be fairly smooth and well shaped with no sprouts, wilting, or soft spots. Avoid any with "light burn," the green discoloration that is caused by too much exposure to light. Green areas should be cut away and discarded.

Storage: Warm temperatures encourage potatoes to sprout and shrivel. If you buy in bulk, a nice, cool, dark, well-ventilated place is best and they will keep at least two weeks. New potatoes should be used as soon as possible. Do not refrigerate. That will cause some of the starch content to convert to sugar. Also, do not store them near onions. They each give off a gas that causes the other to deteriorate faster.

BAPTIZED FRENCH FRIES

What a way to showcase our continued love for all things fried!

YIELD: 6 SERVINGS

4 russet potatoes, unpeeled
Canola or vegetable oil
Kosher salt to taste

Bring water to a boil in a Dutch oven. Cut two potatoes lengthwise into $\frac{1}{4}$-inch slices. Stack a couple of slices and cut into $\frac{1}{4}$-inch sticks. Plunge the potato sticks into the boiling water and cook 3 to 4 minutes, or just until the potatoes are beginning to soften.

Meanwhile, line a large baking sheet with paper towels. Cut the other two potatoes as directed above. Remove the blanched potato sticks with a large slotted spoon from the boiling water and drain on the paper towels. Repeat the process with the remaining potato sticks.

Pour the oil to a depth of 4 inches in another Dutch oven or heavy pot. Place over medium-high heat and bring to 350°F. Add the potato sticks that were blanched first to the hot oil. Fry until golden brown, about 6 minutes. Drain on clean paper towels and repeat with the remaining potatoes. Sprinkle with the salt and serve immediately.
Note: Fries may be kept warm in a 250°F oven up to 10 minutes before serving.

SLOW COOKER POTATO CHEESE SOUP

What could be finer than potatoes in the presence of cheese, onions, and garlic? One thing: The slow cooker does all the cooking!

YIELD: 6 SERVINGS

6 large Yukon gold potatoes, peeled and sliced
$1\frac{2}{3}$ cups chicken stock, divided
2 garlic cloves, minced
$1\frac{1}{4}$ cups shredded sharp Cheddar cheese, divided
$\frac{1}{4}$ cup chopped green onions
$\frac{1}{2}$ teaspoon kosher salt
$\frac{1}{2}$ teaspoon black pepper
1 cup cream or half-and-half
3 slices bacon, cooked and crumbled

Place the potatoes and 1 cup of the stock in a slow cooker. Cover and cook on high 2 hours. Using an immersion blender, purée to the desired consistency. Stir in the garlic, 1 cup of the shredded cheese, the remaining stock, and the onions.

Cover and cook on low 30 minutes. Add more stock if the soup is too thick. Season with the salt and pepper. Add the cream and cook 10 minutes more. Ladle into warm soup bowls and garnish with the remaining cheese and the bacon. Serve immediately.

HOMEMADE POTATO CHIPS

The old advertising slogan of "no one can eat just one" certainly applies to these chips. It's just the reason you need to purchase a mandoline if you don't already have one. You'll never want store-bought chips again.

YIELD: 8 TO 10 SERVINGS

6 white round potatoes, peeled and sliced into very thin wafers.
1 teaspoon kosher salt
Vegetable or canola oil for frying
1 teaspoon ground red pepper

Soak the potato wafers in a large pot of ice water 2 hours. Drain and sprinkle with the salt. Pour the oil 4 inches deep in a large cast-iron pot. Place over medium-high heat and bring to 350°F.

Carefully drop the potatoes a few slices at a time in the hot oil. Stir with a strainer to keep the potatoes circulating in the grease until golden brown, about 2 or 3 minutes

Drain and repeat with the remaining chips, frying only a few at a time. Sprinkle with the red pepper as soon as the potatoes are drained. Serve hot or at room temperature.

Note: Use a mandolin for slicing the potatoes. If you don't have one, try to slice as uniformly as possible for even frying.

LAYERED BAKED POTATO CHIPS

Southerners have been baking this incredible dish for eons. It is fabulously crispy on the top and soft underneath.

YIELD: 6 SERVINGS

8 white round potatoes, peeled and thinly sliced
$1/4$ pound (1 stick) unsalted butter, melted
1 tablespoon kosher salt
1 tablespoon black pepper

Preheat the oven to 350°F. Lightly grease a 2-quart baking dish.

Place one layer of the potato slices in the bottom of the prepared dish. Brush with the melted butter. Sprinkle with the salt and pepper. (You don't have to evenly divide the butter, salt and pepper. Just give each layer a good brushing and sprinkling.) Continue layering, brushing, and sprinkling. Press down each layer with a spatula.

When finished, brush the top with butter and give it another sprinkling of the salt and pepper. Bake 1 hour, or until the top is golden brown and crispy. Serve hot.

"RUN IT THROUGH THE GARDEN" HASH BROWN CASSEROLE

Hash browns were originally called "hashed browned potatoes." By 1945, it was shortened to "hash brown potatoes" and by 1970 simply to "hash browns."

YIELD: 10 SERVINGS

$1/4$ pound (1 stick) unsalted butter
1 (10.75-ounce) can condensed cream of celery soup
1 (8-ounce) container sour cream
1 cup shredded sharp Cheddar cheese, divided
1 (2-ounce) jar diced pimientos, drained
$1/2$ teaspoon black pepper
$1/8$ teaspoon cayenne
1 (30-ounce) package frozen or refrigerated shredded hash browns (thawed if frozen)
1 (10-ounce) can mixed vegetables, drained

Preheat the oven to 350°F. Place the butter in a 13 x 9-inch baking dish and place in the oven to melt.

Meanwhile, in a mixing bowl, combine the soup, sour cream, $1/2$ cup of the cheese, the pimientos, pepper, and cayenne, blending well. Set aside.

Spread the hash browns over the melted butter. Sprinkle the vegetables over the hash browns. Spread the soup mixture over the vegetables.

Bake 40 minutes. Sprinkle with the remaining cheese and bake 5 minutes longer. Let stand 5 minutes before serving.

RUSTIC YUKON GOLD POTATOES

These are not really mashed. They are more like crushed and the oven does all the work.

YIELD: 8 SERVINGS

2 tablespoons vegetable oil

6 Yukon Gold potatoes

6 tablespoons unsalted butter, cut into cubes and softened

$^1/_2$ teaspoon kosher salt

$^1/_4$ teaspoon black pepper

2 teaspoons truffle oil

Preheat the oven to 350°F. Rub the vegetable oil over the potatoes and place, without touching, on a rimmed baking sheet. Bake 1 hour, or until tender.

With a potato masher or fork, coarsely crush the potatoes. Dot with the butter and sprinkle evenly with the salt and pepper. Gently mix and transfer to a serving bowl. Drizzle with the truffle oil. Serve warm.

SOUR CREAM POTATO SALAD

No Southern summer celebration is complete without this on the table.

YIELD: 8 SERVINGS

7 new red potatoes, peeled

3 hard-cooked eggs, chopped

3 green onions, sliced

2 celery stalks, sliced

1 cup mayonnaise

$^1/_2$ cup sour cream

$^1/_3$ cup Italian dressing

$1^1/_2$ teaspoons prepared horseradish

$^1/_2$ teaspoon kosher salt

$^1/_4$ teaspoon celery seeds

Fill a Dutch oven with water and bring to a boil over medium-high heat. Add the potatoes and cook 30 minutes, or until tender. Drain well and cool. Cut the potatoes into cubes and transfer to a serving bowl. Add the eggs, onions, and celery.

In a medium bowl, stir together the mayonnaise, sour cream, mustard, salt, and celery seeds. Gently toss over the potato mixture. Cover and refrigerate at least 2 hours before serving.

SOUTHERN HOME MASHED POTATOES

It's basic, but the best. I would venture to say that this recipe has been served repeatedly in nearly every Southern household.

YIELD: 4 TO 6 SERVINGS

4 russet potatoes, peeled and cut into 4 wedges

4 tablespoons unsalted butter, cut into pieces

$^1/_2$ cup half-and-half

$^3/_4$ teaspoon kosher salt

$^1/_4$ teaspoon black pepper

Fill a large saucepan with water and bring to a boil over medium-high heat. Add the potatoes and cook 25 minutes, or until tender. Drain and return to the saucepan.

Add the butter and with a potato masher, crush the cooked potatoes into very small pieces. Add the half-and-half, salt, and pepper. Continue mashing until you reach the desired consistency. Serve warm.

PUMPKINS

MY HUSBAND IS A PUMPKIN EXPERT. WHEN I MET HIM, HE WAS WELL INTO AN ESTABLISHED hobby of growing massive pumpkins that weighed hundreds of pounds each. They almost didn't even look real and some of them could indeed have been used to chauffeur Cinderella to the ball.

While watching him grow them, I realized that pumpkins are true vegetable heavy hitters that are tough and rugged like Southern men. Even when growing on the vine, these orbs hardly need any pampering or coaxing to produce. They just need some water and plenty of room to grow. Pumpkin vines could give Jack's bean stalk a good run for the money. They like to take over!

If you are ever in a hurry, you do not want to go and pick out pumpkins with us. George is just as bad as I am at needing to pick every single one of them up. Then we look at them from every possible angle, rub them, and quickly eliminate those without an interesting stem. The perfect ones take time to find, and we've been known to go through dozens before we find just the right ones for our front door.

Because pumpkin plants are extremely sensitive to frost, the South provides a great place for growing those that range from miniature to monstrous. It is considered a type of winter squash thanks to the hard outer skin or rind and is among the South's most celebrated foods with lots of legend and lore.

Local farmers have endless choices that range from round to oval, gigantic to teeny tiny, ridged and bumpy to smooth, and snow white to deep orange. So whether you are in search of pumpkins for cooking purposes or to be a fearsome porch ornament, there are plenty of varieties to carve a grin on your face.

Canned vs. Fresh: If you are used to the consistency of canned pumpkin, you'll find that using fresh is completely different. Fresh pumpkin retains more moisture than the heat-processed canned, so you'll have a product that is not as firm in texture thanks to the higher water content. While that high water amount keeps it low in calories, you may actually prefer a firmer texture. If so, substitute up to one-third of the fresh pumpkin required in the recipe with cooked, mashed sweet potatoes. It provides a delicious flavor and firms up fresh pumpkin in a flash. Oh, and just so you'll know: Canned pumpkin is often combined with squash to give it more body!

Nutrition: A one-cup serving of pumpkin contains only around eighty calories and is packed with vitamin A (the color is your key!). It also contains nice amounts of iron, potassium, calcium, and vitamin C.

Selection: The main consideration to look for in selecting a good quality pumpkin is the strength of that outer shell or rind. Mess up here and you'll have yourself a pumpkin that won't even make it to the Halloween carving. Avoid any pumpkins with surface cracks, soft spots, watery areas, or unusually dark areas. Also, those that are stemless have a greater tendency to become soft and rot quickly. You want to select one that is completely firm, heavy for its size, and has a healthy-looking attached stem.

BUTTER BRICKLE PUMPKIN PIE

This pie gives you two options. You can bake the fresh pumpkin for a true indulgence, or substitute canned pumpkin instead. Butter brickle chips are sometimes labeled "toffee chips." They can be found in the baking aisle of the supermarket and add a touch of crunch to this pie. For a traditional pumpkin pie, omit the brickle chips.

YIELD: 8 SERVINGS

2 small pie pumpkins (about 1½ pounds each) or 3 cups canned pumpkin

1 cup sugar

½ teaspoon ground allspice

½ teaspoon ground cinnamon

½ teaspoon ground ginger

½ teaspoon ground nutmeg

¼ teaspoon salt

3 eggs, lightly beaten

1 (12-ounce) can evaporated milk

1 recipe Single Pie Pastry (page 402)

1 cup butter brickle chips

Preheat the oven to 325°F. Lightly grease a jelly-roll pan or a small roasting pan and set aside.

Cut the pumpkins in half crosswise and remove the strings and seeds. Save the seeds for roasting later and discard the strings.

Place the cut sides down on the prepared pan. Bake 45 minutes, or until fork tender. Cool on a wire rack 15 minutes. Increase the oven temperature to 425°F. Peel and purée the pumpkin pulp in a food processor or mash. Set aside.

In a mixing bowl, combine the sugar, allspice, cinnamon, ginger, nutmeg, salt, eggs, and evaporated milk. Blend well. Add the pumpkin purée and stir well to blend.

Place the pastry in a 10-inch deep-dish pie plate.

Flute and crimp the edges as desired. Sprinkle the brickle chips evenly over the bottom of the crust. Pour the pumpkin filling over the chips and spread evenly.

Bake 15 minutes and reduce the oven temperature to 350°F. Bake 50 minutes longer, or until a knife inserted in the center comes out clean. Cool completely on a wire rack before serving.

Note: Store leftovers in the refrigerator and use within four days.

DEEP-FRIED PUMPKIN CHIPS

These crispy chips are slightly sweet and a gorgeous color. You'll have a hard time keeping up with the demand. If you have the proper equipment, fry them outside for the masses.

YIELD: 12 DOZEN CHIPS

Peanut oil

1 pound fresh pumpkin, peeled and seeded

1 to 2 teaspoons kosher salt

Pour the oil to a depth of 4 inches in a Dutch oven. Place over medium-high heat and bring to 375°F.

Meanwhile, cut the pumpkin in very thin slices with a vegetable peeler or mandoline. Carefully place the slices in batches in the hot oil. Fry about 3 minutes or until crisp. Drain on paper towels and repeat with the remaining slices. Sprinkle with the salt and serve immediately or cool to room temperature.

Note: Store leftovers in a tightly closed container and use within two weeks.

FREEZER PUMPKIN BREAD

How nice it is to be able to make bread ahead of when it will be needed. This recipe makes two loaves that freeze beautifully, so make them now while you have time in the kitchen and use them later when you don't!

YIELD: 2 LOAVES

3$\frac{1}{3}$ cups all-purpose flour

2$\frac{1}{2}$ cups sugar

2 teaspoons baking soda

2 teaspoons ground cinnamon

1$\frac{1}{2}$ teaspoons ground nutmeg

1$\frac{1}{2}$ teaspoons pumpkin pie spice

1$\frac{1}{2}$ teaspoons salt

4 eggs

1 cup vegetable oil

$\frac{2}{3}$ cup water

2 cups cooked, mashed pumpkin

Preheat the oven to 350°F. Grease and flour two loaf pans and set aside.

In a mixing bowl, combine the flour, sugar, baking soda, cinnamon, nutmeg, pumpkin pie spice, and salt. Make a well in the center and set aside.

In a separate bowl, whisk together the eggs, oil, water, and pumpkin. Blend well. Add to the flour mixture, stirring until smooth.

Evenly divide between the two prepared pans. Bake 55 minutes, or until a tester inserted in the center comes out clean. Cool 5 minutes in the pans and then cool completely on wire racks.

Note: To freeze, wrap in heavy-duty aluminum foil, label, and freeze. This bread is best if used within three months of freezing.

GINGERSNAP-PUMPKIN CHEESECAKE

Gingersnaps become the crust for this luscious cheesecake that mimics the colors of fall and Thanksgiving. Canned pumpkin gives it a more dense texture than you would have with fresh pumpkin.

YIELD: 12 SERVINGS

30 gingersnaps

3 tablespoons unsalted butter, melted

3 (8-ounce) packages cream cheese, softened

1$\frac{1}{4}$ cups sugar, divided

1 tablespoon pure vanilla or walnut extract

6 eggs, separated

2 (16.25-ounce) cans pumpkin

2 eggs, lightly beaten

Preheat the oven to 300°F. Lightly grease a 12-inch springform pan and set aside.

Place the gingersnaps in the bowl of a food processor and process until ground. Transfer to a mixing bowl and add the butter. Stir until moistened. Press in the bottom and one inch up the sides of the prepared pan. Set aside.

In the bowl of an electric mixer, cream the cheese at medium speed until smooth. Add 1 cup of the sugar and the extract. Beat until smooth. Stir in the egg yolks, blending well. Measure 2$\frac{1}{2}$ cups of the cream cheese mixture and spread into the prepared crust. Set aside.

To the remaining cream cheese mixture, add the pumpkin and 2 whole eggs. Stir well and set aside.

Beat the egg whites at high speed of an electric mixer until foamy. Add the remaining sugar, one tablespoon at a time, until stiff peaks form. Gently fold into the pumpkin mixture and spread evenly over the cream cheese mixture.

Bake 1$\frac{1}{2}$ hours. Turn the oven off and gently run a knife edge around the sides of the pan. Let stand in the oven with the door partially open for $1\frac{1}{2}$ hours. Remove the sides of the pan and serve or cover and refrigerate until ready to serve.

··

HALLOWEEN PUMPKIN CUPCAKES

You have the pumpkin carved and lit on the front porch but you want to serve something made with pumpkin for the neighborhood party. In walks canned pumpkin, which is a worthy substitute until you can get that carved pumpkin into the oven. These are easy to decorate after frosting.

YIELD: 2 DOZEN CUPCAKES

2 cups all-purpose flour

2 cups sugar

1 tablespoon pumpkin pie spice

2 teaspoons baking soda

4 eggs

1 cup vegetable oil

$1\frac{1}{2}$ cups canned pumpkin

Buttercream Frosting (page 399)

Preheat the oven to 350°F. Line 24 muffin cups with paper liners and lightly grease. Set aside.

In a mixing bowl, combine the flour, sugar, pumpkin pie spice, and baking soda. Make a well in the center and set aside.

In a separate bowl, lightly beat the eggs. Add the oil and pumpkin, mixing well. Stir into the flour mixture, blending well. Spoon evenly in the muffin cups, filling two-thirds full.

Bake 25 to 30 minutes, or until a tester inserted in the center comes out clean. Cool completely on wire racks before spreading with the frosting.

HOLIDAY PUMPKIN ROLL

This is a basic sponge cake that is filled with a cream cheese mixture that will have you salivating. The cake is rolled in a clean tea towel that has been dusted with confectioners' sugar. This keeps it from tearing and maintains the perfect shape. It looks difficult but is easy to master and tastes heavenly.

YIELD: 8 TO 10 SERVINGS

3 eggs

1 cup granulated sugar

$\frac{2}{3}$ cup cooked, mashed pumpkin

1 teaspoon lemon juice

$\frac{3}{4}$ cup all-purpose flour

1 teaspoon baking powder

1 teaspoon ground cinnamon

1 teaspoon pumpkin pie spice

$\frac{1}{4}$ teaspoon ground nutmeg

$\frac{1}{4}$ teaspoon salt

1 cup chopped pecans or walnuts

2 tablespoons plus 1 cup confectioners' sugar, divided

1 (8-ounce) package cream cheese, softened

6 tablespoons unsalted butter, softened

1 teaspoon pure vanilla or walnut extract

Preheat the oven to 375°F. Grease and flour a jelly roll pan and set aside.

In the bowl of an electric mixer, beat the eggs until thick, about 1 minute. Gradually add the granulated sugar and beat 4 minutes. Stir in the pumpkin and lemon juice. Set aside.

In a separate bowl, combine the flour, baking powder, cinnamon, pumpkin pie spice, nutmeg, and salt. Add to the pumpkin mixture at low speed of the electric mixer. Blend well and spread evenly into the prepared pan. Sprinkle with the pecans, gently pressing into the batter. Bake 12 minutes.

Meanwhile, sift 2 tablespoons of the confectioners'

sugar on a clean tea towel. When the cake is done, immediately turn out onto the towel. Starting at the narrow end, roll up the cake and towel together. Place on a wire rack to cool completely with the seam side down.

In the bowl of an electric mixer, beat the cream cheese and butter at high speed until light and fluffy. Reduce the mixer speed and gradually add the remaining 1 cup of confectioners' sugar and the extract. Beat until well blended and smooth.

Carefully unroll the cake and remove the towel. Spread the inside of the cake evenly with the cream cheese mixture. Gently reroll the cake and transfer to a serving plate with the seam side down.

Note: Store leftovers in the refrigerator and use within three days.

PUMPKIN WAFFLES

Serve these yummy waffles after a fall hay ride or in November after you've baked the Halloween pumpkin.

YIELD: 10 SERVINGS

2$^1/_4$ cups all-purpose flour

$^1/_4$ cup packed brown sugar

4 teaspoons baking powder

1$^1/_2$ teaspoons ground cinnamon

1 teaspoon ground allspice

$^1/_2$ teaspoon ground ginger

$^1/_2$ teaspoon salt

4 eggs, separated

2 cups milk

1 cup cooked, mashed pumpkin

4 tablespoons unsalted butter, melted

Lightly grease and preheat a waffle iron.

Meanwhile, in a large bowl, combine the flour, sugar, baking powder, cinnamon, allspice, ginger, and salt. Make a well in the center. Add the egg yolks, milk, pumpkin, and butter, stirring just until moistened. Set aside.

In the bowl of an electric mixer, beat the egg whites on high speed until soft peaks form. Gently fold in the batter.

Pour $^1/_2$ cup of the batter on the hot iron and cook until golden brown. Repeat with the remaining batter. Serve warm with butter and butter pecan syrup.

ROASTED PUMPKIN SEEDS

These deliciously roasted seeds will help you continue to enjoy it long after the carved pumpkin has been discarded and the baked flesh turned into goodies. If you want, sprinkle the warm seeds with a teaspoon of Cajun seasoning for a little kick.

YIELD: 1 CUP

1 cup fresh pumpkin seeds

1$^1/_2$ teaspoons canola or vegetable oil

$^1/_2$ teaspoon kosher salt

Wash the pumpkin seeds, removing any bits of clinging string. Dry on paper towels.

Preheat the oven to 325°F. Line a jelly-roll pan with aluminum foil and lightly grease. Set aside.

In a medium bowl, toss the pumpkin seeds with the oil. Make sure to evenly coat the seeds. Transfer to the prepared jelly-roll pan and spread in an even, single layer. Sprinkle with the salt.

Roast 15 minutes, or until crisp and light golden brown. Stir every 5 minutes to evenly roast. Serve immediately or cool on a wire rack for later use.

Note: Store in an airtight container and use within two weeks.

RASPBERRIES

YOU WOULDN'T THINK A SIMPLE RASPBERRY WOULD BE A SOURCE OF MUCH CONFUSION, but it has been for me. When I moved to Tennessee, I immediately began the task of meeting local growers and getting to know the area, particularly the downtown Nashville Farmers' Market.

That's where I met Randy Boone at Barnes Produce. Randy is like having a talking produce dictionary right in front of you. As he was showing me the wide assortment of Southern produce he had, he encouraged me to nibble away, knowing that one bite was all it would take to turn me into a loyal customer.

That's when I grabbed what I thought was a beautiful ripe blackberry and plopped it in my mouth. Very quickly, I realized what I was eating was not a blackberry. Instead, it was a black raspberry. It was a wow moment for my tastebuds.

Quite honestly, your tongue has to be ready for a raspberry on a level that blackberries do not demand. I had not been prepared, much to Randy's amusement. As I was trying to process what was happening in my mouth, Randy handed me a yellow one to enjoy. My eyes were totally confusing me. Back in Mississippi, we only had raspberries available in a very recognizable shade of red.

From that moment on, I have had a renewed respect for this intensely flavored Southern grown fruit. They are truly jewels and the rich assortment of types in varying colors only adds to the charm.

Since then, I have used those unexpected black and yellow fruits to confuse my own dinner guests, but on most occasions, the familiar red ones rule. Their purpose is clear: Tang is the name of the game!

Nutrition: One cup of fresh raspberries contains only fifty calories. Raspberries are an excellent source of vitamin C and dietary fiber. They contain fair amounts of iron, niacin, and potassium.

Preservation: Raspberries do not dry well unless you use them to make fruit leathers, but are excellent when canned or frozen. Freezing is my preferred method of preservation. Place the berries on a jelly-roll pan and freeze until solid. Then pack into freezer containers, label, and use within six months. There is no need to thaw frozen berries before using. Just place the berries in a colander and give them a quick rinse of cold water. Drain and they are ready to use.

Selection: Choose plump, brightly colored raspberries with no hull attached to the fruit. If the hulls are still attached, the berries were picked too early and will be extremely tart. The same rule applies when picking this fruit. If the berry doesn't readily disconnect from the hull, it's not ready to be harvested. Berries that are past their prime are easy to spot. They will appear soft and shriveled, have leaky spots, and will sometimes show evidence of mold.

"AFTER-THE-OPRY" COFFEE CAKE

WSM is the radio home of the Grand Ole Opry—Nashville's premier live country venue—and is over late at night. Here's the perfect dessert to cap off the night as soon as you arrive home. There are some recipes that you find yourself going back to over and over. This is one of mine. It is easy, beautiful, deliciously different, and just sweet enough.

YIELD: 8 TO 10 SERVINGS

1 cup self-rising flour

$\frac{1}{2}$ cup granulated sugar

1 (3-ounce) package cream cheese, softened

5 tablespoons unsalted butter, softened and divided

$\frac{1}{4}$ cup milk

1 teaspoon grated lemon zest

1 egg

1 teaspoon pure vanilla extract

5 ounces raspberry butter or melted seedless raspberry jam

$\frac{1}{2}$ cup confectioners' sugar

1 tablespoon fresh lemon juice

$\frac{1}{4}$ cup chopped pecans, toasted

Preheat the oven to 350°F. Lightly grease and flour an 8-inch round cake pan and set aside.

In a large bowl, combine the flour, granulated sugar, cream cheese, 4 tablespoons of the butter, milk, zest, egg, and extract. Beat on low speed of an electric mixer until moistened. Increase the mixer speed to medium and beat 2 minutes longer. Spread the batter into the prepared pan.

Spoon the raspberry butter by teaspoons over the batter. Using a knife, swirl the butter over the batter to marbleize. Bake 25 to 30 minutes. Cool slightly.

Meanwhile, make the drizzle by combining the remaining butter, confectioners' sugar, and lemon juice in a small bowl. Mix until smooth and drizzle over the warm coffee cake. Sprinkle with the pecans and serve warm or at room temperature.

"IN A JAM" RASPBERRY SHORTBREAD

Use this recipe when you are in a jam and need something delicious, but simple for dessert or brunch. It looks like it took a lot of time, but doesn't!

YIELD: 6 DOZEN

$\frac{1}{2}$ pound (2 sticks) unsalted butter, softened

$\frac{2}{3}$ cup granulated sugar

$2\frac{1}{2}$ cups all-purpose flour

1 (10-ounce) jar seedless raspberry jam, divided

$1\frac{1}{2}$ cups confectioners' sugar

3 tablespoons water

$1\frac{1}{2}$ teaspoons lemon juice

$\frac{1}{2}$ teaspoon pure almond extract

Preheat the oven to 350°F. Lightly grease two baking sheets and set aside.

In the bowl of an electric mixer, beat the butter and granulated sugar until light and fluffy, around 3 minutes. Reduce the mixer speed to low and gradually add the flour. Blend well.

Divide the dough into 6 equal portions and roll each portion into a 12 x 1-inch strip. Place the strips on the prepared baking sheets.

With the handle of a wooden spoon, make a $\frac{1}{2}$-inch-wide by $\frac{1}{4}$-inch-deep indention down the middle of each strip. Spoon half of the jam evenly into the indentions.

Bake 15 minutes. Spoon the remaining jam into the indentions. Bake 5 minutes longer or until lightly browned.

Meanwhile, in a mixing bowl, combine the confectioners' sugar, water, lemon juice, and extract, whisking until smooth. Drizzle over the warm shortbread. Cut each strip into diagonal slices. Cool in the pans on wire racks.

LEMON-RASPBERRY MUFFINS

These light muffins use lemon to accent the tart flavor of fresh raspberries. You'll love the combination.

YIELD: 18 MUFFINS

2 cups sugar
1/4 cup vegetable oil
1 teaspoon grated lemon zest
1 egg
2 egg whites, lightly beaten
1/2 cup cottage cheese
1/2 cup plain yogurt
2 teaspoons fresh lemon juice
2 teaspoons pure vanilla extract
1/2 teaspoon lemon extract
2 cups all-purpose flour
1 tablespoon baking powder
1 pint fresh raspberries

Preheat the oven to 350°F. Line 18 muffin cups with paper liners and set aside.

In a large mixing bowl, combine the sugar, oil, zest, egg, and egg whites. Set aside.

In the container of a blender or food processor, combine the cottage cheese, yogurt, lemon juice, vanilla extract, and lemon extract. Process until smooth and add to the egg mixture, mixing until well combined.

Slowly add the flour and baking powder, mixing until smooth. Gently fold in the raspberries, but do not overmix.

Fill each muffin cup two-thirds full with batter. Bake 25 minutes, or until a tester inserted in the center comes out clean. Cool at least 5 minutes before serving or cool completely.

FRESH RASPBERRY SAUCE

Think chocolate! This sauce is terrific over chocolate pudding, chocolate ice cream, or a chocolate pound cake. When strawberries are in season, substitute them for the raspberries.

YIELD: 1 1/2 CUPS

2 pints fresh raspberries
1/4 cup orange juice
2 teaspoons honey

Place the raspberries, orange juice, and honey in the container of a blender or food processor. Purée until smooth. Strain through a fine-meshed sieve and discard the solids.

Refrigerate, covered, until ready to serve. Use within two days.

RASPBERRY-ALMOND BISCUITS

I'm not quite sure when I began making these lovely biscuits, but I know I'll never stop. They are divine with chicken salad, turkey slices, or brunch.

YIELD: 20 BISCUITS

3 cups all-purpose flour
1 tablespoon baking powder

$^1/_2$ teaspoon baking soda

$^1/_8$ teaspoon salt

$^1/_2$ teaspoon sugar

12 tablespoons (1$^1/_2$ sticks) unsalted butter, cut into pieces

1 cup fresh raspberries

$^1/_2$ cup chopped almonds

1 teaspoon grated orange zest

$^1/_2$ teaspoon pure almond extract

$^3/_4$ cup milk

$^3/_4$ cup plain yogurt

Preheat the oven to 400°F. Lightly grease a baking sheet or cast-iron biscuit baker and set aside.

Combine the flour, baking powder, baking soda, salt, and sugar in a large bowl. Cut in the butter with a pastry blender or two forks until the mixture is crumbly.

Gently stir in the raspberries, almonds, and zest. Add the extract, milk, and yogurt, stirring with a fork until moistened. The dough will be very sticky.

Turn the dough onto a heavily floured surface and knead lightly six times. Roll to a $^3/_4$-inch thickness and cut with 2-inch round cutters. Place on the prepared baking sheet and bake 20 to 25 minutes or until lightly browned. Serve warm with butter.

Storage: The key to extending the shelf life of these fragile fruits is to keep them dry and refrigerated. Excess moisture causes the raspberry to break down and decay quickly. If possible, place them in a single layer in the refrigerator. Handle as little as possible and gently mist or wash them quickly with cold water just before use.

RASPBERRY CHEESECAKE BARS

When finger foods need to be the rule of the occasion, here's your queen. These are also easy to transport in the pan and can be cut into individual servings on site.

YIELD: 15 SERVINGS

1$^1/_4$ cups all-purpose flour

$^1/_2$ cup packed brown sugar

$^1/_2$ cup finely chopped almonds

$^1/_2$ cup vegetable shortening

2 (8-ounce) packages cream cheese, softened

$^2/_3$ cup granulated sugar

2 eggs

$^1/_2$ teaspoon pure almond extract

$^1/_2$ cup shredded coconut

$^1/_2$ cup slivered or sliced almonds

1 cup seedless raspberry jam or preserves, melted

Preheat the oven to 350°F. Lightly grease a 13 x 9-inch baking dish and set aside.

In a mixing bowl, combine the flour, brown sugar, and chopped almonds. Cut in the shortening with a pastry blender or two forks until the mixture resembles fine crumbs. Set aside $^1/_2$ cup of the crumbs. Press the remaining crumbs into the bottom of the prepared pan. Bake 12 to 15 minutes, or until the edges are golden brown.

With an electric mixer, beat the cream cheese, granulated sugar, eggs, and extract until smooth. Spread over the hot crust and bake 15 minutes.

Meanwhile, in a mixing bowl, combine the reserved crumbs with the coconut and slivered almonds. Spread the warmed jam over the cheese. Sprinkle the top evenly with the crumb mixture. Bake an additional 15 minutes. Cool completely in the pan before cutting into squares.

Note: Store leftovers in the refrigerator and use within three days.

"SPECIAL OCCASION" RASPBERRY CHEESECAKE

Creamy, smooth cheesecake provides the perfect resting spot for red raspberries. The presentation is outstanding!

YIELD: 8 SERVINGS

12 ounces cream cheese, softened
$\frac{1}{2}$ cup plus 2 tablespoons sugar, divided
2 eggs
$\frac{1}{2}$ teaspoon pure vanilla extract
1 (9-inch) graham cracker crust pie shell
4 to 5 cups fresh raspberries
2 teaspoons cornstarch

Preheat the oven to 350°F.

In a medium bowl, beat the cream cheese and $\frac{1}{2}$ cup sugar until completely smooth. Add the eggs and extract, beating just until blended. Pour into the pie shell. Bake 30 minutes, or until set. Cool completely on a wire rack and then refrigerate.

Cover the top of the cheesecake with the raspberries placed stem end down. Purée the remaining raspberries in a blender. Strain through a fine-meshed sieve. You should have around $\frac{1}{2}$ cup of raspberry purée.

Place the remaining sugar and cornstarch in a small saucepan over medium heat. Add the raspberry purée, stirring well. Bring to a simmer, stirring constantly. Simmer and continue stirring until the mixture is thick, about 2 minutes. Cool completely and spoon over the cheesecake. Slice and serve cold.

THUMBPRINT COOKIES

Any flavor of jam will work in this recipe, but raspberry is my favorite and looks great against the butter cookie background.

YIELD: 2 DOZEN COOKIES

$\frac{1}{2}$ pound (2 sticks) unsalted butter, softened
$\frac{3}{4}$ cup sugar
2 teaspoons pure vanilla extract
1 teaspoon pure almond extract
$2\frac{1}{4}$ cups all-purpose flour
$\frac{1}{2}$ cup finely chopped almonds
$\frac{1}{3}$ cup seedless raspberry jam

Preheat the oven to 300°F. Line two baking sheets with parchment paper and set aside.

In the bowl of an electric mixer, cream the butter and sugar until light and fluffy, about 2 minutes. Add the vanilla and almond extracts. Reduce the mixer speed to low and gradually add the flour.

Place the almonds in a shallow dish. Roll the dough into 1-inch balls. Roll in the chopped almonds and place on the prepared pans about two inches apart.

With your thumb, press the center of each cookie to form a well. Fill the centers with $\frac{1}{2}$ teaspoon of the jam. Bake 20 to 22 minutes, or until light brown. Cool on the baking sheets 10 minutes. Transfer to a wire rack to cool completely.

Note: Store in an airtight container with wax paper between the layers and use within two weeks.

Celebrations
May 3 is National Raspberry Tart Day.
July 31 is National Raspberry Cake Day.
August 1 is National Raspberry Cream Pie Day.

RHUBARB

THERE'S SOMETHING ABOUT FOOD DELICACIES THAT ARE AVAILABLE TRULY FRESH ONLY FOR short time periods that sparks inspiration. You can witness it in artist's renderings and especially see the evidence of this obsession in the minds of those of us who love working in the kitchen. Every spring, I find myself that way with rhubarb, the produce world's most marvelous way to mark the passage of winter.

I love the old-fashioned tag that goes along with rhubarb. When a friend of mine recently purchased an old home in the country, we found a nice hearty clump of rhubarb growing out back. Likely, it had been growing there for years. It is a plant that just seems to exude memories of good old times.

Perhaps you were the victim of childhood dares to eat it raw, or maybe you really weren't sure what it was, but chances are, if you were raised in the South, you enjoyed it in pie. While it is rarely a stand-alone star, rhubarb shines when matched with fruits that can serve as a show-off point for this vegetable we use as a fruit. In pie, it quite literally is transformed into much more than a red celery look-alike.

So feel free to salute this unique fruit any way you like. Match it with any number of other ingredients and spices and it will routinely rise to the culinary occasion. And while I use rhubarb in many other ways, it will always and forever be my "go-to guy" every spring when homemade pie begins to call my name.

Cooking: Rhubarb is over 90 percent water, so like apples, it takes very little additional water when cooking. It also cooks quickly, so keep that in mind!

Preserving: The easiest way to preserve fresh rhubarb for later use is to freeze it. Prepare the rhubarb as you would for cooking, trimming it into the desired lengths. Drop it in boiling water for one minute and immediately drain and plunge it in ice water for the same length of time. Then drain well and pat dry with paper towels. Pack into freezer containers, label, and freeze up to one year.

Selection: Look for crisp, plump red or pink rhubarb stalks that are medium in size. If the leaves are still attached, promptly remove and discard them as soon as you get home because they are not edible. Avoid rhubarb stalks that are excessively thin, wilted, flabby, or faded in color. Also avoid purchasing any that have obvious scratches or bruises because those are areas of waste you will need to cut away before use.

Storage: Rhubarb can be stored wrapped in a loosely closed plastic bag in the refrigerator crisper drawer for several days. Give it a sprinkle of water because it loves high humidity. When ready to use, just wash it in cold water. Make a fresh cut on the stem end, pat dry, and cut into the desired size. There is no need to peel rhubarb.

CHERRY RHUBARB CRUMBLE

A crumb topping of nutty oats, brown sugar, butter, and pecans gives this mixture of rhubarb and cherries character. Serve it with vanilla ice cream or freshly whipped cream.

YIELD: 12 TO 15 SERVINGS

1 cup water

1 cup granulated sugar

3 tablespoons cornstarch

1 (21-ounce) can cherry pie filling

$\frac{1}{2}$ teaspoon pure almond extract

1 cup all-purpose flour

1 cup old-fashioned (or rolled) oats

1 cup packed light brown sugar

$\frac{1}{8}$ teaspoon salt

$\frac{1}{4}$ pound (1 stick) unsalted butter

4 cups chopped rhubarb

$\frac{1}{4}$ cup chopped pecans

Preheat the oven to 350°F. Lightly grease a 13 x 9-inch baking dish and set aside.

Place the water in a medium saucepan and set over medium-high heat. In a small bowl, mix together the granulated sugar and cornstarch. Add to the water and cook until thick and bubbly, around 4 minutes, stirring frequently. Cook 1 minute longer and add the cherry pie filling and extract. Set aside.

In a mixing bowl, combine the flour, oats, brown sugar, and salt. With a pastry blender or two forks, cut in the butter until the mixture resembles coarse crumbs. Press two cups in the bottom of the prepared pan.

Sprinkle the rhubarb evenly over the crust. Spread the cherry mixture over the rhubarb. Combine the remaining crumb mixture with the pecans. Sprinkle over the top.

Bake 40 minutes, or until golden brown and bubbly. Let stand at least 10 minutes on a wire rack before serving or cool completely before serving.

"A STALK ON THE WILD SIDE" COMPOTE

You will find many uses for this delicious dessert sauce.

YIELD: 3½ CUPS

2 cups finely chopped rhubarb

2 cups quartered strawberries

1 cup sugar

1 (2-inch) vanilla bean, split with the seeds removed

1 teaspoon finely chopped crystallized ginger

In a heavy saucepan over medium heat, combine the rhubarb, strawberries, sugar, vanilla bean, and ginger. Cook 10 minutes, stirring constantly. Cover and cool 10 minutes. Remove and discard the vanilla bean. Cool completely or serve warm.

Note: Store leftovers in the refrigerator and use within one week.

WARM RHUBARB AMBROSIA

In Greek mythology, the ambrosia was the food of those residing on Mt. Olympus. I must admit this warm version is quite heavenly.

YIELD: 6 SERVINGS

5 cups finely chopped rhubarb

1$\frac{1}{3}$ cups sugar

2 tablespoons all-purpose flour

$\frac{1}{8}$ teaspoon salt

1½ teaspoons finely grated orange zest, divided

1 orange, peeled, sectioned, and chopped

4 cups soft bread cubes, divided

4 tablespoons unsalted butter, melted and divided

½ cup flaked coconut

Preheat the oven to 375°F. Lightly grease an 8-inch square baking dish and set aside.

In a mixing bowl, combine the rhubarb, sugar, flour, and salt. Stir in ¾ teaspoon of the zest, the orange sections, 2 cups of the bread cubes, and 2 tablespoons of the butter. Mix well and transfer to the prepared baking dish.

In the same bowl, combine the remaining ¾ teaspoon zest, 2 cups of bread cubes, and 2 tablespoons of butter. Stir in the coconut and sprinkle evenly over the rhubarb mixture. Bake 40 minutes, or until golden brown. Cool 5 minutes before serving.

GINGER CRUMB–TOPPED RHUBARB PIE

Ginger has always been a popular addition to rhubarb desserts and you'll see why with this pie.

YIELD: 8 SERVINGS

4 cups strawberry quarters

¾ cup granulated sugar, divided

4 cups (1-inch pieces) sliced rhubarb

¼ cup water

2 tablespoons cornstarch

¾ cup plus 2 tablespoons all-purpose flour

2 tablespoons fresh lemon juice

1 teaspoon finely grated lemon zest

¾ cup packed light brown sugar

1 teaspoon ground ginger

6 tablespoons unsalted butter, cubed and softened

1 recipe Single Pie Pastry (page 402), baked in a 9-inch pie plate and cooled

Preheat the oven to 375°F.

Place the strawberries in a bowl and sprinkle with ¼ cup of the granulated sugar. Toss well and set aside. In a large saucepan over medium-high heat, combine the rhubarb and water. Bring to a boil, reduce the heat to low, and cover. Cook 4 minutes.

In a small bowl, combine the remaining ½ cup of granulated sugar, the cornstarch, and flour. Add to the rhubarb mixture and cook 4 minutes, or until thick and bubbly. Stir in the lemon juice, zest, and strawberries. Cook 2 minutes longer and set aside.

In a mixing bowl, combine the brown sugar and ginger. Gently cut in the butter with a pastry blender or two forks until the mixture resembles coarse crumbs.

Transfer the rhubarb mixture to the pie pastry. Sprinkle evenly with the ginger mixture. Bake 12 to 15 minutes, or until golden brown. Cool completely on a wire rack and then cover and refrigerate at least 1 hour before slicing and serving.

RHUBARB BARS

Rhubarb doesn't always have to be paired with other fruits. In this instance, it stands all alone and is marvelous.

YIELD: 12 TO 15 SERVINGS

1¼ cups all-purpose flour, divided

½ cup confectioners' sugar

¼ pound (1 stick) unsalted butter, softened

1 cup granulated sugar

¾ teaspoon baking powder

2 eggs, lightly beaten

3 cups finely chopped rhubarb

Preheat the oven to 350°F. Lightly grease a 13 x 9-inch baking dish and set aside.

In a mixing bowl, combine 1 cup of the flour with the confectioners' sugar. Cut in the butter with a pastry blender or two forks until the mixture resembles coarse meal. Transfer to the prepared baking dish and press evenly in the bottom of the pan.

Bake 12 minutes and set aside on a wire rack. Reduce the oven temperature to 325°F.

In the bowl of an electric mixer, combine the remaining ¼ cup of flour with the granulated sugar and baking powder.

Add the eggs and mix well. Stir in the rhubarb and blend. Pour the rhubarb mixture over the prepared crust.

Bake 45 to 50 minutes, or until set. Cool completely on a wire rack before cutting in squares.

STRAWBERRY RHUBARB CRISP

I have always loved any type of crispy topping. This one is exceptional and the one I must bake every year.

YIELD: 8 SERVINGS

6 cups hulled and halved strawberries
4½ cups (½ -inch pieces) sliced rhubarb
1¼ cups granulated sugar
3 tablespoons cornstarch
1 tablespoon lemon juice
Dash of salt
1¼ cups old-fashioned (or rolled) oats
¾ cup all-purpose flour
¾ cup packed light brown sugar
12 tablespoons unsalted butter, cubed
  and softened

Preheat the oven to 425°F. Lightly grease a 13 x 9-inch baking dish and set aside.

In a mixing bowl, gently combine the strawberries, rhubarb, granulated sugar, cornstarch, lemon juice, and salt. Toss to evenly coat and transfer to the prepared baking dish. Set aside.

In the bowl of an electric mixer, stir together the oats, flour, and brown sugar. At low speed, add the butter and blend until moistened and clumps form. Evenly sprinkle the topping over the filling.

Bake 45 to 50 minutes, or until golden brown and bubbly. Let stand at least 10 minutes before serving warm.

TRIPLE FRUIT SPRING PIE

Let no springtime special occasion go by without making this glorious dessert.

YIELD: 8 SERVINGS

1½ cups (½ -inch pieces) sliced rhubarb
1½ cups raspberries
3 Golden Delicious apples, peeled and chopped
1¼ cups plus 1 teaspoon sugar, divided
⅓ cup all-purpose flour
1 teaspoon grated orange zest
1 teaspoon ground cinnamon
1 recipe Double Pie Pastry (page 400)
1 egg, lightly beaten

Preheat the oven to 425°F.

In a mixing bowl, combine the rhubarb, raspberries, apples, 1¼ cups of the sugar, flour, zest, and cinnamon. Toss well to evenly coat and set aside.

Place one pie pastry in the bottom of a 9-inch deep-dish pie plate. Place the remaining pie pastry on a hard surface and with a pastry wheel or a sharp paring knife, cut into strips.

Transfer the rhubarb mixture into the pie plate,

pressing slightly. Use the pastry strips to make a lattice design over the top of the filling. Flute or crimp the edges as desired. Brush the egg over the top pastry. Sprinkle with the remaining sugar.

Place the pie plate on a baking sheet and bake 30 minutes. Cover the edges with aluminum foil and bake an additional 30 minutes. Cool completely on a wire rack before slicing and serving.

NUTRITION: Rhubarb is one of those rare produce items that is not really high in anything nutritionally. It provides fair amounts of vitamins A and C and only moderate levels of calcium and potassium.

BOTANY: Rhubarb belongs to the buckwheat family, with buckwheat and rhubarb being the only two important food plants of the family grown in this country. This herbaceous perennial is a vegetable that we use as a fruit. Plants are usually divided in order to keep production uniform. It frequently doesn't stay true when planted from seeds.

ORIGIN: It is believed that rhubarb originated in northern Asia. We know it was a common medicine in China thousands of years ago. It was the English who first introduced rhubarb to the kitchen as a food.

NICKNAME: In the South, you will often hear rhubarb called "pie plant" because of our frequent use of it in pies.

CONGEALED RHUBARB SALAD

Most Southerners I know grew up with a congealed salad on the table for any occasion. We love them because they are cold and refreshing … just like this one!

YIELD: 6 SERVINGS

1 cup finely chopped rhubarb
$^3/_4$ cup water
1 (3-ounce) package strawberry gelatin
$^1/_2$ cup sugar
1 cup pineapple juice
1 cup finely chopped apple (unpeeled)
$^1/_2$ cup chopped pecans or walnuts

In a heavy saucepan over medium-high heat, combine the rhubarb and water. Cook 10 minutes, or until the rhubarb is tender, stirring occasionally. Remove from the heat and stir in the gelatin, sugar, and pineapple juice. Stir until the gelatin and sugar dissolve completely.

Cover and refrigerate until the mixture has the consistency of unbeaten egg whites (around 20 minutes, depending on how shallow your container is).

Meanwhile, lightly grease a 4-cup mold and set aside. Fold the apples and pecans into the gelatin mixture. Cover and refrigerate until firm, at least one hour. To serve, unmold onto a serving plate.

RICE

THE MISSISSIPPI DELTA IS THE WESTERN REGION OF THE STATE THAT BENEFITS GREATLY from being in close proximity to the mighty Mississippi River. Some people call it the Mississippi Valley, but locals call it simply, "the Delta." It is a beautiful area of the state, and I loved living in the middle of it when I worked in Yazoo City for a while.

If I had to select one word to describe the Mississippi Delta, it would be "flat." You can see for miles and miles, which makes it the perfect place for growing rice. Yes, rice…that pantry staple that too often goes unnoticed underneath a pile of cooked red beans, gumbo, or jambalaya. Rice is a Southern-grown food.

Rice first came to America in 1647 when Sir William Berkeley planted half a bushel of seed on his land in Virginia. But the real beginning happened forty years later when it somehow ended up in South Carolina, where it was farmed with great success.

There are two prominent theories that battle each other as to how America's rice farming began. Some say that in 1685 Captain John Thurber's ship, which was carrying rice, was blown off course and ended up in Charleston.

A second story is that a 1694 Dutch ship, filled with rice from Madagascar, was headed for England. It got horribly lost and ended up docking in South Carolina. No matter how it got there, it flourished and continues to be a widely grown Southern agricultural crop to this day.

So put your stir fry ideas aside. The South has its own unique way of showcasing this subtle dinner star. And while it anchors other foods just fine, it also can handle dessert or main courses. That's the facts of rice.

Cooking: Instead of water, use stock when cooking rice for added flavor. Rice is fully cooked when most of the liquid has been absorbed. To make sure the liquid absorbs without burning, remove the pot from the heat source five minutes before the end of the cooking time. Leave covered and let stand without disturbing.

Nutrition: Rice has no cholesterol, fat, or sodium, all of which many cooks promptly add to this food after it is cooked. Rice is about 80 percent starch, thus providing essential carbohydrates. Enriched or converted rice contains several B vitamins and small amounts of minerals, such as zinc, phosphorus, and iodine.

Storage: Rice has a relatively long shelf life, which makes it a great pantry staple. It likes to be stored in any cool, dry, dark place. Cooked leftovers should be refrigerated and used within three days.

BREAKFAST RICE CROQUETTES

Picture thick, pan-fried croquettes that are creamy on the inside and crispy on the outside. That's what you have here. They are a regular breakfast treat served with warm maple syrup.

YIELD: 20 CAKES

1 cup cooked rice
2 cups milk, divided
1½ cups all-purpose flour
½ teaspoon salt
1¼ tablespoons sugar
2 teaspoons baking powder
1 egg
1 tablespoon vegetable shortening, melted
Maple syrup

Cover the rice with 1 cup of the milk and refrigerate overnight.

In a mixing bowl, combine the flour, salt, sugar, and baking powder. Add the egg, shortening, and the remaining cup of milk. Mix well. Add the rice and stir well to combine.

Heat a large well-seasoned cast-iron skillet or a skillet well coated with cooking spray over medium heat. Drop spoonfuls of the batter into the skillet. Allow to brown on one side, turning only one time. Drain the croquettes on paper towels and serve drizzled with warm maple syrup.

BROWN RICE CONSOMMÉ

Consommé is clarified stock that can be based on either meat or fish. You will find it in the supermarket by stocks and soups. This one uses beef consommé to add unbelievable flavor to this rice side dish.

YIELD: 4 SERVINGS

2 tablespoons unsalted butter
1 white onion, peeled and chopped
2 (10.5-ounce) cans beef consommé
1 cup brown rice
¾ cup sliced mushrooms
½ teaspoon black pepper

In a heavy saucepan over medium-high heat, melt the butter. Add the onion and sauté 1 minute. Stir in the consommé and bring to a boil.

Add the rice, cover, and reduce the heat to low. Simmer 30 minutes. Stir in the mushrooms and pepper. Cover and simmer 20 minutes, or until the liquid is nearly absorbed. Serve warm.

DUAL-DUTY CHICKEN AND RICE

There is something warm and comforting about this old-fashioned casserole. It is simple to prepare and can serve two purposes. Cook the entire amount as a meal for a crowd or split it in half, freeze one, and use later for a smaller dinner.

YIELD: 8 SERVINGS

4 cups cooked chopped chicken
2 (10.75-ounce) cans cream of chicken soup
1 (8-ounce) can sliced water chestnuts, drained and chopped
1 (14.5-ounce) can chicken stock
1 (6.2-ounce) package long-grain and wild rice mix, cooked
1 white onion, peeled and chopped
1 green bell pepper, chopped
½ cup mayonnaise or sour cream
¼ teaspoon black pepper

Preheat the oven to 350°F. Lightly grease a 13 x 9-inch baking dish or two 8-inch square baking dishes and set aside.

In a large bowl, combine the chicken, soup, water chestnuts, stock, rice mix, onion, pepper, mayonnaise, and black pepper. Stir well to blend. Transfer to the prepared baking dish or evenly divide between the two baking dishes.

If using two baking dishes, cover one with heavy-duty aluminum foil, label, and freeze up to one month.

Bake the large baking dish 55 minutes, or until thoroughly heated. Bake the smaller baking dish 40 to 45 minutes, or until thoroughly heated. Serve warm.

Note: When ready to use the frozen casserole, thaw in the refrigerator overnight and bake as directed above.

MAD GOOD RICE

When I made this recipe once for TV, the co-host described it as "Mad Good Rice" and the name has stuck. Everything is done in the oven. This recipe calls for Beau Monde, which is popular in Creole cooking. Look for it in the spice aisle. It is a mixture of salt, dried onions, and crushed celery seeds. It is often called for in Bloody Marys.

YIELD: 8 SERVINGS

4 tablespoons unsalted butter
1¼ cups long-grain rice
1 cup chopped celery
4 green onions, sliced
1 (14.5-ounce) can beef stock
1 (4-ounce) can sliced mushrooms, undrained
1 bay leaf
1 tablespoon chopped fresh parsley

1 teaspoon Beau Monde
½ teaspoon dried tarragon
¼ teaspoon black pepper

Preheat the oven to 350°F. Place the butter in a 13 x 9-inch baking dish. Place in the oven while the desired temperature is reached.

Meanwhile, in a mixing bowl, combine the rice, celery, onions, stock, mushrooms, bay leaf, parsley, Beau Monde, tarragon, and pepper. Stir to blend.

Pour over the melted butter. Cover and bake 50 minutes, stirring occasionally. Remove and discard the bay leaf. Serve hot.

RAISIN RICE PUDDING

I think this could quite possibly be the most misunderstood dessert. Too many have never experienced rice pudding at its best. This one is wonderfully creamy and aromatic.

YIELD: 8 SERVINGS

2 cups water
2 tablespoons unsalted butter
½ teaspoon finely grated lemon zest
¼ teaspoon salt
1 cup long-grain white rice
4 cups milk
½ cup sugar
½ vanilla bean, halved lengthwise
1 cup golden raisins

In a heavy saucepan over medium-high heat, combine the water, butter, zest, and salt. Bring to a boil and add the rice. Return to a boil, cover, and reduce the heat to low. Simmer 15 minutes.

Meanwhile, in a large saucepan, combine the milk, sugar, and vanilla bean over low heat. Stir well to blend and bring just to a simmer. Stir in the rice mixture and raisins. Simmer about 20 minutes, uncovered, stirring frequently until most of the milk is absorbed. Remove and discard the vanilla bean.

Transfer to a serving bowl and cool at least 10 minutes before serving.

··

SOUTHERN PECAN RICE

Pull out this recipe when you are roasting any type of meat. The pecans and celery give it a nice crunch. It doesn't have a lot of overpowering flavors to compete with other dishes.

YIELD: 8 SERVINGS

1$\frac{1}{2}$ cups long-grain rice

1 tablespoon vegetable oil

1 cup chopped celery

1 white onion, peeled and chopped

1 green bell pepper, seeded and chopped

2$\frac{3}{4}$ cups chicken stock

1 teaspoon poultry seasoning

$\frac{1}{2}$ teaspoon salt

$\frac{1}{4}$ teaspoon black pepper

$\frac{1}{4}$ cup chopped pecans, toasted

Preheat the oven to 350°F. Lightly grease a shallow two-quart baking dish. Add the rice and set aside.

Meanwhile, heat the oil in a large skillet over medium-high heat. Add the celery, onion, and pepper. Sauté 3 minutes, stirring frequently. Stir in the stock, poultry seasoning, salt, and pepper. Bring to a boil.

Pour the hot stock mixture over the rice. Cover and bake 30 minutes, or until the liquid is nearly absorbed. Uncover and sprinkle with the pecans. Let stand 5 minutes before serving.

THANKSGIVING RICE DRESSING

This is not your normal cornbread dressing. It is loaded with rice, sausage, and vegetables, but no eggs. Serve it as a non-traditional accompaniment to roasted or grilled turkey.

YIELD: 12 SERVINGS

1 (1-pound) package mild or hot pork sausage

1 tablespoon unsalted butter

1 white onion, peeled and diced

1 red bell pepper, seeded and diced

1 carrot, peeled and diced

4 garlic cloves, minced

2 cups cooked rice

1 recipe Southern Cornbread (page 188), cooked and crumbled

$\frac{1}{2}$ cup chopped fresh parsley

1 tablespoon poultry seasoning

1$\frac{1}{2}$ tablespoons chopped fresh sage

$\frac{1}{2}$ teaspoon salt

$\frac{1}{2}$ teaspoon black pepper

4 cups chicken stock

Lightly grease a 13 x 9-inch baking dish and set aside.

Place the sausage in a large skillet over medium heat. Cook until the sausage is no longer pink, stirring to crumble, around 6 minutes. With a slotted spoon, transfer the sausage to paper towels to drain.

Add the butter to the pan drippings and increase the heat to medium high. When melted, add the onion, pepper, carrot, and garlic. Sauté 3 minutes, or until tender.

In a large mixing bowl, combine the rice, crumbled cornbread, sausage, vegetable mixture, parsley, poultry seasoning, sage, salt, and pepper. Add the stock and stir until moistened. Transfer to the prepared pan. Cover and refrigerate 8 hours or overnight.

Bring the dressing to room temperature 20 minutes. Preheat the oven to 350°F. Bake 45 to 50 minutes, or until thoroughly heated. Serve warm.

WILD ABOUT RICE

This is a good every meal rice recipe. It pulls in a lot of dried herbs and seasonings from your pantry to keep things interesting. This recipe is particularly good with turkey or fried pork chops.

YIELD: 4 SERVINGS

2$\frac{1}{2}$ cups water

$\frac{1}{2}$ cup wild rice

2 tablespoons dried parsley

1 tablespoon dried onion flakes

1 tablespoon chicken bouillon granules

1 teaspoon crushed red pepper

$\frac{1}{2}$ teaspoon garlic powder

$\frac{1}{4}$ teaspoon salt

$\frac{1}{4}$ teaspoon black pepper

1 cup chopped green onions

Bring the water to a boil over medium-high heat. Meanwhile, combine the rice, parsley, onion flakes, bouillon granules, red pepper, garlic powder, salt, and black pepper. Stir in the boiling water, blending well.

Reduce the heat to low and partially cover. Simmer 45 minutes or until the rice is cooked. Stir in the green onions and serve warm.

LONG GRAINS: As a general rule, rice labeled as long grain has grains that are about five times longer than its width. When cooked, it separates easily. Converted rice is long-grain rice that has been soaked and then steamed under pressure to preserve its nutrients. You will sometimes see it labeled as "parboiled" rice. When cooked, one cup of converted rice yields about four cups. The same amount of regular long-grain rice yields three cups.

SHORT GRAINS: Short-grain rice is fat looking and has a higher starch content than long-grain varieties. It is very moist when cooked, which often makes the grains stick together. Sticky rice is made with short-grain rice.

MEDIUM GRAINS: Medium-grain rice is equally placed between long and short. It is more moist than long-grain types but not as starchy as short-grain rice. It stays separated right after cooking, but begins to clump as it cools down.

BROWN RICE: Brown rice has a nutty flavor and chewy texture thanks to the bran layer not being removed. Only the outer husk is removed, giving it a high fiber content. It requires a longer cooking time and more liquid than you would use when cooking white rice.

WILD RICE: Wild rice is actually a long-grain grass seed that is indigenous to the U.S. and grows in shallow water. Wild rice expands three to four times after cooking.

RUTABAGAS

ALL OVER THE SOUTH, YOU WILL FIND RESTAURANTS LABELED BY LOCALS AS A "MEAT and three." This simply means the place will have an ever-changing daily special that routinely includes some kind of meat and three vegetables served on the plate.

The prices for a meat and three are extremely reasonable, and as you travel in the more rural areas, you'll find a meat and three in nearly every Southern town. All you have to do to find it is ask, or look where all the truckers go for lunch.

At a local meat and three in Lawrenceburg, Tennessee, I was served what was labeled on the chalk board as mashed yellow turnips. I had honestly never had yellow turnips before. I thought all turnips were white.

I didn't want to show my ignorance, so I didn't question it. Those yellow turnips were fabulous and I ate every bite. I vowed that day I would purchase some when I returned to Nashville. It took me quite some time to realize those "yellow turnips" were actually rutabagas that had been misidentified!

"Rutabaga" is not a great word from a marketing standpoint. It doesn't inspire much thought, but I must admit it is a fun word to say and spell. While some are a little lackluster when it comes to this root vegetable, I am not.

I really like them and they have become an annual fall and winter reward in my house. They are incredibly inexpensive and wonderfully long-lasting. And to get to the root of the matter, they are delicious no matter what you call them!

Nutrition: Fresh rutabagas are good sources of dietary fiber as well as vitamins A and C. They have a nutty, sweet flavor.

Peeling and Slicing: Most rutabagas are covered with a thin layer of edible wax to increase the shelf life. Since they must be peeled before using, this is removed in that process. To slice, first cut a piece off the top with a sharp knife so you have a flat surface. Then place that surface down and cut several slices from one side. Now you have two flat surfaces to work with. Place the second flat surface on a cutting board to finish slicing the rutabaga.

Selection: Choose roots that are firm, generally smooth, solid, and heavy for their size. Lightweight ones are likely to taste woody. Avoid those with any skin punctures. Size is not a quality factor, but a flavor one. Small ones are sweet tasting, while larger ones have a stronger taste. That's because the root loses water content as it grows and ages, becoming more pronounced in flavor.

Storage: Although rutabagas can be refrigerated, most people I know don't have any extra space there. So instead, they can be kept in a cool, dry, dark place that is well-ventilated. Humid storage areas will cause the roots to become soft and flabby quickly.

BREADCRUMB-TOPPED RUTABAGA CASSEROLE

Chunks of rutabagas are baked with a cheese sauce while nestled under an herb-enhanced breadcrumb topping. Serve this dish for brunch or dinner.

YIELD: 6 SERVINGS

4 cups peeled and diced rutabagas
6 tablespoons unsalted butter, divided
¼ cup all-purpose flour
2 cups milk
1 cup shredded sharp Cheddar cheese
1 teaspoon salt
¼ teaspoon white pepper
½ cup seasoned dry breadcrumbs
1 tablespoon chopped fresh parsley
1 teaspoon chopped fresh chives

Preheat the oven to 400°F. Lightly grease a 1½-quart baking dish. Place the rutabagas evenly in the dish and set aside.

In a heavy saucepan over low heat, combine 4 tablespoons of the butter and the flour. Cook 1 minute, stirring constantly. Gradually whisk in the milk and increase the heat to medium. Cook 7 minutes, stirring constantly until the mixture is smooth and thick.

Remove from the heat and stir in the cheese, salt, and pepper. Stir until the cheese has completely melted. Pour over the rutabagas.

In a small bowl, combine the remaining 2 tablespoons of butter with the breadcrumbs, parsley, and chives. Stir to evenly moisten. Sprinkle evenly over the rutabagas.

Bake 20 to 30 minutes, or until the rutabagas are tender and the casserole is bubbly. Let stand 5 minutes before serving warm.

BROWN SUGAR– GLAZED RUTABAGAS

Who could possibly resist these sugar-crusted roots? Serve them with ham or wild game.

YIELD: 6 SERVINGS

3 cups peeled and cubed rutabagas
2 cups water
2 tablespoons unsalted butter
2 tablespoons brown sugar
2 tablespoons Worcestershire sauce
1 tablespoon lemon juice
1 teaspoon soy sauce

In a large skillet over medium-high heat, combine the rutabagas and the water. Bring to a boil and reduce the heat to medium low. Simmer 15 to 20 minutes, or until tender. Drain and set aside.

Add the butter to the skillet and place over medium heat. When completely melted, stir in the brown sugar, Worcestershire, lemon juice, and soy sauce. Return the rutabagas to the skillet and toss gently with the brown sugar mixture. Cook 3 minutes, stirring constantly. Serve immediately.

CREOLE-ROASTED RUTABAGAS

There are numerous blends on the market labeled as Creole seasoning. Basically, they all contain paprika, garlic powder, onion powder, black pepper, cayenne, oregano, thyme, and salt. The mixture works perfectly to accent this dish.

YIELD: 6 SERVINGS

1 rutabaga, peeled and cut in 2-inch cubes
¼ cup olive oil

2 tablespoons Creole seasoning

2 tablespoons fresh chopped parsley

Preheat the oven to 450°F. Lightly grease a jelly-roll pan and set aside.

Place the rutabaga chunks in a mixing bowl. In a separate bowl, whisk together the oil and Creole seasoning. Drizzle the oil mixture over the rutabagas and toss gently to evenly coat. Transfer to the prepared pan in a single layer.

Roast 25 minutes and stir in the parsley. Roast another 25 minutes and serve warm.

Note: You can substitute five peeled and cubed potatoes for the rutabagas if desired. Reduce the roasting time to a total of 40 minutes, stirring after 20 minutes.

DEEP-FRIED RUTABAGA SLICES

Slices of yellow rutabagas get brined ahead of frying, giving them just the right flavor to enjoy warm.

YIELD: 8 SERVINGS

2 rutabagas, peeled and cut in $1/2$-inch slices

1 tablespoon plus $1/4$ teaspoon kosher salt, divided

Vegetable oil

1 egg

$3/4$ cup milk

1 teaspoon white wine vinegar

1 cup all-purpose flour

1 cup plain cornmeal

$1/2$ teaspoon baking powder

$1/4$ teaspoon black pepper

Place the rutabaga slices in a shallow dish and cover with water. Add 1 tablespoon of the salt and stir gently to dissolve. Cover and soak at room temperature 2 hours. Drain and set aside.

Pour the oil to a depth of 2 inches in a Dutch oven over medium-high heat. Bring to 375°F.

Meanwhile, in a mixing bowl, whisk together the egg, milk, and vinegar until well blended. In a shallow bowl, stir together the flour, cornmeal, baking powder, pepper, and the remaining $1/4$ teaspoon of salt. Dip the rutabaga slices in the egg mixture and dredge in the flour mixture.

Carefully lower into the hot oil in batches. Fry around 4 minutes, or until golden brown on both sides. Drain on paper towels and serve warm.

GOLDEN MIXED AND MASHED RUTABAGAS

I love to mix rutabagas with potatoes in order to demonstrate to those in doubt that rutabagas are delicious. The golden hue of rutabagas mixes beautifully with Yukon Gold potatoes. This dish reheats well over low heat when thinned with a bit of milk.

YIELD: 4 SERVINGS

1 pound rutabagas, peeled and cut in 1-inch cubes

1 pound Yukon Gold potatoes, peeled and cut in 1-inch cubes

$1/4$ cup milk

4 tablespoons unsalted butter, softened

2 tablespoons chopped fresh parsley

2 tablespoons chopped fresh chives

$1/2$ teaspoon salt

$1/4$ teaspoon black pepper

Place the rutabagas and potatoes in a large Dutch oven. Cover with water and place over medium-high heat. Bring to a boil and cook 15 to 20 minutes, or until the vegetables are fork-tender.

Drain and transfer to a large mixing bowl. Add the milk and butter. Coarsely mash with a hand or potato masher to the desired consistency. Stir in the parsley, chives, salt, and pepper. Serve warm.

PAN-DRIPPED RUTABAGAS

I'm fairly certain that bacon goes with everything except dessert. This recipe was in my mother's recipe notebook and is my husband's favorite way to enjoy rutabagas.

YIELD: 4 TO 6 SERVINGS

1 rutabaga, peeled and cubed
1 teaspoon sugar
3 bacon slices, diced

Combine the rutabagas and sugar in a medium saucepan. Cover with water and place over medium-high heat. Bring to a boil and cook 15 minutes or until tender.

Meanwhile, fry the bacon in a skillet over medium heat until crisp, around 5 minutes. Drain the rutabagas and transfer to a serving bowl. Pour the bacon and pan drippings over the rutabagas. Toss to evenly coat and serve warm.

Yields: One pound of rutabagas will give you two and a half cups that are cooked and diced. Allow about one-third pound per person to be generous.

TOUGH AND TENDER STEAMED RUTABAGAS

Rutabagas that are raw are tough. Those that are steamed are as tender as potatoes with a slightly sweet flavor. This is the traditional way of serving rutabagas in the South.

YIELD: 6 SERVINGS

4 cups peeled and cubed rutabagas
3 tablespoons unsalted butter, melted
1 tablespoon chopped fresh parsley
1/2 teaspoon kosher salt
1/4 teaspoon black pepper

Place the rutabagas in a steamer basket and set over boiling water. Cover and steam 30 to 35 minutes or until the rutabagas are tender.

Transfer to a serving bowl and gently toss with the melted butter. Sprinkle with the parsley, salt, and pepper. Toss to evenly coat and serve warm.

SEASON: Rutabagas are winter vegetables, so look for peak supplies and the lowest prices from October through March. Cold storage allows the season to extend into the spring, but supplies are smaller. Ruta-Bits are baby rutabagas that don't need any peeling. They are only available early in the season.

ORIGIN: Rutabagas originated in Eastern Europe and Siberia. They are sometimes labeled as "Swedish Turnips" and get their name from the Swedish word *rotabage*, meaning "round root."

SAUSAGE

NECESSITY HAS DETERMINED MUCH OF THE CULINARY TRADITIONS THAT ARE PREVALENT throughout the South. In the past, many Southerners had little, very little, or next to nothing, and the privilege of being wasteful was simply not an option. Sausage is a good example of this because it has always been a way to utilize all the leftover animal trimmings.

From those humble beginnings, sausage has now evolved into a master class of its own. You can find it in a variety of flavors and forms, yet it remains remarkably inexpensive and easy to use. No longer is it the poor man's leftovers, but a delightful ingredient for appetizers, breads, or main dishes.

In the South, the use of sausage has traditionally been a lot like the use of wine. For years, we were taught that a certain sausage item was meant to go with a certain meal or should only be served at a particular time of the day.

For instance, I always knew that sausage patties were for breakfast and should be served with gravy and biscuits. Every Southern hostess knows that sausage links are for brunch because they marry well with fancier foods. And smoked sausages are made for buns or sliced and used in evening meals. That's simply the way it used to be.

But just as wine connoisseurs will serve the vintage they most enjoy during any meal or at any time of day, sausage lovers have begun to move out of their ruts. Look at a Southern menu these days and you'll see that we now dare to be different.

Although I have tasted some delicious sausages made with chicken, turkey, wild game, and even seafood, my preference is pork. This goes back to my deep Southern roots, I'm sure, but it also provides the flavor I crave when just the word "sausage" is mentioned.

Storage: Fresh sausage must always be kept refrigerated or frozen. Ideally, fresh sausage should be used within a week of purchase. Freezer storage extends the shelf life to a couple of months if it remains raw and uncooked. Cooked leftovers should be consumed within three days or frozen and used within one month. Semi-dry sausages may be kept at room temperature for a couple of days, or refrigerated up to three weeks. Dry sausages may be stored unsliced at room temperature for up to six weeks. After slicing, refrigerate and use within one month. Both dry and semi-dry sausages may be frozen up to three months, but expect to have some texture loss.

BATTER UP SAUSAGE MUFFINS

I love these muffins at breakfast or brunch. But be ready. They all but pull people into your kitchen with their heavenly aroma. You can use any flavor of sausage for this recipe.

YIELD: 12 MUFFINS

$\frac{1}{2}$ pound ground pork sausage

2 cups all-purpose flour

2 tablespoons sugar

1 tablespoon baking powder

$\frac{1}{4}$ teaspoon salt

$\frac{1}{4}$ teaspoon paprika

1 cup milk

1 egg, lightly beaten

4 tablespoons unsalted butter, melted

$\frac{1}{2}$ cup shredded sharp Cheddar cheese

Preheat the oven to 375°F. Lightly grease 12 muffin cups or line with papers and lightly grease the liners. Set aside.

Brown the sausage in a large skillet over medium heat. Crumble the sausage as it cooks. When no pink remains, around 6 minutes, drain on paper towels and set aside.

In a mixing bowl, combine the flour, sugar, baking powder, salt, and paprika. Make a well in the center and set aside.

In a separate bowl, whisk together the milk, egg, and butter. Add to the flour mixture, stirring just until moistened. Stir in the sausage and cheese.

Fill the prepared muffin cups two-thirds full. Bake 20 minutes, or until golden brown. Immediately remove from the muffin pan and serve warm.

FIRECRACKER SAUSAGE BALLS

Every year over the holidays, I can count on having these festive favorites served at a party. I head straight for them because I always know they will be gone fast. My version is spicy hot but can be tamed by using mild sausage, if you like.

YIELD: 7 DOZEN

3 cups all-purpose baking mix

1 pound ground hot pork sausage

2 cups shredded sharp Cheddar cheese

1 teaspoon paprika

1 teaspoon cayenne

Preheat the oven to 400°F. Lightly grease two jelly-roll pans and set aside.

In a large mixing bowl, combine the baking mix, sausage, cheese, paprika, and cayenne. Mix well to evenly blend. Shape into 1-inch balls and place on the prepared pans. Bake 15 to 18 minutes, or until lightly browned. Serve warm or at room temperature.

Note: You can freeze uncooked sausage balls for later use. Bake 19 to 20 minutes without thawing.

LOW-COUNTRY SAUSAGE PILAU

Carolina natives understand the importance of this traditional rice dish (pronounced "pih-LOW"), but also know that variety is the spice of life. Sausage takes the place of shrimp, chicken, or okra in this classic.

YIELD: 4 SERVINGS

2 bacon slices, chopped

$\frac{1}{2}$ pound smoked sausage, cut into
   $\frac{1}{4}$-inch slices

1 white onion, peeled and chopped

2 tablespoons chopped green bell pepper

2 cups water

1 cup uncooked long-grain rice

1 teaspoon salt

1/4 teaspoon paprika

1/8 teaspoon black pepper

In a Dutch oven over medium-high heat, cook the bacon until almost crisp, around 4 minutes. Add the sausage and cook 4 minutes longer, or until lightly browned. With a slotted spoon, remove the bacon and sausage. Drain on paper towels.

Add the onion and pepper to the pan drippings and sauté 2 minutes or until tender. Add the water, rice, salt, paprika, and black pepper. Bring to a boil. Add the bacon and sausage, cover, and reduce the heat to low. Simmer 20 minutes, or until the water is absorbed and the rice is tender. Let stand 5 minutes before serving.

MAPLE SAUSAGE-LENTIL SOUP

This is George's favorite soup and my daddy is quite partial to it as well. I'll admit it is not the prettiest soup you'll ever make, but I guarantee it will be one of the tastiest. Leftovers freeze very well.

YIELD: 6 SERVINGS

1 pound ground maple pork sausage

4 (14-ounce) cans vegetable stock

1 (1-pound) bag lentils

1 white onion, peeled and diced

2 carrots, peeled and diced

2 celery stalks, diced

3 garlic cloves, minced

1/2 teaspoon salt

1/4 teaspoon black pepper

In a large Dutch oven over medium-high heat, brown and crumble the sausage. Stir in the stock, lentils, onion, carrots, celery, garlic, salt, and pepper. Bring to a boil, reduce the heat to low, and cover. Simmer 1 hour, stirring occasionally. If necessary, add water if the soup looks dry. Serve hot.

OVERNIGHT BREAKFAST CASSEROLE

If you ever have company coming for the weekend, chances are you will pull out this recipe. It is prepared and refrigerated overnight, with only the baking left to do at brunch the next morning. Add a side of fruit and you're ready to pass the plates.

YIELD: 4 SERVINGS

1 pound ground mild, hot, or sage pork sausage

3 slices white sandwich bread

1 (8-ounce) package shredded sharp Cheddar cheese, divided

3 eggs

1 cup milk

1 teaspoon prepared mustard

1 teaspoon chopped fresh parsley

1/8 teaspoon black pepper

1/8 teaspoon paprika

Lightly grease an 8-inch square baking dish and set aside.

In a large skillet over medium-high heat, cook the sausage until no pink remains, around 5 minutes. Crumble the sausage as it cooks. Drain on paper towels.

Arrange the bread slices in the prepared baking dish to completely cover the bottom. Sprinkle half of the sausage over the bread. Sprinkle half the cheese over the sausage.

In a mixing bowl, whisk together the eggs, milk, mustard, parsley, pepper, and paprika. Pour over the cheese. Sprinkle with the remaining sausage and then top with the remaining cheese. Cover and refrigerate 8 hours or overnight.

Preheat the oven to 350°F. Bring the casserole to room temperature while the oven preheats. Bake 45 minutes. Let stand 5 minutes before serving.

PIG-OUT SAUSAGE SQUARES

You'll have a hard time keeping your hands off these brunch goodies. Just try and eat only one! Use any flavor of sausage you prefer for this recipe.

YIELD: 15 SERVINGS

1 pound ground pork sausage

1 yellow onion, peeled and chopped

2 cups all-purpose baking mix

$^3/_4$ cup milk

2 eggs, divided

2 teaspoons caraway seeds

$1^1/_2$ cups sour cream

$^1/_2$ teaspoon salt

$^1/_2$ teaspoon paprika

$^1/_3$ teaspoon black pepper

Preheat the oven to 350°F. Lightly grease a 13 x 9-inch baking dish and set aside.

In a large skillet over medium heat, cook the sausage and onion around 8 minutes, or until no pink remains. Crumble the sausage as it cooks. Drain on paper towels and set aside.

In a mixing bowl, combine the baking mix, milk, and one egg. Mix well and spread into the prepared baking dish. Sprinkle evenly with the caraway seeds and top with the sausage mixture.

In a separate bowl, combine the sour cream, salt, paprika, pepper, and the remaining egg. Spread over the sausage.

Bake 25 to 30 minutes, or until bubbly and light brown. Let stand 10 minutes before cutting into squares and serving warm.

QUICK-LINK SAUSAGE PUFFS

Warn your guests that there is a bit of fire nestled in the center of these puffed appetizers. If you don't want to bring on the heat, substitute onion or bell pepper slices.

YIELD: 40 APPETIZERS

2 tablespoons cornmeal, divided

1 (17.25-ounce) package frozen puff pastry, thawed

$^1/_2$ pound smoked link sausage, cut in 20 ($^1/_4$-inch) slices

40 slices pickled jalapeño peppers, drained

Preheat the oven to 400°F. Lightly grease two baking sheets and sprinkle each evenly with $^1/_2$ tablespoon of the cornmeal. Set aside.

Place a pastry sheet on a surface that's sprinkled with $^1/_2$ tablespoon of the remaining cornmeal. Cut into 3-inch squares. Cut each sausage slice in half crosswise and place in the center of each square.

Place a jalapeño slice on top of each sausage slice. Fold the corners to the center, slightly overlapping. Place with the seam side down on the prepared baking sheets. Repeat with the remaining cornmeal, pastry, sausage, and peppers.

Bake 13 to 15 minutes, or until puffed and golden brown. Serve immediately.

SAUSAGE SLAW SOUP

This is one of my favorite slow-cooker soups. It is perfect served with Hot Water Cornbread (page 189).

YIELD: 6 SERVINGS

1 (8-ounce) package fully cooked smoked sausage, halved lengthwise and cut into $1/2$-inch slices

2 cups coleslaw mix

1 cup fresh or frozen green beans (if frozen, do not thaw)

2 (14.5-ounce) cans stewed tomatoes

1 (10.5-ounce) can condensed onion soup

3 cups vegetable stock

1 (9-ounce) package refrigerated fresh cheese-filled tortellini

Shredded Parmesan cheese

Place the sausage, coleslaw, beans, tomatoes, soup, and stock in a slow cooker. Cover and cook on low heat 8 hours or on high heat 4 hours. If using low heat, turn to high heat after the cooking time has passed. Stir in the tortellini, cover, and cook 10 minutes longer. Ladle into warm serving bowls and sprinkle with the cheese. Serve hot.

CURING: Sausage is cured with salt, smoke, or both. As you would expect, curing greatly extends the shelf life of any sausage product. In addition to being cured, some are also dried. Time for drying can range from just a few days to as long as six months. As a general rule, the firmer it is the longer it was dried.

FRESH: Fresh sausage is made from raw ground meat and is typically bound with eggs, breadcrumbs, cereals, and/or fat. The seasonings vary greatly and results in sausage that is labeled as either hot or mild. Mild sausage can also be enhanced with maple or sage flavorings. It may or may not be smoked but must be cooked before it is served.

BOUDIN BLANC: Head to Louisiana and you'll find that sausage takes on a completely different taste and look. Boudin blanc is a delicacy that practically commands you to love it. In addition to pork, it has a main ingredient of cooked rice. Boudin blanc is a sturdy sausage that is highly seasoned with plenty of cayenne and enclosed in a casing. It is a close cousin to boudin rouge, which is a little harder to find. It is enhanced in color with pork blood and is a rare Cajun treat.

HEAD CHEESE: Heat cheese is a sausage, not a cheese. It is composed of the meaty bits from the animal's head and bound with a gelatin-like broth. Head cheese is seasoned with a variety of spices. It is typically sliced very thin and served cold or at room temperature. In the South, it is called souse.

ITALIAN SAUSAGE: Italian sausage was so named thanks to the loads of Italian dishes that utilize this sausage, but don't let the name fool you. It has been made in the Southern sausage factories for years. This sausage is made with ground pork that is seasoned with garlic, fennel seeds (sometimes anise seeds), spices, and even wine. It is available in both hot and mild flavors. The hot version has the addition of cayenne. You can use this sausage as is or remove the casings and crumble the sausage.

SHRIMP

GROWING UP IN NORTHEAST MISSISSIPPI, WE DID NOT ENJOY SHRIMP ON A REGULAR basis at all. It was strictly a treat brought to us by friends and family who had been traveling near the Southern coast. We would always get the shrimp frozen and could hardly wait to put it to use. Waiting for it to thaw in the refrigerator seemed to take forever!

I still look at shrimp as the go-to item for any type of special occasion. It has launched many wonderful gatherings at my house, whether I used it as an appetizer or as the anchor for the meal. Shrimp adds a bit of panache to anything and should be married to champagne!

Shrimp are crustaceans like lobster, crawfish, and crab, but let's face it ... they look like something from outer space. They have ten legs and the first pair is equipped with claws. Long wispy antennae allow them to smell and touch. Protruding on short stalks to provide 360-degree vision, the eyes are multifaceted, like those of an insect.

While you'll hardly find a savory Louisiana dish that doesn't include shrimp, it has a cousin that's just as full of hospitality. As you travel throughout the South, you might notice there are several prawn farms scattered across the landscape. Prawns are relatives of lobster that look like a very large shrimp. You can use them as a substitute for any recipe calling for jumbo or colossal shrimp.

I'm partial to this charismatic seafood because it doesn't need a lot of extra help to taste good. The firm texture of the meat makes it easy to work with and it is equally well suited to dozens of cooking methods. The versatility continues in the way it beautifully pairs with a pantry full of other foods and ingredients.

One of the things I've learned over years of cooking shrimp is the importance of knowing when to stop. Overcooked shrimp is tough and sadly is the fate of many a crustacean. Cook just until they begin to turn pink and then get them off the heat source. You'll be rewarded with perfect shrimp every time!

Deveining: The small dark line that runs down the back of shrimp is its intestinal tract. It is generally removed for aesthetic purposes and is very simple to do. Just slit the shrimp down the back and use the tip of a small paring knife to pull the vein out.

Purchasing: Shrimp are sold according to size. This can range from colossal to small salad shrimp. Keep in mind that the larger the size, the larger the price.

Storage: Cooked leftovers should be used within a couple of days. Frozen shrimp should be used within three months for best quality. Always thaw in the refrigerator overnight and drain before using.

Yields: One pound of whole, raw, headless shrimp yields nearly three-fourths pound of cooked meat. That is enough to generously serve two for a main course or four as an appetizer. When raw and unshelled, they are sometimes called "green shrimp."

HOLY TRINITY SHRIMP CREOLE

Creole cooking always makes good use of tomatoes and is a blend of French, Spanish, and African cuisines. The "holy trinity" of green peppers, onions, and celery is found here as well.

YIELD: 8 SERVINGS

$1/4$ cup bacon drippings or vegetable oil

$1/4$ cup all-purpose flour

$1^1/2$ cups chopped yellow onion

1 cup chopped green onions

1 cup chopped celery

1 green bell pepper, seeded and chopped

2 garlic cloves, minced

1 (16-ounce) can stewed tomatoes

$1^1/2$ teaspoons kosher salt

1 teaspoon black pepper

$1/2$ teaspoon ground red pepper

2 bay leaves

1 tablespoon lemon juice

1 teaspoon Worcestershire sauce

$1/4$ teaspoon hot sauce

5 pounds large or jumbo shrimp, peeled and deveined

$1/2$ cup chopped fresh parsley

Hot cooked rice

Place the drippings and flour in a cast-iron skillet over medium heat. Cook, stirring constantly, 15 minutes, or until the roux is dark brown. Add the yellow onions, green onions, celery, bell pepper, and garlic. Cook another 15 minutes, stirring often.

Transfer to a large Dutch oven. Add the tomatoes, salt, black pepper, red pepper, bay leaves, lemon juice, Worcestershire, and hot sauce, stirring well. Bring to a boil, cover, and reduce heat to low. Simmer 45 minutes, stirring occasionally.

Stir in the shrimp and simmer 5 minutes or until the shrimp turn pink. Remove and discard the bay leaves. Sprinkle the parsley on top and serve immediately over hot cooked rice.

CIDER-GLAZED SHRIMP

Something about this dish makes me want to sit around an outdoor fireplace in the fall, maybe sipping on the extra cider or wine used in this recipe.

YIELD: 4 TO 6 SERVINGS

1 teaspoon vegetable oil

2 garlic cloves, minced

1 teaspoon fresh ginger, peeled and chopped

$1/2$ cup apple wine

$1/2$ cup apple cider

2 tablespoons honey

1 jalapeño pepper, seeded and chopped

2 tablespoons olive oil

1 teaspoon chopped fresh thyme

$1/2$ teaspoon black pepper

24 large raw shrimp, peeled and deveined

Heat the vegetable oil in a sauté pan over medium heat. Add the garlic and ginger. Sauté about 1 minute, or until fragrant,. Increase the heat to medium high and add the wine. Cook until reduced by one-half, about 7 minutes. Add the cider and cook until reduced by half again, about 9 minutes longer.

Add the honey and jalapeños. Cook 2 minutes longer. Add the oil, thyme, and pepper. Stir well and set aside to cool 10 minutes. Divide the glaze in half.

Preheat the grill to medium high. Meanwhile, thread the shrimp on skewers. Place on the grate and generously brush with half of the glaze. Grill 2 minutes, turn, and brush the shrimp again with the glaze. Cook another 2 minutes or until the shrimp turn pink. Serve warm with the remaining glaze.

●●●

BEER-BATTERED SOUTHERN-FRIED SHRIMP

Southerners love beer with fried seafood, so it naturally became part of the batter. For this recipe, buy for the largest shrimp you can find with the tails still attached.

YIELD: 6 SERVINGS

Vegetable oil
½ cup all-purpose flour
½ cup cornstarch
½ teaspoon kosher salt
½ cup beer (not dark)
4 tablespoons unsalted butter, melted
2 egg yolks
2 pounds large or jumbo shrimp, peeled and deveined
Cocktail sauce

Pour the oil to a depth of 2 inches in a large Dutch oven. Place over medium-high heat and bring to 375°F.

Meanwhile, in a large mixing bowl, combine the flour, cornstarch, and salt. Add the beer, butter, and yolks, stirring until the mixture is smooth. Dip the shrimp in the batter and drop a few at a time in the hot oil.

Fry until golden brown, about 1 to 2 minutes, and then remove with a slotted spoon. Repeat with the remaining shrimp. Drain on paper towels and serve warm with cocktail sauce.

FROGMORE STEW

The name is a bit confusing, but the dish is a mixture of everything we love about the coast!

YIELD: 10 SERVINGS

5 quarts water
¼ cup crab and shrimp boil
4 pounds red new potatoes
2 pounds hot smoked sausage, cut into 2-inch pieces
6 ears corn on the cob, cut in half crosswise
4 pounds unpeeled large shrimp
½ cup cocktail sauce

Bring the water and crab seasoning to a boil over medium-high heat in a very large stockpot. Add the potatoes and return to a boil. Cook, uncovered, 10 minutes.

Add the sausage and corn. Return to a boil and cook 10 minutes longer, or until the potatoes are tender. Add the shrimp and cook 4 minutes. Drain.

Serve immediately on a very large platter or bowl with cocktail sauce on the side.

●●●

"LOLLYGAG BY THE WATER" SHRIMP BISQUE

Southerners love to dawdle by any type of water. It demands relaxation and lots of sitting. Serve this soup when you need to do just that. It has surprisingly little cream included in the recipe.

YIELD: 8 SERVINGS

3 tablespoons unsalted butter, divided
1½ pounds medium shrimp, peeled and deveined
3 carrots, peeled and chopped

2 celery stalks, chopped

1 sweet onion, peeled and chopped

2 tablespoons uncooked white rice

2 tablespoons tomato paste

$^{1}/_{8}$ teaspoon cayenne

2 teaspoons kosher salt

8 cups Shrimp Stock (page 397)

$^{1}/_{3}$ cup cream

2 tablespoons lemon juice

Chopped fresh chives for garnish

In a large Dutch oven over medium heat, melt 1 tablespoon of the butter. Add the shrimp and cook, stirring frequently, about 3 minutes, or until nearly cooked through. Remove with a slotted spoon and set aside.

In the same pot, melt the remaining butter. Add the carrots, celery, and onions and cook 10 minutes, stirring frequently. Stir in the rice, tomato paste, cayenne, salt, and stock. Reduce the heat to low and simmer, covered, 20 minutes.

Stir in the reserved shrimp and purée with an immersion blender (or in a regular blender in batches) until smooth. Add the cream and cook 10 minutes. Stir in the lemon juice and adjust the seasonings if necessary. Garnish with the chives and serve immediately.

MY OWN SHRIMP AND GRITS

Southerners are as familiar with this dish as Macaroni and Cheese. And like that tried-and-true dish, there are many versions. This one is a regular on my table.

YIELD: 6 SERVINGS

$1^{1}/_{4}$ cups shrimp stock (page 397)

$1^{1}/_{4}$ cups milk

$1^{1}/_{4}$ cups cream

1 teaspoon kosher salt, divided

$^{3}/_{4}$ teaspoon black pepper, divided

1 cup regular grits

4 tablespoons unsalted butter

1 cup diced sweet onion

2 garlic cloves, minced

$^{1}/_{2}$ cup chopped red bell pepper

$^{1}/_{2}$ cup chopped yellow bell pepper

$^{1}/_{2}$ cup chopped green bell pepper

1 jalapeño pepper, seeded and finely minced

2 Roma tomatoes, seeded and diced

$^{1}/_{4}$ cup sour cream

1 pound large shrimp, peeled and deveined

In a large Dutch oven, combine the stock, milk, and cream. Bring to a boil over medium-high heat. Add the salt and pepper. Slowly whisk in the grits.

Reduce the heat to medium-low and cook 2 minutes, stirring constantly. Reduce the heat to low and cook about 25 minutes, or until the grits are done, stirring every 5 minutes to break up any clumps.

Meanwhile, in a large skillet, melt the butter over medium-high heat. Add the onions and garlic and cook 3 minutes, or until the onions are translucent. Add the red, yellow, and green peppers and cook 4 minutes longer. Add the jalapeños and tomatoes and reduce the heat to low. Simmer 5 minutes longer.

Preheat the grill to medium-high heat (375°F). Thread the shrimp on skewers. Grill 2 minutes on each side, or until the shrimp are cooked. Immediately remove the skewers.

When the grits are done, add the pepper mixture and sour cream, stirring well to blend. Place the grits in each serving bowl and place the shrimp in the center of the grits. Serve immediately.

OVERNIGHT MARINATED SHRIMP

This is a recipe I use all year long. It is so easy to make and looks as good as it tastes.

YIELD: 10 SERVINGS

7$\frac{1}{2}$ cups water

3 pounds unpeeled, large shrimp

1 purple onion, peeled and sliced

1 yellow bell pepper, seeded and sliced

1 cup vegetable or canola oil

1 cup red wine vinegar

3 tablespoons sugar

3 tablespoons fresh lemon juice

1 tablespoon lemon zest

2 garlic cloves, minced

1 tablespoon Worcestershire sauce

1 tablespoon hot sauce

1 tablespoon Dijon mustard

$\frac{1}{2}$ teaspoon salt

$\frac{1}{4}$ cup chopped fresh basil

In a large stockpot, bring the water to a boil. Add the shrimp. Cook 2 to 3 minutes, or until done. Drain and rinse with cold water. Peel and devein. In a shallow serving container, layer the shrimp, onion, and pepper.

In a jar with a tight-fitting lid, combine the oil, vinegar, sugar, lemon juice, zest, garlic, Worcestershire, hot sauce, mustard, and salt. Shake well to emulsify and pour over the shrimp. Cover and refrigerate overnight or up to 24 hours, stirring occasionally.

One hour before serving, add the basil and stir. Bring to room temperature before serving.

SHRIMP STOCK

Use this for making any seafood soups, chowders, or stews.

YIELD: 2 QUARTS

2 pounds unpeeled medium fresh shrimp with heads

3 quarts water

1 carrot, cut in half

2 celery stalks, quartered

1 yellow onion, peeled and quartered

$\frac{1}{2}$ cup fresh thyme with stems

$\frac{1}{3}$ cup fresh parsley

$\frac{1}{2}$ cup fresh basil leaves

$\frac{1}{2}$ cup fresh oregano with stems

1 tablespoon dried savory

Remove the heads from the shrimp and peel. Place the heads and shells in a large Dutch oven. Reserve the shrimp for another use.

Add the water, carrot, celery, onion, thyme, parsley, basil, oregano, and savory. Bring to a boil over medium-high heat. Reduce the heat to low and simmer, uncovered, 45 minutes.

Pour through a fine mesh strainer and discard the solids. Stock can be used immediately or frozen for later use.

Celebrations

May 10 is National Shrimp Day.

October 12 is National Gumbo Day.

December 20 is National Fried Shrimp Day.

SO SOUTHERN!

YOU MAY BE WONDERING WHY THIS CHAPTER IS INCLUDED IN THE BOOK. AFTER ALL, there's a wonderfully extensive list of Southern foods that's already covered individually. What more could there be? Well, a lot, actually.

This chapter is full of recipes that quite didn't fit into any of the other chapters. Upon careful examination, you will notice that every recipe in this chapter has a common ingredient of butter, vegetable shortening, or lard. All three of these are considered balms of goodness in Southern kitchens, but it seemed strange to have an entire chapter under that heading. Hence, "So Southern" was born.

Look again and you see another common thread that runs through this chapter. Most of the recipes help satisfy our prevalent Southern sweet tooth. In addition to basics, such as pie pastry and frosting, you'll find my family's favorite desserts. It is a salute to simplicity and basic Southern baking.

BUTTERCREAM FROSTING

This frosting has been around for years, but nothing can beat it on cakes or cupcakes. You can tint it easily with food coloring, if desired.

YIELD: ENOUGH FOR 1½ DOZEN CUPCAKES OR ONE SHEET CAKE

¼ pound (1 stick) unsalted butter, softened
3 to 4 cups confectioners' sugar
¼ cup milk
½ teaspoon pure vanilla extract

Cream the butter and 3 cups of the sugar on low speed of an electric mixer until light and fluffy, around 3 minutes. Add the milk and extract. If necessary, add the remaining cup of sugar to reach the desired spreading consistency.

Use immediately or tint with a few drops of food coloring.

ICING VS FROSTING: Although some call it "icing," in the South, we call it frosting. It not only delivers additional flavor to a cake, but serves as a protector to keep the cake moist.

TRIVIA: Butterscotch is a mixture of butter and brown sugar. It is believed to have originated in Scotland. The name is believed to have been a mispronunciation of "scorched butter."

BUTTERSCOTCH BARS

This is not your average butterscotch bar with the chips sprinkled on the crust. Instead, the butterscotch chips become part of the crust. I have made these forever and made it even quicker by melting the chips and butter in the microwave.

YIELD: 24 BARS

1 (10.5-ounce) package butterscotch chips
¼ pound (1 stick) unsalted butter
2 cups graham cracker crumbs, divided
1 (8-ounce) package cream cheese, softened
1 (14-ounce) can sweetened condensed milk
1 egg
1 teaspoon pure vanilla extract

Preheat the oven to 325°F. Lightly grease a 13 x 9-inch baking pan and set aside.

In a large microwave-safe bowl, heat the chips and butter on high power around 1 or 2 minutes, or until the chips are melted, stirring every 30 seconds until smooth. Add 1⅓ cups of the cracker crumbs. Press into the bottom of the prepared pan.

In a small mixing bowl, beat the cream cheese until smooth. Add the milk, egg, and extract, mixing well. Pour over the crust and sprinkle evenly with the remaining ⅔ cup of crumbs. Bake 30 to 35 minutes, or until set. Cool completely on a wire rack before cutting into squares.

Note: Store leftovers in the refrigerator and use within one week.

CHITLINS—BOILED AND FRIED

This is spelled Chitterlings by those other than Southerners and is a common use of the intestines of pigs. They are sold only partially cleaned and must be cleaned again before using. The aroma can be pungent, so make sure your exhaust fan is on high or cook them outside. You can use the same boiling instructions for pig's feet.

YIELD: 6 SERVINGS

5 pounds chitterlings (if frozen, thawed)

1 cup cider vinegar

2 white onions, peeled and cut in wedges

1 green bell pepper, seeded and cut in large chunks

3 bay leaves

3 garlic cloves, peeled

1 teaspoon salt

$^1/_2$ teaspoon black pepper

Hot sauce

Using a soft brush, clean the chitterlings thoroughly and rinse in several changes of cold water. Cut in 2-inch pieces and place in a Dutch oven.

Add the vinegar and enough water to completely cover. Place over high heat. Add the onions, pepper, bay leaves, garlic, salt, and pepper. Bring to a boil and reduce the heat to low. Simmer 3 hours or until the chitterlings are tender. Drain well and serve immediately with hot sauce.

Note: For fried chitlins, cut the boiled chitterlings into quarter-sized pieces. Place a lightly beaten egg in a shallow dish and a cup of all-purpose flour or crushed saltine crackers in a separate shallow dish. Pour vegetable oil to a depth of one-inch in a Dutch oven. Place over medium-high heat and bring to 375°F. Dip the chitterlings in the egg and then dredge in the flour. Fry 1 minute or until golden brown. Drain on paper towels and serve warm.

TRIVIA: During pre-Civil War days, Southern slaves were given the pig intestines, pig's feet, and hog jowls after slaughter. This is where these foods originated as Southern "soul" food because it was frequently the only meat they were allowed to have. A disposable soft brush is a must for thoroughly cleaning the intestines before cooking.

DOUBLE PIE PASTRY

This recipe is quick and easy. It is done in one bowl and can be refrigerated until ready to use. For a single pie pastry recipe see page 402.

YIELD: 1 DOUBLE CRUST PIE PASTRY

2 cups all-purpose flour

$^3/_4$ teaspoon salt

$^2/_3$ cup vegetable shortening or lard

6 tablespoons ice cold water

In a mixing bowl, combine the flour and salt. With a pastry blender or two forks, cut in the shortening until the mixture is crumbly. Sprinkle with the water, one tablespoon at a time, stirring with a fork until the pastry is moistened. Divide the pastry in half and shape into two balls. Wrap in plastic and refrigerate until ready to use.

On a lightly floured surface, use your hands to slightly flatten one of the pastry balls. Roll from the center to the edges with a rolling pin to form a circle about 12 inches in diameter. Lightly dust with flour as needed.

Wrap the pastry around the rolling pin and unroll into a 9-inch pie plate. Ease the dough into the pan with as little stretching as possible. Trim the edges of crust to $\frac{1}{2}$-inch beyond the plate. Fill the pastry according to your recipe.

Roll out the second pastry ball and place over the filled pastry. Cut a few slits in the top for venting. Fold the excess dough under the bottom crust. Flute or crimp the edges if desired. Bake as directed in the recipe.

Note: If at all possible, use lard when making pie pastry and you will be rewarded with the most tender, flaky crust imaginable!

HOT BUTTERED RUM

This drink is better than any electric blanket for warming you up! It has the holidays written all over it. Crème de cacao is a chocolate-flavored liqueur with just a hint of vanilla. It can be clear or dark and either can be used in this recipe.

YIELD: 4 SERVINGS

4 tablespoons unsalted butter
1 cinnamon stick
5 whole cloves
$\frac{1}{4}$ to $\frac{1}{2}$ cup packed light brown sugar
2 cups water
2 tablespoons crème de cacao
1 cup dark rum

In a heavy saucepan over medium heat, melt the butter. Add the cinnamon and cloves. Sauté 3 minutes. Stir in the brown sugar and cook 3 minutes, stirring frequently. Add the water and stir until the sugar dissolves.

Increase the heat to medium high and bring the mixture to a boil. Remove from the heat and stir in the crème de cacao and rum. Blend well and let stand 1 minute.

Remove and discard the spices with a slotted spoon. Ladle into mugs and serve warm.

TRIVIA: Hot buttered rum originated in Europe around the 1700s when rum began to be regularly imported from the Jamaican colonies.

MAMA'S CRISPY SUGAR COOKIES

My grandmother kept a supply of these to-die-for cookies in her ceramic cookie jar that had lemons on the lid. I now have the cookie jar and am always happy to fill it with these treats.

YIELD: ABOUT 3 DOZEN COOKIES

$2\frac{1}{2}$ cups all-purpose flour
2 teaspoons cream of tartar
1 teaspoon baking soda
$\frac{1}{2}$ teaspoon salt
$\frac{1}{2}$ pound (2 sticks) unsalted butter, softened
1 cup plus 3 tablespoons sugar, divided
1 teaspoon pure vanilla extract
2 eggs, lightly beaten
3 tablespoons water

In a mixing bowl, combine the flour, cream of tartar, baking soda, and salt. Set aside.

In the bowl of an electric mixer, cream the butter and 1 cup of the sugar 2 minutes, or until light and fluffy. Add the extract and eggs. Gradually add the flour mixture, blending well. Cover and refrigerate one hour.

Preheat the oven to 375°F. Lightly grease two cookie sheets and set aside.

Place the remaining 3 tablespoons of sugar in a small shallow bowl. Place the water in a separate shallow bowl. Shape the dough into small balls. Quickly dip the top in the water and then in the sugar. Flatten each slightly with a greased glass.

Bake 10 minutes, or until lightly browned around the edges. Cool completely on wire racks.

• •

OLD-FASHIONED SHORTBREAD

This is the dessert I make when I have a lot of other things going on in the kitchen. I always have the ingredients on hand and it's so easy!

YIELD: 16 PIECES

$\frac{1}{2}$ cup packed light brown sugar
2 cups all-purpose flour
$\frac{1}{2}$ pound (2 sticks) unsalted butter, softened

Preheat the oven to 325°F. Lightly grease an 8-inch square baking dish and set aside.

Combine the sugar and flour in a mixing bowl. Work the butter into the dry ingredients with your fingers. Don't overwork.

Press the dough into the prepared pan. It will be rough looking. Bake 50 to 60 minutes, or until lightly browned. Cool on a wire rack in the pan. When ready to serve, cut into small squares.

Name: The term "short" is used when you have a high proportion of fat or shortening to flour.

SINGLE PIE PASTRY

A food processor makes this recipe come together in a snap. Make sure the water you use is ice cold, not just cold water from the tap. For a double pie pastry recipe see page 402.

YIELD: PASTRY FOR 1 (9-INCH) PIE

1 cup all-purpose flour
$\frac{1}{4}$ teaspoon salt
$\frac{1}{4}$ cup vegetable shortening or lard
$\frac{1}{4}$ cup ice cold water

In the bowl of a food processor, combine the flour, salt, and shortening. Pulse until the mixture resembles cornmeal but some larger pieces remain.

With the processor running, add the cold water through the feed tube one tablespoon at a time. Stop the processor as soon as all the water is added. Scrape down the sides. Pulse two times. Remove the pastry (even though it may not look completely moistened) and form into a ball.

On a lightly floured surface, use your hands to slightly flatten the pastry. Roll from the center to the edges with a rolling pin to form a circle about 12 inches in diameter. Lightly dust with flour as needed.

Wrap the pastry around the rolling pin and unroll into a 9-inch pie plate. Ease the dough into the pan with as little stretching as possible. Trim the edges of crust to $\frac{1}{2}$ inch beyond the plate. Flute or crimp the edges if desired.

For a baked pastry shell, preheat the oven to 425°F. Prick the bottom and sides of the pastry with a fork. Bake 10 to 12 minutes, or until golden brown.

Note: If at all possible, use lard when making pie pastry and you will be rewarded with the most tender, flaky crust imaginable!

SPRITZ COOKIES

These buttery cookies were always made by my mother during the holidays. They take on fanciful shapes thanks to a cookie press. The cookies can be decorated with sprinkles or the dough can be tinted with food coloring. I cannot make it through the holidays without these cookies!

YIELD: ABOUT 6 DOZEN COOKIES

$^3/_4$ pound (3 sticks) unsalted butter, softened

1 cup sugar

1 egg

1 teaspoon pure almond or vanilla extract

$3^1/_2$ cups all-purpose flour

Colored sugar or sprinkles

Preheat the oven to 375°F.

In the bowl of an electric mixer, cream the butter and sugar 2 minutes at medium speed. Add the egg and extract and blend well. Reduce the mixer speed to low and stir in the flour, one cup at a time, until well blended.

Fill a cookie press with the dough and the desired shaping disk. Press 1-inch apart on ungreased baking sheets. If desired, decorate with colored sugar or sprinkles.

Bake 10 minutes or until very light brown around the edges. Cool completely on wire racks.

TRIVIA: The name of these cookies comes from the German word that means "to squirt."

VINEGAR PIE

The story goes that lemons were at one time very difficult to find, so enterprising Southern cooks substituted vinegar instead. You would never guess it. This pie recipe is from my mother's notebook and is divine!

YIELD: 8 SERVINGS

1 recipe Single Pie Pastry (page 402)

2 tablespoons unsalted butter

$^1/_2$ cup sugar

3 tablespoons all-purpose flour

2 teaspoons ground cinnamon

$^1/_2$ teaspoon ground cloves

$^1/_2$ teaspoon ground allspice

1 egg

2 tablespoons cider vinegar

1 cup water

Preheat the oven to 450°F. Partially bake the pie pastry 3 minutes. Set aside and lower the oven temperature to 350°F. Bring water in the bottom of a double boiler to a boil over medium-high heat.

Meanwhile, in the bowl of an electric mixer, cream the butter and sugar at medium speed 2 minutes, or until light and fluffy.

In a separate bowl, combine the flour, cinnamon, cloves, and allspice. With the mixer speed on low, add to the butter mixture. Stir in the egg, vinegar, and water.

Pour in the top of the double boiler and cook around 4 minutes, stirring constantly. The mixture should be thick and bubbly, coating the back of a spoon. Cook 1 minute longer and pour into the pastry shell.

Bake 30 minutes, or until a knife inserted in the center comes out clean. Cool completely on a wire rack before slicing and serving.

SPINACH

FRESH SPINACH HAS BEEN THE ESTEEMED GREEN OF THE SOUTH FOR YEARS, BUT LIKE MANY people I know, it does not flourish well in really hot weather. It is classified as a very hardy cool season crop. In the South, if spinach is planted too late in the spring, the plant will quickly flower and go to seed after developing only a few leaves. That's why you'll see it as a regular on Southern farm markets only in the early spring and late fall.

Spinach grows best in sandy soils, which explains the groans you often hear when it's time to clean it for use. I wash mine until there is no sand left in the bottom of the sink. That means quite a few water baths because no one likes gritty spinach! When straight from the garden spinach is not available, I enjoy the convenience of the fresh-bagged product. Good-bye sandy water and hello freedom!

I believe I could work a bit of fresh spinach into just about any savory dish. Sometimes I chop it up and work it into my pizza dough or let it wilt under a bed of hot cooked noodles. I regularly throw a bit into soups and stews, but my favorite way to enjoy spinach is steamed. Occasionally I drizzle it with some really good balsamic vinegar, and other times I just let salt and pepper be the only enhancement. It is delicious simplicity at its finest.

When local supplies of fresh spinach diminish, I regularly turn to the frozen product as a good and worthy substitution. Don't purchase it with the salty sauce but just plain. It simply needs to be thawed and well drained. I always remove extra moisture by wringing it between layers of paper towels.

So, if you haven't already, it's time to go green! In either the fresh or frozen form, spinach is a truly great Southern ingredient.

Nutrition: Spinach is loaded with iron, folic acid, and vitamins A and C. It contains only forty calories per one-and-a-half cups raw.

Selection: Look for bright, crisp, solid green leaves. Avoid bunches with leaves that are wilted, slimy, or turning yellow. Smaller, tender leaves are preferred for salads. Larger ones are great to use for wraps. Fresh spinach that has just been harvested will sometimes have smaller heart leaves that are yellowish-green because they have been shaded by the other leaves. They are still fine to eat.

Storage: Keep spinach refrigerated in the crisper drawer and use as quickly as possible. Do not wash until ready to use then be prepared to really wash it thoroughly in several changes of cold water. Remove and discard the tough stems and midribs. Dry it in a colander or salad spinner.

Yields: One pound of raw spinach will yield two cups of cooked or eight cups of coarsely chopped raw greens.

COUNTRY-STYLE FRIED SPINACH

I have only recently discovered this dish and love it. My husband (Mr." I Love Fried!") says it's the best spinach he's ever had.

YIELD: 6 SERVINGS

¼ cup vegetable or canola oil
4 tablespoons unsalted butter
6 garlic cloves, minced
2 (10-ounce) bags fresh spinach leaves
¼ teaspoon black pepper

Place the oil and butter in a Dutch oven over medium-high heat. Add the garlic and sauté 3 minutes. Add the spinach, stirring to evenly coat. Fry 5 minutes, stirring frequently. Sprinkle with the pepper and serve warm.

DELUXE SPINACH SOUFFLÉ

I was a bundle of nerves the first time I made this dish. I had seen too many TV sitcoms where the baked soufflé immediately collapsed into a pancake as soon as it was removed from the oven. This one has never failed me.

YIELD: 4 SERVINGS

2 tablespoons unsalted butter, melted
1 tablespoon all-purpose flour
1 cup milk
½ teaspoon kosher salt
⅛ teaspoon black pepper
4 eggs, separated
1 cup cooked, chopped fresh spinach, pressed dry
⅓ cup freshly grated Parmesan cheese

Preheat the oven to 325°F. Lightly grease a 1-quart soufflé dish and set aside.

In a heavy saucepan over low heat, melt the butter. Blend in the flour, stirring until smooth. Cook 4 minutes, stirring constantly.

Gradually stir in the milk and cook 8 minutes, stirring constantly, until thickened. Stir in the salt and pepper.

In a small bowl, beat the egg yolks. Add a small amount of the hot milk to the yolks, stirring well. Stir the yolks into the saucepan. Add the spinach and cheese, mixing well.

In the bowl of an electric mixer, beat the egg whites at high speed until stiff peaks form. Fold into the spinach mixture. Spoon into the prepared soufflé dish. Bake 50 minutes, or until firm. Serve immediately.

GORGONZOLA-SPINACH CUSTARDS

These savory custards are a lovely addition to a beef-focused dinner party. I have tried it with various other cheeses, but Gorgonzola is the best.

YIELD: 6 SERVINGS

½ cup frozen chopped spinach, thawed
1 tablespoon unsalted butter
1 tablespoon olive oil
2 sweet onions, peeled and thinly sliced
2 teaspoons brown sugar
3 eggs
1½ cups half-and-half
¼ teaspoon kosher salt
¼ teaspoon ground nutmeg
¼ teaspoon black pepper
5 ounces crumbled Gorgonzola cheese

Drain the spinach well, pressing between layers of paper towels and squeezing to remove the excess moisture. Set aside.

Melt the butter and oil in a large skillet over medium heat. Add the onions and sauté 5 minutes. Add the sugar and cook 20 minutes, or until the onions are caramelized. Stir occasionally.

Meanwhile, preheat the oven to 350°F. Lightly grease six custard cups and set aside.

Whisk together the eggs, half-and-half, salt, nutmeg, and pepper until well blended. Stir in the spinach and set aside.

Reserve $\frac{1}{4}$ cup of the onion mixture. Spoon the remaining onion mixture evenly into the prepared cups. Sprinkle the tops evenly with the cheese. Spoon the egg mixture evenly over the cheese.

Carefully place the cups in a 13 x 9-inch baking pan and place in the oven. Add water to a depth of 1 inch in the pan surrounding the cups. Bake 35 to 40 minutes, or until almost set. Remove the cups from the hot water and cool on a wire rack at least 10 minutes. Unmold and top with the reserved onions. Serve warm.

"IT'S HIP TO BE SQUARE" SPINACH BROWNIES

Don't let the name fool you. These marvelous bars are guaranteed to be an instant hit at any neighborhood gathering.

YIELD: 30 SQUARES

1 cup all-purpose flour
1 teaspoon baking powder
1 teaspoon salt
2 eggs
6 tablespoons unsalted butter, melted

2 pounds fresh spinach, cooked, well drained, and finely chopped
$\frac{1}{4}$ cup finely chopped onions
4 cups shredded Monterey Jack cheese

Preheat the oven to 350°F. Lightly grease a 4.8-quart rectangular baking dish (larger than a 13 x 9-inch baking dish) and set aside.

In a medium bowl, combine the flour, baking powder, and salt. In the bowl of an electric mixer, lightly beat the eggs. Add the butter and beat at medium speed until blended. Reduce the mixer speed to low and add the flour mixture just until blended.

With a wooden spoon, fold in the spinach, onions, and cheese. Spread evenly in the prepared pan and bake 40 minutes. Cool on a wire rack at least 5 minutes. Cut into squares and serve warm or cool completely and serve at room temperature.

MISSISSIPPI FLAT LAND CASSEROLE

There is hardly a week that passes when I don't use rice as an anchor for something. I love to watch it being harvested from fields in the flat Mississippi Delta.

YIELD: 6 SERVINGS

4 cups cooked brown rice
1 tablespoon olive oil
2 cups finely chopped onions
2 pounds fresh spinach leaves, finely chopped
5 garlic cloves, minced
1 teaspoon kosher salt
$\frac{1}{4}$ teaspoon ground nutmeg
$\frac{1}{4}$ teaspoon cayenne
$\frac{1}{4}$ teaspoon black pepper

2 teaspoons prepared mustard

$^1\!/_2$ cup sunflower seeds, divided

2 eggs, beaten

1 cup milk

$1^1\!/_2$ cups shredded sharp Cheddar cheese

Paprika for garnish

Preheat the oven to 350°F. Lightly grease a 13 x 9-inch baking dish and set aside. Place the rice in a large mixing bowl and set aside.

Heat the oil in a large skillet over medium heat. Add the onions and sauté 6 to 8 minutes or until soft. Add the spinach, garlic, and salt. Cook 5 minutes more, stirring frequently. Add to the rice, stirring well.

Stir in the nutmeg, cayenne, pepper, mustard, half of the sunflower seeds, eggs, milk, and cheese. Spread evenly in the prepared pan and sprinkle with the remaining sunflower seeds. Dust with the paprika. Bake, uncovered, 35 to 40 minutes, or until lightly browned. Serve hot.

MY FAVORITE STEAMED SPINACH

Ok, here it is … my all-time favorite way to enjoy fresh spinach!

YIELD: 4 SERVINGS

1 bunch fresh spinach leaves, washed

$^1\!/_4$ teaspoon kosher salt

$^1\!/_8$ teaspoon black pepper

Over medium-high heat, bring water to a boil in a large saucepan. Place the spinach in a colander and set over boiling the water. Steam 3 minutes. Transfer to a serving bowl and season with the salt and pepper. Serve warm.

MOCKINGBIRD LANE SPINACH PIE

Muenster was a cheese not regularly found in my refrigerator for a long time. Then I used it to make this dish and I'm a convert. You can use a young mild Muenster or an aged assertive one.

YIELD: 8 SERVINGS

3 (10-ounce) packages frozen chopped spinach, thawed

2 (6-ounce) packages Muenster cheese slices

1 white onion, peeled and finely chopped

1 cup small curd cottage cheese

3 eggs, lightly beaten

$^1\!/_3$ cup grated Parmesan cheese

$^1\!/_2$ teaspoon salt

$^1\!/_4$ teaspoon black pepper

Pimiento strips for garnish

Preheat the oven to 350°F. Drain the spinach well between paper towels, squeezing to remove the excess moisture. Set aside.

Cut 3 cheese slices into small triangles and set aside. Cover the bottom and sides of a lightly greased 9-inch pie plate with the remaining slices, overlapping as needed.

In a medium bowl combine the spinach, onion, cottage cheese, eggs, Parmesan, salt, and pepper. Spoon into the cheese-lined pie plate. Bake 45 minutes, or until set. Immediately top with reserved cheese triangles. Cool 10 minutes on a wire rack. Garnish with the pimiento strips and serve warm.

SPINACH AND ARTICHOKES IN PUFF PASTRY

These flaky spirals of spinach and artichokes can be made ahead and baked at the last minute. They hold well, which means if your dinner guests are late, these pastries are just as good served at room temperature.

YIELD: 24 APPETIZERS

1 (10-ounce) package frozen chopped spinach, thawed

1 (14-ounce) can artichoke hearts, drained and chopped

$\frac{1}{2}$ cup mayonnaise

$\frac{1}{2}$ cup grated Parmesan cheese

1 teaspoon onion powder

1 teaspoon garlic powder

$\frac{1}{2}$ teaspoon black pepper

1 (17.3-ounce) package frozen puff pastry, thawed

Drain the spinach well, pressing between layers of paper towels to remove the excess moisture. In a large bowl, stir together the spinach, artichoke hearts, mayonnaise, cheese, onion powder, garlic powder, and pepper.

Unfold the pastry sheets and spread half of the spinach mixture evenly over each sheet, leaving a $\frac{1}{4}$-inch border. Roll up jelly-roll style, pressing to seal the seams.

Wrap in plastic wrap and freeze 25 minutes. Meanwhile, preheat the oven to 400°F and lightly grease 2 baking sheets. Cut the rolls into $\frac{1}{2}$-inch-thick slices and place on the prepared baking sheets. Bake 20 minutes, or until golden brown. Serve warm.

Note: Uncut rolls may be frozen up to three months. Thaw overnight in the refrigerator before proceeding to bake and serve.

SPINACH GARDEN BURGERS

The addition of spinach keeps these burgers nice and juicy.

YIELD: 8 SERVINGS

1 (10-ounce) package frozen spinach leaves, thawed

2 pounds ground beef

$\frac{1}{2}$ cup plain dry breadcrumbs

$\frac{1}{2}$ cup shredded Swiss cheese

1 teaspoon garlic powder

$\frac{1}{8}$ teaspoon kosher salt

$\frac{1}{8}$ teaspoon black pepper

Mayonnaise

8 hamburger buns

Sliced tomatoes

Preheat the grill to medium-high heat (375°F to 400°F).

Meanwhile, drain the spinach between layers of paper towels, squeezing to remove the excess moisture. Place in a large bowl and add the beef, breadcrumbs, cheese, garlic powder, salt, and pepper. Shape into 8 patties.

Grill, covered, 6 minutes on each side, or until the beef is no longer pink. Serve on mayonnaise-smeared buns with sliced tomatoes.

Celebrations
May is National Salad Month.
Every Year: March 26 is National Spinach Day.

SPOON BREAD

IF YOU HAVEN'T SPENT MUCH TIME IN THE SOUTH, YOU MIGHT NOT BE FAMILIAR WITH A VERY common side dish we called spoon bread. It is not a dressing, nor is it really a type of cornbread that hasn't been baked quite long enough. Spoon bread has a unique identity of its own, and it hardly resembles bread at all.

Spoon bread is only slightly similar to cornbread in that they both use cornmeal. Spoon bread has a softer, moister, sometimes more pudding-like texture than grainy, dense cornbread. In fact it's so soft, a spoon is often required for both serving and enjoying the dish, hence the name.

The reason for the difference between spoon bread and cornbread has a lot to do with how it is baked. Rather than using seasoned cast-iron skillets in a high-temperature oven, spoon bread is baked in a casserole dish in a moderate oven. This, along with several wet ingredients helps keep it soft instead of crispy and bread-like. You would have a really hard time trying to cut it into wedges or squares.

Like most traditional Southern foods, the dish existed long before it was ever put into print, which was 1850 in "The Practical Cook Book." It is believed that spoon bread came from a Native American porridge dish called "suppone" or "suppawn."

By the Revolutionary War, it was a somewhat regularly served dish, but after the Civil War, it exploded and became a staple of the Southern table. The popularity continues today with loads of enhancements as flavoring options.

Spoon bread is usually served with any type of meat. In some of the more "new South" recipes, seafood or meat is included in the spoon bread, which makes it perfect for serving alongside a salad. Either way, get out your spoons and get ready for a Southern treat!

Baking: Spoon bread will yield the best consistency if you bake it in a glass or ceramic casserole or baking dish. Glass is a good insulator, so it will keep the spoon bread warm for quite some time. I like the ones that come with a heavy-duty plastic lid so you can stack other items on top of it in the refrigerator after the leftovers are stored.

Resting: Spoon bread is not like a soufflé that must be served immediately when removed from the oven. Instead, it benefits from resting a few minutes after baking in order for the dish to firm up a bit and not be soupy. Let spoon bread rest a minimum of five minutes after coming out of the oven and up to ten minutes is fine.

"BELLS-ARE-RINGING" SPOON BREAD

Red and green bell peppers give this spoon bread a holiday look. It is a great alternative to traditional dressing.

YIELD: 8 TO 10 SERVINGS

1 recipe Old-Fashioned Cornbread (page 195), cooked and cooled

2 teaspoons cumin seeds

4 tablespoons unsalted butter

2 cups finely chopped celery

$^1/_2$ cup chopped onion

1 red bell pepper, seeded and chopped

1 green bell pepper, seeded and chopped

1 garlic clove, minced

1 (8-ounce) package herb-seasoned stuffing mix

2 (10.5-ounce) cans chicken stock

2 cups water

2 eggs, lightly beaten

$^1/_2$ teaspoon salt

$^1/_2$ teaspoon red pepper

Preheat the oven to 350°F. Lightly grease a 13 x 9-inch baking dish and set aside. Crumble the cornbread in a large mixing bowl and set aside.

Place the cumin seeds in a large skillet over medium heat. Stir constantly until the seeds are fragrant and lightly browned, about 3 minutes. Transfer to a small bowl to cool, crush, and set aside.

In the same skillet, melt the butter over medium heat. Add the celery, onions, red pepper, green pepper, and garlic. Cook 4 minutes, stirring constantly.

Add the pepper mixture to the cornbread, along with the stuffing mix, stock, water, eggs, salt, and pepper. Stir well to blend and evenly mix. Transfer to the prepared baking dish. Bake 1 hour 15 minutes, or until lightly browned. Let stand 5 minutes before serving.

BUTTERMILK SPOON BREAD

Southerners love their buttermilk. It provides a nice tang to this spoon bread recipe. I think it is marvelous with country ham.

YIELD: 8 TO 10 SERVINGS

7 eggs

$^1/_2$ cup cream

4 cups water

$1^1/_2$ cups buttermilk

$^1/_4$ pound (1 stick) unsalted butter, softened

$1^1/_2$ teaspoons salt

$^1/_2$ teaspoon white pepper

2 cups self-rising cornmeal

Preheat the oven to 350°F. Lightly grease a 13 x 9-inch baking dish and set aside.

In a medium bowl, whisk together the eggs and cream. Set aside.

Place the water, buttermilk, butter, salt, and pepper in a heavy saucepan over medium-high heat. Bring to a simmer and gradually add the cornmeal. Remove from the heat and whisk constantly 3 minutes until thick and smooth.

Gradually add 1 cup of the cornmeal mixture to the eggs. Whisk until well blended. Stir the egg mixture into the cornmeal mixture and blend well. Transfer to the prepared baking dish.

Bake 30 minutes, or until a tester inserted in the center comes out clean. Let stand 5 minutes before serving warm.

CORN SPOON BREAD

If you don't have good corn to cut from the cob, you can substitute canned whole-kernel corn that has been drained well. This is particularly light and goes well with fish.

YIELD: 8 SERVINGS

2 cups milk

2 cups chicken stock

1½ cups plain cornmeal

3 cups fresh corn, cut from the cob (5 ears)

6 eggs, separated

1 teaspoon hot sauce

2 garlic cloves, minced

1 teaspoon salt

1 teaspoon black pepper

1 cup shredded Cheddar cheese

¼ cup all-purpose flour

1 teaspoon baking powder

Preheat the oven to 375°F. Lightly grease a 13 x 9-inch baking dish and set aside.

In a large saucepan over medium-high heat, bring the milk and stock to a boil. Reduce the heat to low and gradually whisk in the cornmeal. Cook, whisking often until smooth and creamy, about 5 minutes. Stir in corn and set aside to cool.

In a small bowl, whisk together the egg yolks, hot sauce, garlic, salt, and pepper. Stir in the cheese and add to the corn mixture, blending well.

Whip the egg whites to soft peaks. Combine the flour and baking powder and add to the corn mixture. Fold the egg whites into the batter. Pour into the prepared pan. Bake 50 minutes to 1 hour, or until a tester inserted in the center comes out clean. Let stand 5 minutes and serve warm.

HOT SAUSAGE SPOON BREAD

If the spice of hot pork sausage is too much for you, substitute mild instead. This spoon bread is terrific with a vegetable dinner.

YIELD: 8 SERVINGS

3 cups whole milk

1 cup self-rising cornmeal

2 tablespoons unsalted butter

1 teaspoon sugar

½ teaspoon salt

1 pound hot pork sausage, cooked, crumbled, and drained

4 eggs, separated

Preheat the oven to 350°F. Lightly grease a two-quart baking dish and place in the oven while it reaches the desired temperature.

Meanwhile, place the milk in a large saucepan over medium-high heat. Gradually add the cornmeal and bring to a boil, stirring occasionally. Cook 5 minutes and add the butter, sugar, and salt. Cool 4 minutes and then add the sausage. Beat the egg yolks and add to the cornmeal mixture.

In a separate bowl, beat the egg whites until stiff peaks form. Fold into the cornmeal mixture and transfer to the prepared baking dish. Bake 45 minutes, or until top is golden brown. Let stand 5 minutes and serve warm.

PIMIENTO CHEESE SPOON BREAD

This is a very versatile spoon bread recipe. Sometimes I add a little more cayenne and other times I'll fold in roasted okra or summer squash. It is really nice served with chicken, ham, or turkey.

YIELD: 8 SERVINGS

1 cup water

$\frac{1}{2}$ cup self-rising cornmeal

$\frac{1}{2}$ cup milk

$\frac{1}{2}$ cup shredded sharp Cheddar cheese

$\frac{1}{4}$ cup minced onions

$\frac{1}{4}$ teaspoon salt

$\frac{1}{4}$ teaspoon black pepper

$\frac{1}{4}$ teaspoon cayenne

2 garlic cloves, minced

1 (2-ounce) jar diced pimientos, drained

3 egg whites

Preheat the oven to 375°F. Lightly grease a 1$\frac{1}{2}$-quart baking dish and set aside.

In a large saucepan over medium-high heat, combine the water and cornmeal, whisking well. Bring to a boil and cook 1 minute, stirring constantly.

Remove from the heat and stir in the milk, cheese, onions, salt, pepper, cayenne, garlic, and pimientos. Set aside.

In the bowl of an electric mixer, beat the egg whites at high speed until stiff peaks form. Gently fold in half of the whites into the batter. Fold in the remaining whites and transfer to the prepared pan.

Bake 50 minutes, or until a tester inserted in the center comes out clean. Let stand 5 minutes before serving warm.

SHRIMP SPOON BREAD

I like to serve this flavorful spoon bread with a simple green salad. You can use larger shrimp if you want more impact.

YIELD: 8 TO 10 SERVINGS

4 tablespoons unsalted butter

$\frac{2}{3}$ cup sweet onion, diced

1 (4.5-ounce) can chopped green chiles, undrained

$\frac{1}{2}$ pound cooked salad shrimp, coarsely chopped

1 (20-ounce) package frozen cream-style corn, thawed

1 (16-ounce) container sour cream

2 eggs

1 (6-ounce) package buttermilk cornbread mix

2 cups shredded Monterey Jack cheese, divided

Preheat the oven to 375°F. Lightly grease a 13 x 9-inch baking dish and set aside.

In a medium skillet, melt the butter over medium-high heat. Add the onions and sauté 3 minutes, or until tender. Stir in the chiles and set aside.

In a large bowl, mix together the shrimp, corn, sour cream, and eggs. Add the cornbread mix and stir just until blended. Add the onion mixture and 1$\frac{1}{2}$ cups of the cheese, stirring just until combined.

Pour into the prepared baking dish and sprinkle the top with the remaining cheese. Bake 45 minutes, or until a tester inserted in the center comes out clean. Let stand 10 minutes before serving warm.

SWEET POTATO
SPOON BREAD

If you don't feel like making a boatload of dressing for Thanksgiving, this will be a worthy substitution. It matches well with turkey that has been prepared in any way.

YIELD: 8 TO 10 SERVINGS

2 cups milk

1 cup water

$\frac{1}{4}$ cup self-rising cornmeal

4 tablespoons unsalted butter

$\frac{1}{4}$ cup packed light brown sugar

$1\frac{1}{2}$ teaspoon ground cinnamon

1 teaspoon salt

$\frac{1}{4}$ teaspoon ground nutmeg

$\frac{1}{8}$ teaspoon ground cloves

3 sweet potatoes, baked, peeled, and mashed

4 eggs

1 cup cream

$\frac{1}{2}$ cup all-purpose flour

$\frac{1}{4}$ cup honey

Preheat the oven to 350°F. Lightly grease a 2-quart baking dish and set aside.

In a heavy saucepan over medium heat, combine the milk, water, cornmeal, butter, brown sugar, cinnamon, salt, nutmeg, and cloves. Whisk until smooth. Cook 10 minutes or until slightly thick, stirring frequently.

Meanwhile, place the sweet potatoes, eggs, cream, flour, and honey in the bowl of an electric mixer. Blend until smooth. Stir in the cornmeal mixture and beat at medium speed until smooth.

Transfer to the prepared dish and bake 40 to 45 minutes, or until a tester inserted in the center comes out clean. Let stand 5 minutes before serving warm.

TRADITIONAL
SPOON BREAD

This is the recipe of old and for many, the only one they will use. It is simple and satisfying and perfect for any meal you are serving.

YIELD: 6 SERVINGS

3 cups milk

1 cup self-rising cornmeal

3 eggs, separated

1 teaspoon sugar

$1\frac{1}{2}$ teaspoons salt

1 tablespoon unsalted butter

Place the milk in a large saucepan over medium-high heat. When the milk just begins to bubble around the edges, gradually add the cornmeal. Stir constantly 10 minutes. Set aside to cool 10 minutes.

Meanwhile, preheat the oven to 375°F. Lightly grease a 13 x 9-inch baking dish and set aside.

Beat the egg whites at high speed of an electric mixer until stiff peaks form. Set aside.

Stir the sugar, salt, butter, and egg yolks into the cornmeal mixture. Gently fold in the egg whites. Pour into prepared baking dish and bake 35 to 40 minutes, or until golden brown. Let stand 5 minutes and serve hot.

SAVORY OR SWEET: Since spoon bread was originally a side dish for meat, it was rarely sweetened with any more than perhaps a teaspoon of sugar. In fact, in the old South, it had little if any added sweetener because sugar was such a scarce commodity. Now, you'll commonly see a small amount of sugar added to many spoon bread recipes to accent the salt. Still others have almost become dessert-like with the addition of honey, sorghum, maple syrup, confectioners' sugar, nuts, and fruits.

SQUASH

(EXCLUDING PUMPKINS AND ZUCCHINI)

IF I AM EVER STRANDED ON A DESSERT ISLAND AND GET TO PICK ONE VEGETABLE TO HAVE WITH me, I'm picking squash. I would never go hungry! In addition to the remarkably prolific summer varieties, I would never get bored with the winter types that come barreling in after everything else is practically finished for the year.

I don't usually plant summer squash at my Tennessee house thanks to the space it commands and the soil it prefers. It likes well-drained, sandy loam best (see what I mean about the dessert island?). That's about as far from what I have in my yard as can be. Hence, I'm content to let others with more space and really good Southern soil do the growing for me.

The feast or famine season of summer squash keeps many from growing very much of this vegetable. It starts out slow, but makes up for that slow start quickly. You've heard the saying, "So many books, so little time." Well, if you've ever grown summer squash, you can change that to, "So much squash and so few friends to pawn it off on!" If you have no gardening friends and seek it during the hot weather months, you won't have to search very hard.

Winter squash took some getting used to on my part. Every fall, my eyes practically glaze over at the numerous types found at the farmers' market. For a couple of years after college, I would only use them as fall decorations because I really didn't know how else to use the things.

This is the fate of too many of these bumpy, chunky, lumpy, hunky masses of fall color. Far too often, these beauties are doomed to a life on fireplace mantels and yard displays rather than showing their glorious inner potential in the kitchen.

I'm not saying I don't decorate with winter squash. The fall season practically screams for it, but please keep in mind that these items are sold in the produce department for a reason. They are all delicious foods that can transform your dinner menus as quickly as they enliven your home.

Cutting Winter Squash: Winter squash is not a cinch to cut, but with a heavy-duty sharp knife, it is not impossible and worth the effort. Place the squash on a damp kitchen towel so it remains steady. Using a sawing motion, patiently cut the squash in half. Scoop out the seeds with a large spoon.

Selection: Look for smooth, uncut skins with no sunken areas or watery spots, regardless of the kind of squash you are purchasing. Winter types should feel heavy for the size.

Storage: Summer squash varieties should be kept refrigerated in the crisper drawer. Winter types just like to be kept dry and cool. Use cooked leftovers of either type within a couple of days.

ACORN SQUASH BOURBON BUTTER

Acorn squash, bourbon, and cider form the basis for this spread for everything from biscuits to ham. Southerners like to call lots of things butter that contain no butter, but are used like butter!

YIELD: 2 CUPS

1 (2-pound) acorn squash
1 cup apple cider
$^1/_4$ cup bourbon
$^3/_4$ cup packed brown sugar
$^1/_2$ teaspoon ground allspice
$^1/_4$ teaspoon ground nutmeg
$^1/_4$ teaspoon ground ginger

Preheat the oven to 375°F. Slice the squash in half lengthwise and remove the seeds. Place the cut sides down in a 13 x 9-inch baking dish. Pour hot water around the squash to a depth of 1 inch. Bake 45 minutes, or until the squash is tender. Drain and cool.

Scoop out the pulp and discard the shells. Place the pulp in the bowl of a food processor and process until smooth. Transfer to a heavy saucepan and add the cider and bourbon. Place over medium-high heat and bring to a boil.

Reduce the heat to low and simmer 35 minutes, stirring frequently. Add the sugar, allspice, nutmeg, and ginger. Cook 10 minutes longer, or until thick. Cool before using.
Note: Cool and refrigerate one month or freeze up to six months.

CANNED YELLOW SQUASH PICKLES

This is just the sort of thing you want to do with yellow squash when they are cheap and abundant. Save some to add to your Thanksgiving Day relish tray.

YIELD: 3 PINTS

2 pounds yellow squash, peeled and
    cut into thin slices
2 white onions, peeled and quartered
$^1/_4$ cup salt
2 cups sugar
1 teaspoon celery salt
2 teaspoon turmeric
2 teaspoons mustard seeds
3 cups cider vinegar

Place the squash and onions in a large bowl. Sprinkle with the salt and cover with cold water, stirring to blend. Cover and let stand at room temperature 2 hours, and then drain.

In a small saucepan over medium-high heat, bring the sugar, celery salt, turmeric, seeds, and vinegar to a boil. Pour over the squash mixture. Cover and let stand at room temperature 2 hours.

Transfer the squash mixture to a large saucepan and place over medium-high heat. Boil 5 minutes. Pack the squash mixture into hot sterilized canning jars. Fill with the boiling liquid, leaving $^1/_2$-inch headspace. Remove the air bubbles, wipe the rims, and adjust the lids. Process 15 minutes in a boiling water bath. (See page 12 for detailed canning instructions.) Cool on a wire rack away from drafts. Store at room temperature.

COME AGAIN SQUASH FRITTERS

I always thought these were so named because it would make company want to come back and visit again. My mother told me it was because the squash returned in a different form!

YIELD: 2½ DOZEN

Vegetable oil for frying
2 cups mashed, cooked yellow squash
2 eggs, lightly beaten
1 yellow onion, peeled and chopped
1 jalapeño pepper, seeded and chopped
¼ teaspoon kosher salt
¼ teaspoon black pepper
¼ teaspoon garlic powder
½ cup round buttery crackers, crushed

Pour 2 inches oil in a large cast-iron pan. Place over medium-high heat and bring to 375°F.

Meanwhile, combine the squash, eggs, onion, jalapeño, salt, pepper, powder, and crackers in the bowl of a food processor. Process until smooth.

Carefully drop tablespoons of the batter into the hot oil. Fry 1 minute on each side, or until golden brown. Drain on paper towels. Serve warm.

DAILY PICK SQUASH CASSEROLE

Because it uses quite a bit of squash, make this terrific summertime dish when armloads of yellow squash need to be picked every single day.

YIELD: 8 SERVINGS

3 pounds yellow squash, cut into ¼-inch slices
1 white onion, peeled and chopped

4 teaspoons kosher salt, divided
16 saltine crackers, divided
1½ cups shredded sharp Cheddar cheese, divided
½ cup mayonnaise
1 egg, lightly beaten
2 tablespoons unsalted butter, melted
¼ teaspoon black pepper

Bring water to a boil in a Dutch oven over medium-high heat. Add the squash, onion, and 3½ teaspoons of the salt. Stir often and cook 25 minutes.

Preheat the oven to 350°F. Lightly grease an 11 x 7-inch baking dish and set aside. Crush 10 crackers and set aside.

Drain and coarsely mash the squash mixture with a fork. Add the crushed crackers, ½ cup of the cheese, the mayonnaise, egg, butter, remaining salt, and the pepper. Stir to combine. Transfer to the prepared dish. Crush the remaining crackers and sprinkle evenly over the squash. Top with the remaining cheese. Bake, uncovered, 30 minutes, or until the cheese is melted and the squash is bubbly. Cool on a wire rack 5 minutes before serving.

ROASTED SUMMER SQUASH

This squash is marvelous as a side dish or can be folded into spoonbread batter.

YIELD: 2 SERVINGS

3 yellow squash, sliced
1 tablespoon olive oil
¼ teaspoon paprika
¼ teaspoon kosher salt
¼ teaspoon garlic powder
¼ teaspoon ground red pepper

Preheat the oven to 350°F. Lightly grease a jelly-roll

pan. Place the squash in a single layer on the pan. Sprinkle evenly with the oil and set aside.

In a small bowl, combine the paprika, salt, garlic powder, and red pepper. Evenly sprinkle over the squash. Roast 25 to 30 minutes. Serve warm.

ROASTED WINTER SQUASH

This recipe works equally well with nearly every winter squash type.

YIELD: 4 SERVINGS

2 (1 to 2 pound) acorn or butternut squash
4 tablespoons unsalted butter
2 tablespoons honey
3/4 teaspoon kosher salt
1/4 teaspoon black pepper

Preheat the oven to 400°F. Line a baking sheet with aluminum foil and set aside.

Cut the squash in half lengthwise and remove the seeds. Place the squash with the cut sides up on the baking sheet.

In a small saucepan over medium heat, combine the butter and honey. Stir until the butter is melted and the mixture is well blended. Brush the honey butter on the cut sides of the squash. Sprinkle the tops evenly with the salt and pepper.

Bake, uncovered, 1 hour or until tender. Let stand 10 minutes. Cut into large chunks and serve warm.

SILLY STRING SQUASH

Strands of quirky spaghetti squash are fun to serve. I don't know of anything that undergoes more of a transformation when baked than this squash variety.

YIELD: 8 SERVINGS

1 spaghetti squash
3 tablespoons unsalted butter
2 tablespoons chopped fresh chives
1/2 teaspoon kosher salt
1/4 teaspoon black pepper
1/4 teaspoon garlic powder

Preheat the oven to 350°F. Slice the squash in half lengthwise and scoop out the seeds. Place the cut sides down in a 13 x 9-inch baking dish. Pour hot water around the squash to a depth of 1 inch. Bake 50 to 55 minutes, or until tender. Drain and cool slightly.

Using a fork, remove the strands into a serving bowl. Add the butter, chives, salt, pepper, and garlic powder, tossing gently. Serve immediately.

SOUL FOOD SQUASH AND TOMATO CASSEROLE

The mixture of summer squash and vine-ripe tomatoes could feed anyone's soul. This casserole reheats well.

YIELD: 8 SERVINGS

2 pounds yellow squash, sliced
1 cup water
3 tomatoes, peeled and chopped with juice retained
1 tablespoon all-purpose flour
2 teaspoons sugar
1 teaspoon kosher salt
1 teaspoon paprika
1/2 teaspoon garlic powder
1/4 teaspoon black pepper
2 cups shredded mozzarella cheese, divided
1/2 cup grated Parmesan cheese

Preheat the oven to 350°F. Lightly grease a shallow 2-quart casserole dish and set aside.

Combine the squash and water in a large saucepan over medium-high heat and bring to a boil. Cover, reduce heat to low, and simmer 10 minutes or until the squash is tender, stirring occasionally. Drain and set aside.

In a medium saucepan combine the tomatoes, flour, sugar, salt, paprika, garlic powder, and pepper. Bring to a boil over medium-high heat. Reduce heat to low and simmer 5 minutes.

Place half of the squash in the prepared dish. Pour one-fourth of the tomato mixture over the squash. Top with 1 cup of the mozzarella and another one-fourth of the tomato mixture.

Repeat the layers with the remaining squash, tomato mixture, and mozzarella. Sprinkle the top with Parmesan and bake 30 minutes. Let stand 10 minutes before serving.

TOASTED PECAN AND SQUASH SALAD

This salad has ribbons of squash and zucchini that are nearly too beautiful to eat. Serve as a cool summer side dish.

YIELD: 6 SERVINGS

5 yellow squash
3 zucchini
$1/4$ cup olive oil
4 garlic cloves, minced
$1/4$ cup julienned fresh basil
$1/2$ teaspoon kosher salt
$1/4$ teaspoon black pepper
$1/4$ cup chopped pecans, toasted

Trim the ends of the squash and zucchini. Cut

each in half lengthwise. With a spoon, scrape out the seeds. Slice into $1/4$-inch strips and then slice the strips into matchsticks.

In a large skillet, heat the oil over medium-high heat. Add the squash and garlic. Sauté 3 minutes. Spread on a plate to cool 10 minutes. Transfer to a serving bowl and toss with the basil, salt, pepper, and pecans. Serve at room temperature.

WILD BRANDIED WINTER SQUASH

Winter squash gets a kick from the apple flavor of brandy and cider and then goes crazier with wild rice and pecans. I always serve this dish with turkey. It's a very happy union when matched with a dry red wine.

YIELD: 6 SERVINGS

2 tablespoons olive oil
1 sweet onion, peeled and chopped
2 garlic cloves, minced
$1/2$ cup apple brandy
$1/4$ cup apple cider
3 large acorn squash or 2 butternut squash, halved and seeded
6 cups cooked wild rice
2 egg yolks
1 cup toasted pecans
1 cup grated Gouda cheese
1 tablespoon chopped fresh sage
1 tablespoon Dijon mustard
$1/2$ teaspoon salt
$1/2$ teaspoon black pepper

Heat the oil in a large sauté pan over medium-high heat. Add the onion and garlic, sautéing 2 minutes. Remove from heat and add the brandy and cider. Return to the heat and reduce until the liquid is nearly evaporated, about 6 minutes. Cool to room temperature, about 30 minutes.

Meanwhile place the squash in a large baking dish and set aside. Preheat the oven to 375°F.

Transfer the cooled onion mixture to a large bowl. Add the rice, egg yolks, pecans, cheese, sage, mustard, salt, and pepper. Mix well and divide the stuffing among the prepared squash. Bake 1 hour, or until the squash is tender. Serve warm.

Varieties: Summer squash is harvested before the seeds have a chance to harden and the skins to toughen. That's why the entire portion is edible. It is over 90 percent water, which means it needs very little, if any, additional water for cooking. It also cooks quickly. Some common summer squash types are yellow crookneck, yellow straightneck, zucchini, pattypan, and scallopini.

Winter squash is the mature side of the family. The seemingly endless types of winter squash make fall meals a rainbow for the eyes. Because winter varieties stay on the vine longer than summer types, they develop outer shells that are nice and thick. This greatly increases their shelf life to several months if stored correctly because it becomes a protective coating. Look for acorn, banana, buttercup, butternut, calabaza, carnival, cushaw, delicata, golden nugget, hubbard, kabocha, sweet dumpling, and turban. Spaghetti squash technically straddles the fence between summer and winter, but is usually classified as winter.

BOTANY: Squash belongs to the Curcubita genus, which includes pumpkins, gourds, melons, and cucumbers. All members of this family bear fruit called a "pepo," which is the edible portion. Winter squash is a mature pepo and has seeds in a definite cavity.

NUTRITION: No matter how different squash look on the outside, they are very similar nutritionally. Most are rich sources of vitamins A and C, as well as niacin, phosphorus, and potassium. Squash is high in dietary fiber and naturally low in sodium.

ORIGIN: All squash varieties are natives of the Western Hemisphere.

SERVINGS: One pound of summer squash will serve four people. Thanks to the inedible hard shell and seeds, a winter squash of two pounds will serve the same number.

Celebration
September 7 is National Acorn Squash Day.

STRAWBERRIES

IT'S CERTAINLY TRUE THAT APRIL SHOWERS BRING MAY FLOWERS, BUT IT ALSO BRINGS TO market the South's most eagerly anticipated berry. Vibrantly ripened local strawberries need no sales pitch . . . just a taste. I particularly like to enjoy them cool and raw right off the plant. Just like that, you have spring.

Strawberries have achieved greatness without pretense and are the precursor to everything wonderful from local farms. Before we can harvest any other fruit, we get to enjoy these ruby-red, heart-shaped delights. What a way to begin!

I love to go a farm and pick these exceptional berries for myself. They ripen when the weather is still incredibly comfortable, particularly when I like to go, which is super early in the morning while the dew is still on the ground. Legend says that dreaming about strawberries is a good omen of fruitful days ahead. If that's the case, I'm in for some really fruitful days!

All winter long, I try to pacify myself with strawberries shipped in from someone else's garden far, far away. Their color promises sunshine, but they taste like winter. It is only after Easter that things begin to look up in the produce department around here.

I frequently showcase strawberries in the South's most beautiful way—on shortcakes topped with snowy mounds of freshly whipped cream. However, they are equally delicious just served with a bowl of confectioners' sugar. Simply put, this fruit is candy in the form of a berry.

Preparation: Do not wash or cap the berries until you are ready to use them. Think of strawberries as tiny sponges. Water will be absorbed by the fruit and break down the berry, so keep them unwashed in the refrigerator. Just before using, give them a gentle rinse with cold water. Drain in a colander or on paper towels and then remove their green caps.

Selection: Strawberries do not continue to ripen after harvest. Make sure you select only berries that are completely red from tip to cap with no white or creamy looking shoulders. Size is not an indication of quality or flavor. Don't harvest or buy any berries with sunken soft spots or leaks, which are signs of age. Any that are shriveled or have lost luster should not be purchased or picked.

Storage: Handle strawberries gently to prevent bruising. If possible, place the berries in a single layer on a baking sheet. The refrigerator is their friend. They will maintain high quality for around three days there, but who can keep them that long?

Yields: A one-pint basket will give you a bit over three cups of whole fruit. This same amount is the equivalent of just over two cups of sliced fruit or one and two-thirds cups of strawberry purée.

"BEST EVER" STRAWBERRY FREEZER JAM

Who doesn't love freezer jam? You don't have to have special equipment and it doesn't take a lot of time to prepare. Let the freezer keep it ready for you to enjoy all year.

YIELD: 4 HALF-PINTS

2 cups crushed strawberries

4 cups sugar

$^{3}/_{4}$ cup water

1 (1.75-ounce) box powdered fruit pectin

In a large bowl, combine the strawberries and sugar. Mix well and let stand at room temperature 10 minutes.

Meanwhile, mix the water and pectin in a small saucepan over medium-high heat. Bring to a boil and boil 1 minute, stirring constantly. Stir into the strawberries for 3 minutes.

Quickly ladle into sterilized freezer jars, leaving $^{1}/_{2}$-inch headspace. Seal immediately. Let the jars stand at room temperature until the jam is set (up to 24 hours), and then refrigerate and use within 1 month or freeze up to one year.

BROWN SUGAR STRAW- BERRY JAM SQUARES

This is a great portable dessert that's perfect for picnics or family gatherings.

YIELD: 8 TO 10 SERVINGS

$1^{1}/_{2}$ cups all-purpose flour

$^{1}/_{4}$ cup confectioners' sugar

$^{1}/_{4}$ pound (1 stick) unsalted butter

1 egg, beaten

$^{1}/_{2}$ cup sour cream

2 tablespoons brown sugar

$^{1}/_{2}$ teaspoon pure vanilla extract

$^{1}/_{2}$ cup strawberry jam

Preheat the oven to 350°F. Lightly grease an 8-inch square baking pan and set aside.

In a medium bowl, combine the flour and confectioners' sugar. Using a pastry blender or 2 forks, cut in the butter until the mixture resembles coarse crumbs. Press into the bottom of the prepared pan. Bake 18 to 20 minutes, or until the edges just begin to brown.

Meanwhile, in a small bowl, combine the egg, sour cream, brown sugar, and extract. As soon as the crust is done, immediately spread the jam over the top. Spoon the sour cream mixture over the top of the jam. Bake an additional 18 to 20 minutes, or until the topping is firm. Cool completely on a wire rack. Cut into squares and serve. Store leftovers in an airtight container at room temperature.

FRESH STRAWBERRIES IN VANILLA SYRUP

An elegant, yet simple and quick dessert to end your meal.

YIELD: 4 SERVINGS

1 cup sweet white wine

1 tablespoon lemon juice

$^{1}/_{4}$ cup sugar

1 vanilla bean

1 pint fresh strawberries, washed, hulled, and quartered

Mint sprigs for garnish

In a small saucepan, combine the wine, lemon juice, sugar, and vanilla bean. Bring to a boil, reduce heat to low. Simmer 15 minutes, or until the liquid is reduced by half. Remove the vanilla bean and discard. Stir in the strawberries. Divide evenly among 4 dessert goblets. Garnish with the mint and serve.

HARVEST FRESH STRAWBERRY CAKE

I like cakes that are moist, which partially explains why this cake is so special. I think it should be served on a table full of fresh cut daffodils on a day full of sunshine.

YIELD: 12 SERVINGS

$2^{1}/_{2}$ cups cake flour

$1^{1}/_{4}$ teaspoons baking powder

$^{3}/_{4}$ teaspoon salt

$^{1}/_{2}$ teaspoon baking soda

12 tablespoons plus 8 tablespoons unsalted butter, softened and divided

$1^{1}/_{2}$ cups granulated sugar

$^{3}/_{4}$ cup strawberry jam

$^{3}/_{4}$ teaspoon pure vanilla extract

4 eggs

$^{1}/_{2}$ cup buttermilk

$1^{3}/_{4}$ cups heavy cream

1 (16-ounce) package confectioners' sugar

$^{1}/_{2}$ cup finely chopped strawberries

Halved strawberries for garnish (optional)

Preheat the oven to 350°F. Grease and flour two 9-inch cake pans and set aside.

In a medium bowl, combine the flour, baking powder, salt, and baking soda. Set aside.

In the bowl of an electric mixer, cream 12 tablespoons of the butter with the granulated sugar at medium speed until light and fluffy. Add the jam

and extract, blending well. Add the eggs, one at a time, blending well after each addition.

Reduce the mixer speed to low and add the flour mixture alternately with the buttermilk and heavy cream, beginning and ending with the flour. Evenly pour the batter into the prepared pans.

Bake 22 to 28 minutes, or until a tester inserted in the center comes out clean. Cool in the pans 5 minutes and then cool completely on wire racks.

Meanwhile, beat the remaining butter at medium speed of an electric mixer until fluffy. Reduce the mixer speed to low and add the confectioners' sugar and chopped strawberries. Spread between the layers, on the sides, and top of the cooled cake. Garnish with strawberry halves, if desired.

HOMEMADE STRAWBERRY PRESERVES

Everyone has a tendency to pick too much at the strawberry patch. This puts all those excess berries to good use and makes a marvelous gift.

YIELD: 4 HALF-PINTS

$1^{1}/_{2}$ quarts strawberries, washed and hulled

5 cups sugar

$^{1}/_{3}$ cup lemon juice

Combine the strawberries and sugar in a large saucepan. Cover and let stand at room temperature 3 hours.

Place over medium heat and slowly bring to a boil, stirring occasionally until the sugar dissolves. Add the juice. Cook rapidly until the berries are clear and the syrup thickens, about 12 minutes.

Pour into a shallow pan and let stand 12 to 24

hours in the refrigerator. Shake the pan occasionally to distribute the berries through the syrup.

In a medium saucepan, reheat the berry mixture thoroughly. Pour into hot sterilized canning jars, leaving $1/4$-inch headspace. Wipe the jar rims and then adjust the lids. Process in a boiling water bath 5 minutes. (See page 12 for detailed canning instructions.) Cool completely on a wire rack away from drafts.

HOT MILK CAKES WITH FRESH STRAWBERRIES

These old-fashioned cakes are incredibly moist and a great host for fresh fruit of any kind. They are named for the hot milk added just before the batter goes into the oven.

YIELD: 6 SERVINGS

2 eggs

$2/3$ cup plus $1/2$ cup sugar, divided

$1/2$ teaspoon pure vanilla extract

1 cup plus 2 tablespoons self-rising flour

$2/3$ cup milk

5 tablespoons unsalted butter

1 quart strawberries, capped, hulled and thinly sliced

Whipped cream for garnish

Place the rack in the center of the oven and preheat the oven to 425°F. Lightly grease 6 custard cups and set aside.

In the bowl of an electric mixer, beat the eggs at high speed until thick, about 3 minutes. Gradually add $2/3$ cup of the sugar and beat 1 minute longer. Add the vanilla and then the flour and beat 1 minute.

Place the milk and butter in a small saucepan over medium heat. Bring just to a boil, stirring constantly until the butter is melted. Add the hot milk to the egg batter and beat until smooth, about 1 minute. Divide the batter among the prepared cups and place on a jelly-roll pan.

Bake 16 minutes, or until the cakes are golden brown and firm to the touch. Cool in the cups at least 20 minutes. Meanwhile, toss the strawberries with the remaining $1/2$ cup of sugar and let stand 15 minutes.

Remove the cakes from the cups and cut off the rounded top of each cake. Place the bottom half of the cake on a serving dish and top with the berries and any excess juice. Place the top of each cake over the berries. Garnish with any remaining berries and whipped cream. Serve immediately.

HOT STRAWBERRY MARINADE

This is a delicious "sweet with heat" outcome that enhances pork or chicken.

YIELD: 1¼ CUPS

$1/2$ cup strawberry jam

Zest of 2 limes, grated

Juice of 2 limes

$1/4$ cup soy sauce

2 tablespoons hot sauce

1 tablespoon finely minced fresh ginger

2 tablespoons chopped fresh mint

In a jar with a tight-fitting lid, combine the jam, zest, juice, soy sauce, hot sauce, ginger, and mint. Shake well to emulsify. Refrigerate at least 1 hour before using.

LOADED WITH STRAW-BERRIES MILKSHAKE

Just add a straw or spoon and you've cooled off in a snap!

YIELD: 3 SERVINGS

3 cups strawberry ice cream
1 cup fresh strawberries, capped
1 cup milk
$1/2$ teaspoon pure almond extract

Place the ice cream, berries, milk, and extract in an electric blender and process until smooth. Serve immediately.

NOTHING-BUT-THE-BERRIES STRAWBERRY PIE

It was always a treat for us as kids to share a piece of Shoney's Strawberry Pie. This is my version and it's just as much of a treat!

YIELD: 8 SERVINGS

1 quart strawberries, capped and hulled
1 recipe Single Pie Pastry (page 402), baked
1 cup sugar
3 tablespoons cornstarch
$3/4$ cup water

Arrange half of the strawberries with the stem end down on the baked pastry. Mash the remaining strawberries and combine with the sugar in a medium saucepan. Place over medium heat and bring to a boil, stirring frequently.

In a small bowl, whisk together the cornstarch and water. Gradually add to the strawberry mixture, stirring constantly. Reduce the heat to low.

Continue cooking and stirring constantly until thickened, about 10 minutes.

Pour the hot mixture over the berries in the pie shell. Refrigerate at least 2 hours before cutting into slices and serving. Refrigerate leftovers.

SOUTHERN STRAWBERRY SHORTCAKE

You will not be able to make it through the fresh season without making this classic dish. The presentation is dramatic. You will never buy those spongy, packaged "cakes" (I refuse to call them shortcakes) again!

YIELD: 8 SERVINGS

1 quart strawberries, capped, hulled, and sliced
$1^1/2$ cups granulated sugar, divided
2 cups all-purpose flour
1 teaspoon baking powder
$1/2$ teaspoon salt
$1/4$ pound (1 stick) unsalted butter
2 eggs
1 cup whipping cream
$1/4$ cup confectioners' sugar

Preheat the oven to 350°F. Line an 8-inch round cake pan with parchment paper and set aside.

In a medium bowl, combine the strawberries and $1/2$ cup of the granulated sugar. Toss to evenly coat and set aside.

In a mixing bowl, combine the remaining 1 cup of granulated sugar, the flour, baking powder, and salt. With a pastry blender or 2 forks, cut in the butter until the mixture is crumbly. Add the eggs, stirring just until moistened.

Transfer the dough to a lightly floured surface and knead 6 times (the dough will be grainy).

Press the dough into the prepared pan. Bake 35 minutes, or until golden brown. Cool in the pan on a wire rack 10 minutes, and then remove and cool completely.

Meanwhile, beat the cream at medium speed of an electric mixer until foamy. Gradually add the confectioners' sugar. Beat until soft peaks form. Split the shortcake in half crosswise to form 2 layers. Place 1 layer on a serving plate and drizzle with 2 tablespoons of the liquid from the strawberry mixture. Spread with half of the whipped cream and top with half of the strawberries. Repeat with the remaining shortcake, whipped cream, and strawberries. Serve immediately.

SPARKLING STRAWBERRY TEA FOR A CROWD

This beautiful fruit tea has spring written all over it!

YIELD: 4 QUARTS

1 quart fresh strawberries, washed and capped

1½ quarts boiling water

3 family-size tea bags

½ cup sugar

1 (6-ounce) can frozen lemonade concentrate, thawed

1 (2-liter) bottle lemon-lime carbonated beverage, chilled

Mint sprigs for garnish

Place the strawberries in an electric blender and process until smooth. Set aside.

Pour the boiling water over the tea bags and then cover and steep 10 minutes. Remove the tea bags and squeeze. Add the sugar, lemonade concentrate, and strawberry purée. Stir to blend, cover, and refrigerate.

When ready to serve, add the lemon-lime beverage. Stir and serve over ice. Garnish with the fresh mint sprigs.

SPRING IS HERE HOMEMADE STRAWBERRY ICE CREAM

I love to make this ice cream at the very end of the strawberry picking season. It ushers in the hotter weather with just a bit of spring left on the tongue!

YIELD: 1 QUART

2½ cups half-and-half

4 egg yolks

½ cup granulated sugar

¼ teaspoon pure vanilla extract

1 pint fresh strawberries, capped and quartered

2 tablespoons confectioners' sugar

Fresh strawberries for garnish

Pour the half-and-half into a heavy saucepan and place over medium-high heat. Bring to a boil and set aside.

Meanwhile, in a medium bowl, beat the egg yolks and granulated sugar until pale and smooth. Stir in ½ cup of hot half-and-half, beating well. Pour the yolk mixture back into the warm saucepan.

Cook over medium heat, stirring constantly, until thick enough to coat a spoon, about 4 minutes. Stir in the extract. Cool to room temperature, cover with plastic and refrigerate at least 4 hours.

An hour before making the ice cream, toss the strawberries with the confectioners' sugar and let stand at room temperature 15 minutes. Mash the berries with a fork until they are bite size.

Stir into the chilled custard and freeze in an ice

cream maker according to the manufacturer's directions. Serve in chilled bowls and garnish with fresh strawberries.

STRAWBERRIES AND GRAND MARNIER SAUCE

There is not so much liqueur in this recipe to get the berries drunk, but just enough to make them speak with a charming Southern accent!

YIELD: 6 SERVINGS

5 egg yolks, at room temperature
$3/4$ cup plus 1 tablespoon sugar, divided
$1/4$ cup Grand Marnier
1 cup cream
3 pints fresh strawberries, capped, hulled, and halved

In the top of a double boiler, beat the yolks with a whisk until light yellow. Whisk in $3/4$ cup of the sugar and place over simmering water. Continue to whisk and cook until thick, about 20 minutes. Whisk until cool.

Stir in the Grand Marnier. With an electric mixer on medium speed, beat the cream until thickened, but still pourable. Add the remaining tablespoon of sugar and mix well. Stir into the Grand Marnier mixture, cover, and refrigerate overnight.

To serve, divide the strawberries among 6 dessert bowls. Top with the sauce and serve, or serve the sauce as a dip for whole strawberries.

STRAWBERRY CREAM PIE

Waiting for this pie to chill and set will be one of the hardest things you'll ever do!

YIELD: 8 SERVINGS

1 (8-ounce) package cream cheese, softened
$1/3$ cup sugar
$1/4$ teaspoon pure almond extract
1 cup whipping cream, whipped
1 recipe Single Pie Pastry (page 402), baked
1 quart strawberries, capped

In the bowl of an electric mixer, beat the cream cheese at medium speed until fluffy. Gradually add the sugar, beating well to blend. Gently fold in the extract and whipped cream.

Spread the filling into the pie shell. Arrange the strawberries cut side down over the cheese mixture. Cover and refrigerate 3 hours before slicing and serving.

STRAWBERRY MINT TEA

It's pink and sweet and quite addictive!

YIELD: 1 GALLON

2 pints strawberries, capped
1 gallon water
1 cup sugar
2 family-size or 4 regular-size tea bags
$1/2$ cup fresh mint leaves
Zest of 1 lemon
1 (1 x 3-inch) piece fresh ginger, peeled and chopped
Fresh mint leaves for garnish

Preheat the oven to 350°F. Put the strawberries in

a roasting pan and roast 12 minutes or until very dark red and soft.

Boil the water in a large saucepan and stir in the sugar to dissolve. Add the strawberries, tea bags, mint, zest, and ginger. Stir well and steep 5 minutes.

Remove, squeeze, and discard the tea bags. Pour through a fine mesh sieve and refrigerate. Serve over ice and garnish with fresh mint.

STRAWBERRY PRETZEL SALAD

I know this is called "salad," but it's actually a dessert. I've never had better than when my niece, Loren, would make it for me. The amount of love she added was always just right!

YIELD: 8 TO 10 SERVINGS

2 cups crushed pretzels

12 tablespoons unsalted butter, melted

3 tablespoons plus $^{3}/_{4}$ cup sugar, divided

1 (8-ounce) package cream cheese, softened

1 (8-ounce) container frozen whipped topping, thawed

1 (6-ounce) package strawberry gelatin

2 cups boiling water

2 (10-ounce) packages frozen strawberries, thawed

Preheat the oven to 400°F.

In a medium bowl, combine the pretzels, butter, and 3 tablespoons of the sugar. Press into the bottom of a 13 x 9-inch baking pan. Bake 7 minutes. Cool on a wire rack.

Meanwhile, in the bowl of an electric mixer, combine the cream cheese and the remaining $^{3}/_{4}$ cup of sugar. Blend until smooth. Gently add the whipped topping and spread over the cooled

crust. Cover and refrigerate.

In a small bowl, dissolve the gelatin in the water, stirring well. Set aside to cool 20 minutes. Add the strawberries. Spread over the cream cheese mixture. Cover and refrigerate at least 30 minutes, or until ready to serve.

STRAWBERRY RHUBARB CRISP

These fruits were made for each other, and in most areas throughout the South, they are harvested at the same time.

YIELD: 8 SERVINGS

2 pounds fresh strawberries, capped, hulled, and halved

2 pounds fresh rhubarb, cut into bite-size pieces

2 cups sugar

$1^{1}/_{2}$ cups all-purpose flour, divided

1 cup packed brown sugar

$^{1}/_{2}$ teaspoon ground cinnamon

$^{1}/_{4}$ pound (1 stick) unsalted butter, cut in small pieces

Preheat the oven to 350°F. Lightly grease a 13 x 9-inch baking dish and set aside.

In a large bowl, gently combine the strawberries, rhubarb, sugar, and $^{1}/_{2}$ cup of the flour. Transfer to the prepared dish.

In a small bowl, combine the remaining 1 cup of flour, the brown sugar, and cinnamon. Using a pastry blender or 2 forks, cut in the butter until the mixture resembles coarse crumbs. Sprinkle on top of the strawberry mixture.

Bake $1^{1}/_{2}$ hours, or until bubbly and golden brown. Cool on a wire rack at least 15 minutes before serving. Serve warm or at room temperature.

SUNRISE STRAWBERRY BUTTER

Your morning biscuit, toast, or bagel just found a new pal!

YIELD: 1 CUP

1 cup sliced strawberries
3/4 cup confectioners' sugar
6 tablespoons unsalted butter, softened

In a food processor, purée the strawberries. Transfer to a mixing bowl and add the confectioners' sugar and butter. Beat on medium speed of an electric mixer until fluffy and smooth. Cover and refrigerate at least 1 hour before using.

SWEET STRAWBERRY SAUCE

Perfect for toasted slices of angel food or pound cake—or spooned over vanilla ice cream.

YIELD: 2 CUPS

2 cups strawberries, capped and hulled
1/4 cup sugar
1/2 tablespoon lemon juice

Place the strawberries, sugar, and juice in the bowl of a food processor and purée. If desired, strain through a fine mesh sieve. Use immediately or refrigerate and use within 2 days.

WHITE CHOCOLATE STRAWBERRY PIE

Think chocolate-dipped strawberries without having to go to all the trouble to dip the individual strawberries!

YIELD: 6 TO 8 SERVINGS

5 (1-ounce) squares white chocolate, divided
2 tablespoons milk
4 ounces cream cheese, softened
1/3 cup confectioners' sugar
1 teaspoon grated orange zest
1 cup whipping cream, whipped
1 recipe Single Pie Pastry (page 402), baked
2 cups sliced fresh strawberries

Place 4 squares of the chocolate and the milk in a small glass bowl. Microwave 1 minute on medium power. Stir well. If necessary, microwave 30 seconds more if not completely smooth. Set aside to cool.

Beat the cream cheese, confectioners' sugar, and zest in a mixing bowl until smooth. Fold in the whipped cream and then the melted chocolate. Spread on the bottom of the baked shell.

Arrange the strawberries on the filling. Melt the remaining square of chocolate and drizzle over the top. Refrigerate at least 1 hour before cutting and serving. Store leftovers in the refrigerator.

Celebrations

May is National Strawberry Month.
February 27 is National Strawberry Day.
May 21 is National Strawberries and Cream Day.
June 14 is National Strawberry Shortcake Day.

SWEET POTATOES

IT'S NO WONDER THE SOUTH IS KNOWN FOR GROWING SWEET POTATOES! THEY ARE TROPICAL plants that love hot, humid conditions. That makes our region a natural place for growing boatloads of them, with North Carolina leading the way. But somehow along the line, sweet potatoes got confused with yams and to this day, many use the terms interchangeably.

Being an identical twin, I adore it when people call me the correct name. Maybe that's the reason I do not call sweet potatoes yams or vice versa. The two couldn't be more different. We do not grow true yams in the South ... only sweet potatoes. We just don't have the proper weather conditions to get real yams grown with any kind of marketable success.

Sweet potatoes and yams are totally unrelated from a botanical standpoint. They come from completely different families and originated on two different continents. Sweet potato plants have between four and ten potatoes produced per plant. Yams only produce half that amount even though the growing season is twice as long.

While sweet potatoes have a smooth, thin skin, yams are rough and scaly on the outside. Nutritionally, sweet potatoes are practically a beta-carotene factory, with yams hardly containing any at all. Sweet potatoes taste moist and sweet. Yams are dry and taste starchy.

So pay no attention to labels or marketing materials that say yams. You could possibly find true yams at a premium price in a specialty store, but I doubt you would enjoy the experience. Instead, stick to what we grow so well here in the South and use their correct name ... sweet potatoes!

Nutrition: Sweet potatoes are a powerhouse of vitamins A, C, E, and B6. They also contain iron, potassium, calcium, and dietary fiber. One baked sweet potato contains less than one hundred forty calories.

Selection: Firm sweet potatoes that range from small to medium in size are best. Extremely large spuds can sometimes have a stringy texture. The outer skin should be smooth and unblemished with no soft spots. Check the tips when shopping because that's usually where they will first begin to decay. Although they appear rugged, the outer skins are quite thin and can be easily broken, so handle carefully. If the skin is cut during harvesting, it will exude a heavy, milky juice from the injured cells. It will dry within a few hours and appear to have closed the wound, but it actually takes days for this to occur.

BOURBON-BASTED SWEET POTATOES

For years, Southern ladies had to enjoy their "spirits" thanks to baking. This dish marvelously provides a bit for the dish and a nip for the cook!

YIELD: 4 SERVINGS

3 sweet potatoes
3 tablespoons unsalted butter, melted
3 tablespoons packed light brown sugar
3 tablespoons orange juice
3 tablespoons bourbon
$1/4$ teaspoon ground cinnamon
$1/8$ teaspoon ground cloves
$1/8$ teaspoon ground nutmeg
$1/4$ cup chopped pecans, toasted

Place the whole potatoes in a large saucepan and cover with water. Place over high heat and bring to a boil. Cover and cook 30 to 40 minutes, or until tender. Drain and let cool completely. Peel and cut in $1/2$-inch slices.

Preheat the oven to 350°F. Lightly grease an 8-inch square baking dish and place the sweet potato slices evenly throughout the dish.

In a small bowl, whisk together the butter, brown sugar, orange juice, bourbon, cinnamon, cloves, and nutmeg. Pour over the potatoes and sprinkle with the pecans. Bake 25 minutes or until thoroughly heated. Serve warm.

EVERYONE'S FAVORITE SWEET POTATO PIE

There is no way I could make it through the holidays without this classic Southern pie. It is a must at Thanksgiving and at any fall celebration.

YIELD: 8 SERVINGS

1 recipe Single Pie Pastry (page 402)
2 eggs
$3/4$ cup sugar
1 (5-ounce) can evaporated milk
3 tablespoons unsalted butter, melted
1 teaspoon pure vanilla or walnut extract
Dash of ground nutmeg
$1^1/3$ cups cooked, mashed sweet potatoes

Preheat the oven to 350°F. Line a 9-inch pie plate with the pastry. Flute or crimp the edges as desired. Set aside.

In a mixing bowl, beat the eggs. Whisk in the sugar, milk, butter, extract, and nutmeg until well combined. Add the sweet potatoes and whisk until well blended and smooth.

Pour into the piecrust. Cover the pie edges with aluminum foil to prevent overbrowning. Bake 30 minutes. Uncover and bake 25 minutes longer, or until the filling is set. The pie is done when a knife inserted in the center comes out clean. Cool completely on a wire rack. Serve within 2 hours, or cover and refrigerate until ready to serve.

OVEN-ROASTED SWEET POTATO FRIES

This recipe is as easy as preheating the oven. By not peeling the sweet potatoes, you get a really nice presentation.

YIELD: 6 SERVINGS

3 sweet potatoes, unpeeled and cut into $1/4$-inch slices
$1/4$ cup olive oil
2 garlic cloves, minced
1 teaspoon salt

½ teaspoon coriander

¼ teaspoon cayenne

¼ teaspoon black pepper

1 lime, cut into 4 wedges

Preheat the oven to 375°F. Lightly grease a jelly-roll pan and set aside.

Place the sweet potatoes in a large mixing bowl. In a jar with a tight-fitting lid, combine the oil, garlic, salt, coriander, cayenne, and pepper. Shake to emulsify and pour over the sweet potatoes, tossing to evenly coat. Spread the potatoes in a single layer in the prepared pan. Drizzle any leftover oil mixture from the bowl over the potatoes.

Bake 45 minutes, or until tender. Immediately squeeze the lime wedges and drizzle with the juice. Serve hot.

PAN-FRIED SWEET POTATO CROQUETTES

These are great last minute appetizers. Just before serving, give them a squirt of fresh lime juice and accompany with sour cream.

YIELD: 10 TO 12 SERVINGS

Vegetable oil

4 cups peeled, grated sweet potatoes

1 jalapeño pepper, seeded and minced

¾ cup all-purpose flour

¾ teaspoon salt

¾ teaspoon baking powder

½ teaspoon chili powder

¼ teaspoon cumin

¼ teaspoon black pepper

¼ teaspoon paprika

¼ cup milk

1 egg

Pour the oil to a depth of 1-inch in a large skillet. Place over medium-high heat.

In a mixing bowl, combine the sweet potatoes, jalapeños, flour, salt, baking powder, chili powder, cumin, pepper, and paprika. Blend well.

In a small bowl, whisk together milk and egg. Add to the sweet potato mixture and blend well.

Carefully drop tablespoons of the batter into the hot oil. Press lightly to flatten. Cook 2 minutes on each side, or until golden brown. Drain on paper towels and repeat with the remaining batter. Serve warm.

SOUTH FLORIDA SWEET POTATO CHIPS

While visiting my friend Tara in Miami, we had lunch at a great little sandwich shop that served these chips. I immediately had to duplicate them at home. They are delish!

YIELD: 10 TO 12 SERVINGS

Vegetable oil

2 teaspoons kosher salt

1 teaspoon finely grated lime zest

2 sweet potatoes, peeled

Pour the oil to a depth of 4 inches in a large Dutch oven. Place over medium-high heat and bring to 375°F.

Meanwhile, in a small bowl, stir together the salt and zest. Set aside.

With a vegetable peeler or mandoline, shave the sweet potatoes in long strips. In batches, carefully drop the strips into the hot oil. Fry around 1 minute, stirring frequently until golden brown. Drain on paper towels and sprinkle with the salt mixture. Repeat with the remaining potatoes. Serve warm or at room temperature.

SOUTHERN SURPRISE SWEET POTATOES

I put "surprise" in this title because these do not smother sweet potatoes under a cloud of marshmallows. Instead, you have a crispy pecan topping that is very adult and extra delicious.

YIELD: 6 SERVINGS

3 cups cooked, mashed sweet potatoes

6 tablespoons plus 4 tablespoons unsalted butter, melted and divided

1 cup granulated sugar

1 egg

$\frac{1}{2}$ teaspoon pure vanilla extract

3 tablespoons all-purpose flour

1 cup chopped pecans

$\frac{1}{4}$ cup packed brown sugar

Preheat the oven to 350°F. Lightly grease an 8-inch square baking dish and set aside.

In a mixing bowl, combine the potatoes, 6 tablespoons of the butter, the granulated sugar, egg, extract, and flour. Blend well and transfer to the prepared baking dish.

In a separate small bowl, stir together the remaining 4 tablespoons of butter, the pecans, and brown sugar. Sprinkle evenly on top of the potato mixture.

Bake 25 minutes, or until hot and bubbly. Let stand 5 minutes before serving.

Note: To make the sweet potatoes with a marshmallow topping, omit the 4 tablespoons of the butter, the pecans, and brown sugar. Bake as directed above, but top with $1\frac{1}{2}$ cups miniature marshmallows and bake 5 minutes longer.

SPICY SAUSAGE AND SWEET POTATO KEBABS

This appetizer can be served warm or at room temperature. I prefer it warm with a nice dry red wine.

YIELD: 8 SERVINGS

1 cup mayonnaise

2 tablespoons fresh chopped parsley

3 garlic cloves, minced

2 teaspoons lemon juice

$\frac{1}{4}$ teaspoon white pepper

4 sweet potatoes, peeled and cut into 32 cubes

2 tablespoons olive oil

$\frac{1}{2}$ teaspoon black pepper

$\frac{1}{4}$ teaspoon kosher salt

$\frac{3}{4}$ pound spicy smoked sausage, cut into 32 pieces

In a small bowl, whisk together the mayonnaise, parsley, garlic, lemon juice, and white pepper. Cover and refrigerate.

Preheat the oven to 450°F.

Lightly grease a jelly-roll pan and add the sweet potatoes. Drizzle with the oil and sprinkle with the pepper and salt. Toss gently to evenly coat. Bake 20 minutes, turning the cubes halfway through the cooking time.

Meanwhile, place the sausage in a large skillet over medium-high heat. Cook 4 minutes, stirring occasionally so that each side browns. Drain on paper towels.

To serve, use short skewers to spear a sausage slice and then sweet potato. Serve with the flavored mayonnaise.

SYRUPS

(MAPLE AND SORGHUM)

THE FIRST TIME I SAW SORGHUM BEING MADE, I FELT LIKE I HAD STEPPED BACK IN TIME. IT WAS during a visit with the Guenther family who own Muddy Pond Sorghum Mill in Monterey, Tennessee. I quickly realized their hard work to make this syrup was a gift to those of us who like things pure, natural, and simple.

It was a sight to behold as draft horses (not mules) pulled the mill that was squeezing juice from the sorghum stalks or canes. When I saw the juice, I was surprised that it was green and wondered how this could possibly become the product I saw being sold there.

After a long, slow process of cooking the juice and skimming the boiling residue, thick syrup is the reward. It was all I could do to carry the jars I was purchasing to the checkout. For years, this tangy, sweet syrup has been chased by a product under the name of molasses. Don't fall for the marketing trick and think for even an instant the two resemble each other.

In the South, we are also famous for utilizing maple syrup. In the pure form, it is nothing short of sweet heaven. The mass produced maple-flavored syrups cannot compare on any level. They are merely corn syrups that have been given a little coloring and a smidgen of maple flavoring to make it look the same. It, sadly, is not.

Southerners are experts on flavor, and we like products that are memorable. Both pure maple and sorghum syrups lack nothing there and are regular staples in Southern pantries. At breakfast, we pour maple syrup over pancakes and waffles while sorghum is used as a topping for hot, buttered biscuits. Later in the day, they are used for baking the sweets we are known to pile on every holiday and special occasion table. For years, both have made living in the South a pure delight.

Nutrition: The nutritional content of maple syrup and sorghum syrup is nearly the same. Both are sources of B vitamins, folic acid, calcium, magnesium, iron, and potassium. They also both contain around fifty calories per tablespoon.

Storage: Sorghum syrup can be stored at room temperature. Like honey, it will eventually begin the natural process of crystallizing. All that is needed to return it to the original state is to place it over a low heat or to place the container in a warm water bath.

Maple syrup is fine when stored at room temperature if you use it regularly. If not, store it in the refrigerator and gently warm when ready to use.

MAPLE-BANANA BREAD

Maple syrup keeps this bread nice and moist, so the shelf life is instantly extended, even though it won't last long enough to go stale.

YIELD: 1 LOAF

2 cups all-purpose flour
$\frac{1}{2}$ cup granulated sugar
$\frac{1}{4}$ cup packed brown sugar
$1\frac{1}{2}$ teaspoons baking powder
1 teaspoon baking soda
1 teaspoon salt
1 egg
$\frac{1}{2}$ cup maple syrup
1 teaspoon banana extract
3 tablespoons unsalted butter, melted
$1\frac{1}{2}$ cups mashed bananas
1 cup slivered almonds, toasted

Preheat the oven to 350°F. Lightly grease a loaf pan and set aside.

In a mixing bowl, combine the flour, granulated sugar, brown sugar, baking powder, baking soda, and salt. Make a well in the center and set aside.

In a separate bowl, whisk together the egg, syrup, extract, butter, and bananas. Add to the flour mixture and stir until evenly moistened. Fold in the almonds. Transfer the batter to the prepared pan.

Bake 1 hour 30 minutes, or until a tester inserted in the center comes out clean. Cool in the pan 5 minutes on a wire rack. Cool completely before slicing and serving.

MAPLE-CREAM SCONES

A food processor makes this easy as can be. It also prevents overworking the dough, which will result in tough scones.

YIELD: 8 SERVINGS

2 cups all-purpose flour
2 tablespoons sugar
1 teaspoon salt
1 teaspoon baking soda
1 teaspoon baking powder
$\frac{1}{4}$ pound (1 stick) unsalted butter, cubed
$\frac{3}{4}$ cup maple syrup, divided
$1\frac{1}{2}$ cups cream, divided
1 egg, lightly beaten

Preheat the oven to 350°F. Lightly grease a baking sheet and set aside.

In the bowl of a food processor, combine the flour, sugar, salt, baking soda, and baking powder. Pulse briefly to mix. Add the butter and pulse until the mixture resembles coarse meal. Transfer to a mixing bowl and set aside.

In a small bowl, whisk together $\frac{1}{4}$ cup of the syrup and $\frac{1}{2}$ cup of the cream. Blend well. Add to the dry mixture and stir just until moistened.

Turn onto a lightly floured surface and knead 8 to 10 times. Form into a 7-inch disk and place on the prepared pan. Cut into eight wedges. Brush the tops with the egg. Bake 20 minutes, or until golden brown.

Meanwhile, in a small saucepan over medium heat, combine the remaining $\frac{1}{2}$ cup of syrup and 1 cup of cream. Bring to a simmer and cook 5 minutes, or until slightly thickened. Set aside to cool.

Serve the warm scones with the maple cream as a dipping sauce.

OLD-FASHIONED GINGERBREAD

Even though gingerbread dates back to the Middle Ages, Southerners have been baking this treat every autumn for decades. Sorghum makes this bread exceptional.

YIELD: 8 SERVINGS

1 1/4 cups all-purpose flour

1 teaspoon baking powder

1/4 teaspoon baking soda

1/2 teaspoon salt

1 teaspoon ground cinnamon

1/2 teaspoon ground ginger

1/4 teaspoon ground cloves

3 tablespoons vegetable shortening

5 tablespoons sugar

1/2 cup sorghum syrup

1/2 cup water

2 eggs, lightly beaten

Preheat the oven to 350°F. Lightly grease an 8-inch square baking pan and set aside.

In a medium bowl, combine the flour, baking powder, baking soda, salt, cinnamon, ginger, and cloves. Set aside.

In the bowl of an electric mixer, cream the shortening and sugar on medium speed until fluffy, around 2 minutes. In a separate bowl combine the sorghum, water, and eggs. Add to the shortening mixture alternately with the flour mixture, beating well after each addition until the mixture is smooth.

Spoon the batter into the prepared pan. Bake 35 minutes, or until a tester inserted in the center comes out clean. Cool to room temperature on a wire rack before cutting and serving.

MAPLE-NUT FUDGE

Get ready to stir and then get ready for a sweet treat that is marvelously full of maple flavor.

YIELD: 48 PIECES

2 tablespoons unsalted butter

1 cup sugar

2 cups maple syrup

2/3 cup cream

1/4 teaspoon salt

1 cup chopped walnuts or pecans

Lightly grease a 9-inch square baking pan and set aside.

Coat a deep saucepan with cooking spray. Place over medium-high heat and add the butter. When melted, add the sugar, syrup, cream, and salt. Stir until the sugar has completely dissolved. Bring to a boil and cook without stirring until a candy thermometer registers 235°F (or when a drop of the mixture forms a firm ball in a glass of cold water).

Remove from the heat and stir constantly 8 to 10 minutes, or until almost fully thickened. Stir in the nuts, blending evenly. Transfer immediately to the prepared pan. Cool completely on a wire rack before cutting into squares and serving. Store leftovers in an airtight container between layers of wax paper.

OVEN MAPLE-BACON PANCAKES

Looking for a one-dish breakfast meal that everyone will love? This is it! At first, I was leery of the cheese, but it helps the dish come together beautifully.

YIELD: 8 SERVINGS

2 eggs

1 1/2 cups all-purpose baking mix

1 tablespoon sugar

3/4 cup milk

1/4 cup maple syrup

1 1/2 cups shredded Cheddar cheese, divided

12 bacon slices, cooked and crumbled

Preheat the oven to 425°F. Lightly grease a 13 x 9-inch baking dish and set aside.

In the bowl of an electric mixer, combine the eggs, baking mix, sugar, milk, and syrup. Mix until smooth and then add 1/2 cup of the cheese.

Pour into the prepared dish and bake 12 minutes. Sprinkle with the remaining 1 cup of cheese and the bacon. Bake 5 minutes longer. Cut into squares and serve with additional maple syrup, if desired.

SHAPE-UP MAPLE-BAKED APPLES

You want to make sure to use apples that will hold their shape well for this recipe rather than those that fall apart and turn to sauce.

YIELD: 2 SERVINGS

2 Braeburn or Jonathan apples, cored

2 tablespoons golden raisins

2 tablespoons chopped pecans

1/2 teaspoon ground cinnamon

1/2 cup maple syrup, divided

2 tablespoons unsalted butter, divided

1/4 cup water

Preheat the oven to 350°F. Place the apples in an 8-inch square baking pan and set aside.

In a small bowl, combine the raisins, pecans, and cinnamon. Divide the mixture in half and, pressing firmly, fill in the apple cavities.

Pour 1/4 cup of the syrup over each apple and then top with 1 tablespoon of the butter. Pour the water around the apples. Cover and bake 45 to 50 minutes. Let stand 5 minutes before serving.

SPICED SORGHUM WAFFLES

Sorghum in itself would be perfect folded into waffle batter, but add layers of ginger, cinnamon, and nutmeg and it is autumn on a plate.

YIELD: 8 WAFFLES

6 tablespoons unsalted butter, softened

1/4 cup sorghum syrup

2 eggs, separated

1 3/4 cups all-purpose flour

2 3/4 teaspoons baking powder

1/4 teaspoon baking soda

1/4 teaspoon salt

1 teaspoon ground ginger

1/4 teaspoon ground cinnamon

1/4 teaspoon ground nutmeg

1 1/2 cups plus 2 tablespoons milk

Lightly grease and preheat a waffle iron.

Beat the butter at medium speed of an electric mixer until creamy. Add the syrup and beat well. Add the egg yolks, one at a time, beating well after each addition.

Combine the flour, baking powder, baking soda, salt, ginger, cinnamon, and nutmeg. Add to the sorghum mixture alternately with the milk, beginning and ending with the flour mixture.

Beat the egg whites at high speed of an electric mixer until stiff peaks form. Gently fold into the batter. Pour 1/2 cup of the batter on the hot iron and cook until golden brown. Repeat with the remaining batter. Serve warm with butter.

SORGHUM AND PECAN WINTER SQUASH

It's hard to beat winter squash that is baked with pecans, butter, and sorghum syrup. Serve with turkey, ham, or chicken.

YIELD: 4 TO 6 SERVINGS

3 acorn squash or 2 butternut squash

³/₄ cup chopped pecans

³/₄ cup sorghum syrup

3 tablespoons unsalted butter, melted

1 tablespoon grated orange zest

¹/₂ teaspoon salt

Preheat the oven to 375°F. Slice the squash in half lengthwise and remove the seeds. Place the cut side down in a 13 x 9-inch baking dish. Pour hot water around the squash. Bake 35 minutes. Drain and cool slightly.

Meanwhile, in a medium bowl, combine the pecans, sorghum, butter, zest, and salt, mixing well.

Turn the squash cut side up and spoon the pecan mixture into the cavities. Bake 30 minutes longer, or until the squash is tender. Serve warm.

Celebrations

December 17 is National Maple Syrup Day.

MAPLE SYRUP: Maple syrup is the sap from a maple tree. It is boiled down to evaporate the excess water. The result is a syrup that is simply a must for breakfast lovers. The sugar season (or tapping season) begins in February and was taught to the early American colonists by the Indians. Southerners use it as a pancake and waffle syrup, as well as a prized baking ingredient. Pure maple syrup has a thinner consistency and sweeter taste than imitation table syrups.

SORGHUM SYRUP: Sorghum is made by extracting juice from sorghum canes. It is then boiled down in extremely large, self-contained pans or cookers, while skimming the foam that develops as it cooks. What begins as an oddly green liquid at the start of the cooking process becomes a thick, dark syrup by the time it is done. Southerners use it as a table syrup and a cooking ingredient.

MOLASSES: Molasses is a vastly inferior product to sorghum and is made from a blend of sugarcane, beet cane, and corn syrup. You will sometimes hear it referred to as "black strap molasses" because it tends to be cooked nearly to the point of burning, giving it a bitter flavor and an extremely thick consistency. Never substitute it for sorghum, which has a tangy, clean flavor and is a 100 percent pure product. Some attempt to add to the confusion by labeling their products "sorghum molasses." This is molasses that has been enhanced by a bit of sorghum. Look for products that are labeled as 100 percent pure sorghum.

TEA

IF THERE EVER WAS AN OFFICIAL BEVERAGE OF THE SOUTH, IT WOULD HAVE TO BE SWEET TEA. Countless gallons of this elixir have been made and consumed over the decades. It has quenched many a thirst and cooled off glistening Southerners on front porch rockers and under shade trees our whole lives.

Tea became extremely popular in the South because it could be made quickly and inexpensively. This made it a daily beverage served over ice that was usually poured into leftover canning jars. At my grandmother's house, iced tea was served out of a blue Carnival glass pitcher. My mother knew better with all of us kids and a thirsty husband around and used a tin pitcher that I covet to this day.

It never occurred to me to try tea any other way than sweet and cold. That's how we drank it all year long. If I wanted something hot, I drank hot chocolate or hot cider and the adults around me drank coffee. Tea was always sweetened as it was made and the sugar was never added later. There's a good reason for that. Tea actually holds more dissolved sugar when it is added while the liquid is hot rather than when it is cold or at room temperature.

Unsweetened tea to a Southerner is merely brown water. We like tea sweetened with real sugar, not those sugar substitutes that come in pastel packets. Tea is the anchor of every meal and consistency of how it is made is very important to us. We would never buy tea in a bottle and perish the thought of it being packaged in a can.

The respect we show sweet tea is seen on every menu and you can order it in any restaurant all day long. Tea will always be the uniquely Southern beverage we reach for when our glasses are filled to the rim with ice. May it for forever reign as our sweet beverage king!

Fermented Tea: Black or fermented tea is the most popular tea used in the South. The leaves are withered in the sun and then mechanically bruised to break their leaf cells. They are allowed to ferment, but unlike yeast fermentation, they ferment thanks to the tannins and natural oils on the leaves. The leaves turn very dark during this process, hence the name.

Unfermented Tea: Green or unfermented tea is produced by steaming the leaves immediately after harvest to prevent fermentation and make them pliable. They are rolled to crush the leaf cells and fired or dried with blasts of hot air. The result is a tea with a pale color that has less aroma and flavor than black tea.

Semi-Fermented Tea: Oolong or semi-fermented tea leaves are given an intermediate treatment that is a combination of the fermented and unfermented processes. They are allowed to ferment partially, but then are steamed to stop the process. This produces a tea that is practically in between black and green teas in color and flavor.

"A SIP OF TRADITION" SWEET TEA

My sister and I were allowed to have sweet tea at supper (now called dinner) when we hit the magical age of eleven. It was a memorable moment in our lives! You can make it the traditional way by boiling the water, or place it in the sun to let nature do the brewing. Either way, it's refreshing!

YIELD: 8 CUPS

6 regular-size tea bags
4 cups boiling water
1 cup sugar
4 cups water

Place the tea bags in a large pitcher. Add the boiling water. Cover and let steep 5 minutes. Remove the tea bags, squeeze the excess moisture, and discard. Add the sugar and stir until the sugar has completely dissolved. Add the water and stir until well blended.

Cover and refrigerate until ready to serve. Serve over ice.

Note: For Sun Tea, place the tea bags in a large container. Add 8 cups of water. Cover and place in direct sunlight 5 hours. You may have to move the container to keep it in direct sunlight. Remove and discard the tea bags. Add the sugar and stir until it completely dissolves. Serve over ice.

ALMOND FRUIT TEA

The first time I enjoyed this marvelous fruit tea was at my friend Thelma Barrett's house. We had a lunch of chicken salad and pear halves on her patio and I couldn't get enough of it. I think of her every time I make this tea.

YIELD: 12 SERVINGS

2 quarts plus 2 cups water
6 regular-size tea bags
1 cup sugar
Juice of 3 lemons
1 teaspoon pure vanilla extract
1 teaspoon pure almond extract

Bring 2 cups of the water to a boil in a medium saucepan over high heat. Remove from the heat and add the tea bags. Steep 10 minutes and then remove the bags, squeeze the excess moisture, and discard the bags. Stir in the sugar and lemon juice, stirring until the sugar dissolves.

Transfer to a large pitcher. Add the remaining 2 quarts of water, the vanilla extract, and almond extract, stirring well. Cover and refrigerate until well chilled, at least 4 hours. Serve over ice.

BUNCH OF TEA PUNCH

Even though this makes quite a bit, you'll find it doesn't last very long! Keep a stash of it in your refrigerator for cooling off in the hot summer months.

YIELD: 1 GALLON

1 quart plus 9½ cups water
8 regular-size tea bags
1 cup sugar
1 (6-ounce) can frozen orange juice concentrate, thawed
1 (12-ounce) can frozen lemonade concentrate, thawed

Bring 1 quart of water to a boil over high heat. Place the tea bags in a large pitcher and pour the boiling water over the top. Cover and let steep 5 minutes.

Remove the tea bags, squeeze the excess moisture, and discard. Add the sugar and stir until completely dissolved. Stir in the orange juice and lemonade concentrates. Blend well. Add the remaining $9\frac{1}{2}$ cups of water, cover, and refrigerate until ready to serve. Serve over ice.

"CRUSH ON MINT" TEA

Use whatever mint variety you have growing in your garden. I typically grow spearmint, which is excellent in this tea.

YIELD: 8 CUPS

10 regular-size tea bags
2 quarts boiling water
$1\frac{1}{2}$ cups sugar
12 fresh mint sprigs
$\frac{1}{4}$ cup lemon juice

Place the tea bags in a large pitcher. Pour the boiling water over the tea bags. Cover and let steep 5 minutes. Remove the tea bags and squeeze the excess moisture. Discard.

Add the sugar and stir until it completely dissolves. Add the mint sprigs and juice. Cover and let steep 30 minutes. Strain through a fine-meshed sieve. Cover and refrigerate until ready to serve. Serve over ice.

"ENDLESS SUMMER" GRAPEFRUIT TEA

Sip on this great version of fruit tea all year long, particularly in the winter when we need a bit of sunshine in our glass.

YIELD: 2 QUARTS

1 quart water
3 regular-size tea bags
2 regular-size mint tea bags
$\frac{3}{4}$ cup sugar
$\frac{1}{2}$ cup lemon juice
$\frac{3}{4}$ cup grapefruit juice

Bring the water to a boil in a heavy saucepan over high heat. Add the regular and mint tea bags. Cover and steep 5 minutes. Squeeze the tea bags slightly and discard. Add the sugar, stirring until the sugar dissolves.

Transfer the tea mixture to a 2-quart pitcher. Add the lemon juice and grapefruit juice, stirring to blend. Add enough cold water to make 2 quarts. Cover and refrigerate at least 4 hours. Serve over ice.

TEA JULEPS

If you have a crowd headed your way and want to satisfy them quickly, have a pitcher of these non-traditional juleps ready to pour.

YIELD: 2 QUARTS

1 (.24) ounce package ice tea mix
$\frac{1}{4}$ cup peppermint schnapps
$\frac{1}{4}$ cup bourbon
Mint sprigs for garnish

Prepare the tea mix according to the package directions. Stir in the schnapps and bourbon, mixing well. Cover and refrigerate at least 4 hours.

Stir again when ready to serve. Serve over ice with a garnish of fresh mint.

"LADIES WHO LUNCH" LEMON TEA CAKE

You will never say this cake is dry. The lemon tea syrup keeps it nice and moist.

YIELD: 12 SERVINGS

2 cups all-purpose flour

$^1/_2$ teaspoon cream of tartar

$^1/_4$ teaspoon baking soda

$^1/_4$ teaspoon salt

$^1/_2$ pound (2 sticks) unsalted butter, softened

$2^1/_2$ cups granulated sugar, divided

5 eggs, room temperature

1 teaspoon pure lemon extract

1 tablespoon finely grated lemon zest

$^1/_2$ cup fresh lemon juice

$^1/_2$ cup steeped lemon herb tea

Confectioners' sugar for dusting

Preheat the oven to 325°F. Grease and flour an 8-cup Bundt pan and set aside.

In a mixing bowl, sift together the flour, cream of tartar, baking soda, and salt. Set aside.

Cream the butter and 1$^1/_2$ cups of the granulated sugar in the bowl of an electric mixer until light and fluffy, around 2 minutes. Add the eggs, one at a time, beating well after each addition. Add the extract and zest.

At low speed, gradually add the flour mixture, beating just until the batter is evenly mixed. Pour into the prepared pan and bake 1 hour or until a tester inserted in the center comes out clean.

Meanwhile, combine the lemon juice, tea, and the remaining cup of granulated sugar in a small saucepan over medium-high heat. Bring to a boil and stir constantly 7 minutes or until the mixture thickens. Cool completely.

Cool the cake in the pan on a wire rack 10 minutes. Pierce the cake all over with an ice pick.

Slowly pour the syrup over the cake, allowing it to absorb completely into the cake. Let the cake cool another 15 minutes. Transfer to a serving platter. Dust with confectioners' sugar before serving.

MIND YOUR TEAS AND CUBES

Enhancing the South's favorite beverage has never been nicer. Make sure you have plenty of ice for this party tea.

YIELD: 3 QUARTS

6 regular-size tea bags

$1^1/_2$ cups boiling water

$1^1/_2$ cups sugar

4 cups water

$^3/_4$ cup lemon juice

1 tablespoon pure vanilla extract

1 teaspoon pure almond extract

1 (1-liter) bottle ginger ale, chilled

Place the tea bags in a large pitcher. Pour the boiling water over the top. Cover and steep 5 minutes. Remove the tea bags and squeeze to remove the excess moisture. Discard.

Add the sugar and stir until it has completely dissolved. Add the 4 cups of water, lemon juice, vanilla extract, and almond extract. Cover and refrigerate at least 4 hours.

When ready to serve, stir in the ginger ale. Serve immediately over ice.

TEA PARTY SANGRIA

Don't limit this recipe to only lemon herb tea. Orange, raspberry, or mint work just as well and give it a nice flavor change.

YIELD: 6 CUPS

4 lemon herb tea bags
2 cups boiling water
3 tablespoons sugar
2 cups cranberry juice cocktail
2 cups dry white wine
1 lemon, sliced

Place the tea bags in a large pitcher. Pour the boiling water over the top. Cover and let steep 5 minutes. Remove the tea bags and squeeze to remove the excess moisture. Discard.

Stir in the sugar until it completely dissolves. Set aside to cool 30 minutes.

Stir in the cranberry juice and wine. Serve over ice with a lemon slice as garnish.

I'm trying to eat better.
And I do feel wise after drinking
tea. After eating vegetables,
I just feel hungry."

—CARRIE LATET

TEA-SER POUND CAKE

Shhh! Who would ever guess that the secret ingredient in this pound cake is instant tea? If you don't tell, I won't either!

YIELD: 12 SERVINGS

$1/2$ pound (2 sticks) unsalted butter, softened
$1/2$ cup vegetable shortening
3 cups sugar
5 eggs
3 cups all-purpose flour
$1/2$ teaspoon baking powder
$1/4$ teaspoon salt
$1/2$ cup unsweetened instant tea powder
1 cup milk
1 teaspoon pure almond or vanilla extract

Preheat the oven to 325°F. Grease and flour a 10-inch tube pan or 12-cup Bundt pan and set aside.

In the bowl of an electric mixer, cream the butter and shortening 2 minutes. Add the sugar and beat 5 minutes. Add the eggs, one at a time, beating just until the yellow disappears.

In a separate bowl, combine the flour, baking powder, salt, and tea powder. Reduce the mixer speed to low. Add to the butter mixture alternately with the milk, beginning and ending with the flour mixture. Stir in the extract.

Transfer the batter to the prepared pan. Bake 1 hour 35 minutes, or until a tester inserted in the center comes out clean. Cool in the pan 10 minutes before removing to a wire rack to cool completely.

TOMATOES

I DIDN'T ALWAYS LIKE TOMATOES. THE FIRST TIME I TRIED A BITE WAS OFF MY GRANDFATHER'S dinner plate and my unrefined palette didn't respond favorably. But as we mature and change, so do our tastes and I have loved them for years.

Like most everyone else in the South, I grow my own tomatoes and eat them every day all summer long. In fact, no matter what the calendar says, summer doesn't officially begin until the first ripe tomato is harvested. From that point forward, you've got yourself a Southern summer full of tomatoes every day. That regular harvest comes to a screeching halt whenever the first frost arrives. Until then, anything straight from the vine is mine!

My grandmother used to say that you never picked a tomato until it was "dead ripe." I still use the term and the rule in my own garden. I will not pick a tomato and let it finish ripening on my kitchen countertop. Why? The plant does a much better job!

Technically, tomatoes are fruits, but you wouldn't know it since we use them like vegetables.

While I naturally gravitate to the fire-engine-red types, don't stop there. The colors range from delicate yellow to deep purple and the flavor is just as diverse. You can change a dish dramatically by using tomatoes that are mild and mellow to tart and acidic. Size runs the gamut as well, running from tremendous to tiny. The options are yours for the taking.

I have not included a recipe for the best way to enjoy this summer sensation. That would be sandwiched between slices of very fresh white bread that has been smeared generously with mayonnaise. When you hear people say it's the South in your mouth, that's what they are talking about!

Equivalents: A pound is typically three or four medium-size tomatoes. This will yield about two-and-a-half cups chopped, three cups of wedges, or three cups of slices.

Peeling: For large quantities of tomatoes to peel, bring a large stockpot of water to a boil. Prepare a large pot of ice water. Cut an X in the bottom of each tomato. Add the tomatoes to the boiling water 1 minute. Remove from the boiling water with a slotted spoon and transfer to the ice water. Leave in the ice water one minute and then drain. When cool, peel away the skins.

Seeding: Removing the seeds from tomatoes is especially important for those with digestive problems. It's easy to do. Just cut the tomato in half horizontally. Cup each half in the palm of your hands and give it a gentle squeeze over the sink. The seeds and extra juice will fall out quickly, leaving you with all the tasty pulp.

APPALACHIAN TOMATO MARMALADE

Spoon this old-fashioned marmalade over grilled veggies, pork loin, or chicken breasts.

YIELD: ABOUT 2 CUPS

1 tablespoon olive oil

1 sweet onion, peeled and finely chopped

5 large fresh tomatoes, peeled and finely chopped

2 garlic cloves, minced

3 tablespoons chopped fresh basil

$1/2$ teaspoon kosher salt

$1/2$ teaspoon fennel seeds, toasted

$1/4$ teaspoon black pepper

Preheat the oven to 400°F. Heat the oil over medium-high heat in a large ovenproof saucepan. Sauté the onions until tender and slightly brown, about 10 minutes. Remove from the heat and add the tomatoes, garlic, basil, salt, seeds, and pepper. Stir well.

Cover and bake 45 minutes, or until thick and bubbly, stirring occasionally. Serve warm, at room temperature, or cold.

COLD CUCUMBER TOMATO SALAD

For as long as I can remember, a bowl of this salad was kept in the refrigerator in the summer. It was continually replenished as the cucumber and tomato harvest continued.

YIELD: 2 CUPS

2 cucumbers, peeled and sliced

1 large tomato, cut in small wedges

1 green bell pepper, seeded and julienned

1 purple onion, peeled and thinly sliced

$1/3$ cup vegetable oil

3 tablespoons red wine vinegar

3 tablespoons sugar

$3/4$ teaspoon kosher salt

$1/4$ teaspoon black pepper

Place the cucumbers, tomato, bell pepper, and onion in a medium bowl. In a small jar with a tight-fitting lid, combine the oil, vinegar, sugar, salt, and pepper. Shake to emulsify and dissolve the sugar.

Pour over the vegetables, tossing gently to coat. Cover and refrigerate at least 3 hours before serving.

COOL DOWN TOMATO SOUP

No one wants a steamy bowl of tomato soup during the dog days of summer. Here's what to serve instead.

YIELD: 6 SERVINGS

3 pounds tomatoes, peeled and seeded

$1/2$ teaspoon balsamic vinegar

$1/2$ teaspoon kosher salt

2 green onions, chopped

2 tablespoons red bell pepper, finely chopped

2 tablespoons cucumber, peeled, seeded, and finely chopped

2 tablespoons avocado, finely chopped

2 tablespoons chopped fresh basil

$1/3$ cup plain yogurt

Purée the tomatoes in a blender or food processor until smooth. Transfer to a large mixing bowl and add the vinegar and salt. Stir gently to combine. Cover and refrigerate at least 2 hours.

Just before serving, stir in the onions, bell pepper,

cucumber, avocado, and basil. Place the yogurt in a squirt bottle and garnish each serving with a yogurt swirl. Serve immediately.

●●

"DINNER IN THE GAZEBO" TOMATO TART

Every time I serve this tart, I get raves. The pairing of tomatoes from my vegetable garden and fresh basil from my herb garden is perfect.

YIELD: 8 SERVINGS

1 recipe Single Pie Pastry (page 402)
1 cup shredded mozzarella cheese, divided
4 Roma tomatoes, cut in small wedges
$^3/_4$ cup loosely packed basil leaves,
    coarsely chopped
4 garlic cloves, minced
$^1/_2$ cup mayonnaise
$^1/_4$ cup grated Parmesan cheese
$^1/_4$ cup white pepper
Fresh basil leaves for garnish

Preheat the oven to 375°F. Place the pastry in the bottom of a 9-inch pie pan. Don't prick. Partially bake 5 minutes. Sprinkle with $^1/_2$ cup of the mozzarella. Cool in the pan on a wire rack.

Meanwhile, drain the tomatoes on paper towels. Arrange the wedges over the melted cheese.

In a medium bowl, combine the remaining $^1/_2$ cup of the mozzarella with the basil, garlic, mayonnaise, Parmesan, and pepper. Spread evenly over the tomatoes.

Bake 25 minutes, or until the cheese is golden brown. Let stand 5 minutes before serving. Garnish with additional basil leaves and serve warm.

DIRTY BLOODY MARY

This recipe is from my good friend Laura's father, Tom. It is a delightfully spicy rendition of this lazy weekend morning favorite.

YIELD: 1 SERVING

1 cup tomato juice
$1^1/_2$ ounces vodka
7 dashes Worcestershire sauce
7 dashes seasoned salt or beau monde
5 dashes celery salt
5 dashes Creole seasoning
3 dashes hot sauce
1 teaspoon olive juice
1 lemon wedge
Freshly ground black pepper

In a large empty glass, combine the tomato juice, vodka, Worcestershire, seasoned salt, celery salt, Creole seasoning, hot sauce, olive juice, and the juice from the lemon wedge. Stir and add ice to fill. Top with a sprinkling of black pepper and serve.
Note: Garnish sticks include celery stalks, asparagus spears, or long green beans. Cocktail pick garnishes include lemon, lime, or orange wedges, spring onions, or olives.

●●

DRIED TOMATO QUICK BREAD

I love how this rustic bread is speckled with bits of tomatoes and cheese.

YIELD: 8 TO 10 SERVINGS

$^1/_4$ cup chopped dried tomatoes
2 cups hot water, divided
8 tablespoons unsalted butter

⅛ teaspoon kosher salt

1 cup all-purpose flour

4 eggs

⅔ cup shredded Gruyère cheese

Preheat the oven to 425°F. Lightly grease a round pizza pan or baking sheet and set aside.

Cover the tomatoes with 1 cup of hot water. Set aside to rehydrate 10 minutes and then drain.

In a large saucepan, over medium-high heat, combine the remaining cup of water, the butter, and salt. Bring to a boil and reduce the heat to medium.

Add the flour and cook, stirring continuously until the dough begins to pull away from the sides of the pan, about 2 minutes. Remove from the heat and beat in the eggs, one at a time. Stir in the tomatoes and cheese.

Place heaping tablespoons of the dough so that they are just touching on the prepared baking sheet. Bake 10 minutes and reduce the oven temperature to 350°F. Bake 20 minutes longer, or until golden brown. Serve warm.

FRIED BUTTERMILK GREEN TOMATOES

The buttermilk dressing mix gives this Southern favorite an extra bit of nip!

YIELD: 8 SIDE DISH SERVINGS OR 12 APPETIZER SERVINGS

¼ cup all-purpose flour

2 egg whites, lightly beaten

2 teaspoons dry buttermilk dressing mix

½ cup dry plain breadcrumbs or cornmeal

¼ cup vegetable oil, divided

4 green tomatoes, cut in ¼-inch slices

Freshly grated Parmesan cheese

Place the flour in a shallow dish and set aside. Combine the egg whites and dressing mix in another shallow dish and set aside. Place the crumbs in another shallow dish and set aside. Heat half of the oil in a large skillet over medium heat.

Meanwhile, coat each tomato slice in flour and then dip in the egg mixture and finally in the crumbs. Arrange the slices in a single layer in the hot oil. Cook 2 minutes on each side, or until golden brown. Drain on paper towels. Cook the remaining slices, adding the remaining oil as necessary. Sprinkle the tomatoes with freshly grated Parmesan and serve hot.

HERBED TOMATO HOE CAKES

An easy, deliciously fresh appetizer showcased on the most Southern of savory "cakes."

YIELD: 8 APPETIZER SERVINGS

2 cups seeded, chopped tomatoes

½ teaspoon garlic salt

¼ teaspoon black pepper

2 tablespoons chopped fresh basil

1 tablespoon capers

1 teaspoon chopped fresh oregano

1 recipe Hoe Cakes (page 193)

In a medium bowl, combine the tomatoes, salt, pepper, basil, capers, and oregano. Cover and let stand 30 minutes.

Meanwhile, prepare the Hoe Cakes in small rounds. Top the hot Hoe Cakes with the tomato mixture and serve.

MARINATED FRESH TOMATOES

Layers of fresh sliced tomatoes and onions highlight each other magnificently.

YIELD: 8 TO 10 SERVINGS

1 large purple onion, peeled and thinly sliced

4 cups ice water

³⁄₄ cup balsamic vinegar

¹⁄₄ cup olive oil

2 tablespoons dry white wine

2 teaspoons sugar

¹⁄₂ teaspoon kosher salt

¹⁄₂ teaspoon black pepper

2 garlic cloves, minced

¹⁄₂ cup chopped fresh basil

6 large tomatoes, sliced

In a large bowl, place the onion slices in the ice water. Set aside 30 minutes. Drain and pat dry with paper towels.

In a jar with a tight-fitting lid, combine the vinegar, oil, wine, sugar, salt, pepper, garlic, and basil. Shake to emulsify.

Layer half of the tomato and onion slices in a shallow dish. Drizzle with half of dressing. Repeat, cover, and refrigerate at least 1 hour.

Note: Excellent when served with thin toasted slices of Baked Hot-Water Cornbread (page 189).

SLOW ROASTED TOMATOES

You will be amazed at how the flavor of fresh tomatoes changes in this dish.

YIELD: 12 SERVINGS

6 large ripe fresh tomatoes, halved

6 teaspoons olive oil

¹⁄₂ teaspoon kosher salt

¹⁄₂ teaspoon black pepper

3 garlic cloves, minced

3 tablespoons chopped fresh basil

Preheat the oven to 325°F. Place the tomatoes on a jelly-roll pan with the cut sides up. Drizzle evenly with the oil and sprinkle with the salt and pepper. Bake 2 hours, or until the tomatoes collapse and begin to caramelize.

Sprinkle with the minced garlic halfway through the roasting process. Sprinkle with the fresh basil just before serving. Serve hot or at room temperature.

Note: For variation, top with crumbled goat cheese or feta just before serving.

SMOKY MOUNTAIN GREEN TOMATO PICKLES

These pickles remind me of time in the East Tennessee mountains. I suppose it's because fall is so gorgeous there and these are a great way to utilize all the tomatoes you harvest just before frost arrives!

YIELD: 6 QUARTS

Small green firm tomatoes

6 garlic cloves, peeled

6 celery stalks, cut into 2-inch lengths

6 green bell peppers, seeded and quartered

2 quarts water

1 quart distilled white vinegar

1 cup canning salt

6 sprigs fresh dill

Pack the tomatoes in hot quart jars. To each jar, add 1 garlic clove, 1 celery stalk, and the equivalent of 1 bell pepper. Combine the water, vinegar, and canning salt and bring to a boil. Add the dill and boil 5 minutes.

Pour over the tomatoes, leaving $1/2$-inch headspace. Remove the air bubbles, wipe the jar rims, and adjust the lids. Process 15 minutes in a boiling water bath. Cool on a wire rack away from drafts. Do not use for 6 weeks. Store at room temperature.

* * *

SPICED TOMATO JAM

This old family recipe is back in the spotlight thanks to how it marries so well with grilled fish, chicken, and pork. It even makes scrambled eggs dance!

YIELD: 1 CUP

3 tomatoes, peeled, seeded, and chopped
1 sweet onion, peeled and chopped
$1/3$ cup apple jelly
3 tablespoons cider vinegar
2 tablespoons chopped fresh tarragon
$1/2$ teaspoon red pepper flakes
$1/4$ teaspoon kosher salt

In a heavy saucepan over medium heat, combine the tomatoes, onions, jelly, vinegar, tarragon, pepper flakes, and salt. Bring to a boil, stirring occasionally. Reduce the heat to low and cook 35 to 40 minutes, stirring occasionally. Cool to room temperature before using.

Note: Leftover jam should be refrigerated and used within one month.

Celebration

May is National Salsa Month.
Every Year: January 1 is National Bloody
   Mary Day.

SUN-DRIED TOMATO SALSA

The flavor will make you think there's another base other than tomatoes. The result is an unforgettable salsa that can be made year-round.

YIELD: 3 CUPS

1 cup chopped sun-dried tomatoes
$1/3$ cup olive oil
$1/4$ cup balsamic vinegar
3 large garlic cloves, minced
1 purple onion, peeled and chopped
1 orange or yellow bell pepper, seeded
   and chopped
$1/2$ cup chopped fresh basil
$1/3$ cup capers, rinsed
$1/2$ teaspoon kosher salt
$1/4$ teaspoon black pepper

Place the tomatoes in a glass bowl and toss with the oil and vinegar. Cover and refrigerate 2 hours.

Add the garlic, onion, pepper, basil, capers, salt, and pepper, tossing well. Cover and refrigerate another 2 hours. Bring to room temperature before serving with pita triangles, crackers, or tortilla chips.

> "It's difficult to think of anything but pleasant thoughts while eating a homegrown tomato."
>
> —LEWIS GRIZZARD

TURKEY

I LOVE THANKSGIVING AND THE FACT THAT WE HAVE A NATIONAL HOLIDAY DEVOTED TO GIVING thanks for the bounty. Everything about it reminds me of home and is deliciously comforting. It isn't really that Thanksgiving ushers in the holiday season. It's the traditional meal, including a roasted turkey, my mother's incredible dressing, the gravy, the green bean casserole, the cranberry sauce, the rolls, and the pies.

The anchor of the meal has always been turkey for us, and those leftovers could be stretched through the long weekend with ease. While some try to serve this dinner celebration without turkey, in my house, the bird will always be as necessary as the prayer before the meal.

It is a well-known fact that Benjamin Franklin pushed long and hard to make the turkey our national bird. I'm glad he didn't succeed in that venture. Who would want to eat our national bird?

Southerners have traipsed through the woods and hunted turkeys for decades. Years ago, we were forced to feast on wild turkeys that were tough to chew thanks to well-exercised muscles that were used when they flew.

Today, it's a much different bird that is lean, tender, and juicy thanks to modern breeding and processing. Plus, the whole turkey has winged its way into a whole new generation of products that are available year-round. I love the convenience of using tenderloins, breasts, cutlets, and turkey sausage, just to name a few. These cuts have transformed turkey from a once-a-year specialty to a year-round entrée with all the trimmings.

Size Selection: When purchasing a whole turkey, allow at least one pound of turkey per person. In order to have generous amounts for leftovers, you can go up to one-and-a-half pounds per person. If you are only purchasing a turkey breast, allow three-fourths pound per person.

Storage: Cooked turkey should be kept refrigerated and used within three days. Frozen cooked leftovers should be used within two months. For maximum flavor, thaw and use raw frozen turkey within nine months.

Thawing: All it takes is a little bit of forethought to have a frozen turkey thawed and ready to cook. Let the refrigerator do all of the work for you. Place it unopened and unwrapped with the breast side up on a large, sturdy tray in the refrigerator. The key is to pay attention to the turkey size. Whole turkeys between nine and twelve pounds need two days in the refrigerator to thaw. Those between twelve and sixteen pounds need another day. Those that are even heavier need a day on top of that. It's no problem if you thaw it too soon, because it will easily keep at least three days in the refrigerator.

BLACKENED TURKEY TENDERLOINS

This is terrific served over a cold green salad or hot cooked rice. Or you can serve it as a sandwich meat with kick! This can get smoky, so make sure your exhaust fan is on high.

YIELD: 6 TO 8 SERVINGS

1 (1-pound) package turkey tenderloins
1 tablespoon paprika
1 teaspoon onion powder
1 teaspoon garlic powder
1/4 teaspoon black pepper

Place the tenderloins on a plastic cutting board and with a sharp knife, slice in half horizontally. Place each piece between two pieces or plastic wrap and pound with a meat mallet to an even thickness.

In a small bowl, combine the paprika, onion powder, garlic powder, and pepper. Rub over the tenderloins and set aside.

Coat a cast-iron skillet with cooking spray and place over high heat. Blacken each tenderloin 4 minutes on each side or until no pink remains. Let stand 5 minutes before cutting in thin slices to serve.

CAJUN SPICED GRILLED TURKEY

A spicy dry rub makes this turkey unforgettable. If your grill is large enough, you can easily double the recipe because two take the same amount of time on the grill as one.

YIELD: 8 SERVINGS

1 (3- to 4-pound) turkey breast
Vegetable oil
1 tablespoon onion powder
1 tablespoon garlic powder
1/2 teaspoon dried thyme
1/4 teaspoon cayenne
1/4 teaspoon black pepper
1/4 teaspoon salt

Place the turkey on a sturdy platter and brush with the vegetable oil. In a small bowl, combine the onion powder, garlic powder, thyme, cayenne, black pepper, and salt. Rub all over the turkey and refrigerate 2 to 8 hours.

When ready to prepare, bring the grill to medium heat (350°F). Spray the grill rack with cooking spray. Place the turkey on the grill rack directly over the drip pan and cover. Grill 1 1/2 to 2 1/2 hours or until a meat thermometer registers 170°F. Cover with aluminum foil and let stand 15 minutes before slicing and serving warm.

DAY-AFTER TURKEY SUCCOTASH SOUP

This is a great way to disguise turkey leftovers!

YIELD: 8 SERVINGS

6 bacon slices
3/4 cup sliced celery
1/2 cup sliced green onions
2 garlic cloves, minced
3 1/2 cups cooked, chopped turkey
8 cups turkey or chicken stock
4 tomatoes, seeded and coarsely chopped
1 (10-ounce) package frozen lima beans, thawed
1 1/2 cups whole kernel corn
1/4 cup tomato paste

3/4 teaspoon dried thyme

1 bay leaf

1/4 teaspoon salt

1/4 teaspoon black pepper

Place the bacon in a Dutch oven over medium heat. Fry until crisp, around 4 minutes. Drain on paper towels and crumble when cool enough to handle. Set aside.

Add the celery, onions, and garlic to the pan drippings. Sauté 4 minutes, or until the vegetables are tender. Stir in the turkey, stock, tomatoes, lima beans, corn, tomato paste, thyme, bay leaf, salt, and pepper.

Increase the heat to medium high and bring to a boil. Cover and reduce the heat to low. Simmer 30 to 35 minutes. Remove and discard the bay leaf. Serve in soup bowls and garnish with the bacon.

DEEP-FRIED TURKEY

If have a turkey fryer and like juicy turkey, this is the way to cook it. I especially love the crispy outer skin! My brother is a master turkey fryer!

YIELD: 12 TO 15 SERVINGS

1 (12- to 15-pound) whole turkey

4 to 5 gallons peanut or vegetable oil

Remove the neck and giblets from the turkey cavities. Place the turkey on the fryer rod and place in the sink. Let stand 20 minutes to allow all the liquid to drain from the turkey cavity.

Meanwhile, pour the oil in a deep turkey fryer to the fill line or to 12 inches from the top. Bring the oil to 375°F. Carefully lower the turkey into the hot oil with the rod attachment.

Fry 1 hour or until a meat thermometer registers 170°F when inserted in the breast. Let stand at least 15 minutes before slicing and serving.

FRIED TURKEY CUTLETS

Because cutlets are thin, they are best when cooked fast. Serve this quick dinner with any kind of gravy and some fresh green beans.

YIELD: 4 SERVINGS

1 (1-pound) package turkey cutlets

1/2 teaspoon salt

1/4 teaspoon black pepper

1 1/2 cups seasoned dry breadcrumbs

2 eggs

1/2 cup milk

1/2 cup vegetable oil, divided

Sprinkle the cutlets evenly with the salt and pepper. Set aside.

Place the breadcrumbs in a shallow bowl. In a separate shallow bowl, whisk together the eggs and milk. Dip each cutlet in the egg mixture and dredge in the breadcrumbs.

Heat 1/4 cup of the oil in a large skillet over medium-high heat. Fry half of the cutlets around 2 minutes on each side or until golden brown and completely done. Repeat with the remaining oil and cutlets. Serve warm.

"GOBBLE-IT-UP" TURKEY HASH

Hash has always been a great way to utilize leftover meat. It is most often matched with potatoes and onions. This version is incredible!

YIELD: 6 SERVINGS

1 1/2 pound new potatoes, diced

3 tablespoons unsalted butter

1 yellow onion, peeled and chopped

1 green bell pepper, seeded and chopped

1 red bell pepper, seeded and chopped

2 celery stalks, chopped

2 cups cooked, chopped turkey

$^3/_4$ cup half-and-half or milk

1 tablespoon poultry seasoning

1 tablespoon Worcestershire sauce

$^1/_4$ teaspoon salt

$^1/_4$ teaspoon black pepper

Place the potatoes in a heavy saucepan and cover with cold water. Place over medium-high heat and bring to a boil. Cook 12 minutes, covered or just until the potatoes are tender. Drain and set aside.

In a large skillet over medium heat, melt the butter. Add the onion, green pepper, red pepper, and celery. Sauté 7 minutes, or until the vegetables are nearly tender.

Stir in the turkey, half-and-half, poultry seasoning, Worcestershire, salt, and pepper. Reduce the heat to low and cook 12 minutes longer or until hot. Serve warm.

KENTUCKY HOT BROWNS

The Brown Hotel in Louisville is the original home of this open-faced turkey delight. The intention was for it to be a late dinner, but it is perfect any time of the day.

YIELD: 2 SERVINGS

2 tablespoons unsalted butter

2 tablespoons all-purpose flour

$2^1/_2$ cups half-and-half

$^1/_2$ cup grated Romano cheese

$^1/_4$ teaspoon salt

$^1/_4$ teaspoon black pepper

2 thick slices Texas toast with crusts removed

2 (6-ounce) slices roasted turkey breasts

1 Roma tomato, sliced in 4 wedges

4 slices cooked bacon

1 tablespoon chopped fresh parsley

$^1/_2$ teaspoon paprika

In a heavy saucepan over medium heat, melt the butter. Whisk in the flour and cook 2 minutes, stirring constantly. Add the half-and-half and cook 3 minutes longer. Remove from the heat and stir in the Romano, salt, and pepper. Stir until completely smooth and set aside.

Preheat the broiler.

Place each bread slice in a small oven-proof dish and top with the turkey. Place two tomato wedges on the side of each turkey slice. Evenly divide the sauce between the two dishes and ladle over the top.

Place under the broiler for 1 minute, or until the top is lightly browned and bubbly. Top with two slices of bacon in a crisscross pattern. Sprinkle evenly with the parsley and paprika and serve immediately.

MIXED TURKEY MEATLOAF

Using a mixture of ground turkey and ground turkey sausage gives this recipe a nice flavor punch. Serve it with Tomato Gravy (page 238).

YIELD: 6 SERVINGS

1 pound ground turkey

1 pound ground hot turkey sausage

1 white onion, peeled and chopped

1 cup chopped fresh parsley

2 eggs

2 tablespoons plain dry breadcrumbs

$^1/_2$ teaspoon salt

$^1/_4$ teaspoon black pepper

Preheat the oven to 350°F. Lightly grease a loaf pan and set aside.

In a large mixing bowl, combine the ground turkey, turkey sausage, onion, parsley, and eggs. Stir well to blend. Add the breadcrumbs, salt, and pepper, mixing well.

Transfer to the prepared pan. Bake 45 to 55 minutes, or until a meat thermometer registers 170°F. Let stand at least 5 minutes before slicing and serving with Tomato Gravy (page 238).

OVEN-ROASTED TURKEY

This is how I've been roasting turkey for years. It is simple as can be and deliciously moist.

YIELD: 10 TO 12 SERVINGS

1 (10- to 12-pound) whole turkey, thawed if frozen
Vegetable oil

Preheat the oven to 325°F. Remove the neck and giblets from the turkey cavities. Drain the turkey well.

Turn the wing tips back to hold the neck skin in place. Truss, if desired, by tying the legs together with kitchen twine to maintain a compact shape.

Place the turkey breast side up on a roasting rack in a roasting pan. Insert a meat thermometer in the thickest part of the thigh, next to the body. Rub the outside of the turkey with vegetable oil. Place in the oven so the thermometer face can be seen from the oven window.

Roast 3 hours or until the meat thermometer registers 180°F. Cover with aluminum foil and let stand 15 minutes before carving and serving.

TURKEY AND DUMPLINGS

This is another one of my turkey leftover recipes that is prepared in one pot. Haven't you washed enough dishes by now?

YIELD: 6 TO 8 SERVINGS

2 tablespoons unsalted butter
1 yellow onion, peeled and sliced
2 celery stalks, sliced
1 garlic clove, minced
3 cups cooked, chopped turkey
2 cups shredded green cabbage
1 (16-ounce) can whole tomatoes, undrained and cut up
1 (15.5-ounce) can kidney beans, undrained
$3\frac{1}{2}$ cups turkey or chicken stock
1 cup water
1 teaspoon dried thyme
1 teaspoon salt
2 cups all-purpose baking mix
$\frac{2}{3}$ cup milk

Place the butter in a Dutch oven over medium heat to melt. Add the onions, celery, and garlic and sauté 4 minutes.

Stir in the turkey, cabbage, tomatoes, beans, stock, water, thyme, and salt. Cover and reduce the heat to medium low. Simmer 30 minutes or until the cabbage is tender.

In a mixing bowl, stir together the baking mix and milk to form a soft dough. Drop tablespoons of the dough on top of the stew. Cover and simmer 15 minutes longer. Serve in warmed soup bowls.

TURNIPS

MENTION TURNIPS AND MOST SOUTHERNERS WILL IMMEDIATELY THINK OF THE GREENS simmering away in a pot on the stove. While that part of the plant is certainly a huge part of Southern culinary culture, so are the roots of this plant.

Once again, we see turnips play a role in feeding families throughout the years when finances were dwindling. They were a popular and much-sought-after food item during the Civil War and hit the spotlight again during the Great Depression. When you look at the root closely, it's easy to see why.

Turnips are incredibly easy to grow in the South and aren't too picky about weather conditions. As long as the soil isn't a rock-hard clay, you can grow them. Unlike many vegetables, the entire plant is edible. While the green tops have a limited shelf life, the roots make up for that with long keeping qualities.

That's especially important during the cold winter months, and these root vegetables are credited with keeping many starving Southerners alive during those lean times. While it's very easy not to be picky when you're hungry, turnips have continued to be a favorite in our area in the good times as well.

They are as easy to cook as they are to grow and are quite lovely. The creamy white roots will have a tinge of either green or purple at the top, depending on the variety. Like potatoes, they just require digging out of the ground and brushing off. Then let them add their distinctive mildly sweet flavor to your winter menus and you have a taste of the past right this minute.

Nutrition: Turnips are a good source of vitamin C, potassium, and phosphorus, while being low in calories. A three-and-a-half-ounce serving contains only thirty calories.

Selection: Choose turnips that are firm to the touch and fairly heavy for the size. Usually, the greens are not attached, but if they are, they should look fresh and not wilted. Remove the tops as soon as you get them home because they will pull moisture from the roots, hastening decay. Do not wash turnips until you are ready to use.

Storage: Keep turnips in a cool, dry, dark place or in the refrigerator if you have room.

BACON AND TURNIP TURNOVERS

This surprisingly good appetizer is great served alone or with your favorite dipping sauce.

YIELD: 24 APPETIZERS

1 turnip, peeled and grated
1 cup finely chopped onions
5 bacon slices, cooked and crumbled
$\frac{1}{4}$ teaspoon black pepper
1 recipe Double Pie Pastry (page 400)
2 tablespoons unsalted butter, melted

Preheat the oven to 375°F.

In a mixing bowl, combine the turnips, onions, bacon, and pepper. Toss to combine and set aside.

Roll each pastry on a hard surface and cut in rounds with a 2-inch cutter. Place 1 teaspoon of the turnip mixture on one-half of the round. Fold the other half over and press the edges together to seal. Use the tines of a fork to create a design along the edges.

Place on an ungreased baking sheet and brush the tops with the butter. Bake 15 to 17 minutes, or until lightly browned. Serve warm.

BRAISED TURNIPS

Stove-top braising is a great cooking method that allows flavors to develop by browning the food in fat first and then adding liquid to tenderize. Make sure the skillet has a lid because the final cooking step requires it to be covered.

YIELD: 6 TO 8 SERVINGS

1 tablespoon unsalted butter
5 cups julienned turnips
1 tablespoon sugar
$\frac{1}{8}$ teaspoon salt
$\frac{1}{3}$ cup chicken stock
3 tablespoons chopped fresh parsley
1 tablespoon lemon juice

Melt the butter in a large skillet over medium-low heat. Add the turnips, sugar, and salt. Cook 10 minutes, stirring occasionally.

Stir in the stock, parsley, and lemon juice. Cover and cook 10 minutes or until the turnips are tender. Serve warm.

COMPANY TURNIP CASSEROLE

Maybe you don't think of serving turnips when company is coming. Southerners do! This hearty casserole is just the dish for a crowd.

YIELD: 8 TO 10 SERVINGS

12 turnips, peeled and cubed
6 bacon slices
2 yellow onions, peeled and chopped
1 garlic clove, minced
1 green bell pepper, seeded and chopped
2 egg yolks, lightly beaten
$\frac{1}{3}$ cup evaporated milk
3 bread slices, toasted and crumbled
4 tablespoons unsalted butter, softened
1 tablespoon chopped fresh parsley
$\frac{1}{2}$ teaspoon salt
$\frac{1}{4}$ teaspoon black pepper

Place the turnips in a heavy saucepan and cover with water. Place over medium-high heat and bring to a boil. Cover and reduce the heat to medium low. Simmer 25 to 30 minutes, or until the turnips are tender.

Meanwhile, fry the bacon in a large skillet over medium heat until crisp, around 4 minutes. Drain on paper towels and when cool enough to handle, crumble and set aside. Add the onions, garlic, and bell pepper to the pan drippings and sauté 5 minutes.

Preheat the oven to 350°F. Lightly grease a 13 x 9-inch baking dish and set aside.

Drain the turnips and transfer to a mixing bowl. Crush with a potato or hand masher. Add the onion mixture, egg yolks, milk, crumbled bread, butter, parsley, salt, and black pepper. Blend well and transfer to the prepared baking dish. Top evenly with the bacon. Bake 30 minutes. Let stand 5 minutes before serving.

GLAZED TURNIPS

I cannot describe how well this glaze enhances turnips. I like to serve it with ribs or pork.

YIELD: 4 SERVINGS

2 tablespoons bacon drippings

4 turnips, peeled and cut in wedges

1¼ cups chicken stock

1 teaspoon sugar

¼ teaspoon salt

⅛ teaspoon black pepper

1 green onion, finely chopped

1 tablespoon chopped fresh parsley

Place the drippings in a large saucepan over medium-high heat. Add the turnips and stir to evenly coat. Cook one minute.

Add the stock, sugar, salt, and pepper. Bring to a boil, cover, and reduce the heat to medium low. Simmer 30 minutes. Uncover and continue to simmer until the liquid has reduced to ¼ cup. Stir in the green onions and parsley. Serve warm.

HASH BROWNED TURNIPS

The secret to really good hash browns is to make sure you don't turn them until one side is golden brown.

YIELD: 4 TO 6 SERVINGS

2 tablespoons bacon drippings

3 cups cubed cooked turnips

½ cup chopped onions

½ teaspoon kosher salt

¼ teaspoon black pepper

Place the drippings in a large skillet over medium heat. Add the turnips and onions. Cook 5 minutes undisturbed, or until golden brown. Turn and cook another 3 minutes, pressing down with the spatula. Sprinkle with the salt and pepper. Serve warm.

SOUTHERN BOILED TURNIPS

This recipe has been made in the South for decades. Its simplicity keeps it popular even now.

YIELD: 4 SERVINGS

6 turnips, peeled and cubed

2 tablespoons unsalted butter, softened

½ teaspoon kosher salt

¼ teaspoon black pepper

Place the turnips in a heavy saucepan and cover with water. Place over medium-high heat and bring to a boil. Reduce the heat to medium low, cover, and simmer 20 minutes or until the turnips are tender. Drain and transfer to a serving bowl.

Stir in the butter and toss until completely melted. Sprinkle with the salt and pepper. Serve warm.

TURNIP AND CARROT SLAW

The incredibly crisp texture of this slaw stands up well to any outdoor menu.

YIELD: 8 SERVINGS

3 cups shredded turnips
1$\frac{1}{2}$ cups shredded carrots
$\frac{1}{2}$ cup golden raisins
$\frac{2}{3}$ cup mayonnaise
2 tablespoons chopped fresh parsley
1 tablespoon lemon juice
$\frac{1}{4}$ teaspoon black pepper

In a large bowl, toss the turnips, carrots, and raisins together. In a separate bowl, whisk together the mayonnaise, parsley, lemon juice, and pepper. Pour over the turnip mixture and toss to evenly coat. Cover and refrigerate at least 2 hours or until well chilled. Serve cold.

ORIGIN: No one really knows how old turnips are, but we do know the earliest records take them back to around AD 42. Siberia appears to be the original home, where wild versions of it still grow today.

TURNIPS AND GREENS

This is the most traditional way to serve both the green tops and the roots. It is magnificent. Get the cornbread ready.

YIELD: 8 SERVINGS

1 ham hock
6 cups water
2 pounds turnip greens
3 turnips, peeled and cubed
1 teaspoon sugar
$\frac{1}{2}$ teaspoon salt

Place the ham hock and water in a large Dutch oven over medium-high heat. Cover and bring to a boil. Add the greens a handful at a time. Stir in the turnips, sugar, and salt. Cover and reduce the heat to medium low. Simmer 30 minutes, or until the turnips are tender. Serve warm with a slotted spoon.

BOTANY: Turnips are members of the mustard family and are related to rutabagas, broccoli, Brussels sprouts, cabbage, cauliflower, collards, kale, mustard, and kohlrabi, just to name a few. The roots are essentially cool climate crops, making their most vigorous growth at relatively low growing temperatures. In some areas, turnips are grown as both a spring and fall crop in the same year.

The plant likes fertile soil that is just a bit on the sandy side. Heavy clay soils are undesirable thanks to the bad influence they have on the shape of the roots. Turnips should be harvested before winter freezes begin.

WALNUTS

WHILE PECAN TREES WERE ALL OVER THE PLACE IN MISSISSIPPI WHERE I GREW UP, WALNUT trees are more common where I live now (Tennessee). They seem to be everywhere and all you need to do to have them fall from the tree is park your car underneath one during the fall. You'll instantly see where all the walnuts are!

English walnuts (called Persian walnuts) are by far the most popular walnuts worldwide, but in the good old South, black walnuts are the ones we use. It's easy to see why Southerners stir them into all kinds of good foods. They are easy to gather and even easier to store.

However, walnuts are not without their challenges. The familiar shell we are used to seeing in the supermarket is underneath a hard, thick, almost rubber-like green hull when it falls from the tree. It's enough to leave cars dented and shellers frustrated.

There were a few walnut trees scattered to and fro when we were growing up. It seemed to be the job of kids to take the just-fallen walnuts into the grass and roll them one by one underneath our shoes to loosen the hulls. This seemed to take forever, but I remember our wooden-soled Dr. Scholl's sandals were great for the task.

My mother said that, often, people with gravel driveways would spread them out for no more than a week and just drive the car over the hulls to crack them. That's brilliant, if you ask me!

Freshly harvested walnuts are harder to shell than harvested pecans. You have to remove that outer hull or the walnuts will mold. Then once the hull is removed, they need to dry a couple of months before they are ready to eat.

My grandmother used to spread them out on an old window screen. Now I know why! Once I placed them in a paper grocery sack and the whole lot molded. It's enough to inspire a renewed appreciation for those shelled walnuts in the supermarket. Convenience is certainly a blessing!

Cracking: Careful use of any good nutcracker will enable you to crack the shells and have nice big kernels. If you don't have a nutcracker, place the walnut on the flat end and hold by the seam. Strike the pointed end with a hammer using a sharp, but bouncing, blow.

Nutrition: Walnuts are a highly concentrated source of protein. The fat is mostly polyunsaturated and monounsaturated. Because of their high fiber content, walnuts are quite filling. One ounce of shelled walnuts has 185 calories.

Selection: When purchasing shelled walnuts, look for those that are plump, meaty, and rather crisp. Fresh kernels should snap easily when broken. Shriveled, limp walnuts are old and perhaps rancid so avoid purchasing those. Unshelled walnuts are, in essence, protected by nature to stay fresh. For the longest shelf life, crack open only the amount you need.

BLACK WALNUT POUND CAKE

This is one of the best pound cakes I've ever found as far as preserving well in the freezer. I usually place half of the cake in the freezer and it keeps beautifully up to three months.

YIELD: 12 TO 15 SERVINGS

$^1/_2$ pound (2 sticks) unsalted butter, softened
$^1/_2$ cup vegetable shortening
3 cups sugar
5 eggs
3 cups all-purpose flour
$^1/_2$ teaspoon baking powder
1 cup milk
$^1/_2$ cup black walnuts, coarsely chopped
$^1/_2$ teaspoon pure vanilla extract

Preheat the oven to 325°F. Grease and flour a 10-inch tube pan or Bundt pan and set aside.

In the bowl of an electric mixer, cream the butter and shortening at medium speed 3 minutes, or until light and fluffy. Gradually add the sugar, beating 6 minutes. Add the eggs, one at a time, beating just until the yellow disappears.

In a separate bowl, combine the flour and baking powder. At low speed, add to the creamed mixture alternately with the milk, beginning and ending with the flour mixture. Stir in the walnuts and extract.

Transfer the batter to the prepared pan. Bake 1 hour 30 minutes, or until a tester inserted in the center comes out clean. Cool in the pan on a wire rack 15 minutes. Remove and cool completely on a wire rack before slicing and serving.

BROWN SUGAR ICEBOX COOKIES

The beauty of this monster batch is that the freezer keeps excess amounts ready to bake at a moment's notice.

YIELD: 15 DOZEN COOKIES

$^1/_2$ pound (2 sticks) unsalted butter, softened
$^3/_4$ cup packed brown sugar
1 egg
$^1/_2$ teaspoon pure vanilla extract
$^1/_4$ teaspoon pure almond extract
$1^1/_2$ cups all-purpose flour
$^1/_2$ teaspoon baking soda
$^1/_2$ teaspoon salt
1 cup chopped walnuts

In the bowl of an electric mixer, beat the butter at medium speed until creamy. Gradually add the brown sugar, beating until blended. Add the egg, vanilla extract, and almond extract.

In a separate bowl, combine the flour, baking soda, and salt. Stir into the butter mixture, blending well. Fold in the walnuts.

Divide the dough into 4 equal portions and shape each portion into a log. Wrap in wax paper and freeze 8 hours.

Preheat the oven to 350°F. Lightly grease two baking sheets. Cut each roll into very thin, $^1/_4$-inch slices and place on the prepared baking sheets. Bake 8 minutes, or until lightly browned. Immediately remove to wire racks to cool completely. Store in an airtight container between layers of wax paper.

CRISPY WALNUT WAFERS

I haven't found the spread yet that will be gone before these crackers. They are marvelously addictive alone, which explains my spread problem. Bake a batch and you'll see!

YIELD: 4 DOZEN

2 tablespoons all-purpose flour

$1/2$ teaspoon salt

$1/2$ teaspoon baking soda

$1/4$ pound (1 stick) unsalted butter, softened

1 cup sugar

2 eggs

1 teaspoon pure vanilla extract

$1^1/2$ cups chopped walnuts

Preheat the oven to 375°F. Line two baking sheets with parchment paper and set aside.

In a mixing bowl, sift together the flour, salt, and baking soda. Set aside.

In a separate bowl, cream the butter and sugar on medium speed of an electric mixer until light and fluffy, around 3 minutes. Add the eggs, one at a time, beating thoroughly after each addition. Add the extract. Fold in the flour mixture and then the walnuts.

Place spoonfuls of batter about 3 inches apart (they'll need space to spread) on the prepared baking sheets. Bake until brown around the edges, about 10 minutes. Remove to wire racks to cool completely. Store in airtight containers.

HOLIDAY WALNUT TORTE

Historically, tortes have little flour and lots of nuts and flavorings. This one is superb.

YIELD: 8 SERVINGS

1 recipe Double Pie Pastry (page 400)

$1/2$ cup sugar

4 tablespoons unsalted butter, softened

$1/4$ cup all-purpose flour

$1/2$ teaspoon ground cinnamon

$1/2$ cup finely chopped dates

$1/2$ cup finely chopped walnuts

$1/2$ cup flaked coconut

1 egg, beaten

Prepare the Double Pie Pastry according to the recipe directions.

Preheat the oven to 375°F. Place one pastry crust on a lightly greased pizza pan and set aside.

In a mixing bowl, cream the sugar and butter at medium speed of an electric mixer until light and fluffy, around 2 minutes. Add the flour, cinnamon, dates, walnuts, and coconut, mixing well.

Spoon the filling onto the pastry on the pizza pan. Spread to within an inch of the edges. Brush the edges of the crust with the egg. Top with the second crust and crimp the edges to seal. Brush the top with the remainder of beaten egg.

Bake 20 to 25 minutes, or until golden brown. Cool at least 30 minutes. Serve warm or at room temperature.

"I DO" WALNUT MUFFINS

These muffins are "I do" magnets ... use them to get him to the altar or to get started on that ever-growing honey-do list!

YIELD: 9 MUFFINS

1 cup chopped walnuts

1 cup packed brown sugar

$1/2$ cup all-purpose flour

2 eggs

¼ pound (1 stick) unsalted butter, melted

Preheat the oven to 350°F. Place foil baking cups in 9 muffin cups and coat the insides with cooking spray. Set aside.

In a large mixing bowl, combine the walnuts, brown sugar, and flour. Make a well in the center and set aside.

In a separate bowl, beat the eggs until foamy. Add the butter and blend well. Stir into the dry ingredients just until moistened.

Spoon the batter evenly into the prepared cups, filling two-thirds full. Bake 20 to 25 minutes, or until a tester inserted in the center comes out clean. Immediately remove from the muffin pan and cool on wire racks.

MAPLE WALNUT PIE

This pie is sinful...just the way I like pies to be!

YIELD: 8 SERVINGS

1 recipe Single Pie Pastry (page 402)

1½ cups maple syrup

3 eggs

6 tablespoons unsalted butter, softened

⅓ cup granulated sugar

¼ cup packed brown sugar

2 cups coarsely chopped walnuts, toasted

1 tablespoon pure vanilla extract

2 tablespoons light rum

¼ teaspoon ground nutmeg

Prepare the Single Pie Pastry according to the recipe directions.

Preheat the oven to 450°F. Line a 9-inch pie plate with the pastry. Prick the bottom and sides with a fork. Line the pastry with a double thickness of aluminum foil. Bake 8 minutes. Remove the foil and bake 5 minutes longer, or until crust is lightly browned. Cool on a wire rack. Reduce the oven temperature to 350°F.

In a heavy saucepan over medium-high heat, bring the syrup to a boil. Reduce the heat to low and simmer, uncovered, about 10 minutes, or until the syrup is reduced to 1 cup. Set aside to cool.

In a mixing bowl, beat the eggs until thickened and set aside.

In a separate mixing bowl, beat the butter on medium speed until fluffy, around 2 minutes. Add the granulated and brown sugars and beat well. Add the syrup and eggs. Fold in the walnuts, extract, rum, and nutmeg. Pour into the cooled crust.

Bake in the lower third of the oven 35 minutes, or until set around the edges. Cool 1 hour on a wire rack before slicing and serving.

RIESLING AND WALNUT ICE CREAM

The first time I made this ice cream was for a dinner party with my wine appreciation class members. It was a homerun and continues to be everywhere I take it.

YIELD: 2 QUARTS

1 cup Riesling wine or semi-sweet white wine

1 cup half-and-half

½ cup sugar

6 egg yolks, lightly beaten

½ teaspoon pure vanilla extract

3 cups whipping cream

1 cup chopped walnuts, toasted

In a small saucepan over medium heat, bring the

wine to a simmer. After 5 minutes, set aside to cool.

In a medium saucepan over medium heat, cook the half-and-half and sugar about 4 minutes, stirring constantly until slightly thick. Stir $1/4$ cup of the hot half-and-half mixture into the beaten eggs, whisking well.

Stir the egg mixture into the saucepan and reduce the heat to low. Cook until the mixture thickens, about 15 minutes.

Remove from the heat and cool 15 minutes. Stir in the extract, cream, cooled wine, and walnuts. Cover and refrigerate 1 hour or overnight. Freeze in an ice cream machine, following the manufacturer's directions.

BOTANY: Walnuts are dried fruits that are technically seeds. The botanical name of Persian walnuts is *Juglans regia* and for black walnuts, *Juglans nigra*. These walnuts are interchangeable, so use either for any recipe calling for walnuts.

ORIGIN: The exact origin of walnuts is unknown, but we do know they grew wild in southwestern Europe and central Asia. They can be traced back to 7000 BC and are one of the oldest tree foods known to civilization.

WALNUT PICK-UP STICKS

These slender sticks are perfect for appetizer parties. Think sweet!

YIELD: 4½ DOZEN

$1/2$ pound (2 sticks) unsalted butter, softened
1 cup sugar
1 egg, separated
1 teaspoon pure vanilla extract
2 cups all-purpose flour
1 teaspoon ground cinnamon
1 teaspoon ground nutmeg
$1^1/2$ cups chopped walnuts

Preheat the oven to 325°F. Lightly grease a jelly-roll pan and set aside.

In the bowl of an electric mixer, cream the butter and sugar at medium speed 3 minutes, or until light and fluffy. Add the egg yolk and extract.

In a separate bowl, combine the flour, cinnamon, and nutmeg. Reduce the mixer speed to low and add the flour mixture, beating well. Press in the bottom of the prepared jelly-roll pan and set aside.

Beat the egg white at high speed of an electric mixer until soft peaks form, around 3 minutes. Spread over the dough and sprinkle evenly with the walnuts. Press the walnuts gently into the egg whites.

Bake 25 minutes. Cut into 2 x 1-inch sticks while still warm. Cool on wire racks before serving. Store leftovers in an airtight container.

WATERMELONS

IT'S A SLICE OF PURE SOUTHERN SUMMER SWEETNESS AND WE AFFECTIONATELY CALL IT "FIELD puddin'."** Watermelons were dubbed the king of all fruits on earth and the food of angels by Mark Twain. That man certainly knew what he was talking about.

In the South, watermelons begin to arrive from local fields just in time to become part of our annual July Fourth celebrations. They are a welcome sign that summer is in full swing. Refrigerators all over the area begin to be cleared of extra clutter so that luscious melon has a spot to get cold and ready to slice.

Because watermelon plants require nearly four months of warm weather, the South leads the way in U.S. production. That's why most of us are intimately familiar with melons that come to us straight from the vine. Nearly every producer I know not only grows them, but grows them well as long as summer rains keep us routinely hydrated.

You'll find two camps of watermelon consumers in the South: Those who eat watermelon with a sprinkling of salt and those of us who like it straight. My husband and daddy belong to the salt group, which I just can't quite stomach. In my opinion, a good, fresh watermelon doesn't need a thing except my time and a good napkin.

In the South, watermelons are nearly always consumed outdoors. That's because we are no less than experts at spitting the seeds. Every Southern child was told that if you swallowed the seeds, they would sprout inside you and you did *not* want that! There is not one among us who did not look at a pregnant woman and wonder if she swallowed a watermelon seed!

There are seedless watermelons all over the market these days, and I'm quite sure the convenience is what makes them hot sellers. But there goes half the fun of enjoying this delightful fruit, so we'll keep picking and spitting seeds at our house.

Nutrition: A two-cup serving of watermelon has fewer than eighty calories. The reason the count is so low is because of the high water content. Watermelons are 92 percent water. They are good sources of vitamins A and C, as well as potassium, dietary fiber, calcium, and iron.

Selecting: For some unknown reason, consumers are told to thump a whole melon to check for ripeness. Not one person I've ever met knew what they were listening for when they did the thumping! When shopping for a large whole watermelon, pick it up. It should feel heavy. Turn it over and look at the rind completely. There should be no cracks, cuts, bruises, or soft spots. Finally, look at the belly or the area where it was resting on the ground as it grew. This is where it pays to be a yellow belly! You want a creamy yellow tummy, not one that is white or pale green. Note: Some small melons will not have a noticeable belly!

"BEAT THE HEAT" WATERMELON LEMONADE

You will love this fruity, refreshing beverage that gets color and flavor from ruby red watermelons.

YIELD: 2 QUARTS

1 cup sugar
¼ cup water
2 cups peeled, seeded and diced watermelon
1 cup lemon juice
1 quart carbonated water

In a medium saucepan over medium-high heat, combine the sugar and water. Stirring constantly, bring to a boil. Let cool 10 minutes.

Meanwhile, place the watermelon and lemon juice in the container of a blender or food processor. Process until smooth. Pour through a fine-mesh sieve into a large pitcher. Discard any solids. Add the sugar syrup to the watermelon mixture, stirring to blend. Cover and refrigerate at least 4 hours.

When ready to serve, stir in the carbonated water. Serve immediately over ice.

"DOUBLE DUTY" WATERMELON SPARKLE

Three ingredients give you two different ways to serve the combination. Blend them into a daiquiri or serve as a fruit salad with punch!

YIELD: 6 SERVINGS

6 cups peeled, seeded and cubed watermelon
1 (6-ounce) can frozen limeade concentrate
½ to ¾ cup light rum

For daiquiris: Place the watermelon, frozen limeade, and rum in a blender. Process until smooth. Serve immediately over ice or alone.

For fruit salad: Thaw the limeade concentrate in the refrigerator overnight. Place the watermelon cubes in a large, shallow bowl. Mix the concentrate and rum until smooth. Pour over the watermelon cubes and toss gently to coat. Refrigerate at least 2 hours before serving.

FRESH WATERMELON SALSA

At first glance, this doesn't appear to be ingredients that would get along. They do and you'll love the unique flavor.

YIELD: 4 CUPS

3 cups diced seedless watermelon
1 cup chopped sweet onions
1 cup chopped orange sections
¼ cup chopped jalapeño peppers
¼ cup orange marmalade
2 tablespoons white wine vinegar
1 garlic clove, minced
½ teaspoon salt
¼ cup chopped fresh cilantro

Place the watermelon, onions, orange sections, and jalapeños in a medium serving bowl. In a separate bowl, combine the marmalade, vinegar, garlic, and salt, whisking until smooth. Pour over the watermelon mixture and toss gently to coat. Cover and refrigerate at least 1 hour. Before serving, add the cilantro. Serve with tortilla chips.

"SLICE OF DELIGHT" WATERMELON RIND PICKLES

I don't know who discovered the value of pickling watermelon rind, but blessings to whoever it was. It is the ultimate in recycling!

YIELD: 5 PINTS

3 quarts (about 6 pounds) watermelon rind
$^3/_4$ cup salt
3 quarts water
6 cups ice cubes
9 cups sugar
3 cups white vinegar
1 tablespoon whole cloves
5 cinnamon sticks
1 lemon, thinly sliced with seeds removed

Trim the green outer skin and pink flesh from the watermelon rind. Cut into 1-inch pieces. In a large bowl, combine the salt, water, and ice cubes. Add the watermelon rind and let stand about 4 hours at room temperature. Drain and rinse with cold water. Cover with cold water and place over high heat. Cook until fork tender, about 10 minutes. Do not overcook. Drain and set aside.

Combine the sugar and vinegar in a large pot with three cups of water over medium-high heat. Tie the cloves and cinnamon sticks in cheesecloth and add to the pot. Boil 5 minutes and pour over the watermelon. Add lemon slices and let stand overnight in the refrigerator.

Remove the spice bag and open. Discard the cloves and set the cinnamon sticks aside.

Heat the watermelon in the syrup to boiling over medium-high heat. Reduce the heat to medium low and slowly cook 1 hour. Pack loosely into sterilized, hot pint canning jars. Add 1 stick of cinnamon from the spice bag to each jar.

Cover with the boiling syrup, leaving $^1/_2$-inch headspace. Remove any air bubbles, wipe the jar rims, and adjust the lids. Process 10 minutes in a boiling water bath. Place on a wire rack away from drafts and cool completely. (See page 12 for detailed canning instructions.)

SUMMER OASIS WATERMELON GRANITA

This is for adults only. I love being a grown-up!

YIELD: 4 SERVINGS

6 cups cubed watermelon, seeded
$^1/_2$ cup sugar
2 tablespoons lemon juice
2 tablespoons vodka

Place the watermelon, sugar, lemon juice, and vodka in the container of a blender and process until smooth, stopping once to scrape down the sides. Pour into an 8-inch square pan. Cover and freeze 2 hours, stirring every 30 minutes. Remove from the freezer 5 minutes before serving to soften slightly. Serve in chilled goblets.

WATERMELON AND PURPLE ONION SALAD

This yummy salad is a great way to use up those left-over watermelon chunks sitting in your refrigerator.

YIELD: 6 SERVINGS

2 purple onions, cut into $^1/_4$-inch slices
$^1/_2$ cup water
$^1/_2$ cup red wine vinegar

¼ cup sugar

4 ounces baby arugula

1 head radicchio, chopped

4 pounds seedless watermelon, cut into
   1-inch chunks

¼ cup olive oil

4 ounces feta cheese, crumbled

½ teaspoon salt

¼ teaspoon black pepper

¼ cup pine nuts, lightly toasted

Separate the onion slices into rings and place in a glass bowl. Bring the water, vinegar, and sugar to a boil in a small saucepan over high heat. Pour over the onion rings and let steep 30 minutes, stirring occasionally.

Meanwhile, combine the arugula and radicchio in a large bowl. Add the watermelon and toss gently. Drain the onions, reserving the liquid. Add the onion rings to the salad bowl.

Combine 2 tablespoons of the reserved liquid with the oil, whisking until smooth. Drizzle over the salad and toss gently. Sprinkle with the cheese and season with the salt and pepper. Divide evenly among six chilled salad plates, garnish with pine nuts, and serve immediately.

WATERMELON ICE

This is a great way to cool off from the Southern summer heat. Just keep a batch in your freezer to have on hand for the next scorcher.

YIELD: 4 SERVINGS

3 pounds seedless watermelon, diced

½ cup sugar

1 tablespoon dry red wine

Mint sprigs for garnish

Place the watermelon in a blender and purée until smooth. Strain through a fine-meshed sieve into a mixing bowl. Add the sugar and wine, mixing well. Pour into a 13 x 9-inch baking dish, cover, and freeze. When frozen, chop into fine chips with a blunt pastry scraper. Garnish with fresh mint and serve immediately.

WATERMELON HAM WRAPS

This appetizer is such a winner. It is unusual, easy to make, inexpensive, and marvelous!

YIELD: 16 APPETIZERS

16 fresh watercress or arugula sprigs

16 (1-inch) peeled and seeded watermelon cubes

8 very thin cooked country ham slices, halved

Place a watercress sprig on each watermelon cube. Wrap with a ham slice and secure with a wooden pick. Cover and refrigerate at least 1 hour. Serve cold.

BOTANY: Watermelons are vegetables that we use as fruits. They are cousins of cucumbers, cantaloupes, squash, and pumpkins and are members of the large gourd family. Although those with a red flesh are the most common, there are yellow-and orange-fleshed varieties available as well.

ORIGIN: Watermelons are originally from the Kalahari Desert region.

ZUCCHINI

THE SOUTHERN SUN SEEMS TO DUPLICATE A SUMMER SQUASH VARIETY KNOWN AS ZUCCHINI practically by the minute. Stand for a few minutes beside the plant and you can just about watch it grow. No matter how often you head out to the garden and pick the plant clean, there will always be more waiting for you soon after.

Zucchini is a much anticipated and welcomed treat early every summer. It doesn't take long to be on the heavy end of a zucchini harvest because it is a remarkably prolific vegetable. Even just one plant will provide enough zucchini to feed your family and most of your neighborhood for months.

While some occasionally complain about the excess, that's when I begin to celebrate. Zucchini is so much more than a bread ingredient and a stir-fry item. To me, it prevents the horrible culinary disease known as ingredient boredom.

It doesn't hurt that zucchini is remarkably versatile and is perfectly at home with a host of other foods. Give it a good washing and you are ready to go. You can quickly grate, chop, dice, slice, or matchstick them.

Zucchini can be poached, steamed, fried, roasted, blanched, grilled, baked, broiled, puréed, or microwaved. You can choose to peel them or not. It can be added to either sweet or savory dishes. In short, zucchini is a creative cook's dream come true.

So if you see a fellow gardening neighbor headed your way with an armload of fresh-picked zucchini, clap your hands and shout, "Glory!" You have been given a terrific gift that will bounce from meal to meal and never look or taste the same way twice. Zucchini is abundance at its very finest.

Nutrition: One cup of steamed zucchini contains only twenty two calories and significant amounts of calcium, phosphorus, potassium, and vitamins A and C.

Selection: Choose young, tender zucchini that are not overly large. I prefer those that are no longer than eight inches in length. Allowing them to grow longer than that means you won't get a crisp, fresh taste and it will be tough. It should have no soft spots or pitting of the skin and always feel firm with no shriveling.

Storage: Keep zucchini refrigerated in the vegetable crisper drawer. It keeps longer if placed in a loosely closed plastic bag. Use it within four days of purchase or you'll likely begin to see pitting in the outer skin.

Varieties: Subtly striped zucchini that is glossy green is the most common type. It is slightly smaller at the top (the stem end) than the bottom (the blossom end). There are more exotic ones that are yellow, white, pale green, and really dark green available as well. In certain markets, you may be able to find a spherical Italian variety that is great for stuffing.

SAVORY ZUCCHINI PIE

No need to worry about a crust with this pie. It forms its own, which means this is a quick company dish that can go from brunch to dinner.

YIELD: 8 SERVINGS

2 cups shredded zucchini

2 eggs, lightly beaten

1 white onion, peeled and chopped

3/4 cup all-purpose baking mix

3/4 cup shredded sharp Cheddar cheese

1/4 cup vegetable oil

1/2 teaspoon salt

1/4 teaspoon black pepper

1/4 teaspoon dried sage

1/4 teaspoon paprika

Preheat the oven to 350°F. Lightly grease a 9-inch pie plate and set aside.

In a mixing bowl, combine the zucchini, eggs, onions, baking mix, cheese, oil, salt, pepper, sage, and paprika. Blend well. Transfer to the prepared pie plate.

Bake 45 minutes, or until a tester inserted in the center comes out clean. Cool 10 minutes on a wire rack before slicing and serving.

FRIED ZUCCHINI MATCHSTICKS

I like to slice zucchini into very thin strips for this fried feast. You may like yours a little heftier. This will cause the fry time to vary depending on the thickness, so adjust accordingly.

YIELD: 6 SERVINGS

Vegetable oil

3 zucchini, trimmed

1/2 cup all-purpose flour

1 teaspoon onion salt

1/2 teaspoon black pepper

1/4 teaspoon garlic powder

1 egg

1 tablespoon milk

1 tablespoon olive oil

1 cup crushed corn flakes

Cut the zucchini in half crosswise. Cut each half into at least eight strips or more, if you prefer. Set aside.

Pour the vegetable oil to a depth of 3 inches in a large cast-iron skillet. Place over medium-high heat and bring to 350°F.

Meanwhile, in a mixing bowl, combine the flour, onion salt, pepper, and garlic powder. In a separate bowl, whisk together the egg, milk, and oil. Add to the flour mixture and whisk until smooth. Place the corn flakes in a shallow dish.

Dip the zucchini strips in the batter and dredge in the corn flakes. Fry in the hot oil until golden brown, from 1 to 4 minutes depending on the thickness. Drain on paper towels. Serve warm.

EVERY YEAR ZUCCHINI BREAD

This bread is an annual feast at my house as soon as the first bit of zucchini begins to be harvested. The honey keeps it nice and moist.

YIELD: 2 LOAVES

3 cups all-purpose flour

1 teaspoon baking powder

1 teaspoon baking soda

1 teaspoon salt

1 tablespoon ground cinnamon

1 cup chopped pecans or walnuts

2 zucchini, peeled and shredded

2 eggs, lightly beaten

1$\frac{1}{2}$ cups sugar

$\frac{3}{4}$ cup honey

1 cup vegetable oil

2 teaspoons pure vanilla extract

Preheat the oven to 350°F. Grease and flour two loaf pans and set aside.

In a mixing bowl, combine the flour, baking powder, baking soda, salt, cinnamon, and pecans. Make a well in the center and set aside.

In a separate bowl, combine the zucchini, eggs, sugar, honey, oil, and extract. Add to the flour mixture and stir just until moistened.

Evenly divide the batter between the prepared pans. Bake 65 minutes, or until a tester inserted in the center comes out clean. Cool in the pans 10 minutes before cooling completely on wire racks.

HERB-CRUSTED ZUCCHINI

A garlic-laced herb breadcrumb mixture gives this dish spunk. It's ready for the oven in a flash thanks to the food processor.

YIELD: 6 SERVINGS

4 zucchini, sliced

$\frac{1}{2}$ teaspoon salt

$\frac{1}{4}$ teaspoon black pepper

4 thick slices French bread, torn into pieces

2 garlic cloves, minced

2 teaspoons chopped fresh oregano

1 teaspoon chopped fresh rosemary

1 teaspoon Dijon mustard

2 tablespoons olive oil

Preheat the oven to 375°F. Lightly grease a two-quart baking dish. Arrange the zucchini in the dish and season with the salt and pepper.

Place the bread in the bowl of a food processor and process until fine. Add the garlic, oregano, rosemary, and mustard and process to mix. With the machine running, add the oil and process until smooth. Spread the breadcrumb mixture over the zucchini. Bake 30 minutes, or until the zucchini is tender. Serve warm.

"LET'S MAKE A DILL" ZUCCHINI SOUP

Everything about this soup screams fresh. It is a real summer heat buster since it is served cold, plus that means it can be made ahead of time so there's no sweat!

YIELD: 9 CUPS

2 tablespoons vegetable oil

2 small leeks, sliced

1$\frac{1}{2}$ pounds zucchini, sliced

3 cups chicken stock

1 cup half-and-half

1 (8-ounce) container sour cream

$\frac{1}{2}$ teaspoon salt

$\frac{1}{4}$ teaspoon white pepper

$\frac{1}{4}$ cup chopped fresh dill

Place the oil in a Dutch oven and set over medium-high heat. Add the leeks and sauté 3 minutes. Add the zucchini and stock. Bring to a boil, cover, and reduce the heat to low. Simmer 10 minutes, or until the zucchini is tender.

Cool 20 minutes. With an immersion blender (or in batches in a regular blender), process the soup until smooth. Stir in the half-and-half, sour cream, salt, pepper, and dill. Blend well. Cover and refrigerate at least 4 hours before serving.

OVEN-CRISP ZUCCHINI WEDGES

You will be surprised these weren't deep fried. They have a terrifically crisp outer coating, but are almost like custard on the inside. I love the contrast in texture and you will, too.

YIELD: 6 SERVINGS

3 zucchini, trimmed
$1/4$ cup seasoned dry breadcrumbs
2 tablespoons shredded Parmesan cheese
$1/4$ teaspoon garlic powder
$1/4$ teaspoon black pepper
$1/4$ teaspoon paprika
2 tablespoons water
1 tablespoon vegetable oil

Preheat the oven to 475°F. Grease a baking sheet with cooking spray and set aside.

Cut the zucchini in half lengthwise and cut in half again. Cut each piece in half crosswise. Place in a zip-top bag and set aside.

In a shallow dish, combine the breadcrumbs, cheese, garlic powder, pepper, and paprika. Add the water and oil to the zucchini bag. Seal the bag and shake to evenly coat. Dredge each piece in the breadcrumb mixture.

Place on the prepared baking sheet. Bake 10 minutes, or until golden brown. Serve warm.

SHREDDED ZUCCHINI SQUARES

This is a great summer appetizer to serve when your herb garden is in need of a snip and your zucchini is in need of picking.

YIELD: 12 TO16 APPETIZER SERVINGS

3 eggs, lightly beaten
1 pound zucchini, shredded
$1/4$ cup chopped green onions
1 garlic clove, minced
1 teaspoon chopped fresh thyme
1 teaspoon chopped fresh parsley
1 teaspoon chopped fresh chives
$3/4$ cup cream
$3/4$ pound soft goat cheese
$3/4$ teaspoon salt, divided
$1/2$ teaspoon black pepper, divided
6 Roma tomatoes, peeled, seeded, and diced
2 tablespoons olive oil

Preheat the oven to 350°F. Lightly grease a 13 x 9-inch baking dish and set aside.

In a large mixing bowl, combine the eggs, zucchini, green onions, garlic, thyme, parsley, chives, cream, cheese, $1/2$ teaspoon of the salt, and $1/4$ teaspoon of the pepper. Blend well.

Pour into prepared baking dish and bake 40 minutes, or until a knife inserted in the center comes out clean. Cool to room temperature on a wire rack.

Meanwhile, combine the tomatoes, oil, and remaining $1/4$ teaspoon of salt and $1/4$ teaspoon of pepper in a small bowl. To serve, cut into squares and place on a serving platter. Top with a spoonful of the tomato mixture.

ZUCCHINI PANCAKES

These are not the type of pancakes you would normally serve with maple syrup. Instead, they are welcomed as an appetizer with fresh homemade salsa or as a side dish with anything from pork to fish.

YIELD: 6 SERVINGS

1 (12-ounce) can coconut milk
2 garlic cloves, minced
2 teaspoons chopped fresh basil
2 zucchini, shredded
$\frac{1}{43}$ cup all-purpose flour
2 egg whites
$\frac{1}{4}$ teaspoon salt
$\frac{1}{4}$ teaspoon black pepper
2 tablespoons vegetable oil
Fresh salsa

In a large bowl, combine the coconut milk, garlic, basil, and zucchini, mixing well. Add the flour and mix well. Set aside.

In the bowl of an electric mixer, beat the egg whites at high speed until soft peaks form. Gently fold into the batter and season with the salt and pepper.

Preheat the oven to 250°F. Heat half of oil in a large sauté pan over medium-high heat. Pour $\frac{1}{4}$ cup of the batter into the pan, adding only as many as will comfortably fit in the pan. Cook 3 minutes or until batter bubbles along the edges.

Flip and cook 3 minutes more or until golden brown. Keep warm in the oven while preparing the remaining pancakes. Serve warm with homemade salsa.

NAME: The word *zucchini* comes from the Italian word *zuccherino*, which means sweet.

FREEZING SLICES: Freezing the excess provides an opportunity for you to use it later, when it might be a little more welcome on the dinner table. It can be easily frozen, but must be blanched first. Place the $\frac{1}{2}$-inch slices in boiling water for three minutes. Drain and plunge the slices in ice cold water for the same amount of time (three minutes) in order to stop the cooking process. Drain again, dry on paper towels, and pack into freezer containers. Label the container with the contents and date. Use within one year for the best quality.

FREEZING GRATED ZUCCHINI: Grated zucchini must be steam, rather than water blanched. Place the grated zucchini in a steamer container placed over boiling water. Steam no less than one minute and no longer than two minutes or until the zucchini is translucent. It is easiest to package grated zucchini in premeasured amounts, such as half-cups or cups. Then you only have to thaw the amount you need for a particular recipe. If the zucchini is watery when thawed, just strain and discard the liquid.

ORIGIN: Zucchini is a native of the Western Hemisphere. It is a type of summer squash that is a distinct variety of vegetable marrow. While cylinder shapes are the most common, you can also find zucchini in round shapes that are about the size of a softball.

INDEX